W9-DBO-750

JavaScript
UNLEASHED
Fourth Edition

R. Allen Wyke
Jason D. Gilliam

201 West 103rd Street, Indianapolis, Indiana 46290

JavaScript Unleashed, Fourth Edition

International Standard Book Number: 0-672-32431-8

Library of Congress Catalog Card Number: 2002104072

Printed in the United States of America

First Printing: December 2002

05 04 03 02   4 3 2 1

Trademarks

Warning and Disclaimer

Acquisitions Editor
Shelley Johnston

Development Editors
Heather Goodell

Jon Steever

Managing Editor
Charlotte Clapp

Project Editors
Katelyn Cozatt
Elizabeth Finney
Tricia Liebig

Copy Editor
Margaret Berson

Indexer
Ginny Bess

Proofreader
Suzanne Thomas

Technical Editors
Michael Walston

Martin Honnen

Team Coordinator
Amy Patton

Interior Designer
Gary Adair

Cover Designer
Alan Clements

Contents at a Glance

Table of Contents

About the Authors

R. Allen Wyke, of Durham, North Carolina, is the Vice President of Technology and Services at Blue292. Allen is responsible for ensuring that Blue292 products have the proper technical vision and direction, while at the same time guiding network engineering to deliver on that message and providing services to support them.

Allen participated on the W3C P3P Working Group, which represents a machine-based privacy standard to be used on the Internet. He has published a dozen books on various Internet technologies such as Perl, JavaScript, and XML, and somehow continues to find time for his dogs and routine trips to the beach.

Jason D. Gilliam is a software developer at Blue292 in Durham, North Carolina. At Blue292 he is an active developer on all of the company's products as well as guiding the development teams' coding activities. His development activities cover a range of technologies such as Java, JSP, ASP, HTML, JavaScript, and the .NET Framework, just to name a few.

In addition to his work at Blue292, Jason has also worked in other Web-based arenas such as chat and discussion group software as well as work in the telecommunications industry. Jason is also a co-author of the book *Pure JavaScript*.

Dedications

This one is for Matt, Jeff, and Greg. You guys are not only good friends, but also the greatest brothers-in-law that my sisters could have found.

—R. Allen Wyke

I dedicate this book to my 1-year-old daughter, Presley. Your smiles and hugs kept me going during this project.

—Jason D. Gilliam

Acknowledgments

First, I would like to thank Bob Kern of TIPS Publishing and my co-author, Jason, for their professionalism, hard work, and overall support in the writing of this book. I would also like to thank Shelley Johnston and everyone else behind the scenes at Sams who worked on the book and helped make sure it was the best it could be.

Finally, I would like to thank Susan Acker for allowing me the flexibility and opportunity (as long as nothing else slipped of course) to write during my duties at Blue292.

—R. Allen Wyke

I would like to thank Bob Kern of TIPS Publishing and my co-author, Allen Wyke, for their work on this book. I would also like to thank Shelley, Elizabeth, Heather, Michael, and everyone else at Sams who worked hard to make this book a success.

—Jason D. Gilliam

We Want to Hear from You!

As the reader of this book, *you* are our most important critic and commentator. We value your opinion and want to know what we're doing right, what we could do better, what areas you'd like to see us publish in, and any other words of wisdom you're willing to pass our way.

You can email or write me directly to let me know what you did or didn't like about this book—as well as what we can do to make our books stronger.

Please note that I cannot help you with technical problems related to the topic of this book, and that due to the high volume of mail I receive, I might not be able to reply to every message.

When you write, please be sure to include this book's title and author as well as your name and phone or email address. I will carefully review your comments and share them with the author and editors who worked on the book.

Email: webdev@samspublishing.com

Mail: Mark Taber
            Associate Publisher
            Sams Publishing
            201 West 103rd Street
            Indianapolis, IN 46290 USA

Reader Services

For more information about this book or others from Sams Publishing, visit our Web site at www.samspublishing.com. Type the ISBN (excluding hyphens) or the title of the book in the Search box to find the book you're looking for.

Introduction

Let us first welcome you to the Fourth Edition of *JavaScript Unleashed*—a book that has become a must-have for all people interested in JavaScript. A lot has transpired since the release of the last edition, and we have made every attempt to touch on each new topic, while not compromising the coverage of the founding aspects of the language. That being said, this edition does represent some serious changes since the third edition, including changes in the organization, the removal of dated material, and additional depth in new areas of JavaScript.

JavaScript has emerged as a significant tool for Web development, whether for simple enhancements to XHTML pages or full-fledged Web-based applications. But because its *raison d'être* is not as glamorous, JavaScript will perhaps never be as popular as Java, XML, or even XHTML. Having said that, JavaScript does something none of the others can do: It makes divergent technologies work together seamlessly. Indeed, the jack-of-all-trades nature of JavaScript is perhaps what gives this language its staying power.

Most people probably see JavaScript as a client-side language. That it is—and much of this book focuses on how to embed JavaScript into XHTML documents to run under supporting browsers. However, JavaScript also has a presence as a server-side scripting language as well as uses in building Web Services and performing administrative tasks. Microsoft's Active Server Pages .NET (ASP .NET) and their Windows Script Host (WSH) were among the first to use JavaScript in these non-client-side implementations.

We are developers and technology leaders by trade, and the more we use JavaScript, the more we see its wide-ranging applicability in the applications we design and develop. It is our hope that JavaScript's capability of handling a wide variety of tasks will become evident as you read this book. Here are a few of the many questions this book will answer:

- What is the relationship between JavaScript, XHTML, and Cascading Style Sheets (CSS)?

- What is the difference between JavaScript, JScript, and ECMAScript?

- What are the compatibility issues surrounding the many versions of JavaScript and JScript?

- How can you create special effects with JavaScript?

- What are the core JavaScript objects?

- How can I use JavaScript on my Web server?

- How do I build .NET Web Services using JScript .NET?

Who Should Read This Book?

Because of its status as the primary Web scripting language, JavaScript is used for all sorts of tasks. Those who use it include

- Webmasters
- XHTML authors and designers
- Web application developers
- Dynamic HTML designers and developers
- Power users

We believe that readers in each of these categories will appreciate this book, although we do assume you have basic Web and XHTML knowledge. You don't need JavaScript experience, but you should have some programming experience in a scripting or full language. If you've never programmed before, this doesn't mean that this book isn't for you. But this book doesn't offer much instruction in beginner programming issues that aren't germane to JavaScript.

System Requirements

In order to use JavaScript, you need a capable computer that has access to the Web. The authors of this book primarily used Internet Explorer 6, Netscape 6 and 7, and various builds of the Mozilla browser on Windows 2000 and XP as well as MacOS X and Red Hat Linux 7.3. The same JavaScript code executed on these platforms will work in Opera and on other versions of MacOS, Unix, and other supported platforms (except where noted).

How This Book Is Organized

JavaScript Unleashed, Fourth Edition, provides a whole-hog look at JavaScript and related technologies. We have not only covered the language itself, but also some of the peripheral technologies, such as XHTML, CSS, and XML. The book itself is divided into seven parts, each of which is summarized in the following sections.

Part I   Getting Started with JavaScript

Part I is a complete introduction to JavaScript and related tools. Chapter 1 takes a unique look at JavaScript, focusing on how and where it fits into Web application development. You will also see how it relates to other technologies, on both the client side and the server side. In Chapter 2, you will learn about the relationship between JavaScript and XHTML and how the browser interprets your code at runtime. Chapter 2 also looks at software tools you can use to assist in developing with JavaScript. Chapter 3 steps you through the entire process of writing your first script.

Part II   The Core JavaScript Language

Part II presents a thorough look at the JavaScript language. In Chapters 4 through 7, you will learn about language basics, operators, control structures, and functions. This part of the book really focuses on the semantics of the language and how it is used.

Part III   Core and Client JavaScript Objects

One of the first things you will learn as you go through this book is that JavaScript is made up of a set of objects. These are further organized into core objects, which are core across all implementations, and host objects, which represent objects specific to the host, or environment, of the implementation—like a browser or particular server. In Chapter 8 we go over these core objects, and then spend Chapters 9 through 13 talking about host objects that are present within the browser's implementation. We conclude with Chapter 14, which shows you how you can create your own JavaScript objects within your scripts.

Part IV   DOM Objects

Part IV dives into the heart of the Document Object Model (DOM) with Chapter 15, "Fundamentals of the Document Object Model." We then move into Chapter 16 where we expose you to other DOM objects not discussed in the previous chapter that focus on accessing the DOM. Following these discussions, it is time to put your knowledge to more use in Chapter 17, "Manipulating the DOM," by showing you how to manipulate documents using these DOM objects, methods, and properties.

Part V   Scripting Documents

The last chapter in Part IV provides a great transition into Part V, which focuses on some of the document scripting techniques people are using JavaScript for on the Web. Chapter 18 starts off the educational process by talking about handling events, while Chapter 19 brings you up to speed with Cascading Style Sheets. Chapter 20 concentrates on the implementation of "layers," introduced in the version 4 browsers, and their migration to standardized document layering that is present in today's newest browsers. Chapter 21 shows you how to do rollovers, animations, banners, and other special effects in JavaScript without using any Java applets. Chapter 22 then applies these lessons by showing you how to create menus and toolbars before moving into Chapter 23, where you will learn about creating JavaScript-based site navigation. Part V is then rounded out with Chapters 24 and 25 that take you through forms and data validation as well as personalization and creating dynamic pages.

Part VI   JavaScript on the Server Side

As previously mentioned, client-side implementations of JavaScript are not the only places where JavaScript can be found. As you will learn in Chapter 26, there are also server-side implementations of JavaScript. Chapter 27 will build on this information by exposing you to using JScript .NET to build .NET-powered Web Services, and Chapter 28 will end this section of the book with coverage of Microsoft's Windows Script Host.

Part VII   Essential Programming Techniques

The seventh and final part of the book focuses on tying together what you have learned, and providing you with some helpful tips, hints, and guidance as you begin using JavaScript in the real world. Chapter 29 introduces regular expression pattern matching, while Chapter 30 dives into error handling. Finally, Chapter 31 gives tips on debugging JavaScript applications.

Conventions Used in This Book

This book uses certain conventions to help make the book more readable and helpful:

- JavaScript code listings, JavaScript method names, and screen messages or displays appear in a special `monospace` font.

- Placeholders (words that are substitutes for what you actually type) appear in `monospace italic`.

- Terms being introduced or defined appear in a **special font**.

- Menu selections are separated with a comma. For example, "Select File, Open" means that you pull down the File menu and choose the Open option.

- Sometimes a line of JavaScript code is too long to fit on a single line of this book. When this happens, the line is broken and continued on the next line, preceded by a ➥ character.

In addition, this book uses special sidebars that are set apart from the rest of the text. These sidebars include Notes, Tips, Cautions, and sidebars whose title indicates the topic.

And that does it! That gives you all the information you need to crack the book open and start learning JavaScript. We are very excited about having this opportunity to guide you through this task, and sincerely hope that you will find *JavaScript Unleashed*, Fourth Edition, one of the most useful, beneficial, and helpful books you have read.

R. Allen Wyke

Jason D. Gilliam

PART I

Getting Started with JavaScript

IN THIS PART

CHAPTER 1

Introducing JavaScript

IN THIS CHAPTER

- JavaScript, JScript, ECMAScript, What?

- Web-based Application Development

- What Can You Do with JavaScript?

- Browser Support for JavaScript

- Resources on the Web

As most of you know, the going rate for an Internet year is equal to about three calendar months. With that in mind, we recommend the best way to learn JavaScript is to jump in head first. Sure, you can play with it a little here or a little there, but to get a firm grasp on how it works and operates, you need to embrace it. And as with any other project, you should put forth a solid effort to digest the information and expose yourself to examples and projects.

But before diving into the nuts and bolts of creating JavaScript code, it's important to look at the purpose of JavaScript. JavaScript has grown outside its initial browser boundaries and can now be found on the server side, within the most recent release of the Windows operating system, and as a backbone language used in Microsoft's .NET initiative. JavaScript emerges as a powerful tool as you begin using it with other technologies to provide effective and deliberate solutions.

In this chapter, we provide an overview of JavaScript and look at JavaScript within the context of the Web application framework. After that, we'll look at the major uses of JavaScript today, current browser support for JavaScript, and provide some resources to point you in the right direction when you need help.

JavaScript, JScript, ECMAScript, What?

JavaScript was initially developed by Netscape under the name of LiveScript and was intended to extend the capabilities of basic HTML by providing a partial alternative to Common Gateway Interface (CGI) scripts used to process form information and add dynamics to a user's page. One of the motivations behind JavaScript was the recognition of a need for logic and intelligence to exist on the client, not simply on the server.

With all logic on the server, processing was forced to go back and forth between the client and the server. In fact, with no logic on the front end, the Web environment falls into the outdated terminal architecture that was replaced with the PC revolution in the 1980s. Providing logic within the browser would empower the client to act in a true client/server relationship as well as provide a means to build three-tier (or greater) systems.

Realizing the importance of Web scripting after the initial release, Microsoft wanted to provide support for JavaScript as well. However, when Netscape would only license the technology to Microsoft rather than give it away, Redmond reverse-engineered JavaScript, based on the public documentation, to create its own implementation, JScript, which is supported in Microsoft Internet Explorer versions 3.0 and higher. JScript 1.0 is roughly compatible with JavaScript 1.1, which is supported in Netscape Navigator 3.0 and higher browsers. However, the myriad of these early JavaScript versions and various platform-specific quirks left Web developers with headaches when they tried to deploy JavaScript-enabled Web sites.

Fortunately, help was on the way for frustrated scripters. Netscape, Microsoft, and other vendors agreed to turn over the language to an international standards body named European Computer Manufacturers Association (ECMA). Since that time, ECMA has finalized a language specification, known as ECMAScript, which vendors can support in unity.

Today, ECMAScript is the driving force behind the core language syntax and semantics themselves, and JavaScript and JScript each are very solid implementations. Since Netscape's JavaScript has moved to the open source arena for development, it has stuck very close to standards such as ECMAScript and the Document Object Model (DOM), while Microsoft has pushed JScript into new areas with the Windows Scripting Host and .NET Framework. Given these factors, there is a lot of excitement around JavaScript and what it holds for tomorrow.

> **NOTE**
>
> Because the term "JavaScript" is generally accepted to represent both Netscape/Mozilla.org's and Microsoft's implementation of ECMAScript, we will use it to cover both throughout this book. If there is a situation where we need to distinguish between the two, we will do so explicitly.

Now that we have covered a very brief history of the language, let's look at the Web application framework.

Web-based Application Development

Using the Web as an application deployment environment is a relatively new phenomenon. With the advent of Java, JavaScript, XML, and other technologies, the idea of developing Web-centric applications has many attractive qualities. This can seem rather confusing, because of the distributed nature of the Web, which means that a Web application can be composed of many parts, using a variety of technologies.

For example, in typical LAN-based client/server architected systems, you might have a client application attached directly to a database server on the network. You would often develop the client application using a single tool such as Delphi, C++, or Visual Basic. The server side of the application is typically developed and maintained using SQL Server, Oracle, or other database administrative tools.

The Web development framework is truly an example of the sum being greater than the parts. By itself, each technology is limited and rather narrow in scope. When combined into cohesive applications, the technologies provide an effective means of developing Internet and intranet solutions. Now let's touch on a few items that every JavaScript programmer should know.

Facts Every Scripter Should Know

Trying to learn a new technology such as JavaScript can be challenging, because it can be difficult to understand how it's used and how it fits into the general picture. In Table 1.1 we have boiled down the basics of JavaScript to a list of essential facts that will help get you started. Study this list before you continue, because you will want to apply this knowledge to your understanding of the language and any projects you do.

TABLE 1.1   Essential Facts for JavaScripters

Fact	Description
Can be embedded into XHTML	Code usually contained within XHTML documents and executed there. Most JavaScript objects have XHTML elements they represent, so the code is included at the core client-side level of the language.
Environment-dependent	JavaScript is a scripting language, and the interpreting engine that processes your code is within the environment—whether it's Netscape Navigator, Microsoft Internet Explorer, or a server-side engine.
Interpreted language	JavaScript is interpreted at runtime by the host environment while it's executed.
Loosely typed language	JavaScript is not a strongly typed language such as Java or C++, in which you must declare all variables of a certain type.
Object-based language	Referred to as an object-oriented programming (OOP) language, but it is really an *object-based* language—it does share some of the OOP concepts.
Event-driven	JavaScript can respond to events generated by the user or the system.
Multifunctional	JavaScript can be used in a variety of contexts to provide a solution to a Web-based problem.

TABLE 1.1   Continued

Fact	Description
Continually evolving	As implementation environments, such as browsers, and standards, such as XHTML or XML, continue to evolve, so does the JavaScript language. It is always changing to meet the needs of developers and scripters alike.
Spans contexts	JavaScript can be useful in a variety of contexts, not only by Web developers, but also on the server side in Microsoft Active Server Pages .NET (ASP.NET) and Windows Script Host (WSH) environment.

Now that we have some basic information about JavaScript, let's take a look at some more detailed information.

Client Side

The client side of developing Web applications consists of several building blocks including:

- Browsers
- XHTML (eXtensible Hypertext Markup Language)
- Scripting languages

Here we will touch on each of these and how they work together.

Browsers

Undoubtedly the most important component of a Web application is the browser itself. The browser is the window to the Web for the user and serves as the user interface for your application. Browser technology is relatively simple (reading documents and displaying them appropriately), but previous development of nonstandard enhancements, such as Netscape layers, has made the selection of browser software a critical one when you determine a Web development platform, although this is less of a problem today than two or three years ago.

XHTML

XHTML is obviously one of the primary technologies upon which the Web is built. XHTML and its predecessor HTML are markup languages that are used to provide structure and formatting to content. Although the browser provides the window for displaying this content to the user, the content itself doesn't matter if you're presenting static documents, returning a query result, providing a feedback form, or displaying a JavaScript-based application. Regardless of the means of obtaining this data, it is ultimately converted into XHTML elements for presentation.

Client Scripting Languages

JavaScript is by far the leading scripting language today, but it is not the only language. VBScript and PerlScript, although rarely used, are alternatives, but they should only be considered if there is some very good reason to avoid JavaScript.

Server Side

The server side of application development consists of the Web server itself, along with extensions to the server software. These extensions can take various forms and be employed with a variety of technologies. Within this framework, the server is charged with handling requests for resources, such as XHTML documents, images, or other files from the client and returning them. Popular servers today include Microsoft Internet Information Server (IIS) and Apache's HTTP Server.

By itself, the Web server provides static resources to the client when requested as well as performing a variety of other functions. However, several extensions to servers provide capabilities that the server itself doesn't support. These include, but are not limited to, JavaScript and Java.

JavaScript on the Server Side

Much of the attention given to JavaScript to date has been because of its capabilities on the client side. However, you can use JavaScript as a server-side scripting tool as well. Microsoft is supporting JScript in ASP and ASP.NET (called JScript .NET) as a server-side scripting language.

JavaServer Pages and Servlets

In recent months, we have seen Java on the server side really take off. Sun has its JavaServer Pages (JSP) and most recently its ONE (Open Net Environment). As you might imagine, this is a competitor to ASP and ASP.NET.

Additionally, you may have heard of Java servlets. Servlets are small components, much like ActiveX and COM controls in the ASP environment, that are invoked as pages are being built *or* to build pages. This allows developers to apply their knowledge of the Java language, which is easier to learn than C, to build fast, reliable, platform-independent components to create pages.

What Can You Do with JavaScript?

Now that you have surveyed the technologies that make up Web applications, you can look at the role that JavaScript can play in developing Web applications.

Client-Side Applications

You can use JavaScript to develop entire client-side applications. Although JavaScript isn't an all-encompassing language like Java, it does provide rather substantial capabilities when it comes to working with XHTML elements and associated objects. Trying to design such an application using Java would be much more complex because of the interaction that is required with XHTML. For certain cases, JavaScript provides the ideal programming backbone on which to develop the application.

Data Validation and Interactive Forms

JavaScript gives you, as a Web developer, a basic means of validating data from the user without hitting the server. Within your JavaScript code, you can determine whether values entered by the user are valid or fit the correct format. JavaScript is a much more efficient validation method than throwing unqualified values to a server process. Not only is the process more efficient for the user entering the data, but it's better for the server as well. By the time data is transferred to the server for processing, you can be assured that the data has been qualified in a proper state for submission.

> **NOTE**
>
> The server should always check the information it gets to make sure it fits the correct criteria, even if the client can validate the data first for speed. If you leave off server-side validation completely, you could open up your application to receiving errors and corrupting your data.

Another common use of JavaScript is to liven up XHTML forms. Part of this task might include validating data, but it can also include additional features that are unavailable with straight XHTML, such as providing information to the user on the status bar, opening a second browser window for help information, and so on.

State Maintenance

In the stateless environment of the Web, you can use JavaScript to help maintain state in exchanges between the client and the server. The main use of state maintenance is with cookies (information stored by the browser on the client). JavaScript provides a means for you to store and retrieve cookies on the client. See Chapter 25, "Personalization and Dynamic Pages," for more information on working with cookies in JavaScript.

Server-Side Applications

As we mentioned earlier, client-side JavaScript, although the focus of this book, is not the only place where JavaScript has been implemented. It has also been implemented on the server side in both previous versions of Netscape and iPlanet's Enterprise Server, as well as within Microsoft ASP (and most recently ASP.NET). There are obviously many uses of ASP, but we have included a couple of examples here to show how you might extend your JavaScript programming after completing this book.

> **NOTE**
>
> Because server-side JavaScript is no longer supported within the Netscape/iPlanet line of servers (now called the Sun ONE Web Server), we will focus only on the JScript .NET implementation used by Microsoft within its ASP.NET.

Processing Comments and Feedback

Have a form on your site that collects customer or user feedback or comments? Well, you can use JScript .NET to not only construct the form you want to present to the user, but also to process it. This could be to simply take the information and forward it in an email to an address of your choice, or it could be to start the data in a database. Your imagination is the only limitation of what could be accomplished.

Web Services

As a defined part of the new .NET initiative, JScript can be used to develop .NET Web Services. Web Services, which we will cover in Chapter 27, is based on XML and three other standards as a means to encapsulate, access, and use computing functionality across the Web. For those of you familiar with DCOM (Distributed Component Object Model) or Common Object Request Broker Architecture (CORBA), Web Services is essentially a Web-based version of these technologies. Again, this is covered in Chapter 27, so we will save the detailed explanations until that time.

Browser Support for JavaScript

Compared to other applications, browsers are relatively simple pieces of software, but they are evolving into more powerful applications as Web technology matures. A browser is your window into the Web; no matter what JavaScript's potential is, it does no good if a browser doesn't support it. This section examines the browsers available today and their support for JavaScript.

Because JavaScript is an interpreted language and is embedded in XHTML documents, it's entirely dependent on the browser software to work. If you use an old browser, which is unlikely in today's world, it won't know what to do with the code and will ignore it.

Netscape and Mozilla-Based Browsers

During the mid-1990s, Netscape became perhaps the single most important player in the Web industry. Not only was it the first to market many important technological breakthroughs, but it also teamed up with other industry leaders—such as Sun—to push the technology envelope on many fronts on the Web.

Obviously, because Netscape developed JavaScript, you would expect its phenomenally successful Navigator browser to support the scripting language. Navigator 2.0 was the first browser to support JavaScript. Later versions provide important enhancements to the language itself. Now that Navigator has been turned over to Mozilla.org, an Open Source initiative started by Netscape, developers around the world continue to make it a successful implementation. Figure 1.1 shows Netscape 7.0, based on Mozilla 1.0, displaying the Netscape.com home page.

FIGURE 1.1   Netscape 7.0.

Microsoft Internet Explorer

Microsoft Internet Explorer 3.0 was the first non-Netscape browser to support JavaScript through its own implementation (JScript), but older versions do not support JavaScript. With the release of Internet Explorer 4, Microsoft really started pushing hard on the standards, and we have seen this progress through 5.0 and the most recent 6.0 version.

Opera

At the time this chapter is being written, there is only one other major browser that provides support for JavaScript that is not based on Mozilla.org's Gecko rendering engine. This last browser is Opera, which is developed by Opera Software and is the most popular non-Microsoft and non-Netscape/Mozilla browser available today.

Version Support in Browsers

At this point you are probably a bit confused with the version numbers associated with JavaScript and JScript as well as the version numbers associated with Netscape and Microsoft browsers. Table 1.2 matches browser versions to language versions.

TABLE 1.2 Language Version Versus Browser Version

Browser	Version	Language
Netscape	2.0	JavaScript 1.0
	3.0	JavaScript 1.1
	4.0–4.05	JavaScript 1.2
	4.06–4.7x	JavaScript 1.3
	6.0–7.0	JavaScript 1.4 & 1.5
Internet Explorer	3.0	JScript 1.0
	4.0–4.5	JScript 3.0
	5.0	JScript 5.0
	5.5	JScript 5.5
	6.0	JScript 5.6

From this chart you can see why it is so important to know what browsers your customers will be using to view your Web pages. By deciding up front what browsers your Web pages will support, you can save a lot of development time. On the other hand, if there is some particular JavaScript functionality that you really want to use in your Web pages, you will need to choose your browser support based on the JavaScript version that supports the desired functionality or use a detection technique.

Resources on the Web

At this point, we have covered a lot of ground in terms of explaining what JavaScript is, how it can be used, and what supports it. To conclude this broad coverage, which will lay the foundation for the depth in subsequent chapters, we have included a list of JavaScript resources in Table 1.3 to help keep you on track as you move through the book.

TABLE 1.3 JavaScript Resources

Site	URL	Description
DevEdge	`developer.netscape.com`	Netscape's central Web site for all of its technologies.
Mozilla.org	`www.mozilla.org/js`	Open source project that builds the Gecko rendering engine, which contains the JavaScript implementation found in Netscape 6+ browsers.
Venkman Debugger	`www.mozilla.org/projects/venkman`	Another Mozilla.org project that has now brought a very nice JavaScript debugger to the market.
Microsoft Scripting	`msdn.microsoft.com/scripting`	Microsoft's main Web site for JScript.
Irt.org	`tech.irt.org/articles/script.htm`	Contains a collection of high-quality articles on all kinds of topics, including JavaScript.

TABLE 1.3   Continued

Site	URL	Description
Focus on JavaScript	`javascript.about.com`	Weekly articles on JavaScript, as well as links to the most current information on other sites.
SuperScripter	`http://builder.cnet.com/webbuilding/pages/Programming/Scripter`	Old, but very useful, archive articles and examples of JavaScript.
JavaScripts.com	`webdeveloper.earthweb.com/webjs/`	Contains thousands of cut-and-paste JavaScript code examples for you to use in your own Web pages.
JavaScript Source	`javascript.internet.com`	Library of high-quality scripts.
JavaScript Kit	`www.wsabstract.com`	Large directory of free JavaScript code and JavaScript tutorials.

Summary

This chapter introduced you to JavaScript and looked at Web application development. As you learned in this chapter, JavaScript serves many important functions within this framework, and it has become a standard in the Web development marketplace. Because Netscape/Mozilla, Microsoft, and Opera browsers own the lion's share of the marketplace, JavaScript support is very dependable when considering it as a tool for development. Now that we have covered this foundation, we can begin the next chapter with a look at the details of JavaScript tools, the development process, and how it interacts with XHTML.

CHAPTER **2**

Assembling Your JavaScript Toolkit

Like any development language, JavaScript often best serves developers when a development environment is used. Java sports a variety of Integrated Development Environments (IDEs), but JavaScript doesn't have any IDEs available specifically for it, although several are available that do provide for the easy editing of code and some basic JavaScript scripting support. Nonetheless, with the plethora of Web tools available, you can create a toolkit that works for you.

In this chapter, we examine the various tools that you can add to your toolkit for JavaScript development. We also introduce you to how to place JavaScript within an XHTML document and how a browser then interprets and executes the code.

An Overview of Necessary Tools

To be productive as a developer, you need to assemble a group of tools that you are comfortable with. If you're developing applications in Forte, Visual Studio .NET, or VisualAge for Java, for example, your toolkit probably is relatively small, because these visual tools contain nearly everything you need out of the box. The same definitely can't be said of JavaScript. As a result, you need to work with the following principal tools to build a development environment:

- A JavaScript editor for writing scripts

- An XHTML editor for XHTML page development

- A Web browser for testing your JavaScript scripts and applications

- A script debugger for helping find errors in your scripts

The purpose of this section is to introduce you to a few tools, but it is not meant to provide details on how these tools should be used. We really want to keep the book focused on the JavaScript language itself, and although JavaScript-specific editors and development environments are important, they are not necessary. Let's dig in and see what we can learn.

JavaScript Editors

Choosing an editor is often a very personal choice for a software developer, much like choosing a bat for a baseball player. Although no one can really recommend what's best for you, we'll offer some information to assist in your selection process by outlining three tool options for writing JavaScript code: text editors, XHTML editors, and JavaScript-specific editors.

Text Editors

Because JavaScript code is contained within XHTML documents, all that is really needed in order to develop with JavaScript is a simple text editor. In Windows, we recommend Windows Notepad or TextPad (`http://www.textpad.com`), shown in Figure 2.1. In UNIX-based environments, such as Linux or MacOS X, you most likely will want to use emacs or vi. You can also use TextEdit or BBEdit for MacOS X. For MacOS 9 and lower, SimpleText is a good choice, and there is also a version of BBEdit for these older systems.

The advantage of using an ordinary text editor like Notepad is that you probably already have the software installed on your computer. However, the disadvantage is that it offers few or no features to facilitate learning the JavaScript language or to enhance your productivity (for example, code libraries or wizards).

As you consider the various options, look at what features are available in the editor before you decide. For example, in TextPad you will find search-and-replace commands, especially those that perform regular expression pattern matching, critical when you start doing any serious JavaScript programming. You should also lean toward using one that color-codes your scripts. This makes it easy to see what is code, XHTML, and comments. These features alone make TextPad a much more attractive option than Notepad, for instance.

The more advanced text-based editors, TextPad and BBEdit, let you develop other code in their environments as well. This allows you to use the same tool to create your XHTML code, JavaScript scripts, or even Java code. Additionally, third-party XHTML editors such as Macromedia HomeSite and Dreamweaver are providing support for JavaScript development.

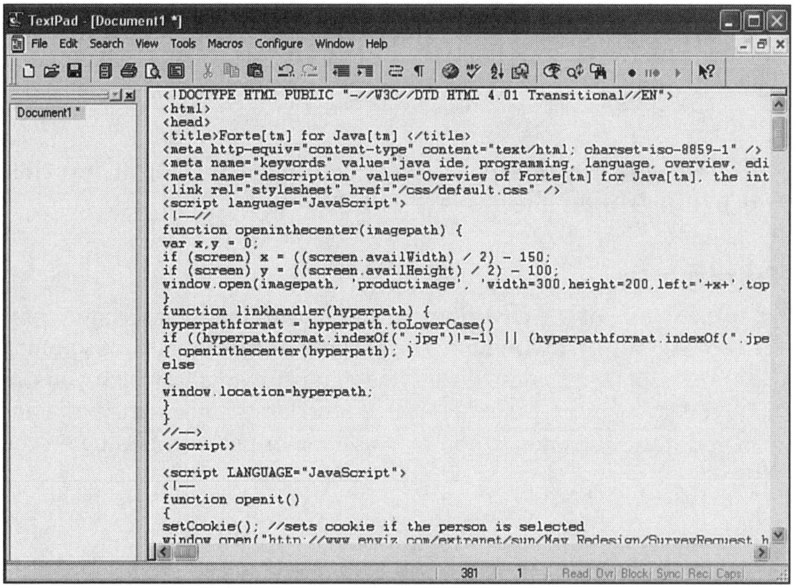

FIGURE 2.1   You can use TextPad as a JavaScript editor.

A single environment eliminates the need to deal with multiple software packages, thereby reducing the number of applications you have to learn. Some of these editors also let you integrate with a Web browser for quick viewing or testing of your pages and scripts.

JavaScript Development Environments

In addition to text editors, there are a few editors specifically devoted to JavaScript script development. ScriptBuilder, originally developed by NetObjects, was one of the first visual editors on the market for JavaScript developers. Since the release of this product, other products have come to the market to allow for easier JavaScript development.

Macromedia's Dreamweaver, for instance, has some of the following features:

- Drag-and-drop text editing
- Drag-and-drop XHTML tags
- Drag-and-drop JavaScript object methods and properties
- Syntax highlighting for JavaScript keywords and XHTML tags
- Search-and-replace functionality
- Integration support for multiple browsers

> **NOTE**
>
> A trial version of Dreamweaver can be downloaded from the Macromedia Web site at `http://www.macromedia.com`.

These tools are not necessarily intended as replacements for an XHTML text editor, but rather to work in concert with one.

XHTML Editors

Lest you forget the nature of the environment you're working in, a second tool you need to add to the toolkit is an XHTML editor. The purpose of this tool is not so much to develop JavaScript scripts but to design the XHTML documents to which you can later add your JavaScript code. The two types of XHTML editors on the market are text and visual. Depending on your tastes and needs, you may use one or both depending on the task at hand.

Text-Based Editors

As discussed earlier in this chapter, text-based editors provide an environment that lets you work with XHTML elements. A text-based editor doesn't try to hide the messy details of these elements. Instead, it provides features supporting XHTML development that make it more productive than a plain text editor.

Visual XHTML Editors

A second type of editor is one that hides the hypertext formatting language from the page creator by providing a visual (or WYSIWYG—What You See Is What You Get) environment that generates code behind the scenes. Therefore, page creation is performed in a point-and-click environment, as you would expect in this graphically based computer world.

> **NOTE**
>
> Because XHTML is new, it is worth mentioning that visual editors may not format the code in the proper XHTML syntax. If this is of concern for you, be sure to read about the specific features of the application before you make a choice about what IDE to use.

Netscape has a visual XHTML editor component called Composer, which is based on the open source Mozilla browser. Composer lets you easily edit XHTML documents within an integrated browser environment, as shown in Figure 2.2. Although Composer's visual environment lets you work with basic XHTML page layout, it doesn't provide sufficient power to work visually with multiframe windows and some other features of XHTML.

> **NOTE**
>
> Check the Mozilla.org home page at `http://www.mozilla.org` for the latest build of the Mozilla browser and Composer.

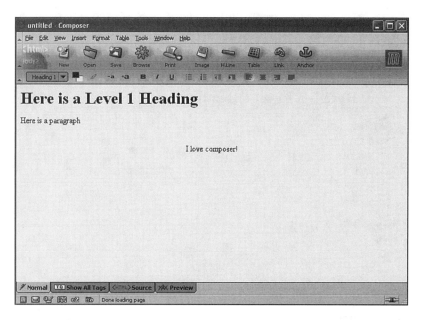

FIGURE 2.2   Mozilla's Composer component.

Microsoft FrontPage, shown in Figure 2.3, is a more sophisticated option. It includes one of the best visual XHTML editors available. Not only does the FrontPage Editor support enhanced options such as framesets and tables, but it also includes an expanded set of templates to speed up the process of developing a Web page.

FrontPage is more than just an editor, however. It lets you build and administer an entire Web site by working closely with Microsoft's Internet Information Server (IIS).

> **NOTE**
>
> Check the Microsoft home page at `http://www.microsoft.com` for the latest information on FrontPage.

A current disadvantage of some visual editors is their inability to let you go into a text-based mode and edit raw XHTML. For the current release of Composer, luckily, you do not need an external editor to do this. Additionally, Composer hardly knows what to do with JavaScript code, so don't even think of using it as your JavaScript editing environment.

Nonetheless, using an XHTML editor will allow you to quickly develop the XHTML documents around your scripts. When you have the XHTML created, you can use a text or JavaScript editor to add to your scripts.

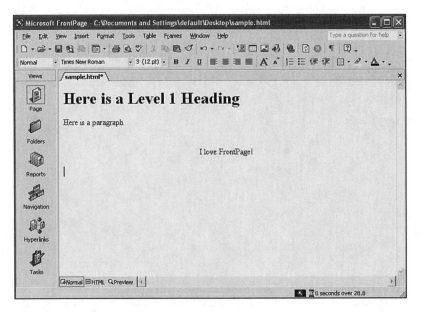

FIGURE 2.3   Microsoft's FrontPage.

Web Browsers

Another component you need is a Web browser that supports JavaScript. Chapter 1, "Introducing JavaScript," discussed the various browsers and their support for JavaScript, so we won't dive into that discussion here. However, because various versions of browsers provide different levels of JavaScript language support, you probably need to have many of these available during your testing phase.

The basic rule of thumb is to test your script using as many of the browsers accessing your pages as possible, within reason. For intranet applications, you might have only a single browser to test. However, for public Internet applications, you need to consider that many types of browsers might access your JavaScript-enabled site.

The best way to tell what browsers are hitting your site is to analyze your Web logs. All browsers send a user-agent string you can use to determine the browsers and operating systems of your users. You should find that they all fall into the following categories:

- Current JavaScript browsers: Netscape 6.0+, Mozilla 1.0 (and other agents built on top of the Gecko rendering engine), and Microsoft Internet Explorer 4.0+

- Early JavaScript browsers: Netscape Navigator 2.0, 3.0, and 4.0 and Internet Explorer 3.0

- Other JavaScript-enabled browsers: HotJava 3+ and Opera 3+

- Browsers that do not support JavaScript

Your JavaScript application doesn't necessarily have to support all browsers. For example, you might need to use a JavaScript feature that was added in the latest version of Netscape, so you require at least that version of the browser to view your pages. However, having previous versions available for testing can be invaluable to providing the best application environment possible.

Script Debuggers

The last tool that you should have as part of your toolkit is a debugger. Currently, the two main debuggers are from Mozilla and Microsoft. You will more than likely want to download both of these so that you can debug scripts in both Mozilla-based browsers, such as Netscape 7, and Internet Explorer browsers. Chapter 31, "Debugging," covers both of these applications, so we will not discuss them here.

The JavaScript Development Process

When you have your toolkit elements, you need to assemble them into a workable development environment. Before you perform this process, it's helpful to understand how the JavaScript application development process is often structured. Figure 2.4 shows a typical scenario, in which basic XHTML document creation is followed by the addition of JavaScript code to the document. The page is then tested iteratively in the Web browser of choice.

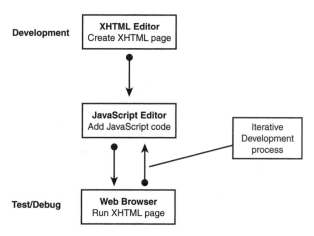

FIGURE 2.4   The JavaScript development process.

The development process itself is broken into several key areas that involve knowing XHTML, how scripts are embedded, the attributes available to the <script> element (where JavaScript code is contained), and viewing JavaScript code. Over the next few pages we are going to go over these in more detail to ensure that you fully understand the concepts.

What Is All This XHTML?

XHTML gives you the capability to create remarkable static Web pages. Although these documents can be creative, interesting, and by all means useful, JavaScript enables you to make these static pages interactive and more responsive to user actions and input. Extending your documents with JavaScript gives your page more power and gives your XHTML more flexibility. But where did this all start?

Well, it all began with HTML—the predecessor to XHTML. It was within HTML documents that JavaScript was first included and browsers first interpreted the code. With the advent of XML, the desire to rewrite HTML as an XML-based language increased. Doing so would allow XML parsers and applications to properly process and validate the markup we have all come to know and love. The end result: XHTML.

Standards of XHTML are changing constantly. The current Recommendation (*aka* standard) is for XHTML 1.1; however, the next generation of XHTML is already being thought up. As we mentioned, XHTML is HTML as an application of XML. Those who follow XML will find that XHTML also allows you to include other dialects (such as MathML) in documents. Details aside, these technologies are evolving with new elements as well as new and refined attributes for elements.

To read more on XHTML, you can visit the W3C at `http://www.w3.org/MarkUp`.

By keeping up-to-date on the latest releases of the popular browsers, an XHTML developer can keep abreast of enhancements and implement them as they become available to the general public. Luckily, for the most part, enhancements included in XHTML and the newest browser releases aren't problematic when displayed in older browsers. However, you should always test your document in older browsers to ensure that the new elements don't have a negative effect on older browsers.

Embedding JavaScript in Your XHTML Documents

JavaScript scripts are integrated into an XHTML document using the `<script>` element. An XHTML document can contain multiple `<script>` elements, and each pair may enclose more than one set of JavaScript statements. The `type` attribute of this element is used to specify the scripting language in which the script is written, and the `src` attribute is used to specify the filename of external source JavaScript files.

To better understand how the `<script>` element works, take a quick look at the various attributes associated with it, in Table 2.1.

TABLE 2.1 Attributes of the `<script>` Tag

Attribute	Description
defer	A `Boolean` attribute whose presence results in a *true*, which is used to tell the browser if the script in this section generates any content. If the attribute is not present, it is *false*.
language	Deprecated attribute that was used to specify the language and version being used inside the tags.

TABLE 2.1 Continued

Attribute	Description
src	Attribute that specifies the URL location of an external source JavaScript file. If this attribute is set, any code present in the body of the element is ignored.
type	Attribute that is being used inside the tags.

The `defer` attribute is a simple attribute that tells the browser if the code between the beginning and ending `<script>` tags generates any content—in other words, whether the `document.write()` method is used.

The `language` attribute, which has been deprecated in the most recent release of HTML and XHTML, was used to specify the language name and version JavaScript included in the `<script>` element. The format of this attribute's value was as follows:

```
<script language="JavaScript">
```

This tells the script to run in JavaScript 1.0–compliant browsers. For other JavaScript versions, such as 1.1, you would use the following:

```
<script language="JavaScript1.1">
```

Table 2.2 shows the values you should use with the `language` attribute. It also points out which browsers will interpret which values.

TABLE 2.2 Current Values of the language Attribute

Language Value	Description
JavaScript	Represents JavaScript 1.0 and is interpreted by Navigator 2+ and Internet Explorer 3+ browsers.
JavaScript1.1	Represents JavaScript 1.1 and is interpreted by Navigator 3+ and Internet Explorer 4+ browsers.
JavaScript1.2	Represents JavaScript 1.2 and is interpreted by Navigator 4+ and Internet Explorer 4+ browsers. Specifying 1.2 or higher rather than 1.1 changes how Navigator handles some of its equality operators.
JavaScript1.3	Represents JavaScript 1.3 and is interpreted by Navigator 4.06+ and Internet Explorer 5+ browsers.
JavaScript1.4	Represents JavaScript 1.4 and is interpreted by HotJava 3+ and Mozilla-based browsers.
JavaScript1.5	Represents JavaScript 1.5 and is interpreted by the Mozilla (M12+) and Netscape 6.0+.

TIP

If the `language` attribute isn't defined, browsers will assume JavaScript 1.0. Additionally, some Opera browser releases ignore this attribute altogether because of its deprecation.

By using this attribute, you can define multiple sets of JavaScript functions. Browsers that support JavaScript 1.1 can take advantage of newer functions, which are hidden from older versions of browsers. The simplest method to take advantage of these options is shown in Listing 2.1.

LISTING 2.1   Using Multiple Versions of JavaScript with the language Attribute

```
<?xml version="1.0" encoding="UTF-8"?>
<!DOCTYPE html
     PUBLIC "-//W3C//DTD XHTML 1.0 Transitional//EN"
    "DTD/xhtml1-transitional.dtd">
<html xmlns="http://www.w3.org/1999/xhtml" xml:lang="en" lang="en">
<head>
  <title>JavaScript version test page</title>
</head>
<body>
<script language="JavaScript" type="text/javascript">
  //Only JavaScript 1.0 browsers read in this section
  document.write('This browser supports JavaScript 1.0<br />');
</script>

<script language="JavaScript1.1" type="text/javascript">
  //Only JavaScript 1.1 browsers read in this section
  document.write('This browser supports JavaScript 1.1<br />');
</script>
<script language="JavaScript1.2" type="text/javascript">
  //Only JavaScript 1.2 browsers read in this section
  document.write('This browser supports JavaScript 1.2<br />');
</script>
<script language="JavaScript1.3" type="text/javascript">
  //Only JavaScript 1.3 browsers read in this section
  document.write('This browser supports JavaScript 1.3<br />');
</script>
<script language="JavaScript1.4" type="text/javascript">
  //Only JavaScript 1.4 browsers read in this section
  document.write('This browser supports JavaScript 1.4<br />');
</script>
<script language="JavaScript1.5" type="text/javascript">
  //Only JavaScript 1.5 browsers read in this section
  document.write('This browser supports JavaScript 1.5<br />');
</script>
</body>
</html>
```

One thing worth noting is that you have two options when integrating JavaScript statements into your document. The method that you choose depends on your requirements when viewing and modifying code. The first option lets you view all your codes simultaneously and involves writing JavaScript statements directly into your document. All your statements are embedded within the <script> element—these are *inline* scripts.

The other option, available only in JavaScript 1.1 and higher, is to include your JavaScript code in an external .js library file. That allows you to call the file from within your document using the src attribute of a single-line <script> element.

Here is the first option for embedding JavaScript in your HTML:

```
<script type="text/javascript">
  function options() {
    document.write("embedding the code");
  }
</script>
```

Here is the second option, including the script in external files:

```
<script src="/jscripts/myscript.js" type="text/javascript"></script>
```

In the second option, you will create a file called myscript.js, which will have one line of code:

```
document.write("calling from a separate file")
```

Best Practices Using External Libraries

Using this methodology, you can modify your JavaScript code without ever opening and risking unwanted changes to your pages. Thus, your code is more modular and portable for use with other documents. Using this option, you may want to include an attribute to see if the .js file is incorrect or not available. Otherwise, the user might see incorrect page behavior and not know why.

A downside to this method is that you might have to modify two sets of code, depending on your JavaScript changes. For example, if you change the name of a function in your JavaScript code, you will also have to remember to change the name in the function call in the XHTML document. Another downside is that external JavaScript files can't contain XHTML elements; they can contain only valid JavaScript-specific statements.

Finally, if you plan on having valid XHTML documents and if your script uses < or & or]]> or --, you must use external scripts. An XML parser will complain if you have these characters present within the document. Additionally, commenting your code out ("hiding") using XHTML comments (<!-- comment -->) will not work either.

> **NOTE**
>
> We want to show you examples of using JavaScript within the body of an XHTML document. However, having valid XHTML documents often means that the code has to be in an external library, so all of our examples may not technically be valid XHTML documents. To turn these into valid XHTML documents, you would simply need to divide the code accordingly between inline and external instances.

Those of you who have written code in JavaScript before may be saying, "What the heck is the `type` attribute? I thought the attribute I was supposed to use was `language`." Well, you are partially correct.

The `language` attribute was the original attribute used not only to define the language, such as `javascript` or `vbscript`, but also the version, as in `javascript1.1` or `javascript1.5`. If you read through the current HTML or XHTML Recommendation, you will find that the `language` attribute has been deprecated in favor of the `type` attribute. The value of this new attribute closely resembles the content type of an external source JavaScript (`.js`) file. So for JavaScript you would use `type="text/javascript"`, and for VBScript you would use `type="text/vbscript"`. Here is how it works.

The HTML 4.01 Recommendation, on which XHTML 1.0 was based, says that you should put a `<meta>` tag in the `<head>` portion of your documents that specifies the default language used in all your scripts. This looks like the following:

```
<meta http-equiv="Content-Script-Type" content="text/javascript">
```

If this setting is not present, the browser should check for a `Content-Script-Type` entry in the header of the HTTP request. The format for this would be

```
Content-Script-Type: text/javascript
```

Now that these are set, the `type` attribute is used to override the default setting. This makes it possible to have multiple scripting languages in the same document. For instance, you may set `Content-Script-Type` to `text/javascript`, but then set `type="text/vbscript"` in a specific instance of a `<script>` tag that uses VBScript as its language.

Obviously, only the newer browsers will even consider looking at this attribute, so you should take care in using it. Give it another couple of years, and all should be fine—the majority of the browsers out there will support this new method. Until then, however, we would recommend that you use both the `type` and `language` attributes in conjunction with the `<script>` tag.

Viewing JavaScript Code

Because you can write JavaScript code inline with your XHTML code, you can easily view and edit it. By now, you should be familiar with the Source menu option available in your browser, which allows you to view the source code of an XHTML document (it's usually under the View menu).

When you view the source of the document, you can also view the JavaScript code that is included in the document, as shown in Figure 2.5. (This is obviously not the case when your JavaScript statements are called from the .js file instead of written into the document. All you will see is the call to the .js file in the <script> tag.) JavaScript doesn't need a special viewer and, because it is just interpreted code and not compiled, it appears in your document source by default.

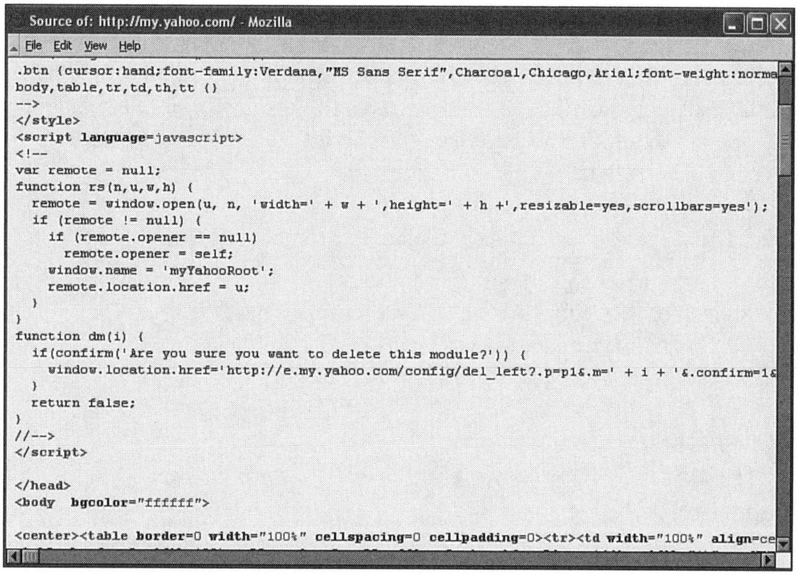

FIGURE 2.5 Viewing JavaScript code.

Creating JavaScript Code

The basics behind creating JavaScript code are simple. Create your basic XHTML page or edit an existing one, and then insert your <script> tags in the <head> or <body> section of the document. Functions and other items that should apply to the entire page are best kept in the <head> of the document. If you need to generate text for the page using JavaScript, this is done or at least called within the <body>.

Executing Scripts

JavaScript execution begins at different times, depending on how it is written. If the script affects the content on the page, such as with the use of the document.write() method for example, the script is executed as it is encountered, assuming it is not within a function.

There is also an event handler, onLoad, that can be used to handle the load event immediately after the document has completely loaded into the browser. If your JavaScript scripts are stored in a separate file, they are also evaluated when the page loads and before any script actions take place.

All JavaScript statements that are contained within a function block are interpreted, and execution does not occur until the function is called from a JavaScript event. JavaScript statements not within a function block are executed as the document loads and while it is being rendered. The execution result of the latter will be apparent to users when they first view the page.

Loading a Page

JavaScript statements that require immediate processing are executed as the page is loaded but before it is displayed. Listing 2.2 demonstrates the display of an alert dialog box as the document is opened. No function is called—JavaScript statements are simply processed in order as the page has loaded.

LISTING 2.2   Calling to Display the Alert Dialog Box Directly

```
<?xml version="1.0" encoding="UTF-8"?>
<!DOCTYPE html PUBLIC "-//W3C//DTD XHTML 1.0 Transitional//EN"
                "DTD/xhtml1-transitional.dtd">
<html xmlns="http://www.w3.org/1999/xhtml" xml:lang="en" lang="en">
<head>
  <title>Dialog Test</title>
  <script type="text/javascript">
    alert("Dialog called");
  </script>
</head>
<body>
  <p>
    Test page of default JavaScript call
  </p>
</body>
</html>
```

The onLoad event handler is an exception to the rule. In this case, the onLoad handler is called not by a user-triggered event but by the event of the document itself loading into the browser. In this instance, the alert dialog box will again appear immediately upon the loading of the page, as shown in Figure 2.6, even though it isn't called directly. Listing 2.3 demonstrates a function named opendoc(), initiated by the onload event. You will have the same end result in both of these listings (2.2 and 2.3), but it is achieved through two scripting methods.

LISTING 2.3 Calling to Display the Alert Dialog onLoad

```
<?xml version="1.0" encoding="UTF-8"?>
<!DOCTYPE html PUBLIC "-//W3C//DTD XHTML 1.0 Transitional //EN"
            "DTD/xhtml1-transitional.dtd">
<html xmlns="http://www.w3.org/1999/xhtml" xml:lang="en" lang="en">
<head>
  <title>Dialog from onLoad</title>
  <script type="text/javascript">
    function opendoc(){
      alert("Dialog called ")
    }
  </script>
</head>
<body onload="opendoc()">
  <p>
    Test page of onLoad JavaScript call
  </p>
</body>
</html>
```

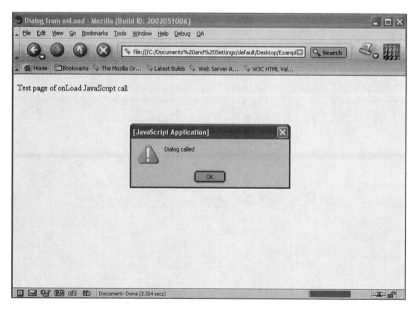

FIGURE 2.6 The alert dialog box in Mozilla called directly from JavaScript.

User Action

The second process by which JavaScript statements can be executed is through function calls. Any statement contained within a function won't be executed until something calls the function. These calls can be triggered in numerous ways, including user action and explicit calls from within the script itself. You can even have events that fire based on set time intervals.

It is worth noting that user actions on your document might trigger events in many instances when you (or the user) are unaware they could happen. Because of this, be sure to fully test your statements to ensure that the user interaction with your page doesn't cause unnecessary or unwanted events to occur.

Chapter 18, "Handling Events," provides a more detailed explanation of JavaScript events and how they're implemented and can be incorporated into your XHTML documents.

As an example, in Listing 2.4 a dialog appears when the pushbutton is clicked.

> **NOTE**
>
> Because XHTML requires the presence of the action attribute of the `<form>` element, we have inserted a value even though it is not used in any of the examples within this chapter. For now, just know it is a placeholder for forms that truly do pass data back to the server. Also, you will find additional information on forms in Chapter 12, "Form Objects."

LISTING 2.4   Calling a Function to Display the Alert Dialog Box

```
<?xml version="1.0" encoding="UTF-8"?>
<!DOCTYPE html PUBLIC "-//W3C//DTD XHTML 1.0 Strict//EN"
              "DTD/xhtml1-strict.dtd">
<html xmlns="http://www.w3.org/1999/xhtml" xml:lang="en" lang="en">
<head>
  <title>Dialog from function call</title>
  <script type="text/javascript">
    function opendoc(){
      alert("Dialog called by Push Button");
    }
  </script>
</head>
<body>
  <p>
    Test page of function called from Push Button
  </p>
  <form action="null">
    <p>
```

LISTING 2.4   Continued

```
      <input type="button" name="BUTTON1" value="PUSH" onclick="opendoc()" />
    </p>
  </form>
</body>
</html>
```

Figure 2.7 shows the results of the function call.

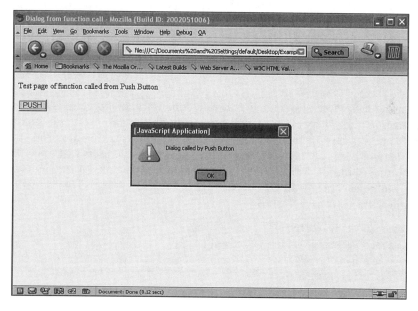

FIGURE 2.7   The alert dialog in Mozilla called from the submit event.

User actions or explicit event calls are the more frequent methods by which JavaScript is executed. One key advantage of JavaScript is that it can increase the amount of user interaction with your document by providing you with a way to process and evaluate user input in a timely manner.

Accommodating Unsupported User Agents

The quick pace of changes in XHTML and JavaScript makes it necessary to be wary of user agents that don't support the documents you're creating. Not all user agents will be current with the newest enhancements, and you, as the programmer, must make your documents as user-friendly as possible for all user agents and environments.

> **NOTE**
>
> The term **user agent** refers to any application that acts as a client to process XHTML documents. In most cases, and generally throughout this book, this refers to browsers. However, with the advancement of wireless devices and Internet-capable phones, pagers, and PDAs, the term user agent has taken on a broader meaning. We are going to use the term user agent in this section of the book because we are specifically talking about applications that do not support JavaScript.

> **TIP**
>
> Testing your XHTML and JavaScript in as many browser environments as possible will give your documents better stability and usability. You should also consider using the various validation services and applications available. For instance, the W3C has validators for HTML, XHTML, CSS, and other standards they have developed and support. You can use these free services by following the appropriate links at http://www.w3.org.

Although using JavaScript allows you to provide enhancements to your users, you must always remember that many older browsers might not be able to make full use of the JavaScript code you have written. By surrounding all statements that are inside the <script> element with XHTML comment tags, you will enable users with older browsers to view your page but not display the JavaScript code. They won't get the full effect of your page, but at least they won't see unwanted text in the browser. The format for using these comments is as follows:

```
<script type="text/javascript">
  <!-- hide your code from older browsers
    // code goes here
  // stop JavaScript code hiding -->
</script>
```

Listing 2.5 shows how to hide JavaScript code from older browsers. You should take the time to notice the use of the beginning and ending XHTML comment identifiers in Listing 2.5 and how they enclose the lines of JavaScript code.

LISTING 2.5   Hiding Scripts from Older Browsers

```
<?xml version="1.0" encoding="UTF-8"?>
<!DOCTYPE html PUBLIC "-//W3C//DTD XHTML 1.0 Transitional//EN"
             "DTD/xhtml1-transitional.dtd">
<html xmlns="http://www.w3.org/1999/xhtml" xml:lang="en" lang="en">
<head>
  <title>Hide From Browser</title>
</head>
```

LISTING 2.5   Continued

```
<body>
<p>
  <script type="text/javascript">
  <!-- Hide
    document.write("I can view JavaScript code")
  // End hide -->
  </script>
  Content goes here.
</p>
</body>
</html>
```

The use of the JavaScript comment tag, //, in the ending XHTML comment keeps JavaScript from interpreting this statement as code during processing. Without these comment markers, some JavaScript implementations will attempt to process the line, and you will receive a JavaScript error upon evaluation.

Writing the Code

As with any other programming language, JavaScript statements can be implemented using various methods and approaches. We have found the practice of defining JavaScript functions in the <head> section and then calling these functions within the <body> is the best way to take advantage of the object-based JavaScript language. And it certainly paves the way for a more object-oriented approach, which appears to be the direction of JavaScript in the future 2.0 version.

The JavaScript language itself isn't difficult and, for developers with an object-based or object-oriented background, the hurdles are few. When you grasp the concepts of object-based development, the creation of JavaScript functions becomes fairly straightforward. Note the following example:

```
document.write("I can view JavaScript code");
```

In plain English, the document.write() method statement says, "On my document, write the following text." Easy enough, right? Well, easy or not, there are a few items that you want to keep in mind. For instance, when beginning to write your code, remember the following principles:

- Code reuse

- Readability

- Ease of modification

As we have mentioned, you can use the `<script>` element in either the `<body>` of a document. Placing the element in the `<head>` ensures that all statements will be evaluated (and executed, if necessary) before the user interacts with the document. The hazards of putting the element in the `<body>` of the document are varied.

For instance, depending on the various elements and the order of the document, you can never know if the user will interact with the script before the page is loaded or will interact with the page before the script has fully loaded and is ready to respond. If either of these situations occurs, problems could occur. (After all your effort, who wants that?)

The practice of defining your JavaScript functions and then calling them from the `<body>` will ensure that all the functions are evaluated before the user can begin interacting with the page. Listing 2.6 shows an example of this practice, and Listing 2.7 shows the alternative.

LISTING 2.6   Calling from a Function

```
<?xml version="1.0" encoding="UTF-8"?>
<!DOCTYPE html PUBLIC "-//W3C//DTD XHTML 1.0 Transitional//EN"
                "DTD/xhtml1-transitional.dtd">
<html xmlns="http://www.w3.org/1999/xhtml" xml:lang="en" lang="en">
<head>
  <title>Page with Pushbutton</title>
  <script type="text/javascript">
  <!--
    function pushbutton(){
      alert("pushed");
    }
  // -->
  </script>
</head>
<body>
  <form action="null">
    <p>
      <input type="button" name="mybutton" value="PUSH" onclick="pushbutton()" />
    </p>
  </form>
</body>
</html>
```

LISTING 2.7   Putting Script Directly in the onclick Event Handler

```
<?xml version="1.0" encoding="UTF-8"?>
<!DOCTYPE html PUBLIC "-//W3C//DTD XHTML 1.0 Transitional//EN"
                "DTD/xhtml1-transitional.dtd">
<html xmlns="http://www.w3.org/1999/xhtml" xml:lang="en" lang="en">
<head>
  <title>Page with Pushbutton</title>
</head>
<body>
  <form action="null">
    <p>
      <input type="button" name="mybutton" value="PUSH"
             onclick="alert('pushed')" />
    </p>
  </form>
</body>
</html>
```

Listing 2.7 demonstrates that it is possible to include JavaScript statements directly into your XHTML elements. To relate the drawbacks of this practice of code-writing we mentioned earlier, remember that modifying and reusing code in the body of documents is difficult. You must search for the element and then cut and paste in the code. Only then can it be reused or redefined in a function call.

You also increase the readability and ease of modification both for yourself and for subsequent developers when you place your JavaScript statements in functions in the <head> section. Endlessly searching for code that could have been easily segregated is tedious and unnecessary.

Programming styles are also important in JavaScript as they are in any programming language. Keeping your styles consistent, your variables defined, and your formatting neat will save future development time.

Creating your JavaScript scripts function by function, piece by piece, will help you build stable interactive documents that have the functionality you want. Because JavaScript is interpreted and not compiled, the debugging process is not always completely straightforward. Many problems or bugs won't be apparent until the document is rigorously tested. We recommend that someone other than the developer test the page to ensure that all situations are encountered when testing the document and integrated JavaScript. (You never know what checking a check box out of order might do to your script.)

Summary

This chapter examined the basic building blocks needed by a JavaScript programmer. We talked about everything from a JavaScript editor, an XHTML editor, a Web browser, to a script debugger.

Although JavaScript is a scripting language separate from XHTML, the two are very closely integrated when it comes to full-scale document design, development, and implementation. JavaScript can be written directly into XHTML documents, expanding its current capabilities.

The enhancements that are continuously arising in XHTML itself make it possible to add more functionality to your JavaScript code. By using these features, you can expand your documents to make them more interactive and user-friendly.

In the next chapter we are going to start getting into JavaScript seriously. Now that you have seen a few simple scripts, it's time to show you how to start writing your own.

CHAPTER **3**

Beginning the Process of Writing Scripts

Over the first two chapters we have taken a look at JavaScript and how it fits into the Internet picture. We have given you insight into what you can do with the language and how it works with XHTML, and have talked about browser support. We have approached the language from a coder's perspective by helping you understand the tools you will need to get started.

Now we are going to tackle the task of writing your first scripts, which is what excites us all. We are going to keep it simple for a specific purpose—to build a solid foundation on good programming practices. We will cover each step of creating this simple example in detail, so that we do not have to cover the longer examples in as much detail later in the book.

To do this, we are going to approach your first script the right way. By *the right way*, we mean that we are going to plan the script, implement it, and test it properly. While doing this, we will also remind you of some of the things you learned in the first two chapters.

Initial Decisions

First, remember that JavaScript is embedded into XHTML documents by using the `<script>` element. As the browser is loading the page, it begins interpreting the code, starting with the first line of the script and processing everything that follows until it reaches the end. This is true whether the code is inline or it is pulled from an external library (`.js`) file.

JavaScript interprets each line of code into instructions it then uses to perform specified tasks. It is the same as following directions to a party, for example. Just as you would read each instruction and act on it by turning or driving your car in the appropriate direction, JavaScript follows each of your instructions in order.

On your way to the party, you might need to stop at a red light, or you might need to pick up a friend. These types of *rules* you can also emulate with JavaScript. For instance, you may want the browser to sit idle until some kind of event, such as a mouse click, happens.

Before you even start writing your code, you do have to make some initial decisions. These decisions will help you better understand what you have to do and how to write your code. The following sections will step you through this process with the objective of helping you understand the questions you should be asking yourself that ultimately lead to the creation of successful code.

What Browsers Do You Want to Support?

The first question you need to ask is, "What browsers do you want or need to support?" This is a huge question because it will determine how much code you need to write. As we said previously, JavaScript has changed drastically over the first several versions of the language. So it is important to know what syntax is available to you when writing your scripts.

In fact, the language had a tendency to be all over the map until the ECMAScript standard was released. Because ECMAScript defines only the core portion of the language, however, it still leaves a lot of gray areas in client-side and server-side implementations. Because of this, you are going to spend a substantial amount of time trying to write scripts that work in all browsers. Hence the question, "What browsers do you want to support?"

In deciding what browsers you want to support, there are several factors that can help. They are as follows:

- Do you have server-side functionality to help you determine the browser before pages are returned to the browser?

- Do unsupported browsers need to fail gracefully?

Help from the Server Side

If you are able to determine the browser making the request, you have a major advantage when creating client-side JavaScript programs. This allows you to avoid potential client-side errors by not sending code that is not supported. This is especially key because many of today's popular browsers have different versions that support different standards.

True, it might mean that you need several versions of your scripts, but the amount of download time for the browser and the chance of error will be greatly reduced. You are no longer sending code to determine the requesting browser because the excess lines needed to perform "client sniffing" are no longer needed. Having this functionality also allows you to better handle known non-supporting browsers gracefully.

Failing Gracefully

The second question has to do with how gracefully you want to handle non-JavaScript browsers. This would include not only browsers that do not have JavaScript support, but also those that have it turned off.

> **CAUTION**
>
> If you have ever taken a look at the preferences of your browser, you will notice that you can turn off JavaScript. See Figure 3.1 for Mozilla 1.0's Preferences dialog box, where you can turn off JavaScript. This is important to keep in mind, because you will need to be able to handle instances with JavaScript turned off gracefully. To do so, simply treat these instances as browsers that do not support JavaScript at all.

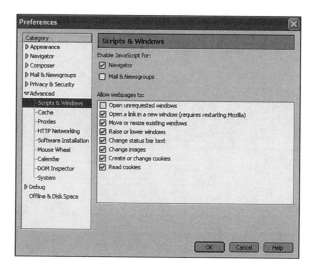

FIGURE 3.1   Turning off JavaScript in Mozilla 1.0.

When asking yourself this question, you need to understand your true objective. Are you building a site that you want all people to access and get the full experience? Maybe you are developing an intranet for a company, and your users will only have one browser. Or you may just be building a sample site to see what you can do with JavaScript.

By going through this exercise, you are determining the type of restrictions that need to be placed on your users. Be sure to make this decision carefully and with the full understanding that leaving out some people may mean leaving out a percentage of potential users. If you have made the decision not to support users who do not have JavaScript enabled, your task will be a bit easier—simply do not provide secondary XHTML for these users. Otherwise, you should try to provide them with as much functionality as possible with the intention of not compromising your content.

How Do You Want to Handle Non-JavaScript Browsers?

Up to this point, we have not talked about how to actually handle browsers that do not support JavaScript or have it turned off. If you have the ability, you can eliminate some of your worries by using the server-side functionality we spoke of earlier; however, this does not solve the problem of those browsers that have JavaScript turned off. But there is hope: the <noscript> element.

The <noscript> element allows you to specify additional XHTML to be displayed when JavaScript is turned off or not supported. This element and its included code usually go directly under any <script> sections you may have. Listing 3.1 shows how you can use this element, and Figure 3.2 shows how this is rendered in Mozilla with JavaScript turned off.

LISTING 3.1   Using the <noscript> Tag

```
<?xml version="1.0" encoding="UTF-8"?>
<!DOCTYPE html
      PUBLIC "-//W3C//DTD XHTML 1.0 Transitional//EN"
      "DTD/xhtml1-transitional.dtd">
<html xmlns="http://www.w3.org/1999/xhtml" xml:lang="en">
<head>
  <meta http-equiv="Content-Script-Type" content="text/javascript" />
  <title>My First JavaScript Script</title>
</head>
<body>
  <h1>What is returned?</h1>
  <p>
    <script type="text/javascript">
      document.write('JavaScript is turned on!');
    </script>
  </p>
  <noscript>
    <p>JavaScript is turned off!</p>
  </noscript>
</body>
</html>
```

If you look at Listing 3.1 and Figure 3.2, you will notice that the <noscript> section tells the user that JavaScript is turned off. If it were turned on, this same page would interpret the JavaScript code and ignore the <noscript> section, as shown in Figure 3.3. This is a great tag to help handle non-supporting browsers gracefully.

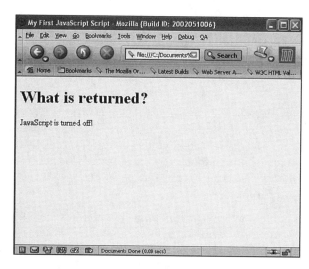

FIGURE 3.2　Rendering the <noscript> tag.

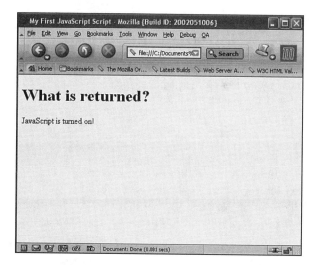

FIGURE 3.3　Listing 3.1 with JavaScript turned on.

CAUTION

Some of the older browsers, such as Navigator 2 and early versions of Internet Explorer, do not support the <noscript> tag. We have also seen problems with using this tag multiple times on a page with older browsers that support JavaScript, but have it turned off.

Inline or src It?

The final question you need to ask is, "How do you want to put it on the page?" The question is a determination of *where* you want to put all of your code. This can either be in external library files that have been included using the src attribute, or directly in the document itself.

As we mentioned before, by placing your code in an external file, you will be able to edit one file to affect scripts on all of your pages. Additionally, if your code contains the characters < or &, it will not properly validate if you are attempting to create valid XHTML documents. Although this is not a problem for most implementations today, the momentum XHTML has in the market, from a standards perspective, could easily make this a requirement in the near future.

We recommend that you put all of your functions in external source files, which solves these problems. We even recommend you split up functions into separate files according to their functionality. For instance, you might have one file called calculations.js that contains reusable calculations, but another file called formhandling.js that contains form handling functions.

> **NOTE**
>
> The src attribute was not supported until JavaScript 1.1, which means that Navigator 3+ and Internet Explorer 4+ support it fully. Additionally, Internet Explorer 3.02 did attempt to support this method of referencing external scripts, but we have had limited success in getting it to work. The good news is that these older browsers represent only some fraction of 1% of users, although we do feel it is important to point out this information.

What Are Your Objectives?

The process of defining objectives is among the most overlooked steps in starting a project. You would expect it to be the first and most thorough step, but often it is not completed successfully or fully. We have all seen many JavaScript programmers approach a script from what we call the *cool* angle rather than the *functional* angle.

JavaScript is definitely "cool," and if the cool factor is your main objective, go for it. However, if your main objective is to provide solid and useful functionality, try to avoid excess and unnecessary coding. In the long run, other programmers and even you will find it hard to follow your code if you have a lot of "cool" features that offer no real value. You will also find it difficult to implement changes and fixes, because you will have to program around your cool code.

When defining your objectives, you fully determine your objectives and ultimately the end result of your program. For instance, you may want it to perform error checking on forms. With this goal in mind, you should work backward to determine what will accomplish this goal. Using the form example, you should ask yourself how many elements are going to be in the form? How many are radio buttons, text fields, selection options, and so on that you want to be able to process?

After you have nailed down this second level of objectives, you can start figuring out how to code your scripts. You will want to write code that handles the radio buttons, text fields, and selection options. You may be able to create a function that will cover all the functionality you need and that simply works from a parameter passed in, such as "radio" to signify the handling of a radio button. Remember that code reuse is a good thing and that you should apply any coding experience you have to reducing the number of lines of code your scripts need.

Starting Your Script

By this time, you should be ready to start coding. You have decided what browsers you want to support, how you want to deal with non-supporting browsers, and where you want to store the scripts. This takes care of all of the technical aspects of writing JavaScript code. Now it is time to begin writing your scripts.

Defining Objectives

In your first script, we are going to create a simple pop-up dialog box that asks the user for a password. If the password is incorrect, the user is redirected to an error page. If the password is valid, the user is sent to the page he is requesting. Those whose browsers do not support JavaScript simply see a message saying they cannot access this page. Because this script is written in very basic JavaScript, it can be used in any supporting browser. For simplicity's sake, we also will keep all of our scripts inline rather than in an external source file.

Here is a quick summary of what we have decided:

- Browser support: Support all.

- Non-supporting browsers: Display a message saying they cannot access this portion of your site.

- Location of script: Inline.

- Objective: Prompt the user for a password when the page is accessed. If the correct password is entered, the user is redirected to the secure page. If an incorrect password is entered, the user is redirected to an error page.

Creating a Code Template

Now that our objectives are defined, the first thing we recommend you do is create a template. We usually include all the necessary <head> information and prepare the <body> portion in this template, which makes it extremely easy to add the necessary scripts and content. Listing 3.2 has a copy of the template I start with.

LISTING 3.2   JavaScript Template File

```
<?xml version="1.0" encoding="UTF-8"?>
<!DOCTYPE html
      PUBLIC "-//W3C//DTD XHTML 1.0 Transitional//EN"
      "DTD/xhtml1-transitional.dtd">
<html xmlns="http://www.w3.org/1999/xhtml" xml:lang="en">
<head>
  <meta http-equiv="Content-Script-Type" content="text/javascript" />
  <title>My First JavaScript Script</title>
  <script type="text/javascript" language="JavaScript">
  <!--

  // Your code will go here...

  //-->
  </script>
</head>
<body>

<!-- Content starts here -->

</body>
</html>
```

Handling Non-Supporting Browsers

The first thing we want to get out of the way in this example is how we will handle non-supporting browsers. Because we are not performing an excessive amount of XHTML for these users, it will be quick and easy to finish. The following snippet shows what will be included in this section.

```
<body>
  <noscript>
    <p>
      <b>
      Sorry, but your browser either does not support JavaScript or you
        have it turned off. For information on JavaScript supporting browsers
```

```
      or how to turn it back on, please see the website of your browser's
      creator.
      </b>
    </p>
  </noscript>
</body>
```

As you can see, this was a very simple task, creating a message that will be displayed to the user. We included the text within bold tags (...) to ensure that it will show up well on the page.

Writing Your Code

At this point the page is ready. Now we just need to write the necessary JavaScript code. By accomplishing all of the other tasks first, such as defining our objectives, creating a template, and handling non-supporting browsers, we have made sure that the page functions properly without any scripting on it. This is an important step; on many occasions we thought that our script had a problem when in fact we had not properly closed an XHTML element, or we had misplaced some comments.

For this example, we will be working in the <head> portion of the page. The first thing we need to do is create a dialog box for the user to enter the password. For this task, we will use the prompt() method. This will give us a dialog like the one shown in Figure 3.4 to pass the entered information back to our script.

FIGURE 3.4   The prompt() dialog box.

The prompt() method is a method of the window object, and it takes two parameters that combine to have the following syntax:

```
prompt("message","default");
```

When using this method, you should replace *message* with instructions for the user. This will be displayed above the field where the user will enter his data. The *default* parameter is used to specify a default set of text for the user. In our first script, we do not want to have a default, so we will simply pass it an empty string.

The key to using this dialog box is that it returns what the user enters. Using the information entered, we can check to see, in our example, if the proper password was typed. Based on this data we can redirect the user's browser appropriately.

In addition to the prompt() method, we will also be using the location property of the window object. We will set this property to redirect the browser to the appropriate page according to the success of the user's entry. The last thing we need to note is that we will include all of this code in a function that is called after the entire page has loaded.

The code that accomplishes this task is relatively short and can be seen in the following block:

```
<script type="text/javascript" language="JavaScript">
<!--
  function passCheck(){
    if(prompt("Please enter your password","") == "letmein"){
      window.location = "/secure.html";
    }else{
      window.location = "/error.html";
    }
  }
//-->
</script>
```

Looking at this code, you see that we have defined a function called passCheck(). Within this function, we use an if..else conditional statement to verify the password entered by the user. Don't worry too much right now about how this works—it is covered in detail in Chapter 6, "Control Structures and Looping." All you need to understand at this point is that it is checking to see if the user entered "letmein" as the password. The == evaluation operator, which will be covered in Chapter 5, "Operators," performs this task.

If the user enters the correct password, he is redirected to the /secure.html page. If the user does not enter the correct password, his browser is redirected to the /error.html page.

Calling the Function

The last step in getting our script to work is to call the function. For this, we will use the onLoad event handler within the <body> element to call the function after the page is loaded. This event handler will be invoked, as mentioned, after the page finishes loading, at which time it will call the passCheck() function we defined. This entire line should look like the following:

```
<body onload="passCheck()">
```

Your First Script

Your first script is now complete and needs only to be assembled into a single document. Listing 3.3 shows you the complete source code.

LISTING 3.3   The Final Script

```
<?xml version="1.0" encoding="UTF-8"?>
<!DOCTYPE html
     PUBLIC "-//W3C//DTD XHTML 1.0 Transitional//EN"
     "DTD/xhtml1-transitional.dtd">
<html xmlns="http://www.w3.org/1999/xhtml" xml:lang="en">
<head>
  <meta http-equiv="Content-Script-Type" content="text/javascript" />
  <title>My First JavaScript Script</title>
  <script type="text/javascript" language="JavaScript">
  <!--
    function passCheck(){
      if(prompt("Please enter your password","") == "letmein"){
        window.location = "/secure.html";
      }else{
        window.location = "/error.html";
      }
    }
  //-->
  </script>
</head>
<body onload="passCheck()">
  <noscript>
    <p>
      <b>
      Sorry, but your browser either does not support JavaScript or you
      have it turned off. For information on JavaScript supporting browsers
      or how to turn it back on, please see the website of your browser's
      creator.
      </b>
    </p>
  </noscript>
</body>
</html>
```

In this listing, you will see that we specified the default language type and our function in the <head> of the page, and we called the function using the onLoad event handler in the

<body> element. Finally, we accommodated non-supporting browsers using the <noscript> element in the <body> portion of the page. To see the result of running this script in a JavaScript-enabled browser, see Figure 3.5. Figure 3.6 shows what users of non-supporting browsers (with JavaScript turned off) see.

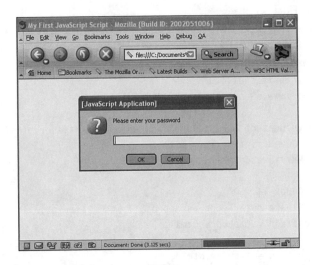

FIGURE 3.5   Running Listing 3.3 in a supported browser.

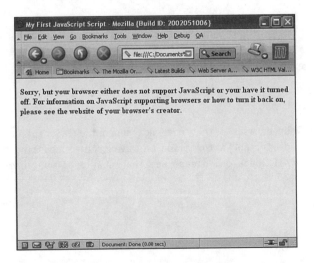

FIGURE 3.6   Running Listing 3.3 in a non-supported browser.

Summary

In this chapter, you had a chance to write your first script. Congratulations on making it this far! We could have done a simple "Hello World" script first, but we wanted to give you something a little more interesting that you might actually use, in a more complex fashion, in the real world.

Although we did not complete any complex examples, you were exposed to a high-level process of how to approach coding. This is an extremely important step as we conclude Part I of the book. In the next section you will learn more about the JavaScript language and how it works at a much deeper level. We will dive into the syntax and semantics of the language and you will learn about the operators and conditional statements we mentioned in this chapter, so it is important that we start off on the solid foundation this chapter laid.

3

PART II

The Core JavaScript Language

IN THIS PART

CHAPTER **4**

Fundamental Language Components

IN THIS CHAPTER

- JavaScript Versions
- Tokens
- Variables
- Constants
- Data Types
- Expressions
- Comments
- Functions
- JavaScript Objects
- Events

This chapter will highlight the fundamental language components of JavaScript as the language stands today. The chapter begins with a quick look at JavaScript versions and then jumps right into the components starting with tokens and eventually wrapping things up with a look at events.

JavaScript Versions

Although the version level of JavaScript is not a fundamental language component, it is important and could be thought of as a fundamental topic, especially if your JavaScript code must run on older browsers.

As Netscape, Microsoft, and other leading companies have been improving the core ECMAScript standard and their individual implementations, JavaScript has seen new versions of the language, along with new versions of the various browsers. This book covers to JavaScript 1.5. For a full list of supported platforms, see Table 4.1.

The next version of JavaScript will be the 2.0 release. Release 2.0 will be a rewrite of the language but keeping backward compatibility in mind. Concepts such as classes, types, and other features more commonly seen in static languages are expected in the 2.0 release.

TABLE 4.1   JavaScript Support

Version	Description
JavaScript 1.0	Supported in Netscape Navigator 2
JavaScript 1.1	Supported in Netscape Navigator 3, Internet Explorer 3, Opera 3, and Netscape Enterprise Server 2
JavaScript 1.2	Supported in Netscape Navigator 4 to 4.05 and Internet Explorer 4
JavaScript 1.3	Supported in Netscape Navigator 4.06 to 4.7 and Internet Explorer 5
JavaScript 1.4	Supported in some pre-alpha versions (before M12) of Mozilla, HotJava 3.0, Netscape Enterprise Server 4.0
JavaScript 1.5	Supported in Navigator 6 (Mozilla) and higher

See Tables 4.2, 4.3, and 4.4 to understand how these versions of JavaScript, JScript, and ECMAScript relate. The relationships of JavaScript, JScript, and ECMAScript to each other are not necessarily the same. There are minor differences that make such comparisons incomplete.

TABLE 4.2   JavaScript's Relationship to JScript

JavaScript	JScript
1.0	1.0
1.1	1.0–2.0
1.2	3.0–4.0
1.3	5.0–5.1
	5.0–5.1
1.5	5.5

TABLE 4.3   JavaScript's Relationship to ECMAScript

JavaScript	ECMAScript
1.0	n/a
1.1	n/a—Foundation for standards submission
1.2	n/a—Contained most of ECMAScript 1.0
1.3–1.4	1.0
1.5	1.0 Edition 3

TABLE 4.4   JScript's Relationship to ECMAScript

JScript	ECMAScript
1.0	n/a
2.0	n/a—Foundation for standards submission
3.0–3.1	1.0
4.0–5.0	1.0
5.5	1.0 Edition 3

In the past, as a JavaScript developer, you had to know the platform you were targeting so that you could develop for the correct version of JavaScript. After you decided, you could specify the version you wanted to use with the language attribute of the <script> tag. But unfortunately this tag has officially been deprecated in HTML 4.01 and XHTML 1.0. Microsoft Internet Explorer has chosen to ignore the JavaScript version numbering above 1.3. Netscape Navigator has taken another approach to be compliant with the HTML standard. They now use <script type="text/javascript; version=1.5">. The bottom line is that there is no longer a standardized tag that allows you to specify the language version.

Now that you have seen the versioning issues associated with JavaScript, let's look at another core component of JavaScript—tokens.

Tokens

Tokens are the smallest individual words, phrases, or characters that JavaScript can understand. When JavaScript is interpreted, the browser parses the script into these tokens while ignoring comments and whitespace.

JavaScript tokens fall into four categories: identifiers, keywords, literals, and operators. As with all computer languages, you have many ways to arrange these tokens to instruct a computer to perform a specific function. The **syntax** of a language is the set of rules and restrictions for the way you can combine tokens.

Identifiers

Identifiers are simply names that represent variables, methods, or objects. They consist of a combination of characters or a combination of characters and digits. Some names are already built into the JavaScript language and are therefore reserved.

Aside from these keywords, you can define your own creative and meaningful identifiers. Of course, there are a few rules to follow:

- You must begin all identifiers with either a letter or an underscore (_).

- You can then use letters, digits, or underscores for all subsequent characters.

- Letters include all uppercase characters, A through Z, and all lowercase characters, a through z. (ECMAScript allows for Unicode characters as well, but use caution when using Unicode characters because older browsers may not support them.)

- The sequence of characters that makes up an identifier should not include any spaces.

- Digits include the characters 0 through 9.

Table 4.5 shows some examples of valid and invalid identifiers.

TABLE 4.5   Examples of User-Defined JavaScript Identifiers

Valid	Invalid
current_WebSite	current WebSite
numberOfHits	#ofIslands
n	2bOrNotToBe
N	return

Notice that `current WebSite` is invalid because it contains a space. JavaScript tries to interpret this as two identifiers instead of one. If a space is needed, it is standard practice to use an underscore in its place.

`#ofIslands` is invalid because the pound sign is not included in the set of characters that are valid for identifiers. `2bOrNotToBe` is not valid because it begins with a number. JavaScript already uses the return identifier for another purpose. Attempting to use it as your own identifier would produce errors when you tried to run the script.

Also, both `n` and `N` are valid identifiers and are different from each other. JavaScript is case sensitive and therefore considers identifiers with different cases to be unique, even though they might be spelled the same.

Keywords and Reserved Words

Keywords are predefined identifiers that make up the core of a programming language. In JavaScript, they perform unique functions, such as declaring new variables and functions, making decisions based on the present state of the computer, or starting a repetitive loop inside your application.

Keywords are built into JavaScript and are always available for use by the programmer, but they must follow the correct syntax. The keyword var is the first keyword that will be described in detail later in this chapter. As you progress through this book, you will learn how to use other keywords to create more dynamic programs.

Reserved words are identifiers that you may not use as names for JavaScript variables, functions, objects, or methods. These include keywords and identifiers that are set aside for possible future use. The following is a complete list of the reserved words for JavaScript:

abstract	else	instanceof	switch
boolean	enum	int	synchronized
break	export	interface	this
byte	extends	long	throw
case	false	native	throws
catch	final	new	transient

char	finally	null	true
class	float	package	try
const	for	private	typeof
continue	function	protected	var
debugger	goto	public	void
default	if	return	volatile
delete	implements	short	while
do	import	static	with
double	in	super	

Literals

Literals are numbers or strings used to represent fixed values in JavaScript. They are values that don't change during the execution of your scripts. The following five sections describe the different types of literals.

Integer

Integers can be expressed in decimal (base 10), octal (base 8), or hexadecimal (base 16) format. An integer literal in decimal format can include any sequence of digits that does not begin with 0 (zero). A zero in front of an integer literal designates octal form.

The integer itself can include a sequence of the digits 0 through 9. To designate hexadecimal, 0x (or 0X) is used before the integer. Hexadecimal integers can include digits 0 through 9 and the letters a through f or A through F. Here are some examples:

Decimal	33, 2139, -33
Octal	071, 03664, 37777777737
Hexadecimal	0x7b8, 0X395, 0xffffffdf

Floating-Point

Floating-point literals represent decimal numbers with fractional parts. They can be expressed in either standard or scientific notation. With scientific notation, use either e or E to designate the exponent. Both the decimal number and the exponent can be either signed or unsigned (positive or negative), as shown in these examples:

3405.673

−1.958

8.3200e+11

8.3200e11

9.98E−12

Boolean

JavaScript implements Boolean data types and therefore supports the two literals `true` and `false`. If you are new to programming, you will soon realize how often `true` and `false` values are needed. This is why JavaScript has built them into the language. The `true` and `false` keywords must appear in lowercase. As a result, the uppercase words `TRUE` and `FALSE` are left open to define as your own identifiers, but doing so is not recommended in order to avoid confusion.

String

A string literal is zero or more Unicode characters enclosed in double quotes (" ") or single quotes (' '). JavaScript gives you this option, but you must use the same type of quote to enclose each string. The following are examples of string literals enclosed in quotes:

```
"Allen's car"

'virtual "communities"'

"#12-6"

"Look, up in the sky!"
```

The use of either type of quotation mark is handy if you have a preference for one or the other. When you learn about JavaScript's built-in methods, be careful to note the guidelines that you must follow when using string literals as parameters. In some instances, in order to use the method properly, you might have to use both types of quotation marks when enclosing one string literal inside another. This is different from using escape codes, which is described in the next section.

Special Characters

When writing scripts, you might sometimes need to tell the computer to use a special character or keystroke, such as a tab or a new line. To do this, use a backslash in front of one of the escape codes, as shown in Table 4.6.

TABLE 4.6 Escape Characters

Escape Sequence	Unicode Value	Description
\b	\u0008	Backspace
\f	\u000C	Form feed
\n	\u000A	Line feed (new line)
\r	\u000D	Carriage return
\t	\u0009	Horizontal tab
\v	\u000B	Vertical tab
\u	\uXXXX	Unicode escape sequences
\\	\u005C	Backslash
\'	\u0027	Single quote
\"	\u0022	Double quote

If you want to emulate a tab key to align two columns of data, you must use the tab character (\t). Listing 4.1 shows how to align text using tabs. The script itself can be harder to read after you add special characters, but as Figure 4.1 shows, the results look much better.

LISTING 4.1   Using Special Characters in JavaScript

```
<html>
<head>
  <title>JavaScript Unleashed</title>
</head>
<body>
<!--
    Notice: Special characters do not take effect unless enclosed in a
    pre-formatted block
-->
  <pre>
    <script type="text/javascript">
    <!--
      document.writeln("\tPersonnel");
      document.writeln("Name\t\tAddress");
      document.writeln("Jeff\t\tjeff@company.com");
      document.writeln("Bill\t\tbill@company.com");
      document.writeln("Kim\t\tkim@company.com");
    // -->
    </script>
  </pre>
</body>
</html>
```

FIGURE 4.1   Aligning text using the tabs in JavaScript.

> **NOTE**
>
> Special characters take effect only when used in a formatted text block; therefore, your script must be within tags such as <pre> and </pre>.

If you need to represent quotation marks within a string literal, precede them with a backslash:

```
document.write("\"Imagination is more important than knowledge.\"");
document.write(", Albert Einstein");
```

The preceding script would display the following line of text:

```
"Imagination is more important than knowledge.", Albert Einstein
```

Operators

Operators are symbols or identifiers that represent the way in which a combination of expressions can be evaluated or manipulated. The most common operator you have used thus far is the assignment operator. In the example x = 10, both 10 by itself and the variable x are expressions. When JavaScript sees an assignment operator between two expressions, it acts according to the rules of the assignment operator. In this case, it takes the value from the expression on the right side and assigns it to the variable on the left side. Along with the common arithmetic operators, JavaScript supports over 30 others. These will be covered more thoroughly in Chapter 5, "Operators."

Variables

A **variable** is the name given to a location in a computer's memory where data is stored. The first computer programmers spent much of their time translating data such as the "Hello World" message into binary data. They would then find an empty area in the computer's memory to put all of the ones and zeros while remembering where the data began and ended. By knowing this location (address), they were able to find, update, or retrieve the data as needed during the rest of the program. This basically meant keeping track of a lot of numbers!

Variables have made this process of storing, updating, and retrieving information much easier for the modern programmer. With variables, you can assign meaningful names to locations where data is stored while the computer handles the rest.

Naming

The name of a JavaScript variable is made up of one or more letters, digits, or underscores. It can't begin with a digit (0 through 9). Letters include not only the English alphabet letters A through Z and a through z but also other characters that Unicode classifies as letters from other alphabets. For example, the German alphabet has ä and ü and the French alphabet has é. JavaScript is case sensitive and therefore considers the following two examples to be different variable names:

```
internetAddress

internetaddress
```

The following are also valid variable names:

```
_lastName

n

number_2
```

When naming variables with a single word in JavaScript, it is common practice to use all lowercase letters. When using two or more words to name a variable, it is common to use lowercase letters for the first word and capitalize the first letter of all words thereafter. I make it a practice to use two or more words when naming variables to give others and myself a better idea of what the variable was created to do.

For example, suppose you need a variable to hold a Boolean value (`true` or `false`) that will let you know if a visitor to your Web page is finished typing his name into a text field. If you use a variable name such as `finish`, another programmer (or you, a couple of months down the road) could look at it and wonder, "Was this a flag that can be checked to find out if the visitor is done? Or was it a string stating what to write when the visitor was done, such as a thank-you message?"

The variable name `isDone` would be a better choice in this case. By using the word `is` as a prefix, you can indicate that this variable is posing a yes-or-no question, which indicates that the variable will store a Boolean value. If the visitor is done entering his name, `isDone` is assigned the value `true`; otherwise, it's assigned the value `false`.

Although the length of a JavaScript variable is limited only by a computer's memory, it's a good idea to keep variables to a practical length. I recommend between 1 and 20 characters or two to three words. Try to prevent running over the end of a line while writing your scripts. Large variable names make this easy to do and can ruin the look and structure of your code.

Some traditional one-word and even single-character variables represent program or mathematical values. The most common are n for any number; x, y, and z for coordinates; and i for a placeholder in a recursive function or a counter in a loop. Again, these methods for using variables are simply traditional, and you may use them for whatever purpose you see fit.

There is a good chance, especially if you are in a professional environment, that at some point your code will need to be read by other people. Using consistent and meaningful naming conventions can be a big help to someone who is maintaining your scripts. Poorly thought-out conventions cause big headaches and can significantly affect a company's bottom line.

Declaring

Declaring a variable lets JavaScript know you're going to use an identifier as a variable. To declare variables in JavaScript, use the keyword var followed by the new variable name. This action reserves the name as a variable to be used as a storage area for whatever data you might want to hold in it. Using the var keyword is not required but is good programming practice. In the following examples, notice that you can also declare more than one variable at a time by using a comma between variable names:

```
var internetAddress;
var n;
var i, j, k;
var isMouseOverLink, helloMessage;
```

After a variable is declared, it is then ready to be filled with its first value. This **initializing** is done with the assignment operator, =.

> **NOTE**
>
> The equal sign (=) is used to assign a value to a variable. You can read more about the assignment operator in Chapter 5.

You can initialize a variable at the same time you declare it or at any point thereafter in your script. Assigning a value when the variable is declared can help you remember what type of value you originally intended the variable to hold. The following shows the previous example, rewritten to include all initializations:

```
var internetAddress = "name@company.com";
var n = 0.00;
var i = 0, j = 0, k;
var isMouseOverLink = false;
var helloMessage = "Hello, thank you for coming!";
k = 0;
```

Notice that all variables have been initialized and declared at the same time except for k, which is initialized soon after. JavaScript reads from the top down, stepping through each line of code and performing the instructions in order. Until the program reaches the initializing step, the variable is said to be **undefined**. JavaScript allows you to check if a variable has been assigned using the typeof operator. This is explained in Chapter 5.

JavaScript offers one other way of declaring a variable: by simply initializing it without using the var keyword. If you assign a value to a new variable before declaring it with var, JavaScript will automatically declare it for you.

> **NOTE**
>
> Declaring variables without the var keyword will automatically declare the variable to be **global** in scope. Although this can be thought of as a shortcut, it's good programming practice to declare all variables specifically. Using the var keyword maintains the scope of the variable.

Types

When storing a piece of data (more commonly known as a **value**), JavaScript automatically categorizes it as one of the five JavaScript data types. Table 4.7 shows the different types of data that JavaScript supports.

TABLE 4.7   JavaScript Data Types

Type	Examples
number	-19, 3.14159
boolean	true, false
string	"Elementary, my dear Watson!", ""
function	unescape, write
object	window, document, null
undefined	undefined

A variable of the number type holds either an integer or a real number. A boolean variable holds either true or false. A string variable can hold any string value (either literal or an expression that yields a string) that is assigned to it, including an empty string. Table 4.7 shows how to represent an empty string with two double quotes. functions are either user-defined or built-in. For example, the unescape function is built into JavaScript. You can learn how to create user-defined functions in Chapter 7, "Functions."

Functions that belong to objects, called **methods** in JavaScript, are also classified under the function data type. Core client-side JavaScript objects such as window or document are of the object data type, of course. object variables, or simply **objects**, can store other objects. A variable that holds the null value is said to be of the object type. This is because JavaScript classifies the value null as an object.

Throughout your program, any value assigned to that variable is expected to be of its defined data type. Furthermore, an error occurs when you attempt to assign a different data type to the variable. This doesn't happen with JavaScript, which is classified as a loosely typed language. You are not required to define data types, nor are you prevented from assigning different types of data to the same variable. JavaScript variables can accept a new type of data at any time, which in turn changes the type of variable it is. The following examples show valid uses of JavaScript variables:

```
var carLength;
carLength = 4 + 5;
document.writeln(carLength);
carLength = "9 feet";
document.writeln(carLength);
```

After you declare the variable, carLength is assigned the value of 4 + 5. JavaScript stores the number 9 as the number type. However, when you reassign carLength to "9 feet", JavaScript lets you store a new type of value, a string, in carLength. This eliminates the extra steps that are usually needed by other computer languages to let the computer know that you are switching data types.

Scope

The **scope** of a variable refers to the area or areas within a program where a variable can be referenced. Suppose you embed one script in the head of an HTML document and another script (using another set of script tags) in the body of the same HTML document. JavaScript considers any variables declared within these two areas to be in the same scope. These variables are considered to be **global**, and they are accessible by any script in the current document. Later in this chapter, I'll more fully introduce functions, which are separate blocks of code. Variables declared within these blocks are considered local and are not always accessible by every script.

Local

A variable declared inside a function is **local** in scope. Only that function has access to the value that the variable holds. Each time the function is called, the variable is created. Likewise, each time the function ends, the variable is destroyed. Another function declaring a variable with the same name is considered a different variable by JavaScript. Each addresses its own block of memory. The exception to this rule is when a function is treated like an object. In this case it is possible for a function variable to persist. More information about this can be found in Chapter 7.

Global

If you want more than one function to share a variable, declare the variable outside of any functions (but, of course, inside the <script> tags). With this method, any part of your application, including all functions, can share this variable.

> **NOTE**
>
> It is recommended that you declare global variables in the <head> of an HTML page to ensure that they are loaded before any other part of your application.

Listing 4.2 demonstrates how global and local variables are declared and implemented. To show the difference between scopes, I included a function in this program. You do not need to understand how functions work, but realize that they are like separate parts of a script, enclosed by curly braces ({}). If you are unfamiliar with functions, you can find more information on functions in Chapter 7.

LISTING 4.2   Global Versus Local Scope of Variables

```
<html>
<head>
<title>Car Specification</title>

<script type="text/javascript" language="JavaScript">
//Initialize global variables
var color = "green";
var numDoors= 4;

//Declare a car specification function
function carSpecs()
{
  //Declare and set variables inside function
  color = "red";
  price = "$25,000";
  var numDoors = 2;
  document.write("The ",numDoors," door ",color);
  document.write(" car is ",price);
}

</script>
</head>

<body>
<h2><u>Car Specifications</u></h2>
<script type="text/javascript" language="JavaScript">

//Display results of carSpecs() function
carSpecs();

//Display variable values outside of function
document.write("<br>The ",numDoors," door ",color);
document.write(" car is ",price);

</script>
</body>
</html>
```

In this example, the global variables, `color` and `numDoors`, are declared in the head of the HTML file as well as the function `carSpecs`. The program begins by calling on the `carSpec` function to display the contents of the variables. One local variable, `numDoors`, is declared in the function. Notice that this variable shares the same name as one of the global variables that was declared in the head of the HTML file but contains the number 2 rather than 4. Also a new global variable, `price`, is defined within the function, and as a side effect of the assignment statement, the global variable price is equal to "$25,000".

At the beginning of the function, the global variable color is changed from `"green"` to `"red"` and the new global variable price is assigned the string `"$25,000"`. When these variables are displayed from within the function, the local variable `numDoors` is used, so the car is said to have two doors.

When the function call is complete, the variables are displayed again but this time outside the function. Because this is outside the `carSpec` function, the global variable `numDoors` is used, so the car is said to have four doors. Even though the variable `price` was declared in the function, it was declared as global, so it is seen outside the function. Figure 4.2 shows these results.

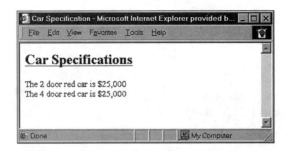

FIGURE 4.2   The difference between local and global scopes.

Constants

A constant is a variable that holds the same value throughout a program's execution. JavaScript uses built-in constants to represent values used by common mathematical operations such as pi. They can be accessed through the `math` object. They are explained in Chapter 8, "Core Language Objects."

User-defined constants are variables that are defined by the programmer and whose values cannot change. Constants are usually represented by capitalized words and are defined at the beginning of a program.

Support for constants only started in JavaScript 1.5 using the keyword `const`. For example, the following line of code

```
const car = "Lamborghini";
```

declares a constant called car. After the constant car is declared, it can be used throughout the code, but its value cannot be changed.

> **NOTE**
>
> const is a JavaScript extension of the ECMAScript edition 3 standard, which is not supported in JScript (the MS implementation of ECMAScript) or Opera's implementation.

Data Types

Although the basic data types that can be assigned to variables have already been discussed, you should know that functions and objects are special types of data. They offer interesting ways to store and act upon the data that your scripts deal with. You will learn how to take advantage of these aspects of the language in Chapter 7.

Expressions

An expression is built by applying operators to operands, which in their simplest form are literal values or variables. JavaScript as one of the following data types can categorize the result of an expression: boolean, number, string, function, object, or undefined.

An expression can be as simple as a number or variable by itself, or it can include many variables, keywords, and operators joined together. For example, the expression x = 10 assigns the value 10 to the variable x. The expression as a whole evaluates to 10, so using the expression in a line of code such as document.writeln(x = 10) is valid.

JavaScript would rather see a string between the parentheses and simply display it, but in this case, it finds some work to do before moving on. It must first evaluate what is between the parentheses and then display the value. In this case, the number 10 is displayed.

After the work is done to assign 10 to x, the following is also a valid expression: x. In this case, the only work that JavaScript needs to do is read the value from the computer's memory; no assignment needs to be performed. In addition to the assignment operator, there are many other operators you can use to form an expression (see Chapter 5).

Comments

So far, HTML comment tags have been used for surrounding scripts, which ensures that old browsers don't display scripts that they can't execute. What if you want to place comments that JavaScript will ignore in your JavaScript code? The two options available to you use the same syntax found in the C/C++ and Java languages. Here is the syntax:

```
// Here is a single line comment
```

The two forward slashes (//) hide text that follows until the end of the current line. For larger blocks of comments, you can use the multiline syntax. To do this, use the following:

```
/* Use this method to contain multiple lines of
comments */
```

Whitespace is ignored in both of these types of comments. Because of this, either of the following is valid:

```
// Comments
/* Multiple lines
comments */
```

Listing 4.3 demonstrates the use of each type of comment. Occasionally you will see the syntax <!-- and //-->. These were used to hide code from older browsers that might not know the <script> tag. This is not really an issue today but is worth pointing out in case you were to run across it in old JavaScript code. Anything that is commented in Listing 4.3 is not output to the display, as shown in Figure 4.3.

LISTING 4.3   Using JavaScript Comment Tags

```
<html>
<head>
  <title>JavaScript Unleashed</title>
</head>
<body>
  <script type="text/javascript">
  <!--
    // Variables
    var firstName = "Jon";
    var lastName = "Simpson";
    var internetAddress = "jsimpson@company.com";


    /*-------------------------------------------
      Display the user's first and last name
      along with their e-mail address.
    -----------------------------------------*/

    // Combine three strings
    document.writeln(firstName + " " + lastName + "<br>");
    document.writeln("e-mail address: " + internetAddress);
  // -->
  </script>
```

LISTING 4.3   Continued

```
</body>
</html>
```

FIGURE 4.3   Comments are not displayed in the browser.

Being able to hide code from JavaScript gives you the ability to document your scripts. It is considered good programming practice to add design notes, friendly reminders, or warnings throughout your program. This can help you and others see what the different sections of your program are meant to do.

Another use of comments is debugging your scripts. You can hide your code to track down problems and then easily replace it when you're done by simply removing comment identifiers. Doing this instead of deleting parts of your script helps save time.

Functions

In its simplest form, a function is a script that you can call by name at any time. This enhances JavaScript in two ways. When an HTML document is read by a JavaScript-enabled Web browser, the browser will find any embedded scripts and execute the instructions step by step. This is fine unless you would rather have part or all of your program wait before executing. Writing this part of your program in a function and assigning it a name is a great way to set up a script to be run at a later time.

When a specific event occurs, you can run this script by using the name that you gave to the function. Another advantage of functions is the ability to reuse scripts without typing in the same code repeatedly. Instead, you can just use the name given to the function to execute the code contained within.

Listing 4.4 shows how JavaScript executes a function. The first thing to notice is where the function is declared. Just as other variables need to be declared, so do functions. Be sure to enclose all function declarations within <script> tags.

> **NOTE**
>
> I recommend declaring your functions in the <head> block of the HTML document. Doing this ensures that the function is loaded by the browser before it is executed by the body.

To call the function, just place the function call in the code where you want the function to be called. The main program is placed within the body and is surrounded by its own set of <script> tags. Take a look at Figure 4.4 to see how this is handled by the browser.

LISTING 4.4   Embedding a JavaScript Function

```html
<html>
<head>
  <title>JavaScript Unleashed</title>
  <script type="text/javascript">
  <!--
    function displayMessage() {
      document.write("JavaScript functions are easy to use!<br>");


    }
  // -->
  </script>
</head>
<body>
  <script type="text/javascript">
  <!--
    document.write("Calling a JavaScript function...<p>");
    displayMessage();
    document.write("<\/p>Done. ");
  // -->
  </script>
</body>
</html>
```

Starting with the main script, JavaScript executes the first statement as always and then arrives at the displayMessage() function call. It looks up the function in memory and begins with the first line of displayMessage(). After writing JavaScript functions are easy to use!, a line break is displayed. The end of the function is reached, and program execution returns to where it left off in the main script.

As you can see in Figure 4.4, each line of text is displayed in this sequence. If you have a lengthy program that displays this message many times, you can insert the function call in each place where you need it. If at a later time there is a need to update the message, you need only change the message in one place. Change it within the function declaration, and your whole application is updated. You can learn more about functions and their advantages in Chapter 7.

FIGURE 4.4   Calling a function in JavaScript.

JavaScript Objects

JavaScript is not an object-oriented language, like Java and C++, because it does not implement the class concept. Although JavaScript lacks class-based inheritance, it does provide prototype-based inheritance. Therefore, JavaScript falls into the category of object-based programming languages. With JavaScript 2 already under development, the language will take on more of an object-oriented feel in the future, but for now we will examine JavaScript objects as they stand today.

This section will take a tour of some of the key components of JavaScript objects. This is not intended to be an exhaustive description of JavaScript objects but rather an overview. Let's begin with a look at the use of dot notation and bracket notation in JavaScript objects.

Dot Notation and Bracket Notation

In JavaScript, you can access the properties and methods of an object in two ways: dot notation or bracket notation. Dot notation and bracket notation, which are demonstrated in the following syntax examples, provide a hierarchy-style method of accessing these properties and implementing the methods.

```
objectName.propertyName
objectName["propertyName"]
objectName.methodName(arguments)
objectName["methodName"](arguments)
```

The current object is addressed through the special variable this. In the method declaration of an object type (class), you address the object itself with the variable this. The object itself, meaning the current object, is the object for which you are declaring the method.

In an object type defining complex numbers, you write a prototype method for adding two complex numbers as follows:

```
// define complex numbers

function Complex(real, img)
{
  this.real = real;
  this.img = img;
}

// get real part
Complex.prototype.getReal = function()
{
  return this.real;
}

// get img part
Complex.prototype.getImg = function()
{
  return this.img;
}

Complex.prototype.add = function(z)
{
  var a;
  var b;
  var rz;

  a = this.real + z.getReal();
  b = this.img  + z.getImg();
  rz = new Complex(a,b);
  return rz;
}
```

Two new complex numbers can now be created by using the Complex object's constructor as demonstrated in the following:

```
var complexNum1 = new Complex(4,1);
var complexNum2 = new Complex(3,2);
```

Once created, the two complex numbers can be added together using the add method that was defined in the Complex object. The following line of code shows how complexNum2 is added to complexNum1 using the add method:

```
complexNum1.add(complexNum2);
```

In the method add, the term this.real addresses the real property of the current object—in this case, complexNum1.real. Similarly, this.img addresses the img property—that is, complexNum1.img, which is the img part of complexNum1.

Exploring the JavaScript Object Model

JavaScript objects are truly objects, in the sense that they have properties and methods and can respond to events. However, as you have learned in this chapter, JavaScript doesn't have the same true OOP capabilities of inheritance, but it does provide prototype-based inheritance. When you look at the JavaScript object model, it is critical that you look at it in that context. Rather than a class hierarchy that is inheritance-based, the JavaScript object model is a containership hierarchy, as shown in Figure 4.5. If you are experienced in object-oriented programming languages such as Java or C++, this might be the biggest adjustment you need to make in your thinking when developing with JavaScript.

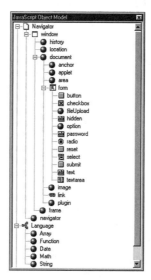

FIGURE 4.5   The JavaScript built-in object model hierarchy.

Containership is the principle of one object containing another object. If you look again at Figure 4.5, you can see that the relationship between the Form object and the Radio object is not one of ancestor and descendant (or class and subclass), but one of container and contained. Stated differently, there is no bloodline between these objects, because one did not descend from the other.

Containership in JavaScript

Containership is an important term to understand as you develop JavaScript scripts and applications—not only in terms of how one object relates to another, but in practical terms of how you reference an object. Recall from the discussion of dot notation earlier in this chapter that when you reference an object's properties or methods, you use a dot to denote ownership. For example, in the following command, the write method is said to be owned by the Document object:

```
document.write("<h1>A cow jumping over the moon.<\/h1>");
```

However, you can extend this to include not only properties and methods of an object but also objects contained by that object. This way of accessing objects is available thanks to the document object model that the browser implements. If you wanted to return the name of a Button object to a variable, you would use the following statement:

```
buttonName = document.formMain.okButton.name;
```

document is the default name of the Document object, and formMain is the name of the Form object, which contains the okButton button.

An important point to understand when you work with objects is knowing when you need to reference a container object and when you don't. For example, the Window object is essentially the highest-level object you work with in your code on the client side. Most of the references you make are to objects within its containership. You could also write the previous document.write example like this:

```
window.document.write("<h1>A cow jumping over the moon.</h1>");
```

Although you can ignore the window reference in most cases, it is necessary when you deal with multiple windows or frames. For instance, Listing 4.5 creates a Window object in the showStats() function and then closes it in the closeWindow() function, which is called when the main document is unloaded. The window.open method opens a new window and returns a reference to the new window. The windowObject.document.open method is then used to open the document for writing. The window.document.close method closes the stream. If the reference is a valid window object, it is then used to close the window, with the close method, when the main document is unloaded.

LISTING 4.5   Creating a New Window and Writing Information to It

```
<html>
<head>
```

LISTING 4.5   Continued

```
   <title>JavaScript Unleashed</title>
   <script type="text/javascript" language="JavaScript">
   <!--
      var windowObject

      //Create a status window
      function showStats() {
        windowObject = window.open("", "ViewStats", "toolbar=0,width=300,
            height=200,resizable=1");
        windowObject.document.open();
        windowObject.document.write("<h2>We outperformed all goals this month.
            Congratulations!</h2>");
        windowObject.document.close();
      }

      //Close status window if status window exists
      function closeWindow(){
        if((typeof(windowObject) == "object") && !windowObject.closed){
          windowObject.close();
        }
      }
   // -->
   </script>
</head>
<body onunload="closeWindow()">
   <h1>
     Click the following button to view the monthly stats.
   </h1>
   <form>
     <input type="button" value="Show Stats" onclick="showStats()">
   </form>
</body>
</html>
```

The Window object is the only one that provides any leniency in object references. For example, if you want to reference a form within an HTML page, you must add its parent object (Document) for JavaScript to understand which object you are referencing within the document object model. If you want to reference the first form within the Document object and retrieve the number of elements in it, you use the following statement:

```
var num = document.forms[0].length;
```

Even if the form had a `name` attribute, you still need to add the parent reference:

```
var num = document.queryForm.length;
```

Properties

Properties in JavaScript resemble the data attributes of an object. The properties of an object explain the characteristics and identity of the given object. In addition to specific characteristics and identifying values, an object's attributes can also represent the state of the object or a role that an object could play at a given time.

When modeling projects, you could define the object type `Project` as follows:

```
function Project(members, leader, currentMilestone, time){
  this.members = members;
  this.leader = leader;
  this.currentMilestone = currentMilestone;
  this.time =  time;
}
```

You would then create the particular software project `myProject` as follows:

```
var memberGroup = new Array();
var currTime = new Date();
var myProject = new Project(memberGroup, "Claudia", "starting", currTime);
```

The object `myProject` consists of a group of persons described in the object `memberGroup`. The project leader is `"Claudia"` and the current milestone is `"starting"` because the project just recently began. The variable `memberGroup` and `currTime` contain an `Array` object and `Date` object, respectively, that are not described here.

In addition to dot notation, you have other ways to access the properties of an object. The following example shows array notation:

```
objectName["propertyName"]
```

The next line demonstrates indexing through ordinal numbers:

```
objectName[integerIndex]
```

This technique returns the attribute of number `integerIndex`.

Methods

A method denotes a service the class offers to other objects. Generally, methods belong to one of the following four categories:

- Modifier: A method that changes the state of an object. This method changes the value of one or more data attributes of the object. A popular modifier method is a set function that sets the value of one particular object attribute.

- Selector: A method that accesses the data attributes of an object but makes no changes. An important selector is a get function that returns (gets) the value of one particular object attribute.

- Iterator: A method that accesses all the parts of an object, such as all the data attributes, in some defined order. As the name denotes, an iterator method iterates over the data attributes of an object.

- Constructor: A constructor is a method of an object type that creates a new object from the class template. A constructor initializes the new object with the given data values in the parameter part of the constructor method.

In JavaScript, object methods are accessed through dot notation or bracket notation:

```
objectName.functionName(arguments)
objectName["functionName"](arguments)
```

Generally, an HTML document is represented by the Document object in JavaScript. The Document object supports the method write(). With this method, you can dynamically extend the text layout of your HTML page through JavaScript. The following statement prints the string "This is sample text":

```
document.write("This is sample text");
```

When constructing new object types in JavaScript, you use a source code template such as the one presented here:

```
function ObjectType (param1, param2, ...) {
  this.property1 = param1;
  this.property2 = param2;
}


ObjectType.prototype.method1 = function (param1, param2, ...)
{
  //Function statements go here
}


ObjectType.prototype.method2 = function (param1, param2, ...)
{
  //Function statements go here
}
```

The implementation for the object methods is given later in a function declaration following the rules for regular JavaScript functions. The arguments of a function can be strings, numbers, Booleans, or complete objects. Listing 4.6 shows an example of defining and using a class representing complex numbers.

LISTING 4.6   Defining and Using a Class Representing Complex Numbers

```html
<html>
<html>
<head>

<title>
Complex Numbers
</title>

<script type="text/javascript">
// define complex numbers

function Complex(real, img){
  this.real = real;
  this.img = img;
}

Complex.prototype.add = function (z) {
  // add this + z  giving rz
  var a;
  var b;
  var rz;

  a = this.real + z.real;
  b = this.img  + z.img;
  rz = new Complex (a,b);
  return rz;
}

Complex.prototype.toString = function () {
  return '(' + this.real + ' + ' + this.img + 'i)';
}
</script>
</head>

<body>
<script type="text/javascript">
```

LISTING 4.6 Continued

```
var a = new Complex(3, 1);
var b = new Complex(1, 2);
var c = a.add(b);
document.write(a + ' + ' + b + ' = ' + c);
</script>
</body>
</html>
```

This code defines an object, called `Complex`, that represents complex numbers. The object definition is made up of a constructor method as well as an `add` method, for adding two `Complex` objects, and a `toString` method for displaying the numbers that make up a complex object.

The code also uses the `Complex` object by first calling on the constructor of the `Complex` object to create two complex numbers, a and b. The `Complex` object b is then added to the `Complex` object a, thanks to the `add` method of the a object. The result of the addition is written into a new `Complex` object and assigned to the c variable.

Finally the `toString` method is automatically called on each of the objects when they are displayed in the HTML document. The result of running the code is shown in Figure 4.6.

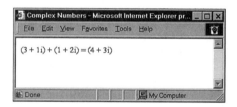

FIGURE 4.6 Adding complex numbers.

Events

Often, JavaScript statements create or manipulate graphical user interface elements such as forms or windows. Figure 4.7 shows a simple graphical user interface.

Listing 4.7 serves only for generating a form shown in Figure 4.7. Other parts are not fully programmed yet and generally produce `Not yet implemented` messages.

LISTING 4.7 A Simple GUI

```
<html>
<head>
  <title>GUI Example</title>
```

LISTING 4.7   Continued

```
  <script type="text/javascript">
  <!--

    // search function not yet implemented
    // here: create display of result list
    function fsearch(aForm){
      alert ("Sorry, search function not yet implemented");
    }

    // display of options not yet implemented
    function foptions(aForm){
      alert ("Sorry, no options available");
    }
    //-->
  </script>
</head>
<body>
  <h3>
    My search form
  </h3>
  <hr>
  <form>
    Find:
    <input type="text" name="tfield" size="40">
    <br>
    <input type="radio" name="search">
    Simple Search
    <br>
    <input type="radio" name="search">
    Extended Search
    <br>
    <input type="button" name="bsearch" value="Search"
      onclick="fsearch(this.form)">
    <input type="button" name="boptions" value="More options"
      onclick="foptions(this.form)">
  </form>
</body>
</html>
```

In the context of a graphical user interface, an event is a result of a user action. It takes place when the user does something. For example, when the user clicks a button on the user interface, a `click` event occurs. Other GUI events include clicking a check box, selecting a string in a list box, double-clicking an item, and opening or closing a window.

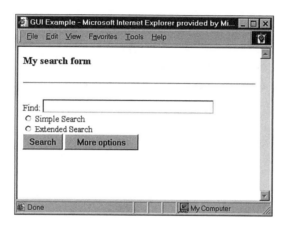

FIGURE 4.7   A graphical user interface.

The best way to control GUIs is through event-driven programming. Events can be **captured** or handled by event handlers in JavaScript. See Chapter 18, "Handling Events," for more information on events.

Summary

This chapter took a high-level look at the fundamental components of JavaScript. We began the chapter by examining the versions of JavaScript and how these versions relate to ECMAScript and JScript as well as some of the more popular browsers on the market. Although standards, such as ECMAScript, have helped pull browsers together, these changes have made versioning of JavaScript a bit confusing. When this discussion was out of the way, we dove into actual JavaScript components.

Starting from the first line of code, the JavaScript interpreter reads a script statement by statement evaluating tokens, the smallest individual words, phrases, and characters that JavaScript can understand. Tokens can be literals, identifiers, or operators.

You learned about the different data types available in JavaScript: `number`, `boolean`, `string`, `function`, and `object`. Variables are used to store one data type at a time. To declare a variable, use the `var` keyword or simply initialize the variable. Always try to use meaningful names for variables to make your scripts easier to read.

You learned that a JavaScript expression is built from simple expressions, like literals or variables, by applying operators to those simple expressions. Expressions evaluate to a single value. The most common expressions assign values to variables. The assignment operator, =, is used to assign the value of its right operand to the variable that is its left operand. JavaScript supports all standard math operations, either through operators or by using the built-in `math` object. You were introduced to functions that are scripts that you can execute at any time before or after the user viewed an HTML document. With functions, you can set aside a script to be executed at any time and as often as you like. Using functions can also make your scripts easier to maintain. Chapter 7 explains functions in greater detail.

You were also introduced to some key aspects of JavaScript objects. Although the discussion was not an exhaustive description of JavaScript objects, you did learn about dot and bracket notation and how they can be used to access properties and methods of objects. You will learn even more about JavaScript objects in later chapters.

Finally, we took a quick glance at events in JavaScript and how they are used to create or manipulate HTML graphical user interface elements.

CHAPTER 5

Operators

IN THIS CHAPTER

- Assignment Operators
- Arithmetic Operators
- Comparison Operators
- String Operators
- Conditional Operators
- Boolean Operators
- The typeof Operator
- Function Operators
- Data Structure Operators
- Bitwise Operators
- Operator Precedence

The whole idea of writing a script is to input, evaluate, manipulate, or display data. Until now, you have concentrated on displaying data with JavaScript. To create more useful programs, you need to evaluate or even change the data that your scripts are dealing with. The tools for this job are called **operators**.

Operators are the symbols and identifiers that represent either the way that the data is changed or the way a combination of expressions is evaluated. The JavaScript language supports both binary and unary operators. Binary operators require two operands in the expression, such as 9 + x, whereas unary operators need only one operand, for example x++.

Both of the examples used here are arithmetic operators, and their use will come naturally to those who have programmed in other languages like C++ or Java. Other types of JavaScript operators deal with strings and logical values. They aren't as familiar, but they're easy to learn and very handy when you're dealing with large amounts of text over the Internet. This chapter takes a close look at each type of JavaScript operator.

Before jumping into the actual operators, it is important to realize that browsers will attempt type conversions on many of the operands of the operators. So if an operator expects a string but a number is entered as an operand, the scripting engine will attempt to convert the string to a number before performing the operator's intended action. Some operators do not automatically do type conversion—those will be mentioned as you go through the chapter.

Assignment Operators

An operator you're already familiar with is the assignment operator. Its most basic function is assigning a value to a variable, thereby placing the value in memory.

For example, the expression x = 20 assigns the value 20 to the variable x. When JavaScript encounters the assignment operator (=), it first looks to the left and ensures that there is a place to store the number. It then looks to the right for a value and then assigns the value. In this case, x holds the value 20. The value to be assigned must always appear on the right, so the expression 20 = x causes an error in JavaScript by trying to assign a new value to 20. This is not allowed, because 20 is not a variable; it is an integer whose value can't be changed.

It is also possible for either side of the assignment operator to be an expression. For example the expression "document.formName.inputName.value" can be assigned the result of the expression "x++" using the following syntax:

```
document.formName.inputName.value = ++x;
```

So if the variable x were equal to 5, the value stored in inputName would be 6.

JavaScript supports 11 other assignment operators that are actually combinations of the assignment operator and either an arithmetic or bitwise operator. These shorthand versions follow:

The Combinations of Assignment and Arithmetic Operators

x += y is short for x = x + y

x -= y is short for x = x - y

x *= y is short for x = x * y

x /= y is short for x = x / y

x %= y is short for x = x % y

The Combinations of Assignment and Bitwise Operators

x <<= y is short for x = x << y

x >>= y is short for x = x >> y

x >>>= y is short for x = x >>> y

x &= y is short for x = x & y

x ^= y is short for x = x ^ y

x |= y is short for x = x | y

Arithmetic Operators

When working with numbers you use arithmetic operators. The most basic operators of the group include the plus sign (+), which adds two values; the minus sign (-), which subtracts one value from another; the asterisk (*), which multiplies two values together; and the forward slash (/), which divides one value by another.

When JavaScript encounters one of these operators, it looks to the right and left sides of the operator to find the values to work on. In the example 7 + 9, JavaScript sees the plus operator and looks to either side of it and finds 7 and 9. The plus operator then adds the two values together, resulting in the expression as a whole equating to 16. When using the arithmetic operators with the assignment operator, you can assign the value of an expression to a variable:

```
x = 7 + 9
```

x will now equal 16 and can be used again, even to give itself a new value:

```
x = x + 1
```

Follow the last two examples in order. x is first assigned the value 16. Next, x is reassigned the present value of x (which, at that moment, is still 16) plus 1. So x ends up being equal to 17.

It is a very common operation to increment the value of a variable and then reassign that value to itself. It is used so often in computer programs that some languages incorporate special shorthand operators to more easily increment and decrement the values that variables hold. JavaScript is one such language. It uses ++ to increment and -- to decrement a value by 1. Note the following syntax:

```
++i is the same as i = i + 1
--i is the same as i = i - 1
```

You can use these operators as either prefixes or suffixes. That way, you can change the order in which a value is returned by the expression and when the new value is assigned. Listing 5.1 demonstrates how increment and decrement operators work.

LISTING 5.1   Examples of Increment and Decrement Operators

```
<html>
<head>
  <title>JavaScript Unleashed</title>
</head>
<body>

  <script type="text/javascript">
  <!--
```

LISTING 5.1   Continued

```
var i = 0;
var result = 0

document.write("If i = 0, ");
document.write("++i returns the value of i");
document.write(" after incrementing  : ");

// Increment prefix
result = ++i;

document.write(result);

// Reset variable
i = 0;
document.write("<br>i++ returns the value of i");
document.write(" before incrementing : ");

// Increment suffix
result = i++;
document.write(result);

// Reset variable
i = 0;
document.write("<br>--i returns the value of i");
document.write(" after decrementing  : ");

// Decrement prefix
result = --i;
document.write(result)

// Reset variable
i = 0;
document.write("<br>i-- returns the value of i");
document.write(" before decrementing : ");

// Decrement suffix
result = i--;

document.write(result);
// -->
```

LISTING 5.1 Continued

```
</script>

</body>
</html>
```

The important thing to notice in Listing 5.1 is whether i is incremented before or after the expression is evaluated.

In the increment prefix section, result is set to the original value of i plus 1. In the increment suffix section, result is immediately set equal to the original value of i before i is incremented. The decrement prefix section and decrement suffix section work the same way but demonstrate the decrement operator.

The results of these four examples are shown in Figure 5.1. Although these might seem like unnecessary ways to use the operator, they can come in handy when writing scripts that repeat a part of the program. This is shown in Chapter 6, "Control Structures and Looping."

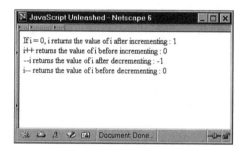

FIGURE 5.1 The increment and decrement operators shown in Listing 5.1.

The unary negation operator (-) is used to change a value from positive to negative or vice versa. It is unary because it operates on only one operand. If, for example, you assign the value 5 to a variable x (x = 5) and then negate x and assign the value to y (y = -x), y will equal -5. The opposite is true when negating a negative number; the result will be positive. In both instances, the negation operator does not negate the value of x. The value of x remains equal to 5.

> **NOTE**
>
> If the operand that appears after the negation operator is a type other than integer, the operand is first converted to an integer before applying negation.

> **NOTE**
>
> In addition to the unary negation operator (+), the ECMAScript edition 3 standard also offers a unary addition operator. This operator simply converts the operand to a number.

The modulus operator is symbolized by the percent sign (%). To find the modulus of two operands is to find the remainder after dividing the first operand by the second. In the example x = 10 % 3, x is assigned the number 1, because 10 divided by 3 is equal to 3 with 1 left over. With the modulus operator, you can easily determine that one number is the multiple of another if the modulus of the two numbers is equal to 0. This would be true for the expression x = 25 % 5. Because 25 divided by 5 is equal to 5 with no remainder; this leaves x equal to 0.

Comparison Operators

As their name implies, comparison operators are used for comparing. Expressions that use comparison operators are essentially asking a question about two values. The answer can be either true or false.

Before going any further, it is important to point out that the comparison operators are not limited to just mathematical comparisons. In fact these operators can compare primitive values (such as integers, Booleans, Strings, and so on) as well as objects. When dealing with primitive values, the actual primitive values are compared. When comparing objects, you are comparing object instances rather than the contents of the objects.

> **NOTE**
>
> As mentioned at the beginning of the chapter, type conversion is applied to most of the operators. The conversion rules for == and != are rather complex, and you can find a thorough explanation of them in Section 11.9.3 of ECMAScript edition 3.

Let's look at the equal operator. Two equal signs (==) make up the equal operator. When you use the equal operator in the middle of two operands, you're trying to determine whether the values of these two operands are equal.

Listing 5.2 shows how to display the result when asking whether two variables are equal.

LISTING 5.2   Using the Equal Operator

```
<html>
<head>
  <title>JavaScript Unleashed</title>
</head>
<body>
  <script type="text/javascript">
```

LISTING 5.2 Continued

```
<!--
  // Declare variables
  var x = 5;
  var y = 5;
  var z = 10;
  // Output to display
  document.write("x = " + x + "<br>");
  document.write("y = " + y + "<br>");
  document.write("z = " + z + "<br>");
  document.write("Is x equal to y,(x == y)? ");
  document.write(x == y);
  document.write("<br>Is y equal to z,(y == z)? ");
  document.writeln(y == z);
// -->
</script>

</body>
</html>
```

Be sure to use the correct operator for the job. Again, the equal operator (==) tests to see whether two values are equal, but the assignment operator (=) sets a variable equal to a value. If you happen to make a mistake and use the wrong one, the JavaScript interpreter is good about letting you know! Figure 5.2 shows the display after Listing 5.2 is executed.

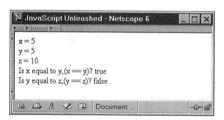

FIGURE 5.2　The equal operator from Listing 5.2.

The equal operator is just one of the operators at your disposal as a JavaScript programmer. Table 5.1 lists the comparison operators.

TABLE 5.1　Comparison Operators

Operator	Description
==	The equal operator. Returns `true` if both of its operands are equal.
!=	The not-equal operator. Returns `true` if its operands are not equal.

TABLE 5.1   Continued

Operator	Description
>	The greater-than operator. Returns `true` if its left operand is greater in value than its right operand.
>=	The greater-than-or-equal-to operator. Returns `true` if its left operand is greater than or equal to its right operand.
<	The less-than operator. Returns `true` if its left operand is less than the value of its right operand.
<=	The less-than-or-equal-to operator. Returns `true` if its left operand is less than or equal to its right operand.
===	The identity operator. Returns `true` if both of its operands are equal. No type conversion is performed on the operands before the comparison is made.
!==	The non-identity operator. Returns `true` if its operands are not equal. No type conversion is performed on the operands before the comparison is made.

NOTE

The strict `===` and `!==` operators are useful when you want to avoid the implicit type conversions that happen with the `==` and `!=` operators. You can also use the type conversion functions `Number`, `Boolean`, and `String` to convert values explicitly to enforce the type comparison you want to occur.

Comparison operators are normally used in JavaScript for making decisions. With them, you can ask, "What path in my script do I want to take?" Chapter 6 goes into detail on this topic.

The Evolution of the Identity and Non-identity Operators

In JavaScript 1.1, the language was very forgiving when comparing operands of different data types. For example, when comparing the number 7 with the string "7", JavaScript would first convert or cast the string operand to a number and then compare the two. JavaScript would then find them equal.

In an attempt to guess what would be in the then-unreleased ECMAScript standard, the decision was made not to do type conversion with comparison operators in JavaScript 1.2. When the ECMAScript was finally released it supported type conversion, so JavaScript 1.3 and up once again attempted to convert operands of the comparison operators before performing the comparison.

For backward compatibility with JavaScript 1.2, the identity and non-identity operators were added in JavaScript 1.3 to perform comparisons without type conversion. Listing 5.3 demonstrates the difference between the standard equal operator and the identity operator as well as the not equal operator and the non-identity operator.

LISTING 5.3   Difference Between Equal and Identity Operators

```
<html>
<head>
  <title>JavaScript Unleashed</title>
</head>
<body>

  <script type="text/javascript">
  <!--
    var x = 3;
    document.write("x = 3");
    document.write("<br><hr>");

    document.write("Equal Operator<br>");
    document.write("(x == 3) returns ");
    document.write(x == 3);
    document.write("<br>");
    document.write("(x == \"3\") returns ");
    document.write(x == "3");
    document.write("<br><hr>");

    document.write("Identity Operator<br>");
    document.write("(x === 3) returns ");
    document.write(x === 3);
    document.write("<br>");
    document.write("(x === \"3\") returns ");
    document.write(x === "3");
    document.write("<br><hr>");

    document.write("Not Equal Operator<br>");
    document.write("(x != 3) returns ");
    document.write(x != 3);
    document.write("<br>");
    document.write("(x != \"3\") returns ");
    document.write(x != "3");
    document.write("<br><hr>");

    document.write("Non-identity Operator<br>");
    document.write("(x !== 3) returns ");
    document.write(x !== 3);
    document.write("<br>");
    document.write("(x !== \"3\") returns ");
```

LISTING 5.3   Continued

```
   document.write(x !== "3");
 //-->
 </script>

</body>
</html>
```

When the script is executed, the string "3" is converted to the number 3 before performing the comparison operation using the equal operator and not equal operator. But when the number 3 is compared to the string "3", false is returned from the identity operator. Similarly, the non-identity operator returns false when comparing the number 3 and the string "3". Figure 5.3 shows the result of running Listing 5.3 in a browser.

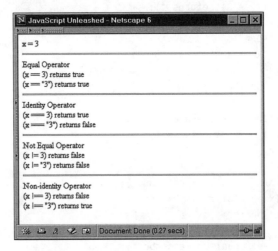

FIGURE 5.3   The difference between equality and identity operators shown in Listing 5.3.

String Operators

The set of string operators available in JavaScript includes all comparison operators and the concatenation operator (+). Using the concatenation operator, you can easily attach strings together to make longer strings. It is even possible to concatenate a string and a number into a string thanks to automatic type conversion. So if you try to concatenate a string and a number using the concatenation operator (+), the number will first be converted to a string and then the two strings will be put together. Listing 5.4 demonstrates the string concatenation operator.

LISTING 5.4   Concatenating Strings

```html
<html>
<head>
  <title>JavaScript Unleashed</title>
</head>
<body>
  <script type="text/javascript">
  <!--
    // Declare variables
    var a = "www";
    var b = "company";
    var c = "com";
    var sumOfParts;
    var address1;
    var address2;
    document.write("Part a is equal to \"" + a + "\".");
    document.write("<br>Part b is equal to \"" + b + "\".");
    document.write("<br>Part c is equal to \""+c+"\".\n");
    sumOfParts = a + "." + b + "." + c;
    address1 = "WWW.COMPANY.COM";
    address2 = "www.company.com";

    // Output to display
    document.write("<br><br>Is sumOfParts equal to " + address1 + "? ");
    document.write(sumOfParts == address1);
    document.write("<br>Is sumOfParts equal to " + address2 + "? ");
    document.write(sumOfParts == address2);
    document.write("<br>Is sumOfParts greater than " + address1 + "? ");
    document.write(sumOfParts > address1);
  //-->
  </script>

</body>
</html>
```

To begin, the script initializes three variables to hold three parts of an Internet Web address. Next, all three parts are added together, separated by the appropriate dots found in all Web addresses. To test if sumOfParts holds a specific Internet address, the script compares it to two possibilities.

Figure 5.4 shows that JavaScript is case sensitive when comparing strings and that it returns true only when comparing addresses with the same case. Because JavaScript strings are Unicode strings, comparison is done at the Unicode code level. So, JavaScript goes from left to right, comparing the Unicode codes (ASCII codes) of each character in both strings. If all character codes match each other, the strings are equal. All uppercase letters have values less than their lowercase equivalents, which explains why the last comparison in Listing 5.3 returns true.

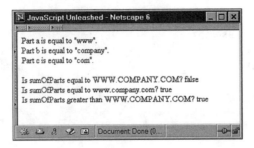

FIGURE 5.4   The concatenation of strings shown in Listing 5.4.

Conditional Operators

JavaScript uses the ternary operator (?:) to form a conditional expression. The JavaScript ternary conditional operator performs the same operation as an immediate if statement (see Chapter 6 for more information on the if statement). The conditional expression, located in front of the question mark (?), is evaluated to be a Boolean value (true or false). If an object is used as an expression, it is converted to a Boolean value, thus allowing the ternary operator to be used for error checking. Then, based on the result of the expression, one of two values is evaluated and returned. If the statement is true, the first value, located between the question mark (?) and the colon (:), is evaluated and returned. If the statement evaluates to false, the second value, located after the colon (:), is evaluated and returned. The syntax looks like this:

```
[condition]?[true expression]:[false expression]
```

For example, you can use the following conditional expression to alert the user if he is the millionth person to view the page:

```
var resultMsg = (numHits == 1000000) ? "Winner!" : "Loser!";
alert(resultMsg);
```

Provided that numHits is set equal to 1000000 elsewhere in the program, this expression returns the string Winner!; otherwise, it returns Loser!. The second line of the previous example displays the result to the user, using the built-in alert() function. If numHits is equal to one million, an alert dialog box pops up to let the visitor know. Otherwise, the expression returns false, and the failure message is displayed.

A conditional expression can be used to return any data type, such as number or boolean. The following expression returns either a string or a number, depending on whether useString evaluates to `true` or `false`. If useString is a string, it will be converted to a Boolean value. If it is an empty string, it will be converted to the Boolean value `false`. If it is a non-empty string, it will be converted to the Boolean value `true`.

```
var result = useString ? "seven" : 7;
document.write(result);
```

Boolean Operators

Boolean operators (also called logical operators) are used in conjunction with expressions that return logical values. The best way to understand Boolean operators is to see them used with comparison operators. Let's examine the three Boolean operators, logical AND, logical OR, and logical NOT.

Logical AND

The logical AND operator (&&) returns `true` if the expression to the left and the expression to the right of the operator evaluate to `true`. If either the left, right, or both expressions evaluate to `false`, the result of the operation is `false`.

The implementation of the logical AND operator in JavaScript is more complex than what was just mentioned. The AND operation actually begins by evaluating the left operand. If the left operand evaluates `false`, the basic logic of the AND operator is complete, so the right operand is never evaluated. But if the left operand evaluates `true`, the right operand must be evaluated to determine the final result of the AND operation. In either case, the final result returned by the AND operation is actually the result of the last operand to be evaluated. Consider the following examples:

```
(1 > 0) && (2 > 1)
```

Because 1 is greater than 0, the second expression must be evaluated. `True` is then returned from the second expression because 2 is greater than 1.

```
(1 > 0) && (2 < 1)
```

Because 1 is greater than 0, the second expression is evaluated. But this time `false` is returned from the second expression because 2 is not less than 1.

Logical OR

The logical OR operator (¦¦) returns `true` if the expression to the left or the expression to the right of the operator evaluates to `true`. If both the left and the right expressions evaluate to `false`, the result of the operation is `false`.

The logical OR operator is similar in complexity to the logical AND operator. The OR operation begins by evaluating the left operand. If the left operand evaluates `true`, the basic logic of the OR operator is complete, so the right operand is never evaluated. But if the left operand evaluates `false`, the right operand must be evaluated to determine the final result of the OR operation. In either case, the final result returned by the OR operation is actually the result of the last operand to be evaluated. Consider the following examples:

`(1 > 0) || (2 < 1)`

Because 1 is greater than 0 and because only one of the two expressions must evaluate to `true`, the second expression is not even evaluated. The result of `true` is returned directly from the first expression.

`(1 < 0) || (2 < 1)`

Because 1 is less than 0, the second expression must be evaluated. The second expression evaluates to `false` because 2 is not less than 1. The result of `false` is returned from the second expression.

Logical NOT

The logical NOT operator (!) is a bit simpler than the other two. The result of the expression following the operator is inverted. If the expression evaluates to `true`, the result of the operation is `false`. If the expression evaluates to `false`, the result is `true`. When the expression evaluates to a non-Boolean value, it is converted to `true` or `false` before performing the inversion based on the rules shown in Table 5.2.

`!(1 > 0)`

Because 1 is greater than 0, `true` is returned from the expression and then inverted, so the final value returned is `false`.

`!(1 < 0)`

Because 1 is not less than 0, `false` is returned from the expression and then inverted, so the final value returned is `true`.

TABLE 5.2   Bitwise Logical NOT Conversion Rules

Input Type	Result
Undefined	false
Null	false
Boolean	No conversion
Number	The result is false if the argument is +0, .0, or NaN; otherwise, the result is true.
String	The result is false if the argument is the empty string (its length is zero); otherwise, the result is true.
Object	true

The typeof Operator

The typeof operator returns a string that contains the name of the type of data that its operand currently holds. This is especially useful for determining whether a variable has been defined. Note the following examples:

typeof aFunction returns the string "function".

typeof undefinedVariable returns the string "undefined".

typeof 33 returns the string "number".

typeof "A String" returns the string "string".

typeof true returns the string "boolean".

typeof null returns the string "object".

Function Operators

Functions are covered in Chapter 7, "Functions." There are two operators you should be familiar with when dealing with functions. The first is the call operator, which is symbolized by a set of parentheses and always follows the function name. For example, a function named displayName would be declared using the following syntax:

```
function displayName(){
    [statements]
}
```

The call operator is also used when calling the function from elsewhere in a script. It would look like this:

```
displayName()
```

The parentheses signify that a function is being called.

Commas are used to separate multiple arguments that a function can accept. The call operator always encloses arguments. The displayName function modified to accept two arguments would look like the following:

```
function displayName(argument1,argument2){
    [statements]
}
```

The function would be called elsewhere in the script by passing two values, represented by a and b, into the function:

```
displayName(a,b)
```

Data Structure Operators

Data structure operators is the term I use to classify two operators that are needed when dealing with data structures. Data structures are frameworks that are set up to store one or more basic pieces of data in an orderly fashion. In JavaScript, objects are used to group pieces of data to serve a more specific purpose.

An operator that you should be familiar with when dealing with objects is commonly referred to as the dot. Symbolized by a period, the use of the dot is often referred to as dot notation. It allows you to refer to a member (a variable, a function, or an object) belonging to the specified object. The syntax is as follows:

```
ObjectName.propertyName
```

or

```
ObjectName.functionName()
```

or

```
ObjectName.anotherObject
```

Using dot notation, the rightmost property can be set or returned and the rightmost function can be called. Thanks to type conversion, it is possible to specify a primitive value in front of the dot. When a primitive value, such as a string, is placed in front of the dot, it is first converted to an object before referring to the member that appears to the right of the dot. The following line of code demonstrates how to uppercase a string directly:

```
"This is a string".toUpperCase();
```

The member operator, also known as the **array subscript operator**, is used to access members of any object. Symbolized by a pair of square brackets, it allows you to refer to any one member of an object, although they are most often associated with arrays. The following is the syntax for using the member operator:

```
objectName[indexNumber]
```

The member operator encloses an arbitrary expression that is evaluated and converted to a string, shown here as indexNumber. indexNumber specifies an index into objectName, allowing access to any one member of the object.

Bitwise Operators

At the lowest level, integers (along with all data) are stored in memory as bits. They are stored using the binary number system, which can represent any integer using the symbols 0 and 1. Depending on placement, a bit set to 1 represents a value equal to 2 raised to n, where n is the number of places from the right of the number.

For example, the integer 12 can be represented by the binary number 1100 and takes a minimum of 4 bits to store in memory. Starting from the right and moving to the left, 1100 can be calculated using the following expression:

```
0 x 2⁰ + 0 x 2¹ + 1 x 2² + 1 x 2³ = 12
```

A larger number such as 237 (11101101 in binary) requires 8 bits of memory to be stored. 11101101 can be calculated in the following way:

```
1 x 2⁰ + 0 x 2¹ + 1 x 2² + 1 x 2³ + 0 x 2⁴ + 1 x 2⁵ + 1 x 2⁶ + 1 x 2⁷ = 237
```

JavaScript sets aside 32 bits per integer when storing numbers in memory. When in memory, 237 conceptually looks like 00000000000000000000000011101101 but is typically written as 11101101, excluding the leading zeros, which are insignificant. You can enter an integer as a decimal, octal, or hexadecimal number, and JavaScript will store it in binary form.

To accommodate negative values, the leftmost bit or highest bit represents a negative value equal to $-(2^{31})$. Using the highest bit, you can start with $-(2^{31})$ and add positive values to it (represented by the remaining 31 bits) to generate any negative number greater than or equal to $-(2^{31})$. Note the following examples:

```
10000000000000000000000000000001 = -2147483648 + 1 = -2147483647

10000000000000000000000000000011 = -2147483648 + 3 = -2147483645

11111111111111111111111111111111 = -2147483648 + 2147483647 = -1

11111111111111111111111111111110 = -2147483648 + 2147483646 = -2
```

JavaScript gives you access to an integer's binary representative through bitwise operators. The simplest of bitwise operators is the unary *one's complement* operator, symbolized by the tilde (~). Its job is to "flip" every bit of its operand. This is classified as a negation operator because it negates each bit. If a bit is a 1, it will become a 0. If a bit is a 0, it will become a 1. Finding the one's complement of the number 6 can be visualized in the following ways:

```
x = ~6

x = ~00000000000000000000000000000110

x =   11111111111111111111111111111001

x = -7
```

Bitwise Logical Operators

When you use bitwise logical operators, JavaScript pairs up each operand bit by bit. It then performs the operation on each pair of bits. For example, using the bitwise AND operator on the numbers 01111 and 11011 results in the number 01011. Their binary equivalents are aligned from right to left to form five pairs of bits. The pairs are then operated on separately, and a new number is generated. The bitwise logical operators are shown in Table 5.3.

TABLE 5.3   Bitwise Logical Operators

Operator	Description
&	The bitwise AND operator evaluates both its operands and converts them to 32-bit signed integers. Then a bitwise AND operation is performed on the two 32-bit values, where in the resulting 32-bit integer value each bit is set to 1 if both operand bits are 1 and to 0 otherwise. For example, 15 & 27 returns 11 (01111 & 11011 returns 01011).
|	The bitwise OR operator evaluates both its operands and converts them to 32-bit signed integers. Then a bitwise OR operation is performed on the two 32-bit values, where in the resulting 32-bit integer value each bit is set to 0 if both operand bits are 0 and to 1 otherwise. For example, 15 | 27 returns 31 (01111 | 11011 returns 11111).
^	The bitwise exclusive OR operator evaluates both its operands and converts them to 32-bit signed integers. Then a bitwise exclusive OR operation is performed on the two 32-bit values, where in the resulting 32-bit integer value each bit is set to 1 if one but not both operand bits are 1 and to 0 otherwise. For example, 15 ^ 27 returns 20 (01111 | 11011 returns 10100).

Bitwise Shift Operators

All bitwise shift operators take two operands. The left operand is an integer whose bits are to be shifted. The right operand is the number of bits to shift the binary representation of the integer. Table 5.4 lists the bitwise shift operators.

TABLE 5.4   Bitwise Shift Operators

Operator	Description
<<	The left-shift operator returns the value of an integer if its bits were shifted a number of places to the left. All void rightmost bits are filled in with zeros. The following examples shift the number 15 to the left by 1 and then by 2.
	15 << 1 returns 30 (1111 << 1 returns 11110)
	15 << 2 returns 60 (1111 << 2 returns 111100)
	Note that shifting a positive integer to the left n times is equivalent to multiplying the value by 2 n times. In most cases, a computer can perform a left-shift faster than it can multiply by 2. For this reason, it is common to see the bitwise left-shift chosen over its higher-level counterpart when performing many multiplications. Any small increase in efficiency could result in a noticeable advantage.

TABLE 5.4   Continued

Operator	Description
	Using the left-shift on a negative integer could result in either a negative or positive integer, depending on the state of the highest bit after the left-shift has been performed.
>>	The sign-propagating right-shift operator returns the value of an integer if its bits were shifted a number of places to the right. All void bits are filled in with a copy of the leftmost bit (also called the *sign bit*). Copying the leftmost bit ensures that the integer will stay either positive or negative. This is also a more efficient way to divide a positive even integer by 2 *n* times. In the case of a positive odd integer, a right-shift is the same as dividing by 2 *n* times, but it throws away remainders. Note the following examples: 15 >> 1 returns 7 (1111 >> 1 returns 0111) -15 >> 1 returns -8 (11111111111111111111111111110001 >> 1 returns 11111111111111111111111111111000)
>>>	The zero-fill right-shift operator returns the value of an integer if its bits were shifted a number of places to the right. All void high-order bits are filled in with zeros. When operating on positive integers, the zero-fill right-shift operator produces the same result as using the sign-propagating right-shift operator. This is because the sign bit being copied is always zero for positive integers. As for negative integers, any zero-fill right-shift will change the highest bit from a 1 to a 0. The result will always be an integer that is greater than or equal to 0. Note the following examples: 15 >>> 1 returns 7 (1111 >>> 1 returns 0111) -15 >>> 1 returns 2147483640 (11111111111111111111111111110001 >> 1 returns 01111111111111111111111111111000)

Why Mess with Bits?

Bitwise operators aren't needed in most scripts. It's possible that you may never have to deal with bits for your entire JavaScript career. However, there are special cases where dealing with data at its lowest level becomes practical or even necessary.

One example of how bitwise operators can be used is when converting a number from base 10 (decimal) to base 16 (hexadecimal). Although this can easily be done with the toString method of the Number object, let's try tackling the problem using bitwise operators. If you store the value 0xDC in a variable x, JavaScript converts it to binary. If you try to display x using the following lines of code, the number is displayed in decimal as 220:

```
var x = 0xDC;

// Will write "220" to the display
document.writeln(x);
```

This is a useful function if you are performing operations on HTML color values that are in hexadecimal. The easiest way to accomplish this is to use the binary value of the integer and translate it into hexadecimal. Hexadecimal values are easily represented in binary.

Four bits of memory can store 16 values. Because hexadecimal uses 16 digits, it takes 4 bits to store the value of each hexadecimal digit. In a 32-bit integer, the rightmost 4 bits of memory represent the rightmost digit of a hexadecimal integer. The next 4 bits store the next digit, and so on. To convert a 32-bit integer into hexadecimal, you can do this eight times, matching each 4-bit value to its hexadecimal equivalent.

To read in only 4 bits at a time, use the & operator with a control value. The control value should have a 1 in each bit location that you would like to copy from the integer being converted. Because you want the value of the first 4 bits, the control value should have a 1 in its first 4 bits. All other bits should be set to 0. The control value in this case must equal 1111 (15 or 0xF). Conceptually, this operation appears as the following:

Control: 00000000000000000000000000001111 &

Integer to convert: 00000000000000000000000011011100 =

Result: 00000000000000000000000000001100

The result is a copy of the first 4 bits of the integer you're converting. You can easily compare this to each of the 16 hexadecimal digits to find that it is equal to C. To find the next hexadecimal digit, copy the next 4 bits out of the integer. I have chosen to do this by shifting all the bits in the integer 4 bits to the right while using the same control. This will work as in the following:

Control: 00000000000000000000000000001111 &

Integer to convert: 00000000000000000000000000001101 =

Result: 00000000000000000000000000001101

Again, you can use the result to match up against the second digit, D. If the original integer was larger, you could continue this process up to six more times.

Listing 5.5 shows this algorithm in action. Using only the operators discussed up to this point, it can convert any 8-bit value into a string representing its hexadecimal equivalent. First I assign to the variable intValue the value to be converted. I then display the value to show that JavaScript will return only the decimal value of DC, which is 220. The program proceeds to translate the binary form of 220 into hexadecimal and displays the result. The output is shown in Figure 5.5.

LISTING 5.5   Converting Base 10 to Base 16 Using Bitwise Operators

```
<html>
<head>
  <title>JavaScript Unleashed</title>
</head>
<body>
  <script type="text/javascript">
  <!--
    // Declare variables
    var originalInt;

    // intValue can be any 8 bit value.
    var intValue = 0xDC;
    var controlValue = 0xF;
    var fourBitValue;
    var hexChar = "";
    var hexString = "";
    document.writeln("When displaying integers from memory,");
    document.writeln("JavaScript always uses their decimal ");
    document.writeln("equivalent: " + intValue);
    originalInt = intValue;
    fourBitValue =  controlValue & intValue;
    hexChar = (fourBitValue == 0x0) ? "0" : hexChar;
    hexChar = (fourBitValue == 0x1) ? "1" : hexChar;
    hexChar = (fourBitValue == 0x2) ? "2" : hexChar;
    hexChar = (fourBitValue == 0x3) ? "3" : hexChar;
    hexChar = (fourBitValue == 0x4) ? "4" : hexChar;
    hexChar = (fourBitValue == 0x5) ? "5" : hexChar;
    hexChar = (fourBitValue == 0x6) ? "6" : hexChar;
    hexChar = (fourBitValue == 0x7) ? "7" : hexChar;
    hexChar = (fourBitValue == 0x8) ? "8" : hexChar;
    hexChar = (fourBitValue == 0x9) ? "9" : hexChar;
    hexChar = (fourBitValue == 0xA) ? "A" : hexChar;
    hexChar = (fourBitValue == 0xB) ? "B" : hexChar;
    hexChar = (fourBitValue == 0xC) ? "C" : hexChar;
    hexChar = (fourBitValue == 0xD) ? "D" : hexChar;
    hexChar = (fourBitValue == 0xE) ? "E" : hexChar;
    hexChar = (fourBitValue == 0xF) ? "F" : hexChar;

    // Build hexString placing digits from right to left
    hexString = hexChar + hexString;
```

LISTING 5.5   Continued

```
    // Shift intValue four bits right
    intValue = intValue >> 4;

    // Extract the next four bit value
    fourBitValue =  controlValue & intValue;
    // Find the matching hex value and assign its string
    // equivalent to hexChar.
    hexChar = (fourBitValue == 0x0) ? "0" : hexChar;
    hexChar = (fourBitValue == 0x1) ? "1" : hexChar;
    hexChar = (fourBitValue == 0x2) ? "2" : hexChar;
    hexChar = (fourBitValue == 0x3) ? "3" : hexChar;
    hexChar = (fourBitValue == 0x4) ? "4" : hexChar;
    hexChar = (fourBitValue == 0x5) ? "5" : hexChar;
    hexChar = (fourBitValue == 0x6) ? "6" : hexChar;
    hexChar = (fourBitValue == 0x7) ? "7" : hexChar;
    hexChar = (fourBitValue == 0x8) ? "8" : hexChar;
    hexChar = (fourBitValue == 0x9) ? "9" : hexChar;
    hexChar = (fourBitValue == 0xA) ? "A" : hexChar;
    hexChar = (fourBitValue == 0xB) ? "B" : hexChar;
    hexChar = (fourBitValue == 0xC) ? "C" : hexChar;
    hexChar = (fourBitValue == 0xD) ? "D" : hexChar;
    hexChar = (fourBitValue == 0xE) ? "E" : hexChar;
    hexChar = (fourBitValue == 0xF) ? "F" : hexChar;
    hexString = hexChar + hexString;
    document.write("<br>" + originalInt + " displayed in");
    document.write(" hexadecimal :");
    document.writeln(hexString);
    // end hiding -->
  </script>
</body>
</html>
```

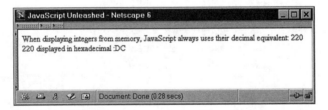

FIGURE 5.5   Converting base 10 to base 16, as shown in Listing 5.5.

NOTE

The previous example uses multiple conditional expressions to find a match. More efficient ways to compare a range of numbers can be accomplished using loops or even a simply indexed array:

```
var hexDigits = ['0', '1', '2', '3', '4', '5', '6', '7', '8', '9', 'A', 'B', 'C', 'D',
➥'E', 'F'];
```

NOTE

As mentioned earlier, it is possible to convert to an alternative base using the toString method of the Numbers object. Simply specify the base as an argument to the toString method. For example, to convert the integer 220 to base 16, simply write:

```
document.write((220).toString(16))
```

This will yield the result "dc".

Operator Precedence

When creating expressions that use more than one operator, you should be aware that JavaScript doesn't necessarily evaluate an expression from right to left or vice versa. Each part of an expression is evaluated in an order based on a predefined precedence for each operator. Note the following example:

```
x = a + b * c
```

b is multiplied by c; the result is added to a. The result of the addition is finally assigned to x. The multiplication operator has a higher precedence than the addition operator and therefore is evaluated first. The assignment operator is evaluated last because it has the lowest precedence. If you need the addition to be evaluated first, you can enclose the expression in parentheses:

```
x = (a *+ b) * c
```

Parentheses are operators that boost the precedence of the expression that they enclose. When an expression has more than one operator of the same precedence, JavaScript evaluates from left to right. The one exception is the assignment operator, which evaluates from right to left.

Table 5.5 shows operators in order of their precedence, from lowest to highest.

TABLE 5.5   Operator Precedence

Operator	Name	Operator
Lowest	Comma	,
	Assignment	= += -= *= /= %= <<= >>= >>>= &= ^= |=
	Conditional	?:

TABLE 5.5   Continued

Operator	Name	Operator
	Logical OR	||
	Logical AND	&&
	Bitwise OR	|
	Bitwise XOR	^
	Bitwise AND	&
	Equality	== != === !==
	Comparison	< <= > >= in instanceof
	Bitwise shift	<< >> >>>
	Addition/subtraction	+ -
	Multiplication/division	* / %
	Negation/increment	! ~ - ++ -- typeof new void delete
Highest	Call, data structure	() [] .

One effect that operator precedence can have is determining the type of value that is returned by an expression. This becomes apparent when trying to concatenate strings and numbers, as shown in Listing 5.6.

LISTING 5.6   Operator Precedence and Different Data Types

```
<html>
<head>
  <title>JavaScript Unleashed</title>
</head>
<body>
  <script type="text/javascript">
  <!--
    //Displays "9"
    var carLength = 4 + 5;
    document.write(carLength);

    //Displays "45 feet"
    carLength = "<br>" + 4 + 5 + " feet";
    document.write(carLength);

    //Displays "Length in feet: 45"
    carLength = "<br>Length in feet: " + 4 + 5;
    document.write(carLength);

    //Displays "Length in feet: 9"
    carLength = "<br>Length in feet: " + (4 + 5);
```

LISTING 5.6 Continued

```
    document.writeln(carLength);
  //-->
  </script>
</body>
</html>
```

When expressions have operators of the same precedence, JavaScript evaluates from left to right. The addition operator has the same precedence as the concatenate operator; therefore, JavaScript will evaluate all additions and concatenations from left to right throughout the statement.

Notice in Figure 5.6 that the first example works as you would expect. The remaining examples show what can happen when JavaScript works as designed. The first example simply adds the numbers 4 and 5 and writes the result (9) to the screen. The second example converts the number 4 to a string and concatenates it to the end of `"<br> "`. The result of this is the string `"<br>4"`. It then does the same with the number 5 to produce `"<br> 45"`.

In the third example the number 4 is converted to a string and concatenated to the end of `"Length in feet: "`. The result of this is the string `"Length in feet: 4"`. It then does the same with the number 5 to produce `"Length in feet: 45"`. If, however, you want to display the sum of 4 and 5 instead, you can use parentheses to increase the precedence of `4 + 5`. In this case, both operands are numbers, and JavaScript performs an addition rather than a string concatenation. Figure 5.6 shows this as the fourth example.

FIGURE 5.6   Operator precedence and different data types, as shown in Listing 5.6.

Summary

Assignment operators assign values to variables. Along with the simple assignment operator, JavaScript supports 11 assignment operators that combine either arithmetic or bitwise operators with the simple assignment operator.

Arithmetic operators let you perform basic math operations in JavaScript. These include addition, subtraction, multiplication, division, and modulus. JavaScript also includes increment and decrement operators as shortcuts to two common math operations. More advanced math operations are also built into JavaScript, but they must be accessed through the Math object, which is discussed in Chapter 8, "Core Language Objects."

Comparison operators compare two values and return a value of true or false. You can check to see whether one value is equal to another, greater or less than another, or any combination of these.

The conditional operators let you return one of two values that you can define to be of any data type. The value returned is decided by the value of a logical expression that you also define.

String operators include the concatenation operator and all comparison operators. The concatenation operator is used to append one string to another to form a new string. Comparison operators can be used with strings to compare character by character based on the Unicode values. Starting with the leftmost character of each string and moving right, a single pair of characters is compared at a time. The returned value is either true or false.

Boolean operators are used with logical expressions to form another logical expression. The AND operator returns the result of the second operand if both of its operands are true. Otherwise, it returns the value of the first operand. The OR operator returns the result of the first operand that is true. Otherwise, it returns the result of the second operand. The NOT operator returns true if its operand is false, and it will return false if its operand is true.

The typeof operator is a built-in operator used to return a string representing the type of data that its operand holds. This is especially useful when determining if a variable has been defined yet.

The call operator always follows a function name and surrounds any arguments that the function might accept. Commas are used to separate arguments if the function accepts more than one.

When you're dealing with arrays and other objects, two operators are needed. The dot is used to reference a member of an object. This is the standard dot notation. The member operator is used to index one element of an object. It follows the object name and encloses an integer or string that refers to the location of the element being accessed.

JavaScript allows access to the binary representation of any integer through its bitwise operators. The one's complement operator is used to flip each bit of an integer. Bitwise logical operators are included to compare two integers. The binary form of each operand is used to pair up the bits in each integer. The logical operation is then performed on each pair of bits to return the resulting integer. Bitwise shift operators shift the bits of an integer to the right or left n number of places. When shifting to the right, JavaScript allows you to specify either sign-propagating or zero-fill shifting.

When all operations in the expression are of the same precedence, JavaScript interprets from left to right when evaluating expressions, except for assignment operators, which work from right to left. Otherwise, the operation with the highest precedence is performed first and then the next highest, and so on. JavaScript predefines the precedence of each operator.

In the next chapter you will learn how to combine these operators with conditional statements and loops to make your script more compact and efficient.

5

CHAPTER **6**

Control Structures and Looping

Designing a script to make decisions during runtime can be the most interesting part of JavaScript. When you have a script make a decision based on its present state, you're simply telling it to ask a question and then choose a path to take based on the answer.

For example, consider my morning commute to work. I can take a couple of different routes, and I choose one based on certain factors. I seldom cook, so the most important question I ask myself in the morning is whether I'm hungry. If I am, I choose the route that passes by the bagel shop. By the time I've finished picking up my breakfast, I'm usually running a little late. To make up for lost time, I drive directly to the highway, where I can quickly accelerate to just under the speed limit. On the other hand, if I'm not hungry, which is hardly ever the case, I choose to drive past the bagel shop and continue driving to work at a steady 10 miles per hour below the speed limit.

Using the same idea, you can design your JavaScript programs to perform specific operations based on one or more factors. For example, in Chapter 5, "Operators," you learned how to test whether a variable is equal to a particular value or even a range of values. Using control structures, you can now make your program take one or more different paths based on the result of such a test. This is the first topic that will be covered in this chapter.

As your programs become larger, one thing to watch for is the length of time it could take for the client to download them.

One way to cut down on the amount of source code in a script is to use looping statements. Using a loop, you can make your scripts perform many similar operations with only a few lines of code. This can help you shrink the size of your scripts and avoid typing the same lines of code repeatedly. This chapter will also demonstrate ways to make your scripts more efficient.

Conditional Statements

In Chapter 5, the `ternary` operator (`?:`) was discussed. This operator is used to create a conditional operation. The conditional expression, located in front of the question mark (?), is evaluated to be either `true` or `false`. Then, based on the result, one of two values is evaluated and returned. If the statement is `true`, the first value, located between the question mark (?) and the colon (:), is evaluated and returned. If the statement evaluates to `false`, the second value, located after the colon (:), is evaluated and returned. The syntax looks like this:

```
[condition]?[true expression]:[false expression]
```

Similarly, you can have scripts make decisions based on an expression using the `if` and `else` statements. However, the result is different. Instead of returning a value based on the result, the program takes one of two paths. With this capability, you can make JavaScript perform many different functions based on any information you have available.

if

The `if` statement is one of the most popular statements you will use. Every programming language has it in one form or another, and its use cannot be avoided. You use the `if` statement in the following way:

```
if (condition)
{
   [statements]
}
```

The `conditional expression` is evaluated and is then converted to a Boolean value. If the Boolean value is `true`, the `statements` are executed, and program execution continues. If the Boolean value is `false`, JavaScript ignores the `statements` and continues.

Before moving on, it is important that you fully understand the way conditional expressions in an `if` statement (as well as the `if..else` and `ternary` statements) are evaluated. The expression in any conditional statement can be of any type because it is first evaluated and then converted to a Boolean value. Table 6.1 describes the precise conversion that takes place depending on the expression type.

TABLE 6.1   Expression Type Boolean Conversion

Type	Result
Undefined	`false`
Null	`false`
Boolean	The result equals the input argument (no conversion).
Number	The result is `false` if the argument is +0, -0, or NaN; otherwise, the result is true.
String	The result is `false` if the argument is the empty string (its length is zero); otherwise, the result is `true`.
Object	`true`

Although the `if` statement tests for a true condition, it is possible to make it test for a false condition as well by placing the negation operator (!) in front of the condition to be tested but within the parentheses. This is useful for throwing errors.

NOTE

More information about using the `if` statement to throw errors can be found in Chapter 30, "Error Handling."

The curly braces are not required if only one statement is to be executed. But if more than one statement is needed, curly braces must be used. In general it is good programming practice to always use curly braces to hold the `if` statement regardless of the number of statements because it improves code readability.

Listing 6.1 emulates the type of influence an overbearing marketing department might have on a company's Web site. The script begins by setting the value of `visitorInterest` to one of two values. I selected `"Technical Support"` for this example and commented out the alternative assignment.

Next, the script reaches the first `if` statement, which checks whether the value of `visitorInterest` is equal to the string `"New Products"`. The resulting value of this expression is `false`, and the block of code immediately following the `if` statement is ignored. The script then reaches the second `if` statement and checks the value of `visitorInterest` against `"Technical Support"`. The expression returns `true`, and the code that is enclosed in curly braces is executed.

Regardless of what value `visitorInterest` is equal to, the last statement always executes, and salesman Frank Zealous sends his pitch to the visitor. The entire display is shown in Figure 6.1. If you switch the value of `visitorInterest`, the output will change.

LISTING 6.1   Using the if Statement to Make Decisions

```
<html>
<head>
  <title>JavaScript Unleashed</title>
```

LISTING 6.1   Continued

```
</head>
<body>
  <script type="text/javascript">
  <!--
    // Declare variables
    var visitorInterest;
    // visitorInterest = "New Products";
    visitorInterest = "Technical Support";

    document.writeln("Hello, my name is Frank Zealous!");

    // Evaluate value of vistorInterest
    if (visitorInterest == "New Products")
    {
      document.writeln("Thank you for inquiring about our products!");
    }

    if (visitorInterest == "Technical Support")
    {
      document.writeln("Technical support is now available.");
      document.write("But first, let me introduce you to our ");
      document.writeln("newest products!");
    }

    document.write("<br>Our newest products will satisfy all of your ");
    document.writeln("business needs!");
  // -->
  </script>
</body>
</html>
```

It's common practice to indent the set of statements enclosed in curly braces. This helps give your scripts a logical look and proves especially helpful when you nest if statements (that is, when you use an if statement within another if statement).

Listing 6.2 demonstrates how you can use logical variables by themselves to determine the path a script can take. The first if statement evaluates the variable needsInfo. needsInfo was set to true, so JavaScript enters the first if block and continues by displaying "Our products are used all over the world". Next, the second, or nested, if block is reached, and needsMoreInfo is evaluated. Again, the value returned is true, and the statements within the second if block are executed. The end of the nested if block is completed, and JavaScript picks up where it left off with the first block. Notice how the indentation helps distinguish the separate blocks of code that may or may not be executed.

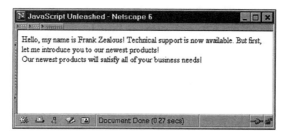

FIGURE 6.1   Frank gives a customized sales pitch.

Figure 6.2 shows that JavaScript performed each line of code in sequence. By resetting the values of needsInfo and needsMoreInfo, you can create three different results. One important thing to realize is that if needsInfo is false, the second if block is never reached. In this case, it doesn't matter if needsMoreInfo is set to true or false, because it will never have a chance to be evaluated. Sorry, Frank, but if they don't need information, they certainly don't need *more* information.

LISTING 6.2   Nested if Statements

```
<html>
<head>
  <title>JavaScript Unleashed</title>
</head>
<body>
  <script type="text/javascript">
  <!--
    // Declare variables
    var needsInfo;
    var needsMoreInfo;

    // Set either of the following to false to see a change in the output.
    needsInfo = true;
    needsMoreInfo = true;

    document.writeln("I work for Best Products International!");
    if (needsInfo)
    {
      document.writeln("Our products are used all over the world.");
      if(needsMoreInfo)
      {
```

LISTING 6.2   Continued

```
        document.write("<br>I don't know how you have managed");
        document.writeln(" without them.");
      }
      document.writeln("<br>Ordering is easy using our on-line service.");
    }
  // -->
  </script>
</body>
</html>
```

FIGURE 6.2   One of three possible outcomes.

if..else

Sometimes using the `if` statement alone is not enough. You can also reserve a set of state-ments to execute if the conditional expression returns `false`. You do this by adding an `else` block of statements immediately following the `if` block:

```
if(condition)
{
  statements
}
else
{
  statements
}
```

Additionally, if you don't want to go straight into a default block, you can combine the `else` portion with another `if` statement. Using this method, you can evaluate several different acceptable scenarios before performing the proper operation. The beauty of using this method is that you can finish it off with an `else` segment as well. The format for this type of statement is as follows:

```
if(condition)
{
```

```
    statements
}
else if (condition)
{
    statements
}
else
{
    statements
}
```

As mentioned earlier in the chapter, the curly braces are not required if only one statement is to be executed. But if more than one statement is needed, curly braces must be used. In general it is good programming practice to always use curly braces to hold the `if` and `else` statements regardless of the number of statements because it improves code readability.

Nothing is worse than a nagging computer, but Listing 6.3 demonstrates how interactive a Web page can be with only a few lines of code. The key value, `purchaseAmount`, is retrieved from the user using the `Window` object's built-in `prompt()` function. The `prompt()` function takes two arguments; the first argument is the question and the second argument is the default value displayed in the prompt entry box. If you use the `prompt` function, `purchaseAmount` can be any value, depending on what the customer orders. Chapter 12, "Form Objects," covers the topic of receiving user input in more detail.

In this example, if the user enters "10.00," he hasn't spent enough money to satisfy Frank. The outer `if` statement first checks to see if any value was entered at all. If no value had been entered, `purchaseAmount` would be null and nothing would be displayed to the browser. Because "10.00" was entered, the outer `if` statement evaluates to `true`. The first, inner `if` condition evaluates to `false`, so the `else if` condition is tested. Similarly, the second `if` condition evaluates to `false`, so the final `else` block is executed. Figure 6.3 shows how the user's purchase is questioned by a pushy salesman.

LISTING 6.3   The else Block Responds to a false Value

```html
<html>
<head>
  <title>JavaScript Unleashed</title>
</head>
<body>
  <script type="text/javascript">
  <!--
    // Declare variable
```

LISTING 6.3   Continued

```
    var purchaseAmount = prompt("Enter your purchase amount.","");

    if(purchaseAmount)
    {
      if(purchaseAmount > 500.00)
      {
        document.write("Thank you for your purchase!");
      }
      else if(purchaseAmount > 100.00 && purchaseAmount <= 500.00)
      {
        document.write("Thank you for your purchase.  Remember if<br>");
        document.write("you spend over $500.00 you get free shipping!");
      }
      else
      {
        document.writeln("Thank you, but surely there is something<br>");
        document.writeln("else you would like to purchase.");
      }
    }
  // -->
  </script>
</body>
</html>
```

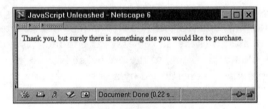

FIGURE 6.3   One of two possible outcomes.

try..catch..finally

The try..catch..finally statement is used to override the default environment handling of errors. This section does not go into a lot of detail about errors. Check out Chapter 30, for more information on try..catch..finally and how to use it to handle errors.

Looping Statements

Creating a loop inside a script can serve many purposes. One simple but very common use of a loop is counting. For example, writing a program that displays the numbers 0 through 9 is a quick and easy task. You could simply write 10 commands to display each number:

```
document.writeln("0");
document.writeln("1");
...
document.writeln("9");
```

This works for counting from 0 to 9, but what if you needed to count to 1,000? You can do this in the same manner, but the code takes much more time to write and download. The best way to count to 1,000 or any number is to use the same display statement with a variable in place of the string literal. By counting like this, the only thing you need is a way to increment the variable and repeat the display statement. JavaScript gives you the tools to handle this and other looping operations. The remainder of this chapter will be devoted to examining each of these looping structures in detail.

for

Use the for statement to start a loop in a script. Before taking a closer look at the for statement in Listing 6.4, examine the following syntax:

```
for ([initializing_expr]; [condition_expr]; [loop_expr])
{
  statements
}
```

The three expressions enclosed in parentheses are optional, but if you omit one, the semicolons are still required. This keeps each expression in its appropriate place. Remember that the curly braces are optional unless there is more than one statement.

You typically use the initializing expression to initialize and even declare a variable to use as a counter for the loop. Next, the condition expression must evaluate to true before each execution of the statements enclosed in curly braces. Finally, the loop expression typically increments or decrements the variable that is used as the counter for the loop.

Listing 6.4 demonstrates the use of a for statement to count from 0 to 99 while displaying each number. To fit the output on a standard page, line breaks were added after each set of 10 numbers. The output is shown in Figure 6.4.

LISTING 6.4   A for Loop Used to Count from 0 to 99

```
<html>
<head>
  <title>JavaScript Unleashed</title>
```

LISTING 6.4   Continued

```
<body>
  <script type="text/javascript">
  <!--
    // Write the header part to the page
    document.write("Numbers 0 through 99:");
    document.write('<hr size="0" width="50%" align="left">');

    for (var i = 0; i < 100; ++i)
    {
      // Put a break in between every 10th number
      if(i%10 == 0)
      {
        document.write('<br>');
      }

      // Write the number to the page
      document.write(i + ",");
    }

    // Finish up with the last number
    document.write("<br><br>After completing the loop, i equals : " + i);

  // -->
  </script>
</body>
</html>
```

FIGURE 6.4   The output after looping through the same code 100 times.

In Listing 6.4, the order of execution is as follows: The initializing expression declares the variable i and sets it to 0. The variable i is then tested to ensure that it's less than 100. Where i is still equal to 0, the condition expression returns true, and the program executes the statements between the curly braces. After the program executes all the statements and reaches the ending curly brace, it evaluates the loop expression, ++i. This increments i by 1, thus concluding the first full loop.

The process now begins again from the top. This time, JavaScript knows not to perform the initializing section of the for loop. Instead, the condition expression is evaluated again. Where i is still less than 100, another loop is allowed to occur. This continues, and the set of statements inside the for block is repeated until i reaches 100.

At 99, the condition expression returns true, and the program executes the statements one last time. Once again, i is incremented and set to 100. When the condition expression is evaluated, it returns false, and the loop breaks. Program execution picks up immediately after the ending curly brace.

Because i was incremented to 100 before the loop was broken, 100 is the resulting value of i after the loop is finished. Notice also that the scope of i extends outside the for loop, obeying the rules of scope discussed in Chapter 4, "Fundamental Language Components."

> **NOTE**
>
> If the condition expression returns false on the first loop, the statements between the curly braces are never executed.

As with if statements, for loops can also be nested. Listing 6.5 shows how to step through each coordinate of a 10×10 grid. For each iteration of the first loop, there are 10 iterations of the nested loop. The result is that the nested loop is executed 100 times.

LISTING 6.5   A Demonstration of a Nested Loop

```
<html>
<head>
  <title>JavaScript Unleashed</title>
</head>
<body>
  <script type="text/javascript">
  <!--
    document.write("All x,y coordinates between (0,0) and (9,9):<br>")

    for (var x = 0; x < 10; ++x)
    {
      for (var y = 0; y < 10; ++y)
      {
```

LISTING 6.5   Continued

```
        document.write("(" + x + "," + y + "),");
    }
    document.write('<br>');
}

document.write("<br>After completing the loop, x equals : " + x);
document.write("<br>After completing the loop, y equals : " + y);
// -->
</script>
</body>
</html>
```

x is first assigned the value of 0. JavaScript reaches the nested loop and also assigns 0 to y. The nested loop displays the values of x and y and then increments y by 1. The nested loop continues until y is no longer less than 10. At this point, 10 sets of coordinates have been generated. The nested loop breaks, and control returns to the outer loop. x is incremented by 1, and again the nested loop starts.

JavaScript knows that the nested loop is starting from the beginning and that the initializing expression must be evaluated again. This resets y to 0, and the statements are run another 10 times. The entire process continues until x is no longer less than 10 and the outer loop finally breaks. This displays 100 sets of coordinates, as shown in Figure 6.5.

You aren't limited to a single nested loop, so you can increase the number of coordinates to three or even four. You can also use this same method to visit each element of a multi-dimensional array. Arrays are discussed in Chapter 8, "Core Language Objects."

FIGURE 6.5   One hundred sets of coordinates generated by two loops.

for..in

You need a basic understanding of JavaScript objects to use a `for..in` loop. After reading Part III, "Core and Client JavaScript Objects," you should be able to use the `for..in` construct with ease.

With `for..in`, you can execute a set of statements for each property in an object. You can use the `for..in` loop with any JavaScript object, regardless of whether it has properties. One iteration is executed for each property, so if the object doesn't have any properties, no loops occur. The `for..in` loop is possible because the enumeration of the properties of objects is performed by the browser. Because the browser determines what is enumerated, it is possible that some properties of an object are not available through the `for..in` statement. So there is no guarantee that all properties of an object will be found. For example, looping through an `Array` object will not yield the length property of the `Array` object. Here is the syntax for the `for..in` loop:

```
for (property in object)
{
  statements
}
```

property is a variable name that is populated with a string value by JavaScript. For each loop, *property* is assigned the next property name contained in *object* until each one is used. Listing 6.6 uses this function to display each property name of the `Document` object, along with each of the property's values. As mentioned earlier, not all of the property names and values are shown, as seen in Figure 6.6.

> **NOTE**
>
> Opera 6 does not enumerate the document properties, so Listing 6.6 will yield nothing in the Opera 6 browser.

LISTING 6.6   Using a for..in Loop in JavaScript

```html
<html>
<head>
  <title>JavaScript Unleashed</title>
</head>
<body>
  <script language="JavaScript1.1" type="text/javascript">
  <!--
    // Declare variables
    var anObject = document;
    var propertyInfo = "";
```

LISTING 6.6 Continued

```
    for (var propertyName in anObject)
    {
      propertyInfo = propertyName + " = " + anObject[propertyName];
      document.write(propertyInfo + "<br>");
    }
  // -->
  </script>
</body>
</html>
```

FIGURE 6.6 Each property and its value for the Document object.

while

The while statement acts much like a for loop but doesn't include the function of initial-izing or incrementing variables in its declaration. You must declare variables beforehand and increment or decrement the variables within the *statements* block. As with other operators, the curly braces are not required if only one statement is needed. The syntax follows:

```
while(condition_expr)
{
  statements
}
```

Listing 6.7 shows how you can use a logical variable as a flag in determining whether to continue looping. This variable, status, is declared ahead of time and set to true. When i is equal to `10`, status is set to `false`, and the loop breaks. The result of Listing 6.7 is the sum of the integers from 0 to 10, as you can see in Figure 6.7.

LISTING 6.7   Using the while Loop in JavaScript

```html
<html>
<head>
  <title>JavaScript Unleashed</title>
</head>
<body>
  <script type="text/javascript">
  <!--
    // Declare variables
    var i = 0;
    var result = 0;
    var status = true;

    document.write("0");
    while(status)
    {
      result += ++i;
      document.write(" + " + i);
      if(i == 10)
      {
        status = false;
      }
    }
    document.writeln(" = " + result);
    // -->
  </script>
</body>
</html>
```

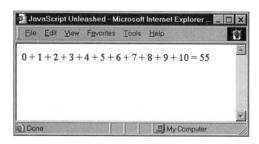

FIGURE 6.7   The result of Listing 6.7: Ten iterations of a while loop.

do..while

Starting with JavaScript 1.2, the language has offered a do..while construct. This works exactly like the while statement, except that it doesn't check the conditional expression until after the first iteration. This guarantees that the script within the curly braces (only required if more than one statement is executed) will be executed at least once.

Listing 6.8 shows an example in which it's unknown what the exact value of userEntry might be (if it were actually entered by the user). A value of 0 is given to userEntry to demonstrate that the user might not enter a value that satisfies the conditional statement. The user's entry is still displayed once because the do..while loop is always executed once before the conditional test is reached. The result of running Listing 6.8 is shown in Figure 6.8.

LISTING 6.8   The do..while Statement Ensures at Least One Iteration

```
<html>
<head>
  <title>JavaScript Unleashed</title>
</head>
<body>
<script language="JavaScript" type="text/javascript">
  <!--
    // Declare variables
    var userEntry = 0;
    var x = 1;

    do
    {
      document.writeln("x=" + x + "  userEntry=" + userEntry + "<br>");
      x++;
    }while(x <= userEntry)
  // -->
  </script>
</body>
</html>
```

break and continue

One thing to note when using a loop is that, by default, it doesn't stop repeating itself until the specified condition returns false. Sometimes, however, you might want to exit or short-circuit the loop before reaching the ending curly brace. This can be accomplished by adding break or continue, respectively, to the *statements* block of the loop.

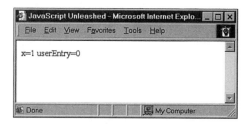

FIGURE 6.8   The result of Listing 6.8: Always one pass through the do..while loop.

break terminates the loop altogether, whereas continue skips the remaining statements for the current loop, evaluates the loop expression (if one exists), and begins the next loop. You can see the difference between these two statements in Listing 6.9. This script takes a very basic approach to finding the approximate square root of a number, n.

LISTING 6.9   Using the continue and break Statements

```
<html>
<head>
  <title>JavaScript Unleashed</title>
</head>
<body>
  <script type="text/javascript">
  <!--
    // Declare variables
    var highestNum = 0;
    var n = 175;          // Sample value

    for(var i = 0; i < n; ++i)
    {
      document.write(i + "<br>");

      //Break out of the for loop all together if n is less than 0.
      if(n < 0)
      {
        document.write("n cannot be negative.");
        break;
      }

      //Go to the next loop iteration if i squared is less than or equal to n
      if (i * i <= n)
      {
        highestNum = i;
        continue;
      }
```

6

LISTING 6.9   Continued

```
      document.write("<br>Finished!");

      //If not caught by one of the if statements then break out of the for loop.
      break;}
   document.write("<br>The integer less than or equal to the Square Root");
   document.write(" of " + n + " = " + highestNum);
  // -->
  </script>
</body>
</html>
```

Starting with i set to 0, the for loop begins by displaying the value of i. Next, the script checks to ensure that n is not negative. If n is negative, the loop is broken, and program execution resumes after the ending curly brace. If n is positive, i is multiplied by itself, and the result is compared to n. If the result is less than n, i is stored as the highest number so far to be equal to or less than the square root of n.

The continue statement then skips the rest of the current loop and resumes from the top of the loop after incrementing i. As soon as i squared is greater than n, the script passes the continue statement and reaches the break statement, which stops the loop completely. The approximate square root of 175 is shown in Figure 6.9.

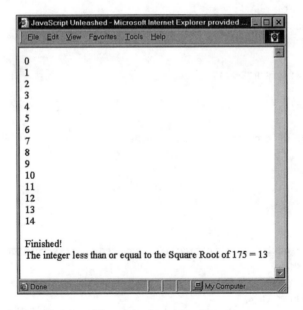

FIGURE 6.9   The display after break is reached and the loop stops.

label Statements

The label statement offers a way to be more specific when using the break and continue statements. The label statement can be placed before any control structure that can nest other statements. This allows you to break out of a conditional statement or loop to a specific location in your code. You can see an example of its use in Listing 6.10.

LISTING 6.10   Using the label Statement

```
<html>
<head>
  <title>JavaScript Unleashed</title>
</head>
<body>
  <script language="JavaScript1.2" type="text/javascript">
  <!--
    // Declare variables
    var stopX = 3;
    var stopY = 8;

    document.write("All x,y pairs between (0,0) and (");
    document.write(stopX + "," + stopY + "):<br>");

  loopX:
    for(var x = 0; x < 10; ++x)
    {
      for(var y = 0; y < 10; ++y)
      {
        document.write("("+x + "," + y +") ");
        if((x == stopX) && (y == stopY))
        {
          break loopX;
        }
      }
      document.write("<br>");
    }
    document.write("<br>After completing the loop, x equals : " + x);
    document.writeln("<br>After completing the loop, y equals : " + y);
  // -->
  </script>
</body>
</html>
```

In Listing 6.10, a `for` loop is "labeled" with the user-defined identifier `loopX`. This lets you break out of or continue in this `for` loop, regardless of how nested the program is at that time. `loopX` is added to the `break` statement to stop both `for` loops from continuing. Without the label, the `break` statement would have stopped only the loop generating values for y. Figure 6.10 displays the result when the x and y values reach 3 and 8, respectively.

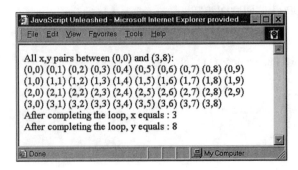

FIGURE 6.10 Using the `label` statement to break out of a nested for loop.

with Statements

The `with` statement is used to avoid repeatedly specifying the object reference when accessing properties or methods of that object. Any property or method in a `with` block that JavaScript doesn't recognize is associated with the object specified for that block. Here is the syntax:

```
with (object)
{
  statements
}
```

object specifies which object reference to use in the absence of one in the *statements* block. This is quite useful when you're using advanced math functions that are available only through the `Math` object. The `Math` object isn't covered until Chapter 8, so instead I'll demonstrate the `with` statement using the `Document` object, which you are probably more familiar with.

When using the `write()` or `writeln()` method associated with the `Document` object, I include the prefix `document.`, as in the following line:

```
document.writeln("Hello!")
```

When you display a large amount of data using this technique, it's not uncommon to use the same `document.writeln()` statement many times over. To cut down on the amount of code needed, enclose all statements that reference the Document object within a with block, as shown in Listing 6.11. This way, you can eliminate the document prefix when using a document's methods or properties.

Notice that title and URL are properties of the Document object and would normally be written as document.title and document.URL. Using the with statement, you need to reference the object only once to produce the same results as typing each line. Figure 6.11 shows the results.

LISTING 6.11   Using the with Statement in JavaScript

```
<html>
<head>
  <title>JavaScript Unleashed</title>
</head>
<body>
  <script type="text/javascript">
  <!--
    with(document)
    {
      write("Hello!");
      write("<br>The title of this document is, \"" + title + "\".");
      write("<br>The URL for this document is: " + URL);
      write("<br>Now you can avoid using the object's prefix each time!");
    }
  // -->
  </script>
</body>
</html>
```

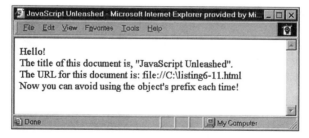

FIGURE 6.11   Displaying information using the with statement.

6

> **NOTE**
>
> Depending on your browser, you may see an encoded format for the URL in this example.

switch Statements

The switch statement is used to compare one value to many others. You might think that this task can be accomplished only by using many if statements, but the switch statement is your answer. It is more readable and allows you to specify a default set of statements to execute in case a match isn't found.

Listing 6.12 assumes that the variable request could change, depending on what the user has asked for. For this example, request is assigned "Names" as the value to compare to each case. The second case is equal to request, and it executes the statements that follow.

LISTING 6.12   The switch Statement

```html
<html>
<head>
  <title>JavaScript Unleashed</title>
</head>
<body>
  <script language="JavaScript" type="text/javascript">
  <!--
    // Declare variables
    var request = "Name";

    switch(request)
    {
      case "Logo" :
        document.write('<img src="logo.gif" alt="Logo">');
        document.write("<br>");
        break;
      case "Name" :
        document.write("Software Inc.");
        document.write("<br>");
        break;
      case "Products" :
        document.write("MyEditor");
        document.write("<br>");
        break;
      default :
        document.write("www.mysite.com");
        break;
    }
  //-->
  </script>
</body>
</html>
```

The break statement is used to stop any further execution of the code remaining in the switch statement. If no break statements were used, the remaining code for each case would be executed, regardless of a match between request and that case. Figure 6.12 simply shows that request matched the value "Name" and displayed the company name.

FIGURE 6.12   Using the switch statement.

> **NOTE**
>
> No type conversion is performed in the case part of a switch statement. In the following code snippet
>
> ```
> switch (0) {
>     case "0": ...
> }
> ```
>
> the string "0" case does not match the integer 0 of the switch.

Summary

To make decisions in JavaScript, use the conditional statement if..else. You can use if by itself to execute a section of code based on the condition of an expression. If the expression returns true, the code will be executed; otherwise, it will not.

Place an else statement immediately after the if block to have JavaScript execute code when the expression from the if block returns false. JavaScript lets you nest if and if..else statements within each other. Using this method, you can ask questions based on the answers to previous questions.

Use for loops to repeat a section of your script. In the declaration, you have the option of initializing a variable to be used inside the loop. You can also specify how to change the variable each time a loop is completed. Based on the conditional expression of the for loop, you can specify the reason for the loop to stop.

Use the for..in loop to perform a set of operations for each enumerated property of an object. JavaScript automatically assigns the name of the property to a variable that you specify. Using this variable, you can perform operations on that property.

Use the `while` loop to repeat a section of your script. You only need to specify a conditional expression that needs to return `true` before each loop is executed.

The `break` and `continue` statements are used to stop the execution of any loop. `break` stops the loop completely, and `continue` stops only the current iteration of the loop and skips to the beginning of the next iteration.

The `with` statement is used in conjunction with JavaScript objects. It allows you to reference an object once rather than each time you access a property or method of the object. Inside the `with` block, you can use the property and method names of an object without their object reference prefix.

And finally, we talked about the `switch` statement. This statement allows you to specify all possible values you would like to see in a given variable to perform the tasks you want. If the value passed is not a value you have specified, it falls through to the `default` section.

In the next chapter you will learn how functions can be also used to make your scripts even more compact and efficient.

CHAPTER **7**

Functions

Performing a function, or many functions, is the purpose of all JavaScript programs. In its simplest form, a script can read or take in data, perform operations on a set of data, or display and send out data. Accomplishing tasks such as these requires many lines of JavaScript code. Some sections of the script might need to execute as soon as a Web page is loaded into the browser. Other parts of the script might be most useful if they are delayed until an HTML form accepts data from the client. Sometimes, you might need parts of a script more than once or even an unlimited number of times, and intermittently repeating a section of code could become necessary.

These issues bring about the idea of splitting a script into smaller parts to serve a specific individual purpose. It makes a lot of sense to split a script logically into sections, each of which serves a single purpose. When the time comes, one particular section of a script can be called to execute. JavaScript gives you this capability through a structure known as a **function**.

Understanding Functions

A JavaScript function is a script that is sectioned off as a separate piece of code and given a name. Using this name, another script can then call this script to execute at any time and as often as it needs to.

Functions can be passed values, called **arguments**. You can then use the arguments as **variables** within the function block. After data is assigned to a variable, you can process the data or use it in calculations and potentially return a result.

Because JavaScript functions are actually JavaScript objects, it is possible to do more with functions than just call them. Functions can be used like any other object. For example, you can assign them, call methods on them, as well as pass functions as arguments to other functions. Function objects are covered in greater detail in Chapter 8, "Core Language Objects."

Creating Functions

The following code fragment shows the syntax for declaring a function in JavaScript:

```
function functionName ([argument1] [...,argumentN])
{
    [statements]
}
```

The keyword function is used to specify a name, *functionName*, which serves as the identifier for the set of statements between the curly braces. Enclosed in parentheses and separated by commas are the argument names, which hold each value that a function receives.

Technically, arguments are variables that are assigned to literal values, other variables, or objects that are passed to the function by the calling statement. If you don't specify any arguments, you must still include an empty set of parentheses to complete the declaration.

The statements, which are the body of the function, are executed each time the function is called. For better readability, statements within the statement block are typically indented.

Where to Declare Functions

Technically, you can declare a function anywhere inside a <script> block. Because script blocks can occur in included JavaScript files (.js files), it is possible for JavaScript functions to be declared outside the current document (see the section "Reusing Functions" later in this chapter for an example of using .js files). Functions can also be declared within other functions, but they will be local to the parent function. However, keep in mind that just as different blocks of an HTML document are loaded ahead of others, so are any scripts that are embedded in these HTML blocks. For this reason, it is recommended that you declare functions in the <head> block of your HTML document. Declaring all your functions here ensures that the functions are available if another script needs to use them immediately. If functions are not placed in <head> tags, at least place them before the code that will call the functions.

Listing 7.1 shows a function named defaultColors() declared inside the <head> block of an HTML document. This function is then called once within the <body> block of the document.

LISTING 7.1   Declaring a Function in the <head> Block

```
<html>
<head>
  <title>JavaScript Unleashed</title>
```

LISTING 7.1   Continued

```
<script type="text/javascript">
<!--
  //Set the document's default colors
  function defaultColors()
  {
    document.writeln("Inside of defaultColors()<br>");
    document.fgColor = "white";
    document.bgColor = "black";
  }
// -->
</script>
</head>
<body>
<script type="text/javascript">
<!--
  document.writeln("<b>Functions are scripts just waiting to run!<br>");
  defaultColors();
  document.writeln("All done.<\/b>");
// -->
</script>
</body>
</html>
```

Functions can also be declared directly in an expression. This is commonly referred to as a "function expression." A function expression does not have a name like a typical expression; rather, the function is assigned to a variable and thus can be used in an expression. For example, the following lines of code create a function expression called `fe` that is evaluated by the `if..else` statement.

```
var fe = function(x,y){return x*y};
if(fe(2,4)==8)
  alert("Equal to 8");
else
  alert("Not equal to 8");
```

Calling Functions

Listing 7.1 shows how the function `defaultColors()` is called from the second script block. This is an example of calling a function that takes no arguments. When the HTML document is loaded, the function is loaded into memory and "put on hold." The function is not executed until the main script block calls it with the statement:

```
defaultColors()
```

At this point, program execution jumps immediately to the first line of the `defaultColors()` function. After executing all three lines of code, the program jumps back to where it left off.

This result has the same effect as if you had inserted all the function's statements directly into that position in your code. Now that a name is assigned to this function, all you need to do to run the same statement is to use its name again. You can view the results of this process in Figure 7.1. Reusing code like this is the ideal way to use functions.

FIGURE 7.1   Reusing code.

Working with Arguments

Setting up functions to accept arguments can also be very useful. Doing so lets you reuse the function in several ways while serving the same general purpose. For example, you might want to create a function to be used many times throughout your program; however, one of the values inside the function might need to change each time the function is called.

One way to solve this problem without arguments is to use global variables that can be modified both outside and inside the function. This can get confusing if you happen to use the same variable names inside more than one function. The best thing to do is set up the function to accept an argument for each value you want it to receive. Listing 7.2 shows a function that takes advantage of using arguments.

LISTING 7.2   Using an Argument with a JavaScript Function

```html
<html>
<head>
  <title>JavaScript Unleashed</title>
  <script type="text/javascript">
  <!--
    function getBinary(anInteger)
```

LISTING 7.2 Continued

```
      {
        var result = "";
        var shortResult = "";
        for(var i=1; i <= 32; i++)
        {
          if(anInteger & 1 == 1)
          {
            result = "1" + result;
            shortResult = result;
          }
          else
          {
            result =  "0" + result;
          }
          anInteger = anInteger >> 1;
        }
        return(shortResult);
      }
    // -->
    </script>
</head>
<body>
  <script type="text/javascript">
  <!--
    var binaryString = "";

    // Define an x variable
    x = 9;
    binaryString = getBinary(x);

    // Write results to the page
    document.write("The number " + x + " in binary form is : ");
    document.writeln(binaryString + "<br>");

    // Redefine x variable
    x = 255;
    binaryString = getBinary(x);

    // Write results to the page
    document.write("The number " + x + " in binary form is : ");
    document.writeln(binaryString + "<br>");
    document.writeln("The variable x is still equal to : " + x);
```

LISTING 7.2   Continued

```
// -->
</script>

</body>
</html>
```

When the function is called with the statement getBinary(x), the function receives a copy of the value that is stored in x. This process is called **passing by value**. The value is then assigned to anInteger, a variable local to the function. You can then use the variable throughout the statement block as a local variable. If anInteger changes value while inside the function, it doesn't affect the value of the variable x, which was passed as an argument, as shown in Figure 7.2.

Notice that you don't need to declare anInteger using the var keyword. JavaScript automatically declares a new variable every time the function is called.

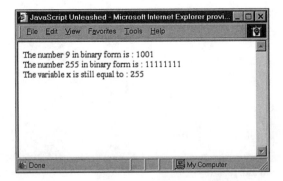

FIGURE 7.2   Passing by value doesn't affect the original variable.

The last statement given in the getBinary() function is return(shortResult). Just as a function can receive a value, it can also return a value. The return statement can return a value to the location in the program that first called the function. If nothing is to be returned from the function, the return statement can be called with no arguments or not even used at all. The actual return statement can occur anywhere within the function body. Returning a value from a function works in the same way as returning a value from an expression. The following statement assigns the value returned by getBinary() to the variable binaryString:

```
binaryString = getBinary(x)
```

In this case, the final value of shortResult is assigned to the binaryString variable.

You can use functions that return values anywhere you use a normal expression. Some functions return the result of a set of calculations, whereas others return a logical value just to let you know if everything went all right. This technique is demonstrated in Listing 7.3.

The function call isPhone(userInput) is used as the condition expression of an if statement. The function isPhone() is a function that returns a logical value. The value returned lets the caller know if a phone number was entered in the correct format. This is useful for validating data that the user has entered in an HTML form. Figure 7.3 shows that the phone number was entered correctly, and an appropriate message is displayed. You can find more information about validating data entry in Chapter 24, "Forms and Data Validation."

LISTING 7.3 Functions That Return Values Can Be Used in Expressions

```html
<html>
<head>
  <title>JavaScript Unleashed</title>
  <script type="text/javascript">
  <!--
    //This function determines if the string represents a valid phone number
    function isPhone(aString)
    {
      var aChar = null;
      var status = true;

      //A valid phone number with dashes is 12 characters long
      if(aString.length != 13)
      {
        status = false;
      }
      else
      {
        //Loop through all the characters in the phone number string
        for(var i = 0; i <= 12; i++)
        {
          aChar = aString.charAt(i);
          //Check for parentheses around area code
          if ( i == 0 && aChar == "(" )
          {
            continue;
          }
          else
          {
```

7

LISTING 7.3   Continued

```
              if( i == 4 && aChar == ")" )
              {
                continue;
              }
              else
              {
                //Check for a dash between phone number
                if( i == 8 && aChar == "-" )
                {
                  continue;
                }
                else
                {
                  //Make sure that only numbers were specified in the string
                  if( parseInt(aChar,10) >= 0 && parseInt(aChar,10) <= 9 )
                  {
                    continue;
                  }
                  else
                  {
                    status = false;
                    break;
                  }
                }
              }
            }
          }
        }
      }
      return(status);
    }
  // -->
  </script>
</head>
<body>
  <script type="text/javascript">
  <!--
    var userInput = "(800)555-1212";
    if(isPhone(userInput))
    {
      document.writeln("Thank you for your phone number.");
      document.writeln("I will have a representative get you");
      document.writeln("more information.");
```

LISTING 7.3   Continued

```
    }
    else
    {
      document.writeln("Please re-enter your phone number");
      document.writeln("using the format (###)###-####");
    }
  //-->
  </script>

</body>
</html>
```

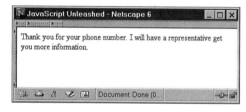

FIGURE 7.3   Using a function call in a conditional expression.

Varying the Number of Arguments

A function is set up to accept a certain number of arguments. Although it's good programming practice to pass the same number of arguments as was declared, it's sometimes practical to allow a different number of arguments. This is common when calling a function that uses the same parameter each time but is set up to handle special cases.

In this case, you might want to use a default value inside the function if no arguments are passed. This lets you use the function without arguments or lets you specify a value other than the default. In Listing 7.4, I set up a function to display a very basic welcome message when the user arrives at a Web page.

LISTING 7.4   Accepting Either One or No Arguments

```
<html>
<head>
  <title>JavaScript Unleashed</title>
  <script type="text/javascript">
  <!--
    // userName is optional
    function welcomeMessage(userName)
```

LISTING 7.4   Continued

```
    {
      if (userName != null)
      {
        document.writeln("\"Hello again, " + userName + ".\"");
      }
      else
      {
        document.writeln("\"Welcome to our Web site!\"");
        document.write("\nIf a value is not passed to this ");
        document.writeln("function, displaying the");
        document.write("variable \"userName\" would show : ");
        document.writeln(userName);
      }
    }
  // -->
  </script>
</head>
<body>
  <script type="text/javascript">
  <!--
    document.writeln("First call to welcomeMessage(),\n");
    welcomeMessage("Mr. President");
    document.writeln("\nSecond call to welcomeMessage(),\n");
    welcomeMessage();
  // -->
  </script>
</body>
</html>
```

Depending on whether it knows the visitor's name, the program displays one of two messages. If userName is not equal to null, the variable was defined. This is possible only if a value, such as Mr. President, was passed to the function. If the variable is equal to null, which means the variable is undefined, the program avoids using the variable in the welcome message altogether. Using it displays unwanted data, as shown in Figure 7.4. Depending on your Web browser, the unwanted data will be displayed as undefined or will be left blank.

Resource

For an up-to-date summary of new JavaScript features, check out Netscape's DevEdge site and look for links leading you to JavaScript documentation. You can access this site at http:// developer.netscape.com.

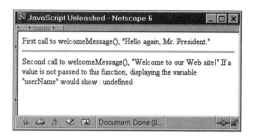

FIGURE 7.4   The result of passing either one of two arguments.

Another possibility is for a function to be passed more arguments than were specified in the declaration. The extra values aren't lost; they're stored in the object named `arguments`. All arguments stored in the object can be extracted within the function's block. For example, to get the first argument passed to the `welcomeMessage` function, you can use the following statement:

```
var firstArg = arguments[0]
```

The first argument is indexed starting at 0. To find the second item in the object, you would use 1, and so on. To find the total number of arguments that were passed, you can access the `length` property as shown following:

```
var numArgs = arguments.length
```

Using these features, I modified the `welcomeMessage()` function to accept an unlimited number of arguments and included it in Listing 7.5. The `welcomeMessage()` function can therefore accept the following syntax:

```
welcomeMessage([userName] [,extraMessage1] [,extraMessage2]...)
```

LISTING 7.5   A Function Can Be Set Up to Accept a Variable Number of Arguments

```
<html>
<head>
  <title>JavaScript Unleashed</title>
  <script type="text/javascript">
  <!--
    // Use this syntax for welcomeMessage function:
    // welcomeMessage([userName] [,extraMessage1] [,extraMessage2]...)
    function welcomeMessage(userName)
    {
      if (userName != null)
      {
        document.writeln("\"Hello again, " + userName + ".\"");
      }
      else
      {
```

LISTING 7.5   Continued

```
        document.writeln("\"Welcome to our Web site!\"");
      }
      var numArgs = arguments.length;
      // If more arguments than the userName were sent,
      // display each one.
      if(numArgs > 1)
      {
        for(var i = 1; i < numArgs; i++)
        {
          document.writeln("\""+arguments[i]+"\"");
        }
      }
    }
  // -->
  </script>
</head>
<body>
  <script type="text/javascript">
  <!--
    var userName = "David", extraMsg = "It has been a long time!";
    var userName2 = null;
    var extraMsg1 = "Would you like to become a member?";
    var extraMsg2 = "You can enroll online!";
    welcomeMessage(userName, extraMsg);
    document.writeln("<hr>");
    welcomeMessage(userName2, extraMsg1, extraMsg2);
  // -->
  </script>
</body>
</html>
```

Notice that Listing 7.5 can still handle the situation in which the userName is unknown but extra messages need to be displayed. The variable userName2 is assigned null to fill the first element in the arguments array, so that the user's name is not displayed in the message. Figure 7.5 shows the resulting output.

TIP

When you're developing with a group of people, it's important to document the intricacies of your scripts so that others can understand the full potential of what you have written. Without descriptive comments, reading through an application and understanding it takes much more time.

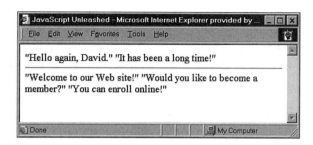

FIGURE 7.5   Accepting multiple arguments to display many messages.

Using Global and Local Variables

Chapter 4, "Fundamental Language Components," described the difference between local and global variables. The chapter demonstrated how a global variable can be modified from anywhere in a document, whereas a local variable can be modified only within the function in which it is declared. You can choose which type of variable to use by following these guidelines:

- If the value of a variable is meant to be used and possibly modified by any part of a program, both inside and outside functions, the variable should be declared outside any function. This has the effect of making it global and modifiable by any part of the program. The best place to declare a global variable is in the <head> block of your HTML document to ensure that it's declared before being used. The variable need not be declared again inside any function.

- If the variable is needed only within a particular function, it should be declared inside that function. Be sure to use the keyword var when declaring the variable. This ensures that its value can be changed only within the function. This also ensures that JavaScript looks at this variable as unique and separate from any global variables that might have the same name. It's not necessary to use the var keyword to declare argument variables. Variables that are specified in the declaration of the function are automatically considered local, as if they were declared with the var keyword.

- If you want to use a variable only in the main script and not within any functions, declare the variable somewhere outside all functions. Unfortunately, nothing prevents the script from using the variable inside functions, because the variable is still considered global. If you aren't careful, this can lead to overwriting values held by variables with the same name. To avoid this problem completely, always follow the preceding guideline.

- If you want the value of a variable to be modifiable by one function, but you need to use the variable in another function, pass the variable as an argument to that function. This has the effect of making a copy of the variable and assigning its value to the argument variable set up to receive it. As the function works and modifies its own copy of the variable, it will not affect the original. Argument variables are automatically declared as local to that function. Even if the argument variable has the same name as the variable being passed, making changes to it doesn't affect the variable that was passed. The one exception to this is objects. When an object is passed as an argument, it's passed by reference, as opposed to being passed by value. Instead of making a copy of the object, the function uses the original object. Changes made to an object's properties within the function have an effect on the original object.

To see examples of passing variables by value, look at Listing 7.6. I made it a point to demonstrate how JavaScript considers some variables with the same name to be different. This is shown when the variable numberB is passed to the function doublePassedVar(). JavaScript automatically creates a local variable also named numberB. Even though this local variable has the same name as the global variable, modifications to it don't affect the global variable. Figure 7.6 shows the results.

LISTING 7.6   The Effects of Local and Global Variables

```
<html>
<head>
  <title>JavaScript Unleashed</title>
  <script type="text/javascript">
<!--
  // Global variable modified in any function
  var numberA;

  // Global variable only modified in main script
  var numberB;

  function doubleGlobalVar()
  {
    // This will change the value of the global variable.
    numberA *= 2;
  }

  function tripleLocalVar()
  {
    // This uses the same name as the global variable, but is considered
    // different by JavaScript.
    var numberA = 1;
    numberA *= 3;
```

LISTING 7.6   Continued

```
    }
    function doublePassedVar(numberB)
    {
      // I purposely gave the argument variable the same name as the
      // variable being passed. This shows that JavaScript considers them
      // to be different.
      numberB *= 2;
    }
  //-->
  </script>
</head>
<body>
  <script type="text/javascript">
  <!--
    numberA = 1;
    document.writeln("Initial value of numberA: " + numberA + "<br />");
    doubleGlobalVar();
    tripleLocalVar();
    document.writeln("Final value of numberA: " + numberA + "<br />");
    numberB = 1;
    document.writeln("Initial value of numberB: " + numberB + "<br />");
    doublePassedVar(numberB);
    document.writeln("Final value of numberB: " + numberB + "<br />");
  // -->
  </script>
</body>
</html>
```

7

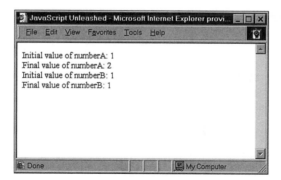

FIGURE 7.6   The resulting values of the numberA and numberB variables.

Passing Objects by Reference

When dealing with functions, it's important to know what happens when you use an object as one of the arguments for a function call.

When a simple data type such as a string, number, or Boolean is passed to a function, it's passed by value. This means that a copy of the variable, instead of the original, is used by the body of the function. Any changes made to the copy do not affect the original.

On the other hand, when an object is passed to a function, it's passed by reference. This allows the function to alter the original version of the object. Listing 7.7 demonstrates the difference between pass by reference and pass by value by passing an Array object and a simple integer into a function.

LISTING 7.7   Passing by Reference Versus Passing by Value

```
<html>
<head>
  <title>JavaScript Unleashed</title>
  <script type="text/javascript">
  <!--
    //Increment all the integers in the array and the lone integer
    function increment(anInt, theArray)
    {
      //Increment the integer
      anInt++;

      //Increment all the integers in the array
      for(var i=0; i<theArray.length; i++)
      {
        theArray[i] = theArray[i] + 1;
      }
    }

    function start()
    {
      // Create an array object and store 4 integers in the array
      var intArray = new Array(4,9,14,19);
      var loneInt = 99;

      //Display the current value in loneInt
      document.write("<h2>Before<\/h2>");
      document.write("loneInt = " + loneInt + "<br>");

      // display current integer values in the array
```

LISTING 7.7 Continued

```
        for(var i=0; i<intArray.length; i++)
        {
          document.write("intArray[" + i + "]=" + intArray[i] + "<br>");
        }

        //Increment the variables
        increment(loneInt, intArray);

        //Display the current value in loneInt
        document.write("<h2>After<\/h2>");
        document.write("loneInt = " + loneInt + "<br>");

        // display current integer values in the array
        for(var i=0; i<intArray.length; i++)
        {
          document.write("intArray[" + i + "]=" + intArray[i] + "<br>");
        }
      }

  //-->
  </script>
</head>
<body>
  <script type="text/javascript">
  <!--
    start();
  //-->
  </script>
</body>
</html>
```

In this example a simple integer, called loneInt, and an Array object, called intArray, are created. The intArray object contains four integers. Both of these variables are passed into a function called increment() whose job it is to increment the simple integer as well as all the integers in the array by 1. When the values are examined after the call to increment() function, we find that loneInt never got incremented whereas the integers in the Array object did get incremented (see Figure 7.7).

So what happened? Because loneInt is a simple integer, it was passed into the increment() function by value, which means that a copy of the integer was made for the body of the function to use. The copy was incremented but the original loneInt variable was untouched. So when the `loneInt` variable was examined after the function call, it still contained the value `"99"`.

The `intArray` on the other hand is an object, and as we learned earlier, objects are passed by reference into functions. So a reference to the `intArray` object was actually passed into the body of the `increment()` function. The result was that the original `intArray` object was actually modified in the function. Thus the integers in the `intArray` were changed after passing through the `increment()` function.

FIGURE 7.7   Passing a JavaScript `Array` object by reference.

More Information on Functions

So far in this chapter, we have covered a lot of ground on functions. Without them, JavaScript would be nothing more than a simple scripting language that could be used only for very simple scripts. In addition to what you have learned so far, functions can be reused, and they can be recursive.

Reusing Functions

A function is great for separating an application into its logical parts, but its best benefit is in promoting the reuse of code.

Unlike sections of code enclosed in loops to be repeated many times in succession, a function can be reused at any given time simply by calling its name. Creating functions that serve one purpose but that are useful in many situations takes practice and a little foresight.

For example, in Listing 7.4, the `welcomeMessage()` function serves one purpose on more than one occasion throughout the execution of the program. By allowing a more flexible argument list in Listing 7.5, the `welcomeMessage()` function became useful in more situations. It still serves the same purpose, but it's a better candidate for reuse in its more flexible form.

Also keep in mind that you can store your functions in external JavaScript source files (.js files). This allows you to include these files using the `src` attribute of the `<script>` tag. Following this approach, it becomes an easy job for a Webmaster to change a function across his entire site, because he has to edit it in only one location.

Listing 7.8 contains a bunch of JavaScript length conversion functions for performing conversions between inches, feet, and yards. By simply including this file in Listing 7.9, it is possible to access these length conversion functions from with in the HTML file using JavaScript. Notice that the `lengthConversions.js` file was included by using the `<script>` `src` attribute at the top of Listing 7.9. Later in the file, additional JavaScript code is used to call these functions. The result of running Listing 7.9 is shown in Figure 7.8.

LISTING 7.8   lengthConversions.js

```
function inchesToFeet(inches)
{
  return(inches/12);
}

function inchesToYards(inches)
{
  return(inches/36);
}

function feetToInches(feet)
{
  return(feet*12);
}

function feetToYards(feet)
{
  return(feet/3);
}

function yardsToInches(yards)
{
  return(yards*36);
}
```

LISTING 7.8   Continued

```
function yardsToFeet(yards)
{
  return(yards*12);
}
```

LISTING 7.9   Using an External JavaScript Source File

```
<html>
<head>
  <title>JavaScript Unleashed</title>
  <script type="text/javascript" src="lengthConversions.js"/>
</head>
<body>
<h2>Length Conversions</h2>

<script type="text/javascript">
  document.write("89 inches = " + inchesToFeet(89) + " feet<br>");
  document.write("89 inches = " + inchesToYards(89) + " yards<br>");
  document.write("89 feet = " + feetToInches(89) + " inches<br>");
  document.write("89 feet = " + feetToYards(89) + " yards<br>");
  document.write("89 yards = " + yardsToInches(89) + " inches<br>");
  document.write("89 yards = " + yardsToFeet(89) + " feet<br>");
</script>

</body>
</html>
```

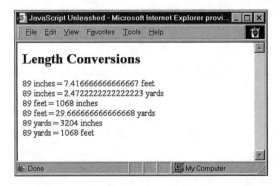

FIGURE 7.8   Performing length conversion using an external JavaScript source file.

Recursive Functions

A JavaScript function can be **recursive**, which means that it can call itself. Solving factorial equations is a common way to demonstrate how recursion works. Because JavaScript doesn't offer a factorial operator, I have included an example of how to solve factorials using a recursive function.

To find the factorial of any positive integer n, you simply find the product of all integers 1 through n. To find the factorial of 6, written 6!, calculate the following:

    6! = 6 × 5 × 4 × 3 × 2 × 1
    = 720

To calculate 7!, you would use the following:

    7! = 7 × 6 × 5 × 4 × 3 × 2 × 1

Comparing these two calculations, you can produce a general formula to use in your function. Notice that 7! is equal to 7 × 6!. For any positive integer n greater than 0, n! = n × (n - 1)!. The first iteration would process this:

    7! = 7 × (7 - 1)!
    = 7 × 6!

From here, you have to stop and calculate 6! before continuing with the rest of the calculation. This occurs six more times before you can back out of each one and find the final solution. Instead of doing that, you can use a recursive function as shown in Listing 7.10. In this example the getFactorial() function calls itself while n is greater than zero.

LISTING 7.10   Generating Factorials Using Recursive Function

```
<html>
<head>
<title>Generating Factorials Using Recursive Function</title>
<script type="text/javascript" language="JavaScript">
function getFactorial(n) {
  var result;
  if(n > 0)
  {
    return(n * getFactorial(n - 1));
  }
  else
  {
    if(n==0)
```

LISTING 7.10   Continued

```
      {
        return(1);
      }
      else
      {
        return(null);
      }
    }
}

</script>
</head>

<body>
<h2>Generating Factorials Using Recursive Function</h2>

<script type="text/javascript" language="JavaScript">
document.write("1!=" + getFactorial(1) + "<br>");
document.write("2!=" + getFactorial(2) + "<br>");
document.write("3!=" + getFactorial(3) + "<br>");
document.write("4!=" + getFactorial(4) + "<br>");
document.write("5!=" + getFactorial(5) + "<br>");
document.write("6!=" + getFactorial(6) + "<br>");
document.write("7!=" + getFactorial(7) + "<br>");
document.write("8!=" + getFactorial(8) + "<br>");
document.write("9!=" + getFactorial(9) + "<br>");
document.write("10!=" + getFactorial(10) + "<br>");
</script>

</body>
</html>
```

The function first checks to see if n is greater than 0, which is the case the majority of the time. If this is true, the function multiplies n by the result returned from calling the function again with a different argument—in this case, n-1. This continues to put many getFactorial functions on hold until n is equal to 0. At this point, the most nested occurrence of the function finishes and returns the first value. JavaScript then backs out and finishes each nested function until it reaches the original call to getFactorial, and then it returns the final result.

Developing useful functions can be one of the most rewarding and interesting aspects of programming. After you see a function in action, it's common to go back and modify it to make it more flexible. If you do this, be sure that the function still serves one purpose and doesn't do more than you expect.

Summary

Becoming experienced in writing functions prepares you for the next exciting step in JavaScript programming—creating custom objects. This is covered in Chapter 14, "Creating Custom JavaScript Objects." For now, there is much to be learned about the objects that are already built into HTML and JavaScript. JavaScript also includes functions that are built into the language and can be used at any time. These are covered in Part III, "Core and Client JavaScript Objects."

JavaScript functions serve several purposes. They let you put code on hold so that it doesn't execute immediately when the document is loaded. Used with arguments, they let you duplicate code easily and use the same code to perform the same operations on different sets of data. Here is a quick list of what functions can do and reminders on how each is accomplished.

- A function is a set of JavaScript code that is grouped and given a name. To declare a function, use the `function` statement, followed by the name you want to give it, a set of parentheses, and the script you want the function to include. Function names must adhere to the rules applied to all variables.

- Functions can be declared anywhere inside an HTML document, as long as the declaration is surrounded by `<script>` tags. It is suggested, though not required, that functions be declared in the `<head>` of the document for clarity.

- To call a function, use its name followed by a set of parentheses. The parentheses enclose any arguments that the function can accept.

- JavaScript arguments are passed by value. Functions can accept a variable number of arguments, regardless of how the function was declared. Each function has an array named `arguments` associated with it. This array can be used to extract an argument that might have been passed to the function.

- JavaScript functions can return values. A function call that returns a value can be used as an expression or inside an expression.

- Argument variables don't need to be declared. They are automatically declared as local variables each time the function is called. To declare a global variable within a function, don't use the `var` keyword. Instead, just initialize the variable.

- Functions that serve one purpose but are flexible enough to deal with different pieces of data are the most reusable functions.

- In JavaScript, functions can call themselves. Functions that do so are called **recursive functions**.

PART III

Core and Client JavaScript Objects

IN THIS PART

CHAPTER **8**

Core Language Objects

Y‌ou could be justified in calling the client-side objects the heart of JavaScript, but an important part of developing sophisticated JavaScript applications comes in working with its core language objects. It is these core objects that are consistent across the various implementations, whether it be Microsoft, Netscape, or Opera software, as well as across the various environments, such as client-side or server-side. These are also the objects that are standardized by the ECMAScript specification.

In this chapter, we'll look at the core String, RegExp, Array, Date, Math, Boolean, Number, Error, and Function objects and their associated properties and methods. The chapter will also explore any differences in working with the various JavaScript versions as well as any ECMAScript additions.

> **NOTE**
>
> Even though we will go over all of the core objects and mention the properties and methods of each, this book will not cover the complete syntax of each object, property, and method. For this information, we recommend you check out http://developer.netscape.com to find information on Netscape's implementation, and http://msdn.microsoft.com/scripting for Microsoft's information. Additionally, you can check out http://www.mozilla.org/js for information on Mozilla-based browsers.

The Global Object

Those of you who have programmed in JavaScript before might ask what in the world the Global object is. This is most likely because you have never heard of it, although you probably have used some of its properties or methods. Before going into these properties and methods, we wanted to give you some background on the Global object.

The Global object seemed to first show its head around the time when ECMAScript was nearing approval as a standard. All of a sudden we noticed that Microsoft grouped some "top-level" properties and methods under this Global object. Netscape also mentioned this object in some of its documentation. This became the birth of the Global object: top-level properties and methods that had no parent object.

There are several methods and properties that fall under this object, which are listed in Table 8.1. As you will see, they are commonly used in many JavaScript scripts and, if you have programmed in JavaScript before, you more than likely have used them.

TABLE 8.1   Methods and Properties of the Global Object

Type	Item	Description
Method	escape()	Returns a String object in which all nonalphanumeric characters are converted to their numeric equivalents
	eval()	Accepts a string of JavaScript statements and evaluates it as source code
	isFinite()	Determines whether a variable has finite bounds
	isNaN()	Determines whether or not a variable is a valid number
	parseFloat()	Converts a string to a number of type float
	parseInt()	Converts a string to an integer
	unescape ()	Takes a hexadecimal value and returns the ISO-Latin-1 ASCII equivalent
Property	Infinity	Keyword that represents positive infinity
	NaN	Represents an object not equal to any number

The String Object

Strings are a fundamental part of any programming language. A string, which is a set of alphanumeric characters, can be either a *literal* string, such as "Push the envelope", or a variable representing a string, such as thePhrase. You learned about strings as data types in Chapter 4, "Fundamental Language Components," but a string in the JavaScript language is also an object, complete with its own suite of methods and properties.

As JavaScript has matured, strings have gained more power. The first version of JavaScript did not treat strings as true objects, but that was quickly corrected. Starting with JavaScript 1.1, you could use the new operator, just like another object, to create an instance of the String object. The following snippet shows how this now works in JavaScript browsers:

```
<script type="text/javascript">
  var str = new String("My name is Allen");
  alert(str.length);
</script>
```

You might be wondering at this point what the purpose is of explicitly declaring a String object. One major benefit is that String objects can be accessed from other frames in a manner that is easier and more reliable than it was originally. For example, if you wanted to access a variable called custName from a parent window, you would use the following:

```
var customer = new String();
customer = parent.custName;
```

Taking the old approach, you would simply have the following, which often proved to be challenging in terms of working correctly:

```
var customer = parent.custName;
```

In addition to some of the simplicity, this is simply good programming practice. As a programmer, you want to be sure that your code uses the proper syntax and semantics so that it will work across implementations as flawlessly as possible. Following the practice of declaring variables as the proper type will help.

To further allow you to handle strings, JavaScript has the properties and methods shown in Table 8.2. Because of the amount of work you will do with strings, you should become familiar with them and how they work.

TABLE 8.2   Methods and Properties of the String Object

Type	Item	Description
Method	anchor()	Creates an instance of the <a> element with the name attribute set to the string passed to the method.
	big()	Converts the string into an instance of the <big> element.
	bold()	Converts the string into an instance of the <bold> element.
	charAt()	Returns the character at the index passed to the method.
	charCodeAt()	Returns the ISO-Latin-1 number of the character at the index passed to the method.
	concat()	Concatenates the two strings passed to return a new string.
	fixed()	Converts the string into an instance of the <tt> fixed-pitch font element.
	fontcolor()	Sets the color attribute of an instance of the <font> element.
	fontsize()	Sets the size attribute of an instance of the <font> element.
	fromCharCode()	Returns the string value of the ISO-Latin-1 number passed to the method.
	indexOf()	Returns the index of the first occurrence of the string passed to the method within an instance of a String object.
	italics()	Converts the string into an instance of the <i> element.
	lastIndexOf()	Returns the index of the last occurrence of the string passed to the method within an instance of a String object.
	link()	Converts the string into an instance of the <a> tag and sets the href attribute with the URL that is passed to the method.
	match()	Returns an array containing the matches found based on the regular expression passed to the method.

8

TABLE 8.2   Continued

Type	Item	Description
	replace()	Performs a search and replace, using the regular expression and replace string passed to the method, on the instance of a String that calls it.
	search()	Returns the index location of the match found in the string passed to the method. A –1 is returned if the string is not found.
	slice()	Returns the string between the beginning and ending indexes passed to the method. If a negative number is passed, the index is referenced from the end of the string passed.
	small()	Converts the string into an instance of the <small> element.
	split()	Returns the string split into segments defined by the string and instance limit passed to the method.
	strike()	Converts the string into an instance of the <strike> element.
	sub()	Converts the string into an instance of the <sub> element.
	substr()	Returns the string beginning with the indexed location and number of characters to return. If a negative number is passed, the index is referenced from the end of the string passed.
	substring()	Returns the string between the beginning and ending indexes passed to the method.
	sup()	Converts the string into an instance of the <sup> element.
	toLowerCase()	Converts all the characters in the string to lowercase.
	toSource()	Returns the string representation of the String passed.
	toString()	Returns the characters passed as type String.
	toUpperCase()	Converts all the characters in the string to uppercase.
Property	length	Returns the length of the string.
	prototype	Provides the capability for a programmer to add properties to instances of the String object.

Because strings are one of the primary types of data you must work with, it is critical to have ways to extract data from strings and obtain information about them. For instance, you can use the length property to determine the size of a string. This snippet, for instance, stores 16 in the len variable:

```
var myString = new String("This is the day.");
var len = myString.length;
```

You can also search for text within strings by using indexOf() and lastIndexOf() methods. Use these when you want to search for a particular character or substring within a string and return the position (or index) of the occurrence within the string. Whereas indexOf() starts at the left of the string and moves right, lastIndexOf() performs the same operation but starts at the right. Both methods start at the 0 position for the first character encountered, and both return a value of -1 if the search text isn't found. For example, the following snippet returns a value of 3, which is stored in the results variable:

```
var myString = new String("Time and time again");
var results = myString.indexOf("e");
```

On the other hand, the following snippet returns a value of 12 in the result variable:

```
var myString = new String("Time and time again");
var result = myString.lastIndexOf("e");
```

Both methods have an optional second parameter that allows you to specify where in the string you want to start the search. For example, the script shown in Listing 8.1 searches through the variable graf and counts the number of occurrences of the letter *e*.

LISTING 8.1   Using the indexOf() Method to Find All Occurrences of the Letter e in a Sentence

```
<?xml version="1.0" encoding="UTF-8"?>
<!DOCTYPE html PUBLIC "-//W3C//DTD XHTML 1.0 Transitional//EN"
                     "DTD/xhtml1-transitional.dtd">
<html xmlns="http://www.w3.org/1999/xhtml" xml:lang="en">
<head>
  <title>JavaScript Unleashed</title>
</head>
<body>
<script type="text/javascript">

  // Declare variables.
  var pos = 0;
  var num = -1;
  var i = -1;
     var graf = "While nearly everyone agrees on the principle of reuse,"
                + "the priority we give it varies wildly.";

  // Search the string and counts the number of e's.
  while (pos != -1) {
    pos = graf.indexOf("e", i + 1);
    num += 1;
    i = pos;
  }

  // Write the response to the page.
  document.write(graf)
  document.write("<hr size='1'>")
```

LISTING 8.1   Continued

```
  document.write("There were " + num + " e's in that paragraph.");
  document.close();
</script>
</body>
</html>
```

Figure 8.1 shows the result of the script.

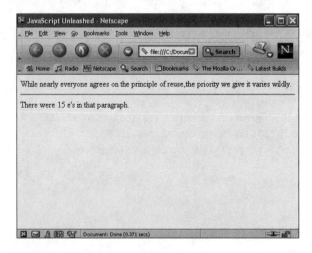

FIGURE 8.1   The result of the indexOf() example.

If you want more than just to find the index of a specific character, you can retrieve a portion of a string variable or literal by using the substring() method. It has two parameters—the start position and the end position of the substring you want to return. Just like indexOf() and lastIndexOf(), this method is also zero-based, such that the first position of the string begins at 0. For example, the following snippet returns Hey:

```
var myString = new String("Hey England");
var results = myString.substring(0,3);
```

If you want to retrieve a single character, you can use charAt(). The charAt() method returns the character at the zero-based position you specify as a parameter. For example, the following snippet returns a value of v:

```
var myString = new String("Denver Broncos");
var results = myString.charAt(3);
```

If you specify a position that is out of the string's range, a value of -1 is returned:

```
var myString = new String("007");
var results = myString.charAt(20102);
```

The true power of these string-handling routines is demonstrated when you combine them to solve a problem. Consider a common routine that you might want in JavaScript: a routine to replace specified text within a string with something else. To do this, you should develop a generic string-replace function that uses the length property, indexOf(), and substring(). Additionally, we will demonstrate both the procedural and the object-oriented approaches to solving this problem.

An Example of String Manipulation

Using a traditional approach, you could develop a stringReplace() function that has three parameters:

- originalString: The original string upon which you want to perform the replacement.

- findText: The string that you want to replace.

- replaceText: The string that you want to insert into the originalString.

The function then uses that information to perform the replacement process. You can see that Listing 8.2 uses the indexOf() method to look for the findText parameter, and the substring() method pulls out the strings that are before and after findText. The function then concatenates preString, replaceText, and postString and assigns the result to the originalString variable. This happens for each occurrence of findText throughout the string. When findText is no longer found, the originalString value is returned to the user.

LISTING 8.2   Creating a Function That Will Search and Replace in Strings

```
<?xml version="1.0" encoding="UTF-8"?>
<!DOCTYPE html PUBLIC "-//W3C//DTD XHTML 1.0 Transitional//EN"
                      "DTD/xhtml1-transitional.dtd">
<html xmlns="http://www.w3.org/1999/xhtml" xml:lang="en">
<head>
  <title>JavaScript Unleashed</title>
  <script type="text/javascript">
    function stringReplace(originalString, findText, replaceText) {
      var pos = 0;
      var len = findText.length;
      pos = originalString.indexOf(findText);
```

LISTING 8.2   Continued

```
      while (pos != -1) {
        preString = originalString.substring(0, pos);
        postString = originalString.substring(pos + len,
            originalString.length);
        originalString = preString + replaceText + postString;
        pos = originalString.indexOf(findText);
      }
      return originalString;
    }
  </script>
</head>
<body>
  <script type="text/javascript">
    // Declare variables.
    var origString = new String("Allen");
    var findString = new String("All");
    var replaceString = new String("Ell");
    var resultString = stringReplace(origString, findString, replaceString)

    // Write results to the page.
    document.write("The original string was: " + origString + "<br>");
    document.write("We searched for: " + findString + "<br>");
    document.write("We replaced it with: " + replaceString + "<hr size='1'>");
    document.write("The result was:  " + resultString);
    document.close();
  </script>
</body>
</html>
```

Another way to code this same function is to take advantage of JavaScript's object proto-type capabilities and add a `replace()` method to the `String` object type. You can restructure the `stringReplace()` code to work within the object framework, the result of which is shown in Listing 8.3.

LISTING 8.3   Adding a replace() Method to the String Object

```
<?xml version="1.0" encoding="UTF-8"?>
<!DOCTYPE html PUBLIC "-//W3C//DTD XHTML 1.0 Transitional//EN"
                    "DTD/xhtml1-transitional.dtd">
<html xmlns="http://www.w3.org/1999/xhtml" xml:lang="en">
<head>
```

LISTING 8.3 Continued

```
<title>JavaScript Unleashed</title>
<script type="text/javascript">

  // Define a new method for the String object.
  String.prototype.replace = stringReplace;

  function stringReplace(findText, replaceText) {

    // Had to add this variable to inherit calling object.
    var originalString = new String(this);

    var pos = 0;
    var len = findText.length;
    pos = originalString.indexOf(findText);
    while (pos != -1) {
      preString = originalString.substring(0, pos);
      postString = originalString.substring(pos + len, originalString.length);
      originalString = preString + replaceText + postString;
      pos = originalString.indexOf(findText);
    }
    return originalString;
  }
</script>
</head>
<body>
  <script type="text/javascript">
    // Declare variables.
    var origString = new String("Allen");
    var findString = new String("All");
    var replaceString = new String("Ell");

    // Notice the difference here.
    var resultString = origString.replace(findString, replaceString)

    // Write results to the page.
    document.write("The original string was: " + origString + "<br />");
    document.write("We searched for: " + findString + "<br />");
    document.write("We replaced it with: " + replaceString + "<hr size='1' />");
    document.write("The result was: " + resultString);
  </script>
</body>
</html>
```

8

As you can see, you can put the `replace()` method into action by creating a `String` object, assigning a value to it, and then calling the newly created method to replace all occurrences of a particular string.

Formatting Strings

JavaScript has several methods you can use to format strings. Most of these methods are simply equivalents of XHTML elements. Using the formatting methods gives you an object-oriented way of dealing with XHTML elements, and it's also easier than continuously concatenating XHTML elements to strings. In other words, if you have a string literal "This is the day" and you want to add bold formatting to it, you can do so by one of two means. You could add XHTML formatting elements:

```
"<b>" + "This is the day" + "</b>"
```

Or you could use the `String` object `bold()` method to add the formatting:

```
var myString = new String("This is the day");
var result = myString.bold();
```

When you use this string, the following XHTML text is returned:

```
<b>This is the day</b>
```

> **NOTE**
>
> Keep in mind the context in which you can use the formatting methods. You can't use them outside a JavaScript script as a substitute for XHTML formatting elements.

To demonstrate how the basic formatting methods are used in JavaScript, let's create a sample JavaScript page that lets you format a user-defined string based on the options set using an XHTML form. In the code behind the form, we will create a single JavaScript method called `showWindow()` that is called when the Show button is clicked. The method assigns the value of the form's text field to a string variable called `txt`. Each of the formatting options shown as check boxes is either `true` or `false`. There will also be code that checks to see if each of the boxes is checked. If so, it calls the appropriate formatting method for the `txt` variable.

None of these formatting options are mutually exclusive—although some might cancel each other out. As a result, you will be able to use as many of the methods at the same time as you want. JavaScript simply processes each of the methods, adding the appropriate XHTML elements in sequential order.

When we try to specify a font color and size, these settings aren't simply logical settings, so they require a parameter to be set. The select boxes on the form are used to specify these settings.

Finally, the txt variable is used in a document.write() method on a new window that is created. This will write the full string to the new window with all the formatting tags around the text.

Listing 8.4 shows the entire source code for this example.

LISTING 8.4   Source Code for Our String-Formatting Script

```
<?xml version="1.0" encoding="UTF-8"?>
<!DOCTYPE html PUBLIC "-//W3C//DTD XHTML 1.0 Transitional//EN"
                      "DTD/xhtml1-transitional.dtd">
<html xmlns="http://www.w3.org/1999/xhtml" xml:lang="en">
<head>
  <title>JavaScript Unleashed</title>
  <script type="text/javascript">

    function showWindow() {

      // Declare your variables.
      var txt = document.form1.stringField.value;
      var clr = "";
      var sze = "";

      // Check to see what options are selected.
      if (document.form1.bigBox.checked) txt = txt.big();
      if (document.form1.boldBox.checked) txt = txt.bold();
      if (document.form1.fixedBox.checked) txt = txt.fixed();
      if (document.form1.italicsBox.checked) txt = txt.italics();
      if (document.form1.smallBox.checked) txt = txt.small();
      if (document.form1.strikeBox.checked) txt = txt.strike();
      if (document.form1.subBox.checked) txt = txt.sub();
      if (document.form1.supBox.checked) txt = txt.sup();

      // Special checking for select box.
      clr = document.form1.colorList.options[document.form1
➥.colorList.options.selectedIndex].text;
      txt = txt.fontcolor(clr);
      sze = document.form1.sizeList.options[document.form1
➥.sizeList.options.selectedIndex].text;
      txt = txt.fontsize(sze);

      // Open a new window to write the results to.
      objWindow = window.open("", "","width=600,height=300");
      objWindow.document.write(txt);
```

8

LISTING 8.4   Continued

```
      objWindow.document.close();
  }
  </script>
</head>
<body>
  <h1>
    String Object Formatting
  </h1>
  <hr />
  <form method="post" name="form1" action="null">
    <p>
      <strong>
        String:
      </strong>
      <input type="text" size="40" maxlength="256" name="stringField" />
    </p>
    <p>
      <strong>
        Style:
      </strong>
      <input type="checkbox" name="bigBox" value="ON" />
      Big
      <input type="checkbox" name="boldBox" value="ON" />
      Bold
      <input type="checkbox" name="fixedBox" value="ON" />
      Fixed
      <input type="checkbox" name="italicsBox" value="ON" />
      Italics
      <input type="checkbox" name="smallBox" value="ON" />
      Small
      <input type="checkbox" name="strikeBox" value="ON" />
      Strike
      <input type="checkbox" name="subBox" value="ON" />
      Sub
      <input type="checkbox" name="supBox" value="ON" />
      Sup
    </p>
    <p>
      <strong>
        Font:
      </strong>
```

LISTING 8.4 Continued

```
      Color:
      <select name="colorList" size="1">
        <option selected="selected">black</option>
        <option>green</option>
        <option>red</option>
      </select>
      Size:
      <select name="sizeList" size="1">
        <option selected="selected">1</option>
        <option>2</option>
        <option>3</option>
        <option>4</option>
        <option>5</option>
        <option>6</option>
        <option>7</option>
      </select>
    </p>
    <input type="button" name="Show" value="Show" onclick="showWindow()" />
  </form>
</body>
</html>
```

Figure 8.2 shows the window with all the options, and Figure 8.3 shows the result window based on the settings selected.

> **TIP**
>
> The toUpperCase() and toLowerCase() methods work just as you would expect. They are useful when you need to compare text without concerning yourself with the case of the text. For example, if you want to compare user-entered text with a string literal, it is helpful to use all uppercase or all lowercase when making the evaluation.

You can also use the String object's anchor() and link() methods to create Anchor and Link objects. These methods make it much easier to work with anchors and links in your code, avoiding painful string concatenations of XHTML elements. To illustrate, we can use an idea similar to the previous formatting example to work with hypertext formatting.

A similar showWindow() method (triggered by the Show button's onClick event handler) processes the user-entered options and calls either the link() or anchor() method of the txt variable.

Listing 8.5 shows the entire source code for our example.

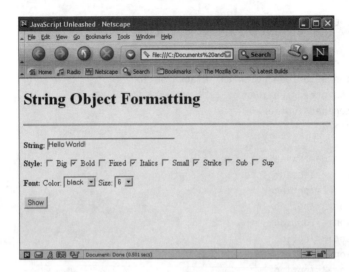

FIGURE 8.2   The initial page that allows you to select the formatting options.

FIGURE 8.3   The result of the string formatting options.

LISTING 8.5   Source Code for a Sample Page That Formats a String Object with the <a> Tag

```
<?xml version="1.0" encoding="UTF-8"?>
<!DOCTYPE html PUBLIC "-//W3C//DTD XHTML 1.0 Transitional//EN"
                     "DTD/xhtml1-transitional.dtd">
<html xmlns="http://www.w3.org/1999/xhtml" xml:lang="en">
<head>
  <title>JavaScript Unleashed</title>
  <script type="text/javascript">

    function showWindow(){
```

LISTING 8.5   Continued

```
      var txt = document.form1.stringField.value

      if (document.form1.hypertext[0].checked){
        txt = txt.link(document.form1.jumptoField.value);
      }else{
        if (document.form1.hypertext[1].checked){
          txt = txt.anchor(document.form1.jumptoField.value);
        }
      }

      // Create and open a window to write the results
      objWindow = window.open("", "","width=600,height=300");
      objWindow.document.write(txt);
      objWindow.document.close();
    }

  </script>
</head>
<body>
  <h1>
    String Object Hypertext Formatting
  </h1>
  <hr />
  <form method="post" name="form1" action="null">
    <p>
      Text:
      <input type="text" size="20" maxlength="256" name="stringField" />
      <input type="radio" name="hypertext" value="Link" checked="checked" />
      Link:
      <input type="radio" name="hypertext" value="Anchor" />
      Anchor:
    </p>
    <p>
      Jump To:
      <input type="text" size="30" maxlength="256" name="jumptoField" />
    </p>
    <input type="button" name="Show" value="Show" onclick="showWindow()" />
  </form>
</body>
</html>
```

Figure 8.4 shows an XHTML form you can use to specify the elements of a hypertext link: text, anchor/link designation, and URL/anchor to associate with the underlined text. Figure 8.5 shows the resulting window with a new hypertext link created.

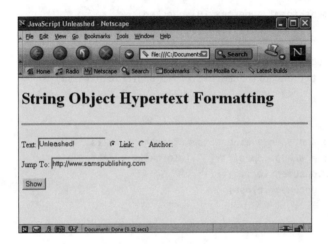

FIGURE 8.4   `String` object hypertext formatting.

FIGURE 8.5   A `link` object created using the `link()` method.

Working with Special Characters

When working with strings in any language, you will discover certain characters that are difficult to use. JavaScript lets you work with these special characters by using a backslash character (\) followed by the character or its code. Table 8.3 lists the JavaScript inline symbols.

TABLE 8.3   Inline Symbols

Symbol	Description
\t	Tab
\n	Newline
\r	Carriage return
\f	Form feed
\\	Backslash
\b	Backspace
\"	Double quote
\'	Single quote

For example, if you want to use a backslash in a string literal, use the following method:

```
var myString = new String("Your file is located in C:\\WINDOWS\\TEMP");
```

When displayed with the `document.write()` method, it looks like this:

```
Your file is located in C:\WINDOWS\TEMP
```

TIP

Use the \r inline symbol to add a carriage return to an `alert()` message box message.

Because these inline symbols can be confusing to use, you might find it helpful to assign variables to them. In fact, if you use them often, you can pull these defined "constants" from a JavaScript code library and use them over and over. Listing 8.6 shows these inline characters treated as constants and shows how to use them in a `document.write()` method.

LISTING 8.6   Defining Special Characters as Variables for Later Use

```
?xml version="1.0" encoding="UTF-8"?>
<!DOCTYPE html PUBLIC "-//W3C//DTD XHTML 1.0 Transitional//EN"
                     "DTD/xhtml1-transitional.dtd">
<html xmlns="http://www.w3.org/1999/xhtml" xml:lang="en">
<head>
  <title>JavaScript Unleashed</title>
</head>
<body>
<script type="text/javascript">
  // Inline Character Constants.
  var TAB = "\t";
  var CR = "\r";
```

8

LISTING 8.6   Continued

```
  var LF = "\n";
  var CRLF = "\r\n";
  var FF = "\f";
  var DQUOTE = '\"';
  var SQUOTE = "\'";
  var BACKSLASH = "\\";
  var BACKSPACE = "\b";

  document.write("Column1" + TAB + "Column2" + TAB + "Column3")
//-->
</script>
</body>
</html>
```

In addition to these inline symbols, you also have other ways of working with nonal-phanumeric values in JavaScript. If you need to convert a nonalphanumeric value to an ASCII-encoded value, you can use the built-in escape() method. One example is the following code:

```
escape("Jim's Favorite ASCII character is the tilde(~)");
```

This code returns the following value:

```
Jim%27s%20Favorite%20ASCII%20character%20is%20the%20tilde%28%7E%29
```

If you need to convert an ASCII-encoded string—perhaps a string retrieved from a server—you can use the unescape() method. The following code is a good illustration:

```
unescape("email%20me%20at%20someone@anywhere.com%21");
```

This code returns the following string value:

```
email me at someone@anywhere.com!
```

Converting Strings and Numbers

JavaScript provides two built-in methods that you can use to convert strings to numbers: parseInt() and parseFloat(). Both functions take strings as their parameters and attempt to convert the string data into a numeric value. parseInt() tries to convert the string to an integer value, and parseFloat() attempts to convert into a floating-point value. For example, the following code returns 123:

```
var myString = new String ("123.88888");
document.write(parseInt(myString));
```

The following code returns 1234.0012121:

```
var myString = new String("1234.0012121");
document.write(parseFloat(myString));
```

Both of these routines start the conversion from the left side of the string and convert until they come to something other than a numeric digit (0 to 9), a decimal (.), or a plus or minus sign (+/-). If the routine encounters a non-numeric character, the rest of the string is ignored. For example, the following code returns 1234.01:

```
var myString = new String("1234.01 is the total price");
document.write(parseFloat(myString));
```

However, the following code returns NaN (Not a Number) because the dollar sign is a non-numeric value:

```
var myString = new String("$1234.01 is the total price");
document.write(parseFloat(myString));
```

These conversion functions are very useful when you're working with text objects. Because the value property of a Text object returns a string, you must convert this data any time you want to treat text entered by the user as a numeric value.

You can also convert numeric values to strings, but in JavaScript versions prior to 1.3, there were no built-in methods to do so. Instead, you could perform this task based on how JavaScript processes the addition (+) operator. If JavaScript encounters a string while it adds elements of an expression, the whole expression is treated as a string from that point on. For example, 35 + 100 returns a numeric value of 135. However, 35 + "100" returns a string value of "35100".

> **NOTE**
>
> If you're working with a Number object and JavaScript 1.3+, you can use its toString() method to convert it to a string value.

Interestingly, because JavaScript processes the addition operator from left to right, you could actually add two numeric digits together before the expression is converted into a string. For example, 10 + 20 + "40" returns a string value of "3040" because the 10 + 20 pair is added before its result is added to the string value. In contrast, "40" + 10 + 20 returns a string value of "401020" because the string is on the left of the numeric values.

In most programming languages, you must convert a numeric value before you can use it in the context of a string value. As you can see, the only thing you need to do is either use it in a string expression with other string values or add an empty string to it. For example, the expression 1300 + "" returns a string value of "1300". Rather than add an empty string each time you want to perform this conversion, you could use a simple conversion function to do this for you:

```
function numToString(number) {
  number += "";
  return number;
}
```

Listing 8.7 shows a sample script that demonstrates this function. The first alert message box displays Number as the data type for the number variable. After the numToString() function is performed, the second alert box displays String as the number's data type.

LISTING 8.7   Converting a Number to a String

```
<?xml version="1.0" encoding="UTF-8"?>
<!DOCTYPE html PUBLIC "-//W3C//DTD XHTML 1.0 Transitional//EN"
                      "DTD/xhtml1-transitional.dtd">
<html xmlns="http://www.w3.org/1999/xhtml" xml:lang="en">
<head>
  <title>JavaScript Unleashed</title>
</head>
<body>
<script type="text/javascript">
  function numToString(number) {
    number += "";
    return number;
  }

  var number = 100;
  alert(typeof number);
  number = numToString(number);
  alert(typeof number);
</script>
</body>
</html>
```

The RegExp Object

As you saw in the previous section, it is possible to create functions that perform string evaluation and searching. The core object RegExp allows you to perform regular expression functions on your strings.

Because Chapter 29, "Pattern Matching Using Regular Expressions," goes into detail on this topic, we will not cover it here. However, Table 8.4 does have a short description of the various properties and methods of the RegExp object.

TABLE 8.4   Methods and Properties of the RegExp Object

Type	Item	Description
Method	compile()	Compiles the regular expression for faster execution
	exec()	Executes the search for a match in a specified string
	test()	Tests for a string match
Property	RegExp,$*	Represents multiline
	RegExp.$&	Represents lastmatch
	RegExp.$_	Represents input
	RegExp.$`	Represents leftContext
	RegExp.$'	Represents rightContext
	RegExp.$+	Represents lastParen
	RegExp.$1,$2,...$9	Represents a substring of matches
	global	Specifies whether to check the expressions against all possible matches
	ignoreCase	Specifies whether case is ignored during a string search
	input	The string that is matched
	lastIndex	Specifies the index at which to start matching the next string
	lastMatch	The last matched characters
	lastParen	The last parenthesized substring match
	leftContext	The substring preceding the most recent match
	multiline	Specifies whether to search on multiple lines
	rightContext	The substring following the most recent match
	source	The string pattern

The Array Object

An array is a programming construct fundamental to nearly all modern languages. JavaScript is no different, providing the capability to construct and work with arrays. An **array** is simply a container holding a set of data elements. Each of the elements in an array is a separate value, but they exist as part of the array and cannot be accessed except by going through the array. Table 8.5 shows all the methods and properties of the Array object.

TABLE 8.5   Methods and Properties of the Array Object

Type	Item	Description
Method	concat()	Concatenates the elements passed into an existing array.
	join()	Concatenates all elements of an array into one string.
	pop()	Deletes the last element of an array.
	push()	Adds elements to the end of an array.
	reverse()	Reverses the order of the elements in the array.
	shift()	Deletes elements from the front of an array.
	slice()	Returns a subsection of the array.

TABLE 8.5   Continued

Type	Item	Description
	sort()	Sorts elements in array.
	splice()	Inserts and removes elements from an array.
	toSource()	Converts elements to a string with square brackets.
	toString()	Converts the elements in an array to a string.
	unshift()	Adds elements to the front of an array.
	valueOf()	Returns an array of elements separated by commas.
Property	index	For an array created by a regular expression match, this property returns the indexed location of the match.
	input	For an array created by a regular expression match, this property returns the original string.
	length	The number of elements in the array.
	prototype	Provides the capability for a programmer to add properties to instances of the Array object.

> **NOTE**
>
> Although strongly typed languages require that all array values be of the same type, JavaScript does not. Consequently, your array can contain mixed data types, just as an object can have properties of varying types.

To define or access a particular element, you need to add brackets and an index value to the array variable. For example, you can define an array called coffee as follows:

```
coffee[0] = "Ethiopian Sidamo"
coffee[1] = "Kenyan"
coffee[2] = "Cafe Verona"
coffee[3] = "Sumatra"
coffee[4] = "Costa Rica"
coffee[5] = "Columbian"
coffee[6] = "Bristan"
```

If you wanted to use any of these elements within a script, you could access them using the array variable along with an index value representing the location of the element within the array. Therefore, if you wanted to write the following line

```
My favorite coffee is Ethiopian Sidamo
```

You would code the following:

```
document.write("My favorite coffee is " + coffee[0])
```

If arrays are new to you, you might find it helpful to think of an array as JavaScript's equivalent of a numbered list. It's really no more complicated than that. For example, suppose you have a list of four items:

- JavaScript

- Java

- C#

- Visual Basic

If you wanted to assemble this group of items in a JavaScript array, it would look like this. Notice, however, that arrays are zero-based—the first element in the array has an index of 0:

```
devTools[0] = "JavaScript"
devTools[1] = "Java"
devTools[2] = "C#"
devTools[3] = "Visual Basic"
```

You can create instances of an Array object using the new operator, and the following statements fill the array with data elements. For example, if you wanted to create the coffee array defined earlier, you would define it as follows:

```
var coffee = new Array();
coffee[0] = "Ethiopian Sidamo";
coffee[1] = "Kenyan";
coffee[2] = "Cafe Verona";
coffee[3] = "Sumatra";
coffee[4] = "Costa Rica";
coffee[5] = "Columbian";
coffee[6] = "Bristan";
```

TIP

An alternative way to define an Array object is to specify the data elements as parameters of the new call. For example, the following line is the functional equivalent of the previous example:

```
var coffee = new Array("Ethiopian Sidamo", "Kenyan", "Cafe Verona",
➥"Sumatra", "Costa Rica", "Columbian", "Bristan");
```

Notice that you didn't specify the size of the array, as is common in many programming languages. JavaScript doesn't require that you specify the size of the array, which allows you to incrementally expand the array as you add each new data element. However, if you want to, you can specify the size of the array initially as a parameter in the new expression:

```
var coffee = new Array(7);
```

Alternatively, you could also resize an array simply by defining a data element at the *n* position. If *n* is the highest number defined in the array, the new array size is expanded to *n* + 1. Note the following example:

```
var javaDrinks = new Array();
javaDrinks[0] = "Regular coffee";
javaDrinks[1] = "Decaf coffee";
javaDrinks[2] = "Cafe Mocha";
javaDrinks[3] = "Cafe au Lait";
javaDrinks[199] = "Cafe Latte";
```

The size of the javaDrinks array is 200, even though only five data elements are defined. Each undefined element returns a null value if you access it.

You can retrieve the size of the array using the Array object's length property. For example, if you wanted to iterate through each element in an Array object, you could use the script shown in Listing 8.8.

LISTING 8.8   Displaying the Contents of an Array

```
<?xml version="1.0" encoding="UTF-8"?>
<!DOCTYPE html PUBLIC "-//W3C//DTD XHTML 1.0 Transitional//EN"
                     "DTD/xhtml1-transitional.dtd">
<html xmlns="http://www.w3.org/1999/xhtml" xml:lang="en">
<head>
  <title>JavaScript Unleashed</title>
</head>
<body>
<script type="text/javascript">
  var coffee = new Array();
  coffee[0] = "Ethiopian Sidamo";
  coffee[1] = "Kenyan";
  coffee[2] = "Cafe Verona";
  coffee[3] = "Sumatra";
  coffee[4] = "Costa Rica";
  coffee[5] = "Columbian";
  coffee[6] = "Bristan";

  document.write("Coffees of the World:<p>");
  for (var i = 0; i < coffee.length; i++) {
    document.write(i + 1 + ". " + coffee[i] + "<br>");
  }
```

LISTING 8.8   Continued

```
  document.write('</p>');
</script>
</body>
</html>
```

Figure 8.6 shows the result.

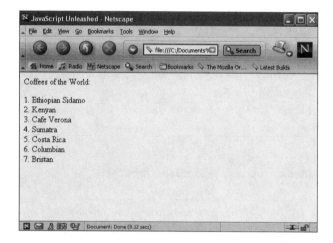

FIGURE 8.6   Using JavaScript to display a coffee list.

> **CAUTION**
>
> The Array object's length property is read-only. As a result, you can't resize an array by assigning a value to the length property.

The Date Object

The Date object is the means by which you work with date and time values in JavaScript. You should understand three significant facts regarding this object before using it:

- Following the UNIX convention, JavaScript considers January 1, 1970, to be the baseline date. Consequently, you can't work with dates prior to that.

- When you create a Date object, the time reflected within the object is based on the client machine. You are thus dependent on the client computer to have a working and accurate clock. Keep this dependency in mind as you consider time-sensitive code in your JavaScript scripts.

- JavaScript keeps track of date/time values in the form of milliseconds since the baseline date (1/1/70).

Encapsulated within the Date object is an impressive array of methods to get and set date values as well as convert them into various forms. Table 8.6 shows all the methods and properties of the Date object.

NOTE

Like almost everything else in JavaScript, relative date values are also zero-based. This is perhaps counterintuitive, because days of the week are 0 to 6 rather than 1 to 7, and months of the year are 0 to 11 rather than 1 to 12. As you process these values in your code, you need to account for these zero-based values.

However, note that the date within the month is an exception (1 to 31), because this is an absolute value.

TABLE 8.6   Methods and Properties of the Date Object

Type	Item	Description
Method	getDate()	Returns the date within month (1 to 31)
	getDay()	Returns the day within the week (0 to 6)
	getFullYear()	Returns the year in local time with four digits
	getHours()	Returns the hour within the day (0 to 23)
	getMilliseconds()	Returns the milliseconds
	getMinutes()	Returns within the hour (0 to 59)
	getMonth()	Returns the month within the year (0 to 11)
	getSeconds()	Returns seconds within the minute (0 to 59)
	getTime()	Returns the number of milliseconds since 1/1/70 00:00:00
	getTimeZoneOffset()	Returns minutes offset from GMT/UTC
	getUTCDate()	Returns the day of the month
	getUTCDay()	Returns the day of the week converted to universal time
	getUTCFullYear()	Returns a four-digit representation of the year converted to universal time
	getUTCHours()	Returns the hour converted to universal time
	getUTCMilliseconds()	Returns the milliseconds converted to universal time
	getUTCMinutes()	Returns the minutes converted to universal time
	getUTCMonth()	Returns the month converted to universal time
	getUTCSeconds()	Returns the seconds converted to universal time
	getYear()	Returns number of years since 1900
	parse()	Converts the passed-in string date to milliseconds
	setDate()	Sets the date within the month (1 to 31)

TABLE 8.6   Continued

Type	Item	Description
	setFullYear()	Sets the year as a four-digit number
	setHours()	Sets hour within day (0 to 23)
	setMilliseconds()	Sets the milliseconds
	setMinutes()	Sets the minutes within the hour (0 to 59)
	setMonth()	Sets the month within the year (0 to 11)
	setSeconds()	Sets the seconds within the minute (0 to 59)
	setTime()	Sets the number of milliseconds since 1/1/70 00:00:00
	setUTCdate()	Sets the day of the month in universal time
	setUTCFullYear()	Sets the year as a four-digit number in universal time
	setUTCHours()	Sets the hour in universal time
	setUTCMilliseconds()	Sets the milliseconds in universal time
	setUTCMinutes()	Sets the minutes in universal time
	setUTCMonth()	Sets the month in universal time
	setUTCSeconds()	Sets the seconds in universal time
	setYear()	Sets the number of years since 1900
	toGMTString()	Returns the date string in universal format
	toLocalString()	Returns the date string in the local system's format
	toSource()	Returns the source of the Date object
	toString()	Returns the date and time as a string in local time
	toUTCString()	Returns the data and time as a string in universal time (UTC)
	UTC()	Converts comma-delimited values to milliseconds of UTC date
	valueOf()	Returns the equivalence of the Date object in milliseconds
Property	prototype	Property that allows you to add methods and properties to the Date object

Creating a Date object is similar to creating a String or Array object. You can create as many of these objects as you want in your scripts. Using the new operator, you can define a Date object as follows:

```
var dateVariable = new Date([parameters]);
```

The various sets of parameters that can be passed in creating these object instances are shown in Table 8.7.

TABLE 8.7   Parameters That Can Be Passed to Create an Instance of the Date Object

Parameter	Description	Example
Nothing	Creates an object with the current date and time.	var today = new Date()
"month dd, yyyy hh:mm:ss"	Creates an object with the specified date and time in the string. (All omitted time values are automatically set to zero.)	var someDate = new Date("September 22, 2000")

TABLE 8.7   Continued

Parameter	Description	Example
yy, mm, dd	Creates an object with the specified date of the set of integer values (zero-based).	var someDate = new Date(00,1,0)
yy, mm, dd, hh, mm,ss	Creates an object with the specified date and time of the set of integer values (zero-based). (All omitted time values are automatically set to zero.)	var someDate = new Date(00,7,12,7,10,29)

After the object is created, you can use one of several methods to either get or set date values. For example, to return the date of the current month, you would code the following:

```
var today = new Date();
result = today.getDate();
```

To change the month defined for the Date object appt, you can use the following:

```
var appt = new Date(1996,06,12);
result = appt.setMonth(7);
```

We discussed earlier how zero-based date values can make it difficult to work with getting dates. You can get around this annoyance by extending the Date object methods by prototyping more user-friendly get methods. If you recall, JavaScript lets you extend the capabilities of built-in objects by letting you prototype new methods or properties. All objects of this type will inherit this new prototype. Add these new methods to the Date object:

- getActualMonth() returns the actual numeric value for the month.
- getCalendarMonth() returns the name of the month.
- getActualDay() returns the actual numeric value of the day of week.
- getCalendarDay() returns the name of the day of week.

Listing 8.9 shows the method definitions for each of these prototype methods. This listing would make a great example of storing commonly used functions in an external JavaScript library or source file that you can load using the src attribute of the <script> tag.

LISTING 8.9   Extending the Date Object to Include Some New Methods

```
<?xml version="1.0" encoding="UTF-8"?>
<!DOCTYPE html PUBLIC "-//W3C//DTD XHTML 1.0 Transitional//EN"
                "DTD/xhtml1-transitional.dtd">
```

LISTING 8.9   Continued

```
<html xmlns="http://www.w3.org/1999/xhtml" xml:lang="en">
<head>
  <title>JavaScript Unleashed</title>
  <script type="text/javascript">
  Date.prototype.getActualMonth = getActualMonth;
  Date.prototype.getActualDay = getActualDay;
  Date.prototype.getCalendarDay = getCalendarDay;
  Date.prototype.getCalendarMonth = getCalendarMonth;

  function getActualMonth() {
    var n = this.getMonth();
    n += 1;
    return n;
  }

  function getActualDay() {
    var n = this.getDay();
    n += 1;
    return n;
  }

  function getCalendarDay() {
    var n = this.getDay();
    var dow = new Array(7);
    dow[0] = "Sunday";
    dow[1] = "Monday";
    dow[2] = "Tuesday";
    dow[3] = "Wednesday";
    dow[4] = "Thursday";
    dow[5] = "Friday";
    dow[6] = "Saturday";
    return dow[n];
  }

  function getCalendarMonth() {
    var n = this.getMonth();
    var moy = new Array(12);
    moy[0] = "January";
    moy[1] = "February";
    moy[2] = "March";
    moy[3] = "April";
```

8

LISTING 8.9   Continued

```
    moy[4] = "May";
    moy[5] = "June";
    moy[6] = "July";
    moy[7] = "August";
    moy[8] = "September";
    moy[9] = "October";
    moy[10] = "November";
    moy[11] = "December";
    return moy[n];
  }
  </script>
</head>
<body>
<script type="text/javascript">
  // Test the new methods you created.
  var today = new Date();

  document.write("<b>I hereby declare that on "
    + today.getCalendarDay() + ", the " + today.getDate()
    + "th day of " + today.getCalendarMonth() + " in the year "
    + today.getFullYear() + " A.D. at the " + today.getHours()
    + "th hour of the day, absolutely nothing is happening.</b>");
</script>
</body>
</html>
```

After the methods are declared, the script creates a `Date` object and then generates an XHTML document using a combination of the prototype methods. Figure 8.7 shows the result.

Given that JavaScript is widely used on the World Wide Web, it is only fitting that it includes some methods to deal with time zones. For instance, `getTimezoneOffset()` returns the number of minutes difference between the client computer and GMT (Greenwich Mean Time). For example, we are in the U.S. Eastern time zone. If we want to return the number of time zone offset hours, we could use the code in Listing 8.10.

LISTING 8.10   Checking the Time Zone Offset

```
<?xml version="1.0" encoding="UTF-8"?>
<!DOCTYPE html PUBLIC "-//W3C//DTD XHTML 1.0 Transitional//EN"
                      "DTD/xhtml1-transitional.dtd">
<html xmlns="http://www.w3.org/1999/xhtml" xml:lang="en">
```

LISTING 8.10   Continued

```
<head>
  <title>JavaScript Unleashed</title>
</head>
<body>
<script type="text/javascript">
  var today = new Date();
  offset = (today.getTimezoneOffset() / 60) + 1;

  if (offset == 5) {
    alert("You are in the Eastern Timezone");
  }
</script>
</body>
</html>
```

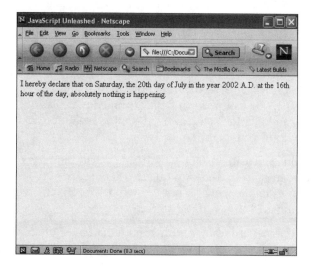

FIGURE 8.7   Using the enhanced Get methods.

Figure 8.8 shows the result when we run the script.

You can also perform calculations between date values, determining such things as the number of days until the end of the next century. When you perform calculations with dates, it's important to keep the dates in their "native" millisecond format during the calculation and then extract the relevant data later.

FIGURE 8.8   Using `getTimezoneOffset()` to determine the time zone.

The Math Object

For mathematical calculations, JavaScript encapsulates a host of mathematical constants and procedures into a single entity—the `Math` object. This object is quite different from the other core objects. First, you can perform basic arithmetic calculations (addition, subtraction, multiplication, and division) outside a `Math` object, so unless you regularly require advanced math functions, you might rarely use it.

Second, although you can create instances of `String`, `Array`, and `Date` objects using `new`, you work with a core instance of the `Math` object. This quality of the object parallels the `navigator` object, for example, which is not created on-the-fly. Consequently, the `Math` object is commonly referred to as a **static** object.

The `Math` object's properties are really nothing more than a list of common mathematical constants. Table 8.8 shows a list of these properties as well as all the methods of the object. Note the case of the constants. Although nearly all JavaScript properties are lowercase or mixed case, these properties are all uppercase.

TABLE 8.8   Methods and Properties of the Math Object

Type	Item	Description
Method	abs()	Absolute value of the value passed
	acos()	Arc cosine, in radians, of the value passed
	asin()	Arc sine, in radians, of the value passed
	atan()	Arc tangent, in radians, of the value passed

TABLE 8.8   Continued

Type	Item	Description
	atan2()	Arc tangent (in radians) of the quotient of the value passed
	ceil()	Next integer greater than or equal to the value passed
	cos()	Cosine of the value passed
	exp()	Euler's constant to the power of the value passed
	floor()	Next integer less than or equal to the value passed
	log()	Natural logarithm, base e, of the value passed
	max()	The highest number of the two values passed
	min()	The lowest number of the two values passed
	pow()	Power of the first number to the second number passed
	random()	A random number between 0 and 1
	round()	The value passed, rounded to the nearest whole number
	sin()	Sine, in radians, of the value passed
	sqrt()	Square root of the value passed
	tan()	Tangent, in radians, of the value passed
	toSource()	A copy of an object
	toString()	A string representation of an object
Property	E	Euler's constant (2.718281828459045)
	LN2	Natural log of 2 (0.6931471805599453)
	LN10	Natural log of 10 (2.302585092994046)
	LOG2E	Log base −2 of E (1.4426950408889633)
	LOG10E	Log base −10 of E (0.4342944819032518)
	PI	Pi (3.141592653589793)
	SQRT1_2	Square root of 0.5 (0.7071067811865476)
	SQRT2	Square root of 2 (1.4142135623730951)

The Boolean Object

Boolean values are an important part of any programming language. The Boolean object is used to convert a non-Boolean value into a Boolean value. You can then use this object as if it were a normal Boolean value (true or false). You can create a Boolean object using the now familiar new operator with the following syntax:

```
var booleanObjectName = new Boolean(initialValue);
```

The initialValue parameter specifies the initial setting of the object. If initialValue is false, 0, null, or an empty string (""), or if it is omitted altogether, a value of false is implied. All other values will set the object to true. Table 8.9 shows a list of all the methods and properties of the Boolean object.

TABLE 8.9   Methods and Properties of the Boolean Object

Type	Item	Description
Method	toString()	This method returns a string representation of the primitive Boolean value stored in the object. If the object contains true, the string "true" is returned. Similarly, if the object contains false, the string "false" is returned.
Property	prototype	This property allows you to add methods and properties to the Boolean object.

The Number Object

The Number object does for number values what the String object does for string values. However, in practice, it is typically used much less. You will find this object useful when you need to access certain constant values, such as the largest and smallest numbers able to be represented, positive and negative infinity, and the Not a Number (NaN) value. JavaScript represents these values as Number object properties. Table 8.10 shows a list of these properties and the methods of the Number object.

TABLE 8.10   Methods and Properties of the Number Object

Type	Item	Description
Method	toSource()	Returns a string representation of the Number object.
	toString()	Returns a string representing the specified Number object.
	valueOf()	Returns the primitive value of a Number object as a number data type.
Property	MAX_VALUE	Largest representable number (1.7976931348623157e+308).
	MIN_VALUE	Smallest representable number (5e-324).
	NaN	Special Not-a-Number value.
	NEGATIVE_INFINITY	Special negative infinite value (-Infinity); returned on overflow.
	POSITIVE_INFINITY	Special infinite value; returned on overflow.
	prototype	Allows you to add properties and methods to the Number object.

Like many of the other core objects, Number instances are instantiated in your script using the new operator, with the following syntax:

```
var numberObjectName = new Number(initialValue);
```

You can create Number objects when you need to add properties to them. For example, the code in Listing 8.11 demonstrates a scenario in which Number objects would be very useful. This avoids the necessity of making several string-to-number conversions.

LISTING 8.11   Creating Number Objects Rather than Performing String-to-Number Conversions

```
<?xml version="1.0" encoding="UTF-8"?>
<!DOCTYPE html PUBLIC "-//W3C//DTD XHTML 1.0 Transitional//EN"
                      "DTD/xhtml1-transitional.dtd">
<html xmlns="http://www.w3.org/1999/xhtml" xml:lang="en">
<head>
  <script type="text/javascript">
    // Add description property to Number objects.
    Number.prototype.description = null;

    // Speed Limit Numbers.
    slHighway = new Number(65);
    slCity = new Number(35);
    slSchoolZone = new Number(25);

    // Add Descriptions.
    slHighway.description = "Interstate Highway Speed Limit";
    slCity.description = "City Speed Limit";
    slSchoolZone.description = "School Zone Speed Limit";

    // Subtract num2 from num1 and display the value of the difference
    // between the two along with the original number descriptions.
    function tellDifference(num1, num2) {
      diff = num1 - num2;
      document.write("The speed difference between " + num1.description +
                    " and " + num2.description + " is " + diff);
    }
  </script>
</head>
<body>
  <script type="text/javascript">
    // Call function
    tellDifference(slHighway,  slCity);
  </script>
</body>
</html>
```

This script will generate the text seen in Figure 8.9.

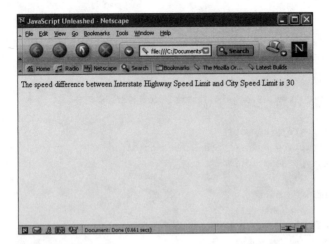

FIGURE 8.9   Using the Number object.

The Error Object

Whenever a runtime error occurs, an instance of the Error object is created. Because we covered the try..catch loop in the last chapter, and we discuss errors in more detail in Chapters 18, "Handling Events," and 30, "Error Handling," we will not cover it here. However, Table 8.11 does have a short description of the various properties and methods of the Error object.

TABLE 8.11   Methods and Properties of the Error Object

Type	Item	Description
Method	toString()	Returns a string representing the specified Error object
Property	description	Descriptive string that describes the error
	message	Error message that is returned and shown to the user
	name	Represents the name or exception type of the error
	number	Numerical value that represents the error

The Function Object

The last core object is the Function object. This object lets you define a string at runtime and compile it as a function. Here is the syntax for declaring a Function object:

functionObjectName = new Function ([*arg1*, *arg2*, ... *argn*], *functionBody*);

Keep in mind that a Function object and a standard JavaScript function are similar but also different. The object name of a Function object is considered a *variable* representing the current value of the function defined with new Function(), whereas a name of a standard JavaScript function is not a variable, just the name of a function.

> **NOTE**
>
> Function objects are evaluated each time they are used. Not surprisingly, they are slower in execution than normal JavaScript functions.

You can use a Function object as an event handler, as shown in the following code:

```
window.onload = new Function("alert('Hello!')");
```

Summary

You can think of the core language objects as the nuts and bolts of JavaScript, because much of the hard programming work is performed within the constructs of these objects. Also remember that it is these core objects that are standardized in the ECMAScript specification.

In this chapter, you learned how to use these core language objects and the differences that exist when working with different versions of browser software. In the next chapter, you will be exposed to the navigator object and the various properties and methods that make up the environment-specific object.

navigator Objects

In the previous chapter we talked about the core JavaScript objects. We mentioned earlier in the book that JavaScript also has "host" objects, methods, and properties that are specific to the host environment of the implementation. One such object is the navigator object.

Boldly named by Netscape, the inventors of JavaScript, the navigator object represents the browser software in use. Using this object, you can retrieve information about the name and version of the browser, as well as some other information. Although all browsers support the navigator object, there are some differences within the implementations.

In this chapter, we cover the subobjects, properties, and methods of the navigator object, and we also provide some examples of using this object to perform browser-specific tasks.

Understanding the Object

The navigator object itself has several different properties and methods, as well as two child objects: the Plugin object and the mimetype object. The information the properties contain range from the user agent string for identifying the browser, to the browser application's internal name. Figure 9.1 provides you a sample of running a script accessing these properties, and as you can see, Netscape 7 does not support all these properties and methods.

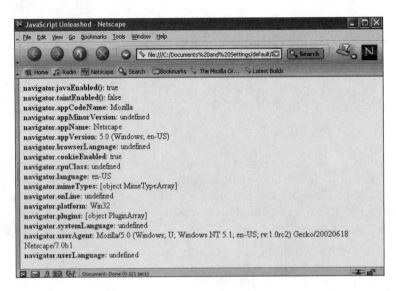

FIGURE 9.1   Using the navigator object to return information about a Netscape 7 browser.

In Figure 9.2 we ran the same script, which you can find in Listing 9.1, in Internet Explorer 6.

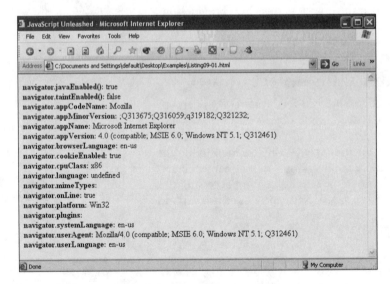

FIGURE 9.2   Running the same script in Internet Explorer 6.

LISTING 9.1   Accessing the Properties of the navigator Object

```
<?xml version="1.0" encoding="UTF-8"?>
<!DOCTYPE html PUBLIC "-//W3C//DTD XHTML 1.0 Transitional//EN"
                      "DTD/xhtml1-transitional.dtd">
<html xmlns="http://www.w3.org/1999/xhtml" xml:lang="en">
<head>
  <title>JavaScript Unleashed</title>
</head>
<body>
  <script type="text/javascript">
    document.write("navigator.javaEnabled(): ".bold() + navigator.javaEnabled()
                + '<br />');
    document.write("navigator.taintEnabled(): ".bold()
                + navigator.taintEnabled()
                + '<br />');
    document.write("navigator.appCodeName: ".bold() + navigator.appCodeName
                + '<br />');
    document.write("navigator.appMinorVersion: ".bold()
                + navigator.appMinorVersion
                + '<br />');
    document.write("navigator.appName: ".bold() + navigator.appName
                + '<br />');
    document.write("navigator.appVersion: ".bold() + navigator.appVersion
                + '<br />');
    document.write("navigator.browserLanguage: ".bold()
                + navigator.browserLanguage
                + '<br />');
    document.write("navigator.cookieEnabled: ".bold() + navigator.cookieEnabled
                + '<br />');
    document.write("navigator.cpuClass: ".bold() + navigator.cpuClass
                + '<br />');
    document.write("navigator.language: ".bold() + navigator.language
                + '<br />');
    document.write("navigator.mimeTypes: ".bold() + navigator.mimeTypes
                + '<br />');
    document.write("navigator.onLine: ".bold() + navigator.onLine
                + '<br />');
    document.write("navigator.platform: ".bold() + navigator.platform
                + '<br />');
    document.write("navigator.plugins: ".bold() + navigator.plugins
                + '<br />');
    document.write("navigator.systemLanguage: ".bold()
```

LISTING 9.1   Continued

```
                + navigator.systemLanguage
                + '<br />');
    document.write("navigator.userAgent: ".bold() + navigator.userAgent
                + '<br />');
    document.write("navigator.userLanguage: ".bold() + navigator.userLanguage
                + '<br />');
    document.close();

  </script>
</body>
</html>
```

As you can see, the information available in this object can be extremely powerful when it comes to determining the capabilities of the browser. Let's move on and take a closer look at what these properties and methods mean, and then we will dive into some examples.

Properties and Methods

The various properties and methods available within the navigator object allow a Web developer to obtain specific information about the user's platform. In today's world of multiple Internet-enabled devices, this can be an extremely beneficial tool in tailoring your content and functionality.

Table 9.1 lists the methods and properties of the navigator object.

TABLE 9.1   The Methods and Properties of the navigator Object

Type	Item	Description
Method	javaEnabled()	Function that tests to see if Java is supported in the browser.
	plugins.refresh()	Used to refresh the list of plug-ins. This is supported in Netscape and Mozilla-based browsers.
	taintEnabled()	Tests to see if data-tainting is enabled.
Property	appCodeName	Represents the code name of the browser.
	appMinorVersion	Refers to the application's minor version value. This is supported in Internet Explorer.
	appName	Refers to the official browser name.
	appVersion	Refers to the version information of the browser.
	browserLanguage	Refers to the language of the browser. This is supported in Internet Explorer.
	cookieEnabled	Specifies if the browser will accept persistent cookies.
	cpuClass	Refers to the CPU class of the machine running the browser. This is supported in Internet Explorer.

TABLE 9.1 Continued

Type	Item	Description
	language	Refers to the language of the browser. This is supported in Netscape and Mozilla-based browsers.
	mimeTypes	Refers to an array of MimeType objects that contains all the MIME types that the browser supports.
	onLine	Retrieves true or false specifying if the browser is in online mode or not. This is supported in Internet Explorer.
	platform	A string representing the platform on which the browser is running.
	plugins	Refers to an array (called a "collection" in Microsoft's implementation) of Plugin objects that contains all the plug-ins installed on the browser.
	systemLanguage	Refers to the default language used by the operating system. This is supported in Internet Explorer.
	userAgent	A string that represents the user-agent header.
	userLanguage	Refers to the operating system's natural language setting. This is supported in Internet Explorer.

The MimeType Object

The MimeType object, which is a subobject of the navigator object, allows you to access information through its properties about the Multipurpose Internet Mail Extensions (MIME) types your browser supports. The properties of the MimeType object are contained in Table 9.2.

TABLE 9.2 Properties of the MimeType Object

Property	Description
description	Contains the description of MimeType
enabledPlugin	Contains the plug-in for a specific MimeType
suffixes	Contains the file extension for MimeType
type	Contains the string representation of MimeType

The Plugin Object

The Plugin object, or collection as it is called in the Microsoft implementation, contains a reference to the plug-ins installed for the browser. This object, which contains an array of elements and MIME types handled by each plug-in, has several properties (shown in Table 9.3). Figure 9.3 shows how you can use this object with the document.write() method to display information on installed plug-ins for Netscape browsers.

9

TABLE 9.3   Properties of the Plug-in Object

Property	Description
description	Refers to a description of the plug-in.
filename	Refers to the filename of a plug-in program.
length	Refers to the number of MIME types contained in the array.
name	Refers to the plug-in's name.

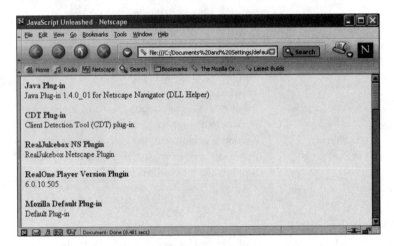

FIGURE 9.3   Displaying the installed plug-ins using the `Plugin` object.

The code that was used to list each of the plug-ins can be seen in Listing 9.2.

LISTING 9.2   Viewing the Plug-ins Installed

```
<?xml version="1.0" encoding="UTF-8"?>
<!DOCTYPE html PUBLIC "-//W3C//DTD XHTML 1.0 Transitional//EN"
                    "DTD/xhtml1-transitional.dtd">
<html xmlns="http://www.w3.org/1999/xhtml" xml:lang="en">
<head>
  <title>JavaScript Unleashed</title>
</head>
<body>
<script type="text/javascript">

navigator.plugins.refresh(false);

var numPlugins = navigator.plugins.length;
```

LISTING 9.2 Continued

```
for (var i = 0; i < numPlugins; i++){
  var plugin = navigator.plugins[i];

  if (plugin) {
    document.write("<b>" + plugin.name + "</b><br />")
    document.write(plugin.description);
    document.write("<br /><br />");
  }
}
</script>
</body>
</html>
```

Using These Objects

Now that we have an understanding of the navigator object, its properties and methods, and the plugin and MimeType subobjects, let's move on to some examples. In this section of the chapter we have picked out some simple examples that help illustrate the importance and flexibility of these objects. After you complete this section, you will not only have some hands-on experience with these objects, but you will also have some good ideas of how to apply these new skills to your own scripts.

Browser Type

The appName property of the navigator object provides your script with the name of the client's browser. The two most popular browsers are Netscape and Microsoft Internet Explorer, and using the following line of code in either of these browsers, in conjunction with a document.write() method call, will display the browser name on the screen:

```
document.write(navigator.appName);
```

If you need to be able to identify other browser types, you will want to use the userAgent property . This property contains a lot of information, but by searching for a specific string using the indexOf() method you learned in the last chapter, you can identify the exact browser name.

> **TIP**
>
> Because this value is a string, it is a good idea to convert it to all lowercase to make comparisons easier.

Table 9.4 lists some of the more common values assigned to the userAgent property and the browsers they represent.

TABLE 9.4   Values of the userAgent Property

Value	Browser
mozilla	Netscape Navigator
msie	Microsoft Internet Explorer
opera	Opera
webtv	Web TV

Would you like to see this in action? The code in Listing 9.3 tests for various browser types using this userAgent property, and writes out what browser the user is using.

LISTING 9.3   Testing for Various Browser Types

```
<?xml version="1.0" encoding="UTF-8"?>
<!DOCTYPE html PUBLIC "-//W3C//DTD XHTML 1.0 Transitional//EN"
                    "DTD/xhtml1-transitional.dtd">
<html xmlns="http://www.w3.org/1999/xhtml" xml:lang="en">
<head>
  <title>JavaScript Unleashed</title>
</head>
<body>
<script type="text/javascript">

var browserType = navigator.userAgent.toLowerCase();

if(browserType.indexOf('mozilla')){
  document.write("Netscape Navigator");
}else if (browserType.indexOf('msie')){
  document.write("Microsoft Internet Explorer");
}else if (browserType.indexOf('opera')){
  document.write("Opera");
}else if (browserType.indexOf('webtv')){
  document.write("Web TV");
}

document.close()
</script>
</body>
</html>
```

Browser Version

The appVersion property of the navigator object provides your script with the version of the client's browser. The following line of code displays the browser version on the screen:

```
document.write(navigator.appVersion);
```

If you convert this property into a floating number (non-integer) with the parseFloat() method, you can do simple mathematical comparisons, rather than having to compare specific strings. Listing 9.4 demonstrates how to create this floating value.

LISTING 9.4   Converting the Application Version into a Mathematical Data Type

```
<?xml version="1.0" encoding="UTF-8"?>
<!DOCTYPE html PUBLIC "-//W3C//DTD XHTML 1.0 Transitional//EN"
                      "DTD/xhtml1-transitional.dtd">
<html xmlns="http://www.w3.org/1999/xhtml" xml:lang="en">
<head>
  <title>JavaScript Unleashed</title>
</head>
<body>
<script type="text/javascript">

document.write(parseFloat(navigator.appVersion));
document.close()

</script>
</body>
</html>
```

Operating System Platform

The platform property of the navigator object provides your script with the client's operating system platform. The following snippet displays the operating system platform:

```
document.write(navigator.platform);
```

You will need this information if, for example, you are on a Macintosh, trying to work around a bug that exists only in Netscape Navigator. In most cases you will not need this information but, should you need it, this is how to get it.

Summary

In this chapter we introduced you to the navigator host object, its properties and methods, and its MimeType and Plugins child objects. As you saw, these are extremely important objects to know and understand, especially if you are creating any content that is specific to the browser or operating system your user is running.

In the next chapter we will move on to the Window object, and cover its various methods and properties.

CHAPTER **10**

Window Object

The host objects are the highest-level objects in the JavaScript object hierarchy in terms of the implementation environment. These objects, one of which (navigator) we covered in the last chapter, don't deal with the nuts and bolts of JavaScript; instead, they deal primarily with the browser, such as opening a new browser window, traversing the history list, or obtaining the hostname from the current URL. When you are writing code that is to be executed within a specific environment, these are often very beneficial objects, methods, and properties. They provide the necessary tools to create code specific for that environment.

This chapter will focus on the Window object, which, as we have said, is at the pinnacle of the object hierarchy in terms of accessing and working with XHTML documents. We'll then descend to some of the other objects, which will be explained in greater detail throughout the rest of the chapter.

The Window Object

The top-level Window object is the parent of all other child objects that are related to the browser window itself, and is present on every page. Of course, a multiplicity of these child objects are possible in a single JavaScript application. The basic methods that surround the operation of the Window object have obvious functionalities and include those described in Table 10.1.

TABLE 10.1   Basic Window Object Methods

Method	Description
open()	Open browser windows; you can specify the size of the window, its content, and whether it has a button bar, location field, and other chrome (GUI) attributes.
close()	Close any open browser windows.
alert()	Show an alert dialog with an appropriate message.
confirm()	Show a confirm dialog with OK and Cancel buttons.
prompt()	Show a prompt dialog with a text entry field.
blur()	Remove focus from a window.
focus()	Add focus to a window.
scrollTo()	Scroll a window to a specified point.
setInterval()	A specified period between a functional call and the evaluation of an expression.
setTimeout()	A single specified period prior to a functional call or the evaluation of an expression.

Unlike other objects that may or may not be present, the Window object is always there within the client-side JavaScript implementations, whether it's in a single or multiframe display. However, the Window object is unusual in that you can often simply ignore it, for two reasons.

First, if you're working in a single-frame environment, you can ignore explicit referencing of the Window object. JavaScript infers the reference to the current window. For example, the following two statements are equivalent and produce the same result:

```
myTitle = window.document.title
myTitle = document.title
```

Second, because of the structure of the JavaScript language, some system-level methods, such as displaying message boxes or setting a timer, are assigned to the Window object. However, you don't need to reference the window itself when calling these methods; the reference to the window is implicit.

Working with Window objects is important when programming in JavaScript because of the way people use browser windows. Although most people browsing the Web typically use only one instance of the browser, having two or more windows open is sometimes beneficial. You can compare pages from different sites, enter information into a form using data from a different Web page, or conduct research from a list on one page and look at the references with another browser instance.

The term **browser window** is often shortened to just **window**, although you should be careful not to confuse separate copies of the browser with frames, which are also referred to as windows (subwindows of the browser window). The browser window is also called the **top window**, because frames are subwindows of the browser. Browsers that support

JavaScript let you programmatically open and close browser windows and navigate through these windows. A site with separate windows can provide several simultaneous views of the site's content, increase access to the information and features, and offer new ways to fully interact with the site.

In many cases, frames might be better for simultaneous viewing, as you'll see in Chapter 13, "Frames." However, multiple browser windows can be individually resized and positioned by the user. Users can also minimize and maximize the window, move the window to the foreground or background as needed, and typically keep all the tools and other features (menu bar, location field, status bar, bookmarks, and so on) with each instance of the browser.

Opening and Closing Windows

You can use JavaScript to open and close browser windows. As a developer, you can create a new window with a particular document loaded into it, based upon specific conditions. You can also specify, for example, the size of the new window and the options that are available in the window, and you can assign names for referencing it.

> **NOTE**
>
> A user can always open a new window by selecting File, New Browser (or a similar option). However, any window opened by a user in this way can't be referenced by JavaScript in other windows.

Although the act of opening a window is similar to creating a new `Window` object, you don't use the `new` constructor. Instead, you use the following syntax:

```
windowVar = window.open(URL, windowName, [, windowFeatures])
```

The parameters for the `open()` method are

- *URL*: The URL of the target window. This parameter is optional. If the URL is an empty string (`""`), the browser opens a blank window, allowing you to use the `write()` method to create dynamic XHTML content.

- *windowName*: The name of the `Window` object. This name is also optional; however, to target the window with a link or a form, you need a name. You can provide a name at a later time by assigning the `window.name` property.

- *windowFeatures*: A list of display attributes for the browser window.

If successful, the `open()` method returns a handle to a `Window` object. If `open()` fails, it returns a null value.

10

NOTE

The two names that can refer to a window aren't the same functionally. Consider the following code:

```
myWindow=window.open("","newWindow");
```

myWindow is a variable that contains an instance of the Window object. The newWindow reference is the new window's name. The new window's properties can be referenced through the variable myWindow. Links and forms can be targeted to the new window with its name newWindow.

Referencing Windows

When working with single and multiple frames in your JavaScript applications, you probably need to use other ways to reference windows. JavaScript provides four references to windows, and each is implemented as a property of the Window object. Chapter 13 provides more information about referencing windows and frames.

Separate browser windows don't have a hierarchy structure; however, the window containing the code that opens another window is often referred to as the **parent window**. The new window is often referred to as the **child window**. Any new window can assign a variable in other windows so that other windows can reference it and its properties. To reference a property in the new window, use *windowName.property*. For instance, consider the following code:

```
newWindow = window.open();
newWindow.location.href = "http://www.samspublishing.com";
```

Although this segment isn't the most efficient way to write the code, it demonstrates referencing a child window's property. The new window is opened and named (in this case, newWindow). Then, the new window's location.href is referenced and assigned.

The Current Window

We have previously discussed how to reference windows; however, what hasn't been covered is that the Window object contains a property called window that can be used as a self-referencing tool. In addition, the self property of the Window object is another means of referring to the current or active window. For example, the following two code lines are functionally the same:

```
window.defaultStatus = "Welcome to the Goat Farm Home Page";
self.defaultStatus = "Welcome to the Goat Farm Home Page";
```

Because both window and self are synonyms of the current window, you might find it curious that both are included in the JavaScript language. As shown in the previous snippet, the rationale is flexibility; you can use window or self as you want.

However, as useful as `window` and `self` can be, it can easily become confusing to think about the logic behind it all. After all, an object's property that is used as an equivalent term for the object itself is rather unusual. Consequently, you might find it helpful to think of `window` or `self` as reserved words for the `Window` object rather than its properties.

Because `window` and `self` are properties of the `Window` object, you can't use both `window` and `self` in the same context. For example, the following doesn't work:

```
window.self.document.write("<h1>Test</h1>");
```

Finally, in multiframe environments, `window` and `self` always refer to the window in which the JavaScript code is executed.

> **NOTE**
>
> In some object-oriented or object-based languages, self might refer to the active object, no matter what type it is. In JavaScript, self refers only to the active `Window` or `Frame` object—nothing else.

Specifying Window Content

The URL parameter specifies what content appears in the new window. If you specify a value, the browser attempts to locate and display the specified document:

```
newWindow = window.open("http://www.samspublishing.com", "Sams", "");
```

Alternatively, you can display a blank page by specifying an empty string (`""`) as the URL parameter. Use this technique if you want to create an XHTML page dynamically using JavaScript:

```
newWindow = window.open("", "DynamicPage", "");
newWindow.document.write("<h1>Document created using JavaScript.</h1>");
newWindow.document.close();
```

See Chapter 11, "Document Objects," for complete details on using the `Document` object's `write()` method to create XHTML dynamically.

Specifying Window Attributes

The *windowFeatures* parameter is important as you display windows, because it lets you customize the look of the window you're opening. The *windowFeatures* parameter is optional; not using it gives you a window with attributes identical to those of the current one. Table 10.2 lists the attributes that you can specify.

10

TABLE 10.2   The open() Method's Window Display Attributes

Attribute	Description
width	Width of the browser client area in pixels.
height	Height of the Navigator client area in pixels, but see innerHeight, which was introduced in JavaScript 1.2.
dependent	When yes, creates a child window of the current window, and when using Windows the child window does not appear on the taskbar. Child windows close in unison with their parent windows.
toolbar	Shows/hides the browser toolbar.
menubar	Shows/hides the browser menu bar.
scrollbars	Shows/hides the browser horizontal and vertical scrollbars.
innerWidth	Specifies the width of a window's content area.
innerHeight	Specifies the height of a window's content area.
resizable	Allows/disallows resizing of the browser window.
screenX	Specifies the distance from the left side of the screen to a new window.
screenY	Specifies the distance from the top of the screen to a new window.
status	Shows/hides the browser status bar.
location	Shows/hides the URL location box.
directories	When yes, shows the personal toolbar.
copyhistory	Copies the current window's Go history for a new window.
outerWidth	Width of the Navigator window in pixels.
outerHeight	Height of the Navigator window in pixels.
left	Distance in pixels from the left side of the screen.
top	Distance in pixels from the top of the screen.
alwaysLowered	Creates a browser window that floats below other windows, regardless of whether or not it is active.
alwaysRaised	When yes, creates a browser window that floats on top of other windows, regardless of whether or not it is active.
z-lock	Creates a new browser window that doesn't rise above other windows when given focus.

The width and height attributes specify the dimensions of the window in pixels, and you might prefer innerWidth and innerHeight. The remaining attributes are set by using Boolean values. The value true can be specified by using 1, yes, or the attribute alone; false can be specified by using 0, no, or leaving the attribute out altogether. For example, if you want to display the new window with only a toolbar and menu bar, use the following syntax:

```
newWindow = window.open("", "myWindow", "toolbar=1,menubar=1")
```

The following syntaxes are also valid:

```
newWindow = window.open("", "myWindow", "toolbar=yes,menubar=yes");
newWindow = window.open("", "myWindow", "toolbar,menubar");
```

As you see, you can simply leave out attributes that aren't specified. They are assumed to have `false` values.

Closing Windows

To close a window, you can use the `Window` object's `close()` method. If you're closing the current window, your method call is simply `window.close()`. Unlike other `Window` object methods such as `alert()` or `setTimer()`, the `close()` method must always accompany an object reference. If you use `close()` by itself, you could close the current document rather than the window, depending on the context of the method call. The reason is that the `Document` object has a `close()` method, too.

Table 10.3 illustrates some typical code scenarios in which we see the `close()` method applied.

TABLE 10.3   The close() Method and Open Windows

Close()/Opener	Description
`window.opener.close()`	Closes the window that opened the current window
`window.opener.name`	Returns the name of the opener window
`top.opener.close()`	Closes the main browser window
`window.opener.document.bgColor`	Refers to the background color of the window that the opener property specifies
`window.opener=null`	Changes the value of the opener property to null, preventing closure of the opener window

If you wanted to create a button that would close the window when clicked, you could use the `window.close()` method in the following way:

```
<form action="null">
  <input type="button" value="Close Window" onclick="top.close()" />
</form>
```

> **NOTE**
>
> For an event handler such as onClick, you must specify a window name such as window, parent, top, self, or an assigned variable name such as myWindow, as in window.close() or myWindow.close(). Simply using close() in an event handler implies documents.close().

You can also close a window by referencing it from the same window that opened it, through the variable assigned to the new window. The following snippet shows how this could be done.

```
<script type="text/javascript">
newWindow = window.open("", "DynamicPage", "");
newWindow.document.write("<h1>Document created using JavaScript.</h1>");
newWindow.document.close();
</script>


<form>
  <input type="button" value="Close Window" onclick="newWindow.close()"/>
</form>
```

A good use of the `window.close()` method is to provide a button or link for users to close a new window when they're finished with it. Some users, especially new ones, might not know how to close the window or might mistakenly exit the browser instead of closing the window. You can use a conditional statement to provide a close button or link if the document is loaded in a window named explicitly (a new window):

```
<script type="text/javascript">

if(top.name == "newWindow"){
  document.write('<a href="javascript:top.close()">Close</a>"'  +
                 ' this window to return to previous window.');
}
</script>
```

The form in Figure 10.1 demonstrates the various aspects of opening and closing windows by creating a form to control the properties. By filling out the form, you can specify how you want the new window to look.

In the first section, you can specify the URL parameter—to use an existing URL or create a page on-the-fly. The second section lets you specify each of the window attributes available. By default, all are unchecked. You can check all the ones you want to display. By checking the Custom Size box, you can specify the dimensions of the new window.

If you select some of these options and then click the Open Window button, you will see something like the new window that is created in Figure 10.2.

Listing 10.1 provides the source code for this example.

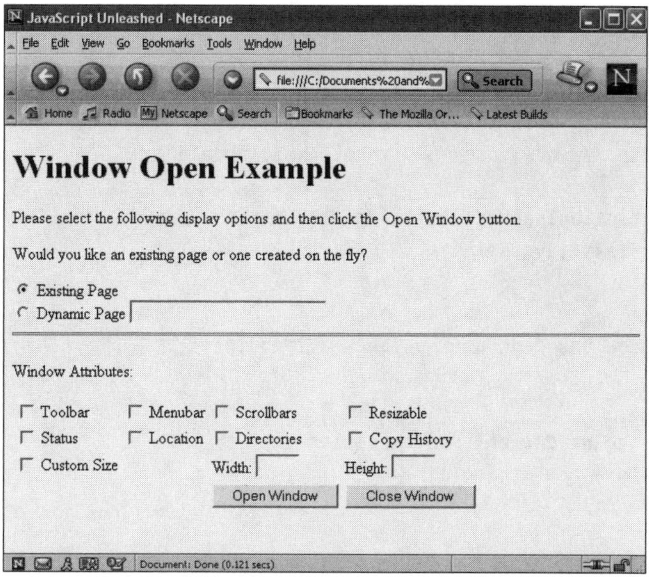

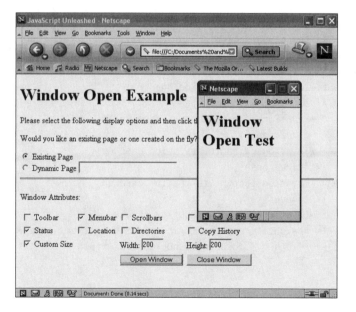

FIGURE 10.1 A window open sample form.

FIGURE 10.2 The new window is displayed.

LISTING 10.1 Code Used to Create Pop-up Window Configuration

```
<?xml version="1.0" encoding="UTF-8"?>
<!DOCTYPE html PUBLIC "-//W3C//DTD XHTML 1.0 Transitional//EN"
                     "DTD/xhtml1-transitional.dtd">
<html xmlns="http://www.w3.org/1999/xhtml" xml:lang="en">
<head>
  <title>JavaScript Unleashed</title>
  <script type="text/javascript">
    var newWindow

    // Open Window based on user defined attributes.
    function openWindow() {

      // Build the windowFeatures parameter list.
      var winAtts = new String()
      winAtts = "";

      if(document.winOptions.toolbarOption.checked){
        winAtts += "toolbar,"}
      if(document.winOptions.menubarOption.checked){
        winAtts += "menubar,"}
      if(document.winOptions.scrollbarsOption.checked){
        winAtts += "scrollbars,"}
      if(document.winOptions.resizableOption.checked){
        winAtts += "resizable,"}
      if(document.winOptions.statusOption.checked){
        winAtts += "status,"}
      if(document.winOptions.locationOption. checked){
        winAtts += "location,"}
      if(document.winOptions.directoriesOption.checked){
        winAtts += "directories,"}
      if(document.winOptions.copyHistoryOption.checked){
        winAtts += "copyhistory,"}
      if(document.winOptions.customSizeOption.checked){
        winAtts += "height=" + document.winOptions.heightBox.value + ","
        winAtts += "width=" + document.winOptions.widthBox.value + ","
      }

      winAtts = winAtts.substring(0, winAtts.length-1);

      // Determine URL and show window.
      if (document.winOptions.pageType[1].checked){
```

LISTING 10.1   Continued

```
      var urlVar = ""
      urlVar = document.winOptions.urlBox.value
      newWindow = window.open(urlVar,"newWindow",winAtts)
    }else{
      newWindow = window.open("","newWindow",winAtts)
      newWindow.document.write("<h1>Window Open Test</h1>");
      newWindow.document.close();
    }
  }

    // Close Window.
    function closeWindow() {
      newWindow.close()
    }
  </script>
</head>
<body>
<h1>Window Open Example</h1>
<p>Please select the following display options and then click
the Open Window button.</p>
<form name="winOptions" method="post" action="null">
  <p>Would you like an existing page or one created on the fly?</p>
  <input type="radio" checked="checked" name="pageType" value="existing" />
  Existing Page
  <br />
  <input type="radio" name="pageType" value="dynamic" /> Dynamic Page
  <input type="text" size="30" maxlength="256" name="urlBox" />
  <hr />
  <p>Window Attributes:</p>
  <table cellpadding="2">
    <tr>
      <td>
        <input type="checkbox" name="toolbarOption" /> Toolbar
      </td>
      <td>
        <input type="checkbox" name="menubarOption" /> Menubar
      </td>
      <td>
        <input type="checkbox" name="scrollbarsOption" /> Scrollbars
      </td>
      <td>
```

10

LISTING 10.1   Continued

```
      <input type="checkbox" name="resizableOption" /> Resizable
    </td>
  </tr>
  <tr>
    <td>
      <input type="checkbox" name="statusOption" /> Status
    </td>
    <td>
      <input type="checkbox" name="locationOption" /> Location
    </td>
    <td>
      <input type="checkbox" name="directoriesOption" /> Directories
    </td>
    <td>
      <input type="checkbox" name="copyHistoryOption" /> Copy History
    </td>
  </tr>
  <tr>
    <td>
      <input type="checkbox" name="customSizeOption" /> Custom Size
    </td>
    <td>
       
    </td>
    <td>
      Width:
      <input type="text" size="5" maxlength="5" name="widthBox" />
    </td>
    <td>
      Height:
      <input type="text" size="5" maxlength="5" name="heightBox" />
    </td>
  </tr>
  <tr>
    <td colspan="2">
       
    </td>
    <td>
      <input type="button" name="OpenButton" value="Open Window"
             onclick="openWindow()" />
    </td>
```

LISTING 10.1   Continued

```
      <td>
        <input type="button" name="CloseButton" value="Close Window"
               onclick="closeWindow()" />
      </td>
    </tr>
  </table>
</form>
</body>
</html>
```

Navigating Between Windows

It's possible to have a number of windows open during a session; however, only one window can be active, or have focus, at a time. Having focus means that the window can directly receive and respond to user input. Also, the window with the focus is typically the top window on the display, the one in the foreground overlapping the other windows.

The user can navigate between the windows by using the mouse. Often, clicking the window gives the window focus. With some varieties of UNIX, moving the mouse cursor on a window is enough to give it focus; conversely, moving the cursor off the window blurs (removes focus or deactivates) the window.

Relying on user action isn't the only way, nor at times the best way, to give focus to a window and blur others. JavaScript and XHTML provide several methods to focus and blur windows automatically through code, as we are sure many of you have experienced with the advertisements that pop up in the background of many Web pages today.

This automatic focusing and blurring allows window navigation with little or no user action. Instead of providing a message to tell the user to click a window, the code can focus the window automatically for the user. The intent isn't to remove user control of the session but to assist the user—as cruise control in an automobile does.

JavaScript provides a good means of controlling windows through the opening and closing techniques previously described and through techniques to apply and remove window focus. All these techniques for controlling windows combine to provide a programmatic window navigation system.

In JavaScript, merely specifying an object of the window or its document or even changing a property in the window doesn't give the window focus. You give focus to a window in two ways:

- Indirectly, by giving focus to an object in the window

- Directly, by giving focus to the window itself

10

Indirect Focus

A window opened with a variable myWindow, containing a document with a form named myForm and an input element named myInput, can receive focus through the window that opened it with the following code:

```
myWindow.document.myForm.myInput.focus();
```

The input element, myInput, gains focus and, as a result, myWindow, which contains myInput, also gets focus.

A new window can give focus to the window that opened it through its opener property:

```
window.opener.focus();
```

To provide focus from a new window to the window that opened it in early versions of JavaScript-capable browsers, the new window needs a variable to reference the opening window:

```
myWindow = window.open("new.html","newWindow");
myWindow.oldWindow = top;
```

The new window can reference the old window and indirectly give it focus:

```
oldWindow.document.myForm.myInput.focus();
```

Direct Focus

A window receives focus directly if you use the window.focus() method. If the window can reference another window through a variable such as myWindow, it can give focus to the other window:

```
myWindow.focus();
```

A new window can give focus to the window that opened it through its opener property:

```
window.opener.focus();
```

A call to a function in a window can provide focus to the window if the function contains window.focus():

```
function focusDemo(){
    top.focus;
    // rest of function
    }
```

Removing Focus

To blur, or remove focus from a window, just give focus to another window. Because only one window at a time can have focus, giving focus to a window directly or indirectly blurs the other windows.

Through the `window.blur()` method, a window can lose focus directly without another window gaining the focus. You can use any of the means that you employ with `window.focus()` for `window.blur()` as well.

Displaying Message Boxes

Dialog boxes are typically an important part of an application environment. JavaScript can display standard dialog boxes to either notify a user or receive information before proceeding. However, because of the nonmodal nature of the Web, we recommend that you not use dialog boxes. You can usually communicate with the user in some other way.

The JavaScript language itself not so subtly enforces this notion by adding a prefix to the messages you display. For alert messages, "JavaScript Alert" appears before the message you specify. For confirm dialog boxes, it's "JavaScript Confirm"; in prompt dialog boxes, you see "JavaScript Prompt." One reason for this is that the user can better determine the source of the dialog box that is displayed.

> **NOTE**
>
> Other than providing the message itself, you can't customize the look of JavaScript message boxes. The title and icons are always the same.

Simple Notification

You use the `Window` object's `alert()` method to display information to the user. The alert dialog box displays a message to the user with a single OK button to close the box. It is modal, so the user must close the dialog box before continuing in the browser, even in multiframe documents. No value is returned when the dialog box closes. Its syntax is as follows:

```
[window.]alert(message)
```

You can display information about the current window in an alert message. To illustrate this, we will need three different XHTML documents. The first document, shown in Listing 10.2, contains the necessary XHTML to create a frameset with two frames.

LISTING 10.2   Creating Our Frameset

```
<?xml version="1.0" encoding="UTF-8"?>
<!DOCTYPE html PUBLIC "-//W3C//DTD XHTML 1.0 Frameset//EN"
```

10

LISTING 10.2   Continued

```
                      "DTD/xhtml1-frameset.dtd">
<html xmlns="http://www.w3.org/1999/xhtml" xml:lang="en">
<head>
  <title>JavaScript Unleashed</title>
</head>
<frameset cols="50%,50%">
  <frame src="one.html" name="one" />
  <frame src="two.html" name="two" />
</frameset>
</html>
```

Listings 10.3 and 10.4 contain the XHTML documents that are loaded into these frames (one.html and two.html respectively). Within each of these documents are JavaScript functions that pop up an alert box showing the name of the window.

LISTING 10.3   Document Loaded in the Left Frame

```
<?xml version="1.0" encoding="UTF-8"?>
<!DOCTYPE html PUBLIC "-//W3C//DTD XHTML 1.0 Transitional//EN"
                      "DTD/xhtml1-transitional.dtd">
<html xmlns="http://www.w3.org/1999/xhtml" xml:lang="en">
<head>
  <title>JavaScript Unleashed</title>
  <script type="text/javascript">
    function displayWindowInfo(){
      var winInfo = new String()
      winInfo = "";

      winInfo += "Window object name: " + window.window.name + "\n"
      winInfo += "URL: " + window.location + "\n"
      alert(winInfo)
    }
  </script>
</head>
<body>
<h1>Frame 1</h1>
<form method="post" action="null">
  <input type="button" value="Display Information"
         onclick="displayWindowInfo()" />
</form>
</body>
</html>
```

LISTING 10.4   Document Loaded in the Right Frame

```
<?xml version="1.0" encoding="UTF-8"?>
<!DOCTYPE html PUBLIC "-//W3C//DTD XHTML 1.0 Transitional//EN"
                       "DTD/xhtml1-transitional.dtd">
<html xmlns="http://www.w3.org/1999/xhtml" xml:lang="en">
<head>
  <title>JavaScript Unleashed</title>
  <script type="text/javascript">
    function displayWindowInfo(){
      var winInfo = new String()
      winInfo = "";

      winInfo += "Window object name: " + window.window.name + "\n"
      winInfo += "URL: " + window.location + "\n"
      alert(winInfo)
    }
  </script>
</head>
<body>
<h1>Frame 2</h1>
<form method="post" action="null">
  <input type="button" value="Display Information"
         onclick="displayWindowInfo()" />
</form>
</body>
</html>
```

In Figure 10.3 you can see both the frames and the alert dialog box that is displayed when the user clicks the button in the document (named "one") on the left side.

The `message` parameter of the `alert()` method is typically a string, although it isn't required to be. Because JavaScript isn't a strongly typed language, you can display other data type information without converting the data to a string. You can even use an object as a parameter, as shown in Listing 10.5. Figure 10.4 shows the result.

LISTING 10.5   DisplayWindowObjectInfo.htm

```
<?xml version="1.0" encoding="UTF-8"?>
<!DOCTYPE html PUBLIC "-//W3C//DTD XHTML 1.0 Transitional//EN"
                       "DTD/xhtml1-transitional.dtd">
<html xmlns="http://www.w3.org/1999/xhtml" xml:lang="en">
<head>
  <title>JavaScript Unleashed</title>
```

LISTING 10.5   Continued

```
<script type="text/javascript">
  function Application(Title, ProgramName, Path, Vendor) {
    this.Title = Title
    this.ProgramName = ProgramName
    this.Path = Path
    this.Vendor = Vendor
  }

  function displayApp() {
    alert(Application)
  }

</script>
</head>
<body>
<form method="post" action="null">
  <input type="button" value="Display Object Definition"
         onclick="displayApp()" />
</form>
</body>
</html>
```

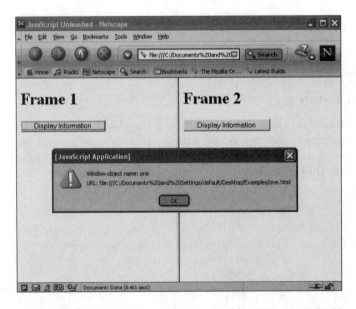

FIGURE 10.3   Alert dialog box showing which frame the button was clicked in.

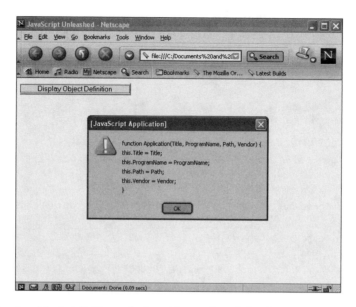

FIGURE 10.4   An object definition, displayed in an alert dialog box.

Confirmations

In addition to simply displaying information in a dialog box, you can ask a question using the `Window` object's `confirm()` method. The confirmation dialog box features OK and Cancel buttons, each returning a value. OK returns `true`, and Cancel returns `false`. As the method's name implies, you typically use a confirmation dialog box to confirm an action the user is about to take. Here is its syntax:

```
returnValue = [window.]confirm(message)
```

A common use of the confirmation dialog box is to ask the user to confirm a form submission or send an email message. Listing 10.6 shows how you can use `confirm()` to return a value to the form's `onSubmit` event handler. If the user clicks OK, the form is submitted. If the Cancel button is clicked, the submit event is canceled.

LISTING 10.6   JavaScriptChronicles.htm

```
<?xml version="1.0" encoding="UTF-8"?>
<!DOCTYPE html PUBLIC "-//W3C//DTD XHTML 1.0 Transitional//EN"
                    "DTD/xhtml1-transitional.dtd">
<html xmlns="http://www.w3.org/1999/xhtml" xml:lang="en">
<head>
  <title>JavaScript Unleashed</title>
  <script type="text/javascript">
```

10

LISTING 10.6   Continued

```
      function confirmAction() {
        return confirm("Do you really want to do this?")
      }
  </script>
</head>
<body>
<form action="/cgi-bin/buy.pl" onsubmit="return confirmAction()"
      method="post">
  <p>What books would you like to order?
    <br />
    <input type="checkbox" name="PJS" value="SKU01" />Pure JavaScript
    <br />
    <input type="checkbox" name="PDD" value="SKU02" />PHP Developer's Dictionary
    <br />
    <input type="checkbox" name="JSU" value="SKU03" />JavaScript Unleashed
  </p>
  <p>Please add some comments
    <br />
    <textarea name="comments" rows="6" cols="46"></textarea>
  </p>
  <p>
    <input type="submit" value="Submit" />
  </p>
</form>
</body>
</html>
```

Figure 10.5 shows the confirmation message box that is displayed when the user clicks the Submit button.

User Input

A third message box that you can use for obtaining user input is invoked with the prompt() method of the Window object. Use the prompt dialog box when you want to obtain a value from a user. This dialog box features a message, an edit box for user input, and OK and Cancel buttons. The prompt() method has the following syntax:

```
returnValue = [window.]prompt(message, defaultReply)
```

As you can see, in addition to specifying the message of the dialog box, you need to specify a *defaultReply* parameter. This value becomes the default text inserted in the edit box of the message box. You should always specify this parameter, even if there is no default value. If you don't add this argument, JavaScript places "Undefined" in the edit box, which can be confusing for users. If you have no default value, use an empty string ("") for the parameter, which will be less confusing.

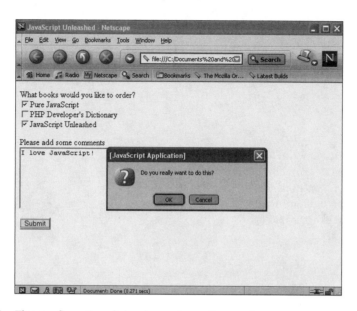

FIGURE 10.5 The confirmation dialog box returns the user's response.

If the user clicks OK, the `prompt()` method returns the string value entered by the user. If nothing is entered in the edit box, an empty string ("") is returned. However, if the user clicks Cancel, a null value is returned.

When using this method, it is important that you don't assume that the user will always click OK in the prompt dialog box. Every time you use the `prompt()` method, you should first ensure that a non-null value is returned before proceeding to evaluate it. Otherwise, if the user clicks Cancel, you will be working with a string value of `"null"` rather than what the user actually entered.

Listing 10.7 shows one example of how you can use the prompt message box.

LISTING 10.7 Prompting the User for Text to Be Written to a Pop-up Window

```
<?xml version="1.0" encoding="UTF-8"?>
<!DOCTYPE html PUBLIC "-//W3C//DTD XHTML 1.0 Transitional//EN"
                  "DTD/xhtml1-transitional.dtd">
<html xmlns="http://www.w3.org/1999/xhtml" xml:lang="en">
<head>
  <title>JavaScript Unleashed</title>
  <script type="text/javascript">
    function showBox() {
```

LISTING 10.7   Continued

```
      userText = prompt("Enter the text for your personalized browser " +
                        "window.","My own browser text");
      if (userText != null) {
        userWindow = window.open("", "userTextWindow", "toolbar=0");
        userWindow.document.write(userText);
        userWindow.document.close();
      }
    }
  </script>
</head>
<body>
<form action="null" method="post">
  <p>Create Your Own HTML Page
    <input type="button" value="Go!"
           onclick="showBox()" />
  </p>
</form>
</body>
</html>
```

The user is asked to enter text in the box, as shown in Figure 10.6. This text is then used in a new window, as shown in Figure 10.7.

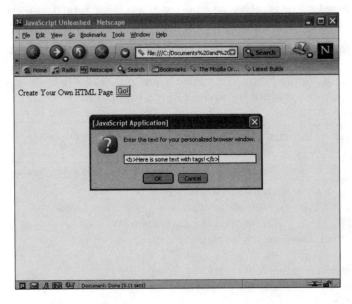

FIGURE 10.6   The prompt message box.

FIGURE 10.7   The new window displays content provided by the user.

The return value is always a string. If you want to treat it as another value, you must convert it first. For example, if you want to calculate a total price based on a user-defined interest rate, you could get that value using the `prompt()` method, as shown in Figure 10.8. Next, you could convert the value into a float using `parseFloat()` before calculating. Listing 10.8 shows the code.

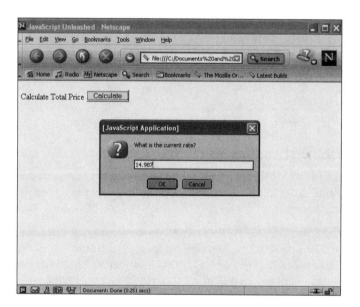

FIGURE 10.8   Retrieving input from the user.

LISTING 10.8   Processing Numerical Input from a User

```
<?xml version="1.0" encoding="UTF-8"?>
<!DOCTYPE html PUBLIC "-//W3C//DTD XHTML 1.0 Transitional//EN"
                "DTD/xhtml1-transitional.dtd">
<html xmlns="http://www.w3.org/1999/xhtml" xml:lang="en">
```

10

LISTING 10.8   Continued

```html
<head>
  <title>JavaScript Unleashed</title>
  <script type="text/javascript">
    function getPercentageRate() {
      percent = prompt("What is the current rate?", "8.5");
      if (percent != null){
        totalPrice = parseFloat(percent) * 20000;
        alert(totalPrice);
      }
    }
  </script>
</head>
<body>
<form action="null" method="post">
  <p>Calculate Total Price
    <input type="button" value="Calculate"
           onclick="getPercentageRate()" />
  </p>
</form>
</body>
</html>
```

Working with Status Bar Messages

The status bar of a browser can be an important means of communicating with the user. You can use two properties of the Window object—defaultStatus and status—to control the text that is displayed.

Generally, there are two ways to use the status bar. First, you can display a default message on the status bar. The user sees this message without performing any action. You can display a default message using the defaultStatus property. The defaultStatus property can be set at any time—either upon loading the window or while the window is already open.

Second, you can display a temporary message that overrides the default text. In practice, this message usually appears when a user performs an event, such as moving a mouse over a link. You can set this message using the status property.

To better understand how this works, let's step through a simple example of using the defaultStatus and status properties. We will create code for three actions that will change the status bar message. First, the following code sets a default message when the window opens:

```javascript
window.defaultStatus = "See, we changed it!!!";
```

Second, when the user passes over the Sams Publishing link, its onMouseOver event handler calls the following function, passing it to "over". This will cause the current status message to change. When the user rolls his mouse off the link, the onMouseOut event handler calls the same function, passing to "out" and changing the message back to the default status.

```
function changeStatus(direction) {
  if(direction == "over"){
    window.status = "Click me to go to Sams";
  }else if(direction == "out"){
    window.status = window.defaultStatus;
  }
}
```

Third, to change the text of the status message based on what option was selected, we will create a select box where the user can select a different message. When the Change button's onClick event handler is triggered, it executes the following function:

```
function changeDefaultStatus() {
    window.defaultStatus = window.document.statusForm.messageList.
            options[window.document.statusForm.messageList.
            selectedIndex].text;
}
```

Listing 10.9 provides the complete source code for this example.

LISTING 10.9   Status.htm

```
<?xml version="1.0" encoding="UTF-8"?>
<!DOCTYPE html PUBLIC "-//W3C//DTD XHTML 1.0 Transitional//EN"
                      "DTD/xhtml1-transitional.dtd">
<html xmlns="http://www.w3.org/1999/xhtml" xml:lang="en">
<head>
  <title>JavaScript Unleashed</title>
  <script type="text/javascript">

    window.defaultStatus = "See, we changed it!!!";

    function changeStatus(direction) {
      if(direction == "over"){
        window.status = "Click me to go to Sams";
      }else if(direction == "out"){
        window.status = window.defaultStatus;
      }
```

10

LISTING 10.9   Continued

```
    }

    function changeDefaultStatus() {
      window.status = window.document.statusForm.messageList.
➥                options[window.document.statusForm.
➥                messageList.selectedIndex].text;
    }

  </script>
</head>
<body>
<p>Let's go to the
  <a href="http://www.samspublishing.com"
    onmouseover="changeStatus('over');return true"
    onmouseout="changeStatus('out');return true">Sams</a>
  home page.
</p>
<form action="null" method="post" name="statusForm">
  <p>To change the  status bar message, select a message from the list
    below and click the Change button. Roll back over the link to see
    it change back to the default.
    <br />
    <select name="messageList" size="1">
      <option selected="selected">Welcome to the large URL page.</option>
      <option>En route to Sams</option>
      <option>This page intentionally left (nearly) blank.</option>
      <option>An exciting example of changing status bar text.</option>
    </select>
    <input type="button" value="Change" name="Change"
           onclick="changeDefaultStatus();return true" />
  </p>
</form>
</body>
</html>
```

Figure 10.9 shows the results of using this example to change the `defaultStatus` and `status` properties.

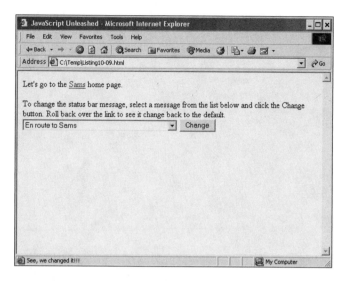

FIGURE 10.9   Setting the `defaultStatus` and `status` properties.

Summary

This chapter dived into the top level of the JavaScript object hierarchy. The `Window` object has much less to do with actual XHTML elements than with various aspects of a browser window.

As the top-level object in the hierarchy, the `Window` object is charged with many responsibilities—in both single and multiframe windows. The `Frame`, `Location`, and `History` objects, which will be discussed in Chapter 13, are all child objects of the `Window` object. This chapter also discussed how to use JavaScript to reference objects and properties in other frames and browser windows.

Now that we have covered the core, browser, and window objects, it's time to move on to the `Document` object, which acts as a container for all methods and properties specific to the document loaded in the browser window.

10

CHAPTER **11**

Document Objects

Although the Window object, which was discussed in Chapter 10, "Window Object," is the top-level object in the hierarchy, the Document object is arguably the most important. After all, the Document object is responsible for all the actual content displayed on a given page. This chapter looks at the Document object in detail as well as three of its "child" objects: Link, Anchor, and Image. In addition to the Document object, this chapter will also examine the Applet object.

The Document Object

The Window object is the highest-level object for client-side JavaScript objects. In this role, it serves as a container, but it doesn't actually have any content associated with it. It leaves the content of a Web document up to the Document object. The Document object serves as the JavaScript equivalent of an HTML document and is used as the method of access to its child objects.

In this role, the Document object is a container for all HTML-related objects that are associated with the <head> and <body> tags. The Document object gets the value of its title property from the <title> tag (located within the <head> section) and several color-related properties from the <body> section, which is shown here:

```
<body
    [background="backgroundImage"]
    [bgcolor="backgroundColor"]
    [text="foregroundColor"]
    [link="unfollowedLinkColor"]
    [alink="activatedLinkColor"]
    [vlink="followedLinkColor"]
    [onload="methodName"]
    [onunload="methodName"]>
</body>
```

> **NOTE**
>
> Although load and unload events can be captured with the onload and onunload event handlers in the <body> tag, they can be scripted through the Window object.

The Document object is critical as you work with JavaScript and HTML, because all the action happens on a Web page within a document. Because of this, you will often refer to the Document object when accessing an object within it. For example, if you want to access a Form object named invoiceForm, you must preface your reference with document:

```
document.invoiceForm.submit();
```

If you don't, JavaScript can't locate the object within the page.

Methods and Properties of the Document Object

The Document object provides access to much of the HTML content within a Web page through various properties. These properties can be a simple attribute, such as the bgcolor attribute of the HTML body tag, or the properties can be an array of objects, such as array of the all the Image objects on the page. In addition, the Document object can perform a number of very important actions through the methods that it offers. Table 11.1 contains a sampling of the methods and properties of the Document object. Document properties and methods are dependent on the object model of the particular browser.

TABLE 11.1   Methods and Properties of the Document Object

Type	Item	Description
Methods	close()	Closes output stream to the document.
	getSelection()	Returns the selected text. This method is only available in NN4+.
	open()	Opens output stream to document.
	write()	Appends text to the document.
	writeln()	Appends text and a newline character to the document.
Property	alinkColor	Color of an activated link.
	all	Array of all HTML tags in the document. This property is only available in IE4+.
	anchors	Array of Anchor objects.
	applets	Array of Applet objects.
	bgColor	Background color of the document.
	cookie	Cookie associated with the document.
	domain	Domain of the document.
	embeds	Array of embedded objects.
	fgColor	Color of text in the document.
	forms	Array of Form objects.
	formName	Specifies Form instance, which is accessed by using the value of the name attribute in the <form> tag.

TABLE 11.1 Continued

Type	Item	Description
	height	Specifies height in pixels of the document. This property is only available in NN4+.
	images	Array of Image objects.
	lastModified	Date when the document was last modified.
	linkColor	Color of links.
	links	Array of Link objects.
	plugins	Array of embedded objects.
	referrer	URL of the document to which the current document was linked.
	title	Title of the document.
	URL	URL of the current document.
	vlinkColor	Color of visited links.
	width	Specifies width in pixels of the document. This property is only available in NN4+.

NOTE

Many of the properties listed in Table 11.1 have subproperties and submethods. You should refer to Netscape's (http://developer.netscape.com) or Microsoft's (http://msdn.microsoft.com) documentation for more information on these.

Creating HTML Documents Programmatically

As you will see throughout this book, you can use JavaScript to react to events generated on static Web pages. You can also use it to generate HTML pages on the fly. In fact, you can use each of the methods of the Document object to alter documents programmatically:

- open() prepares a stream for write() and writeln() statements.

- write(expression1,expression2,…) evaluates the arguments and then passes the results to the method. The method converts its arguments to strings and writes them to the document.

- writeln(expression1,expression2,…) also evaluates the arguments and then passes the results to the method. The method converts its arguments to strings and writes them to the document but appends a newline character to the end of the expression.

- close() closes the stream that was opened by the open() method.

Whereas open() and close() prepare or close a generated document, the write() and writeln() methods give the document content. You can use any valid JavaScript expression as their parameter, including a string literal, a variable, and an integer value. For example, each of the following is a valid use of write():

```
var loc = "Ashford, Kent"
document.write("The castle is located in " + loc)
document.write("I stayed in the Robert Courtneys room.")
document.write("I would like " + 70 + "copies of that report.")
```

Keep in mind that you are writing HTML, not straight text. You can use HTML tags just as if you were writing the document in an HTML editor, as in the following example:

```
document.write('<h3>Return to the <a
➥href="http://www.samspublishing.com">Sams Publishing</a> home
➥page.</h3>');
```

Figure 11.1 shows the result.

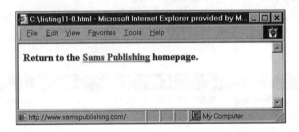

FIGURE 11.1   A link generated using JavaScript.

The one key limitation you need to keep in mind when using `write()` or `writeln()` is that you can't change the contents of the current document without completely reloading the window. The following sections describe the three valid contexts in which you can create HTML documents on the fly.

Creating in the Current Window

You can insert markup into the document of the current window when the document loads. You typically place this code within a `<script>` tag either in the `<head>` section or by itself if it stands alone. For example, if you want to evaluate the browser and change the text based on its type, you can use the script shown in Listing 11.1.

LISTING 11.1   Writing Different Text to a Page Based on the Browser

```
<script type="text/javascript">
<!--
  var browser = navigator.appName;


  if(browser == "Netscape"){
    document.write("<h2>Welcome <a href='http://home.netscape.com'>
```

LISTING 11.1   Continued

```
➡        Navigator</a> user.</h2>");
  }else if(browser == "Microsoft Internet Explorer"){
    document.write("<h2>Welcome <a href='http://www.microsoft.com'>
➡        Internet Explorer</a> user.</h2>");
  }else{
    document.write("<h2>Welcome. But what browser are you using?</h2>")
  }
  document.write("We are glad you came to our Web site. Do you know how");
  document.write(" we knew your browser type?");


//-->
</script>
```

Figure 11.2 shows the result in Navigator 6, and Figure 11.3 shows the result in Internet Explorer 6.

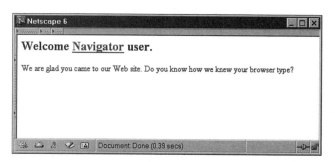

FIGURE 11.2   A customized Navigator page.

FIGURE 11.3   A customized Internet Explorer page.

Creating in a Frame

You can also generate a new document in another frame of a multiframe window. The techniques are similar to those used in the preceding example, but you must reference the correct document using dot notation or bracket notation. For example, to reference the first frame of a frameset, you could use the following code:

```
parent.frames[0].document.write("test");
```

Listing 11.6, which you'll see later in this chapter, has an example of setting a frame document programmatically.

Creating in a Separate Window

The third technique for creating documents on the fly is opening a new window and writing to its document. If you want to enumerate a list of installed Navigator plug-ins for the browser in a separate window, use the code shown in Listing 11.2.

LISTING 11.2   Displaying a List of Navigator Plug-Ins

```
<html>
<head>
  <script type="text/javascript">
  <!--
    function showWindow(){
      var len = navigator.plugins.length;
      newWin = window.open("", "", "height=400,width=500");
      newWin.document.write("<h2>Plug-In Info:</h2>");

      for(var i = 0; i < len; i++){
        newWin.document.write("<li>" + navigator.plugins[i].description +
            "</li>");
      }

      newWin.document.close()
    }
  //-->
  </script>
</head>
<body>
  <form>
    <input type="button"
           value="Show Plug-In Information"
           onclick="showWindow()">
  </form>
</body>
</html>
```

Figure 11.4 shows the result of the script in a Navigator browser.

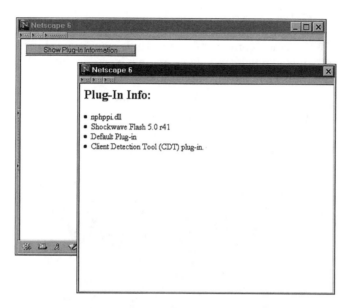

FIGURE 11.4   Generating a new document in a separate window.

Changing Document Colors

Color settings for documents are by default set in the user's browser configuration, but HTML gives you the capability to change these color settings, and with JavaScript you can do it programmatically. The Document object has five properties that reflect the colors of various attributes within the document—alinkColor, bgColor, fgColor, linkColor, and vlinkColor. These are described in Table 11.2.

TABLE 11.2   Document Color-Related Properties

Property	HTML <body> Attribute	Description
alinkColor	alink	The color of an activated link (after mouse down and before mouse up)
bgColor	bgcolor	The background color of the document
fgColor	text	The foreground color (text) of the document
linkColor	link	The color of unvisited links
vlinkColor	vlink	The color of visited links

These properties are expressed either as a string literal or as a string representation of hexadecimal RGB triplet values prefixed by a hash mark. For example, if you want to assign a background color of chartreuse to a document, use the string literal chartreuse:

```
document.bgColor="chartreuse";
```

You could also use the equivalent hexadecimal RGB triplet value:

```
document.bgColor="#7fff00";
```

A hexadecimal RGB triplet is a combination of three hexadecimal values representing red, green, and blue. When combined, the values form a hexadecimal RGB triplet. The number should take the case-insensitive form: #rrggbb.

To see how to set these color settings, look at the example shown in Figure 11.5. The Web page has a selection list of colors and a group of radio buttons associated with the Document attribute color options. You can select a color and the property you want to use and then click the Apply button to make the color change occur.

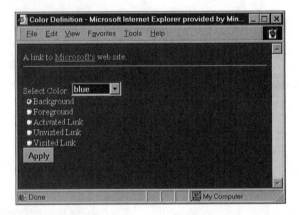

FIGURE 11.5   Changing the color of a document on the fly.

Listing 11.3 provides the HTML source of the document. When the user clicks the Apply button, the ChangeColor method assigns a value to the newColor variable based on the currently selected option in the selection list. Next the color attribute of the document that was specified is changed according to the user's request.

LISTING 11.3   Document Color Selectors

```html
<html>
<head>
  <title>Color Definition</title>
  <script type="text/javascript" language="JavaScript">

    //Change the color of attribute specified
    function ChangeColor() {
      var newColor = document.form1.colorList.options[document.form1.
➥colorList.selectedIndex].text;
```

LISTING 11.3   Continued

```
      if(document.form1.type[0].checked)
      {
        document.bgColor = newColor;
      }
      else if(document.form1.type[1].checked)
      {
        document.fgColor = newColor;
      }
      else if(document.form1.type[2].checked)
      {
        document.alinkColor = newColor;
      }
      else if(document.form1.type[3].checked)
      {
        document.linkColor = newColor;
      }
      else if(document.form1.type[4].checked)
      {
        document.vlinkColor = newColor;
      }
    }
  </script>
</head>

<body>

  A link to <a href="http://www.microsoft.com">Microsoft's</a> web site.<hr>

  <form name="form1">
      Select Color:
      <select name="colorList" size="1">
        <option>black</option>
        <option>blue</option>
        <option>brown</option>
        <option>cyan</option>
        <option>gold</option>
        <option>gray</option>
        <option>green</option>
        <option>indigo</option>
        <option>lavender</option>
        <option>lime</option>
```

LISTING 11.3   Continued

```
        <option>maroon</option>
        <option>navy</option>
        <option>olive</option>
        <option>orange</option>
        <option>pink</option>
        <option>purple</option>
        <option>red</option>
        <option>royalblue</option>
        <option>silver</option>
        <option>slategray</option>
        <option>tan</option>
        <option>teal</option>
        <option>turquoise</option>
        <option>violet</option>
        <option>white</option>
        <option>yellow</option>
    </select>
    <br>
    <input type="radio"
           name="type"
           value="bgColor"
           checked>Background</input><br>
    <input type="radio"
           name="type"
           value="fgColor">Foreground</input><br>
    <input type="radio"
           name="type"
           value="alinkColor">Activated Link</input><br>
    <input type="radio"
           name="type"
           value="linkColor">Unvisited Link</input><br>
    <input type="radio"
           name="type"
           value="vlinkColor">Visited Link</input><br>
    <input type="button"
           name="Apply"
           value="Apply"
           onclick="ChangeColor()">
  </form>
</body>
</html>
```

Although this is a limited example, you can build on this base to develop much more flexible scripts to change colors as well as other properties on the fly.

The Link Object

Perhaps love makes the world go 'round, but links are what make the World Wide Web go 'round. HTML links are the core elements of any Web document, allowing you to jump to another Web page with the click of a mouse. The location of the document is immaterial; it could be on the same Web server or thousands of miles away. All that matters is that the URL is valid. The JavaScript equivalent of the hypertext link is the Link object, which is defined in HTML syntax as follows:

```
<a href=locationOrURL
    [name="objectName"]
    [hreflang="langcode"]
    [type="contentType"]
    [rel="linkTypes"]
    [rev="linkTypes"]
    [charset="charset"]
    [id="idname"]
    [class="classname"]
    [lang="lang"]
    [title="elementTitle"]
    [stype="styleInfo"]
    [shape="shape"]
    [coords="coords"]
    [tabindex="tabNav"]
    [accesskey="accessKeys"]
    [target="windowName"]
    [onclick="methodName"]
    [onfocus="methodName"]
    [onblur="methodName"]
    [ondblclick="methodName"]
    [onmousedown="methodName"]
    [onmouseup="methodName"]
    [onmouseover="methodName"]
    [onmousemove="methodName"]
    [onmouseout="methodName"]
    [onkeypress="methodName"]
    [onkeydown="methodName"]
    [onkeyup="methodName"]
    [onmouseover="methodName"]>
    linkText
</a>
```

The Link object has several properties that are the same as the parameters for the Location object. These include hash, host, hostname, href, pathname, port, protocol, and search.

Referencing Link Objects

Link objects can be referenced a number of different ways. With IE4+, links can be referenced using linkId with document.all as shown following:

```
document.all["linkId"];
```

A link can also be referenced by name using the getElementsByTagName method of the Document object as well as other DOM methods. The getElementsByName method returns a collection, so you must access an individual with the item method of the collection object. The following demonstrates how to get the first link with the name "linkName":

```
document.getElementsByTagName("linkName").item(0);
```

A link can also be referred to by using the document.links array. The document.links array is a collection of all the links within the current document. The order of the array is based on the order in which the links are located within the source file. Consider the following example that demonstrates how to use the document.links array to deal with individual Link objects.

Suppose you want to extract the URLs from each link on a page and list them on another page. Using a triple-frame frameset, you can set the bottom frame to be the "free" window that is used for browsing, the top frame to contain a button to set off the process, and the middle frame to list the URLs. Figure 11.6 shows the triple-frame frameset in an Internet Explorer window after this process is performed.

Listing 11.4 displays the frameset source code; Listing 11.5 shows the code for the bottom frame, which contains all the lines; and Listing 11.6 lists the JavaScript source code for the top frame, which contains the processing power for this example. Clicking the Extract Link Information button triggers the getLinkInfo() method. This method references the links array of the bottom frame (named bFrame) and sets the len variable equal to its length. While writing to the middle frame, the method loops through each element in the links array and retrieves the href property value.

LISTING 11.4   Source Code for the Frameset

```
<html>
<head>
  <title>New Frameset</title>
</head>
<frameset rows="80,*,185">
  <frame src="listing11-6.html"
         name="tFrame"
         marginwidth="2"
```

LISTING 11.4   Continued

```
        marginheight="4">
  <frame src="about:blank"
        name="mFrame"
        marginwidth="5"
        marginheight="2">
  <frame src="listing11-5.html"
        name="bFrame"
        marginwidth="5"
        marginheight="2">
</frameset>
</html>
```

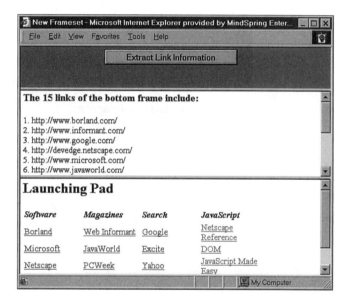

FIGURE 11.6   Getting URL information using the `links` array.

LISTING 11.5   Source Code for the Bottom Frame

```
<html>
<head>
  <title>Links</title>
</head>
<body>
<h2>Launching Pad</h2>
  <table width="80%">
    <tr>
```

LISTING 11.5   Continued

```html
    <td width="25%">
      <em><strong>Software</strong></em>
    </td>
    <td width="25%">
      <em><strong>Magazines</strong></em>
    </td>
    <td width="25%">
      <em><strong>Search</strong></em>
    </td>
    <td width="25%">
      <em><strong>JavaScript</strong></em>
    </td>
  </tr>
  <tr>
    <td width="25%">
      <a href="http://www.borland.com">Borland</a>
    </td>
    <td width="25%">
      <a href="http://www.informant.com">Web Informant</a>
    </td>
    <td width="25%">
      <a href="http://www.google.com">Google</a>
    </td>
    <td width="25%">
      <a href="http://devedge.netscape.com">Netscape Reference</a>
    </td>
  </tr>
  <tr>
    <td width="25%">
      <a href="http://www.microsoft.com">Microsoft</a>
    </td>
    <td width="25%">
      <a href="http://www.javaworld.com">JavaWorld</a>
    </td>
    <td width="25%">
      <a href="http://www.excite.com">Excite</a>
    </td>
    <td width="25%">
      <a href="http://www.w3.org/DOM">DOM</a>
    </td>
  </tr>
```

LISTING 11.5   Continued

```
    <tr>
      <td width="25%">
        <a href="http://home.netscape.com">Netscape</a>
      </td>
      <td width="25%">
        <a href="http://www.pcweek.com">PCWeek</a>
      </td>
      <td width="25%">
        <a href="http://www.yahoo.com">Yahoo</a>
      </td>
      <td width="25%">
        <a href="http://www.jsmadeeasy.com">JavaScript Made Easy</a>
      </td>
    </tr>
    <tr>
      <td width="25%">
         
      </td>
      <td width="25%">
        <a href="http://www.infoworld.com">InfoWorld</a>
      </td>
      <td width="25%">
        <a href="http://www.altavista.com">Alta Vista</a>
      </td>
      <td width="25%">
        <a href="http://www.javascript.com/">JavaScript Reference</a>
      </td>
    </tr>
  </table>
</body>
</html>
```

LISTING 11.6   Source Code for the Top Frame

```
<html>
<html>
<head>
  <base target="middle">
  <script type="text/javascript">
  <!--
    function getLinkInfo() {
```

LISTING 11.6   Continued

```
      var len = parent.bFrame.document.links.length;

    with(parent.mFrame.document){
      open();
      write("<h3>The " + len);
      write(" links of the bottom frame include:</h3><p>");

      for(var i = 0; i < len; i++){
        write((i + 1) + ". ");
        write(parent.bFrame.document.links[i].href + "<br>");
      }
      close()
    }
  }
//-->
</script>
</head>
<body bgcolor="red">
  <form>
    <div align="center">
      <input type="button"
             name="Extract"
             value="Extract Link Information"
             onclick="getLinkInfo()">
    </div>
  </form>
</body>
</html>
```

Executing JavaScript Code Within Links

You can execute JavaScript code within links in several ways. One way is to use
javascript: as the protocol element of the link's href. You can then perform a JavaScript
expression in place of a typical link action, such as jumping to a new Web page or sending
a mail message. You can also assign a JavaScript expression to an event handler such as the
onclick event handler, so long as the href value is set to "#".

For example, you could use a link to evaluate the type of browser in use, such as in the
following code:

```
<a href="#" onclick="if(navigator.appName != 'Netscape')
➡{ alert('You should not have clicked this link!') } else
➡{ alert('Thanks for clicking.')} ">All Netscape users, click me</a>
```

> **NOTE**
>
> `javascript:` hrefs are possible but have many disadvantages because of their original purpose. They are supposed to consist of a JavaScript expression returning some markup to be loaded into the target window of the link. Because of this, when a `javascript:` url is executed, the wait cursor can appear and the status bar in the browser indicates that it is loading a document. Often unwanted side effects include the stopping of GIF animation. If all you want to do is execute JavaScript, the onclick handler with a return false at the end is far more appropriate and has none of the disadvantages.

As a second example, a Web page displays a list of baseball-related deals. Each item has an associated link. For the href attribute of these links, a JavaScript call is made to a predefined JavaScript function located in the header block. When an item is selected, an alert box is used to display the special deal associated with the item. Listing 11.7 shows the HTML code for this example, and Figure 11.7 shows the result of clicking the baseballs link. The first two links (baseballs and baseball glove) use the javascript: protocol, whereas the third link (baseballbat) uses the onclick event handler.

LISTING 11.7 Displaying Baseball Deals with document.alert() Links

```html
<html>
<head>
  <title>JavaScript Unleashed Links Object</title>
  <script type="text/javascript">
    function baseball()
    {
      alert("Buy 4 get 1 free!");
    }

    function baseballglove()
    {
      alert("$2 off the purchase of any baseball glove!");
    }

    function baseballbat()
    {
      alert("Buy any baseball bat and get 2 baseballs for free!");
    }
  </script>
</head>
<body>
  <h2>Michael's Baseball Deals</h2>
  <i>Select item for specials</i><br><br>
```

LISTING 11.7   Continued

```
    <a href="javascript:baseball();">baseballs</a><br>
    <a href="javascript:baseballglove()">baseball glove</a><br>
    <a href="#" onclick="baseballbat()">baseball bat</a>
</body>
</html>
```

FIGURE 11.7   Clicking a link displays a message box.

The Anchor Object

You most often use a Link object to jump to another Web page or another location within the current document. Within the current document, the link locates a specific place in the text, called an **anchor**. This is defined in HTML syntax as

```
<a [href=locationOrURL]
    name="objectName"
    [target="windowName"]>
    anchorText
</a>
```

Anchors can be accessed in JavaScript through the anchors array of the Document object. You can use the document.anchors array to determine the number of anchors in a document and iterate through them as desired.

The Image Object

If you've spent much time on the Web, you probably realize how important graphics are to the Web. You can hardly go to a page without seeing several graphics scattered

11

throughout. The Image object represents an HTML image, which is defined in the following format:

```
<img
    [name="objectName"]
    src="Location"
    [longdesc="uri"]
    [id="idName"]
    [class="className"]
    [alt="alternateText"]
    [lang="lang"]
    [dir="textDirection"]
    [title="elementTitle"]
    [style="style"]

    [height="Pixels"|"Value"%]
    [width="Pixels"|"Value"%]
    [hspace="Pixels"]
    [wspace="Pixels"]
    [border="Pixels"]
    [align="left"|"right"| "top"|
        "absmiddle"|"absbottom"|
        "texttop"|"middle"|"baseline"|
        "bottom"]
    [ismap]
    [usemap="Location#MapName"]
    [onabort="methodName"]
    [onerror="methodName"]
    [onclick="methodName"]
    [ondblclick="methodName"]
    [onmousedown="methodName"]
    [onmouseover="methodName"]
    [onmousemove="methodName"]
    [onmouseout="methodName"]
    [onkeypress="methodName"]
    [onkeydown="methodName"]
    [onkeyup="methodName"]
    [onload="methodName"]>
```

For example, to display an image called dot.gif in HTML, you would use the following syntax:

```
<img src="dot.gif" height="200" width="200">
```

For IE5+ and NN6+ you can create an instance of an `Image` object using the new operator, as shown here:

```
companyLogo = new Image();
companyLogo.src = "logo.gif";
```

You can then set the dimensions of the graphic as a parameter to the `Image()` constructor. For example, if you want to display the logo in a 200×300–pixel format, use the following:

```
companyLogo = new Image(200,300);
companyLogo.src = "logo.gif";
document.body.appendChild(companyLogo);
```

By assigning a value to the `src` property, you can change the image that is displayed. However, if you do this, the new URL or graphic loads in the image area.

Because you still define an image using the `<img>` tag, an `Image` object you create serves a rather limited purpose. You can use it to retrieve an image before it's actually needed for display purposes. Because this image is now in memory, it would be much quicker to display it when a document is reloaded. This is often used to create rollover effects.

> **TIP**
>
> See Chapter 21, "Rollovers and Visual Effects," for more information on how you can use `Image` objects.

The Applet Object

The `Applet` object, which was added in JavaScript 1.1, represents the JavaScript equivalent of the `<applet>` HTML tag. In a generic sense, these JavaScript objects have no methods associated with them, but that is really irrelevant, because you can use JavaScript to access the specific methods of a given Java applet. Because of this, the properties of the `Applet` object are all public fields of a Java applet, and the methods are all public methods.

Accessing Java from JavaScript

JavaScript scripts communicate with Java applets running in an HTML page by accessing members (methods and fields) of the Java objects associated with those applets. Any Java method declared with the `public` modifier is available to be called from JavaScript, and any Java field declared as `public` is available to be examined or modified. The first step in communicating with a Java applet from JavaScript is to obtain a reference to the applet. After that's accomplished, you can directly access any of the applet's public members.

> **NOTE**
>
> You might have heard of LiveConnect in association with JavaScript and Java. Although no longer supported, LiveConnect was a Netscape client-side technology that provided seamless manipulation of data between Navigator's three main client-side development environments—plug-ins, Java, and JavaScript. You can find additional information on LiveConnect at Netscape's DevEdge site at http://developer.netscape.com.

Referencing Applets

Applets running in a document are reflected in JavaScript within the document.applets array. For example, the first applet defined in the current document could be referenced from JavaScript as document.applets[0]. The same applet could also be referenced by name as document.applets["appletName"], or simply document.appletName if its name was specified in the <applet> tag. An applet's name can be specified in the <applet> tag by giving a value to the name attribute. For example, this tag

```
<applet name="myApplet" code="testApplet.class" width="100" height="100"
➡ mayscript></applet>
```

would create an applet of class testApplet named myApplet. If it also happened to be the first applet on the page, it could be referenced by document.applets[0], document.applets["myApplet"], or document.myApplet.

JavaScript scripts can also reference Java applets running in other frames in the same browser window. For example, if a Java applet were running in a frame called frame1, it could be referenced from a sibling frame as parent.frame1.document.myApplet.

Translating Data Types

One of the most difficult and confusing aspects of calling Java methods from JavaScript can be getting the types of the arguments you pass to Java to match up with the types of the arguments the Java method is looking for. If the two sets of arguments don't match exactly, the attempted function call fails, and you get an error message saying that JavaScript couldn't find a Java method that was expecting the arguments you tried to pass.

Java is a strongly typed language (meaning that every variable has a specific, declared type), and all Java methods must declare in advance how many arguments they are expecting, of what type, and in what order. Within a Java program, any attempt to invoke a method with an argument sequence that doesn't exactly match the method's declared argument sequence, type for type, results in a compile-time error.

JavaScript, in contrast, has much more relaxed typing and, as an interpreted language, must do all its checking at runtime anyway. JavaScript variables don't have a declared type; in fact, they don't have to be declared at all, because they can simply come into existence by being referenced. The same JavaScript variable can be assigned a string in one statement, an integer in the next statement, and an array in the next.

How are JavaScript objects converted into Java objects when they're passed to Java methods? How does Java know how to find a Java type that matches exactly the JavaScript object's structure? The short answer is that, in general, it doesn't. There probably is no such object. Unless the object happens to fall into one of certain exceptional cases, Java won't necessarily have a class that exactly mirrors the object's JavaScript type, so it simply assigns it a default type, JSObject, specifically designed to represent JavaScript objects in Java.

Fortunately, the aforementioned exceptional cases encompass some of the most common and useful data types, including JavaScript's three basic data types: strings, numbers, and booleans. JavaScript strings (that is, string constants and variables that have most recently been assigned strings) appear in Java as instances of the Java String type. JavaScript numbers (numeric constants and variables most recently assigned integer or real numeric values) are converted to double Java values. JavaScript Boolean values (true and false) become Java Boolean objects.

One other special case concerns JavaScript objects that are wrappers around Java objects. Such objects are simply "unwrapped" and converted to their original Java types. Although this fact is currently undocumented, there is additional flexibility in passing JavaScript numbers directly to Java methods. An attempt to make a call such as

```
document.myApplet.setNumber(3.7);
```

would succeed if the myApplet applet had a method with a signature of

```
public void setNumber(type x);
```

where *type* is one of the following: Double, double, float, long, int, short, char, or byte, although only Double ought to be acceptable. In cases where the applet has more than one overloaded method expecting one of these types, the first such method (the method closest to the top of the Java source file) is chosen. Tie-breaking by lexicographic location is probably not the best way to resolve conflicts between overloaded methods, and it is very likely that some other mechanism will be devised.

Suppose you wrote a setText() method to be picky about acceptable values for theText, and you wanted a way to find out if a given call to setText() had resulted in theText() being successfully set. If you designed the new function to return a Boolean flag indicating success or failure, it might look something like this:

```
public boolean setText(String s){
  if (s.equals("Hello world!")){

    // I'm sick of that string; don't accept it.
    return false;
  }else{
    theText = s;
```

```
    return true;
  }
}
```

If you wrote a JavaScript script that included this line

```
var changed = document.myApplet.setText("Hello world!")
```

the value returned by `setText()` would be stored in `changed`. The question remains, though: Exactly how will the Java `Boolean` value returned by `setText()` be converted into a JavaScript object? In this particular case, the answer is simple and intuitive: Java `Boolean` values become JavaScript `boolean` values when they're returned to JavaScript.

Passing Java objects to JavaScript isn't always quite so simple—a number of rules govern the exact translation for a given object. The good news is that things often work out just the way you might hope. Java arrays become JavaScript arrays, Java numeric types become JavaScript numbers, Java `Boolean` values become JavaScript `boolean` values, and Java `Strings` become JavaScript `Strings`. For completeness, here is the entire set of rules used to govern the conversion:

- Java numeric types (`byte`, `char`, `double`, `float`, `int`, `long`, `short`) become JavaScript numbers.

- Java `Boolean` values become JavaScript `boolean` values.

- Java `JSObjects` are converted back to their original JavaScript objects.

- Java arrays are wrapped in JavaScript `Array` objects.

- All other Java objects are converted to JavaScript wrapper objects that can be used to access the original Java members.

When an attempt is made to convert a JavaScript wrapper into a JavaScript string, number, or Boolean, the original Java object's `toString()`, `doubleValue()`, or `booleanValue()` method is called, if it exists, and the value of the converted object is the value returned by the corresponding method. If the corresponding method doesn't exist, the conversion fails. Note that Java strings work as expected in JavaScript, even though they are technically passed to JavaScript as wrapper objects. Any attempt to use one in a context where a JavaScript string is expected causes the correct conversion to be applied.

Summary

The document objects discussed in this chapter are the JavaScript equivalent of some of the most basic HTML elements around. These objects include the HTML `Document`, `Link`, `Anchor`, `Image`, and `Applet`. Although you can use JavaScript to enhance or retrieve information from these objects, much of the JavaScript interaction usually comes from working with forms. Therefore, the next chapter looks closely at `Form` objects.

CHAPTER **12**

Form Objects

One of the key milestones in the evolution of the Web was the emergence of HTML forms from the world of static pages. With forms, the Web could actually be more than a one-directional mode of communication. Forms provided a means by which any user on any machine could transfer data to a server for processing.

With JavaScript, HTML forms grow even more powerful. Not only can you preprocess form data before it's sent to the user, but you can also use forms in an application that is contained completely on the client side. This chapter discusses the Form object and the numerous objects it can contain, including Text input objects, Button objects, Radio objects, and Select objects. The aim of this chapter is simply to provide all the information you need to implement forms quickly and at the same time bring your attention to some really useful tips.

You can also **pattern mine** using this chapter, which is fun and saves lots of time when developing sites. With pattern mining, you simply look at the listings and their general structures and then reshape their code to suit your own needs. At the same time, you don't actually copy the code directly. More and more developers are working this way, and this chapter attempts to provide lots of patterns that you can use.

The Form Object

One of the principal uses of JavaScript is to provide a means to interact with the user on the client side. Most of the time, this interaction with the user happens through an HTML form. As a result, the JavaScript Form object is an important object within the JavaScript object model. You don't do that much with a Form object in and of itself. Rather, the Form object provides a container with which you can retrieve data from the user.

In HTML, the Form object is defined as follows:

```
<form
    [name="formName"]
    [action="serverURL"]
    [enctype="encodingType"]
    [accept="contentTypes"]
    [accept-charset="charset"]
    [method=get | post]
    [target="windowName"]
    [id="idName"]
    [class="className"]
    [style="styleName"]
    [title"title"]
    [lang="langCode"]
    [dir="directory"]
    [onclick="script code"]
    [ondblclick="script code"]
    [onmousedown="script code"]
    [onmouseup="script code"]
    [onmouseover="script code"]
    [onmousemove="script code"]
    [onkeypress="script code"]
    [onkeydown="script code"]
    [onkeyup="script code"]
    [onsubmit="script code"]
    [onreset="script code"]
</form>
```

To define a form, follow standard HTML conventions:

```
<form name="form1"
      action="http://www.javascriptunleashed.com/dosomething.jsp"
      method=e"get">
  <!-- Enter form objects here -->
</form>
```

> **NOTE**
>
> For more information on using forms in JavaScript, see Chapter 24, "Forms and Data Validation."

Submitting Forms to the Server

Before JavaScript came along, the only real purpose of an HTML form was to send the data elements gathered on the client side to the server. Because the client side itself wasn't powerful enough to process the data intelligently, it was up to the server to then react to the information it received. JavaScript lets you add a great deal of front-end processing to your HTML forms, but that doesn't eliminate the need to submit a form to a server for more industrial-strength purposes.

You can submit a form using one of two processes. You can call the Form object's submit() method, or you can click a Submit button, which automatically submits the form with which it is associated.

> **NOTE**
>
> See Chapter 18, "Handling Events," for more information on performing validity checks using JavaScript before submitting a form.

Many of the Form object properties deal with additional information that is sent to the server from the form. A sampling of these properties is discussed in the following list:

- action (same as the action= parameter): The action property specifies the server URL to which the form is sent. Depending on the particular browser and version, the URL may be relative or absolute.

```
var form1 = document.forms.forms1;
form1.action = "http://www.javascriptunleashed.com/dosomething.jsp"
```

  This is often a CGI program, a JSP page, an ASP page, or a Perl script.

- enctype (same as the enctype= parameter): The enctype property specifies the MIME encoding of the form. The default is application/x-www-form-urlencoded, although not all browsers show the default value.

- method (same as the method= parameter): The method property defines how the form is sent to the server. The value of GET is used most often, but you can use POST as well. This parameter is based on the server-side process, so as you design the HTML form, you need to check the server program's requirements. The following code shows an example of using the method parameter:

```
var methodType = document.form1.method;
alert("The method type for this form is: " + methodType)
```

- target (same as the target= parameter): The target property specifies the destination window for the browser to choose to display the result of the form submission. If the target property isn't specified, the browser displays results in the window that submitted the form. If you're using a frameset, the target property can be a frame specified by the name parameter of the <frame> tag. You can also use one of the following reserved window names: _top, _parent, _self, and _blank. Keep in mind that you are in HTML for this specification, not JavaScript. You can't use a JavaScript Window object name, such as parent.resultsWindow. The following code shows an example:

```
if (document.form1.newWindowCheckBox.checked) {
     document.form1.target = "resultsForm" }
else {
     document.form1.target = "_self" }
```

The HTML form shown in Listing 12.1 uses a combination of HTML tags and JavaScript code to submit a form. Note that if the user checks the Rush Order check box, the Form's action property changes to a new value during the Form's onSubmit event. The check box is evaluated by using dot notation to access the check attribute of the check box called rush. The action attribute of the form1 form is set using dot notation. Setting the action property programmatically overrides the value given in the markup as the action attribute value.

LISTING 12.1   Submitting a Form

```
<html>
<head>
<title>For More Information</title>
<script type="text/javascript" language="JavaScript">

     function checkType() {
          if (document.form1.rush.checked) {
               document.form1.action = "http://www.acadians.com/js/rush.cgi";
          }
     }
</script>
</head>

<body>
<h1>Order Form</h1>
<hr>
<form name="form1" action="http://www.acadians.com/js/order.cgi"
method="POST" onSubmit="checkType()">
<p>Please provide the following contact information:</p>
<blockquote>
<pre><em>     First name </em><input type=text size=25 maxlength=256
name="Contact_FirstName">
```

LISTING 12.1 Continued

```
<em>       Last name </em><input type=text size=25 maxlength=256
name="Contact_LastName">
<em>          Title </em><input type=text size=35 maxlength=256
name="Contact_Title">
<em>     Organization </em><input type=text size=35 maxlength=256
name="Contact_Organization">
<em>       Work Phone </em><input type=text size=25 maxlength=25
name="Contact_WorkPhone">
<em>            FAX </em><input type=text size=25 maxlength=25
name="Contact_FAX">
<em>           E-mail </em><input type=text size=25 maxlength=256
name="Contact_Email">
<em>            URL </em><input type=text size=25 maxlength=25
name="Contact_URL">
</pre>
</blockquote>
<p>Please provide the following ordering information:</p>
<blockquote>
<pre><strong>QTY     DESCRIPTION
</strong><input type=text size=6 maxlength=6
name="Ordering_OrderQty0">
<input type=text size=45 maxlength=256 name="Ordering_OrderDesc0">
<input type=text size=6 maxlength=6 name="Ordering_OrderQty1">
<input type=text size=45 maxlength=256 name="Ordering_OrderDesc1">
<input type=text size=6 maxlength=6 name="Ordering_OrderQty2">
<input type=text size=45 maxlength=256 name="Ordering_OrderDesc2">
<input type=text size=6 maxlength=6 name="Ordering_OrderQty3">
<input type=text size=45 maxlength=256 name="Ordering_OrderDesc3">
<input type=text size=6 maxlength=6 name="Ordering_OrderQty4">
<input type=text size=45 maxlength=256 name="Ordering_OrderDesc4">

<em>                  </em><strong>BILLING</strong>
<em>Purchase order # </em><input type=text size=25 maxlength=256
name="Ordering_PONumber">
<em>    Account name </em><input type=text size=25 maxlength=256
name="Ordering_POAccount">

<em>                  </em><strong>SHIPPING</strong>
<em>   Street address </em><input type=text size=35 maxlength=256
name="Ordering_StreetAddress">
<em> Address (cont.) </em><input type=text size=35 maxlength=256
```

12

LISTING 12.1 Continued

```
name="Ordering_Address2">
<em>            City </em><input type=text size=35 maxlength=256
name="Ordering_City">
<em>  State/Province </em><input type=text size=35 maxlength=256
name="Ordering_State">
<em> Zip/Postal code </em><input type=text size=12 maxlength=12
name="Ordering_ZipCode">
<em>          Country </em><input type=text size=25 maxlength=256
name="Ordering_Country">
</pre>
<pre><input type=checkbox name="rush" value="ON">Rush Order!</pre>
</blockquote>
<p><input type=submit value="Submit Form"> <input type=reset
value="Reset Form"> </p>
</form>
</body>
</html>
```

> **NOTE**
>
> For more information on the onSubmit event handler, see Chapter 18.

Checking Elements on a Form

The Form object acts as a container object for all objects on a form. Because these types of objects, such as Text or Button objects, are for user interaction, you can refer to them as **user interface objects** or **UI objects**. The Form object has an elements property that you can use to either refer to an element on a form or check all elements on a form to perform a particular task. The order of the array is based purely on the order in which the elements of the HTML form are defined in the source file. The first element listed is elements[0], the second is elements[1], and so on.

You can refer to each Form element either by name or by its index in the elements array. For example, if the Text object named LastName is the first element defined on the form, it can be accessed with the following code:

```
var curLastName = document.form1.elements[0].value;
```

You could also use this:

```
var curLastName = document.form1.LastName.value;
```

You can also use the elements property to do something with each object within the form.

For example, suppose you want to make sure that each field on your form isn't blank. Using the `elements` property, you can use a `for` loop to iterate through each array element and check the values. This code is shown in Listing 12.2.

> **NOTE**
>
> You will notice that the following form validation procedures do not check that the year is a numeric entry. For information on useful validation techniques, refer to Chapter 24.

LISTING 12.2   Check for Blank Fields

```html
<html>
<head>
<title>Online Registration</title>
<script type="text/javascript"language="JavaScript">
    function checkFields() {
        var num = document.form1.elements.length;
        var validFlag = true;
        for (var i=0; i<num; i++)
        {
            if (document.form1.elements[i].value == "" &&
                document.form1.elements[i] == 'text')
            {
                validFlag = false;
                alert("The " + document.form1.elements[i].name +
                    " field is blank. Please enter a value.");
                break;
            }
        }
        return validFlag;
    }
</script>
</head>

<body>
<form name="form1" method="POST" onSubmit="return checkFields()">
<h2>Online Registration</h2>
Username:<br />
<input type="text" size="25" maxlength="256" name="Username"><br />
Category of Interest:<br>
<input type="text" size="25" maxlength="256" name="Category"><br />
Starting Year:<br />
<input type="text" size="25" maxlength="256" name="StartYear"><br />
```

LISTING 12.2   Continued

```
Email address:<br />
<input type="text" size="25" maxlength="256" name="EmailAddress"></p>
<br /><br />
<input type="submit" value="Register"><input type="reset" value="Clear">
</form>
</body>
</html>
```

Notice that the checkFields() method uses the elements.length property to determine the number of iterations in the for loop. Next, because the elements array includes all objects in the form, including the two Button objects, the type and value attributes of each element are checked. If the element is a text input object and it does not contain any value, an alert box is displayed and the submit action is cancelled by returning false from the function. Figure 12.1 shows the alert message box that appears if a field is blank.

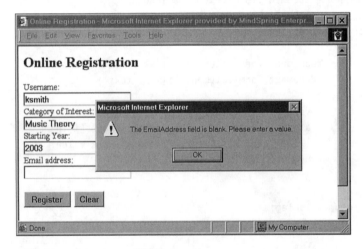

FIGURE 12.1   Checking the values of fields on a form.

The Text Input Object

For most tasks, the Text input object is the element you use most often to gather data entered by the user. The Text object is used for capturing single-line, free-flow information. For information that spans multiple lines, use the Textarea object, discussed in the section "The Textarea Object." As with other Form objects, the Text object is the "objectified" version of an HTML tag, and it has the following syntax:

```
<input
    type="text"
    [name="objectName"]
```

```
[value="value"]
[size="size"]
[maxlength="size"]
[readonly]
[disabled]
[alt="shortdescription"]
[tabindex="number"]
[accesskey="char"]
[id="idName"]
[class="className"]
[lang="language"]
[title="title"]
[style="styleName"]
[align="alignment"]
[onclick="script code"]
[ondblclick="script code"]
[onmousedown="script code"]
[onmouseup="script code"]
[onmouseover="script code"]
[onmousemove="script code"]
[onmouseout="script code"]
[onkeypress="script code"]
[onkeydown="script code"]
[onkeyup="script code"]
[onblur="script code"]
[onchange="script code"]
[onfocus="script code"]
[onselect="script code"]>
```

For example, to define a Text object for a last name, you could use the following:

```
<input type="text" name=LastName size=20 maxlength=25>
```

NOTE

For more information on the Text object events, such as onBlur, onChange, onFocus, and onSelect, see Chapter 18.

Assigning a Default Value to a Text Object

There might be times when you want to assign a default value to a Text object. If you're creating an HTML document on the fly, using JavaScript write and writeln methods, you can do this by setting the value= parameter of the <input type="text"> tag. To illustrate, suppose you wanted to automatically check the type of the Navigator object and enter it in a form. The code shown in Listing 12.3 generates the form shown in Figure 12.2. Notice that the Browser field is automatically filled in for the user when the script checks the appName property of the Navigator object.

LISTING 12.3   Automatically Filling in the Browser Field

```
<html>
<head>
  <title>Online Registration</title>
</head>
<body>
<script type="text/javascript" language="JavaScript">
var browserVar = navigator.appName;
document.write('<form name="form1" method="POST">');
document.write('<h2>Online Registration</h2>');
document.write('Username:<br>');
document.write('<input type=text size=25 maxlength=256 name="Username"><br>');
document.write('Browser used:<br>');
document.write('<input type=text size=25 maxlength=256
        name="Browser" value="' + browserVar + '"><br>');
document.write('Email address:<br>');
document.write('<input type=text size=25 maxlength=256 ');
document.write('name="EmailAddress"><br><br>');
document.write('<input type="submit" value="Register">');
document.write('<input type="reset" value="Clear">');
document.write('</form>');
</script>
</body>
</html>
```

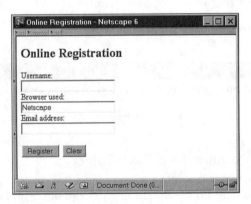

FIGURE 12.2   The default value is set for the user.

A second way to assign a default value to a Text object already generated is to set its `value` property. For example, you could create the same form using the code shown in Listing 12.4. In this example, the window's onLoad event handler assigns a value to the Browser field.

LISTING 12.4   Automatically Filling in the Browser Field

```
<html>
<head>
<title>Online Registration</title>
<script  type="text/javascript" language="JavaScript">
    function findBrowser() {
         document.form1.Browser.value = navigator.appName;
    }
</script>
</head>

<body onLoad="findBrowser()" >
<form name="form1" method="POST">
<h2>Online Registration</h2>
<p>Username:<br>
<input type=text size=25 maxlength=256 name="Username"><br>
Browser used:<br>
<input type=text size=25 maxlength=256 name="Browser"><br>
Email address:<strong> <br>
</strong><input type=text size=25 maxlength=256 name="EmailAddress"></p>
<h2><input type=submit value="Register"> <input type=reset value="Clear"></h2>
</form>
</body>
</html>
```

Paradoxically, the defaultValue property isn't used in this example. Although you can assign a value to the defaultValue property, the form isn't updated in some browsers when you do so (NN6 does update the form when the default value is set). Therefore, it is easier to just use the value property, as shown in Listing 12.4.

Selecting Text upon Focus

By default, when you enter a Text object, the cursor is an insertion point. If the field currently has text you want to type over, you have to select the text, delete it, and retype a value. You can change this behavior by using the select() method of the Text object. Listing 12.5 shows an HTML form with three Text objects, each of which call this.select() when the onFocus event is triggered. As a result, when the user enters each of these fields, any existing text is highlighted automatically. Figure 12.3 shows the result.

LISTING 12.5   Highlighting Text in the Text Field

```
<html>
<head>
<title>Online Registration</title>
</head>

<body>
<form name="form1" method="POST">
<h2>Online Registration</h2>
Username:<br>
<input type=text size=25 maxlength=256 name="Username"
onFocus="this.select()"><br>
Browser used:<br>
<input type=text size=25 maxlength=256 name="Browser"
onFocus="this.select()"><br>
Email address:<br>
<input type=text size=25 maxlength=256 name="EmailAddress"
onFocus="this.select()">
<br><br>
<input type=submit value="Register"><input type=reset value="Clear">
</form>
</body>
</html>
```

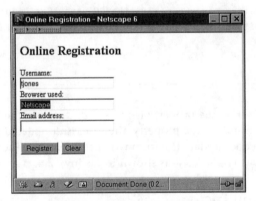

FIGURE 12.3   Highlighting text automatically.

Capturing Data Using the Textarea Object

The Textarea object provides a means for capturing information that doesn't lend itself to simple text fields, radio buttons, or selection lists. You can use the Textarea object to enter free-form data that spans several lines. The `Textarea` object is defined using the standard HTML syntax:

```
<textarea
    name="objectName"
    rows="numRows"
    cols="numCols"
    [wrap="off|virtual|physical"]
    [value="value"]
    [readonly]
    [disabled]
    [tabindex="number"]
    [accesskey="char"]
    [id="idName"]
    [class="className"]
    [lang="language"]
    [dir="directory"]
    [title="title"]
    [style="styleName"]
    [onclick="script code"]
    [ondblclick="script code"]
    [onmousedown="script code"]
    [onmouseup="script code"]
    [onmouseover="script code"]
    [onmousemove="script code"]
    [onmouseout="script code"]
    [onkeypress="script code"]
    [onkeydown="script code"]
    [onkeyup="script code"]    [onblur="script code"]
    [onchange="script code"]
    [onfocus="script code"]
    [onselect="script code"]>
    displayText
</textarea>
```

For example, to define a `Textarea` for submitting online comments, you could define the object as follows:

```
<textarea name="Comments" rows=12 cols=78></textarea>
```

Figure 12.4 shows the result in a form.

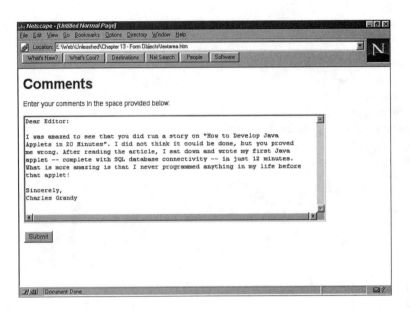

FIGURE 12.4   The Textarea object.

For more information on Textarea events, such as onBlur, onChange, onFocus, and onSelect, see Chapter 18.

Wrapping Text in a Textarea Object

The wrap attribute of the Textarea object allows text wrapping to be turned off and on in individual Textarea objects. Unfortunately, if the wrap attribute is not specified, the state of text wrapping is determined by the particular browser. When text wrapping is turned off, the user must manually enter a new line using the Enter key. However, working with such an element can be frustrating for the user, so you can set text wrapping options with the wrap= parameter of the <textarea> HTML tag. Besides off, the default setting, you have two additional options:

- virtual: If the wrap= parameter is set to virtual, the lines wrap onscreen at the end of the Textarea object, but a new line is defined only when you actually enter a carriage return.

- physical: If the wrap= parameter is set to physical, the lines wrap onscreen, but a carriage return is automatically placed at the end of each onscreen line when it is sent to the server.

The Button Objects: Submit, Reset, Button, and Image

Because graphical operating environments have become dominant over the past decade, the pushbutton is perhaps the most ubiquitous of all user interface components. HTML has four types of buttons you can use in your forms: Button, Submit, Reset, and Image. As you can see, two are specialized forms of the more generic Button object, and one is good for changing the look of a button. Using conventional HTML syntax, a button is defined as follows:

```
<input
    type="button|submit|reset|image"
    [name="objectName"]
    [value="labelText"]
    [disabled]
    [tabindex="number"]
    [accesskey="char"]
    [src="image"]
    [alt="altDescription"]
    [usemap="imageMap"]
    [ismap]
    [id="idName"]
    [class="className"]
    [lang="language"]
    [dir="directory"]
    [title="title"]
    [style="styleName"]
    [onclick="script code"]
    [ondblclick="script code"]
    [onmousedown="script code"]
    [onmouseup="script code"]
    [onmouseover="script code"]
    [onmousemove="script code"]
    [onmouseout="script code"]
    [onkeypress="script code"]
    [onkeydown="script code"]
    [onkeyup="script code"]
    [onblur="script code"]
    [onfocus="script code"]>
```

The button types have different purposes:

- The Submit button submits the form in which it is contained to the server, based on the parameters of the form. No JavaScript code is needed to perform this action, because its behavior is built into the object itself.

- The Reset button clears the values in the fields of the current form, restoring any default values that might have been set. As with the Submit button, no JavaScript code is used for this.

- The Button object is a generic object with no predefined behavior built into it. In order for this object to do anything, you need to add an onClick event handler to the button.

- The Image object is a special Button object that allows a graphic to be used in place of the normal button UI. This object has four attributes—src, alt, usemap, and ismap—that are useful only when dealing with the Image object. These attributes do not apply to the other button types. You will need to define event handlers in order to do things with this special button.

If you're new to HTML, you might be wondering about the reasons for the Submit and Reset buttons, because you could use a Button object to perform these same tasks. These originated before the days of JavaScript, when you couldn't use a generic button because you had no way to make it do anything. Additionally, although not all browsers support JavaScript (and thus the Button object), all modern browsers do support the Reset and Submit buttons. For compatibility reasons, it's usually best to use the Submit and Reset buttons unless JavaScript support is a requirement for accessing your page. In that case, it wouldn't matter.

As for the image button, it is perfect if you are trying to create a flashy form submit button but do not want to be limited by the standard battleship-gray button. Just create an image to represent the button to make your site look more professional.

> **NOTE**
>
> For more information on the onClick event for the Button type objects, see Chapter 18.

Listing 12.6 shows an example of how you can use all four buttons. As you would expect, the Submit and Reset buttons are used to submit or clear the form, although their value= parameters were changed to reflect a more user-friendly wording. The Button object is used to display a Help window that tells users how to fill out the registration form, and the Image object is used to display a Free Gift window that tells the user about a free gift he can receive by just registering.

Additionally, in the Help window that is generated by the showHelp() method, a Button object is defined using the document's write() method. The same is done for the Free Gift window. Figure 12.5 shows the form that is generated by the HTML.

LISTING 12.6 Creating a Help Window

```
<html>
<head>
<title>Online Registration</title>

<script type="text/javascript"language="JavaScript">
    function showHelp() {
        var helpWin = window.open("", "Help", "height=300,width=400");
        helpWin.document.write("<body><h2>Help on Registration<\/h2>");
        helpWin.document.write("1. Please enter your product
information into the fields.<br /><br />");
        helpWin.document.write("2. Click the Register button
to submit your form.<br /><br />");
        helpWin.document.write("3. Click the Clear button to
clear the form and start again.<br /><br />");
        helpWin.document.write("<center><form>");
        helpWin.document.write("<button type=\"button\"
onClick=\"window.close()\">  OK  <\/button>");
        helpWin.document.write("<\/form><\/center><\/body>");
        helpWin.document.close();


    }


    function freeGift() {
        var freeGiftWin = window.open("", "Gift", "height=150,width=400");
        freeGiftWin.document.write("<body><h2>Registration Gift<\/h2>");
        freeGiftWin.document.write("If you register today you will receive
a free backpack!");
        freeGiftWin.document.write("<center><form>");
        freeGiftWin.document.write("<button type=\"button\"
onClick=\"window.close()\">  OK  <\/button>");
        freeGiftWin.document.write("<\/form><\/center<\/body>");
        freeGiftWin.document.close();
    }

</script>
</head>
<body>
<h1>Online Registration</h1>
<form method="POST" action="processForm.jsp">
<p>Please provide the following product information:</p>
<blockquote>
```

LISTING 12.6   Continued

```
<pre><em>    Product name </em><input type="text" size="25" maxlength="256"
name="ProductName">
<em>           Model </em><input type="text" size="25" maxlength="256"
name="Product_Model">
<em>  Version number </em><input type="text" size="25" maxlength="256"
name="Product_VersionNumber">
<em>Operating system </em><input type="text" size="25" maxlength="256"
name="Product_OperatingSystem">
<em>   Serial number </em><input type="text" size="25" maxlength="256"
name="Product_SerialNumber">
</pre>
</blockquote>
<p><input type="submit" value="Register">
<input type="reset" value="Clear">
<button type="button" onClick="showHelp()">Help</button>
<img src="freeGift.gif" onClick="freeGift()"></p>
</form>
</body>
</html>
```

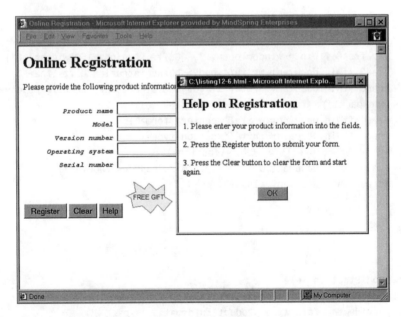

FIGURE 12.5   Display the Help window when the Help button is clicked.

The Checkbox Object

The Checkbox object is the Form object that is best equipped to denote logical (true or false) data. It acts as a toggle switch that can be turned on or off either by the user or by your JavaScript code. To define a Checkbox, use the following HTML syntax:

```
<input
    type="checkbox"
    [name="objectName"]
    [value="value"]
    [checked]
    [disabled]
    [tabindex="number"]
    [accesskey="char"]
    [id="idName"]
    [class="className"]
    [lang="language"]
    [dir="directory"]
    [title="title"]
    [style="styleName"]
    [onclick="script code"]
    [ondblclick="script code"]
    [onmousedown="script code"]
    [onmouseup="script code"]
    [onmouseover="script code"]
    [onmousemove="script code"]
    [onmouseout="script code"]
    [onkeypress="script code"]
    [onkeydown="script code"]
    [onkeyup="script code"]
    [onblur="script code"]
    [onchange="script code"]
    [onfocus="script code"]
    [onselect="script code"]>
    [displayText]
```

For example, the following Checkbox lets users specify their foreign-language proficiencies:

```
<input type=checkbox name="language">I speak multiple languages.
```

Following user interface conventions, a Checkbox shouldn't usually cause a "processing action" to be performed (as do Button objects). As a result, you probably won't use its onClick event handler extensively. However, the exceptions to this rule include changing the state of other objects on the form.

NOTE

For more information on the `onClick` event for the `Checkbox` object, see Chapter 18.

Determining Whether a Checkbox Object Is Checked

Perhaps the most important property of the `Checkbox` object is its `checked` property. You can evaluate this property to determine whether the user has checked a check box. You shouldn't use the `value` property to test a `Checkbox` object, as clarified in the following.

CAUTION

The `value` property can be misleading at first. Unlike similar properties in some environments, the `value` property is static and doesn't change in response to the `Checkbox`'s change of state. Therefore, don't check the `value` property to determine whether a check box is checked.

To illustrate, I'll build on an example used in the discussion of `Text` objects earlier in this chapter. As you'll recall, one of the examples automatically highlighted the contents of a `Text` object by calling the `Text` object's `select()` method. Suppose you want to give users the option of having the text selected or not. You can use a check box to achieve this result. Listing 12.7 shows this code, and Figure 12.6 shows the resulting form.

LISTING 12.7   Selective Highlighting of Text in Text Field

```html
<html>
<head>
<title>Online Registration</title>
<script type="text/javascript" language="JavaScript">

    function selectText(currentObject) {
        if (document.form1.selectBox.checked) {
            currentObject.select();
        }
    }

</script>
</head>

<body>
<form name="form1" method="POST">
<h2>Online Registration</h2>
<p>Username:<br>
<input type=text size=25 maxlength=256 name="Username"
```

LISTING 12.7   Continued

```
onFocus="selectText(this)"><br>
Browser used:<br>
<input type=text size=25 maxlength=256 name="Browser"
onFocus="selectText(this)"><br>
Email address:<strong> <br>
</strong><input type=text size=25 maxlength=256 name="EmailAddress"
onFocus="selectText(this)"></p>
<h2><input type=submit value="Register"> <input type=reset value="Clear"></h2>
<p><input type=checkbox name="selectBox">Activate field selection.
</form>
</body>
</html>
```

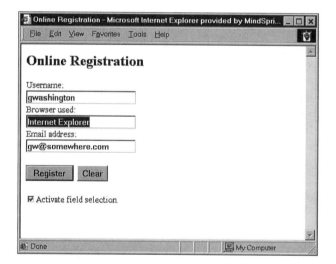

FIGURE 12.6   Using a check box.

The Radio Object

You use the Radio object to let a user select a single option from a group of options. If one option within a set is selected, no others can be selected at the same time. The act of clicking a radio button deselects any other radio button that was selected.

The Radio object is different from the other Form objects you have worked with. Whereas other Form objects have a one-to-one correspondence with an HTML tag, a Radio object has a one-to-many relationship with a set of <input type="radio"> elements within the HTML source code. Each element of a Radio object is defined like this:

```
<input
    type="radio"
    [name="groupName"]
    [value="value"]
    [checked]
    [disabled]
    [tabindex="number"]
    [accesskey="char"]
    [id="idName"]
    [class="className"]
    [lang="language"]
    [title="title"]
    [style="styleName"]
    [onclick="script code"]
    [ondblclick="script code"]
    [onmousedown="script code"]
    [onmouseup="script code"]
    [onmouseover="script code"]
    [onmousemove="script code"]
    [onmouseout="script code"]
    [onkeypress="script code"]
    [onkeydown="script code"]
    [onkeyup="script code"]
    [onblur="script code"]
    [onfocus="script code"]>
    [displayText]
```

You don't group each of these elements as you do with the items in a Select object (discussed later in this chapter). The way they are grouped is based on the name= parameter of the radio buttons. Each element in a Radio object must use the same value in that parameter. For example, the following set of radio buttons is treated as a single Radio object called weekdays:

```
<input type="radio" name="weekdays" value="Monday">Monday
<input type="radio" name="weekdays" value="Tuesday">Tuesday
<input type="radio" name="weekdays" value="Wednesday">Wednesday
<input type="radio" name="weekdays" value="Thursday">Thursday
<input type="radio" name="weekdays" value="Friday">Friday
<input type="radio" name="weekdays" value="Saturday">Saturday
<input type="radio" name="weekdays" value="Sunday">Sunday
```

NOTE

For more information on the onClick event for the Radio object, see Chapter 18.

Determining the Value of the Selected Radio Button

One of the most common programming needs you will have when using a Radio object is retrieving the value of the currently selected radio button. To do so, you must determine which of the radio buttons is selected and then return its value. Rather than custom coding each time you need this routine, you could more easily use a generic function I call getRadioValue(), which returns the value of the Radio object used as the method's parameter.

Look at the code shown in Listing 12.8. The Songs Radio object lists a set of three songs. The Show Selected Button object displays the currently selected object by calling the getRadioValue() method using the Songs object as the function's parameter. The getRadioValue() method performs a for loop to analyze which of the radio buttons is checked (selected). It uses the length property of the Radio object to determine the number of iterations. When the for loop encounters the checked value, it assigns the variable the value of the radio button, breaks the loop, and then returns the value to the Button event handler.

LISTING 12.8 Display Selected Radio Button

```html
<html>
<head>
<title>Using Radio Buttons</title>
<script type="text/javascript" language="JavaScript">
    function getRadioValue(radioObject) {
        var value = null;
        for (var i=0; i<radioObject.length; i++) {
            if (radioObject[i].checked) {
                value = radioObject[i].value;
                break;
            }
        }
        return value;
    }
</script>
</head>
<body>
<form name="form1">
<p><input type=radio name="songs" value="Liquid">Liquid</p>
<p><input type=radio name="songs" value="Flood">Flood</p>
<p><input type=radio name="songs" value="World's Apart">World's Apart</p>
<input type=button value="Show Selected"
onClick="alert(getRadioValue(this.form.songs))">
</form>
</body>
</html>
```

Figure 12.7 shows the result of clicking the Show Selected button.

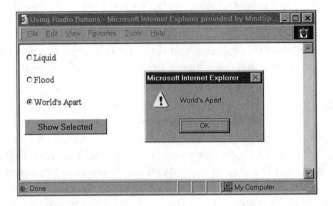

FIGURE 12.7   Determining the value of the Radio object.

The Select Object

The Select object is one of the most useful and flexible of all the Form objects. You can use it in instances where you might otherwise use a Radio object. The Select object can take up less real estate than a Radio object, which needs space for each of its radio buttons. The Select object, unlike Radio objects, also allows multiple selections. Here is the basic HTML syntax for a Select object:

```
<select
    [name="objectName"]
    [size="numberVisible"]
    [multiple]
    [disabled]
    [tabindex="number"]
    [id="idName"]
    [class="className"]
    [lang="language"]
    [dir="directory"]
    [title="title"]
    [style="styleName"]
    [onclick="script code"]
```

12

```
   [ondblclick="script code"]
   [onmousedown="script code"]
   [onmouseup="script code"]
   [onmouseover="script code"]
   [onmousemove="script code"]
   [onmouseout="script code"]
   [onkeypress="script code"]
   [onkeydown="script code"]
   [onkeyup="script code"]
   [onblur="script code"]
   [onchange="script code"]
   [onfocus="script code"]>
   <option
       [selected]
       [disabled]
       [label="text"]
       [value="optionValue"]
       [id="idName"]
       [class="className"]
       [lang="language"]
       [dir="directory"]
       [title="title"]
       [style="styleName"]
       [onclick="script code"]
       [ondblclick="script code"]
       [onmousedown="script code"]
       [onmouseup="script code"]
       [onmouseover="script code"]
       [onmousemove="script code"]
       [onmouseout="script code"]
       [onkeypress="script code"]
       [onkeydown="script code"]
       [onkeyup="script code"]>
   </option>
   [<option...</option>]
</select>
```

The Select object is flexible and can take three different forms: a selection list, a scrolling list, and a multiselection scrolling list.

> **NOTE**
>
> For more information on Select object events, see Chapter 18.

Creating a Selection List

A selection list is a drop-down list of options in which the user can select a single item from the list. A selection list usually displays a single value at a time, as shown in Figure 12.8, but it expands to show a list when the user clicks its arrow, as shown in Figure 12.9. You can't enter a value in the box, as you can with combo boxes in the Windows world; you can only select from an existing array of values.

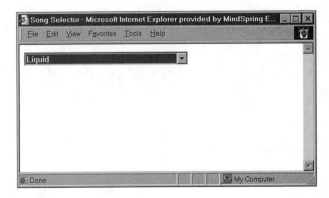

FIGURE 12.8   A selection list in its normal state.

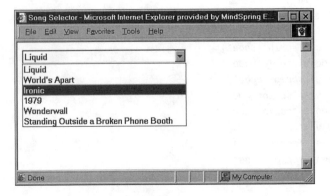

FIGURE 12.9   A selection list in an expanded state.

The selection list shown in Figures 12.8 and 12.9 can be defined like this:

```
<select name="songs" SIZE=1>
  <option value="Liquid">Liquid</option>
  <option value="World's Apart">World's Apart</option>
  <option value="Ironic">Ironic</option>
  <option value="1979">1979</option>
  <option value="Wonderwall">Wonderwall</option>
```

```
<option value="Standing Outside a Broken Phone Booth">
Standing Outside a Broken Phone Booth</option>
```

The key to defining a selection list is to give the size= parameter a value of 1 (or leave it out entirely). This ensures that the list shows only a single line at a time.

Creating a Scrolling List

The second form a Select object can take is a scrolling list—commonly known in many operating environments as a **list box**. Rather than retract all the items in a drop-down list, a scrolling list displays a designated number of items at one time in a list format. The scrolling list includes scrollbars so that the user can scroll up or down to see more than what fits in the space provided.

To define a scrolling list, the only change you make to the HTML <select> definition is in the size= parameter. Making this value greater than 1 transforms the Select object into a scrolling list. For example, when you change the size= parameter of the previously defined Songs object from 1 to 5, the list takes on a new look, as shown in Figure 12.10. As with the selection list, a scrolling list lets you select a single value from the list.

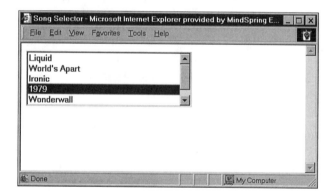

FIGURE 12.10   A scrolling list.

Creating a Multiselection List

The final form a Select object can take is a multiselection list. It looks the same as a normal scrolling list but has different behavior. You can select one or more items from this type of Select object. The task of selecting multiple items depends on the operating environment. In most cases, you can either drag the mouse across multiple contiguous items or hold the Shift or Ctrl key while you click an item.

To define a multiselection list, you simply add the MULTIPLE parameter to the Select object definition:

```
<select name="songs" size=5 multiple>
  <option value="Liquid">Liquid</option>
  <option value="World's Apart">World's Apart</option>
  <option value="Ironic">Ironic</option>
  <option value="1979">1979</option>
  <option value="Wonderwall">Wonderwall</option>
  <option value="Standing Outside a Broken Phone Booth">
Standing Outside a Broken Phone Booth</option>
```

Determining the Value or Text of the Selected Option

In a selection or scrolling list, you can determine the value of the selected option by using a combination of the options and selectedIndex properties of the Select object. For example, if I wanted to determine the song that was selected in our Songs object example, I could use the following:

```
favorite = document.form1.songs.options[document.form1.songs.selectedIndex].
   value;
```

The options property is an array containing each option defined within a Select object. Using this property, you can access the properties of each option. You can use the selectedIndex property to return the index of the selected option. When options and selectedIndex are used in combination, you can return the value of the currently selected option.

With JavaScript's dot notation requirements, trying to retrieve the currently selected value can involve long code lines. You can avoid this by making a generic getSelectValue() method to use instead. Listing 12.9 shows how to define this method. As you can see, the Select object is passed as the getSelectValue() method's parameter when the user clicks the Show Current button. The selectObject variable is treated as an object type variable and retrieves the value of the currently selected option. This value is passed back to the Button object's event handler and displayed in an alert message box.

LISTING 12.9   Display Selected Radio Button

```
<html>
<head>
<script type="text/javascript" language="JavaScript">

    function getSelectValue(selectObject) {
        return selectObject.options[selectObject.selectedIndex].value;
    }
```

LISTING 12.9   Continued

```
</script>
</head>
<body>
<form name="form1">
Songs: <select name="songs" size=1>
<option value="Liquid">Liquid</option>
<option value="World's Apart">World's Apart</option>
<option value="Ironic">Ironic</option>
<option value="1979">1979</option>
<option value="Wonderwall">Wonderwall</option>
<option value="Standing Outside a Broken Phone Booth">
Standing Outside a Broken Phone Booth</option>
</select><p>
<input type=button value="Show Current"
onClick="alert(getSelectValue(this.form.songs))">
</form>
</body>
</html>
```

One important difference between the `Select` and `Radio` objects is that the `Select` object has a `text` property in addition to the `value` property. If the value you want to define is the same as what is being displayed to the user—as in Listing 12.9—you can return the `text` value of the currently selected object rather than the `value` property. If the `Select` object were defined like this

```
<select name="songs" size=1>
  <option>Liquid</option>
  <option>World's Apart</option>
  <option>Ironic</option>
  <option>1979</option>
  <option>Wonderwall</option>
  <option>Standing Outside a Broken Phone Booth</option>
```

you could use the `text` property rather than the `value` property to return the song name:

```
function getSelectValue(selectObject) {
    return selectObject.options[selectObject.selectedIndex].text;
}
```

Determining the Values of Multiselection Lists

In lists where a single option is selected at any given time, the `selectedIndex` property efficiently returns information you need from the currently selected option. If you have a multiselection scrolling list, however, selectedIndex returns only the first option that is selected, not all of them. When you use multiselection lists, you must use the selected property of the options array to determine the status of each option in the list. Listing 12.10 shows an example of this in its showSelection() method. In this function, a for loop iterates through each option in the Select object and tests to see if the selected property is true. If it is, the value of the element's text property is added to the list variable. The result is then presented in a second window, as shown in Figure 12.11.

LISTING 12.10   Select Multiple Items

```
<html>
<head>
<title>Favorite Songs</title>
<script type="text/javascript" language="JavaScript">

    function showSelection(objectName) {
        var list = "";
        for (var i=0; i<objectName.length; i++) {
            if (objectName.options[i].selected) {
                list += objectName.options[i].text + "<p>";
            }
        }
        var selWindow = window.open("", "Selections", "height=200,width=400");
        selWindow.document.write("<h2>You picked the following songs:
    </h2><p><p>");
        selWindow.document.write(list);
        selWindow.document.close();
    }

</script>
</head>
<body>
<form name="form1">
Pick Your Favorite Songs From the List:<p>
<select name="songs" size=5 multiple>
<option>Fortress Around Your Heart</option>
<option>Breakfast at Tiffany's</option>
<option>Flood</option>
<option>The Chess Game</option>
<option>Liquid</option>
<option>World's Apart</option>
<option>Ironic</option>
<option>1979</option>
<option>Wonderwall</option>
```

LISTING 12.10   Continued

```
<option>Standing Outside a Broken Phone Booth</option>
</select><p>
<input type=button value="Show Selection"
onClick="showSelection(this.form.songs)">
</form>
</body>
</html>
```

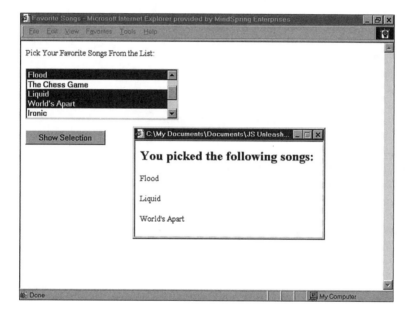

FIGURE 12.11   Displaying multiple selections.

Selecting an Option Using JavaScript

You can select an option programmatically by setting the selected property of a Select object's options array. Suppose you have a Favorite Band field and a list of songs. If the value of the Favorite Band field is Oasis, you want to locate a song written by that group in the Songs field. Listing 12.11 shows this example.

LISTING 12.11   Programmatically Setting the Options Array

```
<html>
<head>
<script type="text/javascript" language="JavaScript">
```

LISTING 12.11   Continued

```
    function quickSelect() {
        var bnd = document.form1.band.value;
        bnd = bnd.toUpperCase();
        if (bnd == "OASIS") {
            document.form1.songs[4].selected = true;
        }
    }

</script>
</head>
<body>
<form name="form1">
Favorite Band: <input type=text name="band" size=20 onBlur="quickSelect()"><p>
Songs: <select name="songs" size=1>
<option value="Liquid">Liquid</option>
<option value="World's Apart">World's Apart</option>
<option value="Ironic">Ironic</option>
<option value="1979">1979</option>
<option value="Wonderwall">Wonderwall</option>
<option value="Standing Outside a Broken Phone Booth">
Standing Outside a Broken Phone Booth</option>
</select><p>
<input type=button value="Show Band's Song" onClick="quickSelect()">
</form>
</body>
</html>
```

Another way to set the selection option is to set the selectedIndex property. This property normally contains the index number of the option in the selection array that the user selected.

The Password Object

As you might guess from its name, the Password object was designed for the purpose of capturing a password value from a user. But the password object is not limited to just passwords. It could be used to get account numbers or other sensitive data that should not be seen. A Password object is similar to a Text object but displays any character the user types in the field as an asterisk (*). It can be defined in HTML syntax like this:

```
<input
   type="password"
   [name="objectName"]
```

```
[value="defaultPassword"]
[size="size"]
[maxlength="size"]
[readonly]
[disabled]
[tabindex="number"]
[accesskey="char"]
[id="idName"]
[class="className"]
[lang="language"]
[title="title"]
[style="styleName"]
[onclick="script code"]
[ondblclick="script code"]
[onmousedown="script code"]
[onmouseup="script code"]
[onmouseover="script code"]
[onmousemove="script code"]
[onmouseout="script code"]
[onkeypress="script code"]
[onkeydown="script code"]
[onkeyup="script code"]
[onblur="script code"]
[onchange="script code"]
[onfocus="script code"]
[onselect="script code"]>
```

The following line shows an example:

```
<input type="password" name="passwordField" size=15>
```

The Hidden Object

As you might infer from its name, the Hidden object is invisible to the user. The Hidden object is a hidden text field that you can use to store values that you don't want to present to the user with a normal text field. You can then pass this information to the server for processing. You can define a Hidden object in HTML using the following syntax:

```
<input
   type="hidden"
   name="objectName"
   [value="value"]>
```

The following line shows an example:

```
<input type="hidden" name="hiddenField1">
```

Hidden fields play an important role in holding specific bits of information on the user side that the server can use later. The following example demonstrates the use of the Hidden object. Figure 12.12 shows a set of radio buttons the user can click. However, you want to add code to the Undo Last button so that the user can undo the last selection he made. You can't use a Reset button for this because that will either clear the radio buttons or return the default value. Instead, you need to add JavaScript code to perform this task. Listing 12.12 uses a set of hidden fields to carry this out. When the form is finally submitted, the values stored in the Hidden objects, as well as the radio button selection, are passed to the server.

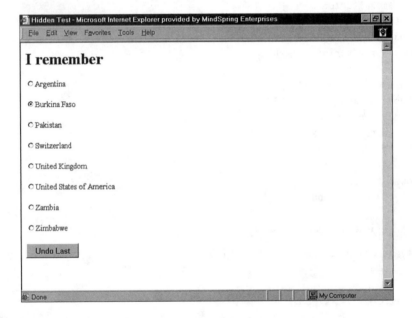

FIGURE 12.12   Using Hidden objects.

LISTING 12.12   Using Hidden Objects

```
<html>
<head>
<title>Hidden Test</title>
<script type="text/javascript" language="JavaScript">

    function postData(value) {
```

LISTING 12.12   Continued

```
            document.form1.holder2.value = document.form1.holder.value;
            document.form1.holder.value = value;
        }

    function resetValue() {
            var len = document.form1.ctyList.length;
            for (var i=0; i<len; i++) {
                if (document.form1.ctyList[i].value ==
                    document.form1.holder2.value) {
                    document.form1.ctyList[i].checked = true;
                    break;
                }
            }
        }

</script>
</head>

<body>
<h1>I remember</h1>
<form name="form1" method="POST" action="doSomething.jsp">
<p><input type=radio name="ctyList" value="Argentina"
onClick="postData(this.value)">Argentina</p>
<p><input type=radio name="ctyList" value="Burkina Faso"
onClick="postData(this.value)">Burkina Faso</p>
<p><input type=radio name="ctyList" value="Pakistan"
onClick="postData(this.value)">Pakistan</p>
<p><input type=radio name="ctyList" value="Switzerland"
onClick="postData(this.value)">Switzerland</p>
<p><input type=radio name="ctyList" value="United Kingdom"
onClick="postData(this.value)">United Kingdom</p>
<p><input type=radio name="ctyList" value="United States of America"
onClick="postData(this.value)">United States of America</p>
<p><input type=radio name="ctyList" value="Zambia"
onClick="postData(this.value)">Zambia</p>
<p><input type=radio name="ctyList" value="Zimbabwe"
onClick="postData(this.value)">Zimbabwe</p>
<p><input type="submit"><input type=button name="UndoLast" value="Undo Last"
onClick="resetValue()"></p>
<input type="hidden" name="holder" value="">
<input type="hidden" name="holder2" value="">
```

12

LISTING 12.12   Continued

```
</form>
</body>
</html>
```

In this first example, each time the user clicks a radio button, the postData() method places the current radio button value in the Hidden object called holder and the current holder value into the holder2 object. This value is then retrieved when the user clicks the Undo Last button and the appropriate radio button is selected. When the Submit button is selected, the values stored in the hidden objects are submitted to the server along with the radio button selection.

The FileUpload Object

The FileUpload object, which was added in JavaScript 1.1, is the equivalent to the HTML file upload element. You can't do much with this object in JavaScript other than reference its properties. You can define a FileUpload object in HTML using the following syntax:

```
<input
    type="file"
    [name="objectName"]
    [value="value"]
    [disabled]
    [accept="contentTypes"]
    [id="idName"]
    [class="className"]
    [lang="language"]
    [title="title"]
    [style="styleName"]
    [onclick="script code"]
    [ondblclick="script code"]
    [onmousedown="script code"]
    [onmouseup="script code"]
    [onmouseover="script code"]
    [onmousemove="script code"]
    [onmouseout="script code"]
    [onkeypress="script code"]
    [onkeydown="script code"]
    [onkeyup="script code"]
    [onblur="script code"]
    [onchange="script code"]
    [onfocus="script code"]
    [onselect="script code"]>
```

The following line shows an example:

```
<form method="POST" enctype="multipart/form-data" action="fileUploadHandler">
  <input type="file" name="theFile">
</form>
```

Summary

Forms play an important role in JavaScript. Not only can you qualify and sharpen data before it's sent to the server for processing, but you can also use HTML forms to create client-side applications using JavaScript. In this chapter, you learned about the `Form` object and the various objects that can exist inside its borders. You also learned how to submit forms to the server and how to work with and check the values of input controls before data is sent on.

CHAPTER **13**

Frames

This chapter discusses the Frame object and its myriad of applications when building Web sites. We will begin by looking at the creation of single and multiframe windows and discuss the methods, properties, and events that surround them. Then we will move on to the History object, a well-known repository for recording user interaction and paths. This is obviously a fairly long chapter, because it has to negotiate many essential topics that relate to frames and windows.

The Frame Object

A **frame** is a subwindow of a full window; its specifications are determined by the designer. Frames quickly became popular because they allow the user to display multiple documents simultaneously in the same window.

Each frame can contain a separate document (HTML, text, image, and so on), each one individually addressable and scrollable. As with windows, you can name and reference frames. You can load documents in a frame without affecting the documents in the other frames.

Frames provide a means to view and interact with a site that isn't accessible otherwise. A frame allows you to have a permanently displayed index that provides quick and effective location of content in the site. You can simultaneously display the input and output of forms and view multiple documents simultaneously. You can select different image files from a menu for viewing. A new window can open to provide an expanded view of a document and close when it's no longer needed. You can give slide show presentations. The uses and implementations of a framed site are limited only by the Web site author's imagination.

For example, a window might hold a number of scrollable frames that point to URLs, and URLs can point at the frame as well. Frame objects are created using `<frame>` tags within `<frameset>` tags or the `<iframe>` tag within a document, and they are essentially `Window` objects, from which they inherit methods and properties. For more information about these methods, properties, and general behaviors, refer to Chapter 10, "Window Object."

CAUTION

Some visitors find frames and new windows distracting. Also, sometimes too much of the display area is lost due to frames, especially with small monitors. The author of a framed site should make sure that using frames provides a benefit to the visitor; he also should make an alternative frameless version of the site available using the `<noframes>` tag.

JavaScript greatly enhances a frame site and adds to the interaction of the site. You can open and close new windows programmatically. You can update and synchronize frames through the script without relying on a server-side program. Imagemaps and links can be dynamic, changing with different configurations and uses of the site. Documents in different frames and windows can interact and pass information to each other.

A real benefit of frames is the capability to provide a permanent navigation menu for the site. Instead of hopping from one page to another to navigate, a user can select a page from the menu and see it appear in another frame (a main display frame). A table of contents might be displayed in one frame and documents displayed in another. You might place a button bar frame along one edge of the window, with which the user can click the buttons to load different portions of the site in the display frame.

TIP

Using frames does have some drawbacks. The major drawback is that the area to display each document is reduced. Users with small monitors, laptop computers, or palmtop computers might have difficulty viewing some of the documents in frames. It's considered a good idea to provide frame and no-frame versions (using the `<noframes>` tag) of a site and give frame-capable users the option of viewing either version (which is fairly easy to accomplish with JavaScript).

The `Frame` object is essentially the same element as a `Window` object, and you can deal with it in a similar manner. If you're working with a single window, the `Window` object is the top-level object. If you're working within a frameset, the top-level window is considered the parent window, whereas its child windows are considered `Frame` objects.

Creating Frames

Frames are created with `<frameset>` tags and specified with `<frame>` tags (inline frames are defined later in the chapter).

```
<html>
<head>
```

```
        <title>Creating frames</title>
</head>
<frameset cols="60%,*,5%">
        <frame src="doc1.html" name="frame1">
        <frame src="doc2.html" name="frame2">
        <frame src="doc3.html" name="frame3">
</frameset>
</html>
```

By adding a few lines of code, you can easily set up a window with four frames, like those following:

```
<html>
<head>
        <title>Window frames: Window One</title>
</head>
<frameset rows="45%,45%" cols="40%,60%"
   onLoad="alert('Windows have frames')">
        <frame src="doc1.html" name="frame1">
        <frame src="doc2.html" name="frame2">
         <frame src="doc3.html" name="frame3">
        <frame src="doc4.html" name="frame4">
</frameset>
</html>
```

TIP

Indenting the <frame> tags isn't necessary but is frequently done to provide the Web author a better view of the tags and the frame hierarchy within the code. Some HTML editors indent automatically, and they may also color certain code segments for improved readability.

<frameset> Tags

The <frameset> tag has attributes that describe how to divide the window into frames. These attributes are cols and rows (for columns and rows). The author can specify the number of rows and columns in the window and the size of each. Each row or column can be specified as an absolute size in pixels, a relative size in percentage of the window, or as the remainder of the window after others are set. The following line creates two frames as columns, one with 60% of the window and the other with the remainder () of the window's width (specified by *, in this case 40%):

```
<frameset cols="60%,*">
```

The next code line creates the two frames as before, but without the percent sign. The width of the first frame is an absolute value of 60 pixels:

```
<frameset cols="60,*">
```

The second frame still has the remainder of the window's width.

The following line creates four frames as columns; three of the frames take 30% of the screen's width each, and the fourth takes the remainder:

```
<frameset cols="30%,30%,30%,*">
```

You could replace the * with 10% in this case. You aren't required to use *. However, if you specify all the frames with percentages, they must add up to 100% of the window's width.

The next code line creates two frames as rows, the first with 70% of the window's height and the second with 30%:

```
<frameset rows="70%,30%">
```

The frame sizes can be a mix of absolute, relative, and remainder, but if the total size of all the frames doesn't equal the window size, the results are unpredictable. Specifying frame sizes with just * might seem obvious; however, you can use * for each frame. The following line creates three equal frames, each with one third of the window's height:

```
<frameset rows="*,*,*">
```

<frame> Tags

The <frame> tag attributes specify the document to be loaded in the frames, the name of the frame, frame margins, scrollbars, and the resizing option. The following list describes each of the attributes of the <frame> tag.

- The src attribute is the URL (relative or absolute) of the document to be loaded in the frame. The document can be from the same server as the frameset file or from another server. If you don't use the src attribute, the frame contains blank space. This blank space might be what you want, especially if you use JavaScript to write content to the frame. This attribute is required because without it no frame is actually specified.

- The name attribute, if specified, provides a means to reference the frame from other frames and with JavaScript. JavaScript can also reference the frame through the frames array, which is covered in the section "Referencing Frames," later in this chapter. The value for the name attribute must begin with an alphanumeric character.

- You set the margins with two attributes, marginwidth and marginheight:

  marginwidth controls the side margins of the frame. Its value, in pixels, can be as low as 1. The maximum value is limited only by the size of the frame. (You can't set the margin in such a way as to leave no room to display the document.)

The `marginheight` attribute is the same as `marginwidth`, except that it controls the top and bottom margins.

Both `marginwidth` and `marginheight`, if not specified, default to a value determined by the browser.

- The `scrolling` attribute controls whether the frame has scrollbars. The values for `scrolling` are `yes`, `no`, and `auto`. `yes` causes scrollbars always to be present in the frame. `no` prevents scrollbars from being displayed. `auto` displays scrollbars only if the document is larger than the frame; otherwise, scrollbars are suppressed. The default value for `scrolling` is `auto`.

- `noresize` prevents the user from resizing the frame. There is no value specified for this attribute. By default, all frames are resizable unless you specify this attribute or set the frameborder equal to `0` because this would mean there is no handle to resize the frame. Frames that border a frame with the `noresize` attribute can't be resized along the common border.

TIP

If possible, it's best to let the user resize the frame by not specifying this attribute.

Use the following code segment to name a frame `frame1`, load the document `doc1.html`, set the side margins to 5 pixels, set the upper and lower margins to 10 pixels, always display scrollbars, and prevent the user from resizing the frame:

```
<frame src="doc1.html" name="frame1" marginwidth="5"
marginheight="10" scrolling="yes" noresize>
```

Netscape and Microsoft are introducing more advanced features for their latest browsers. Visit the Web sites of these companies to find detailed information (`http://developer.netscape.com/` and `http://msdn.microsoft.com/`, respectively).

Tag Placement

You usually place the `<frameset>` and `<frame>` tags in place of the typical `<body>` tags of the document. Place the `<frameset>` tags after the `<head>` section of the document and omit the `<body>` tags, as shown in Listing 13.1.

LISTING 13.1 A Simple Frame Example

```
<html>
<head>
    <title>Simple Frame Example</title>
```

LISTING 13.1 Continued

```
</head>
<frameset cols="60%,*">
    <frame src="frame1.html" name="frame1">
    <frame src="frame2.html" name="frame2">
</frameset>
</html>
```

This code sets up the frames and loads the frames called frame1.html and frame2.html, which are defined in Listings 13.2 and 13.3, respectively. When Listing 13.1 is executed, the two frames are placed side by side according to the column spacing defined in the frameset definition.

LISTING 13.2 frame1.html

```
<html>
<head><title>Simple Frame Example - Frame 1</title></head>
<body style="text-align:center">

<h2>Frame 1</h2>
This is sample frame 1.

</body>
</html>
```

LISTING 13.3 frame2.html

```
<html>
<head><title>Simple Frame Example - Frame 2</title></head>
<body style="text-align:center">

<h2>Frame 2</h2>
This is sample frame 2.

</body>
</html>
```

Actually, you can make the file smaller, because the <html>, <head>, and <body> tags are optional; the file can contain only the <title>, <frameset>, and <frame> tags. (The <title> opening and closing tags are the only tags required by HTML specification to be in every HTML document.) We will still include the <html> tags in Listing 13.4 in order to have a well-formed document.

LISTING 13.4   Simple Frame Example Variation

```
<html>
<title>Simple Frame Example</title>
<frameset cols="60%,*">
    <frame src="frame1.html" name="frame1">
    <frame src="frame2.html" name="frame2">
</frameset>
</html>
```

The <noframes> Tag

Many authors also include a set of <noframes> tags to display a message for browsers that don't use frames:

```
<noframes>
code and text content to display to nonframe-capable browsers
</noframes>
```

The content can contain HTML tags as well as text. A frames-capable browser ignores the content between the <noframes> and </noframes> tags, whereas a frames-incapable browser ignores the <frameset>, <frame>, and <noframes> tags and displays the content between the <noframes> and </noframes> tags. You place the <noframes> tags within <frameset> tags as shown in Listing 13.5.

LISTING 13.5   Simple No-Frame Example

```
<html>
<title>Simple No Frames Example</title>
<frameset cols="60%,*">
    <frame src="frame1.html" name="frame1">
    <frame src="frame2.html" name="frame2">
    <noframes>
        No frames could be displayed!
    </noframes>
</frameset>
</html>
```

> **TIP**
>
> A number of authors actually duplicate the main document of the site in the <noframes> tags for a non-frame version. However, it isn't usually necessary to use this technique, because you can create a framed version of the site with JavaScript from the same pages that are displayed to frames-incapable users.

It's interesting to note that you can include the <body> tags in the <noframes> tags, using the attributes of background, bgcolor, text, and so on for the no-frames version of the document. The frames-incapable browser ignores the <frameset> tags and initiates the body section at the first appropriate content (that is, a <body> tag) in the <noframes> tag. The frames-capable browser initiates the body section at the first <frameset> tag and ignores the contents of the <noframes> tag. Of course, the frames-capable browser loads the documents specified by the <frame> tags, and the <body> tags of these documents are properly recognized by the browser.

Nested Frames

You can create nested frames in which a frame is divided into more frames. Of the two different ways to create nested frames, both appear the same. However, there's a big difference in the frame hierarchy and the way nested frames are referenced.

The code from Listing 13.6 along with Listings 13.2, 13.3, and 13.7 creates frames with multiple framesets in a single window. Figure 13.1 shows the frames, and Figure 13.2 shows the structure (hierarchy).

LISTING 13.6   Simple Nested Frame Example

```
<html>
<frameset cols="30%,*">
      <frame src="frame1.html" name="frame1">
      <frameset rows="*,30%">
            <frame src="frame2.html" name="frame2">
            <frame src="frame3.html" name="frame3">
      </frameset>
</frameset>
</html>
```

LISTING 13.7   frame3.html

```
<html>
<head><title>Simple Frame Example - Frame 3</title></head>
<body style="text-align=:center">

<h2>Frame 3</h2>
This is sample frame 3.

</body>
</html>
```

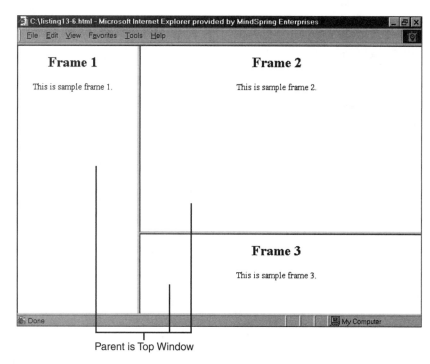

FIGURE 13.1   Creating frames with multiple framesets in a single window.

FIGURE 13.2   The frame hierarchy of multiple framesets in a single window.

Listings 13.8 and 13.9 along with the code from Listing 13.2 and Listing 13.3 create frames with multiple framesets in two windows. (A frame is considered a window.) Figure 13.3 shows these frames, and Figure 13.4 shows the hierarchy.

LISTING 13.8   Another Nested Frame Example

```
<html>
<frameset cols="30%,*">
    <frame src="frame1.html" name="frame1">
    <frame src="subFrame.html" name="subFrame">
</frameset>
</html>
```

The file `subFrame.html` contains the additional frameset information in Listing 13.9.

LISTING 13.9   subFrame.html

```
<html>
<frameset rows="*,30%">
    <frame src="frame2.html" name="frame2">
    <frame src="frame3.html" name="frame3">
 </frameset>
</html>
```

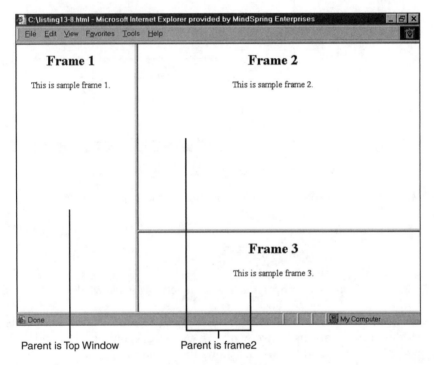

FIGURE 13.3   Creating frames with multiple framesets in two windows.

The two code snippets produce frames that appear exactly the same, as shown in Figures 13.1 and 13.3. However, the structures, as shown in Figures 13.2 and 13.4, are completely different. In the code for Figure 13.2, all three frames have the same parent, the top window. In the code for Figure 13.4, only `frame1` and `subFrame` have the top window as parent; the parent of `frame2` and `frame3` is `subFrame`. This can make a big difference in how the frames are referenced, as discussed in the following sections.

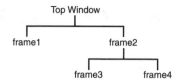

FIGURE 13.4 The frame hierarchy of multiple framesets in two windows.

<iframe> Tags

The <iframe> tag provides a way to put a frame directly inline within a document. Unlike the <frame> tag, an inline frame is defined inside the text of a document rather than inside a <frameset> tag. For example, Listing 13.10 creates a document that contains an inline frame. The inline frame is defined in Listing 13.11, which is called inlineFrame.html.

LISTING 13.10 An iframe Example

```
<html>
<head>
  <title>iframe example</title>
</head>
<body>
  This is a document with an inline
  <iframe src="inlineFrame.html">
    Cannot display inline frame.
  </iframe>
  frame directly in the middle of this text.
</body>
</html>
```

LISTING 13.11 inlineFrame.html

```
<html>
<body>
This is the contents of an inline frame.
</body>
</html>
```

The text that appears between the <iframe> and </iframe> tags is displayed if the user has selected for frames to be turned off. The result of executing Listing 13.10 is shown in Figure 13.5.

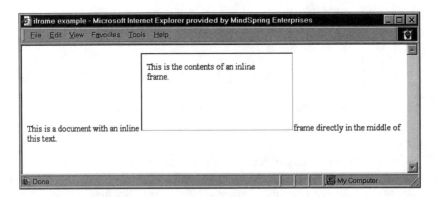

FIGURE 13.5   Creating an inline frame using the `<iframe>` tag.

The `<iframe>` tag has the following attributes that specify the document to be loaded in the inline frame, the name of the inline frame, frame margins, scrollbars, and the resizing option.

- The `src` attribute is the URL (relative or absolute) of the document to be loaded in the frame. The document can be from the same server as the frameset file or from another server. If you don't use the `src` attribute, the frame contains blank space. This blank space might be what you want, especially if you use JavaScript to write content to the frame. This attribute is required in order for the inline frame to work.

- The `name` attribute, if specified, provides a means to reference the frame from other frames and with JavaScript. JavaScript can also reference the frame through the `frames` array, which is covered in the section "Referencing Frames," later in this chapter. The value for the `name` attribute must begin with an alphanumeric character.

- You set the margins with two attributes, `marginwidth` and `marginheight`:

   `marginwidth` controls the side margins of the frame. Its value, in pixels, can be as low as 1. The maximum value is limited only by the size of the frame. (You can't set the margin in such a way as to leave no room to display the document.)

   The `marginheight` attribute is the same as `marginwidth`, except that it controls the top and bottom margins.

   Both `marginwidth` and `marginheight`, if not specified, default to a value determined by the browser.

- The `scrolling` attribute controls whether the frame has scrollbars. The values for `scrolling` are yes, no, and auto. yes causes scrollbars always to be present in the frame. no prevents scrollbars from being displayed. auto displays scrollbars only if the document is larger than the frame; otherwise, scrollbars are suppressed. The default value for `scrolling` is auto.

Adding JavaScript Code to Frames

The frameset files and most of the files of the documents that appear in frames are HTML files. As a result, you can use JavaScript in them, as you do in other HTML files. The only difference is that JavaScript can reference properties of other documents in frames and use certain features to reference those properties.

You can refer to the top window and its frames by their relationships to each other. A window can be referenced with the Window properties top, parent, window, and self. The top property refers to the main window (the browser window); parent refers to the window containing the frameset for a particular frame. For frames inside one frameset with no nesting, parent and top are the same. The properties self and window refer to the particular frame or window.

Consider the following code:

```
<frameset cols="30%,40%,30%">
  <frame src="frameA.html" name="frameA">
  <frame src="frameB.html" name="frameB">
  <frame src="frameC.html" name="frameC">
</frameset>
```

The file frameB.html contains the following additional frameset information:

```
 <frameset rows="50%,50%">
   <frame src="frameD.html" name="frameD">
   <frame src="frameE.html" name="frameE">
 </frameset>
```

The parent of frameA, frameB, and frameC is top because the frameset for each of these frames is in the top window. The parent for frameD and frameE is frameB because the frameset for these two frames is in the window frameB. To reference the top frame from the document in frameD, you use the top property; to reference frameB, you use the parent property; and finally, to reference its own frame, you use self or window.

You can refer to functions, variables, and other properties with the relational Window properties as demonstrated in the following example. This example is made up of a frameset that is defined in Listing 13.12 and a subframeset that is defined in Listing 13.13. Listings 13.14, 13.15, 13.16, and 13.17 define the contents of the frame.

LISTING 13.12   JavaScript and Nested Frameset Demo

```
<html>
<head>
<title>JavaScript and Nested Frameset Demo</title>
<script type="text/javascript" language="JavaScript">
var a = 2;
```

LISTING 13.12   Continued

```
function displayA(){
    alert("a="+a);
}
</script>
</head>

<frameset cols="30%,40%,30%">
    <frame src="frameA.html" name="frameA">
    <frame src="frameB.html" name="frameB">
    <frame src="frameC.html" name="frameC">
</frameset>
</html>
```

LISTING 13.13   frameB.html

```
<html>
<head>
<title>Frame B</title>
<script type="text/javascript" language="JavaScript">
var b = 2;
function displayB(){
    alert("b="+b);
}
</script>
</head>

<frameset rows="50%,50%">
    <frame src="frameD.html" name="frameD">
    <frame src="frameE.html" name="frameE">
</frameset>
</html>
```

LISTING 13.14   frameA.html

```
<html>
<head>
<title>Frame A</title>
</head>

<body>
  <h1>Frame A</h1>
```

LISTING 13.14   Continued

```
  <button type="button" onclick="top.displayA();">
    top.displayA()
  </button><br>
  <button type="button" onclick="top.frameB.displayB();">
    top.frameB.displayB()
  </button>
</body>
</html>
```

LISTING 13.15   frameC.html

```
<html>
<head>
<title>Frame C</title>
</head>

<body>
  <h1>Frame C</h1>
  <button type="button" onclick="parent.displayA();">
    parent.displayA()
  </button><br>
  <button type="button" onclick="parent.frameB.displayB();">
    parent.frameB.displayB()
  </button>
</body>
</html>
```

LISTING 13.16   frameD.html

```
<html>
<head>
<title>Frame D</title>
</head>

<body>
  <h1>Frame D</h1>
  <button type="button" onclick="top.displayA();">
    top.displayA()
  </button><br>
  <button type="button" onclick="top.frameB.displayB();">
```

LISTING 13.16   Continued

```
     top.frameB.displayB()
   </button>
 </body>
 </html>
```

LISTING 13.17   frameE.html

```
<html>
<head>
<title>Frame E</title>
</head>

<body>
  <h1>Frame E</h1>
  <button type="button" onclick="parent.parent.displayA();">
    parent.parent.displayA()
  </button><br>
  <button type="button" onclick="parent.displayB();">
    parent.displayB()
  </button>
</body>
</html>
```

To access function displayA() from frameA or frameC, you could use either
top.displayA() or parent.displayA(). Similarly, to access the function displayB() from
frameA, or frameC, you could use either top.frameB.displayA() or
parent.frameB.displayA(). To access function displayB() from frameD or frameE, you
could use either top.frameB.displayB() or parent.displayB(). However, to access function displayA() from frameD or frameE, you could use top.displayA() or
parent.parent.displayA().

We'll discuss more ways to refer to various frames and windows in the section
"Referencing Frames," later in this chapter.

You must exercise several precautions when dealing with framed documents and
JavaScript. Your script can produce errors if a referenced frame doesn't contain the correct
document or doesn't even exist. Errors will also occur if frames defined in a frameset do
not exist on the same server.

Synchronizing Frames

As I mentioned, not having the right documents or the right frames loaded can cause
errors and other problems. A session can stop dead in its tracks if it can't find one variable.

Furthermore, the problem might be that the documents haven't finished loading. Synchronizing the frames ensures that the frames and documents have finished loading before they are needed or that alternative actions are taken.

Verifying Frames

A common problem occurs when a page contains JavaScript that can be viewed either in or out of frames. The `window` object, designated by `top` as shown following, is quite useful for letting JavaScript determine whether a document is being viewed in frames. You can set a conditional statement that performs an action if frames are being used:

```
if( top != window ){
    document.write("Frames are being used");
    }
```

You usually use `top` or `parent` instead of `window`, because `window` implies the frame containing the code, which doesn't contain frames unless the document is a frameset file.

The short-circuit feature of the `if` statement is useful for preventing a document that isn't in the frames from trying to access a variable in another frame or frameset. If the top frameset contains an `a1` variable that is used in a conditional statement by a framed document, an error is produced if the document is viewed as a standalone (no-frame) document. However, if the `length` property is checked first in the conditional and found to be `false`, the statement ends, which prevents accessing a nonexistent variable.

The first part of the following statement, `parent.length != 0`, is `false` when frames aren't used, so further evaluation is stopped:

```
if( (parent.length != 0) && (top.a1 == x ) )
```

Verifying Documents Loaded

Various techniques have been developed to synchronize frames—some rather simple, others rather complex. One of the easiest techniques is to use JavaScript to verify that a particular document is present in a certain frame before proceeding with the rest of the code. The `frames` array lets you specify a frame as an element of the array. (Refer to the section "Referencing Frames," later in this chapter, for information on the `frames` array.) Consider the following code line:

```
if( (parent.length == 3)&&(parent.frames[1].title == "My Page") )
```

The `if` statement verifies that the correct frame structure is present (in this case, three frames) and that the document in the second frame (which, in this case, is to be referenced) is the correct one. If the frame structure is incorrect, the conditional evaluation stops, and no further action is taken or an alternative action is taken. If the frame structure is correct but the wrong document is present, the script initiates either no action or an alternative action. Initiating no further action simply maintains the session at its current position, allowing the user to proceed with other actions or retry a failed action.

(Perhaps the page wasn't finished loading and another attempt will be successful.) Alternative actions could include providing an alert to the user, loading the correct page and proceeding, or proceeding with the action but skipping the steps that require the missing document.

The previous example checked a simple frame structure (three frames). You can check more complex structures using the `frames` array of various windows in a multipart `if` statement. The multipart `if` statement has to verify the structure from the top down; otherwise, referencing a missing frame causes an error. Note the following line of code:

```
if(top.length==3)&&(top.frames[1].length==2)&&(top.frames[1].frames[1]==3)...
```

If a portion of the frame structure isn't present, the `if` statement stops at that point, and the script can perform an alternative action by using an `else` statement or perform no action at all.

In verifying that the correct document is present, the code can check other properties besides the title, such as the frame's `location.href`. You can assign a common variable in each document a unique name or number and then check that document identity variable instead of the document title or other property.

Registering Documents

Simply verifying that the required document is present can get complicated with larger sites and doesn't necessarily verify that the document is loaded. Another technique involves having the documents indicate when they are loaded and unloaded. Using the `onLoad()` and `onUnload()` events, documents record their presence in a top `Window` variable or a cookie. The following code shows that you don't have to use the title to identify the document; you could use another property or an identity variable:

```
<body onLoad="top.funRecord(document.title)"
   onUnload="top.funRemove(document.title)">
```

The following code shows a simple document registration scheme. The first code segment contains some of the code that might appear in the top frameset file:

```
<script type="text/javascript" language="JavaScript">
<!--
var a4 = "";   // Variable for document registration string.

function funRecord(a){ // Add the document to the registration string on load.
   a4 += a;
}

function funRemove(a){       // Remove document registration on unload.
   a4 = a4.substring( 0,a4.indexOf(a) ) +
         a4.substring(a4.indexOf(a)+a.length,a4.length);
```

```
}

function funCheck(a){    // Check whether document is registered or not.
  if( a4.indexOf(a) != -1)  return true;
  else  return false;
 }
// -->
</script>
```

The next code segment shows code that might appear in the document file:

```
<html>
<title>The Harley FXSTC</title>
<script type="text/javascript" language="JavaScript">
<!--
function funRegister(a){
  // Check that top frameset is present to register document, else ignore.
  if( ( top.length != 0 )&&(top.document.title == "Main Frameset") )
     if( a =="R") top.funRecord(document.title);
     else top.funRemove(document.title);
 }
function funCheck(a){    // Check whether document is registered or not.
  if( ( top.length != 0 )&&(top.document.title == "Main Frameset") )
     return top.funCheck(a);
 else return false;
}
// -->
</script>
<body onLoad="top.funRecord(document.title)"
    onUnload="top.funRemove(document.title)">
```

The following code checks whether the document is registered:

```
if( funCheck("The Softtail Series") )
       top.frames[2].fxnames();   // Document registered, proceed with action.
else                         // Document not registered, take alternative action.
       top.location.href = "http://www.foo.com/fx.html";
```

Using Extensive Registration Schemes

More complex schemes not only register the document but also register the document's position in the frame structure hierarchy. If a document position changes due to different possible loading scenarios or a site update, the code dependent on referencing the document can locate the document through the document's registration information. Instead of using a single variable or a cookie to hold registration information, some schemes employ an array of variables with each element (variable) containing identity and position information for a registered document. These schemes are complex to set up; however, they do provide great benefit in very large sites where a small change in the structure could throw off the code references in many of the documents.

Updating Frames

A significant benefit of frames is the capability to update or change the document in a frame while other frames remain unchanged. Whether a frame gets updated from user input in another frame or gets updated programmatically, you can provide the means to direct the changes to the appropriate frame through several techniques. These techniques can employ HTML, JavaScript, or a combination of both.

Links

Perhaps the simplest updating technique is using a link to update its own frame (by loading a new document). To direct the new document into another frame, the anchor tag has a target attribute for which you can specify either the value of a frame name or a relational name. The relational words correspond to the relational window properties discussed previously. The relational names used for targeting links all begin with an underscore and are always lowercase. These names are _top, _parent, and _self, which correspond to the window properties top, parent, and self. There is no window, however.

The following code represents frames in which a link in one frame must update another frame:

```
<frameset cols="30%,*">
        <frame src="doc1.html" name="doc1">
        <frame src="doc2.html" name="doc2">
        <frame src="doc3.html" name="doc3">
</frameset>
```

The file doc2.html contains the following additional frameset information:

```
<frameset rows="*,20%">
                <frame src="doc4.html" name="doc4">
                <frame src="doc5.html" name="doc5">
  </frameset>
```

To load a new document in doc2 from a link in doc4.html (in doc4), write the link as follows:

```
<a href="new.html" target="parent">
```

Use the following line to load the document in the top window and clear all the frames:

```
<a href="new.html" target="_top">
```

Dynamic Links

Because links are objects in JavaScript and `href` and `target` are properties of links, you can create a dynamic link by reassigning the values of `href` and `target`:

```
<a href="#" target="_top" onClick='this.href="new.html";this.target="_self";'>
```

For JavaScript-enabled browsers, the document `new.html` loads in the current frame; otherwise, the current document loads in the top window. (A fragment specifier, #, without a URL and an anchor name, or fragment identifier, refers to the current document.) This reassignment of the link's `href` and `target` properties can be more dynamic if you combine the assignment statements with conditional and other statements. For example, load a frameset file in the parent if frames are being used; otherwise, load the main document of the frameset:

```
<a href="main.html" target="_top"
   onClick='if( top.length != 0 ){this.href="frameset1.html";
                                  this.target="_parent";}'>
```

> **CAUTION**
>
> Watch those quotes; the event handler must be enclosed in a set of quotes (either double or single).

You don't need to reassign both the `href` and `target` properties for every dynamic link. The previous example could have had the `target` attribute set to _parent.

For the no-frames user, _parent and _top are equivalent. If the user doesn't have a frames-capable browser, the `target` attribute is ignored. The example could be written this way:

```
<a href="main.html" target="_parent"
   onClick='if( parent.length != 0 ){this.href="frameset1.html";}'>
```

The link tag can get pretty long and cumbersome as you add more statements to the event handler. To simplify the link, you can use function calls:

```
<a href="main.html" target="_top" onClick='this.href=theHref();
                                  this.target=theTarget();'>
```

`theHref()` is a user-defined function that determines the conditions and returns the appropriate value for the `href` property. Likewise, `theTarget()` returns the appropriate value for the `target` property. These functions must return a value regardless of whether the evaluated condition is `true` or `false`; only the non-JavaScript–enabled browser uses the default values set by the `href` and `target` attributes. For our frame-to-noframe examples, consider the following code:

```
function theHref(){
    var a;
```

```
if( top.length != 0 )
    a = "frameset1.html";
else
   a = "main.html";
return a;
}
```

theTarget() would be similarly constructed. You could also use the functions for other links on the page by passing the appropriate URLs and target names in the function calls. You could use one or two generic functions for a number of links.

You will often find that dynamic links aren't necessary. Typically, a page is loaded into the current frame or the links appear on a navigational menu that isn't seen by no-frames users and can always be targeted to a particular frame. However, for the few circumstances when they're necessary, dynamic links can be quite effective. Also, the frames/no-frames condition isn't the only case where dynamic links might be necessary; you can set up these links for any circumstance you can imagine.

The location.href Property

Another way to update a frame that doesn't necessarily require a link is by using the href property of the Location object. You can also use the href property in conjunction with a form button event handler or a function. The following statements are equivalent and update the current frame with the home page of http://www.samspublishing.com/:

```
location.href = "http://www.samspublishing.com/";
self.location.href = "http://www.samspublishing.com/";
window.location.href = "http://www.samspublishing.com/";
```

The following statements update the parent and top frames, respectively:

```
parent.location.href = "http://www.samspublishing.com/";
top.location.href = "http://www.samspublishing.com/";
```

Instead of using relational Window properties, you can use a frame name:

```
parent.frame3.location.href = "http://www.samspublishing.com/";
```

In addition to writing the href property, you can also write the pathname property of the Location object, which lets you specify the path or filename from the server root. (Of course, the host name, as well as the protocol and port, remains unchanged from the current location.) Use the following code to load the document http://www.abc.com/foo/doc2.html in frame1, which currently has http://www.abc.com/index.htm:

```
frame1.location.pathname="/foo/doc2.html";
```

However, if the current document is `http://www.def.org/home.html` or `ftp://ftp.abc.com/pub/abc.txt`, you must use the `href` property.

The write() Method

A third way to update a frame is using the document `write()` or `writeln()` method as well as the document `open()` and `close()` methods. JavaScript can dynamically generate a document in a frame by starting with a frameset as shown in Listing 13.18.

LISTING 13.18   Updating a Frame by Writing to It

```
<html>
<head>
<title>Updating Demo Frameset</title>
</head>
<frameset cols="40%,*">
    <frame src="frameWriter.html" name="frame1">
    <frame src="about:blank" name="frame2">
</frameset>
</html>
```

The second frame, named `frame2`, can be any file or `"about:blank"` to ensure an empty document initially.

Dynamically uploading a frame can be interactive with the user through links or forms as shown in Listing 13.19.

LISTING 13.19   frameWriter.html

```
<html>
<head>
<title>Updating Demo frame1</title>
<script type="text/javascript" language="JavaScript">
<!--
function docWrite(){
    top.frame2.document.open();
    top.frame2.document.write("<html><head>" +
        "<title>Updating Demo frame2<\/title>");
    top.frame2.document.write(" <\/head><body bgcolor=\"" +
                    document.form1.bginput.value + "\">");
    top.frame2.document.write("<h1>Updated Page<\/h1>");
    top.frame2.document.write("Update by " + document.form1.input1.value);
    top.frame2.document.write("<\/body><\/html>");
    top.frame2.document.close();
}
```

LISTING 13.19   Continued

```
// -->
</script>

</head>
<body>
<form name="form1">
<input type="text" name="input1">
<p>
Select a Background Color</br>
<input type="radio" name="radio1" value="white" checked
    onClick='document.form1.bginput.value="white"'>White<br />
<input type="radio" name="radio1" value="red"
    onClick='document.form1.bginput.value="red"'>Red<br />
<input type="radio" name="radio1" value="blue"
    onClick='document.form1.bginput.value="blue"'>Blue<br />
<input type="radio" name="radio1" value="green"
    onClick='document.form1.bginput.value="green"'>Green<br />
<p><input type="hidden" name="bginput" value="white"></p>
<p><input type="button" value="Update frame2" onClick="docWrite()"></p>
</form>
</body>
</html>
```

The JavaScript code used to update a frame can be very sophisticated. You can use conditional statements, calculations, or any script imaginable to create a document to update the frame. Games, slide shows, highlighted maps, and database query result (returned as HTML content) are some examples of what you can use to update the frame.

Caching Files

Image files to be included in an updated frame can be cached ahead of time to prevent the download from delaying the update. You use the Image object to cache an image until it's needed. Another technique is to use a document in a hidden frame to download the image:

```
<html>
<head>
<title>Hidden Frame to Cache Images</title>
</head>
<frameset cols="100%,*">
    <frame src="doc1.html" name="frame1">
    <frame src="cache.html" name="frame2">
```

```
</frameset>
</html>
```

The following is an undisplayed document just for downloading images so that the image files are stored in the cache:

```
<html>
<head>
<title>Updating Demo frame1</title>
<script type="text/javascript" language="JavaScript">
<!--
var loaded = false;
// -->
</script>
</head>
<body onLoad="loaded = true;">
<img src="image1.gif" width=100 height=200>
<img src="image2.jgp" width=300 height=120>
<img src="image3.gif" width=200 height=200>
</body>
</html>
```

> **TIP**
>
> You should size the image tags to prevent problems when the script executes in certain browser versions.

Although good practice usually dictates that you use the `alt` attribute with image tags, the attribute isn't necessary here because the document isn't displayed in any browser—let alone a nongraphical browser.

Variable a1 is a flag that is set when the images are downloaded. You aren't required to use this flag, but it's useful to prevent the execution of a frame update script until the images are downloaded:

```
if(top.frame2.loaded != true ){
    alert("Please wait, images are still downloading");
  }
else{
    ...continue with rest of script
```

Referencing Area Objects

You can reference the `Area` objects with the `links` array. The `links` array consists of all the `Link` and `Area` objects in the document. The elements are numbered from zero to one less than the total number of link and area tags. The following code is an example of a document with a link and a client-side imagemap.

```html
<html>
<head>
<title>Client-side Imagemap Demo</title>
</head>
<body>
<a href="doc1.html" target="frameA">The Softtails</A>
<map name="map1">
<a id="areaA" coords="20,20,80,80" href="doc2.html" target="frameA">
<a id="areaB" coords="100,20,180,80" href="doc3.html" target="frameA">
<a id="areaC" coords="20,100,80,180" href="doc4.html" target="frameA">
<a id="areaD" coords="100,100,180,180" href="doc5.html" target="frameA">
</map>
<img src="map1.gif" width=200 height=200 alt="Menu" usemap="#map1">
<!-- Code for alternative server-side map and a text menu for
non-graphical browsers omitted for clarity in the above example -->.
</body>
</html>
```

In the preceding example, the link is referenced by document.links[0] because it's the first link or area tag in the document. Area areaA is referenced by document.links[1] because it's the second link or area tag. areaB is document.links[2], areaC is document.links[3], and areaD is document.links[4].

The href and target properties of the Area objects, as with the Link objects, can be referenced and assigned new values through the links array. The following line changes the value of areaB's href property so that when its area of the imagemap is clicked, the document doc6.html loads instead of doc3.html:

```
document.link[2].href="doc6.html"
```

Likewise, you can change the target property:

```
document.link[2].target="frameB"
```

The target attribute and property must be specified as a frame name or one of the special relational frame words (_top, _parent, _self, or _blank) and not with a JavaScript property (top, parent, and so on).

You can open and name new windows by assigning to the target a name that isn't already in use. A new window opened in this manner has the name specified as the value of the target attribute.

Calling Functions

The area tags don't always have to reference a document. You can make function calls by using the `onClick` event handler:

```
<a name="areaA" coords="20,20,80,80" onClick="fun1()">
```

The script calls the user-defined function `fun1()` instead of a document. You can also use JavaScript methods and statements. This technique is particularly suited for a framed version of a site in which the imagemap server is a navigation button bar. The function can perform various statements to determine whether frames are used and certain flags are set, or perform a calculation or evaluation. The function can then take the appropriate action, such as loading a certain document, or take no action at all.

The following example contains a rather simple slide show script with a button bar imagemap that allows the user to cycle forward and backward through slides. The imagemap also contains a button so the user can return to the home page. Each slide show has a sequence name that forms the first part of the filenames of the slides in the sequence. The second part of the filename is a sequential number unique to each slide in the sequence. Each of the slide files has three variables: the sequence name, the sequential number of the slide, and the total number of slides in the sequence. The script reads these three variables to load the next slide file based upon which portion of the imagemap was clicked. Listing 13.20 creates a frameset in which the slide show will live. Listings 13.21 and 13.22 create two slides for the slide show. Listing 13.23 contains the button bar, which is created using an imagemap. Finally, Listing 13.24 contains the home page to load when the user exists the slide show.

LISTING 13.20   Frameset for Slide Show

```
<html>
<head>
<title>Slide Show Main Frameset</title>
</head>
<frameset rows="*,150">
    <frame src="slide1.html" name="frameA">
    <frame src="buttonBar.html" name="frameB">
</html>
```

LISTING 13.21   slide1.html

```
<html>
<head>
<title>Slide Show - First Slide</title>
<script type="text/javascript" language="JavaScript">
<!--
```

LISTING 13.21   Continued

```
var slideName = "slide";      // First portion of slide file names.
var slideNumber = 1;          // Sequential number of the slide.
var totalNumSlides = 2;       // Total number of slides.
// -->
</script>
</head>
<body>
<h1>Slide 1</h1>
</body>
</html>
```

LISTING 13.22   slide2.html

```
<html>
<head>
<title>Slide Show - Second Slide</title>
<script type="text/javascript" language="JavaScript">
<!--
var slideName = "slide";      // First portion of slide file names.
var slideNumber = 2;          // Sequential number of the slide.
var totalNumSlides = 2;       // Total number of slides.
// -->
</script>
</head>
<body>
<h1>Slide 2</h1>
</body>
</html>
```

LISTING 13.23   buttonBar.html

```
<html>
<head>
<title>Slide Show Demo Image Map</title>
<script type="text/javascript" language="JavaScript">
function move(action){
  // Root file name for series of slides.
  var slideName = top.frames[0].slideName;
  // Sequential slide number.
  var slideNumber = top.frames[0].slideNumber;
```

LISTING 13.23   Continued

```
  // Number of slides.
  var totalNumSlides = top.frames[0].totalNumSlides;
  if( action == "f" )
    if(slideNumber == totalNumSlides)
      slideNumber = 0;
  if( action == "r" )
    if(slideNumber == 1)
      slideNumber = totalNumSlides - 1;
    else
      slideNumber = slideNumber - 2;
  slideNumber = slideNumber + 1;
  slideName += slideNumber;
  slideName += ".html";
  top.frames[0].location.href = slideName;
 }
</script>
</head>
<body bgcolor="000000" style="text-align:center">

<map name="map1">
  <area coords="1,1,100,100" href='javascript:move("r")'
   onMouseOver='window.status="Cycle reverse through slide show";
   return true'>
  <area coords="101,1,200,100" href="slideShowHome.html" target="_top"
    onMouseOver='window.status="Quit Slide Show and Return to Home Page";
    return true'>
  <area coords="201,1,300,100" href='javascript:move("f")'
    onMouseOver='window.status="Cycle forward through slide show";
    return true'>
</map>
<img src="buttons.gif" width="300" height="50" usemap="#map1">

</body>
</html>
```

LISTING 13.24   slideShowHome.html

```
<html>
<head>
<title>Slide Show Home</title>
</head>
```

LISTING 13.24   Continued

```
<body>
<h1>Slide Show Home</h1>
</body>
</html>
```

Working with Frame URLs

There are no real differences between framed and unframed documents regarding URLs. Within the entire window, however, you can use different sites and base hrefs. One frame might contain a document from a certain directory on a server, another frame might have a document from another directory, and a third frame could have a document from a different server. Regardless of which frame is targeted, a relative URL in a link is referenced from the document containing the link. You can use the <base> tag <base href="http://www.foo.com/some.html"> in a document to set all links relative to the base href, if needed. You can override the base href by specifying an absolute URL in the link.

As with the href attribute of the <base> tag, you can also specify a base target. <base target="frameA"> directs all links in the document to the specified frame. You can also override the base target with the target attribute in the link. For example, <a href="some.html" target="_self"> overrides the base target and loads the document into its own frame.

> **NOTE**
>
> You must place the <base> tag <base href="some.html" target="someframe"> in the <head> section of the document. No content or closing tag is associated with the <base> tag. The <base> tag with both the href and target attributes is shown in the following example:
>
> ```
> <html>
> <head>
> <title>Base Demo</title>
> <base href="http://www.foo.com/home.html" target="frameA">
> </head>
> <body>
> ...
> ```

You can find additional information on using URLs in frames throughout this chapter, especially in the next section and the section "Updating Frames" found earlier in this chapter.

Referencing Frames

When working with single and multiple frames in your JavaScript applications, you probably need to use other ways to reference windows. JavaScript provides four references to windows. Each is implemented as properties of the `Window` object.

> **NOTE**
>
> Separate browser windows don't have a hierarchy structure; however, the window containing the code that opens another window is often referred to as the parent window. The new window is often referred to as the child window. Any new window can assign a variable in other windows so that other windows can reference it and its properties. To reference a property in the new window, you simply use `windowName.property`.
>
> Consider the following code:
>
> ```
> newWindow = window.open();
> newWindow.location.href = "http://www.samspublishing.com/";
> ```
>
> Although this segment doesn't exhibit the most efficient way to write the code, it demonstrates referencing a child window's property. The new window is opened and assigned to a variable called `newWindow`. Then, the new window's `location.href` is referenced and assigned.

Referencing the Current Window

The `Window` object also contains a property called `window` that can be used as a self-referencing tool. In addition, the `self` property of the `Window` object is another means of referring to the current or active window. For example, the following two code lines are functionally the same:

```
window.defaultStatus = "Welcome to the Goat Farm Home Page"
```

```
self.defaultStatus = "Welcome to the Goat Farm Home Page"
```

Because `window` and `self` are both synonyms of the current window, you might find it curious that both are included in the JavaScript language. As shown in the previous example, the rationale is flexibility; you can use `window` or `self` as you want.

However, as useful as `window` and `self` can be, it can easily become confusing to think about the logic behind it all. After all, an object's property that is used as an equivalent term for the object itself is rather unusual. Consequently, you might find it helpful to think of `window` or `self` as "reserved words" for the `Window` object rather than its properties.

Finally, in multiframe environments, `window` and `self` always refer to the window in which the JavaScript code is executed unless another frame is chosen using syntax similar to the following:

```
parent.frames[2].window.document
```

> **NOTE**
>
> In some object-oriented or object-based languages, self might refer to the active object, no matter what type it is. In JavaScript, self refers only to the active Window or Frame object—nothing else.

Parent to Child

A child frame is referenced by the parent in one of two ways. First, you can use a frame's name, which is defined by the name parameter of the <frame> tag. For example, in the following code, the FrameName variable references the name of the frameA frame:

```
<html>
<head>
<title>Parent to Child Demo</title>
<script type="text/javascript" language="JavaScript">
function showFrameName(){
    var frameName = self.frameA.name;
    alert("frameName: " + frameName);
}
</script>
</head>
<frameset cols="50%,*">
    <frame src="doc1.html" name="frameA" onLoad="showFrameName();">
    <frame src="doc2.html" name="frameB">
</frameset>
</html>
```

You can also reference child frames using the frameset's frames array. Every frame in the window, or parent frame, is an element of the array. The frames array elements are referenced by frames[i], where i is the number corresponding to the order in which the frame is created in the parent window. The frames are numbered from zero to one less than the total number of frames. For example, in the following code, the frameName variable references the name of the frame specified:

```
<html>
<head>
<title>Parent to Child Demo</title>
<script type="text/javascript" language="JavaScript">
function showFrameName(frameNumber){
    var frameName = self.frames[frameNumber].name;
    alert("frameName: " + frameName);
}
</script>
</head>
```

```
<frameset cols="50%,*">
    <frame src="doc1.html" name="frameA" onLoad="showFrameName(0);">
    <frame src="doc2.html" name="frameB" onLoad="showFrameName(1);">
</frameset>
</html>
```

The frameset above contains two frames, which are contained in the window's frames array as shown following:

frames[0] for frame frameA

frames[1] for frame frameB

> **NOTE**
>
> Note the plural, frames, when referring to an element in the frames array.

Child to Parent

As you've learned in this chapter, frames are the same as Window objects within a frameset. Within this multiframe setting, you need to distinguish between the various frames displayed in the browser. The parent property of a Window object helps you do that by referencing its parent—the window containing the <frameset> definition. For example, if you want to retrieve some information about the current window's parent, such as the title, your code for the child window might look something like that shown in Listing 13.25.

LISTING 13.25   childWindow1.html

```
<html>
<head>
<title>Child Window</title>
</head>
<script type="text/javascript" language="JavaScript">
<!--
    function getParentInfo() {
        myParentTitle = parent.document.title
        alert("My Dad's name is " + myParentTitle)
    }
// -->
</script>
<form>
<input
    type="button"
```

LISTING 13.25   Continued

```
      value="Get Info"
      onClick="getParentInfo()">
</form>
</body>
</html>
```

Not only can you retrieve property values, but you can also access the parent's methods. For example, Listing 13.26 shows the HTML source for a parent window in a frameset with a showInfo() method defined with no means of implementation in it. Listing 13.27 shows how the child window accesses this method. When the user clicks the childButton Button object, its onClick event handler calls runDadMethod() using the this keyword as its parameter. The runDadMethod() in turn calls the parent object's showInfo() method, passing the current object's name as the parameter. Figure 13.6 shows the result.

LISTING 13.26   parentWindow.html

```
<html>
<head>
<title>Parent Window Title</title>
<script type="text/javascript" language="JavaScript">

    function showInfo(objectName) {
        alert(objectName)
    }

</script>
</head>
  <frameset cols="50%,50%">
    <frame name="childWindow1" src="childWindow1.html">
    <frame name="childWindow2" src="childWindow2.html">
  </frameset>
</html>
```

> **TIP**
>
> To define a blank frame, simply leave off the src attribute in the <frame> definition. In Netscape Navigator 4, you have to set src to "about:blank".

LISTING 13.27   childWindow2.html

```
<html>
<head>
```

LISTING 13.27   Continued

```
<title>Child Window</title>
</head>
<script type="text/javascript" language="JavaScript">
<!--
     function runDadMethod(curObject) {
          parent.showInfo(curObject.name)
     }

// -->
</script>
<form>
<input
     type="button"
     name="childButton"
     value="Run Dad's Method"
     onClick="runDadMethod(this)">
</form>
</body>
</html>
```

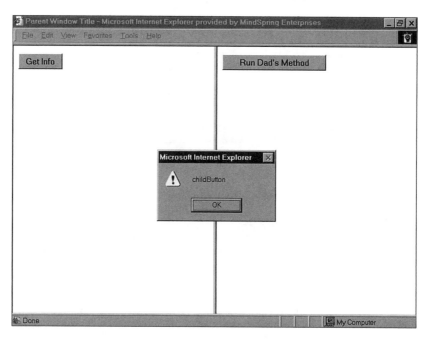

FIGURE 13.6   Calling a method of a parent.

The parent is often the topmost window within a multiframe window environment, but not necessarily. You can have nested levels of framesets, as you will see in the following discussion on the top property. Therefore, the parent property refers to the current window's immediate parent. If you want to access the parent's parent (the "grandparent" window), you could use the following:

```
myGranddadTitle = parent.parent.document.title
```

In more complex frame structures, all the frames can still be referenced by their positions in the structure, as shown in Figure 13.7 and Table 13.1.

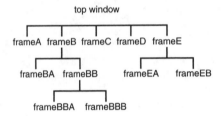

FIGURE 13.7   The hierarchy of a complex nested frame site.

TABLE 13.1   Referencing Other Frames from frameBBB

Frame	Reference
frameA	`top.frameA` or `top.frames[0]`
frameBA	`top.frames[1].frameBA` or `top.frames[1].frames[0]`
frameBB	`parent`, `top.frames[1].frameBB`, or `top.frames[1].frames[1]`
frameEA	`top.frames[4].frameEA` or `top.frames[4].frames[0]`

Use the following line to reference the title of the document in frameEA and assign it to a variable a1:

```
a1 = top.frames[4].frames[0].document.title;
```

Other properties are referenced similarly.

> **NOTE**
>
> It's important to note the hierarchy differences that can exist between two similar-looking frame structures, as mentioned in the section "Creating Frames," earlier in this chapter.

The opener property is used to reference the window (the parent) that opened the current window. From the new (child) window, you can reference a property of the opener (parent) window with the top.opener.property.

You can also use an assignment technique to reference the opener window from the new window. The samples here use the Window property top; however, you can use self, parent, or window instead of top if necessary. The top property is used in the following code segment because the code might appear in any frame of the windows. Using top ensures that the appropriate property of the top window is identified. self, parent, or window could be any frame in the top window.

```
newWindow = window.open("doc1.html");
newWindow.oldWindow = top;
```

Use the following syntax to reference a property in the opener window from the new window:

```
top.oldWindow.property
```

Using Child-to-Child References

The parent property is important not only for accessing a child window's parent window, but also for referencing another object in one of its "sibling" windows. As shown in Figure 13.8, any communication between child frames can go through their parent.

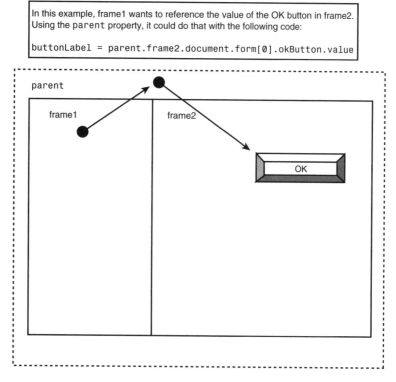

FIGURE 13.8 Using the parent property to reference siblings.

Frames on the same level with different parents must be referenced by the absolute position in the frame structure:

```
<frameset cols="50%,*">
    <frame src="doc1.html" name="frameA">
    <frame src="doc2.html" name="frameB">
</frameset>
```

The following segment contains doc1.html:

```
<frameset rows="50%,*">
    <frame src="doc3.html" name="frameAA">
    <frame src="doc4.html" name="frameAB">
</frameset>
```

The next segment contains doc2.html:

```
<frameset rows="50%,*">
    <frame src="doc5.html" name="frameBA">
    <frame src="doc6.html" name="frameBB">
</frameset>
```

frameAB is referenced by frameBB as in the following:

```
top.frames[0].frameAB
```

You can also use the following line:

```
top.frames[0].frames[0]
```

There is no intermediate level between top and parent, such as grandparent, to reference frames. It's probably a good thing that parent is the only term borrowed from genealogy; imagine referring to a frame as third.cousin.twice.removed.

If browser windows are always assigned a name when opened, it's no problem for one of the new (child) windows to reference another child window through the opener (parent window). The name of the window is simply referenced as described in the previous sections. If a window is assigned a variable name of myWindow when it is opened, another child window can reference it like this:

```
top.opener.myWindow
```

You can synchronize the window with the same techniques employed for frames. However, because there is no one top browser window or window hierarchy, one window, such as the opener for the other windows, has to serve as the synchronization point. The following code segment is an example of a script used to synchronize windows:

```
<html>
<title>The Harley FXSTC</title>
<script type="text/javascript" language="JavaScript">
<!--
function funRegister(a){
  // Check that page is in its own window and that the opener
  // window contains the correct document.
 if( (top.name=="newWindow1") && (top.opener.document.title=="Main Frameset") )
     if( a =="R") top.opener.funRecord(document.title);
     else top.opener.funRemove(document.title);
 }
function funCheck(a){    // Check whether document is registered or not.
 if( (top.name=="newWindow1") && (top.opener.document.title=="Main Frameset") )
     return top.opener.funCheck(a);
 else return false;
}
// -->
</script>
<body onLoad="top.funRecord(document.title)"
    onUnload="top.funRemove(document.title)">
...
```

The following code checks whether the document is registered. This code would appear in the same file as the previous code snippet so that the function funCheck can be accessed.

```
if( funCheck("The Softtail Series")
   newWindow2.frames[2].fxnames(); // Document registered, proceed with action.
else                     // Document not registered, take alternative action.
     top.location.href ="http://www.foo.com/fx.html";
...
```

As with frames, you can use more complex schemes to register the location information for the document. Those schemes employ the same scripts as those for frames but would extend one level to incorporate separate browser windows.

The Top Window
Similar in function to the parent property, the Window object's top property allows you to reference the topmost window within a frameset or set of framesets. If you're working with a single frameset, the top and parent properties refer to the same window. However, if you have nested levels of framesets, top refers to the highest level window, whereas parent may or may not refer to that same window.

This difference is best illustrated through an example. Suppose you have two framesets. The first frameset divides the window horizontally using 65%, 35% (as shown in Figure 13.9). Divided into four quadrants, the second frameset (shown in Figure 13.10) is intended for the lower 35% of the top-level frameset.

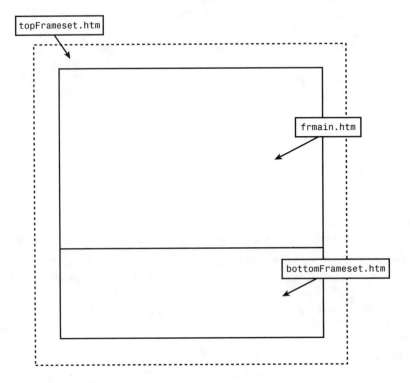

FIGURE 13.9   A top-level frameset.

For each child frame, suppose you want to get the titles of its top and parent windows. To do so, you can define a common function called getName() that returns this information to the calling window. Just as child windows can access a method in a parent window, all frames in a multiframeset window can access methods in the top window. Therefore, the top window serves as a good repository for functions you want to be globally available to all windows. The getName() method is defined as follows:

```
function getName(callingObject, relation, parentName) {
  callingObject.document.write("My " + relation + "'s name is " +
```

```
    parentName +".")
}
```

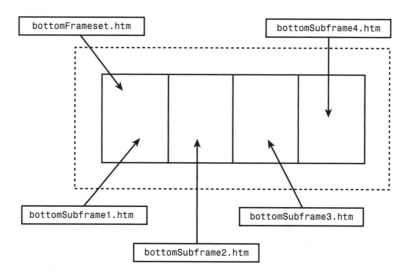

FIGURE 13.10   A lower-level frameset.

The `callingObject` parameter represents the window that is calling the function. Using dot notation, you can then assign the `document.write` command to be performed within the window in question. The `relation` and `parentName` parameters are strings provided by the calling window but aren't manipulated in this function.

This `getName()` method is called by the child frames upon loading. You can do this by putting the following code in each of the child frames:

```
<script type="text/javascript" language="JavaScript">
    top.getName(self, "parent", parent.document.title)
    document.write("<p>")
    top.getName(self, "top", top.document.title)
</script>
```

The script uses `top` to access the `getName()` method, `self` to identify itself as the calling window, and `parent` and `top` to retrieve the titles for both windows. Figure 13.11 shows the result when the frameset is loaded.

Listings 13.28, 13.29, 13.30 and 13.31 provide the source code for the top-level frameset (`topFrameset.html`), lower-level frameset (`bottomFrameset.html`), and one of the bottom child frames (`bottomSubframe1.html`).

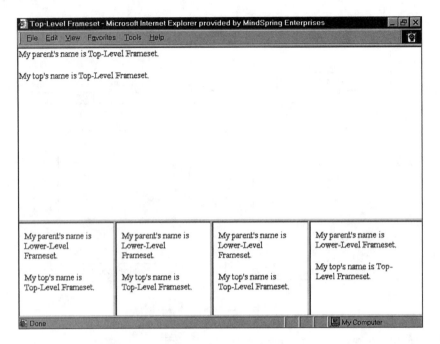

FIGURE 13.11   The top and parent properties.

LISTING 13.28   topFrameset.html

```
<html>
<head>
<title>Top-Level Frameset</title>
<script type="text/javascript" language="JavaScript">

    function getName(callingObject, relation, parentName) {
     callingObject.document.write("My " + relation +
       "'s name is " + parentName +".")
    }

</script>
</head>
<frameset rows="65%,35%">
  <frame src="frmain.html"
         name="main"
         marginwidth="1"
         marginheight="1">
  <frame src="bottomFrameset.html"
```

LISTING 13.28   Continued

```
        name="footnotes"
        marginwidth="1"
        marginheight="1">
  <noframes>
Warning text should go here for browsers with no frame support.
<body>
</body>
</noframes>
</frameset>
</html>
```

LISTING 13.29   frmain.html

```
<html>
<head>
<title>Main Frame</title>
<script type="text/javascript" language="JavaScript">
    top.getName(self, "parent", parent.document.title)
    document.write("<p>")
    top.getName(self, "top", top.document.title)
</script>
</head>
<body>
</body>
</html>
```

LISTING 13.30   bottomFrameset.html

```
<html>
<head>
<title>Lower-Level Frameset</title>
</head>
<frameset cols="24%,24%,24%,28%">
  <frame src="bottomSubframe1.html">
  <frame src="bottomSubframe2.html">
  <frame src="bottomSubframe3.html">
  <frame src="bottomSubframe4.html">
</frameset>
</html>
```

LISTING 13.31   bottomSubframe1.html, bottomSubframe2.html, bottonSubframe3.html, and bottomSubframe4.html

```
<html>
<head>
<title>Footnotes Frame in Bottom Frameset</title>
<script type="text/javascript" language="JavaScript">
    top.getName(self, "parent", parent.document.title)
    document.write("<p>")
    top.getName(self, "top", top.document.title)
</script>
</head>
<body>
</body>
</html>
</html>
```

The Location Object

The Location object encapsulates the URL of the current page. Its purpose is twofold, allowing you to do the following:

- Set the Location object to move to a new URL.

- Extract specific elements of the URL and work with them. Without the Location object, you would be forced to perform string manipulations on a URL string to get at the information you needed.

The basic structure of a URL is as follows:

protocol//*hostname*: *port pathname search hash*

A typical URL could look something like the following:

```
http://www.acadians.com/javascript/search/Hats?qt=RFC+1738+&col=XL
```

The Location object has the properties shown in Table 13.2, each of which is an element in the URL.

TABLE 13.2   Location Object Properties

Attribute	Description
href	Complete URL
protocol	Initial element of a URL (before and including colon)
hostname	Host and domain name or IP address
host	*Hostname:port* element of a URL

TABLE 13.2   Continued

Attribute	Description
port	Communications port of the server
pathname	Path element of a URL
search	Query definition portion of a URL (begins with ?)
hash	Anchor name of a URL (begins with #)

Opening a New URL

Instead of using a specific method to go to a new URL in a window, you can open a new URL by setting the value of the Location object. Interestingly, you can do this by either assigning a URL to the object itself or assigning a URL to the Location object's href property. For example, the following two lines perform the same action:

```
window.location = "http://www.acadians.com/"
```

```
window.location.href = "http://www.acadians.com/"
```

For example, to simulate a browser's location edit box using JavaScript, you could use the code in Listing 13.32.

LISTING 13.32   Simulating a Browser's Location Box

```
<html>
<head>
<script type="text/javascript" language="JavaScript">

function moveon() {
  var urlAddress = ""
  urlAddress = document.forms[0].newURL.value
  if(urlAddress != "")
    window.location = urlAddress
}

</script>
</head>
<body>
<form>
Please enter URL:<input type="text" name="newURL">
<input type="button" value="move" onClick="moveon()">
</form>
</body>
</html>
```

In multiframe windows, you can specify the value of the Location object in other frames by referring to the appropriate window name. For example, the code in Listing 13.33 creates two frames. The lower frame, whose code is shown in Listing 13.34, provides an interface for changing the URL of the upper frame.

LISTING 13.33   Example frameset for Specifying URL of Another Frame

```
<html>
<frameset rows="50%,50%">
  <frame name="upperFrame">
  <frame src="lowerFrame.html" name="lowerFrame">
</frameset>
</html>
```

LISTING 13.34   Example for Specifying URL of Another Frame

```
<html>
<html>
<head>
<script type="text/javascript" language="JavaScript">

function moveon() {
  var urlAddress = ""
  urlAddress = document.forms[0].newURL.value
  if(urlAddress != "")
    parent.upperFrame.location = urlAddress
}

</script>
</head>
<body>
<form>
Please enter URL:<input type="text" name="newURL">
<input type="button" value="move" onClick="moveon()">
</form>
</body>
</html>
```

Working with the protocol Property

The protocol property of the Location object lets you specify the type of URL with which you're working. Table 13.3 lists the most common protocols used.

TABLE 13.3   Location Object Protocols

URL Type	Protocol
Web	`http:`
File	`file:`
FTP	`ftp:`
MailTo	`mailto:`
Usenet	`news:`
JavaScript	`javascript:`
Navigator	`about:`

The History Object

If you've done much Web surfing, you're probably very familiar with a browser's History list. Just as the History list lets a user traverse where they have been, JavaScript's `History` object lets you as a JavaScript developer maneuver through previously visited Web pages (but only when a signed script requests permission). The `History` object has no events and only the properties and methods that are shown in Tables 13.4 and 13.5.

TABLE 13.4   History Object Properties

Property	Description
`current`	The URL of the current document
`length`	The History list's length
`next`	The History list's next URL
`previous`	The History list's previous URL

TABLE 13.5   History Object Methods

Method	Description
`Back()`	Loads the History list's previous document
`Forward()`	Loads the History list's next document
`Go()`	Goes to a specific document
`Go(n)`	If n>0, loads the document that is n entries ahead in the History list
`Go(string)`	Loads the History list document whose URL contains the specified string

Determining the Size of the List

You can use the `length` property of the `History` object to determine the number of entries in the list. For example, suppose you want to track the number of History list entries in the right frame of a multiframe window. The left frame contains the following code:

```
<html>
<head>
```

```
<script type="text/javascript" language="JavaScript">

    function moveon() {
        var urlAddress = ""
        urlAddress = document.forms[0].Edit1.value
        parent.frames[1].location = urlAddress
        document.forms[0].Edit2.value = parent.frames[1].history.length
    }

</script>
</head>

<body>
<form>
<input type="text" name="Edit1">
<input type="button" value="move" onClick="moveon()">
<input type="text" name="Edit2">
</form>
</body>
</html>
```

The user can use the Edit1 text object to enter a destination URL. As the user clicks the Move button to move to the URL, the Edit2 text object is updated to provide the length of the History list for the right frame.

Navigating the History List

Just knowing the length of the History list is rarely useful, but it can become useful if you want to navigate a list using the History object methods back(), forward(), and go().

Moving Back a Page

The back() method is the functional equivalent of clicking the Back (left-arrow) button on the browser's toolbar (assuming of course that the window that is referenced is the outermost window or frame). For example, the following code moves a specified window or frame to its previous position:

```
window.history.back()
```

Moving Forward a Page

As you would expect, the forward() method is the same as clicking the right-arrow button on the browser's toolbar (assuming of course that the window that is referenced is the outermost window or frame). It is used as follows:

```
window.history.forward()
```

Going to a Specific Page Based on a Number

The `go()` method jumps to a specific place in the History list. Its syntax follows:

```
[window.]history.go(delta | "location")
```

The `delta` parameter is a positive or negative integer that can specify the number of places to jump. For example, the following line moves to the next document in the History list (the equivalent of using the `forward()` method):

```
window.history.go(1)
```

Table 13.6 lists the possible `delta` values.

TABLE 13.6   delta Values

Values	Description
delta < 0	Moves backward *delta* number of entries
delta > 0	Moves forward *delta* number of entries
delta = 0	Reloads the current document

Going to a Specific Page Based on a String

Alternatively in Netscape, you can use the `location` parameter to specify a specific URL in the list. Note that this doesn't have to be an exact URL—only a substring. The following example moves to the URL in the History list that contains `www.acadians.com/filenew`:

```
window.history.go("www.acadians.com/filenew")
```

You could add the `back()`, `forward()`, and `go()` to the earlier example to provide a more fully functional multiframe navigating system.

Summary

This chapter dived into single and multiframe windows. The `Frame`, `Location`, and `History` objects provide a means to work with their respective browser counterparts.

This chapter also discussed how to use JavaScript to reference objects and properties in other frames and browser windows. Basic window creation and frame setup were covered as well as references to properties in different frames and windows. The chapter also explained updating frames and synchronizing frames and windows, providing a few examples of windows and frames interacting with each other through JavaScript.

Although using JavaScript in a framed site might be a little more complex than using it in a no-frames site, the benefits are often worth the small amount of added complexity. This chapter only touched on a few examples of JavaScript with frames and windows. The possible uses and implementations of a framed site are limited only by the Web site author's imagination and the depth of his perseverance.

Creating Custom JavaScript Objects

This chapter's discussion is a natural follow-up to the previous chapters in this section. The previous chapters introduced objects such as the Navigator object, the Window object, and the Document object, as well as a number of other built-in objects that are readily available as built-in objects within the JavaScript language. But if you stop there, you limit a great deal of the power that JavaScript has: letting you create your own custom objects. In this chapter, I discuss how to create custom objects in JavaScript, one of the major capabilities of JavaScript, and the limitations of custom objects.

Creating an Object

An object contains both data, known as **properties**, and behavior, known as **methods**. Our mission, then, is to create an entity that can encapsulate data elements and responses to methods.

To create a JavaScript object, you need to create a **constructor**. A constructor is a special JavaScript function that defines what the object will look like and how it will act. The constructor doesn't actually create the object; instead, it provides a template for what an instantiated object will look like. (Creating an instance of an object is called **instantiating** an object.) The following is the basic structure of an instantiated object:

```
function object(parameter1, parameter2,...)
{
  this.property1 = parameter1
  this.property2 = parameter2
```

```
    this.property3 = parameter3
    this.property4 = parameter4
    this.method1 = function1
    this.method2 = function2
}
```

As you can see, the actual structure of the constructor is relatively straightforward.

1. Name the method itself. The name of the function will serve as the name of your object type. Therefore, it's critical for clarity's sake to give your constructor method a descriptive name. If you're creating an object to represent an invoice, call it `invoice`. I've seen some people name their constructors in a verb format, such as `createInvoice`. This practice can lead to confusing and hard-to-read code, because a property of the object would look like this:

   ```
   myDate = createInvoice.date;
   ```

   Even worse, if you had `create()` as a method of the object, your code would look like this:

   ```
   createInvoice.create();
   ```

   A much clearer method of presentation is to use a noun-based approach, which would make the preceding two lines much more readable:

   ```
   myDate = invoice.date;
   ```

   and

   ```
   invoice.create();
   ```

2. Add parameters to the function for all the properties of the object. With this approach, when you instantiate the object, you pass the property values to the function as parameters. You can also create functions that have no parameters; this is represented by an empty set of parentheses. It is important to note that even though a function might specify parameters, you do not have to pass in any parameters when instantiating the object; just make sure the function can handle parameters being empty.

3. Assign the value of the incoming parameters to the properties of the object. The `this` keyword comes in handy here; it's used to represent the object as you define the properties.

4. Define the methods that the object type will have. Whereas properties are assigned values by parameters of the constructor itself, methods are created as functions outside of the constructor and are assigned to the method definition of the object.

To illustrate, suppose I want to create a custom object in which I can store information on my favorite books. In particular, I want to track a book's title, author, ISBN, subject, and a personal rating. The constructor can be defined as follows:

```
function book(title, author, ISBN, subject, rating)
{
  this.title = title;
  this.author = author;
  this.ISBN = ISBN;
  this.subject = subject;
  this.rating = rating;
}
```

Also, I want to add a method called show(), which displays the information on the instantiated object to the user. Therefore, I need to create a function, separate from the constructor itself, to do this:

```
function show()
{
  objWindow = window.open("", "", "width=600,height=300");
  objWindow.document.write("<html><body>");
  objWindow.document.write("<h1>Object Description<\/h1>");
  objWindow.document.write("Book Title: " + this.title + "<br \/>");
  objWindow.document.write("Author: " + this.author + "<br \/>");
  objWindow.document.write("ISBN: " + this.ISBN + "<br \/>");
  objWindow.document.write("Subject: " + this.subject + "<br \/>");
  objWindow.document.write("Allen's Rating: " + this.rating + "<br \/>");
  objWindow.document.write("<\/body><\/html>");
  objWindow.document.close();
}
```

Even though this code is outside of the constructor, you can consider it a part of the object declaration. Therefore, you can use the this keyword and have it refer to the object instance that is being called.

I can then add a new entry to my constructor for the method:

```
function book(title, author, ISBN, subject, rating)
{
  this.title = title;
  this.author = author;
  this.ISBN = ISBN;
  this.subject = subject;
  this.rating = rating;
  this.show = show; // New method to display
}
```

Notice two details about the show() method declaration. First, although the object method name is the same as the associated external function, it doesn't have to be. You can name each object method anything you like. For readability, some developers prefer to use identical names, and others prefix the external function with the object name, such as book_show(). Second, the external function doesn't include parentheses in the constructor, only the function name itself.

I find it helpful to place any method definitions immediately under the object constructor to make the code easier to follow. I also use comments to keep the set of functions together and treated as a unit. The final complete object declaration for the Book object would look like the following:

```html
<script type="text/javascript">
  function book(title, author, ISBN, subject, rating)
  {
    this.title = title;
    this.author = author;
    this.ISBN = ISBN;
    this.subject = subject;
    this.rating = rating;
    this.show = show;
  }

  function show()
  {
    objWindow = window.open("", "", "width=600,height=300");
    objWindow.document.write("<html><body>");
    objWindow.document.write("<h1>Object Description<\/h1>");
    objWindow.document.write("Book Title: " + this.title + "<br \/>");
    objWindow.document.write("Author: " + this.author + "<br \/>");
    objWindow.document.write("ISBN: " + this.ISBN + "<br \/>");
    objWindow.document.write("Subject: " + this.subject + "<br \/>");
    objWindow.document.write("Allen's Rating: " + this.rating + "<br \/>");
    objWindow.document.write("<\/body><\/html>");
    objWindow.document.close();
  }
</script>
```

Instantiating Objects

To use the object I have declared in the book() constructor method, I need to create an instance of it in my JavaScript code. The new operator is used for this purpose. It has the following syntax:

```
objectInstance = new objectType(parameter1, parameter2, parameter3,...)
```

Using the new operator, I create a Book object using the following code:

```
dbBook = new book("Cost of Discipleship", "Dietrich Bonhoeffer",
➥"1-57521-118-1", "Grace", 5);
```

I can now refer to this object anywhere in my code using the dbBook variable. The instance will exist in memory as long as the page is loaded in my browser. After the user moves to a new page or closes the browser, the instance of the object disappears. This is important to understand when you start assigning values to object properties. If you want persistent objects, you will need to pass them to the server for processing.

> **NOTE**
>
> Persistence is a buzzword of the object community. In a nutshell, it means the capability to create an object instance and save the state of the object, so that the next time the object is accessed, it is retrieved in its saved state.
>
> You can't store objects persistently using client-side JavaScript.

To demonstrate what has been developed so far, Listing 14.1 has all the code necessary to create an instance of the Book object and call its show() method. Figure 14.1 shows the result of loading this page in a browser.

LISTING 14.1   Using the Book Object Constructor

```html
<html>
<head>
  <title>Using the book object</title>
  <script type="text/javascript">
  function book(title, author, ISBN, subject, rating)
  {
    this.title = title;
    this.author = author;
    this.ISBN = ISBN;
    this.subject = subject;
    this.rating = rating;
    this.show = show;
  }

  function show()
  {
    objWindow = window.open("", "", "width=600,height=300");
    objWindow.document.write("<html><body>");
    objWindow.document.write("<h1>Object Description<\/h1>");
    objWindow.document.write("Book Title: " + this.title + "<br \/>");
```

14

LISTING 14.1   Continued

```
    objWindow.document.write("Author: " + this.author + "<br \/>");
    objWindow.document.write("ISBN: " + this.ISBN + "<br \/>");
    objWindow.document.write("Subject: " + this.subject + "<br \/>");
    objWindow.document.write("Allen's Rating: " + this.rating + "<br \/>");
    objWindow.document.write("<\/body><\/html>");
    objWindow.document.close();
  } </script>
</head>
<body>
  <script type="text/javascript">    // Book object defined here
    dbBook = new book("Cost of Discipleship", "Dietrich Bonhoeffer",
➡        "1-57521-118-1",  "Grace", 5);
    dbBook.show(); </script>
</body>
</html>
```

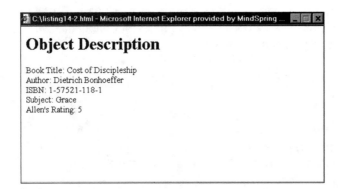

FIGURE 14.1   Book object information is displayed in a new window.

Working with Object Instances

After an object instance is created, you can work with it by assigning values to it or by performing one of its methods. You can also connect objects to user interface elements.

For example, suppose you want to create a form that will let you change the rating for books, as well as display the book information form for each of the Book objects you have instantiated. You can define the Book object as shown earlier and create five instances using the following code:

```
dbBook = new book("Cost of Discipleship", "Dietrich Bonhoeffer",
➡    "1-57521-118-1","Grace", 5);
```

```
fkBook = new book("The Once and Future King", "T.H. White", "1-57521-112-1",
➡  "Camelot", 5);
olBook = new book("On Liberty", "John Stuart Mill", "1-53221-118-1",
➡  "Political Philosophy", 4);
iaBook = new book("Icarus Agenda", "Robert Ludlum", "1-53221-118-1",
➡  "Political Thriller", 2);
cnBook = new book("Chronicles of Narnia", "C.S. Lewis", "1-53231-128-1",
➡  "Children's Fiction", 5);
```

For the form element defined for each of the books, as well as one for the rating (a range of 1 to 5). Add two buttons—one for the rating assignment and another for displaying the book information form. The form code looks like the following (and the result is shown in Figure 14.2):

```html
<html>
<body>
  <h1>Book Objects</h1>
  <form name="form1">
    <h2>Select a book:</h2>       <select name="bookList" size="1">
        <option value="dbBook">Cost of Discipleship</option>
        <option value="fkBook">The Once and Future King</option>
        <option value="olBook">On Liberty</option>
        <option value="iaBook">Icarus Agenda</option>
        <option value="cnBook">Chronicles of Narnia</option>
    </select>       <h2>
    Assign a rating:</h2>
    <select name="rating" size="1">
      <option>1</option>
      <option>2</option>
      <option>3</option>
      <option>4</option>
      <option>5</option>
    </select>
  <h2>Click to assign:</h2>
    <input type="button" name="Assign" value="Assign" onClick="assignRating()">
  <h2>Click to show:</h2>
    <input type="button" name="Show" value="Show" onClick="showBook()">
  </form>
</body>
</html>
```

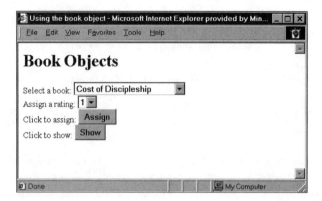

FIGURE 14.2   The Book object form.

The heart of this example will be in the event handlers for the Assign and Show buttons. The assignRating() method assigns the value of the selected rating to the selected book:

```
function assignRating()
{
  selectedBook = document.form1.bookList.options[document.form1.bookList.
       selectedIndex].value;
  selectedBook = eval(selectedBook);
  selectedBook.rating = document.form1.rating.options[document.form1.
       rating.selectedIndex].text;
}
```

Looking at this more closely, you can see that the method retrieves the value of the selected bookList option and assigns it to the selectedBook variable. To get this value, I use the bookList object's options property, along with its selectedIndex property. I now have the name of the Book object contained in the selectedBook variable, but JavaScript looks at this as a string value, not as a reference to an object instance. Therefore, the eval() method is used to convert the variable to an object reference.

The last line of the method uses the selectedBook variable to assign its rating property the value of the currently selected option in the rating Select object.

> **NOTE**
>
> You can use the typeof operator to test a variable's type during a method's execution. For example, you could display an alert message box showing the selectedBook variable's type, using the following code:
>
> ```
> alert(typeof selectedBook);
> ```

The showBook() method uses the same techniques to call the object's show() method:

```
function showBook()
{
  selectedBook = document.form1.bookList.options[document.form1.bookList.
        selectedIndex].value;
  selectedBook = eval(selectedBook);
  selectedBook.show();
}
```

Listing 14.2 gives the entire source code for this example.

LISTING 14.2   Source Code for the showBook() Example

```
<html>
<head>
  <title>Using the book object</title>
  <script type="text/javascript">
  function book(title, author, ISBN, subject, rating)
  {
    this.title = title;
    this.author = author;
    this.ISBN = ISBN;
    this.subject = subject;
    this.rating = rating;
    this.show = show;
  }

  function show()
  {
    objWindow = window.open("", "", "width=600,height=300");
    objWindow.document.write("<html><body>");
    objWindow.document.write("<h1>Object Description<\/h1>");
    objWindow.document.write("Book Title: " + this.title + "<br \/>");
    objWindow.document.write("Author: " + this.author + "<br \/>");
    objWindow.document.write("ISBN: " + this.ISBN + "<br \/>");
    objWindow.document.write("Subject: " + this.subject + "<br \/>");
    objWindow.document.write("Allen's Rating: " + this.rating + "<br \/>");
    objWindow.document.write("<\/body><\/html>");
    objWindow.document.close();
  }

  function assignRating()
  {
```

14

LISTING 14.2   Continued

```
    selectedBook = document.form1.bookList.options[document.form1.bookList.
        selectedIndex].value;
    selectedBook = eval(selectedBook);
    selectedBook.rating = document.form1.rating.options[document.form1.
        rating.selectedIndex].text;
  }

  function showBook()
  {
    selectedBook = document.form1.bookList.options[document.form1.bookList.
        selectedIndex].value;
    selectedBook = eval(selectedBook);
    selectedBook.show();
  }

  // Execute on loading
  dbBook = new book("Cost of Discipleship", "Dietrich Bonhoeffer",
      "1-57521-118-1", "Grace", 5);
  fkBook = new book("The Once and Future King", "T.H. White",
      "1-57521-112-1", "Camelot", 5);
  olBook = new book("On Liberty", "John Stuart Mill",
      "1-53221-118-1", "Political Philosophy", 4);
  iaBook = new book("Icarus Agenda", "Robert Ludlum",
      "1-53221-118-1", "Political Thriller", 3);
  cnBook = new book("Chronicles of Narnia", "C.S. Lewis",
      "1-53231-128-1", "Children's Fiction", 5);
  </script>
</head>
<body>
  <h1>Book Objects</h1>
  <form name="form1">
    Select a book:
      <select name="bookList" size="1">
        <option value="dbBook">Cost of Discipleship</option>
        <option value="fkBook">The Once and Future King</option>
        <option value="olBook">On Liberty</option>
        <option value="iaBook">Icarus Agenda</option>
        <option value="cnBook">Chronicles of Narnia</option>
      </select>
    <br />Assign a rating:
      <select name="rating" size="1">
```

LISTING 14.2 Continued

```
        <option>1</option>
        <option>2</option>
        <option>3</option>
        <option>4</option>
        <option>5</option>
      </select>
    <br />Click to assign:
      <input type="button" name="Assign"
➥value="Assign" onClick="assignRating()">
    <br />Click to show:
      <input type="button" name="Show" value="Show" onClick="showBook()">
  </form>
</body>
</html>
```

Creating Complex Objects

The objects covered so far have been **simple objects**, those with a single level of properties and methods. JavaScript also supports **complex objects**, with which an object's property can itself be an object. Complex objects let you structure your code in a more logical manner rather than being forced to dump all data into a single-level object.

Suppose you would like to track information on employees, their current projects, and their related clients. Obviously a client address really shouldn't be part of an employee object definition, so JavaScript's complex objects let you structure the data around three separate but related entities: employee, project, and client.

In the `employee` constructor, define the basic properties (name, phone, and email address) and a method called `showSummaryInfo()`. However, for project information, define a `project` property in the `employee` object. You would define this in much the same way you would a normal property, except that the `project` parameter is actually a reference to another object rather than a string value:

```
function employee(FirstName, LastName, HomePhone, Ext, EmailAddress, project)
{
  this.FirstName = FirstName;
  this.LastName = LastName;
  this.HomePhone = HomePhone;
  this.Ext = Ext;
  this.EmailAddress = EmailAddress;
  this.Project = project;
  this.showSummaryInfo = summaryInfo;
}
```

Define the `project` object in a similar manner, using the `client` object as a property:

```
function project(ProjectName, client, DevTool)
{
  this.ProjectName = ProjectName;
  this.Client = client;
  this.DevTool = DevTool;
}

function client(ClientName, Address, City, State, Zip)
{
  this.ClientName = ClientName;
  this.Address = Address;
  this.City = City;
  this.State = State;
  this.Zip = Zip;
}
```

To show how these nested objects can be referenced, define the `showSummaryInfo()` method of the `employee` object. This method opens a new window to display an employee summary information sheet—essentially a listing of all the properties for the `employee` object and the objects contained within it.

```
function summaryInfo()
{
  objWindow = window.open("", "", "width=600,height=400");
  objWindow.document.write("<html><body>");
  objWindow.document.write("<h1>Employee Summary Information Sheet<\/h1>");
  objWindow.document.write("<h2>" + this.FirstName);
  objWindow.document.write(" " + this.LastName + "<\/h2>");

  objWindow.document.write("<h3>Contact Information<\/h3>");
  objWindow.document.write("Home Phone: " + this.HomePhone + "<br \/>");
  objWindow.document.write("Ext.: " + this.Ext + "<br \/>");
  objWindow.document.write("Email: " + this.EmailAddress + "<br \/>");

  objWindow.document.write("<h3>Project Information<\/h3>");
  objWindow.document.write("Current Project: ");
  objWindow.document.write(this.Project.ProjectName + "<br \/>");
  objWindow.document.write("Client: ");
  objWindow.document.write(this.Project.Client.ClientName + "<br \/>");
  objWindow.document.write("Client: ");
  objWindow.document.write(this.Project.Client.Address + "<br \/>");
  objWindow.document.write("Client: ");
  objWindow.document.write(this.Project.Client.City + ", ");
```

```
    objWindow.document.write(this.Project.Client.State + " ");
    objWindow.document.write(this.Project.Client.Zip + "<br \/>");
    objWindow.document.write("Development Tool Used: ");
    objWindow.document.write(this.Project.DevTool + "<br \/>");
    objWindow.document.write("<\/body><\/html>");
    objWindow.document.close();
}
```

Child objects are referenced using familiar dot notation, so that the client's address is referenced with `this.Project.Client.Address`. The dot notation makes it easy to follow the code, because it specifies the path to the actual method or property being used. You can follow the parent object (before the first dot) down through the child objects, until you hit the final method or property.

Now that the constructors are defined for each of these object types, you can instantiate sample `employee`, `project`, and `client` objects:

```
CoastTech = new client("Coastal Technology", "100 Beacon Hill",
                       "Boston", "MA", "01220");
Coastal = new project("Coastal01", CoastTech, "JavaScript");
Allen = new employee("Allen", "Wyke", "617/555-1212", "100",
                     "allen@anywhere.com", "Coastal");
```

The `project` parameter in the employee definition and the `client` parameter in the project definition are not strings; they are the names of the newly created objects. Also, notice the order in which these objects are created. Because the `Allen` object uses the `Coastal` project object as a parameter, `Coastal` must be instantiated first, or you will get an error. The same principle applies to creating the `CoastTech` instance of the `client` object before creating the `Coastal` project.

After the object instances are created, call `Allen.showSummaryInfo()` to display the window shown in Figure 14.3.

Listing 14.3 provides the entire source code for this example.

LISTING 14.3   Complete Example of Using the employee, client, and project Objects

```
<html>
<head>
  <title>Using the book object</title>
  <script type="text/javascript">

  function employee(FirstName, LastName, HomePhone, Ext, EmailAddress, project)
  {
    this.FirstName = FirstName;
    this.LastName = LastName;
    this.HomePhone = HomePhone;
```

LISTING 14.3   Continued

```
  this.Ext = Ext;
  this.EmailAddress = EmailAddress;
  this.Project = project;
  this.showSummaryInfo = summaryInfo;
}

function summaryInfo()
{
  objWindow = window.open("", "", "width=600,height=400");
  objWindow.document.write("<html><body>");
  objWindow.document.write("<h1>Employee Summary Information Sheet<\/h1>");
  objWindow.document.write("<h2>" + this.FirstName);
  objWindow.document.write(" " + this.LastName + "<\/h2>");

  objWindow.document.write("<h3>Contact Information<\/h3>");
  objWindow.document.write("Home Phone: " + this.HomePhone + "<br \/>");
  objWindow.document.write("Ext.: " + this.Ext + "<br \/>");
  objWindow.document.write("Email: " + this.EmailAddress + "<br \/>");

  objWindow.document.write("<h3>Project Information<\/h3>");
  objWindow.document.write("Current Project: ");
  objWindow.document.write(this.Project.ProjectName + "<br \/>");
  objWindow.document.write("Client: ");
  objWindow.document.write(this.Project.Client.ClientName + "<br \/>");
  objWindow.document.write("Client: ");
  objWindow.document.write(this.Project.Client.Address + "<br \/>");
  objWindow.document.write("Client: ");
  objWindow.document.write(this.Project.Client.City + ", ");
  objWindow.document.write(this.Project.Client.State + " ");
  objWindow.document.write(this.Project.Client.Zip + "<br \/>");
  objWindow.document.write("Developmnt Tool Used: ");
  objWindow.document.write(this.Project.DevTool + "<br \/>");
  objWindow.document.write("<\/body><\/html>");
  objWindow.document.close();
}

function project(ProjectName, client, DevTool)
{
  this.ProjectName = ProjectName;
  this.Client = client;
  this.DevTool = DevTool;
```

LISTING 14.3   Continued

```
  }

  function client(ClientName, Address, City, State, Zip)
  {
    this.ClientName = ClientName;
    this.Address = Address;
    this.City = City;
    this.State = State;
    this.Zip = Zip;
  }

  </script>
</head>
<body>
  <script type="text/javascript">
  CoastTech = new client("Coastal Technology", "100 Beacon Hill",
                    "Boston", "MA", "01220");
  Coastal = new project("Coastal01", CoastTech, "JavaScript");
  Allen = new employee("Allen", "Wyke", "617/555-1212", "100",
                    "allen@anywhere.com", Coastal);
  Allen.showSummaryInfo();
  </script>
</body>
</html>
```

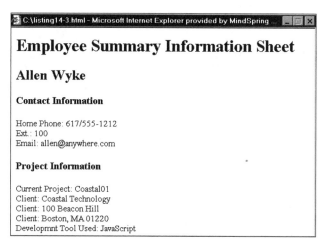

FIGURE 14.3   The employee summary information sheet.

Creating Objects Dynamically

The capability to create objects in code gives the JavaScript developer power and flexibility, but all the examples I've shown so far have dealt with objects being created as the window loads using the new operator. You might be wondering what capability you have to dynamically create objects at runtime. After all, with other object-oriented programming environments, you can create object instances on-the-fly.

JavaScript allows you to create object instances on-the-fly, but with certain definite limitations. Initially, my plan was to create a generic instantiation function that created an object instance each time it was called. If this were successful, you could avoid using new statements that have already been defined and create objects based on input from the user. The idea was that the method would look like this:

```
function addEmployee(ObjectName,FirstName, LastName)
{
  ObjectName = new employee(FirstName, LastName);
}
```

Ideally, this method would instantiate an object and give the object's name based on the ObjectName parameter. Unfortunately, no matter what was tried, JavaScript wouldn't allow the name of the object instance to be a variable. Instead, it used ObjectName as the name of the object. In contrast, the following is valid as long as Frank has already been defined as the object reference:

```
function addFrank(FirstName, LastName)
{
  Frank = new employee(FirstName, LastName);
}
```

Although you can't dynamically name an object being instantiated, you can create an object as an element of a container array. You could, therefore, have an employeeList array that stores each employee object that is created. Therefore, if you modify the addEmployee() method, you could use the following:

```
function addEmployeeObject(FirstName, LastName, HomePhone, Ext, EmailAddress)
{
  empList[i] = new employee(FirstName, LastName, HomePhone, Ext, EmailAddress);
}
```

Using this method, you can actually create object instances based on user input and dynamically create the object by calling the addEmployeeObject() method. For example, the form shown in Figure 14.4 allows a user to enter basic employee information. When the user clicks the Add button, a new object instance is created. Listing 14.4 shows the source code for this sample form.

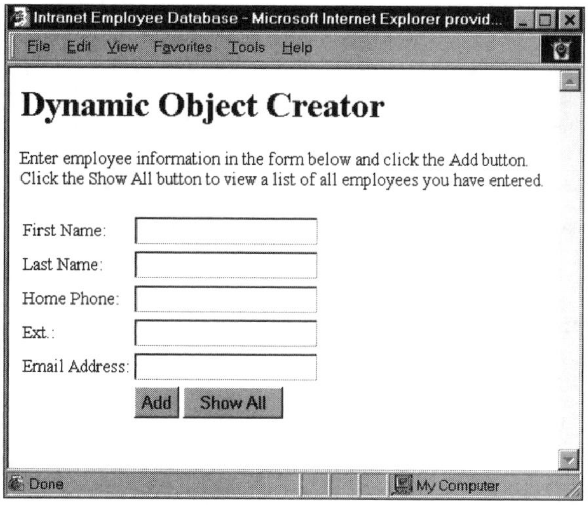

FIGURE 14.4   Dynamic object creation.

LISTING 14.4   Creating Objects Dynamically

```html
<html>
<head>
  <title>Intranet Employee Database</title>
  <script type="text/javascript">

    // Global variables
    var i = 0;

    // Create Array objects
    var empList = new Array();

    // Employee object constructor
    function employee(FirstName, LastName, HomePhone, Ext,  EmailAddress)
    {
      this.FirstName = FirstName;
      this.LastName = LastName;
      this.HomePhone = HomePhone;
      this.Ext = Ext;
      this.EmailAddress = EmailAddress;
      this.show = show;
    }


    function show()
```

LISTING 14.4   Continued

```
{
  alert(this.FirstName + "/n" +
        this.LastName + "/n" +
        this.HomePhone + "/n" +
        this.Ext + "/n" +
        this.EmailAddress);
}

function addEmployeeObject(FirstName, LastName, HomePhone,
                          Ext, EmailAddress)
{
  empList[i] = new employee(FirstName, LastName, HomePhone, Ext,
      EmailAddress);
}

function insertRecord()
{
  FirstName = document.form1.FirstName.value;
  LastName = document.form1.LastName.value;
  HomePhone = document.form1.HomePhone.value;
  Ext = document.form1.Ext.value;
  EmailAddress = document.form1.EmailAddress.value;
  i++;
  addEmployeeObject(FirstName, LastName, HomePhone, Ext, EmailAddress);

  //Clear fields
  document.form1.FirstName.value = "";
  document.form1.LastName.value = "";
  document.form1.HomePhone.value = "";
  document.form1.Ext.value = "";
  document.form1.EmailAddress.value = "";
}

function showAll()
{
  objWindow = window.open("", "", "width=600,height=300,scrollbars=yes");
  objWindow.document.write("<html><body>");
  objWindow.document.write("<h1>Object Description<\/h1>");
  for (var q=1; q<empList.length; q++)
  {
    objWindow.document.write("<h3>" + empList[q].FirstName + " ");
```

LISTING 14.4　Continued

```
            objWindow.document.write(empList[q].LastName + "<\/h3>");
            objWindow.document.write(empList[q].HomePhone + "<br \/>");
            objWindow.document.write(empList[q].Ext + "<br \/>");
            objWindow.document.write(empList[q].EmailAddress + "<br \/>");
            objWindow.document.write("<\/body><\/html>");
        }
        objWindow.document.close();
    }
  </script>
</head>
<body>
  <h1>Dynamic Object Creator</h1>
  <p>Enter employee information in the form below and click the Add button.
  Click the Show All button to view a list of all employees you have
  entered.</p>
  <form name="form1">
    <table>
      <tr>
        <td>First Name:</td>
        <td><input type="text" size="20" maxlength="256" name="FirstName"></td>
      </tr>
      <tr>
        <td>Last Name:</td>
        <td><input type="text" size="20" maxlength="256" name="LastName"></td>
      </tr>
      <tr>
        <td>Home Phone:</td>
        <td><input type="text" size="20" maxlength="256" name="HomePhone"></td>
      </tr>
      <tr>
        <td>Ext.:</td>
        <td><input type="text" size="20" maxlength="256" name="Ext"></td>
      </tr>
      <tr>
        <td>Email Address:</td>
        <td><input type="text" size="20" maxlength="256"
➥name="EmailAddress"></td>
      </tr>
      <tr>
        <td></td><td><input type="button" name="Add" value="Add"
                onClick="insertRecord()">
```

LISTING 14.4   Continued

```
            <input type="button" name="ShowAll" value="Show All"
                onClick="showAll()"></td>
      </tr>
    </table>
  </form>
</body>
</html>
```

The Show All button lets you see all the objects that have been created during that session. Figure 14.5 shows a list of employee objects that have been instantiated.

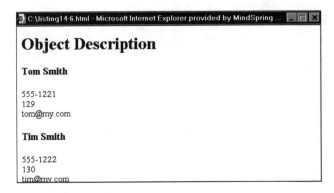

FIGURE 14.5   A list of objects created dynamically.

Extending Instantiated Objects

Just as JavaScript is a loosely typed language in terms of data types, it's also flexible in terms of object definitions. You can extend the definition of any object instance by declaring the new property and assigning it a value. Using the Book object example from earlier in this chapter, suppose you wanted to add a Series property to the cnBook object after it has been defined. As you recall, it is defined as follows:

```
cnBook = new book("Chronicles of Narnia", "C.S. Lewis",
➥   "1-53231-128-1", "Children's Fiction", 5);
```

JavaScript lets you extend objects you already created using an object prototype. Its syntax is as follows:

```
objectType.prototype.propertyName;
```

An object prototype lets you add a property or method to each instance of an object type. Therefore, if you wanted to add a new `recommend` property to each `Book` object and it had the value of `true`, you could use the following line:

```
book.prototype.recommend = true;
```

Listing 14.5 demonstrates how to prototype a new book property called `recommend`. This property is then available in the `dbBook` object instance. Based on the value of the `recommend` property, an alert box is displayed to recommend the book to the user, as shown in Figure 14.6.

LISTING 14.5   Adding a Property to an Object Using a Prototype

```
<html>
<head>
  <title>Using the book object</title>
  <script type="text/javascript">
  function book(title, author, ISBN, subject, rating)
  {
    this.title = title;
    this.author = author;
    this.ISBN = ISBN;
    this.subject = subject;
    this.rating = rating;
    this.show = show;
  }

  function show()
  {
    objWindow = window.open("", "", "width=600,height=300");
    objWindow.document.write("<html><body>");
    objWindow.document.write("<h1>Object Description<\/h1>");
    objWindow.document.write("Book Title: " + this.title + "<br \/>");
    objWindow.document.write("Author: " + this.author + "<br \/>");
    objWindow.document.write("ISBN: " + this.ISBN + "<br \/>");
    objWindow.document.write("Subject: " + this.subject + "<br \/>");
    objWindow.document.write("Allen's Rating: " + this.rating + "<br \/>");
    objWindow.document.write("<\/body><\/html>");
    objWindow.document.close();
  } </script>
</head>
<body>
  <script type="text/javascript">    // Book object defined here
    book.prototype.recommend = true; // Add a new attribute to book
```

14

LISTING 14.5   Continued

```
    dbBook = new book("Cost of Discipleship", "Dietrich Bonhoeffer",
                        "1-57521-118-1",  "Grace", 5);

    // If this book is recommended then let the user know
    if(dbBook.recommend)
    {
      alert("I recommend this book.");
    }

    dbBook.show();
  </script>
</body>
</html>
```

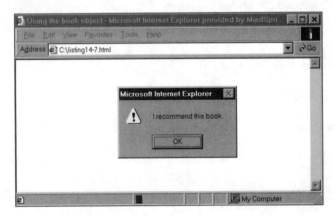

FIGURE 14.6   Displaying an alert based on a prototyped property.

Summary

JavaScript supports the capability to create custom objects in your client-side scripts. This adds a great deal of power and flexibility to JavaScript and allows you to structure your code in an object-based manner.

In this chapter, you learned all about the various aspects of creating and instantiating object types. You also learned about how to extend the power of normal objects by creating complex objects, which can also be referred to as "objects within objects." You can use complex objects to encapsulate data that spans multiple levels, much in the same way a relational database does with one-to-many table relationships. Finally, you learned how to extend objects that have already been instantiated by using the prototype operator.

PART IV

DOM Objects

IN THIS PART

CHAPTER **15**

Fundamentals of the Document Object Model

The next few chapters of this book are going to be devoted to learning about the Document Object Model, which is often referred to as the DOM. This chapter will begin by examining the evolution of the DOM from Netscape layers to Internet Explorer's DHTML. After the review of the history, the chapter will then begin to introduce you to the DOM and its relationship to JavaScript.

Understanding the Document Object Model

When HTML was introduced, its purpose was to be a markup language for documents. This markup would allow standard formatting (such as bold and italics) that could be presented on various platforms. HTML pages were basically static. The only dynamic aspect was the ability to jump, via links, to other HTML documents or to other locations within the same document.

With the addition of JavaScript, HTML documents took on a bit more life. With this addition, HTML documents could do more than just present markup data; they could manipulate form data and even generate new HTML documents. This was a big improvement, but an entire document had to be reloaded if any aspect of the HTML document needed to change. What was lacking was a way to display, move, and hide HTML content without having to load an entirely new HTML page. Netscape's solution to this problem was the <layer> and <ilayer> tags, which were introduced in Navigator 4.

Netscape Layers

Netscape layers could contain most any kind of HTML content. By using JavaScript layers, HTML content could be positioned, moved, and hidden within the browser without ever having to load a new page. This was an exciting step forward, and developers quickly started dreaming of ways to present dynamic pages with changing content without ever needing to pull new content from the server. This was especially important given that it took much longer to pull pages than it does today.

Netscape layers were defined by placing HTML content between the <layer> and </layer> tags or the <ilayer> and </ilayer> tags. The <layer> tags used absolute positioning, which allowed the position within the HTML document to be specified. On the other hand, the <ilayer> tags used relative positioning, which allowed layers to appear in their natural location in the flow of the HTML content. A simple layer would have looked like the following:

```
<layer name="myLayer" width="300" height="200" bgcolor="red"
       top="150" left="100" visibility="show">
  This is a Netscape Layer!
</layer>
```

In the preceding code snippet, a layer would be created that was 300 pixels wide by 200 pixels high. It would be positioned 150 pixels from the top of the document and 100 pixels from the left of the document. The layer would have a red background with the text "This is a Netscape Layer!" displayed inside.

Access to the layer tag was provided to JavaScript by way of the layers array of the document object. Netscape required a name attribute to be specified in the <layer> and <ilayer> tags in order for the layer to be accessed by JavaScript. After the attributes of the layer tag were accessed, they could then be dynamically altered, thus providing the ability for layers to be moved, hidden, and displayed on the fly. For example, the layer defined earlier could be repositioned slightly to the right within the document using the following line of JavaScript:

```
document.layers["myLayer"].left="200";
```

Although layers were useful, they left Web developers wanting more functionality. After all, HTML content still could not be altered on the fly. What was really needed was a way to get to the actual HTML content that existed within the browser via JavaScript. Microsoft provided this with Dynamic HTML.

IE Dynamic HTML

In response to Netscape's layers, Microsoft introduced Dynamic HTML, also called DHTML, into its IE browsers. To counter Netscape's <layer> and <ilayer> tags, IE provided the <div> tag. Like the <layer> and <ilayer> tags, HTML content could be placed within the <div> and </div> tags. But unlike the <layer> and <ilayer> tags, the <div> tag used the standardized id attribute that was available for all HTML tags to identify <div> tags. A simple div might look like the following:

```
<div id="myDiv" width="300" height="200" background-color="red"
     position="absolute" top="150" left="100" visibility="visible">
  This is an IE Div!
</div>
```

When it came time to access <div> tags using JScript, IE provided access through the all collection of the document object. The code to adjust the height of the div would look like this:

```
document.all["myDiv"].height="400";
```

The IE solution was much broader than that provided by Netscape because the all collection could be used to access the majority of the HTML tags that were in a document by way of the id attribute of each tag. Each HTML tag had different properties, methods, and events, some of which could be manipulated and some could not. But even this solution didn't provide a way to dynamically add, remove, or generally manipulate the HTML structure on the client side (browser). To be able to do this would require some type of structured representation of a Web page, which is what the DOM provides.

The DOM

The DOM, or Document Object Model, is a way of modeling HTML documents in a very logical fashion. The DOM also defines ways to access, navigate, and manipulate HTML documents within the confines of the model. The DOM gives you full control by allowing you to access and modify the content, structure, and style of a document.

Unlike the DHTML, which only provided access to individual HTML tags, the document object model is much more general in that it provides a model for the whole document. The Document Object Model represents a document as a tree. The tree structure completely describes the entire HTML document by representing every HTML tag and textual entry inside a tag as a node in the tree. Because it is a tree structure, there is a child-parent-sibling relationship that allows you to navigate through the entire tree and thus the entire HTML document.

Another difference between the DOM and DHTML is that the DOM makes it truly possible for Web pages to be dynamic. After all, DHTML was really nothing more than a means of changing object attributes. With the DOM you can manipulate the document tree in any way you need by creating new nodes, deleting existing nodes, and moving nodes around the tree. This is equivalent to adding new tags, deleting existing tags, and moving existing tags around. In addition to tags, you can update every textual entry as well.

DOM Browsers

The DOM is a product of the World Wide Web Consortium (W3C). When Netscape rewrote the core of its browser for Navigator 6, the basis was none other than the DOM. At this point the `<layer>` and `<ilayer>` tags and associated JavaScript layers array were completely dropped as there was no longer a need for them. It wasn't long before IE also came into compliance with the DOM starting with its IE 5 browser. There was a period of time during the infancy of DOM support when cross-browser code and browser sniffing were necessary. But those days are fading fast, so with newer browsers you can be confident that the DOM will be supported.

The Document Object Model Specification

There's really not a lot to the DOM. It merely defines a logical and standardized document structure. This lets you build, edit, and browse elements and content in XHTML or XML documents. The DOM structure is nothing more than an object hierarchy that is comparable to that of JavaScript or any other object-based language. The difference is that DOM has a useful API that is language-neutral and defines a standard set of interfaces. That's not to say that all DOM applications will be based on the same objects; they might define their own interfaces and objects. This might be the case if you renovate an application so that it can become DOM-compliant, for example.

There are two DOM specifications: Level 1 and Level 2. Level 2 is the more recent specification. The information contained in the specification is not pitched directly at JavaScript or other ECMA-compliant scripting languages. To provide a bridge between the DOM specification and JavaScript, a special ECMAScript language binding specification was created. This language binding defines an API to the DOM through JavaScript. There are also a number of DOM tutorials on the Web, and numerous articles and papers to accompany them.

> **NOTE**
>
> You can obtain the W3C Document Object Model (DOM) Level 2 specification from `http://www.w3.org/TR/1999/CR-DOM-Level-2-19991210`. The earlier Level 1 specification can also be obtained from this site.

Structure of the DOM

As mentioned earlier, the real power of the DOM is its tree-like structure. If you have taken any classes on data structures and algorithms, you are probably already familiar with the concept of trees. If you are not familiar with representing relationships with trees, don't worry. We will look at a simple tree structure and learn what it means to navigate and modify tree structures.

Tree Structure

A tree structure is very much like the object for which it was named, a tree. Think of the trunk of a tree as the base and the limbs as nodes. In the case of the DOM tree, there is a node for every tag and for every textual entry.

So what would the tree structure of a simple XHTML page look like? The code in Listing 15.1 creates a very simple page that contains a title and a paragraph.

LISTING 15.1   Simple DOM Structure

```
<html>
<head>
  <title>Simple DOM Structure</title>
</head>
<body id="theBody">
  <p>This is a simple DOM example</p>
</body>
</html>
```

Figure 15.1 shows what the DOM tree structure would look like. Notice that the `<html>` tag has two children, which are the `<head>` tag and the `<body>` tag. The `<head>` tag and `<body>` tag are siblings and their parent is, of course, the `<html>` tag. The `<title>` tag is the child of the `<head>` tag, and the `<p>` tag is a child of the `<body>` tag. Finally, the `<title>` tag has a child node that is simply the text contained within the `<title>` and `</title>` tags. Likewise, the `<p>` tag has a child node that is simply the text contained within the `<p>` and `</p>` tags.

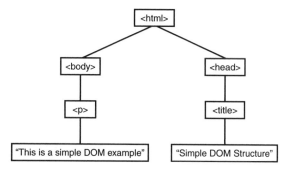

FIGURE 15.1   The DOM tree structure of a simple Web page.

Navigating Documents

The key to navigating documents is the parent-child-sibling relationship. This relationship makes it possible to move through any tree structure. The parent and child relationship makes moving up and down a tree possible, whereas the sibling relationship allows movement from side to side. You can only start "climbing" the tree from those nodes that have been assigned the id attribute. However, because the tree can be navigated, every node of the tree can be reached.

So looking back at Listing 15.1, if you wanted to reach the text in the paragraph <p> tag, you would start at the <body> tag because it can be accessed via its id tag. From the <body> tag, you traverse to its children, which is simply the <p> tag in this case. From the <p> tag, you would transverse to its children, which is the actual text in the paragraph.

If you wanted to reach the text in the title, you would once again start at the <body> tag. From the <body> tag you would look for its sibling, the <head> tag. After the <head> tag is found, it could be traversed to get to its children, which is simply the <title> tag in this case. From the <title> tag, you would traverse to its children, which is the actual title text.

To actually navigate the Document Object Model using JavaScript requires the objects defined in the ECMAScript Binding. These objects have methods that actually perform the navigation described in the preceding two paragraphs. For details on how to actually navigate the DOM using JavaScript, see Chapter 16, "Accessing the DOM."

Manipulating Documents

Now that you have a feel for how you might navigate a tree structure, let's talk about manipulating a tree structure. There are a number of aspects of the DOM that can be manipulated. First, many of the XHTML tags have attributes. It is possible to change these attributes by accessing the corresponding node in the tree and changing the value of the attribute.

The other way to manipulate the DOM is to change the layout of an XHTML document by deleting existing nodes as well as adding new nodes to the tree. For example, we could dynamically change the text in the <title> tag of Listing 15.1 to say "Simple Document Object Model Structure." Or we could delete the existing paragraph tag and its contents. Then we could add an XHTML table as a child of the <body> tag. The end result would be an XHTML document that resembles the code shown in Listing 15.2.

LISTING 15.2   Result of Manipulating an XHTML Document

```
<html>
<head>
  <title>Simple Document Object Model Structure</title>
</head>
<body id="theBody">
  <table>
    <tr><th>Name</th><th>Age</th></tr>
    <tr><td>Paul</td><td>32</td></tr>
```

LISTING 15.2   Continued

```
  </table>
</body>
</html>
```

Of course, to actually manipulate the Document Object Model using JavaScript requires the objects defined in the ECMAScript Binding. These objects have methods that actually provide the needed functionality to perform the changes to the tree structure described in the previous paragraph. For details on how to actually manipulate a document using JavaScript, see Chapter 17, "Manipulating the DOM."

Summary

This chapter introduced you to the Document Object Model, which is commonly referred to as the DOM. The chapter started with a bit of a history lesson on the evolution of the DOM. The first attempt at dynamic content was Netscape's <layer> and <ilayer> tags. Microsoft quickly countered using the <div> tag and its own DHTML model. Neither of these solutions quite met the needs of the Web development community. But, thanks to the World Wide Web Consortium (W3C), we now have the DOM and the ECMAScript Bindings. These standards have been adopted by both Netscape and IE, thus making them a viable solution.

The DOM defines XHTML documents as trees. Thanks to the ECMAScript Bindings, it is possible to traverse the tree and manipulate its contents using JavaScript. The end result is the ability to change a physical XHTML document on the client side.

In the next few chapters you will learn about the objects defined in the ECMAScript Binding and how these objects and their methods can be used to navigate and manipulate the Document Object Model.

15

CHAPTER **16**

Accessing the DOM

In the previous chapter you learned about the evolution of the DOM from Netscape layers to Internet Explorer's DHTML. You were also introduced to the tree structure that the DOM utilizes. With the history and theory behind us, it is time to answer the question you have probably been asking, "How do I access the DOM using JavaScript?"

This chapter will explore all of the objects defined in the ECMAScript Language Binding document as well as the object's associated methods and properties. Armed with these properties and objects, you will try your hand at accessing and navigating the DOM.

The ECMAScript Language Binding

The ECMAScript Language Binding document defines a number of DOM objects that can be accessed from JavaScript. In fact, the ECMAScript Language Binding document is an appendix to the Level 2 Document Object Model Core definitions. From the JavaScript perspective, the ECMAScript Language Binding can be thought of as an add-on to ECMAScript.

So what is a binding? Basically the ECMAScript Language Binding document contains definitions for two dozen JavaScript objects that provide all the functionality needed to navigate and manipulate the DOM. So what is needed to begin using this great funtionality? Not much, just a browser that represents HTML content as a tree structure and provides JavaScript and the objects defined in the ECMASCript Language Binding. All the leading browsers support the DOM, JavaScript, and the bindings, so there is nothing to do other than continue using JavaScript as you always have but with a few additional objects in your toolbox.

Table 16.1 lists all the objects defined in the ECMAScript Language Binding document.
The combination and interaction of all these objects will provide you with everything you
need to interact with the DOM using JavaScript. The objects provided allow JavaScript to
work with HTML and XML documents.

TABLE 16.1   ECMAScript Language Binding Objects

Objects
Attr
CDATASection
CharacterData
Comment
Document
DocumentFragment
DocumentType
DOMException
DOMImplementation
Element
Entity
EntityReference
NamedNodeMap
Node
NodeList
Notation
ProcessingInstruction
Text

Node-Related Objects

The Node object is the primary data type for the entire Document Object Model. As
mentioned in the previous chapter, the DOM is a tree-like structure. In this structure every
limb is called a node. A node can be an element, text, attribute, and so on. In fact, quite a
few of the objects defined in the ECMAScript Language Binding inherit from the Node
object. The Node object provides everything that one would need to navigate through the
DOM. Table 16.2 lists all the attributes of the Node object. Notice that there are quite a few
constants associated with the Node object. Because other objects inherit from the Node
object, the property nodeType can be used to determine the type by comparing to the
constants.

TABLE 16.2   Node Object's Attributes

Type	Name	Description
Constants	`ELEMENT_NODE`	Value is 1.
	`ATTRIBUTE_NODE`	Value is 2.
	`TEXT_NODE`	Value is 3.
	`CDATA_SECTION_NODE`	Value is 4.
	`ENTITY_REFERENCE_NODE`	Value is 5.
	`ENTITY_NODE`	Value is 6.
	`PROCESSING_REFERENCE_NODE`	Value is 7.
	`COMMENT_NODE`	Value is 8.
	`DOCUMENT_NODE`	Value is 9.
	`DOCUMENT_TYPE_NODE`	Value is 10.
	`DOCUMENT_FRAGMENT_NODE`	Value is 11.
	`NOTATION_NODE`	Value is 12.
Properties	`attributes`	A `NamedNodeMap` object containing all the attributes of this node.
	`childNodes`	A `NodeList` that contains all of the children of this node.
	`firstChild`	The first child of this node.
	`lastChild`	The last child of this node.
	`localName`	The local part of the qualified name of this node.
	`namespaceURI`	The namespace URI of this node.
	`nextSibling`	The node immediately following this node.
	`nodeName`	Name of this node.
	`nodeType`	The type of the underlying object of this node. This corresponds to one of the constants defined in the `Node` object.
	`nodeValue`	The value of this node.
	`ownerDocument`	The `Document` object associated with this node.
	`parentNode`	The parent node of this node.
	`prefix`	The namespace prefix of this node.
	`previousSibling`	The node immediately preceding this node.
Methods	`appendChild(N)`	Adds the node, *N*, to the end of the list of children of this node.
	`cloneNode(deep)`	Returns a duplicate of this node. If *deep* is true, the current node and all nodes under it are copied.
	`hasAttributes()`	Returns `true` if this node has attributes, else returns `false`.
	`hasChildNodes()`	Returns `true` if current node has children, else returns `false`.
	`insertBefore(N,E)`	Inserts the new node, *N*, before existing child node, *E*.

16

TABLE 16.2   Continued

Type	Name	Description
	isSupported(F,V)	Determines if the feature, F, version, V, is supported by this node.
	normalize()	Puts Text nodes in the full depth of the subtree underneath this node.
	removeChild(N)	Removes and returns child node, N, from the list of children.
	replaceChild(N,E)	Replaces and returns existing child node, E, with the new node, N.

There are also two other objects that are closely related to the Node object. They are the NodeList object and the NamedNodeMap object.

NodeList Object

The NodeList object is really nothing more than a container for a list of Node objects. Quite a few of the language binding objects return this object from their methods. The NodeList object provides a property and method for accessing the list of nodes that it contains. The properties and methods are described in Table 16.3.

TABLE 16.3   NodeList Object's Properties and Methods

Type	Name	Description
Property	length	The number of nodes contained in the list
Method	item(index)	Returns a particular node from the list

NamedNodeMap Object

The NamedNodeMap object represents a collection of nodes that can be accessed by name. Unlike the NodeList object, the NamedNodeMap does not maintain its nodes in any particular order. But the NamedNodeMap does provide an ordinal index that allows for convenient enumeration of its contents. A few of the language binding objects return this object from their methods. The properties and methods associated with the NamedNodeMap are described in Table 16.4.

TABLE 16.4   NamedNodeMap Object's Properties and Methods

Type	Name	Description
Property	length	The number of nodes in the container.
Methods	getNamedItem(name)	Returns the named node from the container.
	getNamedItemNS(URI,name)	Returns the node from the container that has the specified namespace URI and local name.
	item(index)	Returns a particular node from the container.

TABLE 16.4   Continued

Type	Name	Description
	`removedNamedItem(name)`	Removes the named node from the container.
	`removeNamedItemNS(URI,name)`	Removes the node from the container that has the same namespace URI and local name.
	`setNamedItem(node)`	Adds a node to the container. If the container already contains a node with the same nodeName attribute, it is replaced by the new one.
	`setNamedItemNS(node)`	Adds a node to the container. If the container already contains a node with the same namespace URI and local name, it is replaced by the new one.

Element-Related Objects

The `Element` object represents an element in an HTML or XML document. An example of element in an HTML document would be a `<table>` tag. Elements can have attributes associated with them, so the `Element` object provides a number of methods for working with the element's attributes. The properties and methods associated with the `Element` object are described in Table 16.5. Because the `Element` object inherits from the `Node` object, the `attributes` property of the `Node` object may also be used by the `Element` object to retrieve the set of all attributes for the element.

TABLE 16.5   Element Object's Properties and Methods

Type	Name	Description
Properties	`tagName`	The name of this element
Methods	`getAttribute(name)`	Returns an attribute value based on the attribute's *name*
	`getAttributeNode(name)`	Returns an `Attr` object based on the attribute's *name*
	`getAttributeNodeNS(UR,name)`	Returns an `Attr` object based on the local *name* and namespace *URI*
	`getAttributeNS(URI,name)`	Returns an attribute value based on the local *name* and namespace *URI*
	`getElementsByTagName(name)`	Returns a `NodeList` of all descendant elements with a given tag *name*
	`getElementsByTagNameNS(URI,name)`	Returns a `NodeList` of all descendant elements based on the local *name* and namespace *URI*
	`hasAttribute(name)`	Returns *true* if element has an attribute of the specified *name*

16

TABLE 16.5   Continued

Type	Name	Description
	hasAttributeNS(*URI*,*name*)	Returns true if element has an attribute of the specified local *name* and namespace *URI*
	removeAttribute(*name*)	Removes the attribute with specified *name*
	removeAttribute(*URI*,*name*)	Removes the attribute with specified local *name* and namespace *URI*
	removeAttributeNode(*attr*)	Removes and returns the specified Attr object
	setAttribute(*name*,*value*)	Adds new attribute *name*/*value* pair to this element
	setAttributeNode(*attr*)	Adds the specified *Attr* object, *attr*, to this element
	setAttributeNodeNS(*attr*)	Adds the specified Attr object, *attr*, to this element
	setAttributeNS(*URI*,*name*,*value*)	Adds new attribute *name*/*value* pair to this element based on the specified local *name* and namespace *URI*

Attr Object

The Attr object represents an element's attribute in an HTML or XML document. An example of an attribute in an HTML document would be the width attribute of the <table> tag. Table 16.6 describes the properties associated with the Attr object.

TABLE 16.6   Attr Object's Properties

Name	Description
name	The name of this attribute.
ownerElement	The element to which this attribute is associated.
specified	If this attribute was explicitly given a value in the original document, this is *true*; otherwise, it is *false*.
value	The value of this attribute.

> **NOTE**
>
> The Attr object inherits from the Node object, but because it is not actually a child node of the element it describes, the DOM does not consider it part of the document tree. Thus, the node attributes parentNode, previousSibling, and nextSibling have a null value for Attr objects.

Text and CharacterData Objects

The Text object represents the textual content of an Element object or Attr object. The Text object only contains one method called splitText(offset). This method breaks the current text node into two nodes at the specified offset, keeping both in the tree as siblings of each other. The Text object also inherits additional functionality from the CharacterData object. The properties and methods associated with the CharacterData object are described in Table 16.7.

TABLE 16.7   CharacterData Object's Properties and Methods

Type	Name	Description
Properties	data	The string itself
	length	Length of the string
Methods	substringData(*offset*,*count*)	Extracts and returns a range of data based on the *offset* and *count*
	appendData(*string*)	Appends *string* to the end of the character data of the node
	insertData(*offset*,*string*)	Inserts *string* at the specified offset
	deleteData(*offset*,*count*)	Deletes a range of data based on the *offset* and *count*
	replaceData(*offset*,*count*,*string*)	Replaces the characters specified by *offset* and *count* with the specified *string*

Document-Related Objects

In Chapter 11, "Document Objects," you learned about the Document object and its importance to JavaScript. The ECMAScript Language Binding extends the Document object by adding additional methods and properties. From the perspective of the DOM, the Document object represents the entire XHTML or XML document. As you learned in the previous chapter, the Document Object Model is a tree-based structure. The Document object serves as the root of the tree.

Because HTML and XML elements must exist inside the context of a document, the Document object contains the methods needed to create these objects. Additional methods and properties provide the primary access to the document's data. Table 16.8 lists all the properties and methods associated with the Document object as defined by the ECMAScript Language Binding.

TABLE 16.8   Document Object's Properties and Methods

Type	Name	Description
Properties	doctype	A DocumentType object associated with this document.
	documentElement	An Element object representing the document.
	implementation	A DOMImplementation object associated with this document.

16

TABLE 16.8   Continued

Type	Name	Description
Methods	createAttribute(*name*)	Creates and returns an Attr object of the given *name*.
	createAttributeNS(*URI*,*name*)	Creates and returns an Attr object of the given qualified *name* and namespace *URI*.
	createCDATASection(*str*)	Creates and returns a CDATASection object whose value is the specified string, *str*.
	createComment(*str*)	Creates and returns a Comment object with the specified string, *str*.
	createDocumentFragment()	Creates and returns an empty DocumentFragment object.
	createElement(*tagName*)	Creates and returns an Element object of the type specified by *tagName*.
	createElementNS(*URI*,*name*)	Creates and returns an Element object given the qualified *name* and namespace *URI*.
	createEntityReference(*name*)	Creates and returns an *EntityReference* object referencing the *name* entity.
	createTextNode(*string*)	Creates and returns a Text object with specified *string*.
	getElementById(*id*)	Returns the Element object based on the element id specified.
	getElementsByTagName(*name*)	Returns a NodeList object that contains all the elements with specified tag *name*.
	getElementsByTagName(*URI*,*name*)	Returns a NodeList object that contains all the elements with a given local *name* and namespace *URI*.
	importNode(*N*,*deep*)	Imports the node, *N*, from another document to this document. If *deep* is true, all the nodes under it are imported.

DocumentFragment Object

The createDocumentFragment method of the Document object returns a DocumentFragment object. A DocumentFragment object is considered a "lightweight" or "minimal" Document object because it simply acts as a container for holding other nodes. For example, it is common to want to be able to extract a portion of a document's tree or to create a new fragment of a document. The beauty of the DocumentFragment object is that when inserted into a Document object (or into any other node that can take children), only the children of the DocumentFragment are inserted into the node and not the DocumentFragment itself. This is useful when you want to create nodes that are siblings. In this case the DocumentFragment acts as the parent of these nodes so that you can use the standard methods from the Node object, such as insertBefore and appendChild.

DOMImplementation

The `implementation` property of the `Document` object returns a `DOMImplementation` object. A `DOMImplementation` object provides a number of methods for performing operations that are independent of any particular instance of the Document Object Model. The methods associated with the `DOMImplementation` object are described in Table 16.9.

TABLE 16.9   Document Object's Methods

Name	Description
`createDocument(URI,name,type)`	Creates and returns a `Document` object with the specified namespace URI, qualified name, and document type.
`createDocumentType(name,publicID,sysID)`	Creates and returns an `DocumentType` object with the specified qualified name, public id, and system id.
`hasFeature(feature,version)`	Tests if DOM implementation has a certain *feature* and feature *version*.

CDATASection

CDATA sections are used to escape blocks of text containing characters that would otherwise be regarded as markup. The only delimiter that is recognized in a CDATA section is the]]> string that ends the CDATA section. Their primary purpose is for including material such as XML fragments, without needing to escape all the delimiters.

The `createCDATASection` method of the `Document` object returns a `CDATASection` object. The `CDATASection` object represents the text of a CDATA section. Because the `CDATASection` object does not have any properties or methods of its own, it inherits from the `CharacterData` object through the `Text` object.

Comment

The `createComment` method of the `Document` object returns a `Comment` object. A `Comment` object represents the content of a comment. For example, all the characters between the starting `<!--` and ending `-->`. Because the `Comment` object does not have any properties or methods of its own, it inherits from the `CharacterData` object.

XML-Specific Objects

So far we have looked at objects in the ECMAScript Language Binding that represent aspects of just HTML documents or a combination of HTML and XML documents. But there are a few more objects that are specific to just XML and available to JavaScript.

Entity Object

The `Entity` object represents an entity, either parsed or unparsed, in an XML document. This object models the entity itself, not the entity declaration. The `Entity` object inherits from the `Node` object but also defines some properties of its own. These properties are described in Table 16.10. It is also important to point out that an entity node does not have a parent node.

16

TABLE 16.10   Entity Object's Properties

Name	Description
notationName	The name of the notation of an unparsed entity
publicId	The public identifier associated with the entity
systemId	The system identifier associated with the entity

EntityReference Object

The createEntityReference method of the Document object returns an EntityReference object. Because the EntityReference object does not have any properties or methods of its own, it inherits from the Node object.

ProcessingInstruction Object

The ProcessingInstruction object represents a processing instruction that is used in XML as a way to keep processor-specific information in the text of the document. This object inherits from the Node object but also defines some properties of its own. These properties are described in Table 16.11.

TABLE 16.11   ProcessingInstruction Object's Properties

Name	Description
data	The content of the processing instruction. This is from the first non-white-space character after the target to the character immediately preceding the ?>.
target	The target of the processing instruction.

Notation Object

The Notation object represents a notation declared in the DTD. A notation either declares, by name, the format of an unparsed entity, or is used for formal declaration of processing instruction targets. This object inherits from the Node object but also defines some properties of its own. These properties are described in Table 16.12.

TABLE 16.12   Notation Object's Properties

Name	Description
publicId	The public identifier associated with the entity
systemId	The system identifier associated with the entity

DocumentType Object

The doctype property of the Document object contains a DocumentType object. The DocumentType object provides an interface to the list of entities that are defined for the document. Table 16.13 describes the properties associated with this object.

TABLE 16.13   DocumentType Object's Properties

Name	Description
entities	A NamedNodeMap containing the general entities, both external and internal, declared in the DTD
internalSubset	The internal subset as a string
Name	The name of the DTD
notations	A NamedNodeMap containing the notations declared in the DTD
publicId	The public identifier associated with the entity
systemId	The system identifier associated with the entity

DOM Exceptions

The ECMAScript Language Binding also defines exceptions that are returned from many of the methods when an operation is impossible to perform. These exceptions are defined by the DOMException object and are shown in Table 16.14.

TABLE 16.14   DOM Exceptions

Exception	Value
INDEX_SIZE_ERR	1
DOMSTRING_SIZE_ERR	2
HIERARCHY_REQUEST_ERR	3
WRONG_DOCUMENT_ERR	4
INVALID_CHARACTER_ERR	5
NO_DATA_ALLOWED_ERR	6
NO_MODIFICATION_ALLOWED_ERR	7
NOT_FOUND_ERR	8
NOT_SUPPORTED_ERR	9
INUSE_ATTRIBUTE_ERR	10
INVALID_STATE_ERR	11
SYNTAX_ERR	12
INVALID_MODIFICATION_ERR	13
NAMESPACE_ERR	14
INVALID_ACCESS_ERR	15

16

Accessing the DOM

Now that you know what the ECMAScript Language Binding provides, it is time to start using some of those objects to access the Document Object Model.

Initial Entry Points

The ECMAScript Language Binding provides three entry points into the DOM via the Document object. The first way is to access the Document element itself by simply referencing the documentElement property of the Document object. The next way is to specify the unique id attribute of the desired element with the getElementById method. Of course, this requires that a unique id be assigned to the element within the HTML. Finally, the getElementsByTagName method returns a list of HTML nodes or XML nodes, based on the arguments supplied.

Listing 16.1 uses each of these approaches to gain access to the DOM. When the Display Number of h2 Tags button is clicked, the getElementsByTagName method is used to retrieve a list of h2 tags stored in a NodeList object. The length of the list, which happens to be two in this case, is displayed in an alert box. When the "Display Id header2 Tag" button is clicked, the getElementById method is used to retrieve the <h2> tag element with an id of "headerB". Because the actual text of the <h2> tag is stored in a child node, the firstChild property of the Node object must be used to access the actual string. The string "This is Header B" is then accessed with the nodeValue property. Finally, the documentElement property is used to access the document element and display its tag name, which is <html>.

LISTING 16.1   Initial Entry Points to the DOM

```
<html>
<head>
<title>Initial Entry Points to the DOM</title>
<script type="text/javascript">
//Display the number of <h2> tags
function displayNumH2s()
{
  var aNodeList = document.getElementsByTagName("h2");
  alert("There are " + aNodeList.length + " H2 tags in this document.");
}

//Display contents of the headerB tag
function displayIdHeaderB()
{
  var headerBnode = document.getElementById("headerB");
  var headerBtextNode = headerBnode.firstChild;
  alert(headerBtextNode.nodeValue);
}

//Display the document element's tag name
```

LISTING 16.1   Continued

```
function displayDocumentTagName()
{
  alert(document.documentElement.tagName);
}

</script>
</head>
<body>

<h2 id="headerA">This is Header A</h2>
<h2 id="headerB">This is Header B</h2>

<input type="button"
       onclick="displayNumH2s()"
       value="Display Number of H2 Tags"><br />
<input type="button"
       onclick="displayIdHeaderB()"
       value="Display Id headerB Tag"><br />
<input type="button"
       onClick="displayDocumentTagName()"
       value="Display Document Tag Name">

</body>
</html>
```

Accessing Nodes and Elements

Now that access to the DOM has been attained, it is time to access the actual nodes and elements. The Node object provides a few properties that describe itself. These properties are nodeName, nodeValue, and nodeType. In addition to the properties provided by the Node object, the Element object provides a property called tagName that contains the name of the tag that the element holds.

Listing 16.2 creates a simple paragraph using the <p> tag and then uses the properties that were just mentioned to access the paragraph node/element. Because the actual text of the <p> tag is stored in a child node, the firstChild property of the Node object must be used to access the actual string. As you can see in Figure 16.1, the tag name and node name of the paragraph tag is P. The value is null and the type is 1, which is Node.ELEMENT_NODE. The child node of the paragraph tag, of course, contains the actual text of the paragraph. The child node does not have a tag name but has a node name of "#text" indicating it is the text of the parent node. Once again, the child node is of type Node.ELEMENT_NODE.

LISTING 16.2   Accessing Nodes and Elements

```html
<html>
<head><title>Accessing Nodes and Elements</title></head>
<body>

<p id="pTag">This is text in a paragraph tag</p>

<script type="text/javascript">
  //Access the pTag element
  var pTagNode = document.getElementById("pTag");
  document.write("<h2>P Tag Node<\/h2>");
  document.write("Tag Name: " + pTagNode.tagName + "<br \/>");
  document.write("Node Name: " + pTagNode.nodeName + "<br \/>");
  document.write("Node Value: " + pTagNode.nodeValue + "<br \/>");
  document.write("Node Type: " + pTagNode.nodeType + "<br \/>");

  //Access the text of the pTag node
  var pTagTextNode = pTagNode.firstChild;
  document.write("<h2>P Tag Text Node<\/h2>");
  document.write("Tag Name: " + pTagTextNode.tagName + "<br \/>");
  document.write("Node Name: " + pTagTextNode.nodeName + "<br \/>");
  document.write("Node Value: " + pTagTextNode.nodeValue + "<br \/>");
  document.write("Node Type: " + pTagNode.nodeType + "<br \/>");
</script>

</body>
</html>
```

> **NOTE**
>
> Even though XHTML specifies that all tags should be lowercase, the tag and node names
> returned in Figure 16.1 are returned as uppercase by the browser.

Accessing Element Attributes

Now that you have seen how to access nodes and elements, it is time to turn our attention
to element attributes. Element attributes are name/value pairs that exist inside the angle
brackets (<>) of a tag. For example, the <input> tag has an attribute called type that
describes the type of input. The value associated with the type attribute could be
"button", "checkbox", and so on.

The ECMAScript Language Binding also provides a number of ways to access the attributes
of elements through methods provided in the Element object as well as the Node object.

The easiest way to access an attribute value is with the getAttribute method of

the Element object. You simply specify the name of the attribute that is associated with the element. The method will then return the value of the attribute. Listing 16.3 uses the getAttribute method to display the value of the type attribute of the <input> tag as shown in Figure 16.2.

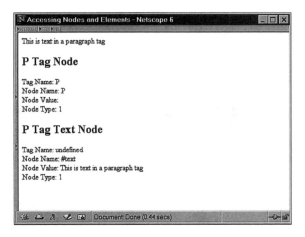

FIGURE 16.1   Accessing a <p> tag.

LISTING 16.3   Accessing an Attribute of an Element

```
<html>
<head><title>Accessing an Attribute of an Element</title></head>
<body>

<form>
First Name<input type="text" id="firstName"><br />
Last Name<input type="text" id="lastName"><br />
<input type="submit">
</form>

<h2>Type Attribute of Input Tags</h2>
<script type="text/javascript">

  //Access the firstName element
  var theElement = document.getElementById("firstName");
  document.write("firstName type=" +
                 theElement.getAttribute("type") +
                 "<br \/>");
```

LISTING 16.3   Continued

```
//Access the lastName element
theElement = document.getElementById("lastName");
document.write("lastName type=" +
               theElement.getAttribute("type") +
               "<br \/>");

</script>
</body>
</html>
```

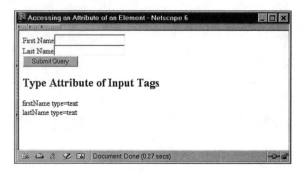

FIGURE 16.2   Accessing the value of the type attribute.

The getAttribute method has limits. What if you want to know more about an attribute other than just its value? The Element object provides another method called getAttributeNode that returns an Attr object representing an attribute. The Attr object provides additional XML-related information about an attribute, such as the parent element node and whether or not the attribute was initially specified. The Attr object is handy when working with a NamedNodeMap. A NamedNodeMap object is returned when the attributes property of the Node object is used to retrieve a list of attributes associated with a particular node. Listing 16.4 uses the attributes property to return a list of attributes associated with the first name <input> tag. The name and value of each node in the list are then displayed in a table by iterating through the nodeMap variable and accessing each Attr object.

LISTING 16.4   Accessing a List of Attr Objects

```
<html>
<head><title>Accessing Attributes of an Element</title></head>
<body>

<table>
```

LISTING 16.4   Continued

```
  <tr>
    <td>First Name</td>
    <td><input type="text" name="firstName" ></td>
  </tr>
  <tr>
    <td>Middle Name</td>
    <td><input type="text" name="middleName"></td>
  </tr>
  <tr>
    <td>Last Name</td>
    <td><input type="text" name="lastName"></td>
  </tr>
</table>

<h2>All Attributes of the firstname Input Tags</h2>
<table border="1">
<tr><th>NAME</th><th>VALUE</th></tr>
<script type="text/javascript">

  //Access all the attributes of the firstName input tag
  var theElement = document.getElementById("firstName");
  var nodeMap = theElement.attributes

  for(var i=0; i<nodeMap.length; i++)
  {
    var aAttr = nodeMap.item(i);
    document.write("<tr><td>" + aAttr.name + "<\/td><td>" +
                   aAttr.value + "<\/td><\/tr>");
  }

</script>
</table>
</body>
</html>
```

Navigating the DOM

The key to navigating through the Document Object Model is the parent-child-sibling relationship that was discussed in the previous chapter. It is this relationship that makes it possible to move through the tree structure. The parent and child relationship makes moving up and down a tree possible, and the sibling relationship allows movement from side to side.

Sibling Nodes

To navigate through sibling nodes, the Node object provides the nextNode and previousNode attributes. These attributes provide access to the neighboring nodes. Listing 16.5 demonstrates how to use these two properties to navigate the siblings of the <h1> tag. A global variable, called currentNode, is provided to keep track of the current node. Two JavaScript functions, next and previous, use the nextNode and previousNode properties to move through the siblings. During each move the displayNode function displays the name, type, and value of the current node in the HTML form fields. When the page is first loaded, the current node is set to the <h1> tag and its contents are displayed. Figure 16.3 shows the result of stepping through a couple of the siblings.

LISTING 16.5   Navigating Sibling Nodes

```
<html>
<head>
<title>Navigating Siblings</title>

<script type"text/javascript">

var currentNode;

//Get the next node in the tree
function next()
{
  //See if current node has a sibling node.
  if(currentNode.nextSibling)
  {
    currentNode=currentNode.nextSibling;
    displayNode(); //Display information about current node
  }
  else
  {
    alert("This is the last sibling");
  }
}

function previous()
{
  //See if current node has a sibling node.
  if(currentNode.previousSibling)
  {
    currentNode=currentNode.previousSibling;
```

LISTING 16.5   Continued

```
    displayNode(); //Display information about current node
  }
  else
  {
    alert("This is the first sibling.");
  }
}


//Display the tag name and type and any text that it contains.
function displayNode()
{
  document.displayForm.NameTextBox.value=currentNode.nodeName;
  document.displayForm.TypeTextBox.value=currentNode.nodeType;
  document.displayForm.TextTextBox.value=currentNode.nodeValue;
}
</script>
</head>


<body>
<h1 id="h1Node">Navigating Siblings</h1>

This example demonstrates how to navigate through sibling
nodes using JavaScript. The starting node is the header tag above.

<form name="displayForm">
Name: <input type="text" name="NameTextBox"><br />
Type: <input type="text" name="TypeTextBox"><br />
Text: <input type="text" name="TextTextBox"><br />
<input type="button" value="PREVIOUS" onclick="previous()">
<input type="button" value="NEXT" onclick="next()">
</form>

<script type="text/javascript">
//Set current node to the h1 node and display the node's attributes.
currentNode = document.getElementById("h1Node");
displayNode();
</script>

</body>
</html>
```

16

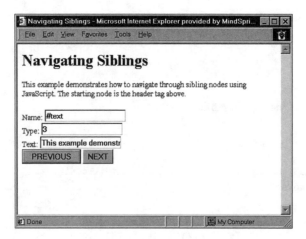

FIGURE 16.3   Navigating through sibling nodes.

Child Nodes

For navigating child nodes, the Node object provides the firstChild and lastChild properties for quick access to the first and last node. The Node object also provides the
childNodes properties. This property returns a NodeList object, which contains a list of
child nodes. The Node object also provides a handy hasChildNodes method for testing for
the existence of child nodes.

Listing 16.6 demonstrates how to use these properties and methods to navigate the child
nodes of an HTML table. A simple HTML table representing a multiplication table is
displayed using traditional HTML tags. The JavaScript function next is called and passed
the multiplication table object and a starting level of 1. Within the next function, the
current method hasChildNodes is used to determine if the current node has children. If it
does, a list of the immediate children is retrieved using the childNodes property. For each
of the children the next function is called recursively. Regardless of whether a node has
children or not, the displayNode function is called to display the name, type, value, first
child, and last child values in a HTML table. The level indicates how deep each node is in
the tree. Figure 16.4 shows the result of running Listing 16.6.

LISTING 16.6   Navigating Child Nodes

```
<html>
<head>
<title>Navigating Child Nodes</title>
<script type"text/javascript">
```

LISTING 16.6   Continued

```
//Get the next node in the tree.
function next(currentNode,level)
{
  //See if current node has child nodes.
  if(currentNode.hasChildNodes())
  {
    //Display information about current node.
    displayNode(currentNode,level);

    //Loop through children of currentNode.
    var children = currentNode.childNodes;
    for(var i=0; i<children.length; i++)
    {
      next(children.item(i),(level+1));
    }
  }
  else
  {
    displayNode(currentNode,level);
  }
}

//Display the tag name and type and any text that it contains.
function displayNode(aNode,level)
{
  document.write("<tr><td>" + level + "</td><td>");
  document.write(aNode.nodeName + "</td><td>");
  document.write(aNode.nodeType + "</td><td>");
  document.write(aNode.nodeValue + "</td><td>");
  if(aNode.hasChildNodes())
  {
    document.write(aNode.firstChild.nodeName + "</td><td>");
    document.write(aNode.lastChild.nodeName + "</td></tr>");
  }
  else
  {
    document.write("</td><td></td></tr>");
  }
```

LISTING 16.6   Continued

```
}
</script>
</head>


<body>
<h1>Multiplication Table</h1>
<table id="multiplicationTable" border="1">
  <tr><td></td><td>1</td><td>2</td><td>3</td></tr>
  <tr><td>1</td><td>1</td><td>2</td><td>3</td></tr>
  <tr><td>2</td><td>2</td><td>4</td><td>6</td></tr>
  <tr><td>3</td><td>3</td><td>6</td><td>9</td></tr>
</table>

<hr />

The following chart shows all the children of the
multiplication table using JavaScript.

<table border="1">
<tr><td>LEVEL</td><td>NAME</td><td>TYPE</td><td>VALUE</td>
<td>FIRSTCHILD</td><td>LASTCHILD</td></tr>

<script type="text/javascript">
  //Start at the multiplication table.
  next(document.getElementById("multiplicationTable"),1);
</script>

</table>
</body>
</html>
```

Parent Nodes

The final navigation property we are going to look at is the parentNode property of the Node object. This property provides access to the parent node. Listing 16.7 demonstrates how to use the parentNode property, as well as others that were discussed earlier, to navigate all the nodes of an HTML document. A global variable, called currentNode, is provided to keep track of the current node. The JavaScript function, next, changes the current node by testing for child and sibling nodes. After all child and sibling nodes have been explored, the parentNode property is used to navigate back up the tree. Along the way the displayNode function displays the name, type, and value of the current node in the HTML form fields. When the page is first loaded, the current node is set to the <body> tag and its contents are displayed. When the top of the tree is reached, the user is alerted that the top of the tree has been reached. Figure 16.5 shows the result of stepping through a couple of the tags.

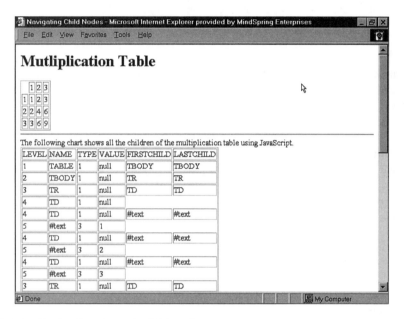

FIGURE 16.4   Navigating through child nodes.

LISTING 16.7   Navigating Parent Nodes

```
<html>
<head>
<title>Navigating Parent Nodes</title>
<script type"text/javascript">

var currentNode;

//Get the next node in the tree.
function next()
{
  //See if current node has a child node first.  If no
  //child node see if current node has a sibling.
  if(currentNode.firstChild)
  {
    currentNode=currentNode.firstChild;
```

LISTING 16.7　Continued

```
  }
  else if(currentNode.nextSibling)
  {
    currentNode=currentNode.nextSibling;
  }
  else if(currentNode.parentNode)
  {
    //If no child or sibling node then go back up the
    //tree until a sibling node is found or top of
    //tree is reached.
    while(currentNode.parentNode)
    {
      currentNode=currentNode.parentNode;
      if(currentNode.nextSibling)
      {
        currentNode = currentNode.nextSibling;
        break;
      }
    }

    if(currentNode==bodyNode)
    {
      alert("You have reached the top of the tree!");
    }
  }
  displayNode(); //Display information about current node.
}

//Display the tag name and type and any text that it contains.
function displayNode()
{
  document.displayForm.NameTextBox.value=currentNode.nodeName;
  document.displayForm.TypeTextBox.value=currentNode.nodeType;
  document.displayForm.TextTextBox.value=currentNode.nodeValue;
}
</script>
</head>


<body id="bodyNode">
<h1>Navigating Parent Nodes</h1>
```

LISTING 16.7   Continued

This example demonstrates how to navigate the parent nodes using JavaScript.

```
<form name="displayForm">
Name: <input type="text" name="NameTextBox"><br>
Type: <input type="text" name="TypeTextBox"><br>
Text: <input type="text" name="TextTextBox"><br>
<input type="button" value="NEXT" onclick="next()">

</form>

<script type="text/javascript">
//Set current node to the body node and display the nodes attributes.
currentNode = document.getElementById("bodyNode");
displayNode();
</script>

</body>
</html>
```

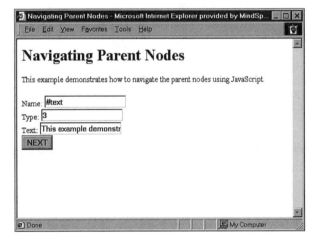

FIGURE 16.5   Navigating through parent nodes.

Summary

This chapter covered a lot of ground. The chapter began with a complete overview of the ECMAScript Language Binding document. All of the objects defined in this document were described along with tables that list their associated methods and properties.

With an understanding of the available tools at our disposal, the chapter jumped into a discussion about accessing the Document Object Model. This discussion started with ways to initially enter the DOM tree. After this you learned about how to access the `Node` and `Element` objects. You also learned how to access the attributes associated with elements.

After you learned how to access the DOM, the discussion shifted to how to navigate the DOM. The chapter introduced you to ways to navigate sibling nodes, child nodes, and parent nodes.

Now that you know about the ECMAScript Language Binding and how to access and navigate the Document Object Model, it is time to have some fun! In the next chapter you will take what you learned in this chapter and extend it to learn how to manipulate the DOM.

CHAPTER **17**

Manipulating the DOM

The last chapter introduced the ECMAScript Language Binding objects and their associated properties and methods. The chapter also demonstrated how to use many of the methods of the various objects to access the Document object and navigate through its tree structure. This chapter builds on what you learned in the last chapter with the focus of this chapter on manipulating the Document Object Model. The ability to manipulate the DOM is the real power of the DOM/JavaScript combination.

This chapter will look at three primary ways to manipulate the DOM. The first way is to simply delete nodes. The second way is to create new content by creating nodes and placing them into an existing structure. Finally, the chapter will be rounded out with a discussion on copying nodes.

Deleting Nodes

The easiest way to manipulate the DOM is to simply delete elements. The ECMAScript Language Binding provides a method called removeChild that is part of the Node object. The method takes one argument—the child node to be deleted from the parent node.

Listing 17.1 creates a basic online shopping cart list. Imagine that you have gone shopping online for drum equipment. You have loaded your cart up with all the items that you need. But before you check out, you are shown the list of items in your shopping cart and given the ability to remove items. When you are satisfied with your selection, you can proceed to the checkout.

So how do you remove items from the list without making a trip to the server but still keeping the form intact? If you could just remove entire form elements, those items would not be sent to the server during checkout. Using the removeChild method, it is possible to do just that!

When the Remove Selected Items button is clicked, the removeItems function is called. Using the forms.elements array, it is possible to loop through all the form elements looking for ones that have been checked. For any item that is checked, the element representing the associated <input> tag is retrieved. The <tbody> and <tr> tags that house the input element are also retrieved. Armed with these elements, the removeChild method is called to remove the table record for the selected item. Figure 17.1 shows the action of removing drum sticks from the shopping cart.

LISTING 17.1   Deleting Items from an Online Shopping Cart

```html
<html>
<head>
<title>Deleting Nodes</title>

<script type="text/javascript">
function removeItems()
{
  var cart = document.cart;

  // Loop through all items in the shopping cart.
  for(var i=0; i<cart.length; i++)
  {
    // If item is checked then remove it.
    if(cart.elements[i].checked)
    {
      // Since element is in a <tr> get the tr and tbody node.
      var inputTag = document.getElementById(cart.elements[i].id);
      var tr = inputTag.parentNode.parentNode;
      var tbody = tr.parentNode;

      // Remove the table record node and everything under it.
      tbody.removeChild(tr);
    }
  }
}
</script>
</head>

<body>
<h2>Music Store Shopping Cart</h2>
```

LISTING 17.1 Continued

```
<form name="cart" id="cart" action="checkout.jsp">
<table border="1">
  <tr><th>Select</th><th>Description</th><th>Price</th></tr>
  <tr>
    <td><input type="checkbox" name="item_456" id="item_456"></td>
    <td>1 pair Pro-Mark 5B drum sticks.</td>
    <td>6.99</td>
  </tr>
  <tr>
    <td><input type="checkbox" name="item_005" id="item_005"></td>
    <td>Remo Pre-Pack Pinstrip Drum Heads.</td>
    <td>39.99</td>
  </tr>
  <tr>
    <td><input type="checkbox" name="item_769" id="item_769"></td>
    <td>Beato II Club Drum Set Bag Set</td>
    <td>149.99</td>
  </tr>
  <tr>
    <td><input type="checkbox" name="item_142" id="item_142"></td>
    <td>Seiko SQ-50 Quartz Metronome</td>
    <td>24.99</td>
  </tr>
</table>

<br />
<button onclick="removeItems()">Remove Selected Items</button>
<input type="submit" value="Proceed to checkout">
</form>

</body>
</html>
```

The ECMAScript Language Binding also defines methods for the Element object for deleting attributes of elements. The removeAttribute method allows an attribute to be removed by name, and the removeAttributeNode removes an Attr object that is associated with an element.

Listing 17.2 demonstrates how to use both of these methods to remove attributes from a table. The listing displays a simple multiplication table in an XHTML table. When the Remove Border button is clicked, the border attribute is removed from the <table> tag element with one simple call to the removeAttribute method.

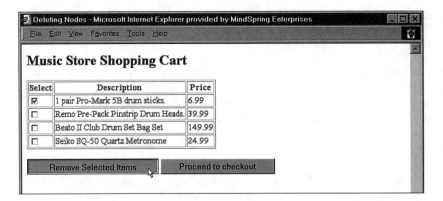

FIGURE 17.1   Deleting drum sticks.

Each of the <td> tags has a background color defined. When any of the color-related buttons are clicked, a NodeList object is created. The list contains all the <td> tags associated with the table. Each tag is checked for a bgcolor attribute and Attr objects are returned. If an attribute has a color match, the associated attribute object is removed from the table data element using the removeAttributeNode method.

Unfortunately, this example does not quite yield the desired results. As I found out while building this example, Internet Explorer 6.0 does not necessarily refresh the table in the browser when the background color attributes are deleted. The Document Object Model in memory does change, but what is seen on the screen does not. There is a way to make it change the colors, and that is to click some of the Delete Color buttons first and then click the Delete Border button. The table is then refreshed and the background colors change. Netscape 6.2 is even worse in that it does not change the colors or remove the border. The good news is the DOM is truly changed, but unfortunately, those changes are not necessary reflected on the screen.

> **CAUTION**
>
> Even though the removeAttribute and removeAttributeNode methods of the Element object delete attributes from the Document Object Model, the graphical ramifications of removing attributes vary between browsers.

LISTING 17.2   Deleting Element Attributes

```
<html>
<head>
<title>Deleting Element Attributes</title>

<script type="text/javascript">
// Remove the border from the table.
```

LISTING 17.2   Continued

```
function removeBorder()
{
  document.getElementById("multiplicationTable").removeAttribute("border");
}

// Remove the green background color from the table header.
function removeColor(color)
{
  // Get list of <td> elements in table.
  var table = document.getElementById("multiplicationTable");
  var tdList = table.getElementsByTagName("td");

  // Loop through list <td> elements.
  for(var i=0; i<tdList.length; i++)
  {
    var tdElement = tdList.item(i);

    // Get the attribute.
    var colorAttr = tdElement.getAttributeNode("bgcolor");

    // If the attribute matches the color then delete attribute.
    if(colorAttr.value == color)
    {
      tdElement.removeAttributeNode(colorAttr);
    }
  }
}
</script>
</head>

<body>
<h2>Multiplication Table</h2>

<table id="multiplicationTable" border="1">
  <tr>
    <td></td>
    <td bgcolor="#ff0000">1</td>
    <td bgcolor="#008000">2</td>
    <td bgcolor="#ffff00">3</td>
  </tr>
  <tr>
    <td bgcolor="#ff0000">1</td>
```

17

LISTING 17.2   Continued

```
      <td bgcolor="#ff0000">1</td>
      <td bgcolor="#008000">2</td>
      <td bgcolor="#ffff00">3</td>
    </tr>
    <tr>
      <td bgcolor="#008000">2</td>
      <td bgcolor="#008000">2</td>
      <td bgcolor="#008000">4</td>
      <td bgcolor="#ffff00">6</td>
    </tr>
    <tr>
      <td bgcolor="#ffff00">3</td>
      <td bgcolor="#ffff00">3</td>
      <td bgcolor="#ffff00">6</td>
      <td bgcolor="#ffff00">9</td>
    </tr>
</table>

<br />
<button onclick="removeBorder()">Remove Table Border</button><br />
<button onclick="removeColor('#ff0000')">Remove Red Background</button><br />
<button onclick="removeColor('#008000')">Remove Green Background</button><br />
<button onclick="removeColor('#ffff00')">Remove Yellow Background</button>

</body>
</html>
```

Creating Nodes

Now that we have looked at the basics of deleting nodes, it is time to turn our attention to adding new nodes to the Document Object Model. The ECMAScript Language Binding provides methods for creating a number of different objects. In this section we are going to look at how two of these functions can be used to create new nodes.

Creating New Elements

The Document object provides a method called createElement that makes creating new elements a breeze. Simply pass the name of the tag to be created and out pops a new Element object. For example, the following line of code creates a new <h2> tag and stores the new element in the newH2 variable:

```
var newH2 = document.createElement("h2");
```

Now that we have an element representing a header 2 tag, we need to place some text into the tag. Normally text would be placed between the <h2> and </h2> tags. In order to do this in the DOM, a new Text object will need to be created using the createTextNode method of the Document object. Simply pass the text in to the method. For example, the following line of code creates a new Text object and stores the new element in the newH2Text variable:

```
var newH2Text = document.createTextNode("This is text for a header 2 tag");
```

Similarly, a new Attr object can be created using the createAttribute method of the Document object. The name of the attribute is passed in to the method. The following two lines of code create a new attribute called age with a value of "34" and store the new Attr object in the newAgeAttr variable:

```
var newAgeAttr = document.createAttribute("age");
newAgeAttr.value = "34";
```

Notice that although we created three new objects, they are not part of the Document Object Model nor are they connected to each other yet. In order to create a relationship between the objects and to make them part of the current document, we must enlist the help of some additional methods, specifically the replaceChild, insertBefore, and appendChild methods of the Node object as well as the setAttribute and setAttributeNode methods of the Element object.

Setting Element Attributes

The ECMAScript Language Binding defines two methods for associating attributes with an element. These methods are part of the Element object. The first, setAttribute, simply takes a name and value and automatically creates an attribute for the given element. The other method, called setAttributeNode, takes an Attr object and associates it with the given element.

Listing 17.3 demonstrates how to use both of these methods to add attributes to a <table> tag. The listing displays a simple multiplication table in an XHTML table. When the Add Border button is clicked, the setAttribute method of the table element is passed the name "border" and the value "1". Now the table tag has a border attribute set to 1. You can see the result of this action as a border is now placed around the table cells.

When the Add Background Color button is clicked, the addBackgroundColor function is passed the string "green". A new Attr object is created for the bgcolor attribute. The attribute is then set to green by accessing the value property of the Attr object. The new bgcolor attribute is then associated with the table element thanks to the setAttributeNode method.

LISTING 17.3   Adding Element Attributes

```html
<html>
<head>
<title>Adding Element Attributes</title>

<script type="text/javascript">
// Add border to the table.
function addBorder()
{
  document.getElementById("multiplicationTable").setAttribute("border","1");
}

// Add background color to the table.
function addBackgroundColor(color)
{
  // Get table element.
  var table = document.getElementById("multiplicationTable");

  // Create an Attr object for the bgcolor attribute and assign it "green".
  var bgColorAttr = document.createAttribute("bgcolor");
  bgColorAttr.value = "green";

  // Associate the attribute with the table.
  table.setAttributeNode(bgColorAttr);
}
</script>
</head>

<body>
<h2>Multiplication Table</h2>

<table id="multiplicationTable">
  <tr><td></td><td>1</td><td>2</td><td>3</td></tr>
  <tr><td>1</td><td>1</td><td>2</td><td>3</td></tr>
  <tr><td>2</td><td>2</td><td>4</td><td>6</td></tr>
  <tr><td>3</td><td>3</td><td>6</td><td>9</td></tr>
</table>

<br />
<button onclick="addBorder()">Add Table Border</button><br />
<button onclick="addBackgroundColor()">Change Background Color</button>

</body>
</html>
```

Inserting Elements into DOM

Now that we know how to associate attributes with an element, let's turn our attention to the three methods (replaceChild, insertBefore, and appendChild) used to create a relationship between objects and make them part of the current document.

The appendChild Method

The appendChild method of the Node object simply appends the specified node to the end of the list of child nodes associated with the calling node. For example, if we had an XHTML table that represented a database table that held first name, last name, and age of users and we wanted to add new rows to the XHTML table, we could use the appendChild method. First, a new element representing the <tr> tag would need to be created as shown following:

```
var newTR = document.createElement("tr");
```

Three new elements representing the <td> tags would need to be created:

```
var newTD1 = document.createElement("td");
var newTD2 = document.createElement("td");
var newTD3 = document.createElement("td");
```

Three new Text elements representing the text to appear within each table cell would need to be created:

```
var newText1 = document.createTextNode("Jason");
var newText2 = document.createTextNode("Gilliam");
var newText3 = document.createTextNode("28");
```

With the elements created, it is now time to start building the relationships between these objects. First, we want to associate the Text objects with their corresponding table record tags. Simply use the appendChild method to connect the objects:

```
newTD1.appendChild(newText1);
newTD2.appendChild(newText2);
newTD3.appendChild(newText3);
```

Now we need to associate the table data objects (<td> tags) with the row object (<tr> tag). Once again the appendChild method is used to connect the objects:

```
newTR.appendChild(newTD1);
newTR.appendChild(newTD2);
newTR.appendChild(newTD3);
```

Assuming you have a <table> object handy, simply access the tbody child element of the table. The new row can then be appended to the end of the list of child rows associated with the tbody element:

```
var tbody = document.getElementById("dbRowsTable").firstChild;
tbody.appendChild(newTR);
```

Now that we have walked through the process of connecting objects using the appendChild method, let's put this method to use in a real example. Listing 17.4 creates an interface for adding new entries to a table representing a database table. The idea is that after all the users have been added within the XHTML page, the data in the table could then be submitted and stored in a database. We will not concern ourselves with the database aspect in this example but will rather focus our attention on dynamically adding new rows to a XHTML table.

LISTING 17.4   Using the appendChild Method to Add a New Row to the Table

```
<html>
<head>
<title>Append Child Node Example</title>
<script type="text/javascript">
function addNewRow()
{
  // Get new row data.
  var newFirstName = document.getElementById("newFirstName").
➥getAttribute("value");
  var newLastName = document.getElementById("newLastName").
➥getAttribute("value");
  var newAge = document.getElementById("newAge").getAttribute("value");

  // Create new table row elements.
  var newTR = document.createElement("tr");
  var newTD1 = document.createElement("td");
  var newTD2 = document.createElement("td");
  var newTD3 = document.createElement("td");
  var newText1 = document.createTextNode(newFirstName);
  var newText2 = document.createTextNode(newLastName);
  var newText3 = document.createTextNode(newAge);

  // Connect the new row elements.
  newTD1.appendChild(newText1);
  newTD2.appendChild(newText2);
  newTD3.appendChild(newText3);
  newTR.appendChild(newTD1);
  newTR.appendChild(newTD2);
```

LISTING 17.4   Continued

```
  newTR.appendChild(newTD3);

  // Get tbody element of dbRowsTable.
  var tbody = document.getElementById("dbRowsTable").firstChild;

  // Insert new row at end of list.
  tbody.appendChild(newTR);
}
</script>
</head>
<body>
<h1>User Database Table</h1>

Add a new row:
<table>
  <tr><td>First Name:</td><td><input type="text" name="newFirstName"></td></tr>
  <tr><td>Last Name:</td><td><input type="text" name="newLastName"></td></tr>
  <tr><td>Age:</td><td><input type="text" name="newAge"></td></tr>
</table>
<button onclick="addNewRow()">Add To Bottom</button>

<br /><hr /><br />

<table id="dbRowsTable" border="1">
<tr>
  <th>FIRST NAME</th>
    <th>LAST NAME</th>
    <th>AGE</th>
</tr>
</table>

</body>
</body>
</html>
```

As you can see in Figure 17.2, the user is presented with three text boxes for collecting user data. After the data is entered and the Add To Bottom button is clicked, the addNewRow function is called. This function creates a new row that contains the first and last name and age of a user. The new row is then appended to the bottom of the dbRowsTable using the appendChild method.

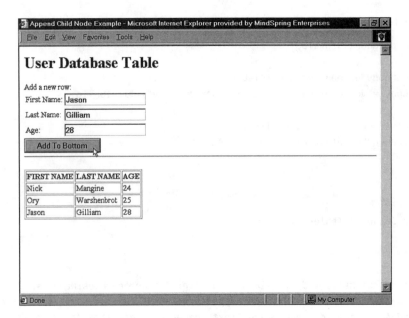

FIGURE 17.2 New rows are added to the bottom of the table.

The insertBefore Method

In the previous example new rows could only be appended to the end of the list of child objects associated with the <tr> tag element. What if you want to be able to insert the row in the middle of the table or at the top of the table? The Node object provides a method for this very purpose. The insertBefore method allows you to specify what child node a new node should be placed in front of. The first argument takes the new node, and the second argument of the method takes the node in front of which the new node should be placed.

Listing 17.5 extends Listing 17.4 by providing an additional button for putting new rows at the top of the table rather than just appending them to the bottom. An argument, where, is passed to the addRow function to instruct the code where to place the new row. If the new row is to be placed at the top of the table, the first data row

```
tbody.firstChild.nextSibling
```

is used to get the reference node for the insertBefore method. Figure 17.3 shows user information getting inserted into the top data row of the table.

LISTING 17.5   Using the insertBefore Method to Add a New Row to Top of the Table

```
<html>
<head>
<title>Insert Before Node Example</title>
```

LISTING 17.5   Continued

```
<script type="text/javascript">
function addNewRow(where)
{
  // Get new row data.
  var newFirstName = document.getElementById("newFirstName").
➡getAttribute("value");
  var newLastName = document.getElementById("newLastName").
➡getAttribute("value");
  var newAge = document.getElementById("newAge").getAttribute("value");

  // Create new table row elements.
  var newTR = document.createElement("tr");
  var newTD1 = document.createElement("td");
  var newTD2 = document.createElement("td");
  var newTD3 = document.createElement("td");
  var newText1 = document.createTextNode(newFirstName);
  var newText2 = document.createTextNode(newLastName);
  var newText3 = document.createTextNode(newAge);

  // Connect the new row elements.
  newTD1.appendChild(newText1);
  newTD2.appendChild(newText2);
  newTD3.appendChild(newText3);
  newTR.appendChild(newTD1);
  newTR.appendChild(newTD2);
  newTR.appendChild(newTD3);

  // Get tbody element of dbRowsTable.
  var tbody = document.getElementById("dbRowsTable").firstChild;

  // Insert new row into the dbRowTable where user specified.
  if(where == "top")
  {
    // Insert new row before the first data row.  Must skip over the header row.
    tbody.insertBefore(newTR,tbody.firstChild.nextSibling);
  }
  else
  {
    // Insert new row at end of list.
    tbody.appendChild(newTR);
  }
```

17

LISTING 17.5   Continued

```
}
</script>
</head>
<body>
<h1>User Database Table</h1>

Add a new row:
<table>
  <tr><td>First Name:</td><td><input type="text" name="newFirstName"></td></tr>
  <tr><td>Last Name:</td><td><input type="text" name="newLastName"></td></tr>
  <tr><td>Age:</td><td><input type="text" name="newAge"></td></tr>
</table>
<button onclick="addNewRow('top')">Add To Top</button>
<button onclick="addNewRow('bottom')">Add To Bottom</button>

<br /><hr /><br />

<table id="dbRowsTable" border="1">
<tr>
  <th>FIRST NAME</th>
  <th>LAST NAME</th>
  <th>AGE</th>
</tr>
</table>

</body>
</body>
</html>
```

The replaceChild Method

Now we can add rows to the top and bottom of the users table, but what happens if the same user is entered again? In Listing 17.5 a duplicate row would be inserted into the table. Ideally we would like for a duplicate entry to act more like an update where the age of the user would be updated. The replaceChild method of the Node object can help with this task. The replaceChild method takes two arguments. The first is the new node to be inserted in place of some existing child node. The second argument is the child node to be replaced.

Listing 17.6 extends Listing 17.5 by providing an additional function called getExistingRow. This function takes the first name and last name and tries to find it in the existing table. If a match is found, the matching row is returned; otherwise, null is returned. In the addRow function, a call is made to the new getExistingRow function. If a matching row node is returned, the replaceChild is used to replace the old row with the new one. If no match is found, the new row will be inserted at either the top or bottom of the table based on the user's selection.

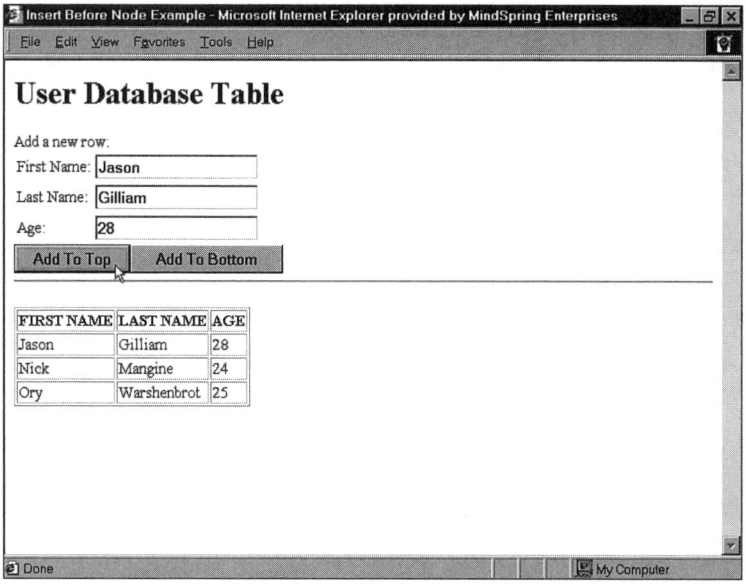

FIGURE 17.3   New row inserted into the top data row of table.

LISTING 17.6   Using the replaceChild Method to Replace a Row in the Table

```
<html>
<head>
<title>Replace Child Node Example</title>
<script type="text/javascript">
function addNewRow(where)
{
  // Get new row data.
  var newFirstName = document.getElementById("newFirstName").
➥getAttribute("value");
  var newLastName = document.getElementById("newLastName").
➥getAttribute("value");
  var newAge = document.getElementById("newAge").getAttribute("value");

  // Create new table row elements.
  var newTR = document.createElement("tr");
```

LISTING 17.6   Continued

```
var newTD1 = document.createElement("td");
var newTD2 = document.createElement("td");
var newTD3 = document.createElement("td");
var newText1 = document.createTextNode(newFirstName);
var newText2 = document.createTextNode(newLastName);
var newText3 = document.createTextNode(newAge);

// Connect the new row elements.
newTD1.appendChild(newText1);
newTD2.appendChild(newText2);
newTD3.appendChild(newText3);
newTR.appendChild(newTD1);
newTR.appendChild(newTD2);
newTR.appendChild(newTD3);

// Get tbody element of dbRowsTable.
var tbody = document.getElementById("dbRowsTable").firstChild;

// If row already exists then replace it otherwise insert it into table.
var existingTR = getExistingRow(tbody,newFirstName,newLastName);
if(existingTR != null)
{
  tbody.replaceChild(newTR,existingTR);
}
else
{
  // Insert new row into the dbRowTable where user specified.
  if(where == "top")
  {
    // Insert new row before the first data row.
    // Must skip over the header row.
    tbody.insertBefore(newTR,tbody.firstChild.nextSibling);
  }
  else
  {
    // Insert new row at end of list.
    tbody.appendChild(newTR);
  }
}
}
```

LISTING 17.6   Continued

```
// Find row with same first name and last name.
function getExistingRow(tbody,firstName,lastName)
{
  var row = tbody.firstChild //Skip header row

  // Loop through rows in oldTable.
  while(row.nextSibling)
  {
    row = row.nextSibling;
    if(firstName == row.childNodes[0].firstChild.nodeValue &&
       lastName == row.childNodes[1].firstChild.nodeValue)
    {
      return(row);
    }
  }
  return(null);
}
</script>
</head>
<body>
<h1>User Database Table</h1>

Add a new row:
<table>
  <tr><td>First Name:</td><td><input type="text" name="newFirstName"></td></tr>
  <tr><td>Last Name:</td><td><input type="text" name="newLastName"></td></tr>
  <tr><td>Age:</td><td><input type="text" name="newAge"></td></tr>
</table>
<button onclick="addNewRow('top')">Add To Top</button>
<button onclick="addNewRow('bottom')">Add To Bottom</button>

<br /><hr /><br />

<table id="dbRowsTable" border="1">
<tr>
  <th>FIRST NAME</th>
  <th>LAST NAME</th>
  <th>AGE</th>
</tr>
</table>
```

17

LISTING 17.6   Continued

```
</body>
</body>
</html>
```

Copying Nodes

The final DOM manipulation functionality we are going to discuss in this chapter is copying nodes. The ECMAScript Language Binding provides a method called `cloneNode` through the `Node` object. This function creates an exact replica of itself. The method accepts one optional parameter called `deep`. If the `deep` parameter is set to `true`, all of the node's children are recursively copied. If this parameter is `false` or not specified, none of the children of the node are copied.

It is important to understand the implications of performing a deep copy versus a shallow copy on elements. Many elements contain text, for example, the `<h1>` tag. In the case of the `<h1>` tag, the shallow copy would only copy the `<h1>` tag itself along with any associated attributes. Remember, attributes are not considered children of elements but rather part of the element. But text that might appear between the `<h1>` and `</h1>` tags is stored in a `Text` object as a child of the `<h1>` element. So in order to copy a tag, such as the `<h1>` tag, and the text that appears within it, you are required to perform a deep copy.

Now that you have an understanding of the `cloneNode` method, let's look at an example that uses the method. Listing 17.7 extends the database row creation page, from earlier in the chapter, by providing the ability to dynamically sort the rows in the XHTML table based on the contents of a particular column.

LISTING 17.7   Table Sorting Example

```
<html>
<head>
<title>Sorting Table Example</title>
<script type="text/javascript">
function addNewRow(where)
{
  // Get new row data.
  var newFirstName = document.getElementById("newName").
➥getAttribute("value");
  var newLastName = document.getElementById("newLastName").
➥getAttribute("value");
  var newAge = document.getElementById("newAge").getAttribute("value");
```

LISTING 17.7   Continued

```javascript
// Create new table row elements.
var newTR = document.createElement("tr");
var newTD1 = document.createElement("td");
var newTD2 = document.createElement("td");
var newTD3 = document.createElement("td");
var newText1 = document.createTextNode(newFirstName);
var newText2 = document.createTextNode(newLastName);
var newText3 = document.createTextNode(newAge);

// Connect the new row elements.
newTD1.appendChild(newText1);
newTD2.appendChild(newText2);
newTD3.appendChild(newText3);
newTR.appendChild(newTD1);
newTR.appendChild(newTD2);
newTR.appendChild(newTD3);

// Get tbody element of dbRowsTable.
var tbody = document.getElementById("dbRowsTable").firstChild;

// If row already exists then replace it otherwise insert it into table.
var existingTR = getExistingRow(tbody,newFirstName,newLastName);
if(existingTR != null)
{
  tbody.replaceChild(newTR,existingTR);
}
else
{
  // Insert new row into the dbRowTable where user specified.
  if(where == "top")
  {
    // Insert new row before the first data row.
    // Must skip over the header row.
    tbody.insertBefore(newTR,tbody.firstChild.nextSibling);
  }
  else
  {
    // Insert new row at end of list.
```

LISTING 17.7   Continued

```
        tbody.appendChild(newTR);
    }
  }
}

// Find row with same first name and last name.
function getExistingRow(tbody,firstName,lastName)
{
  var row = tbody.firstChild //Skip header row

  // Loop through rows in oldTable.
  while(row.nextSibling)
  {
    row = row.nextSibling;
    if(firstName == row.childNodes[0].firstChild.nodeValue &&
       lastName == row.childNodes[1].firstChild.nodeValue)
    {
      return(row);
    }
  }
  return(null);
}


function sortTable(columnId,sortOrder)
{
  // Get column position.
  var colPosition = 0;
  var tempNode = document.getElementById(columnId).previousSibling;
  while(tempNode)
  {
    colPosition++;
    tempNode = tempNode.previousSibling;
  }

  // Set sort order.
  if(sortOrder != "descending")
  {
    sortOrder = "ascending";
  }
```

LISTING 17.7   Continued

```
// td -> tr -> tbody.
var oldTableBody = document.getElementById(columnId).parentNode.parentNode;
var newTableBody = oldTableBody.cloneNode();

// Only sort table if there are 2 or more rows (plus the header row).
if(oldTableBody.childNodes.length<=2)
{
  return;
}

// Get the header row.
var headerRow = oldTableBody.firstChild;

// Seed the newTableBody with the first data rows from oldTableBody.
var oldRow = headerRow.nextSibling;
newTableBody.appendChild(oldRow.cloneNode(true));
oldRow = oldRow.nextSibling;

// Loop through rows in oldTable.
while(oldRow)
{
  var addedRowFlag = false;
  var curNewRow = newTableBody.firstChild;

  // Loop through rows in new table.
  while(!addedRowFlag && curNewRow)
  {
    var curNewRowValue = curNewRow.childNodes[colPosition].
➥firstChild.nodeValue;
    var oldRowValue = oldRow.childNodes[colPosition].firstChild.nodeValue;

    // If ascending and old row value is greater than or equal to new row
    // value then move to next item and compare.  If descending and old row
    // value is less than or equal to new row value then move to next item
    // and compare. If neither of these cases are true then the item should
    // be inserted before the current new row. This will allow the table to
    // be sorted indirectly by multiple rows.
    if((sortOrder=="ascending" &&
```

LISTING 17.7   Continued

```
              greaterThanOrEqual(oldRowValue,curNewRowValue)) ||
              (sortOrder=="descending" &&
              lessThanOrEqual(oldRowValue,curNewRowValue)))
        {
          curNewRow = curNewRow.nextSibling;
        }
        else
        {
          newTableBody.insertBefore(oldRow.cloneNode(true),curNewRow);

          // Break out of loop and get next row in old table.
          addedRowFlag = true;
        }
      }

      // If no match was found above then item
      // should be added to bottom of list.
      if(!addedRowFlag)
      {
        newTableBody.appendChild(oldRow.cloneNode(true));
      }

      oldRow = oldRow.nextSibling;
    }

    // Add deep copy of header row to top of newTableBody.
    newTableBody.insertBefore(headerRow.cloneNode(true),newTableBody.firstChild);

    // Replace the old <tbody> with the new <tbody>.
    var oldTable = oldTableBody.parentNode;
    oldTable.replaceChild(newTableBody,oldTableBody);
}

function greaterThanOrEqual(left, right)
{
  return(left>=right);
}

function lessThanOrEqual(left, right)
```

LISTING 17.7 Continued

```
{
  return(left<=right);
}


</script>
</head>
<body>
<h1>User Database Table</h1>

Add a new row:
<table>
  <tr><td>First Name:</td><td><input type="text" name="newFirstName"></td></tr>
  <tr><td>Last Name:</td><td><input type="text" name="newLastName"></td></tr>
  <tr><td>Age:</td><td><input type="text" name="newAge"></td></tr>
</table>
<button onclick="addNewRow('top')">Add To Top</button>
<button onclick="addNewRow('bottom')">Add To Bottom</button>

<br /><hr /><br />

<table id="dbRowsTable" border="1">
<tr>
  <th id="tableColumn1">FIRST NAME
    <img src="ascending.gif"
        alt="Sort Ascending"
        onclick="sortTable('tableColumn1','ascending')">
    <img src="descending.gif"
        alt="Sort Descending"
        onclick="sortTable('tableColumn1','descending')">
  </th>
  <th id="tableColumn2">LAST NAME
    <img src="ascending.gif"
        alt="Sort Ascending"
        onclick="sortTable('tableColumn2','ascending')">
    <img src="descending.gif"
        alt="Sort Descending"
        onclick="sortTable('tableColumn2','descending')">
  </th>
  <th id="tableColumn3">AGE
```

LISTING 17.7   Continued

```
        <img src="ascending.gif"
             alt="Sort Ascending"
             onclick="sortTable('tableColumn3','ascending')">
        <img src="descending.gif"
             alt="Sort Descending"
             onclick="sortTable('tableColumn3','descending')">
      </th>
    </tr>
  </table>

  </body>
</html>
```

As you can see in Listing 17.7, a few additional functions are needed along with some event handlers and some graphics to make a dynamically sorting table. First, two methods, called greaterThanOrEqual and lessThanOrEqual, are created for comparing two string or number values that are passed into the functions. A Boolean value is returned from both functions. These two functions will be used in a new function called sortTable.

The new sortTable function does most of the work of reordering the rows of the table. The function takes in two parameters, the id given to the column and the sort order. The column id is used to determine which column is to be examined for sorting. The cloneNode method is used to create a shallow copy of the tbody element of the table. If there are fewer than two data rows, there is nothing to sort, so break out of the function without doing anything.

If there are at least two data rows, the new tbody element is seeded with an initial row, from the old table, for performing comparisons. Each row in the original table is then compared and placed into the new tbody element based on the user's sorting instructions. The header row from the original table is deep copied and added to the top of the tbody element. Finally, the old tbody element is replaced with the new sorted tbody element using the replaceNode method. Now all that is needed are event handlers to call on this new sortTable function. First, two graphics, representing ascending and descending, are added to each column head cell in the table. These will allow the user to choose the order and column to sort by. Next, onclick event handlers are added to these graphics to call on the sortTable function. In order to know which column should be used for comparing, each <th> table header tag is given an id, which is passed to the sortTable function.

The end result of this example is an XHTML table that can be dynamically sorted different ways all on the client's browser without ever making a trip to the server. Figure 17.4 shows the finished product in action.

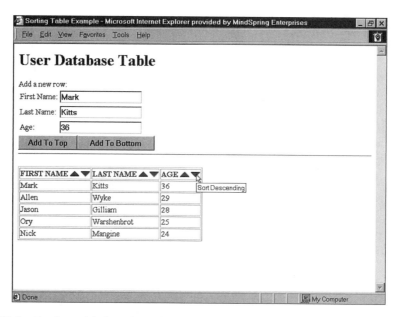

FIGURE 17.4   Sorting table based on descending age.

Summary

This chapter is the last of three chapters dealing with the Document Object Model (DOM). In this chapter you were introduced to three fundamental ways to manipulate the DOM.

The first technique covered was how to delete nodes from the DOM. You learned how to use the `removeChild` method of the `Node` object to remove nodes. You also learned how to remove attributes from `Element` objects using the `removeAttribute` and `removeAttributeNode` methods.

Next you learned about adding new nodes to the DOM. This discussion was broken down into three parts. The first part talked about how to create new objects, such as the `Element`, `Attr`, and `Text` objects. The second part showed you how to add new attributes to elements. The third part demonstrated how to create a relationship between objects and make them part of the current document using the `appendChild`, `insertBefore`, and `replaceChild` methods.

The chapter wrapped up with a discussion on copying nodes using the `cloneNode` method. You learned the difference between a deep copy and a shallow copy.

The JavaScript/DOM combination truly makes XHTML pages dynamic. The possibilities are endless, and it is my hope that this chapter has sparked your interest to dive even deeper into the DOM!

PART V

Scripting Documents

IN THIS PART

Handling Events

If you have programmed a lot over the past several years, chances are you've worked with an event-driven programming language. Procedural programs of the past dictated which task a user could perform at any given time. However, the graphical, windowed environments of today have a completely different paradigm and require applications to respond to events initiated by users rather than the other way around.

Given JavaScript's object-based nature, it should come as no surprise that JavaScript is primarily an event-driven language. This chapter discusses JavaScript events and how you can respond to them and thus create interactive scripts for your site.

Understanding Events and Event Handlers

Much of the code you write in JavaScript will respond to an event performed by either the user or the browser software. This event-driven environment lets you focus only on the events that affect your application; what the browser performs between events is its burden, not yours. In addition, you don't need to concern yourself with all the events performed by the user—only those to which you have access and to which you want to respond.

Each event has a corresponding **event handler** that is charged with the responsibility of automatically responding to the event when it occurs. For instance, when a person clicks on a link within an XHTML page, the click itself is the event. Behind the scenes there is an event handler that processes that event, and in this case, tells the browser to request a new page or other resource. When you work with an event, you never add code to it or modify the event itself; rather, you work with the event handler to which that event corresponds.

JavaScript Event Handlers

If you've created XHTML pages, you know that each element on a form has an element and attributes associated with it. For example, you would define text input in the following way:

```
<input type="text" size="30" maxlength="30" name="LastName" />
```

JavaScript can interface with the browser's event handlers by using attributes within these XHTML elements. For example, suppose you want to call a JavaScript function each time the value of a text field in a form changes. To do so, assign the function (called, for example, checkField()) to the element's onchange attribute (also known as event handler interface). Building on our last snippet of code, this would look like the following:

```
<input type="text" size="30" maxlength="30" name="LastName"
        onchange="checkField()" />
```

Within the quotes, you can either write in-place JavaScript code or call a function, as in the preceding code snippet. Although the previous example calls the checkField() function, the following code, which illustrates in-place JavaScript, would also be valid:

```
<input type="text" size="30" maxlength="30" name="LastName"
        onchange= "alert('Something Changed' )" />
```

> **TIP**
>
> If you use in-place code, you can place multiple lines within the event handler assignment by using a semicolon to separate each JavaScript command. However, use multiple lines of code with caution. It's much easier when code is encapsulated as a function than as the value of the event handler attribute. For example, if the code is located in a central location, it becomes much easier to make changes to it over the life of your Web site.

As you proceed through this chapter, you will examine the most common events supported by browsers. We will pay particular attention to the events for which you will most often want to trap. In doing so, you will take a typical XHTML form (shown in Figure 18.1) and add life to it by adding code to its event handlers. The form you will use initially is a customer information form, and the code used to create this form can be found in Listing 18.1.

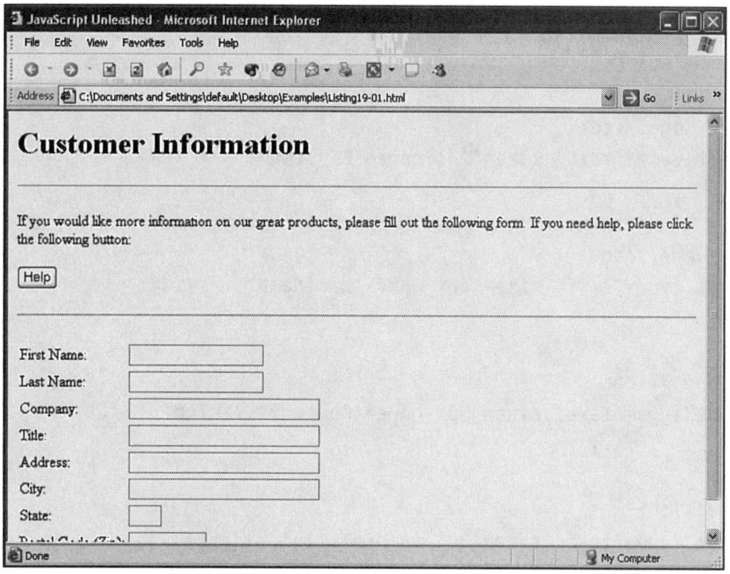

FIGURE 18.1   A sample XHTML form.

LISTING 18.1   Code for Sample Form

```
<?xml version="1.0" encoding="UTF-8"?>
<!DOCTYPE html PUBLIC "-//W3C//DTD XHTML 1.0 Transitional//EN"
                      "DTD/xhtml1-transitional.dtd">
<html xmlns="http://www.w3.org/1999/xhtml" xml:lang="en">
<head>
  <title>JavaScript Unleashed</title>
</head>
<body>
<h1>Customer Information</h1>
<hr />
<p>If you would like more information on our great products, please fill out
the following form. If you need help, please click the following button:
</p>
<form action="null">
  <p>
    <input type="button" value="Help" />
  </p>
</form>
<hr />
<form action="/cgi-bin/process_customer_info.cgi">
```

18

LISTING 18.1   Continued

```html
<table>
  <tr>
    <td>First Name:</td>
    <td><input type="text" size="20" name="FirstName" /></td>
  </tr>
  <tr>
    <td>Last Name:</td>
    <td><input type="text" size="20" name="LastName" /></td>
  </tr>
  <tr>
    <td>Company:</td>
    <td><input type="text" size="30" name="Company" /></td>
  </tr>
  <tr>
    <td>Title:</td>
    <td><input type="text" size="30" name="Title" /></td>
  </tr>
  <tr>
    <td>Address:</td>
    <td><input type="text" size="30" name="Address" /></td>
  </tr>
  <tr>
    <td>City:</td>
    <td><input type="text" size="30" name="City" /></td>
  </tr>
  <tr>
    <td>State:</td>
    <td><input type="text" size="2" name="State" /></td>
  </tr>
  <tr>
    <td>Postal Code (Zip):</td>
    <td><input type="text" size="10" name="Zip" /></td>
  </tr>
  <tr>
    <td colspan="2"><input type="submit" value="Submit" /></td>
  </tr>
</table>
</form>
</body>
</html>
```

Clicking an Object

One of the most common uses of JavaScript is to enhance XHTML forms to provide a greater degree of interactivity. If that is true, perhaps the single most common event many developers will work with is the click event. As you have come to see throughout this book, the click event is triggered when the user clicks within the browser window. There are event handlers for everything from clicking the window itself to clicking specific elements, such as a button, within an XHTML document.

As is standard for most computer environments, the click event is triggered only after the default mouse button, usually the left one, is pressed and released. A user holding the mouse button down without releasing it on the object will not cause the object's click event to be triggered.

When a click event occurs, the onClick event handler for the object that is clicked executes one or more commands. By using the onclick attribute, you can intercept, or "handle," what happens next with JavaScript. For example, in Figure 18.1, there is a button for users to access additional help if needed. Let's suppose you want to add some JavaScript code to open a second browser window with the help information when the button is clicked.

To accomplish this task, you must first create a JavaScript function to pop up the new window and load the necessary help page. This is done within the <head> section of the XHTML document. For this purpose, you will write a displayHelp() function that will be called when the button's onClick event handler is triggered. The JavaScript code used to perform this task is as follows:

```
<script type="text/javascript">
  function displayHelp() {
    helpWindow = window.open("help.html", "myHelp",
                            "toolbar=0,width=300,height=200,resizable=0");
  }
</script>
```

What this function does is create a window (referenced as helpWindow from JavaScript) and open the window (named myHelp from a browser perspective) with the help.html page loaded. The final list of arguments passed to the window.open() method tells the browser to open a window that has no toolbars, is 300 pixels wide, 200 pixels high, and is not resizable.

After this function has been created, we need to add the appropriate attribute to our button element to call the function. If you remember, we created the Help button using the <input> element with the type attribute set to button. We just need to add the onclick attribute and have it call our function, which can be accomplished with the following:

```
<input type="button" value="Help" onclick="displayHelp()" />
```

When the user clicks the button, the event handler calls the JavaScript function containing the `window.open()` method, which displays a new window showing our help message. This window can be seen in Figure 18.2.

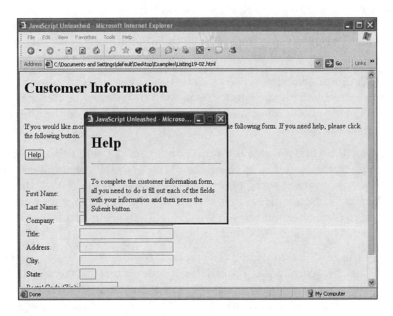

FIGURE 18.2   The second window is displayed using the `open()` method.

The final and updated document that contains the code used to define and call our function can be found in Listing 18.2. We have also included the XHTML document needed for our help window in Listing 18.3.

LISTING 18.2   Updated Code for Our Sample Form

```
<?xml version="1.0" encoding="UTF-8"?>
<!DOCTYPE html PUBLIC "-//W3C//DTD XHTML 1.0 Transitional//EN"
                     "DTD/xhtml1-transitional.dtd">
<html xmlns="http://www.w3.org/1999/xhtml" xml:lang="en">
<head>
  <title>JavaScript Unleashed</title>
  <script type="text/javascript">
    function displayHelp() {
      helpWindow = window.open("help.html", "myHelp",
                          "toolbar=0,width=300,height=200,resizable=0");
    }
  </script>
```

LISTING 18.2   Continued

```
</head>
<body>
<h1>Customer Information</h1>
<hr />
<p>If you would like more information on our great products, please fill out
the following form. If you need help, please click the following button:
</p>
<form action="null">
  <p>
    <input type="button" value="Help" onclick="displayHelp()" />
  </p>
</form>
<hr />
<form action="/cgi-bin/process_customer_info.cgi">
<table>
  <tr>
    <td>First Name:</td>
    <td><input type="text" size="20" name="FirstName" /></td>
  </tr>
  <tr>
    <td>Last Name:</td>
    <td><input type="text" size="20" name="LastName" /></td>
  </tr>
  <tr>
    <td>Company:</td>
    <td><input type="text" size="30" name="Company" /></td>
  </tr>
  <tr>
    <td>Title:</td>
    <td><input type="text" size="30" name="Title" /></td>
  </tr>
  <tr>
    <td>Address:</td>
    <td><input type="text" size="30" name="Address" /></td>
  </tr>
  <tr>
    <td>City:</td>
    <td><input type="text" size="30" name="City" /></td>
  </tr>
  <tr>
    <td>State:</td>
```

18

LISTING 18.2　Continued

```
    <td><input type="text" size="2" name="State" /></td>
  </tr>
  <tr>
    <td>Postal Code (Zip):</td>
    <td><input type="text" size="10" name="Zip" /></td>
  </tr>
  <tr>
    <td colspan="2"><input type="submit" value="Submit" /></td>
  </tr>
</table>
</form>
</body>
</html>
```

LISTING 18.3　Code for Our Help Window

```
<?xml version="1.0" encoding="UTF-8"?>
<!DOCTYPE html PUBLIC "-//W3C//DTD XHTML 1.0 Transitional//EN"
                       "DTD/xhtml1-transitional.dtd">
<html xmlns="http://www.w3.org/1999/xhtml" xml:lang="en">
<head>
  <title>JavaScript Unleashed</title>
</head>
<body>
<h1>Help</h1>
<hr />
<p>
  To complete the customer information form, all you need to do is fill out
  each of the fields with your information and then click the Submit button.
</p>
</body>
</html>
```

The onClick event handler isn't just for capturing click events for buttons; you can use it to respond to clicks on check boxes, radio buttons, links, and other items as well. Because of the nature of these controls, a customized click event for them may be less common, because check boxes and radio buttons are often used for data entry and evaluated at the server. Links, on the other hand, are used primarily to link to other resources on the Web, but code is often added to modify or verify this default behavior.

NOTE

For check boxes, links, radio buttons, reset buttons, and submit buttons, you can return a false value from handling a click event to cancel the triggered action. For example, if you wanted to confirm whether or not to check a check box, you could use the following code:

```
<input type="checkbox" name="myCB" value="DeluxeRoom"
onclick="return confirm('Are you sure?')" />Deluxe Room
```

Because the appearance of a Web page is important, you might want to use images rather than buttons. Although an image, by default, does not have the inherent ability to respond to click events, you can imitate this action by wrapping it with a link. To illustrate this point, we'll replace the button in our example with an image. Like the button, however, this image will be used to call the `displayHelp()` function. To do this, you simply replace your `<form>` element and its child elements (`<p>` and `<input>`) and define your button with the following:

```
<a href="javascript:displayHelp()">
  <img src="help.gif" alt="Help" border="0" width="17" height="17" />
</a>
```

One of the things you might notice is that we use the `javascript:` as the URL for the `href` attribute of the `<a>` element. Using this format, `javascript:JavaScriptExpression`, tells the browser to execute the `JavaScriptExpression` rather than request a specific resource, which is what most links are used for.

Submitting a Form

As discussed in Chapter 1, "Introducing JavaScript," one of the advantages of using JavaScript in XHTML forms is that you can perform data validation on the client side rather than pass this task onto an overloaded server. You can perform validation on a field-by-field basis or on a form-wide basis. Depending on the context, you might want to use one or both methods.

For form-wide data validation, as well as for other tasks, the submit event is the one to focus on from an event standpoint. This event occurs after a submit button has been clicked, but just before the submission of a form. You can intercept and process this event by adding the `onsubmit` attribute to the `<form>` element. This enables you to perform any desired checks before the submission of the form as well as either allow it to proceed or block it. The submit event will occur unless a `false` value is returned from your code, which is how you can block or prevent the submission. Any other value (`true` or otherwise) will cause the submission to occur.

For example, suppose you want to display a simple confirmation message to the user of our customer information form before submission. To accomplish this simple task, you first need to create the necessary function to prompt the user for confirmation. The function you can use is

18

```
function confirmSubmit() {
  return confirm('Are you certain you wish to submit?');
}
```

Next, you need to add the onsubmit attribute and a value specifying your function to your <form> instance. The following snippet shows what this would look like after adding this attribute:

```
<form action="/cgi-bin/process_customer_info.cgi"
      onsubmit="return confirmSubmit()">
```

When the submit button is clicked, the confirmSubmit() method displays a confirmation dialog box allowing the user to accept the submission or cancel it. If the user clicks OK, the dialog box is closed, and a true value is returned to the form, which then passes on the true value to the submit event and the submission proceeds as normal. If the user clicks Cancel, false is returned and the user is simply returned to the page with no submission.

The onSubmit event handler of a form is similar to an onClick event handler tied to a submit button. Both of these can be used to trap a form before it's processed. If you have attempted to capture both the click event of the Submit button and the submit event of the form, the Submit button's onClick event handler is triggered first, followed by the form's onSubmit, as shown in Figure 18.3.

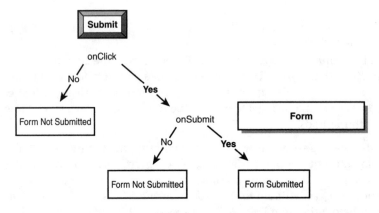

FIGURE 18.3   Event sequencing on a form submission.

The onSubmit event handler is an ideal method of processing the submission of a form, which means that it is the best place to perform data validation on the form before it is sent to a server.

Our form, now complete with using an image to display our help and confirmation of submission, can be found in Listing 18.4 and seen in Figure 18.4.

LISTING 18.4   Final Form with Image and Submission Confirmation

```
<?xml version="1.0" encoding="UTF-8"?>
<!DOCTYPE html PUBLIC "-//W3C//DTD XHTML 1.0 Transitional//EN"
                      "DTD/xhtml1-transitional.dtd">
<html xmlns="http://www.w3.org/1999/xhtml" xml:lang="en">
<head>
  <title>JavaScript Unleashed</title>
  <script type="text/javascript">
    function displayHelp() {
      helpWindow = window.open("help.html", "myHelp",
                            "toolbar=0,width=300,height=200,resizable=0");
    }

    function confirmSubmit() {
      return confirm('Are you certain you wish to submit?');
    }
  </script>
</head>
<body>
<h1>Customer Information</h1>
<hr />
<p>If you would like more information on our great products, please fill out
the following form. If you need help, please click the following button:
  <a href="javascript:displayHelp()">
    <img src="help.gif" alt="Help" border="0" width="17" height="17" />
  </a>
</p>
<hr />
<form action="/cgi-bin/process_customer_info.cgi"
      onsubmit="return confirmSubmit()">
<table>
  <tr>
    <td>First Name:</td>
    <td><input type="text" size="20" name="FirstName" /></td>
  </tr>
  <tr>
    <td>Last Name:</td>
    <td><input type="text" size="20" name="LastName" /></td>
  </tr>
  <tr>
```

LISTING 18.4   Continued

```
    <td>Company:</td>
    <td><input type="text" size="30" name="Company" /></td>
  </tr>
  <tr>
    <td>Title:</td>
    <td><input type="text" size="30" name="Title" /></td>
  </tr>
  <tr>
    <td>Address:</td>
    <td><input type="text" size="30" name="Address" /></td>
  </tr>
  <tr>
    <td>City:</td>
    <td><input type="text" size="30" name="City" /></td>
  </tr>
  <tr>
    <td>State:</td>
    <td><input type="text" size="2" name="State" /></td>
  </tr>
  <tr>
    <td>Postal Code (Zip):</td>
    <td><input type="text" size="10" name="Zip" /></td>
  </tr>
  <tr>
    <td colspan="2"><input type="submit" value="Submit" /></td>
  </tr>
</table>
</form>
</body>
</html>
```

Resetting a Form

You might have to trigger an event when a form is reset, as well as when it is submitted. The onReset event handler triggers code when a reset event occurs. Just as with onSubmit, onReset is an event handler that can be used with a <form>.

To illustrate, look again at our form. Using this example, we can capture the reset event by placing an onreset attribute into our <form>, which would look like this:

```
<form action="/cgi-bin/process_customer_info.cgi"
      onsubmit="return confirmSubmit()"
      onreset="return confirmReset()">
```

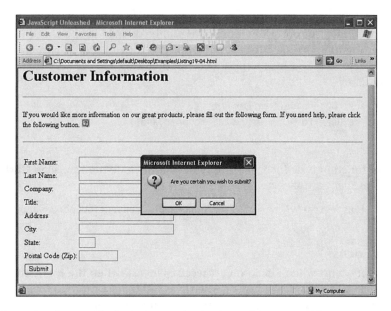

FIGURE 18.4   Our form with the image and submit confirmation additions.

As you might imagine, the confirmReset() function referenced in the onreset attribute of the <form> will need to be defined in the <head>. If we use a similar approach to our submission message, we come up with the following:

```
function confirmReset() {
  return confirm('Are you certain you wish to reset?');
}
```

Finally, we need to add the Reset button to our form, which we will add next to (within the same table cell) our Submit button. The code used to add the Reset button is

```
<input type="reset" value="Reset" />
```

Modifying Data

As mentioned with the submit event, when your JavaScript applications deal with user-entered data, you'll typically want to preprocess the data to avoid validation problems at the server. Although submit is designed for form-wide verification, the change event is typically the most important event for field-level validation. The change event occurs after the value of a field changes and it loses focus.

You use the onChange event handler to capture and execute JavaScript code or call a function to handle these events. Suppose you want to add a basic validity-checking routine to the example form. Specifically, you want to ensure that the State field is always uppercase.

In order to do this, you must first create the appropriate function to call after the user has entered the data. Like our other functions, this will be defined in the <head> of the document. Converting to uppercase is relatively simple, because of the `toUpperCase()` method of the `String` object. Using this method, you can perform the necessary check with the following function:

```
function convertToUppercase(formElement) {
  formElement.value = formElement.value.toUpperCase()
}
```

Now that our function is defined, we simply need to include the `onchange` attribute with the text field element as follows:

```
<input type="text" size="2" name="State" onchange="convertToUppercase(this)" />
```

Receiving Focus

The focus event occurs when a field object receives focus—when the user either tabs into the object or clicks it with the mouse or when you call the appropriate `focus()` method and explicitly assign focus. As you might imagine, only one object can receive focus at a given time. Also, you can access the `onFocus` event handler for these objects. For example, let's enhance the standard behavior of the text fields on the form.

When you move into a text field, an insertion point appears by default. However, it is standard in many applications that if the field already has a value, the contents are selected when the object receives focus. To create this behavior in our example, we first need to create a function. This simple function, contained in the following snippet, calls the `select()` method.

```
function selectContents(formElement) {
    formElement.select();
}
```

Next, we need to add an `onfocus` attribute to each of the text fields. The following snippet of code shows what this would look like for the field that collects a person's first name:

```
<input type="text" size="20" name="FirstName" onfocus="selectContents(this)"/>
```

Although you could write separate functions for each of these fields, it would not be wise to do so unless the processes were completely different. In this case, however, they are not—it is the same process for each text field. This is accomplished by taking advantage of the `this` keyword, which passes a reference to the current object making the call. We have made a lot of additions to our example since we last included it in the chapter, so Listing 18.5 includes the up-to-date version of our code. You can see the functions we have added, as well as the attributes and their values, to capture and process the various events we have been talking about.

LISTING 18.5   Up-to-Date Version of Our Code

```
<?xml version="1.0" encoding="UTF-8"?>
<!DOCTYPE html PUBLIC "-//W3C//DTD XHTML 1.0 Transitional//EN"
                      "DTD/xhtml1-transitional.dtd">
<html xmlns="http://www.w3.org/1999/xhtml" xml:lang="en">
<head>
  <title>JavaScript Unleashed</title>
  <script type="text/javascript">
    function displayHelp() {
      helpWindow = window.open("help.html", "myHelp",
                              "toolbar=0,width=300,height=200,resizable=0");
    }

    function confirmSubmit() {
      return confirm('Are you certain you wish to submit?');
    }

    function confirmReset() {
      return confirm('Are you certain you wish to reset?');
    }

    function convertToUppercase(formElement) {
      formElement.value = formElement.value.toUpperCase()
    }

     function selectContents(formElement) {
       formElement.select();
    }
  </script>
</head>
<body>
<h1>Customer Information</h1>
<hr />
<p>If you would like more information on our great products, please fill out
the following form. If you need help, please click the following button:
  <a href="javascript:displayHelp()">
    <img src="help.gif" alt="Help" border="0" width="17" height="17" />
  </a>
</p>
<hr />
<form action="/cgi-bin/process_customer_info.cgi"
      onsubmit="return confirmSubmit()"
```

LISTING 18.5   Continued

```
        onreset="return confirmReset()">
<table>
  <tr>
    <td>First Name:</td>
    <td>
      <input type="text" size="20" name="FirstName"
             onfocus="selectContents(this)" />
    </td>
  </tr>
  <tr>
    <td>Last Name:</td>
    <td>
      <input type="text" size="20" name="LastName"
             onfocus="selectContents(this)" />
    </td>
  </tr>
  <tr>
    <td>Company:</td>
    <td>
      <input type="text" size="30" name="Company"
             onfocus="selectContents(this)" />
    </td>
  </tr>
  <tr>
    <td>Title:</td>
    <td>
      <input type="text" size="30" name="Title"
             onfocus="selectContents(this)" />
    </td>
  </tr>
  <tr>
    <td>Address:</td>
    <td>
      <input type="text" size="30" name="Address"
             onfocus="selectContents(this)" />
    </td>
  </tr>
  <tr>
    <td>City:</td>
    <td>
      <input type="text" size="30" name="City"
             onfocus="selectContents(this)" />
```

LISTING 18.5   Continued

```
        </td>
      </tr>
      <tr>
        <td>State:</td>
        <td>
          <input type="text" size="2" name="State"
                 onchange="convertToUppercase(this)" />
        </td>
      </tr>
      <tr>
        <td>Postal Code (Zip):</td>
        <td>
          <input type="text" size="10" name="Zip"
                 onfocus="selectContents(this)" />
        </td>
      </tr>
      <tr>
        <td colspan="2">
          <input type="submit" value="Submit" />
          <input type="reset" value="Reset" />
        </td>
      </tr>
    </table>
  </form>
</body>
</html>
```

Losing Focus

The blur event, which is the inverse of the focus event, is triggered when an object loses focus. For example, suppose on our form we wanted to ensure that a person's postal code was not left blank. We could add a check using the onBlur event handler of that particular element instance. Because this affects a single field of the form, we will add the necessary JavaScript code right into the body of the <input> element itself, as shown in the following snippet.

```
    <input type="text" size="10" name="Zip"
           onfocus="selectContents(this)"
           onblur="if(this.value == ''){
                       alert('Please Enter A Postal Code');
                       this.focus();
                   }" />
```

> **NOTE**
>
> After the user tabs into the field, he will be required to enter a value in the field before he clicks somewhere else. Obviously, this could be very frustrating for users, so if you plan on using this approach on your live site, be sure this is the effect you want.

If the user tries to tab out of this text field without entering any information, an alert dialog box will notify her not to leave the field blank, as shown in Figure 18.5. After the notification, the next command returns focus to the text field. If we had not included this step, the cursor would have been allowed to move to another part of the page.

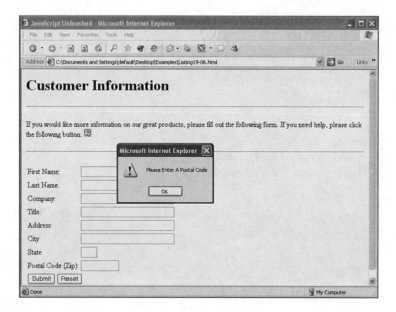

FIGURE 18.5   Preventing the user from avoiding the Postal Code data entry.

Selecting Text

The next event is the select event, which occurs when the user selects text from a text or textarea element. For this event, the `onSelect` event handler is accessed to either execute your own JavaScript code or call a predefined function. Regardless, this event's scope is rather limited for most purposes, and most developers will have little occasion to use it.

Moving the Mouse over Objects

If you are an experienced Web user, you have come to expect that the act of moving your mouse over a link will display the destination URL in the status bar of the browser. Using a couple of the mouse-oriented events, you can change this default text in the status bar. Let's look more closely at these events before doing this.

The mouseOver event takes place when the user moves the mouse cursor over an element. As you might expect, mouseOut behaves in much the same way, except that it occurs each time a mouse pointer leaves an element. Using the corresponding event handlers, we can capture and then change the default behavior of the browser and what it displays in the status bar.

For example, suppose you want to display the words "Get Help" in the status bar when a user rolls her mouse over the help image. To accomplish this task, you can simply set the window.status property using the onmouseover attribute of the <a> element wrapped around the image. This, however, will permanently change the text in the status bar, so you will need to change it back to something else when the mouse moves off that area. This will be accomplished using the mouseOut event handler, as you can see in the following snippet.

```
<a href="javascript:displayHelp()"
   onmouseover="alert(window.status='Get Help'; return true"
   onmouseout="window.status='Done'; return true">
```

> **TIP**
>
> If you're capturing multiple mouseOver and mouseOut events within an <area> element, it is worth noting that mouseOut will be fired when you leave an <area>, followed by mouseOver when you enter the next <area>.

Loading a Document

The initial opening of a window or frameset can be an important time to perform an action controlled through JavaScript. In this case as we have seen before, the load event, which is executed when the browser finishes loading a window or all frames within a frameset, can be captured by the onLoad event handler. This is done by adding the onload attribute to a single window's <body> element or to a multiframe's <frameset> element.

To illustrate, suppose you want to ensure that all intranet users in your company are using the correct version of the Netscape browser. You could evaluate the browser's user agent string when the page finishes loading and then, if necessary, notify the user that his software version is incorrect. In this example, if the user is not using a Netscape browser, or if her browser is older than Netscape 6, an alert message will be displayed.

The function we have created to handle this process is

```
function checkBrowser(){
  if((navigator.appName != 'Netscape') ||
             (parseInt(navigator.appVersion.substring(0,1)) <= 4)){
```

```
      alert('Your Web Browser needs to be updated')
   }
}
```

Now that the function is defined, all we need to do is call it using the onload attribute of the <body> element as seen following:

```
<body onload="checkBrowser()">
```

When the document is loaded, the JavaScript function is called, and as in Figure 18.6, the alert message is displayed for browsers or versions that don't pass the test.

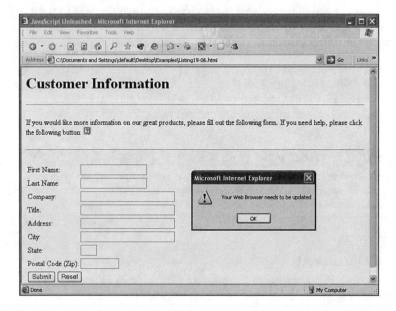

FIGURE 18.6   The alert is displayed by the onLoad event handler.

NOTE

Images also have an onLoad event handler. This event is triggered after an image is loaded by the browser. Note that this event does not occur during the loading of an image to a client, but during the display of that image.

Exiting a Document

The unload event, which is the counterpart to the load event, is triggered just before the user exits a document. As with the onLoad event handler, you can use the onUnload event handler to capture unload events from a single window's <body> element or a multiframe <frameset> element. If you have a frameset and multiple onUnload event handlers, the <frameset> event handler always happens last.

One example of how you can use the unload event is cleaning up the browser environment before continuing to the next page. For instance, suppose you want to close the Help window when leaving our customer information page. To do this, you can create a function that explicitly closes our window:

```
function clean(){
  helpWindow.close();
}
```

The helpWindow is a variable declared when we created the window and it references the Help window. If the Help window is open when the user exits the current page, it will automatically close because this function is called by adding the onunload attribute to the <body> element as follows:

```
<body onload="checkBrowser()" onunload="clean()">
```

Our completed code, with all of the additions we have applied in this chapter, can be seen in Listing 18.6.

LISTING 18.6   The Completed Form Example with All Code Changes

```
<?xml version="1.0" encoding="UTF-8"?>
<!DOCTYPE html PUBLIC "-//W3C//DTD XHTML 1.0 Transitional//EN"
                      "DTD/xhtml1-transitional.dtd">
<html xmlns="http://www.w3.org/1999/xhtml" xml:lang="en">
<head>
  <title>JavaScript Unleashed</title>
  <script type="text/javascript">
    function displayHelp() {
      helpWindow = window.open("help.html", "myHelp",
                              "toolbar=0,width=300,height=200,resizable=0");
    }

    function confirmSubmit() {
      return confirm('Are you certain you wish to submit?');
    }

    function confirmReset() {
      return confirm('Are you certain you wish to reset?');
    }
```

18

LISTING 18.6   Continued

```
    function convertToUppercase(formElement) {
      formElement.value = formElement.value.toUpperCase();
    }

    function selectContents(formElement) {
       formElement.select();
    }

    function checkBrowser(){
      if((navigator.appName != 'Netscape') ||
           (parseInt(navigator.appVersion.substring(0,1)) <= 4)){
        alert('Your Web Browser needs to be updated')
      }
    }

    function clean() {
       helpWindow.close();
    }

  </script>
</head>
<body onload="checkBrowser()" onunload="clean()">
<h1>Customer Information</h1>
<hr />
<p>If you would like more information on our great products, please fill out
the following form. If you need help, please click the following button:
  <a href="javascript:displayHelp()"
     onmouseover="window.status='Get Help'; return true"
     onmouseout="window.status='Done'; return true">
    <img src="help.gif" alt="Help" border="0" width="17" height="17" />
  </a>
</p>
<hr />
<form action="/cgi-bin/process_customer_info.cgi"
      onsubmit="return confirmSubmit()"
      onreset="return confirmReset()">
<table>
  <tr>
    <td>First Name:</td>
    <td>
      <input type="text" size="20" name="FirstName"
```

LISTING 18.6   Continued

```
             onfocus="selectContents(this)" />
      </td>
   </tr>
   <tr>
      <td>Last Name:</td>
      <td>
         <input type="text" size="20" name="LastName"
                onfocus="selectContents(this)" />
      </td>
   </tr>
   <tr>
      <td>Company:</td>
      <td>
         <input type="text" size="30" name="Company"
                onfocus="selectContents(this)" />
      </td>
   </tr>
   <tr>
      <td>Title:</td>
      <td>
         <input type="text" size="30" name="Title"
                onfocus="selectContents(this)" />
      </td>
   </tr>
   <tr>
      <td>Address:</td>
      <td>
         <input type="text" size="30" name="Address"
                onfocus="selectContents(this)" />
      </td>
   </tr>
   <tr>
      <td>City:</td>
      <td>
         <input type="text" size="30" name="City"
                onfocus="selectContents(this)" />
      </td>
   </tr>
   <tr>
      <td>State:</td>
      <td>
```

18

LISTING 18.6   Continued

```
      <input type="text" size="2" name="State"
             onchange="convertToUppercase(this)" />
   </td>
  </tr>
  <tr>
    <td>Postal Code (Zip):</td>
    <td>
      <input type="text" size="10" name="Zip"
             onfocus="selectContents(this)"
             onblur="if(this.value == ''){
                        alert('Please Enter A Postal Code');
                        this.focus();
                     }" />
    </td>
  </tr>
  <tr>
    <td colspan="2">
      <input type="submit" value="Submit" />
      <input type="reset" value="Reset" />
    </td>
  </tr>
</table>
</form>
</body>
</html>
```

Handling Errors

The window and image objects also have an onerror event handler that lets you trap for errors occurring during the loading of a document or image. The error that will be trapped will be either a JavaScript syntax error or a runtime error, not a browser error. As you might have thought, this event handler is accessed by using the onerror attribute with the <body> and <img> elements.

For example, in the following snippet if the image is not available, an alert box will pop up:

```
<img onerror="alert('Error loading image')" alt="Home" src="home.gif" />
```

Aborting an Image Load

Loading an image can be a time-intensive process, depending on the size of the image, especially for people who are still accessing the Web via dial-up modem. As a result, users may become impatient and stop the image load before it is complete. For example, a user may abort the loading process by clicking a link to another page or the browser's stop button.

However, having the user work with a partially downloaded file might not be what you would like to occur and will probably have some ramifications on any image-specific code in your script. The onabort event lets you react to this aborting of a load and potentially call a JavaScript function as a response. For example, suppose you wanted to alert your user that the entire XHTML document or a given image hasn't been downloaded. If you wanted to display an alert, you could add the following event handler to an <img> element instance to be called if he stopped the download of an image:

```
<img alt="World Map" src="global.gif"
    onabort="alert('You have not downloaded the entire image.')">
```

Other Event Tricks

In addition to the events and event handlers that are tied to XHTML elements, there are several other aspects that we want to share with you. Over the next few sections we are going to touch on these and show you further how you can tap the power of capturing events and performing your own processing.

Changing Event Handlers

It is also possible to change the function to handle an event previously defined within your XHTML element. For example, in Listing 18.7, the optionA() function is assigned within the <input> instance. However, the second script evaluates the choice variable, and depending on how it is defined, it will potentially change this assignment. If choice is equal to "A", the code changes the event handler assignment to the optionB() function. In this example, if you click the button, you will notice that the optionB() function is in fact called.

LISTING 18.7   An Example of Changing Event Handlers

```
<?xml version="1.0" encoding="UTF-8"?>
<!DOCTYPE html PUBLIC "-//W3C//DTD XHTML 1.0 Transitional//EN"
                    "DTD/xhtml1-transitional.dtd">
<html xmlns="http://www.w3.org/1999/xhtml" xml:lang="en">
<head>
  <title>JavaScript Unleashed</title>
  <script type="text/javascript">

    var choice = "A"

    function optionA(){
```

18

LISTING 18.7   Continued

```
      alert("Option A");
    }

    function optionB(){
      alert("Option B");
    }
  </script>
</head>
<body>
<form action="null" name="myForm">
  <input type="button" name="myButton" value="Click Here"
         onclick="optionA()" />
</form>

<script type="text/javascript">
  if (choice == "A"){
    document.myForm.myButton.onclick = optionB;
  }
</script>
</body>
</html>
```

> **NOTE**
>
> When you use this syntax to call the event handlers, the values themselves are function references and therefore do not have parentheses added to them.

Triggering Events in Code

So far, this chapter has discussed responding to events generated either by the user, such as a click, or the system, such as an unload event. In most cases, these types of events are the ones you are most concerned with. However, as a JavaScript developer, you don't have to rely on external forces to cause an event to happen. In fact, you can trigger some events automatically with your code.

For example, you can simulate a click event for a button by calling the click() method of that particular Button object instance. Although this is valid for a Button object, a link—which has an onClick event handler—doesn't have a click() method. So, check to make sure that the event you want to fire is actually a valid event for that element or object instance.

Timer Events

Many event-driven programming environments use timer events, which are events that can be triggered every time a given time interval elapses. Although core JavaScript language offers no such method to control events, you can use the `window.setInterval()` method to serve the same function.

The `setInterval()` method repeatedly calls a function or evaluates an expression each time a time interval (in milliseconds) has expired. This method continues to execute until the window is destroyed or the `clearInterval90` method is called.

For example, in Listing 18.8, the `setInterval()` method is executed when the document opens and begins to call the `dailyTask()` function every 10,000 milliseconds (10 seconds). The `dailyTask()` function evaluates the time each time it is called, and when it is 8:30 a.m., the code within the `if` statement is called, alerting the user and then clearing the interval. After the `clearInterval()` method is called, `setInterval()` halts execution.

LISTING 18.8 Source Code for Timer12.htm

```
<?xml version="1.0" encoding="UTF-8"?>
<!DOCTYPE html PUBLIC "-//W3C//DTD XHTML 1.0 Transitional//EN"
                  "DTD/xhtml1-transitional.dtd">
<html xmlns="http://www.w3.org/1999/xhtml" xml:lang="en">
<head>
  <title>JavaScript Unleashed</title>
  <script type="text/javascript">
  function dailyTask(){
    var tdy = new Date();
    if((tdy.getHours() == 8) && (tdy.getMinutes() == 30)){
      alert('Good morning sunshine!');
      clearInterval(timerID);
    }
  }

  timerID = setInterval('dailyTask()', 10000)
  </script>
</head>
<body>
<p>
Task Reminder
</p>
</body>
</html>
```

18

Summary

Given JavaScript's event-driven nature, a solid understanding of events, event handlers, and how JavaScript can be used to control these events is key to maximizing its power. This chapter discussed events, their associated event handlers, and how to intercept these events directly from XHTML elements. We focused on the most useful events and provided specific examples of how to use these. Having this foundation in place will assist you over the next few chapters as we look in depth at using events for other tasks.

CHAPTER **19**

Cascading Style Sheets

The introduction of Cascading Style Sheets (CSS) into HTML gave developers a more powerful way to express style, enhance presentation, and have more consistent control within documents. Before CSS, one of the major disadvantages of publishing information to the Web was the fact that it was nearly impossible to have the control the traditional desktop publishing world had. You had to use all kinds of workarounds to have items placed in the right locations or for fonts to be of the right type and size. Often, you were forced to use XHTML tables or rely on browser bugs to position your elements the way you wanted.

This all ended when CSS became a formalized Recommendation from the World Wide Web Consortium (W3C). CSS enabled developers to specify the exact fonts and sizes they wanted their text to be, as well as the exact location (CSS positioning, or CSS-P) of elements, and dozens of other items, such as backgrounds and colors.

In this chapter, we am going to introduce you to CSS and touch on some Netscape-only JavaScript arrays that allow you to work with styles in older version 4 browsers. If this were a perfect world and no one were using these older browsers, we would be able to remove this chapter from the book. However, many of you probably will have version 4 browsers accessing your site, so we felt it was necessary to leave it in for one more edition of the book.

It is also worth pointing out that this chapter is not meant to be a complete coverage of CSS, but rather a primer, so that you are familiar with CSS when we go over Dynamic HTML (DHTML) in Chapter 22, "Menus and Toolbars." We will also touch on CSS in terms of positioning in Chapter 20, "Layers."

NOTE

Complete coverage of CSS and its variations is beyond the scope of this book. If you would like more information on CSS, please visit the W3C Web site at `http://www.w3.org`.

Basic Style Sheet Concepts

A style sheet consists of one or more style definitions (font sizes, font styles, text alignment, font and background colors, margins, padding, line height, and so on) for XHTML elements that can be either linked or embedded in documents. This functionality was created to give developers and Web designers the ability to have consistent styles and positioning throughout the document.

Over the next few pages, you are going to take an introductory look at this technology and how it applies to JavaScript. Additionally, you will get into some of the details of using CSS because it is an integral piece of technology in the implementation of DHTML.

Standards

To successfully implement any kind of technology on a wide scale, there must be some kind of standard or formalized method of implementation. Like many of the standards being used by Internet developers today, CSS was created and is maintained by the W3C. In this section of the chapter we will take a quick look at the various releases of the CSS Recommendations, so that you have a better understanding of the history and direction of this technology. We will go into more detail on these standards throughout the rest of the chapter, but right now we want to first introduce them to you at a high level.

CSS Level 1

In December 1996, the first version of CSS was made an official Recommendation by the W3C, often referred to as CSS1. This was the first attempt to create a standardized method of applying styles to Web documents, which started down the path of separating content from presentation.

It was obviously a giant step for developers and companies, because they were being given the flexibility and formatting they needed for their documents. However, this Recommendation, which was last updated in January 1999, did not contain everything that was needed by developers. Primarily it lacked the capability to position elements on a page and functions that would be needed for future uses, such as handheld and wireless devices.

CSS-P

In August 1997, the W3C issued the Positioning with Cascading Style Sheet (CSS-P) Recommendation. This Recommendation contained a subset of properties that allowed developers to explicitly specify the location of their elements on a page. This, combined with CSS, gave developers the majority of the control, down to the pixel, that they needed to create stylish pages. It was also the combination of CSS1 and CSS-P that was first implemented in browsers, such as Navigator 4, Internet Explorer 4, and Opera 3.5.

Level 2 Enhancements

The second version of CSS (Level 2 or CSS2 for short) accomplished several primary tasks. First and foremost, it combined the CSS1 and CSS-P Recommendations into a single Recommendation. It also implemented the concept of media types to best accommodate the need for styling print material or data delivered to Internet appliances or devices. CSS2 even added a property that specified the type of cursor that the application should use as the pointing device.

Proposal for Level 3

The CSS group of the W3C is currently working on CSS Level 3 (CSS3), which breaks up the Recommendation into a set of modules, such as text, fonts, value and units, and lists. This latest edition, which has not been officially released as a W3C Recommendation yet, is attempting to provide not only support for scaleable vector graphics and international layout, but many other user interface enhancements as well. It will be this version that will take CSS to a more globally supported Recommendation, in much the same manner that HTML 4 and XHTML 1.0 did for HTML.

Inheritance

It's important to remember the concept of inheritance when defining styles. The term **inheritance** is used to describe the concept by which a child has the same properties as the parent. For the definitions used here, **parent** and **child** refer to XHTML elements that are grouped or contained within other elements. Style sheets give you the ability to set global styles for your documents and allow those styles to be passed to other elements within the document, thus saving you the time of defining styles for each element.

For example, the <body> element can have many children within it, including <h1> and <p>, whereas the <p> element will have fewer children (<em> is an example). For the majority of styles, the style of a parent is inherited by the child if the child has the same properties. You can safely assume that a <p> within the <body> will reflect the font size of the <body>, unless the <p> specifically overrides it. Styles are inherited inside containers for which they are defined. This functionality gives the document a more consistent look and feel.

Font sizes, text placement, and margins are excellent examples of how style sheets can help give a Web site consistency. When you define these styles generically in the parent elements, the styles will be inherited in the children of the document. Each document can have the same look and feel, while still giving the developer the option of manipulating and overriding the styles during runtime if desired.

19

> **NOTE**
>
> For the most part, styles that aren't inherited will be obvious. If the child doesn't have the same CSS property as the parent, the child can't inherit the style.

Margins and Padding

Not only can text properties be defined with CSS, but padding, borders, and margins for block-level elements can also be defined. Block-level elements are elements such as <h1> and <p>, which always start on a new line. These properties allow you to specify everything from the margins and padding around elements to borders.

Comments

As in all coding, comments are important in your code. Writing comments in CSS is similar to defining comments in other well-known programming languages, except that it only officially supports what are commonly known as multiline comments. For example, the following snippet is an acceptable comment format in CSS:

```
/* comment */
```

Using Styles in Your Document

There are several different methods of using styles in your documents. They can be placed inline using the `style` attribute, defined within a <style> section, or linked in using the <link> tag. In addition to the methods of placing styles in your documents, there are also several ways to apply them. Styles can be applied globally, by assigning a class with the `class` attribute, or even on an individual basis with the `id` attribute.

Defining Styles

As mentioned, styles are defined in one of three ways. By "defining a style," we mean that there are three locations where you can place a style. When creating a document that is using style sheets, you should use these methods to define your styles. There is not an exact rule on how you should do this; just try to implement it in a way that makes the most sense to you and those editing your documents.

<style>

The first location for defining styles is within the <style> tag. This tag takes a single attribute (`type`) that tells the browser what kind of style is being defined. The value of this attribute for CSS is `text/css`. Within the element are the actual style definitions. Listing 19.1 gives an example of using this method of defining styles.

LISTING 19.1   Defining Styles in the <style> Tag

```
<?xml version="1.0" encoding="UTF-8"?>
<!DOCTYPE html PUBLIC "-//W3C//DTD XHTML 1.1//EN"
    "http://www.w3.org/TR/xhtml11/DTD/xhtml11.dtd">
<html xmlns="http://www.w3.org/1999/xhtml" xml:lang="en" >
<head>
  <title>Sample Styles</title>
  <style type="text/css">
    h1{
      color: green;
      font-style: italic;
      font-size: 12pt;
    }

    h1.special{
      font-size: 24pt;
    }

    .newheader{
      color: red;
    }

    #caps{
      font-variant: small-caps;
    }
  </style>
</head>
<body>
  <h1>Green, italic, and a point size of 12</h1>
  <h1 class="newheader">Red, italic, and a point size of 12</h1>
  <h1 class="special">Point size of 24</h1>
  <p>
    Here is some <span id="caps">capitalized</span> text.
  </p>
</body>
</html>
```

In this example, you will see four different styles that are being applied to the text in the body of the document. Figure 19.1 shows the result of loading this example in a browser. Don't worry about the different types at this moment. We will cover them shortly.

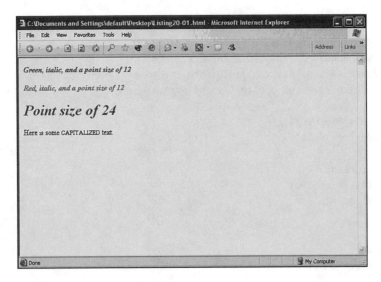

FIGURE 19.1   Header text overridden with class for Internet Explorer browsers.

<link>

If you prefer to store all or a set of your styles in a single location so that changes are applied globally across your site, you can use the <link> element. This element is used to link external style sheets to a document. The attributes of the <link> element, type and href, are used to define the type of link and the URL where the external style sheet can be located, as in the following snippet.

```
<link rel="stylesheet" type="text/css" href="/styles/tables.css" />
```

External style sheets are created similarly to inline style definitions. The style sheet is stored as a URL containing the style definitions, but the <style> element is not needed. The <link> element should be contained in the <head> section of your document. The following snippet of code shows how you might include the style sheet named chapters.css in a given document:

```
<head>
  <title>Same Call For An External Style Sheet</title>
  <link rel="stylesheet" type="text/css"
        href="http://www.mcp.com/stylesheets/chapters.css" />
</head>
```

The style Attribute

The final method to define styles and include them in your documents is through the use of the style attribute of any XHTML text element. style defines a new style to be used for that particular element instance only. This allows each element to have its own style, independent of any style defined in the current style sheet.

This lowest-level method of applying a style involves defining it for a particular instance of an element. This allows for very specific style definitions for each element. Styles are not often defined in this manner because of the difficulty of editing the style in the future. However, defining styles in this manner becomes extremely useful when the need to override a style occurs for only one particular instance of an element in the document.

For example, the following code line will make this particular <h3> a point size of 36:

```
<h3 style="font-size: 36pt;">Hello</h3>
```

Applying Styles

After you have defined styles, you can apply them by using the id or class attributes or at a global level. Of course, the last method of defining styles discussed, using the style attribute, could also be a method of applying a style. It is actually a one-step method of defining and applying a style.

Applying Styles Globally

To apply a style globally across all instances of an element, you have to specify the element and the corresponding style changes in your definition. For example, if we wanted to change all instances of the <p> element to be displayed in an italic 16-point font, we would put the following in the <head> portion of our document. When we use this method, these styles will be applied every time we use the <p> element in this document.

```
<style type="text/css">
<!--
  p{
    font-style: italic;
    font-size: 16pt;
  }
-->
</style>
```

The id Attribute

The second method of applying a style is with the id attribute. When you use this method, you will define your style and prepend the name with a #. Listing 19.2 shows an example of creating a "heading" style that we then use on a <p> element. Notice that only the <p> element with the id="heading" value is affected. See Figure 19.2 for the result of loading this page in a browser.

LISTING 19.2   Using the id Attribute

```
<?xml version="1.0" encoding="UTF-8"?>
<!DOCTYPE html PUBLIC "-//W3C//DTD XHTML 1.1//EN"
    "http://www.w3.org/TR/xhtml11/DTD/xhtml11.dtd">
<html xmlns="http://www.w3.org/1999/xhtml" xml:lang="en" >
<head>
  <title>Sample Styles</title>
  <style type="text/css">
  <!--
    #heading{
      font-style: italic;
      font-size: 24pt;
    }
  -->
  </style>
</head>
<body>
  <p id="heading">
    Welcome to my page!
  </p>
  <p>
    Here is some text.
  </p>
</body>
</html>
```

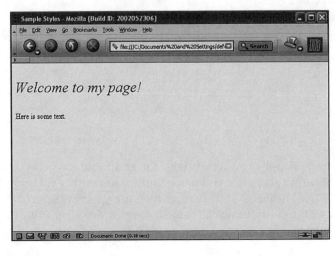

FIGURE 19.2   Specifying styles with the id attribute.

The class Attribute

Styles that are defined by class are explicitly called with the XHTML elements at each use. Style classes, as shown in Listing 19.3, are a way to group together style properties that you are going to use in several locations in your document. Defining styles to the document in classes rather than generically gives you more control over the use of the styles and allows for more flexibility on an element-by-element basis. This method can also make CSS more complicated because the XHTML document has now become more complex, with much interwoven CSS class usage.

Defining classes of styles can be especially useful when styles need to apply to more than one element. It would be extremely tedious to define a style that set the color to yellow for each element. You can use classes to define one yellowClass and then use that class with any element that has the color property. Defining classes is the most effective method for making use of the flexibility of style sheets. Listing 19.3 shows an example of defining two classes of styles and applying them to different instances of the <p> element.

LISTING 19.3   Using the class Attribute to Select a Style

```
<?xml version="1.0" encoding="UTF-8"?>
<!DOCTYPE html PUBLIC "-//W3C//DTD XHTML 1.1//EN"
    "http://www.w3.org/TR/xhtml11/DTD/xhtml11.dtd">
<html xmlns="http://www.w3.org/1999/xhtml" xml:lang="en" >
<head>
  <title>Sample Styles</title>
  <style type="text/css">
  <!--
    .heading{
      font-style: italic;
      font-size: 24pt;
    }

    .content{
      font-size: 12pt;
    }
  -->
  </style>
</head>
<body>
  <p class="heading">
    Welcome to my page!
  </p>
  <p class="content">
    Here is some text.
  </p>
```

19

LISTING 19.3   Continued

```
</body>
</html>
```

<span> Tags

The final method of applying a style is through the use of the <span> element. This element is used to mark a specific piece of text, not the entire parent element, to which a style will be applied. This allows you to apply a style to content that has already had a style applied. Listing 19.4 shows an example of how you can override default styles using this tag.

LISTING 19.4   Using the <span> Element

```
<?xml version="1.0" encoding="UTF-8"?>
<!DOCTYPE html PUBLIC "-//W3C//DTD XHTML 1.1//EN"
    "http://www.w3.org/TR/xhtml11/DTD/xhtml11.dtd">
<html xmlns="http://www.w3.org/1999/xhtml" xml:lang="en" >
<head>
  <title>Sample Styles</title>
  <style type="text/css">
  <!--
    p{
      font-style: italic;
      font-size: 24pt;
    }

    #smaller{
      font-size: 12pt;
    }
  -->
  </style>
</head>
<body>
  <p>
    Here is some text that has global styles applied, but
    <span id="smaller">here is some smaller text</span> in
    the middle of this paragraph.
  </p>
</body>
</html>
```

Mixing Selectors

The implementation of multiple style sheets brings up the possibility of multiple style definitions for XHTML elements. Generally, style definitions in a style sheet will take precedence over any styles that have been previously defined for the document. The use of multiple style sheets can be beneficial when generic styles apply to the entire document and certain styles need to be overwritten for only a portion of the document. This is helpful when a corporate style is defined for the beginning of a document and the developer would like different styles to take precedence.

The exception to this rule is the use of the !important marker. For instance, if you have the following snippet, the later declaration of red will not apply:

```
p { color: blue !important; }
p { color: red; }
```

Listing 19.5 mixes selectors of different types, to achieve the effect shown in Figure 19.3. This includes applying attributes of different selector types (one class and one id attribute) and using the <span> element inside another element with a class defined.

LISTING 19.5   Combining Styles in a Single Style Definition

```
<?xml version="1.0" encoding="UTF-8"?>
<!DOCTYPE html PUBLIC "-//W3C//DTD XHTML 1.1//EN"
    "http://www.w3.org/TR/xhtml11/DTD/xhtml11.dtd">
<html xmlns="http://www.w3.org/1999/xhtml" xml:lang="en" >
<head>
  <title>Sample Styles</title>
  <style type="text/css">
  <!--
    h1{
      color: gray;
    }

    #ital{
      font-style: italic;
    }

    .newheader{
      color: red;
    }

    #myid{
```

LISTING 19.5   Continued

```
      font-size: 12pt;
    }
  -->
  </style>
</head>
<body>
  <h1>Gray</h1>
  <h1 class="newheader" id="myid">Red and point size 12</h1>
  <h1 class="newheader">Red and <span id="ital">italic</span></h1>
  <h2>This will be default text</h2>
</body>
</html>
```

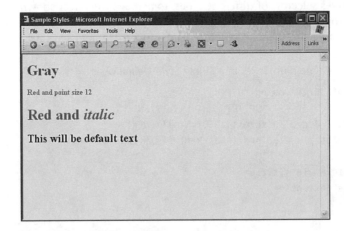

FIGURE 19.3   Mixed and matched selectors.

Determining Style Precedence

To find the value or precedence of a style for an element (and property), you must adhere to the following rules:

1. Locate all references to the element by any selector.

2. Sort the references by explicit weight.

3. Sort by origin of style sheet. Default values are overridden, if applicable, by user style sheets, which are overridden by author style sheets unless the user style sheet has !important declarations.

4. Sort by specificity. Give one point for each of the following three options, and then sum the points to get specificity:

- The number of `id` attributes

- The number of `class` attributes

- The number of element names referenced

5. Sort by the order specified. For two rules with identical weights, the latter rule will take precedence.

Using these five rules, you can accurately determine and account for the style that will be applied for an element when you're developing documents using CSS.

JavaScript Style Objects

In JavaScript 1.2, Netscape added three JavaScript objects—`tag`, `class`, and `id`—for use with style sheets. These objects, which were removed in JavaScript 1.5 (Netscape 6 and Mozilla-based browsers), are used to define the types of styles that can be applied to style definitions. These style definitions can be in external style sheets that are linked to the XHTML document, or they can be defined in the document itself, within the `<style>` element.

> **NOTE**
>
> JavaScript Style Sheets (JSSS) was created as an alternative to CSS within Netscape Navigator 4. NN4's CSS implementation is actually a layer on top of JSSS and is the foundation of these Style objects. This is painfully clear when you find out that disabling JavaScript in Netscape Navigator 4 disables both JavaScript and CSS style sheets.

> **NOTE**
>
> Currently, only Navigator 4 supports the method of accessing styles through these objects. Although other browsers may or may not provide a method to do so, take special care if you use these tags to assign styles. However, this is useful information when creating cross-browser DHTML that includes Netscape Navigator 4, but consider phasing this approach out because it is no longer supported in the newer browsers.

document.tags

The `document.tags` array is a reference to XHTML elements and, in truth, is a subobject of the `Document` object. Following the definition is the element to which it applies. After the element definition is the style property that is being defined (which does not necessarily have the same name as defined in CSS). The full syntax of a definition specifying that all <p> tags should have a font size of 20 is as follows:

```
document.tags.p.fontSize = "20pt";
```

> **NOTE**
>
> You can statically define the style only once in the document—while it loads. Although this syntax seems to imply the ability to change this style, this is not possible using document.tags.

document.classes

document.classes is also an array and a subobject of the Document object. This array contains access to tags with the class attribute specified. A style class can apply to one particular element:

```
document.classes.fontclass.blockquote.fontSize = "20pt";
```

Or it can be defined to be accessible to all elements:

```
document.classes.fontclass.all.fontSize = "20pt";
```

Following the object in the dot notation is the name of the class and then the element for which the class is defined. Classes defined as all can be applied to all elements, as shown in the second example.

document.ids

The document.ids object is similar to document.classes, except that any element that references that id will be rendered with the style defined.

```
document.id.myid.fontSize = "20pt";
```

The document.ids object is followed by the name of the id and, unlike the document.classes and document.tags objects, it doesn't take the element name (or all) as part of the definition. document.ids objects can be used with any element to which they apply.

Properties

Table 19.1 shows the properties available through the JavaScript style objects that you can use to define styles on your pages for Netscape Navigator 4 browsers.

TABLE 19.1   JavaScript Style Object Properties

Property Name	What It Applies To	Possible Values	Value Definitions
Font Properties			
fontSize	All elements	Absolute sizes	xx-small, x-small, small, medium, large, x-large, xx-large, point size
		Relative sizes	smaller, larger
		Percentage	150% bigger
fontStyle	All elements		normal, italic
Text Properties			
lineHeight	Block-level elements	Number	Units to increase height by
		Length	Absolute value of line height
		Percentage	Percentage of element's font size
textDecoration	All elements		none, underline, line-through, blink
textTransform	All elements		capitalize, uppercase, lowercase, none
textAlign	Block-level elements		left, right, center, justify
textIndent	Block-level elements	Length	Numerical units to indent
		Percentage	Percentage of parent
Block-Level Properties			
paddings()	All elements	Number	Number of units of padding
		Percentage	Percentage of parent
borderWidths()	All elements	Number	Number of units for width of border
margins()	All elements	Length	Margins in number of units
		Percentage	Percentage of parent
		Auto	Document autosizes margins
borderStyle	All elements		none, solid, double, inset, outset, groove, ridge
width	Block-level elements	Length	Width in units
		Percentage	Percentage of parent
		Auto	Document autosizes width
align	All elements		left, right, none
Color Properties			
color	All elements	Color	color names, RGB colors
backgroundImage	All elements		URL
backgroundColor	All elements	Color	color names, RGB colors

19

TABLE 19.1 Continued

Property Name	What It Applies To	Possible Values	Value Definitions
Classification Properties			
display	All elements		block, inline, list-item, none
listStyleType	Elements with display property		disc, circle, square, decimal, lower and upper-roman, lower and upper-alpha, none
whiteSpace	Block-level elements	Normal and pre	

Summary

Over this chapter we have talked about how CSS offers Web developers greater control over the styling of XHTML documents. It provides a means by which developers can define default styles both internally and externally to the document, which is an incredibly powerful tool when it comes to where the Web is today, not only when accessed from normal computers, but also wireless devices.

Because of CSS, styles can then be applied to a wide range of elements. Developers have at their disposal many different style properties available to control how their content looks. This gives them the flexibility and power that their publishing challenges demand.

In the next chapter we are going to put some of that styling to use by looking at layers, how to position them, and how to use them in your documents.

CHAPTER **20**

Layers

Until recently, one of the fundamental limitations of Web pages has been the inability to position text or images on a page precisely. Additionally, there was no way to overlap XHTML elements on a page. One of the most innovative aspects of the newer browsers is the support for **layers**. Layers let you define overlays of transparent or solid content in an XHTML document, which can be positioned precisely where you want them.

Layers originally could be implemented using several different techniques, and those of you who are knee-deep in the Web publishing world know this was often a cause of confusion. But with the adoption of HTML, XHTML, CSS, and DOM standards, the issues around layers have been greatly improved and reduced. Layers can be created using an XHTML element and applying several cascading style sheet (CSS) properties to position, show, and control the stacking of the element. Simply by the nature of what the <div> element represents (a division of data), it is the most logical choice for creating layers, and it is what is commonly used.

These are all the specifics we are going to cover on layers for now. The specific elements and approaches will be covered in more detail later in the chapter, so we are going to move on to assessing the use and benefits of layers from a higher level. In this chapter we are going to look at not only some universal practices, but also at using the <div> and <iframe> (a second useful element) methods for deploying layers.

NOTE

Although Netscape's version 4 browsers had a second method of creating layers, we will not be focusing on that approach in this book. However, we do offer some basic information near the end of the chapter in the "What About <layer> and <ilayer>?" sidebar.

Universal Practices

Despite the early differences in the implementation of layers we mentioned, things have moved toward a more universal implementation. In this section of the chapter, we will look at some of the universal practices and theories that apply no matter what method you use to deploy layers on your pages.

Using Style Sheets for Layering

As we mentioned in the introduction of this chapter, the proper and standardized way of implementing layers is to control them through the use of style sheets. This would include everything from the positioning and styling of the data included in the layer to the stacked location and visibility of the layer. The properties of CSS that we are going to focus on are

- position

- left, right, top, and bottom

- height and width

- z-index

- visibility

> **NOTE**
>
> Please note that we will not go into all the properties of CSS in this chapter. Please refer to Chapter 19, "Cascading Style Sheets," for more information on style sheets.

position

The position property is used to tell the browser how and where to place applicable elements. There are four different values of this property, all of which are listed and described in Table 20.1.

TABLE 20.1   Values of the position Property

Value	Description
absolute	This value tells the browser that you will be specifying the absolute coordinates of the element. When you use this value, you also use the top and left properties. If these are not specified, the browser assumes the x and y coordinates are 0 (the top-left corner of the browser window).
fixed	This value is the same as absolute, except that it does not move when the window is scrolled.
relative	This value lets you offset the element based on the preceding element.
static	This is the default value that is used in rendering XHTML in today's browsers.

To help you understand how this property works, look at Listing 20.1. In this listing, we placed three <p> elements within the body of the document. Each of these has been provided a unique ID. In the <head> of the document, we have given each of the IDs a different background-color (for ease of seeing the difference), left, and top value. You will also notice that we have set the position property to absolute. Figure 20.1 shows what this looks like when loaded in a browser.

> **NOTE**
>
> Although we mentioned it at the beginning of the chapter, we purposely did not use the <div> element in this example to demonstrate that these types of styles can be applied to any element.

LISTING 20.1   Specifying the Absolute Positioning of HTML Elements with CSS Properties

```
<?xml version="1.0" encoding="UTF-8"?>
<!DOCTYPE html PUBLIC "-//W3C//DTD XHTML 1.0 Transitional//EN"
                     "DTD/xhtml1-transitional.dtd">
<html xmlns="http://www.w3.org/1999/xhtml" xml:lang="en">
<head>
  <title>JavaScript Unleashed</title>
  <style type="text/css">
<!--
#first{
background-color: green;
left: 0px;
position: absolute;
top: 0px;
}

#second{
background-color: red;
left: 30px;
position: absolute;
top: 30px;
}

#third{
background-color: blue;
left: 60px;
position: absolute;
top: 60px;
}
-->
</style>
```

20

LISTING 20.1   Continued

```
</head>
<body>
  <p id="first">
    Layer 1
  </p>
  <p id="second">
    Layer 2
  </p>
  <p id="third">
    Layer 3
  </p>
</body>
</html>
```

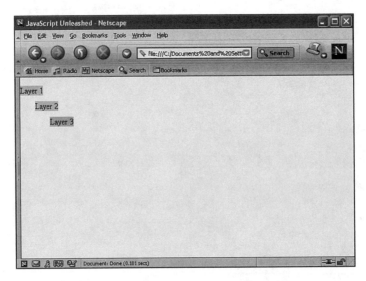

FIGURE 20.1   Specifying the absolute positioning of XHTML elements.

left, right, top, and bottom

As you saw in the preceding example, certain CSS properties allow you to specify the exact location of an element. When using these properties, which take numerical values for coordinates, you will not use all of them at once. For instance, an element cannot have the `right` property set at the same time a `left` property is set. The same is true for `top` and `bottom`. If you try to do this, most browsers default to the property that is last in your style definition to be applied.

For example, look at Listing 20.2. I have expanded on the preceding listing and added a fourth layer and style definition. I have used the various combinations of the `right`, `left`, top, and bottom properties to place squares in each of the four corners of the browser window, as shown in Figure 20.2.

LISTING 20.2   Using the right, left, top, and bottom Properties

```
<?xml version="1.0" encoding="UTF-8"?>
<!DOCTYPE html PUBLIC "-//W3C//DTD XHTML 1.0 Transitional//EN"
                      "DTD/xhtml1-transitional.dtd">
<html xmlns="http://www.w3.org/1999/xhtml" xml:lang="en">
<head>
  <title>JavaScript Unleashed</title>
  <style type="text/css">
  <!--
  #first{
  background-color: green;
  left: 0px;
  position: absolute;
  top: 0px;
  }

  #second{
  background-color: red;
  position: absolute;
  right: 0px;
  top: 0px;
  }

  #third{
  background-color: blue;
  bottom: 0px;
  position: absolute;
  right: 0px;
  }

  #fourth{
  background-color: yellow;
  bottom: 0px;
  left: 0px;
  position: absolute;
  }

  -->
  </style>
```

LISTING 20.2   Continued

```
</head>
<body>
  <p id="first">
    Layer 1
  </p>
  <p id="second">
    Layer 2
  </p>
  <p id="third">
    Layer 3
  </p>
  <p id="fourth">
    Layer 4
  </p>
</body>
</html>
```

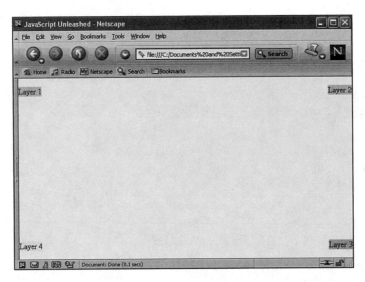

FIGURE 20.2   Specifying the right, left, top, and bottom positions of XHTML elements.

height and width

The next two properties allow you to specify the height and width of your layers. Understandably, these properties are called `height` and `width`. Like the properties that allow you to specify the location of layers, these two properties take numerical values for how tall and wide a layer should be. In Listing 20.3, we have worked even more on our example by giving our four layers specified `height` and `width` values. You can see the result in Figure 20.3.

LISTING 20.3   Using height and width to Specify the Size of Your Layers

```
<?xml version="1.0" encoding="UTF-8"?>
<!DOCTYPE html PUBLIC "-//W3C//DTD XHTML 1.0 Transitional//EN"
                      "DTD/xhtml1-transitional.dtd">
<html xmlns="http://www.w3.org/1999/xhtml" xml:lang="en">
<head>
  <title>JavaScript Unleashed</title>
  <style type="text/css">
  <!--
  #first{
  background-color: green;
  height:20px;
  left: 0px;
  position: absolute;
  top: 0px;
  width: 60px;
  }

  #second{
  background-color: red;
  height:100px;
  position: absolute;
  right: 0px;
  top: 0px;
  width: 35px;
  }

  #third{
  background-color: blue;
  bottom: 0px;
  height:100px;
  position: absolute;
  right: 0px;
  width: 50px;
  }

  #fourth{
  background-color: yellow;
  bottom: 0px;
  height:100px;
  left: 0px;
  position: absolute;
```

LISTING 20.3   Continued

```
width: 200px;
}


-->
</style>
</head>
<body>
  <p id="first">
    Layer 1
  </p>
  <p id="second">
    Layer 2
  </p>
  <p id="third">
    Layer 3
  </p>
  <p id="fourth">
    Layer 4
  </p>
</body>
</html>
```

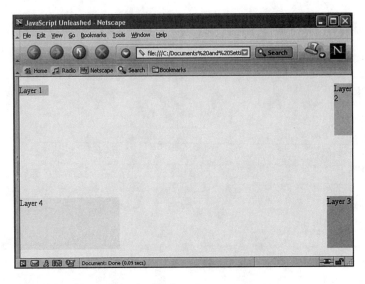

FIGURE 20.3   Specifying how tall and wide layers are.

z-index

Now it is time to get into the good stuff in terms of layers. Up to this point, we have only been defining how the layer looks—its style characteristics. Now we are going to start stacking those layers so that we can get the effect of overlapping layers. To do this, we will use the z-index property.

The z-index property contains a numerical value that specifies the location of the layer relative to the browser window, which is zero (0). Setting z-index to a value of 1 would mean that you place the layer above the browser window. This is how they appear on a page. However, if you have overlapping layers and one of them has a z-index of 1, it will overlap the other. Remember that the browser window is 0, which is below 1.

Before we jump into an example, look at Listing 20.4. It has four layers that overlap. This is not because they have z-index values set, but because of the order in which they appear in the document. The first layer is at the bottom, then the second, third, and fourth. Figure 20.4 shows what this looks like.

LISTING 20.4   Layers That Have Overlapping Coordinates

```
<?xml version="1.0" encoding="UTF-8"?>
<!DOCTYPE html PUBLIC "-//W3C//DTD XHTML 1.0 Transitional//EN"
                  "DTD/xhtml1-transitional.dtd">
<html xmlns="http://www.w3.org/1999/xhtml" xml:lang="en">
<head>
  <title>JavaScript Unleashed</title>
  <style type="text/css">
  <!--
  #first{
  background-color: green;
  height: 100px;
  left: 0px;
  position: absolute;
  top: 0px;
  width: 100px;
  }

  #second{
  background-color: red;
  height: 100px;
  left: 20px;
  position: absolute;
  top: 20px;
  width: 100px;
  }
```

LISTING 20.4   Continued

```
#third{
background-color: blue;
height: 100px;
left: 40px;
position: absolute;
top: 40px;
width: 100px;
}

#fourth{
background-color: yellow;
height: 100px;
left: 60px;
position: absolute;
top: 60px;
width: 100px;
}

-->
</style>
</head>
<body>
  <p id="first">
    Layer 1
  </p>
  <p id="second">
    Layer 2
  </p>
  <p id="third">
    Layer 3
  </p>
  <p id="fourth">
    Layer 4
  </p>
</body>
</html>
```

As you can see, the order of the layers plays an important role in how they are displayed. Are they really stacked on top of each other? No—they just appear to be. However, we can order them by specifying the z-index property. Of course, if we place them in the same order, they will look exactly the same, so this property is most often used to change the order, rather than to specify them in the default order when building your pages.

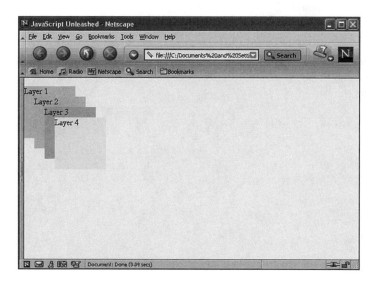

FIGURE 20.4   Layers overlapping due to their order in the document.

Let's now take a look at Listing 20.5. As you can see in this listing, we have given both the first and third layer a z-index value. Because we want the first layer to be on top, we have given it a value of 2 and the third layer a value of 1. Look at Figure 20.5 to see the result of loading this listing in a browser.

LISTING 20.5   Changing the z-index of the Layers

```
<?xml version="1.0" encoding="UTF-8"?>
<!DOCTYPE html PUBLIC "-//W3C//DTD XHTML 1.0 Transitional//EN"
                    "DTD/xhtml1-transitional.dtd">
<html xmlns="http://www.w3.org/1999/xhtml" xml:lang="en">
<head>
  <title>JavaScript Unleashed</title>
  <style type="text/css">
  <!--
  #first{
  background-color: green;
  height: 100px;
  left: 0px;
  position: absolute;
  top: 0px;
```

20

LISTING 20.5   Continued

```
width: 100px;
z-index: 2;
}

#second{
background-color: red;
height: 100px;
left: 20px;
position: absolute;
top: 20px;
width: 100px;
}

#third{
background-color: blue;
height: 100px;
left: 40px;
position: absolute;
top: 40px;
width: 100px;
z-index: 1;
}

#fourth{
background-color: yellow;
height: 100px;
left: 60px;
position: absolute;
top: 60px;
width: 100px;
}

  -->
  </style>
</head>
<body>
  <p id="first">
    Layer 1
  </p>
  <p id="second">
    Layer 2
```

LISTING 20.5   Continued

```
    </p>
    <p id="third">
      Layer 3
    </p>
    <p id="fourth">
      Layer 4
    </p>
</body>
</html>
```

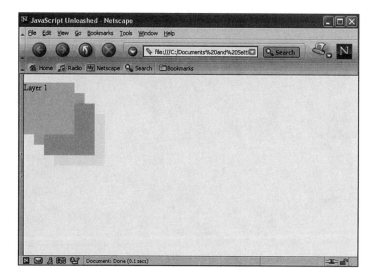

FIGURE 20.5   Changing the overlap of the preceding example.

visibility

The final property that we are going to look at is the `visibility` property. This property has four possible values, which are listed and defined in Table 20.2. As you might guess, this property is responsible for hiding and exposing layers.

TABLE 20.2   Values of the visibility Property

Value	Description
collapse	Same as `hidden`, except when used on tables
hidden	Hides the element
inherit	The browser's default value; takes the same value as its parent
visible	Makes the element visible

To demonstrate this property, we are going to take the code from the preceding example and add two lines to it. Remember the two layers that we gave a z-index value to? This brought them to the front of the page. In their style definition, we are going to set their visibility to hidden. Listing 20.6 shows the code that we used, and Figure 20.6 shows that these two layers are no longer seen.

LISTING 20.6   Using the visibility Property to Hide Elements

```
<?xml version="1.0" encoding="UTF-8"?>
<!DOCTYPE html PUBLIC "-//W3C//DTD XHTML 1.0 Transitional//EN"
                      "DTD/xhtml1-transitional.dtd">
<html xmlns="http://www.w3.org/1999/xhtml" xml:lang="en">
<head>
  <title>JavaScript Unleashed</title>
  <style type="text/css">
<!--
#first{
background-color: green;
height: 100px;
left: 0px;
position: absolute;
top: 0px;
width: 100px;
z-index: 2;
visibility: hidden;
}

#second{
background-color: red;
height: 100px;
left: 20px;
position: absolute;
top: 20px;
width: 100px;
}

#third{
background-color: blue;
height: 100px;
left: 40px;
position: absolute;
top: 40px;
width: 100px;
```

LISTING 20.6 Continued

```
  z-index: 1;
  visibility: hidden;
  }

  #fourth{
  background-color: yellow;
  height: 100px;
  left: 60px;
  position: absolute;
  top: 60px;
  width: 100px;
  }

  -->
  </style>
</head>
<body>
  <p id="first">
    Layer 1
  </p>
  <p id="second">
    Layer 2
  </p>
  <p id="third">
    Layer 3
  </p>
  <p id="fourth">
    Layer 4
  </p>
</body>
</html>
```

Managing Overlying Layers

Using the CSS properties that we have talked about allows you to perform some interesting visual effects. For example, suppose you wanted to display some chart report data on a Web page. Your goal is to display one chart at a time and to give the user the option of viewing one of the other charts. Perhaps if you were working in a Windows environment, you could imagine the use of a tabbed window for this purpose, with each chart being shown on a separate tab. Layers make it possible to have a similar effect on a Web page.

20

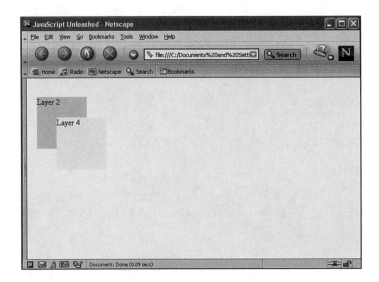

FIGURE 20.6   Hiding layers.

In creating these layers, however, it is important to remember that you need to manage them effectively. Reproducing tabs, lists, or other menu style items you see in everyday applications is not easy. You have to remember the previous state of an element or an entire set of elements, so that when one changes, they all do. For instance, if you click outside a cascading menu, you want the menu to go away—which means you also have to capture clicks. We will not discuss these items here; they are covered in more detail in Chapter 22, "Menus and Toolbars."

Creating Animation Effects

Another intriguing aspect of layers is the way you can use them to create animations. Because JavaScript lets you position layers dynamically, you can create recursive routines in which layers can appear to slide or jump across the document. It is this combination of XHTML and JavaScript that allows you to create Dynamic XHTML (DHTML).

Using layers, JavaScript, and style sheets, you can create (with XHTML), design (with CSS), and manipulate (with JavaScript) elements on a page. With advancements such as better support of the Document Object Model (DOM) and XML (eXtensible Markup Language) in browsers around the corner, the possibilities are endless.

\<div> and \<iframe>

Now that we have covered the basics of creating layers, it is time to get into the specifics. As we mentioned, Netscape had an old method of using \<layer> and \<ilayer> for implementing layers, but that method has been deprecated, so we will look at the more universal method of implementing them, using the <div> and <iframe> elements. This approach not only works in Internet Explorer 4+ browsers, but also in Netscape 6+.

Defining Data Blocks

One of the first steps in creating layers is to define the block of data that you consider to be a layer. If you think of a regular application such as a browser, the window might be considered the first layer. When you click on a menu, however, the menu itself is displayed above the window—this would be a second layer on top of the first layer. If you click on a submenu that cascades out, this is another layer (it might or might not be of the same level as the first).

The current method of defining these blocks of data is through the use of the <div> element. This tag creates a defined block-level structure in a document. In terms of rendering, it is similar to the <p> element, except that <p> is supposed to not only dictate the start of a new paragraph but also define the data within it as part of a paragraph. The <div> element, on the other hand, defines the data more than it tells the browser how to render it.

Before we get into moving layers, or <div> blocks, in this method, we are going to take a look at the attributes of this element and what they mean. These attributes are all shown in Table 20.3.

TABLE 20.3   Attributes of the <div> Element

Value	Description
align	Used to align the data contained inside the <div> element; can take values of left, right, center, and justify. Deprecated in favor of using CSS to align elements.
class	A comma-separated list of style classes that make the element an instance of those classes.
dir	Specifies the text direction of any text contained in the element. Value ltr means *left to right* and rtl means *right to left*.
id	Often used by style sheets to define the type of style that should be applied to the data in the element.
lang	Identifies the human language code of the data within the element.
style	Allows you to specify a style definition within the tag, rather than in a style sheet.
title	Allows you to provide a more informative title for the tag than the <title> element, which applies to the whole document.

Defining a Data Block

Using the <div> element is easy. All you have to do is place it around the elements you want to define as a block of data. Listing 20.7 shows how this is done. As you see, there are two <div> blocks in this example. Within the first one are two horizontal rules (<hr> tags), and the text DIV 1. In the second block, we have included a level 3 heading (<h3> tag) and a paragraph (<p> tag). We have also included some text before and after each

<div> block so that you can see where they start and end. Figure 20.7 shows what this looks like when loaded in a browser.

LISTING 20.7   Using the <div> Element

```
<?xml version="1.0" encoding="UTF-8"?>
<!DOCTYPE html PUBLIC "-//W3C//DTD XHTML 1.0 Transitional//EN"
                      "DTD/xhtml1-transitional.dtd">
<html xmlns="http://www.w3.org/1999/xhtml" xml:lang="en">
<head>
  <title>JavaScript Unleashed</title>
</head>
<body>
  Before the first block.
  <div id="layer1">
    <hr />
    DIV 1
    <hr />
  </div>
  After the first block.
  <br />
  Before the second block.
  <div id="layer2">
    <h3>
      DIV 2
    </h3>
    <p>
      Inside the second DIV block.
    </p>
  </div>
  After the second block.
</body>
</html>
```

Positioning Your <div> Blocks

The next thing is to apply positioning to these blocks of data. To do this, we take advantage of the id property of these elements and define style properties for each. We are going to define the location, size, and background colors first, so that they are readily apparent. These are all items we looked at earlier in the chapter. Listing 20.8 shows the code to do this, and Figure 20.8 shows what it looks like.

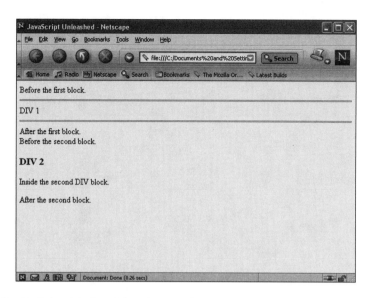

FIGURE 20.7   Defining blocks of data in your documents.

LISTING 20.8   Applying Style Sheets and Position to Your <div> Blocks

```
<?xml version="1.0" encoding="UTF-8"?>
<!DOCTYPE html PUBLIC "-//W3C//DTD XHTML 1.0 Transitional//EN"
                    "DTD/xhtml1-transitional.dtd">
<html xmlns="http://www.w3.org/1999/xhtml" xml:lang="en">
<head>
  <title>JavaScript Unleashed</title>
  <style type="text/css">
  <!--
    #first{
    background-color: green;
    height: 100px;
    left: 275px;
    position: absolute;
    top: 30px;
    width: 150px;
    }

    #second{
    background-color: red;
    height: 100px;
    left: 100px;
```

LISTING 20.8   Continued

```
    position: absolute;
    top: 55px;
    width: 150px;
    }
  -->
  </style>
</head>
<body>
  Before the first block.
  <div id="first">
    <hr />
    DIV 1
    <hr />
  </div>
  After the first block.
  <br />
  Before the second block.
  <div id="second">
    <h3>
      DIV 2
    </h3>
    <p>
      Inside the second DIV block.
    </p>
  </div>
  After the second block.
</body>
</html>
```

As you see in the figure, we have set the positioning so that the second block appears to the left of the first one, and the first one also overlaps some of the text.

Manipulating with JavaScript

Now that we have had a primer in creating layers and specifying their characteristics, we can start to add the power of JavaScript to the mix. In this section, we are going to introduce you to the JavaScript capability to dynamically change the presentation of layers and move them.

The first thing you need to remember in accessing layers in JavaScript is the syntax that should be used. The method used in today's world of browsers is to access and manipulate layers using the DOM, which was first supported in Netscape 6, Internet Explorer 5, and Opera 5 browsers.

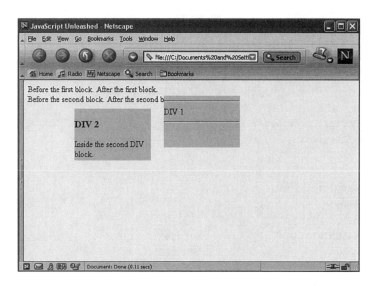

FIGURE 20.8   Positioning blocks of data.

For our examples in this chapter, we are going to use the getElementById() method. Because you have the id attribute set in the <div> element, we can uniquely identify the layer. From our previous example, the following line of code could be used to access the first layer:

```
document.getElementById('layer')
```

Now that we have access to the layer, we need to change its specific properties. After we have returned a pointer to the element, using the snippet of code we just listed, we can then access the style.visibility property to hide or show a layer.

In Listing 20.9 we have an example of doing this. As you will see, we have created a single layer that appears, using some CSS properties, under two buttons. Each of the buttons makes a call to a changeState() function, passing it a value and a layer reference. The

20

value tells the function whether it should show or hide the layer that was passed. The id reference tells it the specific layer to hide or show.

LISTING 20.9   Accessing Layers with JavaScript

```
<?xml version="1.0" encoding="UTF-8"?>
<!DOCTYPE html PUBLIC "-//W3C//DTD XHTML 1.0 Transitional//EN"
                       "DTD/xhtml1-transitional.dtd">
<html xmlns="http://www.w3.org/1999/xhtml" xml:lang="en">
<head>
  <title>JavaScript Unleashed</title>
  <style type="text/css">
  <!--
    #layer1{
    background-color: green;
    height: 100px;
    left: 10px;
    position: absolute;
    top: 50px;
    width: 100px;
    }
  -->
  </style>
  <script type="text/javascript">
    // Take the state passed in, and change it.
    function changeState(layerRef, state){
      var blockElement = document.getElementById(layerRef);
      blockElement.style.visibility = state;
    }
  </script>
</head>
<body>
  <div id="layer1">
    DIV 1
  </div>
  <form action="null">
    <input type="button" value="Hide"
           onclick="changeState('layer1','hidden')" />
    <input type="button" value="Show"
           onclick="changeState('layer1','visible')" />
  </form>
</body>
</html>
```

Figure 20.9 shows what the page looks like before the Hide button is clicked. This example works in both Internet Explorer and Navigator.

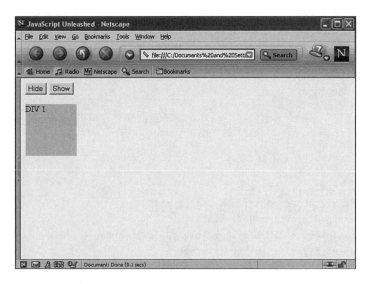

FIGURE 20.9   The contents of the page before a button is clicked.

Pulling in External Files

Using the <iframe> element, you can pull in external files. This allows you to manage your content better and provides a mechanism to include content from a different location. A good example of the use of this element would be a Current News section on your site. Suppose you want to change the news daily, but you don't want to update every page on which it appears every day. Using the <iframe> element, you can reference a single page that contains the news for that day. This allows you to make the change in a single location and effect the change on all of your pages.

To clarify, let's take an example. As you see in Listing 20.10, we will call in an external page called news.html (see Listing 20.11). The tag will reference this page using its src attribute and apply other attributes. In Figure 20.10, I have given <iframe> a border so that you can see it more easily. Also, Table 20.4 lists the attributes of the <iframe> tag.

LISTING 20.10   Using the <iframe> Tag to Load External Files

```
<?xml version="1.0" encoding="UTF-8"?>
<!DOCTYPE html PUBLIC "-//W3C//DTD XHTML 1.0 Transitional//EN"
                "DTD/xhtml1-transitional.dtd">
<html xmlns="http://www.w3.org/1999/xhtml" xml:lang="en">
<head>
```

LISTING 20.10   Continued

```
<title>JavaScript Unleashed</title>
<style type="text/css">
<!--
  #layer1{
  height: 100px;
  left: 10px;
  position: absolute;
  top: 50px;
  width: 100px;
  }
-->
</style>
<script type="text/javascript">
  // Take the state passed in, and change it.
  function changeState(layerRef, state){
    var blockElement = document.getElementById(layerRef);
    blockElement.style.visibility = state;
  }
</script>
</head>
<body >
  <iframe id="layer1" src="news.html" frameborder="1" scrolling="no"></iframe>
  <form action="null">
    <input type="button" value="Hide"
           onclick="changeState('layer1','hidden')" />
    <input type="button" value="Show"
           onclick="changeState('layer1','visible')" />
  </form>
</body>
</html>
```

LISTING 20.11   The Contents of the External File

```
<?xml version="1.0" encoding="UTF-8"?>
<!DOCTYPE html PUBLIC "-//W3C//DTD XHTML 1.0 Transitional//EN"
                      "DTD/xhtml1-transitional.dtd">
<html xmlns="http://www.w3.org/1999/xhtml" xml:lang="en">
<head>
  <title>JavaScript Unleashed</title>
</head>
<body bgcolor="red">
```

LISTING 20.11   Continued

```
  <p>
    This is the news page!
  </p>
</body>
</html>
```

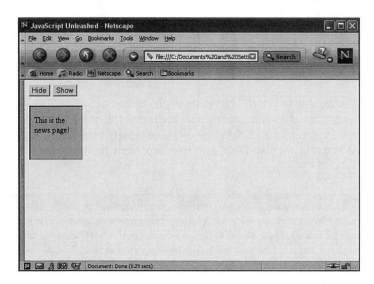

FIGURE 20.10   Viewing an inline frame with a different document loaded.

TABLE 20.4   Attributes of the <iframe> Element

Value	Description
align	Used to align the data inside the <iframe> element. Takes values of left, right, top, middle, and bottom. Deprecated in favor of CSS.
class	A comma-separated list of style classes that instantiate the tag as an instance of the defined classes.
frameborder	Takes a value of 0 or 1 to determine whether a border should be drawn around the frame.
height	Specifies the height of the <iframe>.
id	Often used by style sheets to define the style that should be applied to the data in the element.
longdesc	Links to a longer description of the contents of the element.
marginheight	The number of pixels between the content of the frame and the top and bottom borders.

TABLE 20.4   Continued

Value	Description
marginwidth	The number of pixels between the content of the frame and the right and left borders.
scrolling	Takes the value of auto, yes, or no to determine whether scrollbars are to be shown.
src	Specifies the URL containing the content of the <iframe>.
style	Allows you to specify a style definition within the tag, rather than outside in a style sheet.
title	Allows you to provide a more informative title for the <iframe> than does the <title> element, which applies to the whole document.
width	Specifies the width of the <iframe>.

As you can see, being able to control layers through the use of JavaScript can be very powerful. However, there are some inconsistencies across the older versions of the major browsers. Internet Explorer 5+ and Netscape 6+ more closely implement the HTML 4, XHTML 1.0, and ECMAScript standards, and they represent the majority of the browsers used today.

What About <layer> and <ilayer>?

When Netscape Navigator 4 was released, it included two new elements: <layer> and <ilayer> (the "i" stands for *inflow*). These elements took a different path from the standardized use of <div> elements for creating layers, which Navigator supported as well. This, of course, caused some confusion and frustration in the Web publishing world.

Unlike the <div> element, the <layer> and <ilayer> elements had attributes that allow you to "style" them. You could create a layer that included the absolute positioning, for instance, right within the <layer> element.

These two elements also had the ability to reference and load external XHTML documents for their content. This was accomplished using the src attribute of the element. But as we know, the <iframe> element has the same functionality and it is part of the HTML 4 Recommendation. Additionally, it can be styled with CSS, so you essentially have the same functionality. Unfortunately, Navigator 4 did not support this tag, so there was a fork in the implementation of layers for the version 4 browsers. But as we know now, this is no longer an issue starting with Netscape 6 and the Mozilla-based browsers that do in fact support <iframe>.

Because there are still some version 4 Netscape browsers being used, we decided to leave in a table of the attributes for the <layer> and <ilayer> elements (see Table 20.5). But this will probably be the last edition of this book that will retain this information.

TABLE 20.5   <layer> and <ilayer> Element Attributes

Property	Description
above	A Layer object higher in z-order of all layers in the document (null if the layer is topmost).
background	The URL of an image to use as the background for the layer.

TABLE 20.5   Continued

Property	Description
below	A Layer object lower in z-order of all layers in the document (null if the layer is lowest).
bgcolor	The background color for the layer.
clip	Defines the clipping rectangle, which is the visible region of the layer. Anything outside of this rectangle is clipped from view.
height	The height of the layer in pixels.
left	The x-axis position of the layer in pixels, relative to the origin of its parent layer.
name	The name of the layer.
src	The URL for the layer's content source.
top	The y-axis position of the layer in pixels, relative to the origin of its parent layer.
visibility	Defines the layer's visibility attributes. show displays the layer, hide hides the layer, and inherit causes the layer to inherit the visibility of its parent layer.
width	The width of the layer in pixels.
z-index	The relative z-order of the layer, relative to its siblings and parent.

Summary

Layers are potentially one of the most significant advancements in Web publishing. They let you move beyond the sequential word processor–like world of XHTML and into the world of graphical layout and design. JavaScript significantly adds to the power of layers by giving the developer full control over their behavior. The results can be powerful and stunning.

In this chapter we discussed layers and how they can be created with the <div> and <iframe> elements. We also discussed some of the differences in earlier browser implementations, and provided some cross-browser examples. In the next chapter we will put this newly found knowledge to use by showing you how to create rollovers and visual effects.

20

CHAPTER **21**

Rollovers and Visual Effects

W eb technologies, such as JavaScript, are important because of the practical purposes they serve in the realm of Web application development. At the same time, some of the primary reasons JavaScript is so popular are the "cool" things you can do with it within your Web site. Remember when Java was gaining popularity? How many meaningless Java marquees and other applets did you see spread across the Web? And, in the JavaScript realm, as the language has matured, you can do many more exciting things with JavaScript.

For instance, a rollover is a common method of spicing up a site's pages with JavaScript. In fact, it was one of the first globally used JavaScript functions that are still in use. Others, such as scrolling status bar messages and text fields, have gone by the wayside. Using rollovers is a fairly easy task and does not involve a lot of code, which is one of the reasons we want to introduce you to this powerful design mechanism.

In addition to rollovers, there are other visual effects that you can add to your Web pages—everything from scrolling text to animated pushbuttons. Each of these areas can enhance your site.

In this chapter we are going to go over some of the important events and event handlers that allow you to interact with your users and make dynamic changes to your pages. We are also going to show you how to create rollover effects, both with images and with layers. Finally, we are going to go through several additional examples to ensure that you not only understand the concepts discussed in the chapter, but you also have hands-on experience with implementing these concepts.

Knowing Your Events

The first items we are going to look at are events. When creating rollover or other effects on your site, you will need to fully understand the related events that can be used in JavaScript. Although these events were discussed more fully in Chapter 18, "Handling Events," we will take another quick look at those events related to rollovers and visual effects in this chapter.

onMouseOver

The onMouseOver event handler indicates when the mouse cursor has been moved over an element. The newer browsers allow the capturing of this event in almost all elements on a page. We will use the onMouseOver event, in conjunction with the <a> element, to trigger most of the "over" events in our examples. A sample follows:

```
<a href="http://www.sams.com" onmouseover="alert('You rolled over!')">Here</a>
```

onMouseOut

The onMouseOut event handler is very similar to the onMouseOver event handler. This event indicates when the mouse cursor has been moved off a particular element. The newer browsers allow the capturing of this event in most elements on a page. A sample follows:

```
<a href="http://www.sams.com" onmouseout="alert('You rolled off!')">Here</a>
```

onMouseDown

The onMouseDown event handler indicates when a mouse button has been pressed down on an element. We will use the onMouseDown event handler, in conjunction with the <a> element, to trigger most of the "down" events in our examples. A sample follows:

```
<a href="http://www.mcp.com" onmousedown="alert('You pressed!')">Here</a>
```

onMouseUp

The onMouseUp event handler indicates when a mouse button has been released after being pressed down on an element. We will use this event, in conjunction with the <a> element, to trigger most of the "up" events in our examples. A sample follows:

```
<a href="http://www.mcp.com" onmouseup="alert('You released!')">Here</a>
```

Now that we have had a very quick refresher on the events we will be using in this chapter, let's move on and take a look at rollovers.

Types of Rollovers

As a Web developer, the first thing you need to decide is what kind of rollover your application needs. You also need to decide how you want to implement the rollover. Many of these rollovers can simulate the others, so your choice will most likely reflect what your users' browsers support or what you know how to do.

In today's world, there are primarily two types of rollovers—image rollovers and layer rollovers. You often see these used for buttons or menus on sites or Web-based applications. Over the next couple of sections we are going to show you how both of these work, and provide you with some examples.

Image Rollovers

There are several methods of implementing image rollovers, but the easiest is to create two arrays that contain the images, and then reference their indexed location within the document, using the document.images array. Rather than talk through all the various concepts, let's dive right into the specific snippets of code that allow us to accomplish this task.

In our example we will store all of the images in an array of Image objects. As you can see in Figure 21.1, we will have two images on a single page. When the user rolls over an image, the image is replaced with the "rollover" version of the image. The array of images can be created with the following code:

> **NOTE**
>
> Don't worry about having all the code for this example right now. We will provide the entire listing when we finish creating the code.

```
// Create arrays to hold images.
var overImg = new Array();
overImg[0] = new Image(24,24);
overImg[1] = new Image(24,24);

var defaultImg = new Array();
defaultImg[0] = new Image(24,24);
defaultImg[1] = new Image(24,24);

// Preload images in the array.
overImg[0].src = "back-over.gif";
overImg[1].src = "forward-over.gif";

defaultImg[0].src = "back.gif";
defaultImg[1].src = "forward.gif";
```

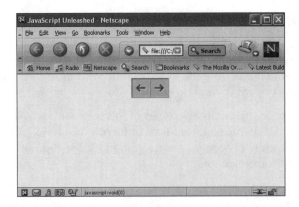

FIGURE 21.1   Our rollover page.

The next thing we need is a function to do the actual swapping of the images. The function that we are going to use will take two parameters: One is the indexed location of the image that needs to be swapped, and the second is the type of swap ("over" or "out") that is occurring. After these parameters are passed in, a `switch` statement will be used to determine which array to pull the replacement image from. After this has been determined, the actual assignment, or replacement, of the image is accomplished through the use of the `src` property of the `Image` object. The following function is used:

```
function rollImage(img,type){
  switch(type){
    case "over":
      document.images[img].src = overImg[img].src;
      break;
    case "out":
      document.images[img].src = defaultImg[img].src;
      break;
  }
}
```

The last task we need to accomplish in our example is the capturing of the `MouseOver` and `MouseOut` events. As indicated before, this is accomplished through the use of the `<a>` element and the `onMouseOver` and `onMouseOut` event handlers (implemented through the `onmouseover` and `onmouseout` attributes). Listing 21.1 shows the complete source code for the capturing of these events, and Figure 21.2 shows the replaced image with the mouse over one of the buttons.

NOTE

Using the newest browsers from Microsoft and Netscape would allow us to avoid the use of the `<a>` element in this example. However, for backward compatibility, we will use it here.

LISTING 21.1   Complete Source Code for Our Image Rollover

```
<?xml version="1.0" encoding="UTF-8"?>
<!DOCTYPE html PUBLIC "-//W3C//DTD XHTML 1.0 Transitional//EN"
                    "DTD/xhtml1-transitional.dtd">
<html xmlns="http://www.w3.org/1999/xhtml" xml:lang="en">
<head>
  <title>JavaScript Unleashed</title>
  <script type="text/javascript">

    // Create arrays to hold images.
    var overImg = new Array();
    overImg[0] = new Image(24,24);
    overImg[1] = new Image(24,24);

    var defaultImg = new Array();
    defaultImg[0] = new Image(24,24);
    defaultImg[1] = new Image(24,24);

    // Preload images in the array.
    overImg[0].src = "back-over.gif";
    overImg[1].src = "forward-over.gif";

    defaultImg[0].src = "back.gif";
    defaultImg[1].src = "forward.gif";

    // Change the state of image depending on the event that fired.
    function rollImage(img,type){
      switch(type){
        case "over":
          document.images[img].src = overImg[img].src;
          break;
        case "out":
          document.images[img].src = defaultImg[img].src;
          break;
      }
    }
  </script>
</head>
<body>
  <table border="1" cellpadding="5" cellspacing="0" align="center"
        bgcolor="#c0c0c0">
    <tr>
      <td align="center">
```

LISTING 21.1   Continued

```
      <a href="javascript:void(0)"
          onmouseout="rollImage('0','out')"
          onmouseover="rollImage('0','over')">
        <img border="0" src="back.gif" width="24" height="24" alt="Back" />
      </a>
    </td>
    <td align="center">
      <a href="javascript:void(0)"
          onmouseout="rollImage('1','out')"
          onmouseover="rollImage('1','over')">
        <img border="0" src="forward.gif" width="24" height="24"
          alt="Forward" /></a>
    </td>
  </tr>
  </table>
</body>
</html>
```

> **NOTE**
>
> The use of `void(0)` in this example simply tells the browser not to perform any action, such as loading a new page, when the link is clicked.

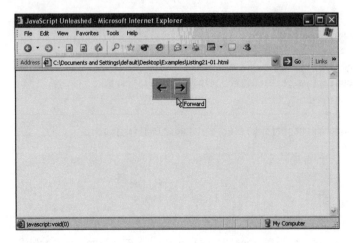

FIGURE 21.2   Rolling over one of our images.

As you can see, creating image rollovers is actually a pretty easy task, yet we all know how powerful it can be. We are going to move on to look at layer rollovers now, but don't worry—we will cover more on image rollovers in Chapter 22, "Menus and Toolbars."

Layer Rollovers

Now that we have covered image rollovers, let's look at layer rollovers. These are generated by hiding and exposing layers within a document. We covered layers in the last chapter, but here we want to specifically focus on accessing the visibility property of an element, using JavaScript, and controlling whether or not it is shown. Unlike the example in Chapter 20, "Layers," we are going to write code that allows this to work in older version 4 (Netscape and Internet Explorer) browsers as well.

Creating the Layer

The first thing we are going to do is create the XHTML that makes up our example. In this example we are going to have a simple link and an initially hidden layer. As you would imagine, our XHTML is very simple. We have also included the necessary JavaScript function calls, which we will detail out later.

```
<div name="layer" id="layer">
  Hello World!
</div>
<p>
  <a href="javascript:void(0)"
     onmouseout="changeState('layer','hidden')"
     onmouseover="changeState('layer','visible')">
     Rollover to show and hide the layer.
  </a>
</p>
```

One of the things you will notice in this snippet of code is that we use the name attribute with the <div> element. When creating scripts to run in all DHTML-supporting browsers, we will want to use the same value for both name and id in the <div> element as we have done in our example. Although this is not part of the XHTML Recommendation, it is required for Netscape version 4 browsers (remember our sidebar in the last chapter).

As with image rollovers, we will be using the <a> element to capture the MouseOver and MouseOut events. In the <a> element, you see three JavaScript interactions. The first is located in the href attribute. This call (javascript:) tells the browser that nothing should happen (void(0)) if the user clicks the link. The second and third instances call a changeState() function and pass it two variables. As you can see, one is name (for Navigator browsers) or id (for Internet Explorer browsers) of the layer instance, and the second is an indicator of whether to hide or show the layer.

> **TIP**
>
> It is possible to use this same syntax, commonly referred to as a "JavaScript URL," to call functions or even execute other JavaScript code—all contained within the href attribute.

Styling Our Layer

The next step is to set up the style sheet for the layer so that it is hidden. To make it easier to see and position properly, we have also included several other CSS properties and values. Chapter 19, "Cascading Style Sheets," and Chapter 20 went over the use of these properties, so for now we will only focus on the use of the visibility property. As you can see, it is set to hidden.

```
<style type="text/css">
<!--
  #layer{
    background-color: red;
    height: 100px;
    left: 10px;
    position: absolute;
    top: 50px;
    width: 100px;
    visibility: hidden;
  }
-->
</style>
```

Accessing the Layer

The next section of code is here only because the older implementation of accessing layers in Navigator and Internet Explorer browsers was different. As you learned in Chapter 20, this is no longer an issue for new browsers—we can use the getElementById() method to access layers. But for our example to work in the version 4 browsers from Netscape and Microsoft, we need to add some additional code to determine what browser is loading the page and perform different actions to manipulate the layers.

Because of this, we have to determine which one is accessing the page and set variables that will allow us to use a single function to process the rollovers. The first thing you need to understand in accessing layers in JavaScript is the syntax that should be used. Because of the differences, we will have to access layers using different methods.

In Navigator 4 browsers, you access them via the layers array. Because you have the name attribute set in the <div> element, you can specify the name of the layer. From our previous example, the following line of code could be used to access the layer:

```
document.layers['layer']
```

Internet Explorer 4 was a bit different, in that you accessed layers through the all collection. The value you pass to specify the layer you are accessing is not held in the name attribute of the <div> element, but rather in the id attribute. For our example, we will use the following line of code to access the layer:

```
document.all['layer']
```

Now that we know how to get to the layer for all of our browsers (Navigator 4 uses `document.layers`, Internet Explorer 4 uses `document.all`, and the newer browsers use `getElementById()`), we need to know how to access the appropriate property to change the layer's visibility.

In Navigator 4, you access the properties of a layer immediately after the `document.layers['`*`layerName`*`']` declaration. For Internet Explorer 4, however, you access it through the `style` array, which means your syntax will be something like `document.all['`*`layerName`*`'].style`. For example, the following would hide our layer in Internet Explorer 4 browsers:

```
document.all['layer'].style.visibility = "hidden";
```

And this snippet would hide our layer in Netscape Navigator 4 browsers:

```
document.layers['layer'].visibility = "hidden";
```

Next we want to create some code that will allow us to use a single function to change layers in both of these browsers. If you look at the syntax, you see that they both take a layer reference and a state (hidden or visible). It is how the layer is referenced and the method to access the styling property that changes. The following code is the first step in taking care of this issue:

```
var layer = new String();
var style = new String();

if(isIE4){
  layer = ".all";
  style = "style";
}else if(isNav4){
  layer = ".layers";
  style = "";
}
```

In this snippet we have created two variables to hold the browser-specific syntax. Depending on what browser executes the script, we will set the variables appropriately. To create the necessary code to apply the appropriate syntax, we will use the `eval()` method for these older version 4 browsers.

Using the `eval()` method, we will take a string and evaluate it as if it were a JavaScript function. This allows us to "build" the proper call to access and change a property of a layer, such as `visibility`, in both of these browsers. Because we have set the appropriate variables, we can use the following statement, where *`layerRef`* and *`state`* are passed as arguments, to handle this situation:

```
eval("document" + layer + "['" + layerRef + "']" + style
    + ".visibility = '" + state + "'");
```

The use of `eval()` in this context will, in our example, turn the statement into

```
document.layers['layer'].visibility = "hidden";
```

when hidden on Navigator 4 browsers, and

```
document.all['layer'].style.visibility = "hidden";
```

when hidden on Internet Explorer 4 browsers.

To this point, we have relied pretty heavily on being able to identify the browser itself, so that we can apply the correct syntax. In other words, we need to look at properly setting our `isIE4` variable to true if an Internet Explorer 4 browser is accessing the page, and setting the `isNav4` variable to true if a Netscape Navigator 4 browser is accessing the page. Additionally, we want to set a third DOM variable to true if a Gecko-based (Netscape 6+ and Mozilla) or Internet Explorer 5+ browser is accessing the page, so that we can use the appropriate `getElementById()` syntax for these newer browsers.

NOTE

Gecko is the name of the rendering engine in the Mozilla-based browsers, including Netscape 6+.

To accomplish this task, we will use a script provided by our friends at Netscape: the "Practical Browser Sniffing Script." This script, which is available at `http://developer.netscape.com/evangelism/docs/api/ua`, can be used to determine several things about the browser itself, including

- The operating system (Windows, Mac OS, UNIX, or other)

- The organization that released the browser (Opera, Netscape, Microsoft, CompuServe, Sun, or other)

- The version number (4, 5, 6, and so on)

- The family (HotJava, Opera, Internet Explorer 3, Internet Explorer 4+, Gecko, Navigator 3, Navigator 4, or AOL)

We will use a combination of these items to determine the values for our previously mentioned variables.

To include this code into our example, we will load the `ua.js` external JavaScript library from Netscape's developer site. The following line of code will accomplish this task:

```
<script type="text/javascript"
        src="http://developer.netscape.com/evangelism/lib/js/ua.js"></script>
```

> **NOTE**
>
> As a safety precaution, you might want to download this file and store it locally in case its location changes on the DevEdge site. This will allow you to reference it on your own servers without having to make changes in case it moves.

Next, we need to set the values of our variables using these scripts. We can do this by following the documentation on the script's site and applying some of our own logic. The following snippet will properly set our variables:

```
// Create global variables for browser type.
var isIE4 = new Boolean(false);
var isNav4 = new Boolean(false);
var isDOM = new Boolean(false);


// determine browser type.
isIE4 = navigator.family == "ie4" && navigator.version == 4;
isNav4 = navigator.family == "nn4";
isDOM = ((navigator.family == "ie4" && navigator.version > 4) ||
         navigator.family =="gecko");
```

We now have all the information we need to build a cross-browser function that will handle layers in Netscape 4+ and Internet Explorer 4+ browsers. Listing 21.2 contains the complete source code for our example, with everything arranged in the appropriate order, including the definition of the `changeState()` function. Figure 21.3 shows the page loaded in the browser. Figure 21.4 shows the result of rolling over the link and exposing the layer.

LISTING 21.2   Our Layer Rollover Example

```
<?xml version="1.0" encoding="UTF-8"?>
<!DOCTYPE html PUBLIC "-//W3C//DTD XHTML 1.0 Transitional//EN"
                      "DTD/xhtml1-transitional.dtd">
<html xmlns="http://www.w3.org/1999/xhtml" xml:lang="en">
<head>
  <title>JavaScript Unleashed</title>
  <style type="text/css">
  <!--
    #layer{
      background-color: red;
      height: 100px;
      left: 10px;
      position: absolute;
      top: 50px;
      width: 100px;
```

LISTING 21.2   Continued

```
      visibility: hidden;
    }
  -->
  </style>

  <script type="text/javascript"
          src="http://developer.netscape.com/evangelism/lib/js/ua.js"></script>
  <script type="text/javascript">

    // Create global variables for browser type.
    var isIE4 = new Boolean(false);
    var isNav4 = new Boolean(false);
    var isDOM = new Boolean(false);

    // determine browser type.
    isIE4 = navigator.family == "ie4" && navigator.version == 4;
    isNav4 = navigator.family == "nn4";
    isDOM = ((navigator.family == "ie4" && navigator.version > 4) ||
              navigator.family =="gecko");

    function changeState(layerRef, state){
      if(isIE4 || isNav4){
        eval("document" + layer + "['" + layerRef + "']"
              + style + ".visibility = '" + state + "'");
      }else if(isDOM){
        var blockElement = document.getElementById(layerRef);
        blockElement.style.visibility = state;
      }
    }

  </script>
</head>
<body>
<div name="layer" id="layer">
  Hello World!
</div>
<p>
  <a href="javascript:void(0)"
     onmouseout="changeState('layer','hidden')"
     onmouseover="changeState('layer','visible')">
```

LISTING 21.2   Continued

```
    Rollover to show and hide the layer.
  </a>
</p>
</body>
</html>
```

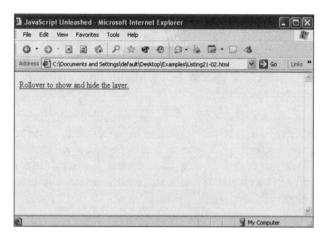

FIGURE 21.3   The example without rolling over the link.

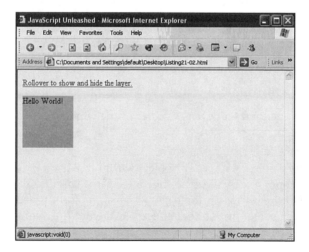

FIGURE 21.4   The layer while rolling over the link.

Visual Effects

We have covered some very interesting and exciting concepts and examples so far in this chapter. We have learned how to create rollovers for both images and layers, and we have learned more about creating cross-browser DHTML that even includes the older browsers.

The rest of the chapter will focus on putting these newfound skills to work. We are going to look at some other visual effects that can be used on your site, and how to spice up even the most boring content.

Scrolling Marquees

A scrolling marquee is a popular effect for Web site developers. Its purpose is to relay the latest news or tidbit to visitors of your Web site. The marquee, or "ticker tape," was first popularized with Java applets.

You can create a scrolling marquee in JavaScript as well, although the visual appearance is typically less stunning than a Java applet. This is because you're forced to use a `Text` object as the container for the scrolling text, and none of the XHTML form objects are going to dazzle you with their appearance. Nonetheless, JavaScript marquees don't require a separate applet and can be created quickly and easily, so you may find them very useful in a variety of situations.

> **NOTE**
>
> Internet Explorer does have a `<marquee>` element that can be used to scroll text, but this is not supported in any other browser. For that reason, we will not be using it for our example here.

To create a JavaScript marquee, you need to do three things:

1. Create an XHTML form with an embedded `Text` object.

2. Write a function that scrolls text within the `Text` object.

3. Associate this function as an event handler of the window's `load` event, to set the wheels in motion.

To begin, create a `Form` object with a `Text` object within it. As you do so, it's helpful to name these objects appropriately. Because they are created specifically for the marquee and are irrelevant to other forms on the page, we label the form `"marqueeForm"` and the text `"marqueeText"`, or something to that effect. Next, enter the marquee message as the value attribute of the `<input>` tag. Here is the `<form>` definition code:

```
<form name="marqueeForm" action="null">
  <input name="marqueeText" size="50" value="THIS JUST IN...
        JavaScript is selected as official scripting language of the
        2004 Summer Olympics" />
</form>
```

After we define the marquee container, we want to define two global constants to use in the marquee: the rate (in milliseconds) at which to scroll and the number of characters to scroll at a time. Also, we will create a String object called marqueeMessage:

```
var scrollRate = 100;
var scrollChars = 1;
var marqueeMessage = new String();
```

The next task is to create a function called JSMarquee(), which gives your ordinary Text object the look of a marquee. Because a marquee requires continuous updating, you will need to make JSMarquee() recursive by calling setTimeout() at the start of the function. The global variable scrollRate is used as the method parameter to determine how often to call the function.

The heart of the JSMarquee() function is first to get the value of the Text object and assign it to the marqueeMessage string. You can then simulate word wrapping by chopping off a chunk of the message at the front and placing it on the end of the string. The String object's substring() method is used to do this, as shown here:

```
function JSMarquee(){
  setTimeout('JSMarquee()', scrollRate);
  marqueeMessage = document.marqueeForm.marqueeText.value;
  document.marqueeForm.marqueeText.value =
                    marqueeMessage.substring( scrollChars ) +
                    marqueeMessage.substring( 0, scrollChars );
}
```

The complete source code for the marquee example is shown in Listing 21.3.

LISTING 21.3   A Marquee Using JavaScript

```
<?xml version="1.0" encoding="UTF-8"?>
<!DOCTYPE html PUBLIC "-//W3C//DTD XHTML 1.0 Transitional//EN"
                    "DTD/xhtml1-transitional.dtd">
<html xmlns="http://www.w3.org/1999/xhtml" xml:lang="en">
<head>
  <title>JavaScript Unleashed</title>
  <script type="text/javascript">
    // Declare variables.
    var scrollRate = 100;
    var scrollChars = 1;
    var marqueeMessage = new String();

    function JSMarquee(){
      setTimeout('JSMarquee()', scrollRate);
```

LISTING 21.3   Continued

```
      marqueeMessage = document.marqueeForm.marqueeText.value;
      document.marqueeForm.marqueeText.value =
                        marqueeMessage.substring( scrollChars ) +
                        marqueeMessage.substring( 0, scrollChars );
  }

  </script>
</head>
<body onload="JSMarquee()">
<form name="marqueeForm" action="null">
  <input name="marqueeText" size="50" value="THIS JUST IN...
  JavaScript is selected as official scripting language of the
  2004 Summer Olympics " />
</form>
</body>
</html>
```

Figure 21.5 shows the scrolling effect of the marquee as it runs continuously while you are on the page.

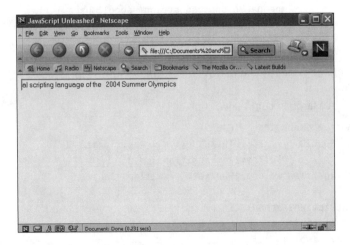

FIGURE 21.5   The start of the scrolling marquee.

Animated Pushbuttons

The look-and-feel of the Web has come a long way over the past three years. Originally, the Web was a text-based technology medium, but the Web today sports graphics, multimedia, and sophisticated page layouts. However, one aspect of the old "ugly" look is form objects, such as text input boxes and pushbuttons. After all, you can't even specify the font for those controls yet.

It isn't surprising, therefore, that many Web developers are looking to JavaScript to provide alternatives to one of the most common UI (user interface) controls today: buttons. Although no graphical button objects are available yet, with the Image object, JavaScript does a remarkably good job of simulating the behavior of a pushbutton.

In this example, we'll show you how to use JavaScript to simulate the look-and-feel of the Windows-style buttons, as an extension of the first example we included in the chapter. A button of this style looks flat until you place the mouse cursor on top of it, at which point it takes on a three-dimensional appearance. To create animated pushbuttons like these, you need to do the following:

1. Create image placeholders on your Web page for each of the buttons.

2. Define Image objects and associate a GIF or JPG file with these language constructs.

3. Create a routine to display images on demand.

4. Add handlers for MouseOver and MouseOut events.

5. Add handler code for the Link object's click event.

To use Image objects to serve as button replacements, you can define the <img> element. Because Image objects can respond to events in the newer browsers, as we previously mentioned, we will not encapsulate each of the images in a Link object as we did with our first example. This is shown in the following code:

```
<img src="back.gif" width="24" height="24" alt="Back"
    border="0" onmouseout="rollImage('0','out')"
    onmouseover="rollImage('0','over')"
    />
<img src="forward.gif" width="24" height="24" alt="Forward"
    border="0" onmouseout="rollImage('1','out')"
    onmouseover="rollImage('1','over')"
    />
```

Within a <script> tag in the <head> section of the XHTML document, we will define the same Image objects for each of the four images to be used as we did in our first example. We will have two representing the flat button look and two representing the 3D look.

```
// Create arrays to hold images.
var overImg = new Array();
overImg[0] = new Image(24,24);
overImg[1] = new Image(24,24);
```

```
var defaultImg = new Array();
defaultImg[0] = new Image(24,24);
defaultImg[1] = new Image(24,24);

// Preload images in the array.
overImg[0].src = "back-over.gif";
overImg[1].src = "forward-over.gif";

defaultImg[0].src = "back.gif";
defaultImg[1].src = "forward.gif";
```

So far we have defined placeholder <img> elements for both the Previous and Next buttons and instantiated the associated Image objects for both their "off" and "on" states. Next, we will add our rollImage() function to change the state of the image.

But these buttons do not perform any task, as currently defined. They just change state when they are rolled over. Because we want this example to be more functional, we need to add the appropriate code to move forward and backward in our history list. This means we need to adjust our code to include an <a> wrapper with the appropriate JavaScript. This includes the addition of the javascript: protocol in the <a> element's href attribute. The JavaScript will use the History object's back() and forward() methods to provide the desired capabilities.

Listing 21.4 provides the complete working source code for this example.

NOTE

As in the first example, we used a table to help with the formatting of our buttons.

LISTING 21.4   Animating Buttons with JavaScript

```
<?xml version="1.0" encoding="UTF-8"?>
<!DOCTYPE html PUBLIC "-//W3C//DTD XHTML 1.0 Transitional//EN"
                       "DTD/xhtml1-transitional.dtd">
<html xmlns="http://www.w3.org/1999/xhtml" xml:lang="en">
<head>
  <title>JavaScript Unleashed</title>
  <script type="text/javascript">

    // Create arrays to hold images.
    var overImg = new Array();
    overImg[0] = new Image(24,24);
    overImg[1] = new Image(24,24);
```

LISTING 21.4   Continued

```
    var defaultImg = new Array();
    defaultImg[0] = new Image(24,24);
    defaultImg[1] = new Image(24,24);

    // Preload images in the array.
    overImg[0].src = "back-over.gif";
    overImg[1].src = "forward-over.gif";

    defaultImg[0].src = "back.gif";
    defaultImg[1].src = "forward.gif";

    // Change the state of image depending on the event that fired.
    function rollImage(img,type){
      switch(type){
        case "over":
          document.images[img].src = overImg[img].src;
          break;
        case "out":
          document.images[img].src = defaultImg[img].src;
          break;
      }
    }
  </script>
</head>
<body>
  <table border="1" cellpadding="5" cellspacing="0" align="center"
        bgcolor="#c0c0c0">
    <tr>
      <td align="center">
        <a href="javascript:history.back()">
          <img src="back.gif" width="24" height="24" alt="Back"
              border="0" onmouseout="rollImage('0','out')"
              onmouseover="rollImage('0','over')"
              /></a>
      </td>
      <td align="center">
        <a href="javascript:history.forward()">
          <img src="forward.gif" width="24" height="24" alt="Forward"
            border="0"onmouseout="rollImage('1','out')"
            onmouseover="rollImage('1','over')"
            /></a>
```

LISTING 21.4   Continued

```
      </td>
    </tr>
  </table>
</body>
</html>
```

As you can see when you load this example in your Netscape 6+ or Internet Explorer 5+ browser, the look-and-feel is the same as in our first example where we included the onMouseOver and onMouseOut event handlers in the <a> element.

Be sure to load a different page before and after you load this page, so that your history has something to move back and forward to. Otherwise, the buttons will not perform any action because there is nothing before or after in the history.

Summary

We have covered some very important JavaScript in this chapter. We not only took a look at some very important events and how to create rollovers, but we also took you through several examples.

Implementing rollover effects is one of the easiest and safest applications of JavaScript you can perform. But do not limit yourself to what you have learned here. To demonstrate this, we even provided coverage of several different types of rollovers. The effect of rollovers lays the foundation for many other tasks that you can accomplish with JavaScript. It familiarizes you with events and accessing elements on a page and introduces you to user interface design. We have also seen some of these other methods in action, which should help your understanding of how they work.

In the next chapter we are going to apply the lessons we learned here and use these methods to create more feature-rich menus and toolbars in DHTML.

CHAPTER **22**

Menus and Toolbars

So far, in this section of the book, we have really focused on the various technologies that allow you to script documents. We have looked into JavaScript events, CSS, layers, and how to create rollovers and other visual effects. At the same time, knowing how to program in JavaScript and knowing how to apply your programming skills are two completely different things. Many people are able to pick up a programming language and learn how to use its syntax and understand its semantics. However, few truly learn the art of applying what they have learned in real-world applications.

In this chapter, we are going to take you deeper into creating and using DHTML. We are going to create a DHTML-driven menu and a toolbar. In a very real-world manner, we are going to decide what browsers to support and code around any differences in browser implementations for our examples. Our objective with this chapter is to take all the skills you have learned so far and apply them to these two examples. We want to give you a break on learning new information, and give you a chance to apply some of that knowledge.

Initial Considerations

When you start a DHTML project, there are several questions that you want to ask yourself.

- What browsers do you want to support? Remember that only Navigator 4+ and Internet Explorer 4+ currently have all the functionality you need to create DHTML applications.

- Do you want to accommodate non-supporting browsers?

- How gracefully do you want to fail in non-supporting browsers?

We have discussed these questions before, so we will not go into detail here. Just remember that picking your supported browsers is a very big decision, and in doing so you must select and design not only for current releases but for future releases as well.

In addition to these questions, you should also ask yourself the following:

- Can you do it?
- How do you plan for the future?
- Is there a better way?

We will not focus too much of our time on talking about the subject of initial considerations because we have covered it before, but there is some additional information we want to make sure you take into account.

Making Sure It Is Possible

This question is often one that is overlooked. JavaScript is perceived as a simple language that anyone can learn. This might have been true in the early versions of the language, but JavaScript 1.2 specifically brought a whole new beast to the table. Since its release, JavaScript has truly stepped up by providing even more objects to support XHTML and the Document Object Model (DOM). Creating a DHTML application is not as easy as you would think, and as you learned in the last chapter, different browser implementations can make it a very tedious task.

Planning for the Future

Another point you must consider is planning for the future. Netscape and Microsoft are releasing browsers every year or so, which means you may have to update your code often.

In planning for the future, you should consider everything from upcoming standards to new browser releases. You should also try to stay on top of the technologies you are working with, so that you will be exposed to any bugs or issues with the various implementations. Designing DHTML applications can be tough, but the payoff can be seen as soon as you get your application working.

Considering APIs

Another thing to think about is using an Application Programming Interface (API). When creating your DHTML, you are going to come to a point at which you say, "There has to be an easier way to do this; someone else has to have done this before." And you are probably right.

The great thing about the Internet is that if you search around a bit, you will find that several individuals have created functions that you want to use—such as moving layers. You will also find that many of these developers have created their own objects, such as a cascading menu or a graphing object. If you find that someone has done this and made the code available, do not reinvent the wheel—learn from the code and use it on your site.

Designing Menus

Now that we have made our initial considerations, let's get down to business. When you design your DHTML menu, there are obvious questions such as what menus and items you want to appear and what overall functionality you are trying to provide. Additionally, you need to decide what look-and-feel you want. What are the colors and dimensions of your menus? How tall do you want the menu bar to be, and where would you like the menu to appear?

These are all things you need to ask yourself so that you can apply the appropriate formatting and styles to create the look you want. For our menu, we have the following design objectives:

- Work with Internet Explorer 5+ and Netscape 6+ browsers.
- Provide a gray menu bar at the top of the browser window.
- Provide two menu options: Go and Help.
    - The Go menu will have three links to popular developer sites for Netscape and Microsoft.
    - The Help menu will have a single item, About, that when selected will pop up a dialog box with information about the menu.
    - The About dialog box will contain an image and a Close button.

Because we do not have to write the necessary code to work with older browsers, our job is a little easier when it comes to creating the layers as well as manipulating them.

Defining Layers

The first thing we are going to do in creating our menu is define our layers and the menu bar itself. For this, we are going to use a combination of XHTML and CSS. Within the XHTML, we will use `<div>` elements to define the layers and a `<table>` for a dialog box. We will also make use of the `<a>` element to handle click events on the items in the menu. You can see the code for these layers here:

```
<div id="menubar"></div>

<div id="go" onmousedown="changeState('helpmenu','hidden')"
```

```
        onmouseup="changeState('gomenu','visible')">
  Go
</div>

<div id="help" onmousedown="changeState('gomenu','hidden')"
      onmouseup="changeState('helpmenu','visible')">
  Help
</div>

<div id="gomenu">
  <a href="http://developer.netscape.com">DevEdge</a>
  <hr size="1">
  <a href="http://www.mozilla.org">Mozilla.org</a>
  <hr size="1">
  <a href="http://msdn.microsoft.com">MSDN</a>
</div>

<div id="helpmenu" onclick="changeState('helpmenu','hidden')"
      onmouseup="changeState('about','visible')">About...</a>
</div>

<div id="about">
  <table border="0">
    <tr>
      <td>
        <img src="info-icon.gif" width="32" height="32" />
      </td>
      <td>
        This DHTML Menu was created by R. Allen Wyke for JavaScript
        Unleashed.
      </td>
    </tr>
    <tr>
      <td colspan="2" align="right">
        <form name="form1" action="null">
          <input type="button" value="Close"
                  onclick="changeState('about','hidden')" />
        </form>
    </tr>
  </table>
</div>
```

For our styles we need several definitions. The following is a description of what we have to define:

- No underlining of <a> elements
- Coloring and positioning of the menu bar
- Coloring and positioning of Go and Help items on the menu bar
- Coloring, positioning, and hiding of Go and Help menus
- Coloring, positioning, and hiding of the About dialog box

The following code contains the style sheet definitions that we will need for this formatting.

```
<style type="text/css">
<!--
  /* Global styles */
  a{
    text-decoration: none;
    font-size: 8pt;
  }

  /* Properties of the menus on the menubar */
  #help{
    background-color: #c0c0c0;
    position: absolute;
    right: 0px;
    top: 0px;
  }

  #go{
    background-color: #c0c0c0;
    left: 0px;
    position: absolute;
    top: 0px;
    width: 100%;
  }

  /* Properties of the actual menus that are hidden until clicked */
  #gomenu{
    background-color: #c0c0c0;
    left: 10px;
    position: absolute;
    top: 20px;
```

```
      visibility: hidden;
      width: 80px;
    }

  #helpmenu{
      background-color: #c0c0c0;
      right: 10px;
      position: absolute;
      top: 20px;
      visibility: hidden;
      width: 80px;
      font-size: 8pt;
    }

  /* Properties of About Dialog box */
  #about{
      background-color: gray;
      border: 2px solid black;
      height: 100px;
      left: 100px;
      position: absolute;
      top: 50px;
      visibility: hidden;
      vertical-align: left;
      width:  200px;
    }
  -->
  </style>
```

Now that everything has been laid out and layers have been defined, it is time to put the D in DHTML.

Handling Actions

The first thing we need to do in the script portion of our menu is check to see if the browser making the request is actually a browser we intend to support. As in the last chapter, we will be using the Practical Browser Sniffing Script. We will also include the necessary checks for Internet Explorer 5+ and Netscape 6+. The code to accomplish this task is relatively simple. As you can see, if the browser is not supported, we pop up a quick message and then direct the user back to the page he came from.

```
// Create global variables for browser type.
var isDOM = new Boolean(false);
```

```
// make sure it's IE 5+ or Netscape 6+.
if((navigator.family == "ie4" && navigator.version > 4) ||
    navigator.family =="gecko"){
  isDOM = true;
}else{
  isDOM = false;
}


if(!isDOM){
  alert("Your browser does not support this menu");
  window.back();
}
```

The last piece of coding we need to include handles the hiding and showing of layers. Again, because we are only supporting the newer browsers, we can use our getElementById() method within a custom changeState() function.

```
function changeState(layerRef, state){
  var blockElement = document.getElementById(layerRef);
  blockElement.style.visibility = state;
}
```

This completes the code for our menu, which can be seen in its entirety in Listing 22.1.

LISTING 22.1   Code for the Menu

```
<?xml version="1.0" encoding="UTF-8"?>
<!DOCTYPE html PUBLIC "-//W3C//DTD XHTML 1.0 Transitional//EN"
                      "DTD/xhtml1-transitional.dtd">
<html xmlns="http://www.w3.org/1999/xhtml" xml:lang="en">
<head>
  <title>JavaScript Unleashed</title>
  <style type="text/css">
  <!--
    /* Global styles */
    a{
      text-decoration: none;
      font-size: 8pt;
    }

    /* Properties of the menus on the menubar */
    #help{
      background-color: #c0c0c0;
      position: absolute;
```

LISTING 22.1   Continued

```
    right: 0px;
    top: 0px;
}

#go{
    background-color: #c0c0c0;
    left: 0px;
    position: absolute;
    top: 0px;
    width: 100%;
}

/* Properties of the actual menus that are hidden until clicked */
#gomenu{
    background-color: #c0c0c0;
    left: 10px;
    position: absolute;
    top: 20px;
    visibility: hidden;
    width: 80px;
}

#helpmenu{
    background-color: #c0c0c0;
    right: 10px;
    position: absolute;
    top: 20px;
    visibility: hidden;
    width: 80px;
    font-size: 8pt;
}

/* Properties of About Dialog box */
#about{
    background-color: gray;
    border: 2px solid black;
    height: 100px;
    left: 100px;
    position: absolute;
    top: 50px;
    visibility: hidden;
```

LISTING 22.1 Continued

```
      vertical-align: left;
      width:  200px;
   }
 -->
 </style>
 <script type="text/javascript"
      src="http://developer.netscape.com/evangelism/lib/js/ua.js"></script>
 <script type="text/javascript">
   // Create global variables for browser type.
   var isDOM = new Boolean(false);

   // make sure it's IE 5+ or Netscape 6+.
   if((navigator.family == "ie4" && navigator.version > 4) ||
      navigator.family =="gecko"){
     isDOM = true;
   }else{
     isDOM = false;
   }

   if(!isDOM){
     alert("Your browser does not support this menu");
     window.back();
   }

   function changeState(layerRef, state){
     var blockElement = document.getElementById(layerRef);
     blockElement.style.visibility = state;
   }
 </script>
</head>
<body>
 <div id="go" onmousedown="changeState('helpmenu','hidden')"
   onmouseup="changeState('gomenu','visible')">
   Go
 </div>

 <div id="help" onmousedown="changeState('gomenu','hidden')"
   onmouseup="changeState('helpmenu','visible')">
   Help
 </div>

 <div id="gomenu">
```

LISTING 22.1   Continued

```
    <a href="http://developer.netscape.com">DevEdge</a>
    <hr size="1" />
    <a href="http://www.mozilla.org">Mozilla.org</a>
    <hr size="1" />
    <a href="http://msdn.microsoft.com">MSDN</a>
  </div>

  <div id="helpmenu" onclick="changeState('helpmenu','hidden')"
    onmouseup="changeState('about','visible')">About...
  </div>

  <div id="about">
    <table border="0">
      <tr>
        <td>
          <img src="info-icon.gif" width="32" height="32" alt="Info" />
        </td>
        <td>
          This DHTML Menu was created by R. Allen Wyke for JavaScript
          Unleashed.
        </td>
      </tr>
      <tr>
        <td colspan="2" align="right">
          <form name="form1" action="null">
            <input type="button" value="Close"
                   onclick="changeState('about','hidden')" />
          </form>
        </td>
      </tr>
    </table>
  </div>
</body>
</html>
```

After you have completed the menu, you are ready to load it into a browser for testing. The menu at this point should look like the one in Figure 22.1. As you can see, CSS and JavaScript allow you to place the menu items at the very top of the browser window and provide clickable items without defining true links. You will also notice that by defining the go item at a width of 100%, you allow the user to resize and still have the proper distribution of the gray menu background.

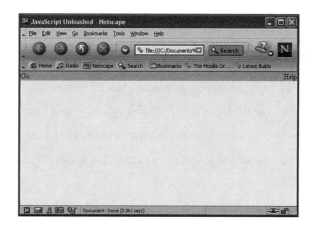

FIGURE 22.1 The menu, loaded in a browser.

If you click on the Go menu in the upper-left corner, the menu of sites is exposed. As you can see in Figure 22.2, the URL of the link is still displayed in the browser's status bar.

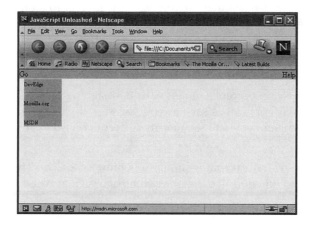

FIGURE 22.2 Accessing the Go menu.

The final menu item that we created was a Help item. If you click on it, you will see the About option, which you can select to display the dialog shown in Figure 22.3.

FIGURE 22.3 The About dialog box.

Exploring Other Things You Can Do

Now that we have built our menu, we are sure that you want to extend it to do more. The following is a quick list of things to implement to get a better feel for building your own DHTML menus. You also can check out Netscape's DevEdge site (http://developer.netscape.com) for a free Menu object.

- Adding support for older browsers, such as Navigator 4 and Internet Explorer 4

- Adding code so that clicking outside the currently expanded menu closes it

- Repositioning the About dialog box to the center of the window

- Adding cascading submenus

Building Toolbars

Building a toolbar is one of the coolest things you can learn to do in DHTML. You may have to tap all your skills to make a toolbar work and interact with other toolbars the way you want. Building a toolbar requires not only the use of JavaScript but CSS and layers as well. The key thing is to determine what you want the toolbar to look like and how you want it to work. Then you can work backward and design the layout, code, and style you want.

Applying Events

The first thing you need to become familiar with in designing toolbars is the events you will use. In an everyday application such as your browser, if you watch the buttons as you roll your mouse over them, you will see that these events trigger changes in the state of the button.

We are going to create a toolbar that is similar to a browser toolbar. The one we are going to create will look and function like the newer toolbars, such as those in Internet Explorer.

What Should Happen?

The first thing we need to do is document what should happen in the toolbar. Open your browser and watch how the state of the buttons changes as you roll your mouse over them and click them. Figures 22.4 through 22.6 show how the Refresh button state changes on Internet Explorer browsers.

FIGURE 22.4   A normal toolbar.

FIGURE 22.5   Rolling over a button with the mouse.

FIGURE 22.6   Pressing a toolbar button.

As you can see, there are three states that we will want to simulate. When the user allows the mouse button to come up, we should invoke an event to perform a certain task. Additionally, we should restore the state of the button when the user's mouse moves off the button and a click is not occurring.

What Can Happen?

Looking at this from a Web-development perspective, all of the necessary functionality for our toolbar can be created. There are events for the mouse rolling over and off an element and for pressing and releasing a button. In conjunction with the Image.src property, which can replace an image on the page with another image, we will be able to simulate rolling over a button and pressing it. This takes care of the visual effects.

We also need for these buttons to perform a task. For this we will use the onClick event handler in an <a> element. If the user clicks a button, we can capture that click and process it. The following list describes the buttons we will use and what they will do.

> **NOTE**
>
> Because we want this example to run in older and newer browsers, we are using the <a> element to handle the click events instead of putting them right inside the <img> elements themselves.

- Back: This button simulates the Back or Previous button on a browser.

- Forward: This button simulates the Forward or Next button.

- Home: This button simulates the Home button on Navigator browsers. Internet Explorer does not support this method.

- Reload/Refresh: This button simulates the Reload or Refresh button on a browser to reprocess and render the current page. We will include a call to the Date.getTime() method on the page so you can see that it has been reloaded.

- Find: This button simulates the Edit, Find menu option, which lets you search the text in the browser window. Internet Explorer does not support this method.

- Print: This button simulates the Print button on a browser to bring up the Print dialog box for printing the current page.

In addition to these six buttons, we will also have a form with a text field that allows the user to enter a URL and click a Go button to load the URL in the browser window.

Now that we know our requirements, let's build the application. We will look at designing the images and writing the code as well.

Considering Design Issues

Before you start writing any code, you need to make some decisions about how you want to actually write and store your code. Most of the functionality of the menu could be included with the XHTML elements themselves—it is not a lot of code. However, the functionality that our example represents could be used elsewhere, so we want to use a more modular approach.

Code Storage

Before we start building our application, we need to decide where the code will be stored. You will have to decide this based on what it is you are building. For our application, we will store all the code within the XHTML document. If you take this example and implement it on your site in multiple locations, you should consider storing the code in an external JavaScript source file (.js).

Modular Programming

We are going to plan this application to be as modular as possible. We want the code to be useable elsewhere if needed. To accomplish this, we are going to create as many functions as necessary to process information.

For our application, there are three different sets of functionality that will be occurring. These are listed and described in the following list:

- Image State Change: This function, which we will call rollImage(), will be responsible for changing the image when it is rolled over or clicked.

- Button Processing: This function, which we will call process(), will perform the button's tasks. When a user clicks a button, this function will react appropriately.

- URL Handling: This function, which we will call takeBrowser(), will take the data entered on the form and direct the browser to that location.

Creating Our Toolbar

Now that we have performed all the preliminary steps, we can really get into creating our toolbar. In this section of the chapter, we are going to cover everything from designing our images, to creating the appropriate XHTML, CSS, and JavaScript to handle not only the design but the functionality of our project.

Designing Images

Unlike other applications, with a Web-based application you have to provide most of the components that make up any kind of interface. Other than the subobjects of the Form object, you will have to provide all of your own images and interface components. Because of the nature of your task, you will also have to provide versions for when the mouse is over the image and when it is pressed.

Earlier we said that a button on a toolbar should change state when the user rolls his mouse over it and when it is pressed. For our example to work properly, we will need the following images:

- Normal: The default image.

- Rollover: The default image with a 1-pixel white border on the left and top and 1-pixel gray border on the right and bottom to give the appropriate look.

- Pressed: The default image with a 1-pixel gray border on the left and top, and a 1-pixel white border on the right and bottom to give the appropriate look.

Designing the XHTML

The first thing we are going to design is the XHTML that will contain the layout of our toolbar. There are several components to the toolbar interface we are going to design, which can be seen in Figure 22.7.

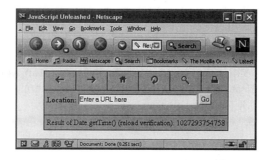

FIGURE 22.7   The interface we are going to build.

For simplicity we are going to use a table to hold and arrange our buttons. There will be three rows in our table, with six cells in the top row and a single cell in the second and third rows. The background of the table will be gray.

The first row of the table will contain the images that make up our toolbar. Each image will be surrounded by <a> elements so that we can apply mouse events. Older browsers do not allow you to apply these events to <img> elements, even though the newer browsers do, so we must wrap the image. The following is an example of what an individual image cell will look like.

```
<td align="center">
  <a href="javascript:process('back')"
    onmouseup="rollImage('0','up')"
    onmousedown="rollImage('0','down')"
    onmouseout="rollImage('0','out')"
    onmouseover="rollImage('0','over')">
  <img border="0" src="back.gif" width="24" height="24" alt="Back" /></a>
</td>
```

In the second row of our toolbar, we have a text box in which the user enters a URL. When the user clicks the Go button, the browser will attempt to load the URL. The XHTML for this is a fairly straightforward use of the `<form>` element. The button makes use of the `onClick` event handler to call a function that will redirect the browser. You will also see that we used the `colspan` attribute to properly implement a cell all the way across the width of the table. The XHTML for this is as follows:

```
<td colspan="6">
  <form name="netsite" action="null">
    <b>
      Location:
    </b>
    <input type="text" size="40" value="Enter a URL here" name="where" />
    <input type="button" value="Go" onclick="takeBrowser(this.form)" />
  </form>
</td>
```

The last row simply contains the result of calling the `getTime()` method of an instance of the `Date` object. This is so that the user can see the Reload button work. When the user clicks Reload, the numerical value displayed in this cell will change, confirming the actual reload of the page. The XHTML for this row is as follows:

```
<td colspan="6">
  Result of Date.getTime() (reload verification):
  <script type="text/javascript">
    document.write((new Date()).getTime());
  </script>
</td>
```

These three rows, in combination with the `<body>` element, make up the entire interface part of the toolbar.

Implementing Image Rollovers
To get the image rollovers working properly, we are going to make use of the `Image` object. We are primarily interested in the `src` property, which will allow us to change the image.

As you saw in the XHTML we have already created for this example, each of the <a> elements around our images calls a rollImage() function, which we will define here.

In building image rollovers, first we need to declare the images we are going to use. We showed you how to do this in the last chapter, so we are going to spare you the details. Just as a reminder, the best way is to store the images in an array. This allows us to access the images in the array and in the document with the same index numbers. If we store the "over" and "pressed" versions of our images in two different arrays in the same indexed position, [0], we can pass a single position variable to the function to perform image swapping.

Because we will also need to return the image to its previous state, the default, we need three arrays. The following shows the code you use to create these arrays and store images in them:

```
// Create array to hold the "over" images.
var overImg = new Array();
overImg[0] = new Image(24,24);
overImg[1] = new Image(24,24);
overImg[2] = new Image(24,24);
overImg[3] = new Image(24,24);
overImg[4] = new Image(24,24);
overImg[5] = new Image(24,24);

// Create array to hold the "down" images.
var downImg = new Array();
downImg[0] = new Image(24,24);
downImg[1] = new Image(24,24);
downImg[2] = new Image(24,24);
downImg[3] = new Image(24,24);
downImg[4] = new Image(24,24);
downImg[5] = new Image(24,24);

// Create array to hold the default images.
var defaultImg = new Array();
defaultImg[0] = new Image(24,24);
defaultImg[1] = new Image(24,24);
defaultImg[2] = new Image(24,24);
defaultImg[3] = new Image(24,24);
defaultImg[4] = new Image(24,24);
defaultImg[5] = new Image(24,24);

// Preload "over" images in the array.
overImg[0].src = "back-over.gif";
```

```
overImg[1].src = "forward-over.gif";
overImg[2].src = "home-over.gif";
overImg[3].src = "reload-over.gif";
overImg[4].src = "search-over.gif";
overImg[5].src = "print-over.gif";

// Preload "down" images in the array.
downImg[0].src = "back-down.gif";
downImg[1].src = "forward-down.gif";
downImg[2].src = "home-down.gif";
downImg[3].src = "reload-down.gif";
downImg[4].src = "search-down.gif";
downImg[5].src = "print-down.gif";

// Preload default images in the array.
defaultImg[0].src = "back.gif";
defaultImg[1].src = "forward.gif";
defaultImg[2].src = "home.gif";
defaultImg[3].src = "reload.gif";
defaultImg[4].src = "search.gif";
defaultImg[5].src = "print.gif";
```

Next we need to define our function to swap the images. Because we have built this function before, this will be an easy task for us. We just need to extend it to include more possible conditions. As a reminder, the function will take two parameters. The first parameter is the index number of the image we are processing. The function call, which is contained in the <a> element, will pass a numerical value that represents its location in the document.

The second parameter is the type of rollover that is occurring. For our purposes, there are four types: over, out, up, and down. Based on what is passed, we will use a switch statement to evaluate the value and perform the proper swapping of images. This is done by accessing the src property of instances of the Image object—both in the document and in the arrays. The entire function definition will look like the following:

```
function rollImage(img,type){
  switch(type){
    case "over":
      document.images[img].src = overImg[img].src;
      break;
    case "out":
      document.images[img].src = defaultImg[img].src;
      break;
```

```
    case "up":
      document.images[img].src = defaultImg[img].src;
      break;
    case "down":
      document.images[img].src = downImg[img].src;
      break;
  }
}
```

This completes the rollover functionality we need.

Implementing a Location Field

On the second row of our toolbar is a text area that will allow the user to enter a URL and then click Go to redirect the browser. As you saw in the XHTML, this button calls a `takeBrowser()` function, passing it the `this.form` object. After the function is invoked, it will use the `Form` object reference that was passed, assign it to a variable, and access the value of the text field. Then it uses the `location.href` property to change the page currently loaded in the browser, thereby redirecting it to the URL that the user entered.

This function does not perform error checking so, if the user enters an incorrect value, the browser will simply complain that it cannot load the page. You will also see in the code that follows that it accesses the value of the text field through the name of the field, which is specified by the `name` attribute.

```
function takeBrowser(ref){
  var form = ref;
  location.href = form.where.value;
}
```

Processing Button Events

The last function to write will take care of the processing. This function, which we will call `process()`, will take a single parameter. We will evaluate this parameter using a `switch` statement for the six possible buttons.

The Find and Home buttons do not work in Internet Explorer, so we have to return an alert dialog informing the user. To do this, we will check our `navigator.org` variable to see if it equals `"microsoft"`. As a reminder, this variable is set using our Practical Browser Sniffing Script from Netscape. The code for this function looks like the following:

> **NOTE**
>
> Don't forget that you need to load the external Practical Browser Sniffing Script JavaScript file before you can use the variables it sets.

```
function process(item){
  switch(item){
    case "find":
      if(navigator.org == "microsoft"){
        alert("Internet Explorer does not support this method");
        break;
      }
      window.find();
      break;
    case "print":
      window.print();
      break;
    case "home":
      if(navigator.org == "microsoft"){
        alert("Internet Explorer does not support this method");
        break;
      }
      window.home();
      break;
    case "reload":
      document.location.reload();
      break;
    case "forward":
      history.forward();
      break;
    case "back":
      history.back();
      break;
    }
}
```

Examining the Result

We have stepped through the XHTML and all of the JavaScript, so now we can test our application. The final code is in Listing 22.2, and Figures 22.8 and 22.9 show the position of the buttons when moused over and down. As you test the program, watch the time string change as you hit the Reload button. The result of clicking the Find and Home buttons is obvious, because a dialog box pops up for Internet Explorer and the appropriate dialogs pop up for Netscape browsers. If you want to test the Forward and Back buttons, you will need to load several pages into your browser so that you have something to go forward and back to.

LISTING 22.2   The Complete Source of the Toolbar

```xml
<?xml version="1.0" encoding="UTF-8"?>
<!DOCTYPE html PUBLIC "-//W3C//DTD XHTML 1.0 Transitional//EN"
                      "DTD/xhtml1-transitional.dtd">
<html xmlns="http://www.w3.org/1999/xhtml" xml:lang="en">
<head>
  <title>JavaScript Unleashed</title>
  <script type="text/javascript"
       src="http://developer.netscape.com/evangelism/lib/js/ua.js"></script>
  <script type="text/javascript">

    // Create arrays to hold images.
    var overImg = new Array();
    overImg[0] = new Image(24,24);
    overImg[1] = new Image(24,24);
    overImg[2] = new Image(24,24);
    overImg[3] = new Image(24,24);
    overImg[4] = new Image(24,24);
    overImg[5] = new Image(24,24);

    var downImg = new Array();
    downImg[0] = new Image(24,24);
    downImg[1] = new Image(24,24);
    downImg[2] = new Image(24,24);
    downImg[3] = new Image(24,24);
    downImg[4] = new Image(24,24);
    downImg[5] = new Image(24,24);

    var defaultImg = new Array();
    defaultImg[0] = new Image(24,24);
    defaultImg[1] = new Image(24,24);
    defaultImg[2] = new Image(24,24);
    defaultImg[3] = new Image(24,24);
    defaultImg[4] = new Image(24,24);
    defaultImg[5] = new Image(24,24);

    // Preload images in the array.
    overImg[0].src = "back-over.gif";
    overImg[1].src = "forward-over.gif";
    overImg[2].src = "home-over.gif";
```

22

LISTING 22.2   Continued

```
overImg[3].src = "reload-over.gif";
overImg[4].src = "search-over.gif";
overImg[5].src = "print-over.gif";

downImg[0].src = "back-down.gif";
downImg[1].src = "forward-down.gif";
downImg[2].src = "home-down.gif";
downImg[3].src = "reload-down.gif";
downImg[4].src = "search-down.gif";
downImg[5].src = "print-down.gif";

defaultImg[0].src = "back.gif";
defaultImg[1].src = "forward.gif";
defaultImg[2].src = "home.gif";
defaultImg[3].src = "reload.gif";
defaultImg[4].src = "search.gif";
defaultImg[5].src = "print.gif";

// Change the state of image depending on the event that fired.
function rollImage(img,type){
  switch(type){
    case "over":
      document.images[img].src = overImg[img].src;
      break;
    case "out":
      document.images[img].src = defaultImg[img].src;
      break;
    case "up":
      document.images[img].src = defaultImg[img].src;
      break;
    case "down":
      document.images[img].src = downImg[img].src;
      break;
  }
}

// Process the URL that was entered in the text box.
function takeBrowser(ref){
  var form = ref;
  location.href = form.where.value;
```

LISTING 22.2   Continued

```
    }

    // Process the buttons as they are pressed.
    function process(item){
      switch(item){
        case "find":
          if(navigator.org == "microsoft"){
            alert("Internet Explorer does not support this method");
            break;
          }
          window.find();
          break;
        case "print":
          window.print();
          break;
        case "home":
          if(navigator.org == "microsoft"){
            alert("Internet Explorer does not support this method");
            break;
          }
          window.home();
          break;
        case "reload":
          document.location.reload();
          break;
        case "forward":
          history.forward();
          break;
        case "back":
          history.back();
          break;
      }
    }
  </script>
</head>
<body>
  <table border="1" cellpadding="5" cellspacing="0" align="center"
        bgcolor="#c0c0c0">
    <tr>
      <td align="center">
```

22

LISTING 22.2   Continued

```
        <a href="javascript:process('back')"
            onmouseup="rollImage('0','up')"
            onmousedown="rollImage('0','down')"
            onmouseout="rollImage('0','out')"
            onmouseover="rollImage('0','over')">
          <img border="0" src="back.gif" width="24" height="24"
              alt="Back" /></a>
    </td>
    <td align="center">
      <a href="javascript:process('forward')"
            onmouseup="rollImage('1','up')"
            onmousedown="rollImage('1','down')"
            onmouseout="rollImage('1','out')"
            onmouseover="rollImage('1','over')">
          <img border="0" src="forward.gif" width="24" height="24"
              alt="Forward" /></a>          </td>
    <td align="center">
      <a href="javascript:process('home')"
            onmouseup="rollImage('2','up')"
            onmousedown="rollImage('2','down')"
            onmouseout="rollImage('2','out')"
            onmouseover="rollImage('2','over')">
          <img border="0" src="home.gif" width="24" height="24"
              alt="Home" /></a>
    </td>
    <td align="center">
      <a href="javascript:process('reload')"
            onmouseup="rollImage('3','up')"
            onmousedown="rollImage('3','down')"
            onmouseout="rollImage('3','out')"
            onmouseover="rollImage('3','over')">
          <img border="0" src="reload.gif" width="24" height="24"
              alt="Reload" /></a>
    </td>
    <td align="center">
      <a href="javascript:process('find')"
            onmouseup="rollImage('4','up')"
            onmousedown="rollImage('4','down')"
```

LISTING 22.2   Continued

```
                    onmouseout="rollImage('4','out')"
                    onmouseover="rollImage('4','over')">
              <img border="0" src="search.gif" width="24" height="24"
                    alt="Search" /></a>
        </td>
        <td align="center">
          <a href="javascript:process('print')"
                  onmouseup="rollImage('5','up')"
                  onmousedown="rollImage('5','down')"
                  onmouseout="rollImage('5','out')"
                  onmouseover="rollImage('5','over')">
              <img border="0" src="print.gif" width="24" height="24"
                    alt="Print" /></a>
        </td>
      </tr>
      <tr>
        <td colspan="6">
          <form name="netsite" action="null">
            <b>
              Location:
            </b>
              <input type="text" size="40" value="Enter a URL here"
                    name="where" />
              <input type="button" value="Go" onclick="takeBrowser(this.form)" />
          </form>
        </td>
      </tr>
      <tr>
        <td colspan="6">
          Result of Date.getTime() (reload verification):
          <script type="text/javascript">
            document.write((new Date()).getTime());
          </script>
        </td>
      </tr>
    </table>
</body>
</html>
```

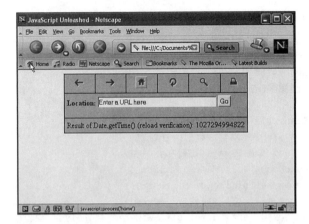

FIGURE 22.8   Rolling over a button with the mouse.

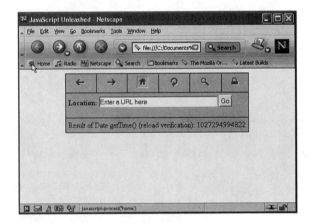

FIGURE 22.9   Pressing a toolbar button.

Summary

In this chapter we applied what we have learned about implementing DHTML on your site. We took what you have learned in Chapter 18, "Handling Events"; Chapter 19, "Cascading Style Sheets"; Chapter 20, "Layers"; and Chapter 21, "Rollovers and Visual Effects," and applied it to our examples. At this point you should be well on your way to implementing dynamic pages using not only JavaScript but other XHTML elements and CSS as well.

In the next chapter we are going to explore various navigation techniques, and create a dynamic toolbar.

CHAPTER 23

JavaScript-Based Site Navigation

Exploring Navigation Techniques

JavaScript transfers much of the burden of content delivery and formatting to the browser rather than having the server deal with it. One of the benefits of this client-side control is improved navigation. Instead of merely providing static links that connect Web pages within a site, Webmasters can use JavaScript to control the display of a site's information.

Frames provide the ability to add navigational aids to Web pages without limiting the site's layout and content. This is accomplished by splitting the browser into more than one window so that a site map can be visible at all times while the user scrolls through the many pages of an XHTML document. Using links on the site map, a new page can be displayed in the other frame. It doesn't take JavaScript to do this. Simply use the target attribute of the anchor tag to point to any frame you want. However, what if the page currently being displayed contains a data entry form and needs to be submitted before moving on to another page? Submitting the form using a submit button is fine, but it brings the user to a new page, leaving him somewhere off the map. In some cases, it may be ideal to allow the user to move throughout the site entering data without requiring him to click a submit button on each page. This can be done using JavaScript by submitting the forms across frames.

If your site map is rather large, you may prefer to display only part of the map at a time. Updating the map then becomes necessary. How do you update a map, submit a form, display the resulting document, and keep track of where the user is with one click? Using JavaScript is the easiest way. The navigation techniques in this chapter demonstrate how to create and use a dynamic navigation toolbar as well as how to use the JavaScript History object.

Scripting a Dynamic Toolbar

A navigation toolbar is a common user interface used to navigate through items in a software program. For example, many database programs use a navigation toolbar to move through database records. Relative to JavaScript, a dynamic toolbar is one that can change when the user interacts with it. The example in this chapter uses a navigation toolbar that controls a simple slide show. Four buttons on the toolbar are used to move forward or backward through an array of slides. Two other buttons are used to start or stop an automatic slide show. One logical way to program this is to create two custom objects—a Button object and a Toolbar object.

Writing a Custom Toolbar Object

A toolbar can be thought of as a set of buttons, so the Toolbar object is named buttonSet. Listing 23.1 shows the buttonSet constructor used to set up all the properties and methods available to a toolbar.

LISTING 23.1   The buttonSet Object Constructor

```
function buttonSet(name)
{
    /*
     * Description: button object constructor.
     * Arguments: name - The variable name of the buttonSet.
     */

    // Properties
    this.name = name;
    this.startIndex = 7;
    this.length = 7;
    this.isBusy = false;

    // Methods
    this.addBtn = addBtn;
    this.print = print;
    this.clear = clear;
    return this;
}
```

The addBtn method creates and adds a new Button object to the buttonSet. The print method writes the buttonSet to an XHTML document. The clear method resets all buttons

contained within the buttonSet to their original states, either disabled or enabled. These
methods are described in detail in the following sections.

Using the Button Object

The buttonSet object is used to keep track of one or more Button objects. Each Button object
holds the information needed for when it is clicked or displayed as an XHTML <img>
element. Listing 23.2 shows the two functions used to create a new Button object.

LISTING 23.2   The Button Object's click Method and Constructor

```
function click()
{
   /*
   * Description: Method of button. Executes command for this button.
   * Arguments: None.
   */


   eval(this.command);
}


function button(name, file, alt, url, spacer, condition, command)
{
   /*
   * Description: button object.
   * Arguments:
   *    name - The name used as this button's XHTML element name.
   *    file - The button image's source url.
   *    alt  - The alt attribute for the button.
   *    url - The url which can reference (across frames) the
   *          buttonSet that holds this button.
   *    spacer - number of pixels of horizontal spacing used
   *             after the button being added.
   *    condition - conditional statement that determines
   *                whether or not to display this button.
   *    command - The command to be executed by this button.
   */

   // Properties
   this.name = name;
   this.file = file;
   this.alt = alt;
   this.url = url;
   this.spacer = spacer;
   this.condition = condition;
   this.command = command;
```

LISTING 23.2   Continued

```
    // Methods
    this.click = click;
    return this;
}
```

The name property becomes its XHTML name. The button's file property is the source URL for the button's image. The alt property is used as the XHTML alt attribute. The url property is used as the href property of the anchor associated with the button's image. Using a transparent graphic file, the spacer property specifies how much space to leave before placing another button image to the right of this one. This allows you to create different sections within the toolbar or compensate for button images with different widths. A Button will be displayed only if its conditional expression evaluates to true. This is the key to knowing which buttons are displayed and available to the user. Whenever a buttonSet object is written to an XHTML page, it looks at each Button's conditional expression to determine if the Button is enabled. If it is enabled and the user clicks it, the command is executed. The command string can be any JavaScript statement, as long as it can be executed from the document where the buttonSet is created.

Instantiating a Toolbar

Using the following lines of code, the slide show program creates a new buttonSet object and resets its current state.

```
Toolbar = new buttonSet("Toolbar");
Toolbar.clear();
```

It is important when creating a new buttonSet that the argument passed to the constructor be equal to the variable name of the object being created. This allows the buttonSet object to create JavaScript commands using its own name. The clear method is used to set or reset the global variables used by the buttonSet to determine which of its buttons are enabled. Listing 23.3 shows the clear method that was written for the Slide Show application.

LISTING 23.3   The clear Method of the buttonSet Object

```
function clear()
{
    /*
    * Description: Method of buttonSet object. Used to reset any global
    *              variables on which any buttons in the buttonSet rely
    *              for their condition statements.
    * Arguments: None.
    */

    gIsRunning=false;
}
```

After the new `buttonSet` has been created, the Slide Show application creates each button by using the `addBtn` method. The first button created is shown in the following code:

```
Toolbar.addBtn("First","graphics/first.gif","First Picture",0,"true",
➥    "changeSlide('first')");
```

Listing 23.4 shows the complete `addBtn` method, which simply creates a new `Button` object and then adds it to the `buttonSet`.

LISTING 23.4   The addBtn Method of the buttonSet Object

```
function addBtn(name, file, alt, spacer, condition, command)
{
    /*
     *   Description: Method of the buttonSet object used to add a new button to
     *                the end of the button set.
     *   Arguments: name - (string) Name used as button's XHTML element name.
     *              file - (string) The button image's source url.
     *              alt  - (string) The alt attribute for the button.
     *              spacer - (integer) number of pixels of horizontal spacing used
     *                       after the button being added.
     *              condition - (string) conditional statement determines
     *                          whether or not to display the button.
     *              command - (string) The command to be executed.
     */

    var i = this.length;
    this[i] = new button(name,file,alt,
            "javascript:parent."+this.name+"["+i+"]"+".click()",
            spacer,condition,command);
    this.length++;
}
```

The `file` argument specified for the `button` constructor in Listing 23.4 is worth noting. This string will be used as the `href` property of the button's image. The following example is the XHTML generated for the first Slide Show button:

```
<a href="javascript:parent.Toolbar[7].click()">
<img src="graphics/first.gif" alt="First Picture" width="24"
➥ height="24" border=0>
</a>
```

When the user clicks this image, the `click` method of the seventh property of the `Toolbar` object is called. The seventh item in the `Toolbar` object (essentially an array) is where the first `Button` object was stored using the `addBtn` method. This is the best way to call the `click` method across frames while working in both Netscape and Microsoft browsers. The `buttonSet` object is set up in such a way that the programmer using it doesn't need to keep track of how the buttons are indexed.

Displaying the Toolbar

The global variable `gIsRunning` is `true` when the slide show is automatically stepping through each slide; otherwise, it is `false`. This variable is used by four `Button` objects to display two buttons at a time. One is for an active state, and the other is for its disabled state (its face is grayed out). The following examples show two buttons that depend on `gIsRunning`:

```
Toolbar.addBtn("Start", "graphics/auto.gif", "Start Slideshow", 0,
               "gIsRunning==false", "changeSlide('start')");
Toolbar.addBtn("StartGray", "graphics/autoGray.gif", "Start Slideshow", 0,
               "gIsRunning==true", "");
```

The `StartGray` button will be displayed only if `gIsRunning` is equal to `true`. On the other hand, if `gIsRunning` is equal to `false`, the `Start` button will be displayed. If the `Start` button is enabled and the user clicks it, the following code is executed within the `changeSlide` function:

```
if(command == "start") {
    gIsRunning = true;
    Toolbar.print(window.frames[2].document);
    gTimer = window.setTimeout("startAuto()",1500);
}
```

`gIsRunning` is set to `true`, and the toolbar is printed to the `Document` object specified. The current toolbar is eliminated, and a new XHTML page is created containing a new toolbar, which then takes into account the new state of `gIsRunning`. This means that the `StartGray` button will be enabled, while the `Start` button is never even written into the new page. This gives the illusion of graying out the `Start` button when, in fact, it is a different button. Listing 23.5 shows the `print` method, which is responsible for writing the new XHTML page.

LISTING 23.5   The print Method of the buttonSet Object

```
function print(dObj)
{
    /*
    * Description: Method of buttonSet object.
    * Arguments: dObj - document object receiving buttonSet.
    */
    this.isBusy = true;
    var spaceInt;
```

LISTING 23.5   Continued

```javascript
var DQUOTE = '\"';
var topBase = "";
var basePath = ""+window.location.pathname;
var baseDir = "";
var baseFile = basePath.substring(basePath.length-10,basePath.length);

baseDir = basePath.substring(0,basePath.length-12);
topBase=window.location.protocol+"//"+window.location.host+baseDir;

dObj.open();
dObj.bgColor = parent.frames[0].document.bgColor;
dObj.writeln('<html><head>');
dObj.writeln('<title>Toolbar<\/title>');
dObj.writeln('<base href = '+DQUOTE+topBase+DQUOTE+'>');
dObj.writeln('<script type="text/javascript">');
dObj.writeln('<\/script>');
dObj.writeln('<\/head>');
dObj.writeln('<body bgcolor="'+
    parent.frames[0].document.bgColor.toUpperCase()+'">');
dObj.writeln('<center>');
dObj.writeln('<table width="100%" border="0">');
dObj.writeln('<tr><td align="center">');

//Print each button. Start at property index i.
for(var i = this.startIndex; this.length > i; i++)
{
    if(eval(this[i].condition))
    {
        dObj.write('<a href="'+this[i].url+'">');
        dObj.write('<img src="'+this[i].file+'" alt="'+this[i].alt+
            '" width="24" height="24" border="0">');
        dObj.write('<\/a>');
        // Add space if specified.
        spaceInt = 0 + this[i].spacer;
        if(spaceInt != 0)
        {
            dObj.write('<img src="graphics/space.gif" width="'+spaceInt+
                '" height="24" border="0">');
        }
    }
}
```

LISTING 23.5   Continued

```
    dObj.writeln('<\/td><\/tr><\/table>');
    dObj.writeln('<\/center>');
    dObj.writeln('<\/body><\/html>');
    dObj.close();
    this.isBusy = false;
}
```

The print method begins by setting the isBusy flag to true to prevent the user from clicking other buttons while the toolbar is refreshing. Next, a base URL is formed that is equal to the base URL of the current window. This is stored in the topBase variable and is used to generate a <base> tag for the new toolbar document.

The print method continues by opening access to the destination document. It then writes each line of XHTML required to build a Web page that looks like a toolbar. This example uses a table to center all the buttons. A for loop is used to print each button that is stored within the buttonSet. If a space was specified, a blank graphic will be inserted and "stretched" to the designated number of pixels. Finally, the document is closed, and the browser window is refreshed.

Refreshing the Toolbar

As you can see, refreshing the toolbar is as easy as calling its print method. Simply set the global variables on which the buttons depend, and call print. Documents within other frames can also refresh the toolbar. For example, you can modify the Slide Show application so that the user cannot start the slide show from the last slide. To do this, add a new global variable called gCanStart to the clear method, and set it equal to false. Modify the addBtn calls for the Start and StartGray buttons to take gCanStart into account. The new code would look like this:

```
Toolbar.addBtn("Start", "graphics/auto.gif", "Start Slideshow", 0,
    "gIsRunning==false && gCanStart==true", "changeSlide('auto')");
Toolbar.addBtn("StartGray", "graphics/autoGray.gif", "Start Slideshow", 0,
    "gIsRunning==true || gCanStart==false", "");
```

Then insert the following script into the <head> block of the last slide document:

```
<script type="text/javascript">
  var savedState;
  savedState = parent.gCanStart;
  parent.gCanStart=false;
  parent.Toolbar.print(parent.frames[2].document);
  parent.gCanStart=savedState;
</script>
```

Next, add another call to `Toolbar`'s `print` method when the document unloads. This would look like the following:

```
<body onUnload="parent.Toolbar.print(parent.frames[2].document)">
```

This will return the toolbar to its previous state after moving to another slide.

If you have every slide set the global variables and reset the toolbar, you can eliminate the need to refresh the toolbar using the `onUnload` event handler. Using this approach, you can have every document specify which buttons to display, knowing that it will be reset the next time a different document is loaded.

Using the Slide Show Application

On the Web site for this book (`www.samspublishing.com`) you will find all the files needed for the Slide Show application. Simply load `slideshow.htm` into the browser to activate the frameset. The toolbar is used to move through each slide and its corresponding description. Figure 23.1 shows what the Slide Show application looks like when loaded into the browser.

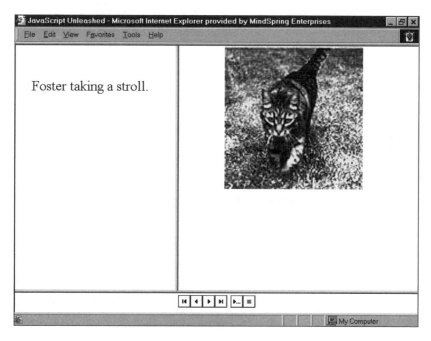

FIGURE 23.1   A toolbar used with the Slide Show application.

Five slides are included with the program. You can use the toolbar to advance or move back by one slide using the third and second buttons, respectively. You can also use the first and fourth buttons to move to the first and last slides, respectively, in the slide show. The last two buttons on the right will start and stop the program from stepping through each slide for you. Notice how the last button is grayed out. This is the `StartGray` button. After the `Start` button, shown as a right-pointing arrow followed by an ellipse, is clicked, the slide show begins to cycle through each pair of XHTML documents. Figure 23.2 shows a snapshot of the browser during the show. Notice how the `Stop` button is enabled while the show is running, and the `Start` button is grayed out.

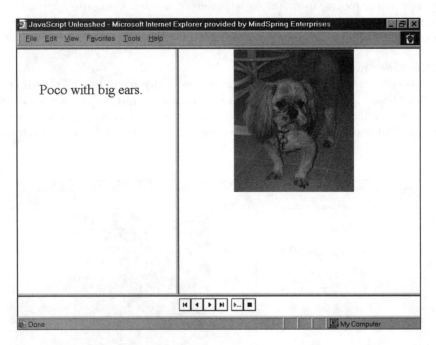

FIGURE 23.2   A snapshot of the slide show in progress.

Examining the Extra Features

The core `buttonSet` object could be altered even more. For example, it could be modified to support vertical toolbars instead of horizontal ones, or even both. Simply modify the `print` method to add the `<br />` tag after each button. You could create the toolbar in a separate browser window. It could be used as a navigation tool or even a help menu. No modifications would be necessary. Simply pass the `Document` object of the new window to the `print` method.

Using the History Object

So far you have seen how to navigate through some predefined Web pages. What if you want to provide navigation controls on your Web page that have the same functionality as those found on your browser's toolbar? Fortunately, JavaScript provides a special History object that allows you to navigate through the Web sites that your browser has already displayed. This includes Web pages that you did not create. The History object is able to do this because it stores all of the URLs that you have visited in a list.

To utilize this list of URLs, the History object has some built-in methods for navigating forward and backward. The back method loads the URL of the previously visited Web site. The forward method loads the next URL from the History list.

In addition, the History object has another method and some properties. Unfortunately, for security reasons, many browsers do not let you use the additional method and properties. This is not really a big drawback, because most of the usefulness of the History object comes from the back and forward methods.

To demonstrate the use of the History object, let's create a very simple page that contains two buttons for navigating. One button will take you back to the previous URL in the History list, and the other button will take you to the next URL in the History list. These buttons will use their onClick event handlers to call the two History methods discussed earlier. The code for this Web page is shown in Listing 23.6.

LISTING 23.6   Using the History Object to Navigate

```
<html>
<head>
<title>Using the History object</title>
</head>

<body style="text-align:center">

<h1>Navigating with the History object</h1>

Click one of the following buttons to navigate.
<hr />

<form>
  <input type="button"
         value="Back"
         onClick="window.history.back()">
  <input type="button"
         value="Forward"
         onClick="window.history.forward()">
</form>

</body>
</html>
```

23

To see how the buttons work, begin by loading one of your favorite Web sites. After that Web site is loaded, load Listing 23.6. Then enter the URL of another favorite site that is different from the first site you loaded. Now click the Back button on your browser. At this point you should see a Web page like the one shown in Figure 23.3. Now you can use the navigation buttons to navigate to either of the Web sites you just visited.

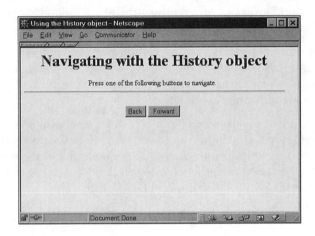

FIGURE 23.3   Navigating with the History object.

Summary

With JavaScript's capability to perform many actions at once, it's possible to create more sophisticated navigation aids. With one click from the user, JavaScript can validate data, submit a form, regenerate a frame, and change the contents of another frame.

The toolbar example showed how to refresh an XHTML page in order to give the illusion that buttons are being disabled or enabled as the user interacts with them. A method for changing the contents of three frames with one button click was also shown. The buttonSet object can easily be used in other page designs with little modification.

The History object allows you to provide the functionality of your Web browser's Forward and Back buttons in your Web pages. This can be very useful if you create a window that does not have the normal browser toolbars but needs the capability to load pages that have already been visited.

Forms and Data Validation

Hᴛᴍʟ enables Web page developers to create online forms. The HTML forms capability has several advantages as a mechanism for creating online forms:

- Client/server model: The Web browser supplies a generic graphical user interface (GUI) driven by the specific HTML script. Domain-specific processing is handled on the server side.

- Platform independence: Web browsers run on multiple platforms. The developer need not be concerned about platform-specific issues when developing forms.

- Network transparency: Network communications are built into the Web browser/Web server pair and implemented through the HTTP protocol.

- Standardized GUI: A user who is familiar with form elements can apply that knowledge to any form on the World Wide Web or corporate intranet.

The HTML forms interface in itself has a few deficiencies:

- Dynamic user feedback: HTML forms have no means of providing dynamic information on required input on a per-form-element basis.

- Client-side form validation: HTML forms can't validate a form element, a group of elements, or an entire form on the client side.

- Dialog boxes: HTML forms can't alert the user dynamically about an input error or request additional input.

- User confirmations: HTML forms have no way to ask for confirmation before taking irrevocable types of action.

- Interactivity among form or window elements: In HTML forms, the interactivity is limited to processing on the server side.

The JavaScript language addresses each of these deficiencies. JavaScript builds on the basic capabilities of HTML and produces a more powerful client-side GUI interface. In this chapter, you will learn how to implement these additional capabilities in JavaScript.

The code in this chapter makes extensive use of JavaScript event handlers. You can view event handlers as callbacks associated with a form or form element. They are explicitly specified as part of a form or form element tag. Event handlers are called when a user-triggered event occurs and, in turn, they call an appropriate JavaScript code fragment or function. Table 24.1 contains a list of JavaScript handlers.

TABLE 24.1   JavaScript Event Handlers

Event Handler	Description
onload	Occurs when the user agent finishes loading a window or all frames within a FRAMESET. This attribute can be used with BODY and FRAMESET elements.
onunload	Occurs when the user agent removes a document from a window or frame. This attribute can be used with BODY and FRAMESET elements.
onclick	Occurs when the pointing device button is clicked over an element.
ondblclick	Occurs when the pointing device button is double-clicked over an element.
onmousedown	Occurs when the pointing device button is pressed over an element.
onmouseup	Occurs when the pointing device button is released over an element.
onmouseover	Occurs when the pointing device is moved onto an element.
onmouseout	Occurs when the pointing device is moved away from an element.
onfocus	Occurs when an element receives focus either by the pointing device or by tabbing navigation.
onblur	Occurs when an element loses focus either by the pointing device or by tabbing navigation.
onkeypress	Occurs when a key is pressed and released over an element.
onkeydown	Occurs when a key is pressed down over an element.
onkeyup	Occurs when a key is released over an element.
onsubmit	Occurs when a form is submitted. It only applies to the FORM element.
onreset	Occurs when a form is reset. It only applies to the FORM element.
onselect	Occurs when a user selects some text in a text field.
onchange	Occurs when a control loses the input focus and its value has been modified since gaining focus.

Gathering User Feedback

With a well-designed form, the user should be able to determine rapidly what information is required. In very simple forms, you can accomplish this with well-thought-out labels adjacent to each form element. In complex forms, you should include a help facility that offers a detailed explanation of how to fill out the form. With JavaScript, you can add user prompting on a per-field basis. This allows you to supply additional information about the requirements or function of a form element at the moment when the information is needed. By doing so, you can reduce the amount of text required in the form element label and simplify the form's appearance.

The following example illustrates how to provide user feedback in a tooltip using the `<div>` tag and JavaScript. Imagine for a moment that you are creating an HTML form interface to a very advanced automated toaster. The goal is to produce an interface so easy to use that the most naive user can instruct it to produce savory toasted bread. Figure 24.1 shows the interface.

FIGURE 24.1   The automated toaster form.

The user can set the values of four input objects:

- A `Selection` object representing the type of bread
- A `Text` object representing the quantity of toasted bread desired
- A `Text` object indicating the amount of toasting (as a numeric quantity)
- A pair of radio buttons indicating whether the bread should be buttered

Each of the `Selection` and `Text` objects has associated `onfocus` and `onblur` event handlers. These handlers display and remove appropriate context-sensitive help that is associated with a given input object. The `onclick` event handler is used to associate user feedback with the radio buttons.

The actual help is dynamically written into a `<div>` block depending on the user's focus on the input objects. When the user focuses on something other than the toaster settings, such as the Reset button, the context-sensitive help is hidden.

The code for the toaster example is shown in Listing 24.1. Because you don't really have an automated toaster, the code sends email after the form is filled in. In this listing, you need to substitute your actual email address for the text *your_mail_ID*.

LISTING 24.1 Automated Toaster That Provides Context-Sensitive Help

```
<html>
<head>
<title>The Amazing Automated Toaster</title>

<script type="text/javascript">
function displayHelpBox(text)
{
  var theHelpBox = document.getElementById("helpBox");
  theHelpBox.style.visibility="visible";
  theHelpBox.firstChild.nodeValue = text;
}
function hideHelpBox()
{
  document.getElementById("helpBox").style.visibility="hidden";
}
</script>
</head>

<body>
<h2>The Amazing Automated Toaster</h2>

<form action="mailto:your_mail_ID" method="post">
<table>
<tr>
<td nowrap="true">

Bread Product:
<select name="product"
        onfocus="displayHelpBox('Select desired bread product from list.')"
        onblur="hideHelpBox()">
<option>Bread
```

LISTING 24.1   Continued

```
<option>Waffle
<option>Bagel
<option>Roll
<option>Muffin
<option>Croissant
<option>Scone
</select>
<br />

Quantity:
<input type="text" name="quantity" value="1" size=4 maxlength=4
     onfocus="displayHelpBox(
          'Enter quantity of bread products desired (1-1000).')"
     onblur="hideHelpBox()">
<br />

Toastiness:
<input type="text" name="toastiness" value="50" size="3" maxlength="3"
     onfocus="displayHelpBox(
'Enter degree of toastiness from 0-100 (0=untoasted 100=burnt).')"
     onblur="hideHelpBox('')">
<br />

Buttered:
Yes
<input type="radio" name="buttered" value="yes" checked
      onclick="displayHelpBox(
          'Do you want butter on the bread product?')">
No
<input type="radio" name="buttered" value="no"
      onclick="displayHelpBox(
          'Do you want butter on the bread product?')">

</td>
<td>
<div id="helpBox"
     style="visibility:hidden; background-color:yellow; height:100; width:100">
No help is available at this time.
</div>
</td>
</tr>
```

LISTING 24.1   Continued

```
</table>
<hr />
<input type="submit" value="Start Toaster" onclick="hideHelpBox()">
<input type="reset" onclick="hideHelpBox()">

</form>
</body>
</html>
```

Validating User Input

Without JavaScript, form validation would have to be handled on the server side. This would mean that the entire form would need to be completed by the user and transmitted to the server prior to validation. By waiting until the form is submitted for validation, the user doesn't receive feedback until after the entire form is completed. Feedback before the form is submitted is desirable because it saves time by letting the user know he did not enter valid data and by giving him the chance to correct it before making a trip to the server only to find out that the data is not valid. Immediate feedback might also influence later behavior and reduce user errors in responding to subsequent form elements. Thankfully, JavaScript is a great way to validate user input before form data is submitted to the server.

Validating Free Form Input

You can use two event handlers to validate text and `textarea` form elements. The `onblur` event handler is called when a text or `textarea` form element loses input focus. The `onchange` event handler is called when the content of a text or `textarea` form element is modified.

A form element is said to have **focus** when any user input will be directed to that element. When a text or textarea form element has focus, a text cursor appears in that element. When the user switches to another element (using the mouse or the Tab key), the original element is said to **lose focus**.

The `onblur` handler is called any time the input field loses focus. The user may or may not have changed the data in the field. The event handler could call the validation code for unchanged data or the default values in the field. You should design the validation code to deal with this possibility.

The `onchange` event handler is called only when the content of the field is modified. If the user momentarily selects the field (perhaps to view feedback in the status bar) and then chooses another field, the user-defined callback code is not invoked. Although this is more efficient, there is a downside. Suppose that you warn a user about erroneous data in a field. If he clicks the field and then declines to modify it, or if he retypes the same erroneous data, this is not considered a change. The onchange event handler is not triggered. For this reason, if you choose to use onchange, you should also validate the input at the time of submission (through the onsubmit or onclick event handler).

Listing 24.2 provides a text field for the user to input the quantity of an item. Valid values are 100 to 1000. The onblur event handler is used to call a validation function. The text input object is passed to the event handler. If the input is invalid, the following occurs:

- An alert box pops up to inform the user.

- Input focus is returned to the text field.

- The text is selected (and highlighted) so that it can be easily modified.

LISTING 24.2   Validating Minimum and Maximum Orders

```html
<html>
<head><title>Minimum and Maximum Orders</title></head>
<script type="text/javascript">
function validateQuantity(quantObj)
{
    if (quantObj.value < 100)
    {
        alert("Minimum order is 100 units.");
        quantObj.focus();
        quantObj.select();
    }
    else if (quantObj.value > 1000)
    {
        alert("Quantities greater than 1000 "
            + "units require special order.");
        quantObj.focus();
        quantObj.select();
    }
    return;
}
</script>
<body>
<h2>Enter number of units:</h2>
<form action="doSomething.jsp">
<input type="text" name="quantity" value="100" length="4"
    maxlength="4" onblur="validateQuantity(this)">
<input type="submit">
```

24

LISTING 24.2   Continued

```
</form>
</body>
</html>
```

Ensuring Consistency

Sometimes there are dependencies between several input fields. Figure 24.2 illustrates part of a form used by a business for entering a department budget. The user is prompted to enter a total budget and then allocate portions of that budget to three different categories.

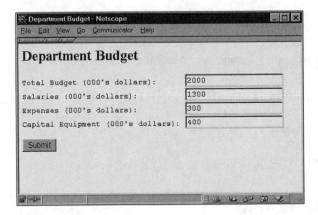

FIGURE 24.2   A form for entering a budget.

The sum of the three categories should add up to the total budget. Without JavaScript, the sum could not be verified until after the form was submitted and processed on the server. Using JavaScript, the data can be validated prior to submission, saving the user time and preserving context (that is, the same Web page is present before and after validation). The following code segment is an implementation of the budget entry form:

```
<form name="myform" method="post" action="actionURL"
    onsubmit="return validateBudget(myform)">
<h2>Department Budget</h2>

<pre>
Total Budget (000's dollars):        <input type="text"
    name="totalBudget" value="0" onblur="validateNumeric(this)">
Salaries (000's dollars):            <input type="text"
    name="salaries" value="0" onblur="validateNumeric(this)">
Expenses (000's dollars):            <input type="text"
    name="expenses" value="0" onblur="validateNumeric(this)">
```

```
Capital Equipment (000's dollars): <input type="text"
    name="capital" value="0" onblur="validateNumeric(this)">
</pre>

...

<input type="submit" name="submit" value="Submit">
</form>
```

onblur event handlers call a user-supplied validation routine to ensure that the user enters valid numeric input in each field. You must supply the following function to verify that the sum of the allocations adds up to the total amount budgeted:

```
function validateBudget(formObj)
{
    var calcBudget = parseInt(formObj.salaries.value,10)
        + parseInt(formObj.expenses.value,10)
        + parseInt(formObj.capital.value,10);
    var totalBudget = parseInt(formObj.totalBudget.value,10);

    if (calcBudget != totalBudget) {
        alert("Error: total budget is not equal to "
            + "sum of allocations.");
        return false;
    }
    else return true;
}
```

This function pops up an alert box in the event of an error and prevents the form submit input tag from being processed.

Enforcing Policy Statements

Policies associated with a form should be indicated to the user through explanatory text within the form, a separate help document (appropriately linked to the form), or both. You can use JavaScript to verify that user input conforms to these policies.

Suppose the form allows the user to specify a ship date but contains a policy statement that orders can't be shipped on the weekend. You can use JavaScript code to verify that the ship date is not on a weekend, thus enforcing the policy. The following code segment implements these policies:

```
// Compute ship date from
//   user input.  Returns
//   date object.
function calcShipDate(formObj)
```

```
{
    var day = parseInt(formObj.shipDay.value);
    var month = parseInt(formObj.shipMonth.value);
    var year = parseInt(formObj.shipYear.value);
    var hrs = 0;
    var min = 0;
    var sec = 0;
    shipDate = new Date(year,month,day,hrs,min,sec);
    return shipDate;
}

// Validate shipping policy - don't
//    ship on weekends.  Make sure
//    date is not in past or current date.
function shippingPolicy(formObj)
{
    var shipDate = calcShipDate(formObj);
    var day = shipDate.getDay();
    var currentDate = new Date();

    if (shipDate.getTime() < currentDate.getTime()) {
        alert("Error: ship date must be future date.");
        formObj.shipDay.focus();
        formObj.shipDay.select();
        return false;
    }

    if (day == 0) {
        alert("Sorry, we cannot ship on Sunday.");
        formObj.shipDay.focus();
        formObj.shipDay.select();
        return false;
    }
    else if (day == 6) {
        alert("Sorry, we cannot ship on Saturday.");
        formObj.shipDay.focus();
        formObj.shipDay.select();
        return false;
    }
    else return true;
}

...
```

```
<form name="myform" method="post" action="actionURL"
    onsubmit="return shippingPolicy(myform)">
```

If the user enters a date corresponding to a Saturday or Sunday, he is reminded of the shipping policy, focus and selection are set to the date input field, and the form is not submitted. The code also enforces the implicit policy of disallowing same-day shipping.

> **NOTE**
>
> When processing dates using JavaScript, be aware that the date and time are based on the setting of the user's computer. It's likely that the client software and server software are running in different time zones. It's also possible that the time setting on the client side is incorrect, perhaps due to the user setting the wrong time and date on his computer. The server should still validate the data even if using JavaScript to do Client Side checking.

Ensuring Completeness

Forms frequently consist of a set of mandatory and optional fields. The form can't be properly processed if the mandatory fields aren't supplied. Again, you can use JavaScript to ensure that they are present.

The next example is a form requesting customer contact information (see Figure 24.3). The name, address, and home phone number are considered mandatory fields. All other fields are optional.

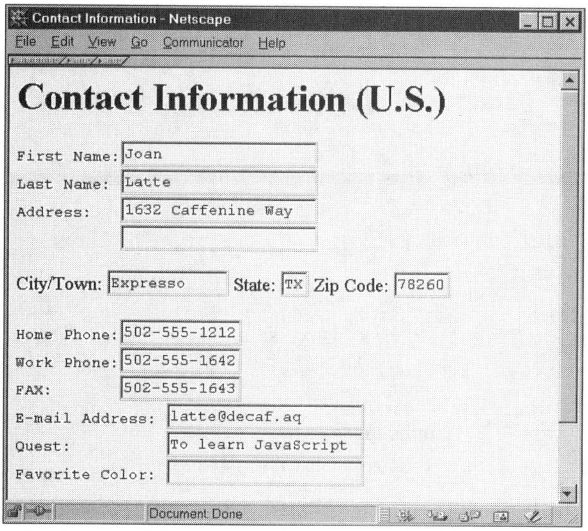

FIGURE 24.3   The contact information form.

When the form is submitted, a validation function is called. If any of the mandatory fields are empty, the user is notified, and the form is not submitted. The code for the contact information form is shown in Listing 24.3.

LISTING 24.3   Validating Mandatory Form Fields on a Contact Information Form

```html
<html>
<head>
<title>Contact Information</title>
<script type="text/javascript">
// Ensure that mandatory fields of
// form have been completed.
function validateComplete(formObj)
{
    if (emptyField(formObj.firstName))
        alert("Please enter your first name.");
    else if (emptyField(formObj.lastName))
        alert("Please enter your last name.");
    else if (emptyField(formObj.address1)
        && emptyField(formObj.address2))
        alert("Please enter your address.");
    else if (emptyField(formObj.city))
        alert("Please enter your city or town.");
    else if (emptyField(formObj.state))
        alert("Please enter your state.");
    else if (emptyField(formObj.email))
        alert("Please enter your E-mail address.");
    else return true;

    return false;

}

// Check to see if field is empty.
function emptyField(textObj)
{
    if (textObj.value.length == 0) return true;
    for (var i=0; i<textObj.value.length; ++i)
    {
        var ch = textObj.value.charAt(i);
        if (ch != ' ' && ch != '\t') return false;
    }
    return true;
```

LISTING 24.3 Continued

```
}

</script>
</head>
<body>
<h1>Contact Information (U.S.)</h1>
<form name="myform" action="actionURL" method="post"
    onsubmit="return validateComplete(document.myform)">
<pre>
First Name:<input type="text" name="firstName">
Last Name: <input type="text" name="lastName">
Address:   <input type="text" name="address1">
           <input type="text" name="address2">
</pre>

City/Town:
<input type="text" name="city" size="12">
State:
<input type="text" name="state" size="2">
Zip Code:
<input type="text" name="zip" size="5">

<pre>
Home Phone:<input type="text" name="homePhone" size="12">
Work Phone:<input type="text" name="workPhone" size="12">
FAX:       <input type="text" name="FAX" size="12">
E-mail Address: <input type="text" name="email">
Quest:          <input type="text" name="quest">
Favorite Color: <input type="text" name="favColor">
</pre>
<hr />
<input type="submit" name="submit" value="Submit">
</form>
<body>
<html>
```

The code performs a very basic validation—a field is present if it is not blank. No attempt is made to determine whether the fields contain reasonable data or gibberish. You could include some additional, simple validation. For example, you could validate that the state is a two-letter abbreviation or that the phone number contains the correct number of digits. In general, you should perform simple validations on the client side and more complex validations on the server side.

> **NOTE**
>
> The preceding example is a contact form for English-speaking users in the United States. The Internet is a worldwide network. In some countries, the family name precedes the given name, states are not a political subdivision, ZIP codes don't exist, and the user's language is not English. People still have a favorite color, however. The issue of internationalization is well beyond the scope of this book; nevertheless, you should be cognizant of the potential user base when designing forms.

Creating Interactive Forms

With JavaScript, you can create interactive forms in which the interaction is handled entirely on the client side without requiring a round trip to the server. JavaScript allows you to create interactions between the following items:

- Form elements on the same page
- Form elements and another window
- Form elements and another frame

You can use any of the techniques described earlier in this chapter—user feedback, message boxes, and input validation—to enhance a form. You can alter the entire page by completely rewriting it. In that case, the browser erases the current page and reformats an entire new page from scratch. You can also change the background color of the page (a Document property) but not the foreground color.

Using Calculated Fields

The next example, shown in Figure 24.4, is a different implementation of the budgeting example from earlier in this chapter. This example has a new text field named remainder. Although you can't update regular text or graphics on a page after it's written, you can update a form element. In this case, you update the remainder text element based on the values in the other elements. As the user enters the total budget and allocations, the remainder text field shows the amount of money left after the allocations are subtracted from the total budget.

This example uses the onchange event handler to update the remainder field whenever one of the values of the other text fields is modified. When the user submits the form, the script recalculates the remainder. If it is zero, the form is submitted; otherwise, an alert dialog box is displayed. The code for this interactive budget is shown in Listing 24.4.

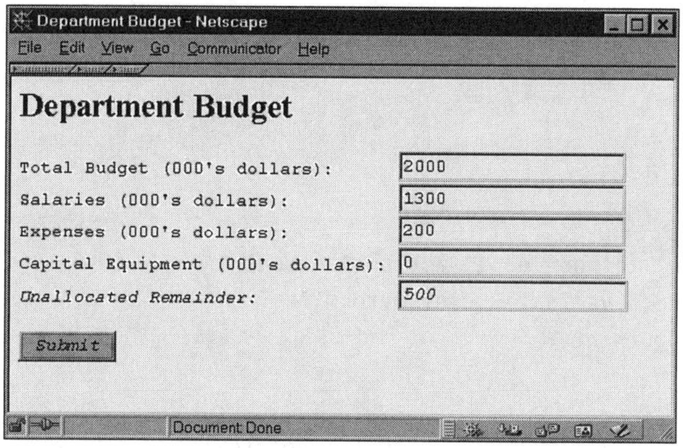

FIGURE 24.4   The calculated budget example.

LISTING 24.4   Automatically Updating Remainder Field Using onchange Event Handler

```
<html>
<head>
<title>Department Budget</title>

<script type="text/javascript">
function calcRemainder(formObj)
{
    var calcBudget = parseInt(formObj.salaries.value,10)
        + parseInt(formObj.expenses.value,10)
        + parseInt(formObj.capital.value,10);
    var totalBudget = parseInt(formObj.totalBudget.value);
    var unalloc = totalBudget - calcBudget;
    formObj.remainder.value = unalloc;
}

function validateBudget(formObj)
{
    calcRemainder(formObj);
    var unalloc = formObj.remainder.value;
    if (unalloc != 0)
    {
        alert("Error: Total budget is not equal "
            + "to sum of allocations.");
        return false;
    }
    return true;
```

LISTING 24.4   Continued

```
}
</script>
</head>

<body>
<form name="myform" method="post" action="actionURL"
     onsubmit="return validateBudget(myform)">
<h2>Department Budget</h2>

<pre>
Total Budget (000's dollars):        <input type="text"
     name="totalBudget" value="0"
     onchange="calcRemainder(myform)">
Salaries (000's dollars):            <input type="text"
     name="salaries" value="0" onchange="calcRemainder(myform)">
Expenses (000's dollars):            <input type="text"
     name="expenses" value="0" onchange="calcRemainder(myform)">
Capital Equipment (000's dollars): <input type="text"
     name="capital" value="0" onchange="calcRemainder(myform)">
<em>Unallocated Remainder:<em>            <input type="text"
     name="remainder" value="0">
</pre>

<input type="submit" name="submit" value="Submit">
</form>
</body>
</html>
```

You can use JavaScript to write small interactive applications where all the processing is done on the client side. Listing 24.5 calculates the future value of an investment. The user supplies the initial amount, an interest rate, and the number of years that the investment is compounded. Figure 24.5 shows the screen after the script has been loaded into the browser. Note that the output of the JavaScript `calculate()` function is displayed through text input objects, as described earlier.

No server-side work is required, because all processing is done on the client side. Note that instead of using a Submit input object, the form uses a Button object. Also, instead of using an onsubmit event handler, the script uses an onclick event handler. The Submit object and onsubmit event-handler semantics are used when the Web browser transmits a form to the server side. Because you want to do the processing on the client side, you use the onclick event handler and the calculate() function when the button is clicked. The button was labeled Calculate for clarity but could have been labeled Submit. Unless the user views the source code for the page, it will be indistinguishable from a page that uses XHTML on the client side and a CGI script on the server side. The code for the compound interest form is shown in Listing 24.5.

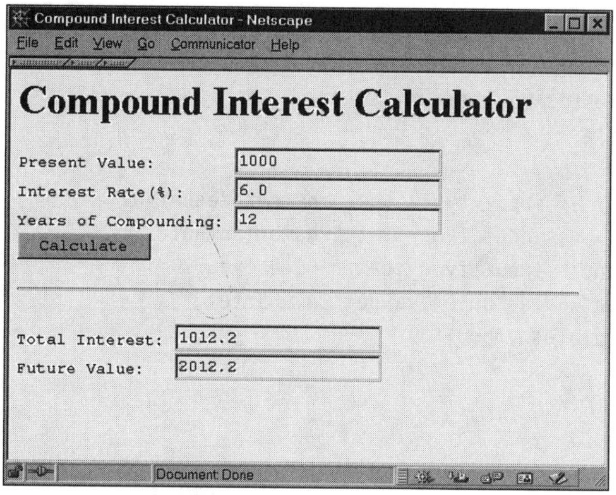

FIGURE 24.5   The compound interest form.

LISTING 24.5   A Compound Interest Calculator That Performs All Calculations on the Client Side

```
<html>
<head>
<title>Compound Interest Calculator</title>
<script type="text/javascript">
function calculate(formObj)
{
    var presentVal = parseFloat(formObj.presentVal.value);
    var intRate = parseFloat(formObj.intRate.value)/100.;
    var years = parseFloat(formObj.years.value);

    var futureVal = presentVal * Math.pow((1.0+intRate),years);
    var totalInt = futureVal - presentVal;
    futureVal = Math.round(futureVal*100.0)/100.0;
    totalInt  = Math.round(totalInt*100.0)/100.0;

    formObj.futureVal.value = futureVal;
    formObj.totalInt.value = totalInt;

    return;
```

LISTING 24.5   Continued

```
}
</script>
</head>

<body>
<h1>Compound Interest Calculator</h1>
<form name="myform">
<pre>
Present Value:         <input type="text" name="presentVal">
Interest Rate(%):      <input type="text" name="intRate">
Years of Compounding: <input type="text" name="years">
<input type="button" name="calc" value="Calculate"
     onclick="calculate(myform)">
</pre>
<hr>
<pre>
Total Interest: <input type="text" name="totalInt">
Future Value:   <input type="text" name="futureVal">
<pre>
</form>
</body>
<html>
```

Creating Reusable Validation Code

The following sections demonstrate ways to validate the most common types of data asked for over the Internet. The examples are especially easy to use in a code library that is stored in a separate file or in the frameset parent document. All examples accept a text element object as one of their arguments. This allows you to update the text field during data validation when necessary. For more specific data validation, incorporate JavaScript regular expressions, which are covered in Chapter 29, "Pattern Matching Using Regular Expressions," into the techniques discussed in this section.

Integer

Listing 24.6 is used to ensure that only whole numbers are accepted as input. The script is called when the user clicks the Validate button. The result, either `true` or `false`, is then displayed in the Result text field. This specifies whether the data passed the validation process.

LISTING 24.6 Integer Validation

```
<html>
<head>
<title>Integer Validation</title>
<script type="text/javascript">
function isInt(textObj) {
   var newValue = textObj.value;
   var newLength = newValue.length;
   for(var i = 0; i != newLength; i++)
   {
      aChar = newValue.substring(i,i+1);
      if(aChar < "0" || aChar > "9")
         return false;
   }
   return true;
}
</script>
</head>

<body>
<h1>Integer Validation</h1>
<form name="form1">
<input type="text"
       size="16"
       maxlength="16"
       name="data">
<input type="button"
       name="CheckButton"
       value="Validate"
       onclick="document.form1.result.value = '' +
       isInt(document.form1.data)">
<br />
Result <input type="text"
              size="16"
              maxlength="16"
              name="result">
</form>
</body>
</html>
```

String

Listing 24.7 shows how to ensure that the user has entered a string of allowable characters, which means alphabetic characters and a few others. The others are specified with the extraChars variable. If the user enters any character that is not in the alphabet or the extraChars variable, the function returns false. Listing 24.7 might be used to validate names, because some names contain periods, spaces, hyphens, and commas.

LISTING 24.7   String Validation

```html
<html>
<head>
<title>String Validation</title>
<script type="text/javascript">
function isString(textObj)
{
   var newValue = textObj.value;
   var newLength = newValue.length;
   var extraChars=". -,";
   var search;
   for(var i = 0; i != newLength; i++)
   {
      aChar = newValue.substring(i,i+1);
      aChar = aChar.toUpperCase();
      search = extraChars.indexOf(aChar);
      if(search == -1 && (aChar < "A" || aChar > "Z") )
         return false;
   }
   return true;
}
</script>
</head>

<body>
<h1>String Validation</h1>
<form name="form1">
<input type="text"
       size="16"
       maxlength="16"
       name="data">
<input type="button"
       name="CheckButton"
       value="Validate"
       onclick="document.form1.result.value = '' +
```

LISTING 24.7 Continued

```
        isString(document.form1.data)">
<br />
Result <input type="text"
                size="16"
                maxlength="16"
                name="result">
</form>
</body>
</html>
```

Date

Listing 24.8 shows how to ensure that a user has entered a date in a format that is acceptable for server side processing. In this particular example a person's first name, last name, and birth date are collected for the purpose of being inserted into a row in a database table. Since databases often expect dates to be in a certain format it is a perfect place for JavaScript to validate the date before making a trip to the server. If the date is not in the proper format, an alert box is displayed and the form submission is canceled by returning `false` to the event handler. The actual date format validation is accomplished using a regular expression that verifies a format of "mm/dd/yyyy." (You can learn more about regular expressions in Chapter 29.) Since this is just an example, no action was specified for the form in order to prevent an error page from being displayed because there is no server-side process.

LISTING 24.8 Date Validation

```
<html>
<head>
<title>Database Row Creator</title>
<script type="text/javascript">
function validateDate(str)
{
  //Date format test.
  var dateFormat = /^\d{1,2}\/\d{1,2}\/\d{4}/;
  if(!dateFormat.test(str))
  {
    alert("The date is not in the correct format.");
    return(false);
  }

  return(true);
```

LISTING 24.8   Continued

```
}
</script>
</head>

<body>
<h1>Database Row Creator</h1>

<form name="newDatabaseRow">
<table>
<tr>
  <td>First Name</td>
  <td><input type="text" name="firstName"
          size="16" maxlength="16"></td>
</tr>
<tr>
  <td>Last Name</td>
  <td><input type="text" name="lastName"
          size="16" maxlength="16"></td>
</tr>
<tr>
  <td>Birth Date</td>
  <td><input type="text" name="birthDate"
          size="16" maxlength="16"></td>
  <td>( mm/dd/yyyy )</td>
</tr>
</table>
<input type="submit"
      value="Add"
      onclick="return(validateDate(document.newDatabaseRow.birthDate.value))">
</form>
</body>
</html>
```

Dollar

Listing 24.9 uses a technique that is somewhat different from the integer and string valida-tion examples. Instead of performing a straightforward validation, it formats a value to be displayed as an amount of money to two decimal places. This is also an example of how the function uses the Text object it was given to update the object's value. If the function can't convert the data it was given into money, it defaults to an amount of 0.

LISTING 24.9   Validating and Money Format Conversion

```html
<html>
<head>
<title>Money Format</title>
<script type="text/javascript">
function moneyFormat(textObj)
{
   var newValue = textObj.value;
   var decAmount = "";
   var dolAmount = "";
   var decFlag = false;
   var aChar = "";

   // Ignore all but digits and decimal points.
   for(i=0; i < newValue.length; i++)
   {
      aChar = newValue.substring(i,i+1);
      if(aChar >= "0" && aChar <= "9")
      {
         if(decFlag)
            decAmount = "" + decAmount + aChar;
         else
            dolAmount = "" + dolAmount + aChar;
      }
      if(aChar == ".")
      {
         if(decFlag) {
            dolAmount = "";
            break;
         }
         decFlag=true;
      }
   }

   // Ensure that at least a zero appears for the dollar amount.
   if(dolAmount == "") {
      dolAmount = "0";
   }
   // Strip leading zeros.
   if(dolAmount.length > 1) {
      while(dolAmount.length > 1 && dolAmount.substring(0,1) == "0") {
         dolAmount = dolAmount.substring(1,dolAmount.length);
```

LISTING 24.9   Continued

```
        }
    }

    // Round the decimal amount.
    if(decAmount.length > 2)
    {
        if(decAmount.substring(2,3) > "4")
        {
            decAmount = parseInt(decAmount.substring(0,2)) + 1;
            if(decAmount < 10)
                decAmount = "0" + decAmount;
            else
                decAmount = "" + decAmount;
        }
        else {
            decAmount = decAmount.substring(0,2);
        }
        if (decAmount == 100) {
            decAmount = "00";
            dolAmount = parseInt(dolAmount) + 1;
        }
    }

    // Pad right side of decAmount.
    if(decAmount.length == 1) {
        decAmount = decAmount + "0";
    }
    if(decAmount.length == 0) {
        decAmount = decAmount + "00";
    }

    // Check for negative values and reset textObj.
    if(newValue.substring(0,1) != '-' ||
            (dolAmount == "0" && decAmount == "00")) {
        textObj.value = dolAmount + "." + decAmount;
    }
    else{
        textObj.value = '-' + dolAmount + "." + decAmount;
    }
}
</script>
</head>
```

LISTING 24.9   Continued

```
<body>
<h1>Money Format</h1>
<form name="form1">
<input type="text"
       size="16"
       maxlength="16"
       name="data">
<input type="button"
       name="CheckButton"
       value="Format"
       onclick="moneyFormat(document.form1.data)">
</form>
</body>
</html>
```

Credit Cards

Accepting credit card orders is an important aspect of doing business over the Web. With JavaScript, you can run a preliminary check on a credit card number before it's stored on the server for final validation. Listing 24.10 demonstrates how you can run this test on credit card numbers to ensure that the card number follows the basic rules set by credit card companies. If the card number fails this validation, you can inform the user that he may have entered the wrong number and should check again. If the user chooses not to update the card number, you can still accept it and perform the final check on the server side using an electronic commerce service.

> **CAUTION**
>
> Listing 24.10 should only be used as a preliminary check for credit card validation. Using an electronic commerce service on the server side is the only way to properly validate credit cards at this time.

The isCreditCard function begins by ignoring any dashes that the user entered. It then runs the number through an algorithm that calculates a code, known as a **checksum,** for the credit card number. If the checksum is equal to the last digit of the credit card number, the number is valid. However, passing this test doesn't necessarily mean that an account exists for the number or that the account hasn't expired. It simply means that the number follows the rules for being a credit card number.

LISTING 24.10   Validating Credit Card Numbers Using a Checksum

```
<html>
<head>
<title>Credit Card Validation</title>
```

LISTING 24.10   Continued

```
<script type="text/javascript">
function isCreditCard(textObj) {
 /*
  *  This function validates a credit card entry.
  *  If the checksum is ok, the function returns true.
  */
  var ccNum;
  var odd = 1;
  var even = 2;
  var calcCard = 0;
  var calcs = 0;
  var ccNum2 = "";
  var aChar = '';
  var cc;
  var r;

  ccNum = textObj.value;
  for(var i = 0; i != ccNum.length; i++)
  {
     aChar = ccNum.substring(i,i+1);
     if(aChar == '-') {
        continue;
     }
     ccNum2 = ccNum2 + aChar;
  }

  cc = parseInt(ccNum2);
  if(cc == 0) {
     return false;
  }
  r = ccNum.length / 2;
  if(ccNum.length - (parseInt(r)*2) == 0) {
     odd = 2;
     even = 1;
  }

  for(var x = ccNum.length - 1; x > 0; x--)
  {
     r = x / 2;
     if(r < 1) {
        r++;
```

LISTING 24.10   Continued

```
      }
      if(x - (parseInt(r) * 2) != 0) {
         calcs = (parseInt(ccNum.charAt(x - 1))) * odd;
      }
      else {
         calcs = (parseInt(ccNum.charAt(x - 1))) * even;
      }
      if(calcs >= 10) {
         calcs = calcs - 10 + 1;
      }
      calcCard = calcCard + calcs;
   }

   calcs = 10 - (calcCard % 10);
   if(calcs == 10) {
      calcs = 0;
   }

   if(calcs == (parseInt(ccNum.charAt(ccNum.length - 1)))) {
      return true;
   }
   else {
      return false;
   }
}
</script>
</head>

<body>
<h1>Credit Card Validation</h1>
<form name="form1">
<input type="text"
       size="16"
       maxlength="16"
       name="data">
<input type="button"
       name="CheckButton"
       value="Validate"
       onclick="document.form1.result.value = '' +
                isCreditCard(document.form1.data)">
<br />
```

24

LISTING 24.10   Continued

```
Result <input type="text"
              size="16"
              maxlength="16"
              name="result">
</form>
</body>
</html>
```

Summary

JavaScript greatly enhances the basic form capability of HTML. Much of the processing that can be performed on the server can be done on the client side using JavaScript. The capabilities can be summarized as follows:

- User feedback: JavaScript lets you provide feedback to the form user through a combination of event handlers and message boxes. By using JavaScript alert and dialog boxes, you can display a pop-up message to the user, request confirmation prior to submitting a form, and query the user for additional information.

- Validating user input: You can validate input fields, groups of fields, or the entire form by using event handlers and JavaScript functions. Users can receive feedback in the context of the current form (that is, the page is not replaced by a new page with an error message).

- You can build interactive forms in which part or even all of the processing is performed on the client side.

You can use JavaScript to create forms that are easier to use and less prone to error. In turn, you can create forms that respond far more quickly than server-oriented programs, particularly when the user has a low-bandwidth connection to the server.

CHAPTER **25**

Personalization and Dynamic Pages

If you have spent any time surfing the Internet, you know that more and more sites are trying to become a one-stop shop for everyone's Internet-related needs. To keep those who use the Internet from being overwhelmed with every piece of news and information from around the world, sites are personalized to match each individual's particular interests. A Web site knows that a certain individual wants to read only the sports page, see certain stock prices, and order groceries online. Today's Web page wants to be everyone's best friend, grocer, or personal financial advisor. Gone are the days of cold, static Web pages. Today's Web pages are dynamic!

When an individual goes to her favorite online bookstore, she is not presented with just a list of books; she is referred to other books that she might like, based on her past purchases. Although many online stores and Web site portals use massive server-side databases to keep track of an individual's personal interests and buying history, so as to provide a personalized and dynamic experience, there are a number of things you, as a Web designer, can do with JavaScript to make your Web site warm and inviting.

In this chapter, I am going to show you how to use JavaScript to manipulate cookies, URL query string parameters, and hidden form variables to make your site more dynamic and personal. To better understand how to make Web pages dynamic, let's take a moment to understand why Web pages are static by nature.

Understanding the Static Web Page

Web servers have very short memories. When you request a page, the server doesn't really know who you are, what you entered on a form three pages ago, or whether this is your first visit to the site or your seventy-fifth. One of the challenges of using the Hypertext Transfer Protocol (HTTP) is that it doesn't track the state of your interactions with the server. **State** refers to any information about you or your visit to a Web site. It's maintained as you move from page to page within the site, and it can be used by the Web server or a JavaScript program (or both) to customize your experience at the site. With this information in hand, you can set user preferences, fill in default form values, track visit counts, and do many other things that make browsing easier for users and give you more information about how your pages are used.

There are a number of ways to maintain state information:

- Store it in cookies

- Encode it in URL links

- Send it in hidden form variables

- Store it in variables in other frames

- Store it on the Web server

There are some technical challenges regarding state maintenance. While browsing a site, a user might suddenly zoom off to another Web site and return minutes, hours, or days later, only to find that any saved state information is out of date or has been erased. He might return by clicking his browser's Back button, by using a bookmark, or by typing in the URL directly, causing state information encoded in the URL to be overwritten or lost.

The Web developer must maintain state information regardless of whether the user navigates through the site using buttons on a form or a URL link on a page. This could mean adding information to both hidden form variables and every URL with the `<a href...>` tag that appears on the page.

With all these difficulties to overcome, these state maintenance mechanisms had better be useful. Luckily, they are. There are many advantages to maintaining state, both within a single site visit and from one visit to the next. Consider the following scenarios:

- A shopping cart application: A user browses through the site, selecting items and adding them to a virtual shopping cart. At any time, the user can view the items in the cart, change the contents of his cart, or take the cart to the checkout counter to purchase. Keeping track of which user owns which shopping cart is essential.

- Personalized portals: Many Web sites provide portals where the user can customize what he sees when he arrives. After the user chooses a layout, a color scheme, news setting, and so on, the preferences are stored on the user's computer through the use of cookies. The user can return to the site any time and get her previously configured page.

- Frequent visitor bonuses: By storing information on the client computer, an application can track how many times a browser has hit a particular page. When the user reaches a certain level of hits, he gets access to more or better services.

- Change banners: You can change graphic banners and text each time the user hits a page. This technique is often used to cycle through a list of advertisements.

- Bookmarks: You can use bookmarks to track where a user was when he last visited the site. Was he reading a story, filling out a questionnaire, or playing a game? Let him pick up where he left off.

- Games: Your game application can remember current or high scores and present new challenges based on past answers and performance.

Introducing Cookies

Cookies let you store information on the client browser's computer for later retrieval. Although they have drawbacks, cookies are the most powerful technique available for maintaining state on the client side.

> **NOTE**
>
> Netscape came up with the original cookie specification. Although they are called **cookies**, there doesn't seem to be any good reason why Netscape chose that particular name. The cookie specification page admits that "the state object is called a cookie for no compelling reason."

In their simplest form, cookies store data in the form of *name=value* pairs. You can pick any name and value combination you want. More advanced cookie features include the capability to set an expiration date and to specify what Web pages may see the cookie information.

> **NOTE**
>
> Netscape and Internet Explorer, as well as most other browsers, provide the ability for the user to turn off all cookies, so there is no guarantee that cookies will be available to you.

Advantages of Cookies

One of the most powerful aspects of cookies is their persistence. When a cookie is set on the user's browser, it can persist for days, months, or even years. This makes it easy to save visit information and user preferences and have them available every time the user returns to your site.

Cookies are especially helpful when used in conjunction with JavaScript. Because JavaScript has functions for reading, adding, and editing cookies, your JavaScript programs can use them to store global information about a user as he surfs through your Web site.

25

Limitations and Disadvantages of Cookies

Some limitations of cookies could prove problematic. Cookies are stored on the user's computer, usually in a special cookie file. As with all files, this cookie file might be accidentally (or purposefully) deleted, taking all the browser's cookie information with it. The cookie file could be write-protected, thus preventing cookies from being stored there. Browser software can impose limitations on the size and number of cookies that can be stored, and newer cookies can overwrite older ones.

Because cookies are associated with a particular browser, problems come up if a user switches from one browser to another. If you use Netscape Navigator and have a collection of cookies, they will no longer be available if you switch to Microsoft Internet Explorer.

Finally, if several people use the same computer and browser, they might find themselves using cookies that belong to someone else. The reason for this is that cookie information is stored in a file on the computer, and the browser has no way to distinguish between multiple users.

There are also some problems, both real and imagined, concerning the use of cookies. Because many browsers store their cookie information in an unencrypted text file, sensitive information, such as a password, should never be stored in a cookie. Anyone with access to the computer could read it.

Some Web browsers have a feature that alerts the user when an attempt is made to set a cookie. The browser can even be configured to prevent cookies from being set at all. This sometimes results in confusion on the user's part when a dialog box informs him that something is happening involving something called a "cookie." If cookies are disabled, your carefully designed Web application might not run at all.

You cannot set an infinite number of cookies on every Web browser that visits your site. Here are the limitations on the number of cookies you can set and how large they can be:

- Cookies per server or domain: 20

- Total cookies per browser: 300

- Largest cookie: 4KB (including both the *name* and *value* parameters)

If these limits are exceeded, the browser might attempt to discard older cookies by tossing the least recently used cookies first.

Cookie Myths

The biggest problem with cookies might be psychological. Some Web users believe that cookies are a tool used by "Big Brother" in order to discover their innermost secrets. Perhaps I exaggerate a bit. However, considering that cookies are capable of storing information about pages the user has visited on a Web site and how many times he has been there, what advertising banners he has viewed, and what he has selected and entered on forms, some people think that their privacy is being invaded whenever a cookie gets on their computers.

In reality, cookies are seldom used for these purposes. Although technically these things are possible, there are now better and easier ways of getting the same information without using cookies. I guess this means that you can still be paranoid—just not about cookies.

Another user might complain about Web sites writing information to her computer and taking up space on her hard drive. This is a legitimate concern. Web browser software limits the total size of the cookies stored to 1.2MB, with no more than 80KB going to any one Web site. Consider, though, that this number is small when compared to the size of the pages and graphic images that a Web browser routinely stores in its page cache.

Other users are concerned that cookies set by one Web site might be read by other sites. This is completely untrue. Your Web browser software prevents this from happening by making a cookie available only to the site that created it.

If your users understand the usefulness of cookies, this "cookie backlash" shouldn't be a problem.

> **TIP**
>
> Because cookies potentially stir up concerns about privacy with those who visit your site, it is a good idea to add a privacy policy link to a page that explains the limitations of cookies and your site's use of cookies.

Using Cookies

By now you have considered the pros and cons of cookies and have decided that they are just what you need to make your JavaScript application a success. In this section, you will find a number of handy functions for reading and setting cookies, which will help you make your Web sites dynamic and more personal. Also included in this section are Internet references for finding additional information concerning cookies.

Retrieving Cookie Values

Cookie names and values are stored and set using the `cookie` property of the `Document` object. To store the raw `cookie` string in a variable, you would use a JavaScript command such as this:

```
var myCookie = document.cookie;
```

To display it on a Web page, use the following command:

```
document.write ("Raw Cookies: " + document.cookie + "<br>");
```

JavaScript stores cookies in the following format:

```
name1=value1; name2=value2; name3=value3
```

Individual *name=value* pairs are separated by a semicolon and a blank space. There is no semicolon after the final value. To make it easier to retrieve a cookie, you should use a JavaScript routine such as the one in Listing 25.1.

LISTING 25.1   The GetCookie Function

```
function GetCookie (name) {
  var result = null;
  var myCookie = " " + document.cookie + ";";
  var searchName = " " + name + "=";
  var startOfCookie = myCookie.indexOf(searchName);
  var endOfCookie;
  if (startOfCookie != -1) {
    startOfCookie += searchName.length; // skip past cookie name.
    endOfCookie = myCookie.indexOf(";", startOfCookie);
    result = unescape(myCookie.substring(startOfCookie, endOfCookie));
  }
  return result;
}
```

In Listing 25.1, the myCookie string helps avoid annoying boundary conditions by making sure all cookie string names start with a space and end with a semicolon. From there, it's easy to find the start of the name= portion of the string, skip it, and retrieve everything between that point and the next semicolon.

Setting Cookie Values

The *name=value* combination is the minimum amount of information you need to set up a cookie. However, there is more to a cookie than that. Here is the complete list of parameters used to specify a cookie:

- *name=value*
- expires=*date*
- path=*path*
- domain=*domainname*
- secure

Cookie Names and Values

The *name* and *value* can be anything you choose. In some cases, you might want it to be explanatory, such as `FavoriteColor=Blue`. In other cases, it could just be code that the JavaScript program interprets, such as `CurStat=1:2:1:0:0:1:0:3:1:1`.

In its simplest form, a routine to set a cookie looks like this:

```
function SetCookieEZ (name, value) {
  document.cookie = name + "=" + escape(value);
}
```

Notice that the value is encoded using the `escape()` function. If there were a semicolon in the string, it might prevent you from achieving the expected result. Using the `escape()` function eliminates this problem.

Also notice that the `document.cookie` property works rather differently from most properties. In most cases, using the assignment operator (=) causes the existing property value to be completely overwritten with the new value. This isn't the case with the `cookie` property. With cookies, each new *name* you assign is added to the active list of cookies. If you assign the same *name* twice, the first assignment is replaced by the second.

There are some exceptions to this last statement. These are explained in the "path" section, later in this chapter.

Expiration Date

The `expires=date` parameter tells the browser how long the cookie will last. The cookie specification page at Netscape states that dates are in the form of

```
Wdy, DD-Mon-YY HH:MM:SS GMT
```

Here's an example:

```
Mon, 08-Jul-96 03:18:20 GMT
```

This format is based on Internet RFC 822, which you can find at `http://www.w3.org/hypertext/WWW/Protocols/rfc822/#z28`.

The only difference between RFC 822 and the Netscape implementation is that in Netscape Navigator the expiration date must end with GMT (Greenwich Mean Time). Happily, the JavaScript language provides a function to do just that. Using the `toGMTString()` function, you can set a cookie to expire in the near or distant future.

TIP

Even though the date produced by the `toGMTString()` function doesn't match the Netscape specification, it still works under JavaScript.

If the expiration date isn't specified, the cookie remains in effect until the browser is shut down. This code segment sets a cookie to expire in one week:

```
var name="foo";
var value="bar";
var oneWeek = 7 * 24 * 60 * 60 * 1000;
var expDate = new Date();
expDate.setTime (expDate.getTime() + oneWeek);
document.cookie = name + "=" + escape(value) +
   "; expires=" + expDate.toGMTString();
```

path

By default, cookies are available to other Web pages within the same directory as the page on which they were created. The `path` parameter allows a cookie to be made available to pages in other directories. If the value of the `path` parameter is a substring of a page's URL, cookies created with that `path` are available to that page. For example, you could create a cookie with the following command:

```
document.cookie = "foo=bar1; path=/javascript";
```

This would make the cookie `foo` available to every page in the `javascript` directory and those directories beneath it. If the command looked like this

```
document.cookie = "foo=bar2; path=/javascript/sam";
```

the cookie would be available only to pages in the `/javascript/sam` directory and those beneath it but would not be available to pages in the `/javascript` directory.

Finally, to make the cookie available to everyone on your server, use the following command:

```
document.cookie = "foo=bar3; path=/";
```

What happens when a browser has multiple cookies on different paths but with the same name? Which one wins?

Actually, they all do. In this situation, it's possible to have two or more cookies with the same name but different values. For example, if a page issued all the commands listed previously, its `cookie` string would look like this:

```
foo=bar3; foo=bar2; foo=bar1
```

To stay aware of this situation, you might want to write a routine to count the number of cookie values associated with a cookie name, as shown in Listing 25.2.

LISTING 25.2   The GetCookieCount Function

```
function GetCookieCount (name) {
  var result = 0;
  var myCookie = " " + document.cookie + ";";
  var searchName = " " + name + "=";
  var nameLength = searchName.length;
  var startOfCookie = myCookie.indexOf(searchName);
  while (startOfCookie != -1) {
    result += 1;
    startOfCookie = myCookie.indexOf(searchName, startOfCookie + nameLength);
  }
  return result;
}
```

Of course, if there is a GetCookieCount function, there would need to be a GetCookieNum function to retrieve a particular instance of a cookie. That function would look like Listing 25.3.

LISTING 25.3   The GetCookieNum Function

```
function GetCookieNum (name, cookieNum) {
  var result = null;
  if (cookieNum >= 1) {
    var myCookie = " " + document.cookie + ";";
    var searchName = " " + name + "=";
    var nameLength = searchName.length;
    var startOfCookie = myCookie.indexOf(searchName);
    var cntr = 0;
    for (cntr = 1; cntr < cookieNum; cntr++)
      startOfCookie = myCookie.indexOf(searchName, startOfCookie + nameLength);
    if (startOfCookie != -1) {
      startOfCookie += nameLength; // skip past cookie name.
      var endOfCookie = myCookie.indexOf(";", startOfCookie);
      result = unescape(myCookie.substring(startOfCookie, endOfCookie));
    }
  }
  return result;
}
```

To delete a cookie, the name and the path must match the original name and path used when the cookie was set.

domain

After a page on a particular server creates a cookie, that cookie is usually accessible only to other pages on that server. Just as the path parameter makes a cookie available outside its home path, the domain parameter makes it available to other Web servers at the same site.

You can't create a cookie that anyone on the Internet can see. You can only set a path that falls inside your own domain. This is because the use of the domain parameter dictates that you must use at least two periods if your domain ends in .com, .edu, .net, .org, .gov, .mil, or .int (for example, .mydomain.com). Otherwise, it must have at least three periods (.mydomain.ma.us). Your domain parameter string must match the tail of your server's domain name.

secure

The final cookie parameter tells your browser that this cookie should be sent only under a secure connection with the Web server. This means that the server and the browser must support HTTPS security. (HTTPS is a protocol for transferring encrypted information over the Internet.)

If the secure parameter is not present, it means that cookies are sent unencrypted over the network.

Now that you have seen all the cookie parameters, it would be helpful to have a JavaScript routine set cookies with all the parameters. Such a routine might look like Listing 25.4.

LISTING 25.4   The SetCookie Function

```
function SetCookie (name, value, expires, path, domain, secure) {
  var expString =
            ((expires == null) ? "" : ("; expires=" + expires.toGMTString()));
  var pathString = ((path == null) ? "" : ("; path=" + path));
  var domainString = ((domain == null) ? "" : ("; domain=" + domain));
  var secureString = ((secure == true) ? "; secure" : "");
  document.cookie = name + "=" + escape (value) +
                  expString + pathString + domainString + secureString;
}
```

To use this routine, you call it with whatever parameters you want to set and use null in place of parameters that don't matter.

Deleting a Cookie

To delete a cookie, set the expiration date to some time in the past; how far in the past doesn't generally matter. To be on the safe side, a few days should work. Listing 25.5 shows the ClearCookie routine that is used to delete a cookie.

LISTING 25.5   The ClearCookie Function

```
function ClearCookie (name) {
  var ThreeDays = 3 * 24 * 60 * 60 * 1000;
  var expDate = new Date();
  expDate.setTime (expDate.getTime() - ThreeDays);
  document.cookie = name + "=ImOutOfHere; expires=" + expDate.toGMTString();
}
```

When deleting cookies, it doesn't matter what you use for the cookie value. Any value will do. When a cookie is deleted or expires, it is simply removed from the user's cookie file.

> **CAUTION**
>
> Some older versions of Netscape do a poor job of converting time to GMT. Some common JavaScript functions for deleting a cookie consider the past to be one millisecond behind the current time. Although this is true, it doesn't work on all platforms. To be on the safe side, use a few days in the past to expire cookies.

A Cookie Example

The JavaScript program in Listing 25.6 provides an example of cookies in use. This program allows the user to create a personalized "News-of-the-Day" page containing links to sites of general interest in a number of different categories. The user's favorite links are stored in cookies. Figure 25.1, which follows the listing, shows what the Favorites page looks like.

LISTING 25.6   The Favorites Script

```
<html>
<head>
<script type="text/javascript">

//=================================================================
// Here are our standard Cookie routines
//=================================================================
//-----------------------------------------------------------------
// GetCookie - Returns the value of the specified cookie or null
//             if the cookie doesn't exist.
//-----------------------------------------------------------------
function GetCookie(name)
{
  var result = null;
  var myCookie = " " + document.cookie + ";";
```

LISTING 25.6   Continued

```
  var searchName = " " + name + "=";
  var startOfCookie = myCookie.indexOf(searchName);
  var endOfCookie;
  if (startOfCookie != -1)
  {
    startOfCookie += searchName.length;
    // skip past cookie name.
    endOfCookie = myCookie.indexOf(";", startOfCookie);
    result = unescape(myCookie.substring(startOfCookie,endOfCookie));
  }
  return result;
}


//----------------------------------------------------------------
// SetCookieEZ - Quickly sets a cookie which will last until the
//               user shuts down his browser.
//----------------------------------------------------------------
function SetCookieEZ(name, value)
{
  document.cookie = name + "=" + escape(value);
}


//----------------------------------------------------------------
// SetCookie - Adds or replaces a cookie. Use null for parameters
//             that you don't care about.
//----------------------------------------------------------------
function SetCookie(name, value, expires, path, domain, secure)
{
  var expString = ((expires == null)? "" : ("; expires=" +
                    expires.toGMTString()));

  var pathString = ((path == null) ? "" : ("; path=" + path));
  var domainString = ((domain == null)? "" : ("; domain=" + domain));
  var secureString = ((secure == true) ? "; secure" : "");
  document.cookie = name + "=" + escape(value)+ expString + pathString +
                    domainString + secureString;

}


//----------------------------------------------------------------
// ClearCookie  - Removes a cookie by setting an expiration date
```

LISTING 25.6 Continued

```
//                three days in the past.
//----------------------------------------------------------------
function ClearCookie(name)
{
  var ThreeDays = 3 * 24 * 60 * 60 * 1000;
  var expDate = new Date();
  expDate.setTime (expDate.getTime() - ThreeDays);
  document.cookie = name + "=ImOutOfHere; expires="+ expDate.toGMTString();
}


//================================================================
// Here are the object and the routines for our Favorites app.
//================================================================
//----------------------------------------------------------------
/* Here is our "favorite" object.
   Properties: fullName - The full descriptive name.
               cook     - The code used for the cookie.
               urlpath  - The full url (http://...) to the site.
      Methods: Enabled - Returns true if the link's cookie is
                          turned on.
               Checked  - Returns the word "CHECKED" if the
                           link's cookie is turned on.
               WriteAsCheckBox - Sends text to the document in a
                                  checkbox control format.
               WriteAsWebLink  - Sends text to the document in a
                                  <a href...> format.
-------------------------------------------------------------*/
function favorite(fullName, cook, urlpath)
{
  this.fullName = fullName;
  this.cook     = cook;
  this.urlpath  = urlpath;
  this.Enabled = Enabled;
  this.Checked = Checked;
  this.WriteAsCheckBox = WriteAsCheckBox;
  this.WriteAsWebLink = WriteAsWebLink;
}


//----------------------------------------------------------------
// Enabled - Checks to see if the cookie exists.
// returns - true if the cookie exists
```

25

LISTING 25.6   Continued

```
//              false if it doesn't.
//------------------------------------------------------------
function Enabled()
{
  var result = false;
  var FaveCookie = GetCookie("Favorites");
  if (FaveCookie != null)
  {
    var searchFor = "<" + this.cook + ">";
    var startOfCookie = FaveCookie.indexOf(searchFor);
    if (startOfCookie != -1)
      result = true;
  }
  return result;
}


//------------------------------------------------------------
// Checked - Checks to see if the cookie exists (using Enabled).
// returns - 'CHECKED ' if the cookie exists
//           "" if it doesn't.
//------------------------------------------------------------
function Checked ()
{
  if (this.Enabled())
    return "CHECKED ";
  return "";
}
//------------------------------------------------------------
// WriteAsCheckBox - The favorite may be either a regular URL or
//                   a section title.  If the urlpath is an empty
//                   string, then the favorite is a section title.
//                   The links will appear within a definition
//                   list, and are formatted appropriately.
//------------------------------------------------------------
function WriteAsCheckBox ()
{
  // Check to see if it's a title or regular link.
  if (this.urlpath == "")
  {
    // It's a section title.
    result = '<dt><strong>' + this.fullName + '<\/strong>';
```

LISTING 25.6 Continued

```
  }
  else
  {
    // It's a regular link.
    result = '<dd><input type="checkbox" name="' +
             this.cook + '" ' + this.Checked() +
             'onClick="SetFavoriteEnabled(this.name,this.checked);">' +
             this.fullName;

  }
  document.write(result);
}


//------------------------------------------------------------
// Global Variable:
// NextHeading - Sometimes we only want to print a heading if one
//               of its favorites is turned on.  The NextHeading
//               variable helps us to do this. See WriteAsWebLink.
//------------------------------------------------------------
var NextHeading = "";


//------------------------------------------------------------
// WriteAsWebLink - The favorite may be either a regular URL or
//                  a section title.  If the urlpath is an empty
//                  string, then the favorite is a section title.
//                  The links will appear within a definition
//                  list, and are formatted appropriately.
//------------------------------------------------------------
function WriteAsWebLink()
{
  var result = '';
  if (this.urlpath == "")
  {
    NextHeading = this.fullName;    // It must be a Title.
  }
  else
  {
    if (this.Enabled() || (GetCookie("ViewAll") == "T"))
    {
      if (NextHeading != "")
      {
```

LISTING 25.6   Continued

```
            result = '<p><dt><strong>' + NextHeading+ '<\/strong>';
            NextHeading = "";
        }
        result = result + '<dd><a href="' + this.urlpath + '">'+
                this.fullName + '<\/a>';


    }
  }
  document.write(result);
}


//================================================================
// Global Variables
//================================================================
/*----------------------------------------------------------------
FaveList will be a list of all favorite objects, which are
then declared below.  Favorites with an empty urlpath property
are section headings.
----------------------------------------------------------------*/
var FaveList = new Array();
// Comics Section ------------------
FaveList[1] = new favorite("Comics", "", "");
FaveList[2] = new favorite("Dilbert", "cdilb",
                            "http://www.unitedmedia.com/comics/dilbert/");


FaveList[3] = new favorite("Doonesbury", "cdoon",
                            "http://www.doonesbury.com");


FaveList[4] = new favorite("Mr. Boffo", "cboff",
                            "http://www.mrboffo.com");


// General News Section ------------
FaveList[5] = new favorite("General News", "", "");
FaveList[6] = new favorite("CNN", "ncnn", "http://www.cnn.com/");
FaveList[7] = new favorite("NPR", "nnpr","http://www.npr.org/news/");
FaveList[8] = new favorite("Boston Globe", "nbos","http://www.boston.com/");
// Computer Industry Section --------
FaveList[9] = new favorite("Computer Industry", "", "");
FaveList[10] = new favorite("W3", "w3","http://www.w3.org");
FaveList[11] = new favorite("JavaScript.com", "js",
                            "http://www.javascript.com");
```

LISTING 25.6   Continued

```
FaveList[12] = new favorite("Netscape", "ntsc","http://devedge.netscape.com/");
FaveList[13] = new favorite("Microsoft", "micr","http://msdn.microsoft.com/");
// Search Engines Section ----------
FaveList[14] = new favorite("Search Engines", "", "");
FaveList[15] = new favorite("Yahoo!", "syah","http://www.yahoo.com/");
FaveList[16] = new favorite("Alta Vista", "sav","http://www.altavista.com/");
FaveList[17] = new favorite("Google", "goog","http://www.google.com/");
// Auction Section ----------------
FaveList[18] = new favorite("Auctions", "", "");
FaveList[19] = new favorite("ebay", "ebay","http://www.ebay.com/");
FaveList[20] = new favorite("Yahoo Auctions", "yhac",
                            "http://auctions.yahoo.com/");

// Misc. Section -------------------
FaveList[21] = new favorite("Misc.", "", "");
FaveList[22] = new favorite("Today in History", "mtih",
                            "http://www.thehistorynet.com/today/today.htm");

FaveList[23] = new favorite("Merriam-Webster's Word of the Day","mwod",
                            "http://www.m-w.com/cgi-bin/mwwod.pl");

FaveList[24] = new favorite("Quotes of the Day", "mquot",
➥"http://www.starlingtech.com/quotes/qotd.html");


//================================================================
// Page Writing Routines
//================================================================
//----------------------------------------------------------------
// SendOptionsPage - Writes a page allowing the user to select
//                   their favorite preferences.
//----------------------------------------------------------------
function SendOptionsPage()
{
  document.write('<h1>Select Favorites<\/h1>');
  document.write('<form method=post>');
  // Here's the button for viewing the Favorites page.
  document.write('<input type=button value="Show Favorites" ' + 'onClick="' +
                 'ReloadPage()'+';">');

  // The links will look nicer inside a definition list.
```

LISTING 25.6   Continued

```
  document.write('<dl>');

  for (var i = 1; i < FaveList.length; i++)
    FaveList[i].WriteAsCheckBox();
  // Write each checkbox.
  document.write('<\/dl><p>');
  ClearCookie("ViewAll");
  document.write('<\/form>');
}


//-----------------------------------------------------------------
// LoadOptions - Sets the ShowOptions cookie, which makes the
//               option selection page appear when the page is
//               then reloaded.
//-----------------------------------------------------------------
function LoadOptions()
{
  SetCookieEZ("ShowOptions", "T");
  window.open(document.location.href, "_top", "");
}


//-----------------------------------------------------------------
// ToggleView - Toggles ViewAll mode on and off.  When on, all
//              links will be displayed.  When off, only the
//              user's favorite selections will be displayed.
//-----------------------------------------------------------------
function ToggleView()
{
  if (GetCookie("ViewAll") == "T")
  {
    ClearCookie("ViewAll");
  }
  else
  {
    var fiveYears = 5 * 365 * 24 * 60 * 60 * 1000;
    var expDate = new Date();
    expDate.setTime (expDate.getTime() + fiveYears );
    SetCookie("ViewAll", "T", expDate, null, null, false);
  }
  window.open(document.location.href, "_top", "");
}
```

LISTING 25.6   Continued

```
//-------------------------------------------------------------
// SendPersonalPage - Writes a page showing the categories and
//                    links which the user prefers. Only shows a
//                    heading if one of its favorites is enabled.
//-------------------------------------------------------------
function SendPersonalPage()
{
  if (GetCookie("ViewAll") != "T")
    document.write('<h1>Your Favorites:<\/h1>');
  else
    document.write('<h1>Links:<\/h1>');
  // Here are the buttons for viewing the options or
  // "View All" pages.
  document.write('<form method=post>');
  if (GetCookie("ViewAll") == "T")
  {
    document.write('<input type=button value="View Favorites" ' +
                   'onClick="ToggleView();">');

  }
  else
  {
    document.write('<input type=button value="View All" ' +
                   'onClick="ToggleView();">');

  }
  document.write('<input type=button '+ 'value="Select Personal Favorites" ' +
                 'onClick="LoadOptions();">');

  document.write('<\/form>');
  // The links will look nicer inside a definition list.
  document.write('<dl>');
  for (var i = 1; i < FaveList.length; i++)
    FaveList[i].WriteAsWebLink();    // Write each link.
  document.write('<\/dl><p>');
}


//=============================================================
// Helper Functions
//=============================================================
```

LISTING 25.6   Continued

```
//---------------------------------------------------------------
// isEnabled - Returns True if the favorite identified by the
//             name parameter is enabled.
//---------------------------------------------------------------
function isEnabled(name)
{
  var result = false;
  var FaveCookie = GetCookie("Favorites");
  if (FaveCookie != null)
  {
    var searchFor = "<" + name + ">";
    var startOfCookie = FaveCookie.indexOf(searchFor);
    if (startOfCookie != -1)
      result = true;
  }
  return result;
}


//---------------------------------------------------------------
// AddFavorite- Enables the favorite identified by the name
//              parameter.
//---------------------------------------------------------------
function AddFavorite(name)
{
  if (!isEnabled(name))
  {
    var fiveYears = 5 * 365 * 24 * 60 * 60 * 1000;
    var expDate = new Date();
    expDate.setTime (expDate.getTime() + fiveYears );
    SetCookie("Favorites", GetCookie("Favorites")+ "<" + name +
             ">", expDate, null, null, false);

  }
}


//---------------------------------------------------------------
// ClearFavorite- Disables the favorite identified by the name
//                parameter.
//---------------------------------------------------------------
function ClearFavorite(name)
{
```

LISTING 25.6   Continued

```
  if (isEnabled(name))
  {
    var FaveCookie = GetCookie("Favorites");
    var searchFor = "<" + name + ">";
    var startOfCookie = FaveCookie.indexOf(searchFor);
    var NewFaves = FaveCookie.substring(0, startOfCookie)+
                   FaveCookie.substring(startOfCookie+searchFor.length,
                                        FaveCookie.length);
    var fiveYears = 5 * 365 * 24 * 60 * 60 * 1000;
    var expDate = new Date();
    expDate.setTime (expDate.getTime() + fiveYears );
    SetCookie("Favorites", NewFaves, expDate, null, null, false);
  }
}


//----------------------------------------------------------------
// SetFavoriteEnabled - Turns the favorite identified by the name
//                      parameter on (SetOn=true) or off
//                      (SetOn=false).
//----------------------------------------------------------------
function SetFavoriteEnabled(name, SetOn)
{
  if (SetOn)
    AddFavorite(name);
  else
    ClearFavorite(name);
}


//----------------------------------------------------------------
// ReloadPage - Reloads the page.
//----------------------------------------------------------------
function ReloadPage()
{
  window.open(document.location.href, "_top", "");
}

</script>
</head>
<body>
<script type="text/javascript">
/*--------------------------------------------------------------
Here's where we select the page to send.  Normally we send the
```

LISTING 25.6   Continued

```
personalized favorites page (by calling SendPersonalPage). However,
If the cookie ShowOptions is set, we'll send the options selection
page instead (by calling SendOptionsPage).
------------------------------------------------------------*/
if (GetCookie("ShowOptions") == "T")
{
  ClearCookie("ShowOptions");
  SendOptionsPage();
}
else
{
  SendPersonalPage();
}
</script>
<center>
This is a very dull page unless you have a JavaScript
enabled browser.<br />
</center>
</body>
</html>
```

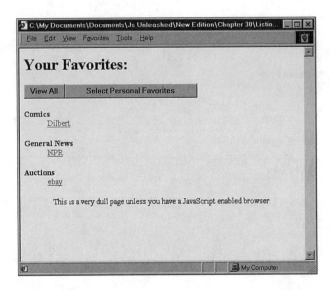

FIGURE 25.1   The Favorites page.

Without JavaScript, a task like this would have been handled at the server. Each hit would have involved having the server run some type of script or program to read the user's cookies and generate his page on-the-fly. With JavaScript, all this processing takes place on the client's browser; the server just downloads the static page. It might not even do that, because the page might come from the client's local cache. When the page is loaded, all the links, selected or not, are sent. With the help of cookies and JavaScript, the client decides which ones to show the user.

This program makes use of three different cookies. The `Favorites` cookie contains a unique code for each favored link. The `ViewAll` cookie toggles between showing the user's favorites and all possible links. The program may also display either of two pages: one for the selected links and the other for changing the configuration and options. When the `ShowOptions` cookie is set, the Options selection page is displayed. Otherwise, the regular page is shown. Figure 25.2 shows what the configuration page looks like.

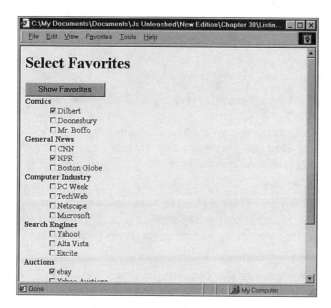

FIGURE 25.2   The Favorites configuration page.

The program creates objects called—you guessed it—"favorites." Each favorite is, in essence, a Web link to another page. The favorite contains information on the link's URL, a user-friendly page description, and the code that identifies it in the `Favorites` cookie string. The favorite also knows how to print itself on a Web page as a regular link for the Favorites page or in a check box format for the Options page.

Using Other State Maintenance Options

As mentioned earlier in this chapter, there are a few drawbacks to using cookies. Perhaps you would rather just avoid the controversy and find some other way to maintain state from one page to the next. There are two ways of doing this. Which one you use depends on how you will have users get from one page of your site to the next.

The main limitation of these methods is that they work only from one page to the page immediately following. If state information is to be maintained throughout a series of pages, these mechanisms must be used on every page.

Query String

If most of your navigation is done through hypertext links embedded in your pages, you need to add extra information to the end of the URL. This is usually done by adding a question mark (?) to the end of your Web page URL, followed by information in an encoded form, such as that returned by the escape() method. To separate one piece of information from another, place an ampersand (&) between them.

For example, if you want to send with your link the parameters color=blue and size=extra large, use a link like the following:

```
<a href="/mypage.html?color=blue&size=extra+large">XL Blue</a>
```

This format is the same as the format used when submitting forms with the get method. A succeeding page can read this information by using the search property of the Location object. This property is called search because many Internet search engines use this part of the URL to store their search criteria.

The following is an example of how to use the location.search property. In this example, the name of the current page is sent as a parameter in a link to another page. The other page reads this property through the search property and states where the browser came from.

Listing 25.7 shows the first page that contains the link.

LISTING 25.7   page1.html—Sending Current Page as Part of Link

```
<html>
<head>
<title>Where Was I? - Page 1</title>
</head>
<body>
<h1>Where Was I? - Demonstration</h1>
This page sets information which will allow the page it is linked
to figure out where it came from. It uses values embedded in the link
URL in order to do this.
```

LISTING 25.7   Continued

```
<p>
We'll assume that any URL parameters are separated by an ampersand.
<p>
Notice that there doesn't need to be any JavaScript code in this page.
<p>
And now,
<a href="page2.html?camefrom=page1.html&more=needless+stuff">
Let's go to Page 2.</a>
</body>
</html>
```

Listing 25.8 shows the second page, demonstrating how to use location.search to find where the browser came from.

LISTING 25.8   page2.html—Using location.search to Get Name of Previous Page

```
<html>
<title>Where Was I? - Page 2</title>
<head>
</head>
<body>
<h1>Where Was I? - Demonstration</h1>
This page reads information which allows it to figure out where it came from.
<p>
<script type="text/javascript">
// WhereWasI
// Reads the search string to figure out which link brought it here.
function WhereWasI() {
  // Start by storing our search string in a handy place (so we don't
  // need to type as much).
  var handyString = window.location.search;
  // Find the beginning of our special URL variable.
  var startOfSource = handyString.indexOf("camefrom=");
  // If it's there, find the end of it.
  if (startOfSource != -1) {
    var endOfSource = handyString.indexOf("&", startOfSource+9);
    var result = handyString.substring(startOfSource+9, endOfSource);
  }
  else
    var result = "Source Unknown"; // Could not find the "camefrom" string.
  return result;
```

LISTING 25.8   Continued

```
}
if (WhereWasI() != "Source Unknown")
  document.write ("You just came from <b>" + WhereWasI() + "<\/b>.<br />")
else
  document.write ("Unfortunately, we don't know where you came from.<br />");
</script>
</body>
</html>
```

Hidden Form Variables

The method used in the preceding section works as long as the user navigates from one page to another using links. To do the same thing with forms, you can use hidden form variables instead of the location.search parameter.

Hidden form variables have the following format:

```
<input type="hidden" name="HiddenFieldName" value="HiddenFieldValue">
```

You can specify whatever you like for *HiddenFieldName* and *HiddenFieldValue*. The value parameter is optional.

Using hidden fields doesn't necessarily require the use of JavaScript code. They are defined instead in the <input> tag of normal HTML documents. However, you do need some sort of server-based script or program in order to read the values of these hidden fields.

Summary

In this chapter, you learned a number of ways to make your Web pages more dynamic and personal by maintaining state between pages of a Web application. Of all the ways we looked at, cookies are the most powerful method.

Cookies allow you to store information on the client computer and use it from within your Internet application to store values and other critical information. Because of the nature of cookies, they can be used for everything from the simplest form of name=value pairs to the more advanced forms.

Although cookies represent the most powerful method of accomplishing state maintenance, other approaches are available, such as URL query string parameters and hidden fields.

PART VI

JavaScript on the Server Side

IN THIS PART

CHAPTER **26**

Server-Side Environment Introduction

Although JavaScript plays a key role on the client side, it can also be used to create server-based applications within Microsoft's Active Server Pages (ASP) environment. Like its client-side counterpart, using JavaScript on the server side has a set of host-specific objects, functions, and methods that extend the environment's core ECMAScript objects. JavaScript is often used as a server-based scripting language in place of CGIs and other technologies to build Web-based applications.

What About Netscape's Server-Side JavaScript?

For those of you who purchased the third edition of *JavaScript Unleashed*, you probably remember that we had dedicated an entire chapter to Netscape's Server-Side JavaScript (SSJS). Since that time, not only did Netscape team with Sun to create the iPlanet alliance and a host of new servers, but we have also seen the end of SSJS (we have actually seen the end of the alliance as well).

SSJS was dropped in version 6 of the Enterprise Server in favor of using Java servlets and JavaServer Pages (JSP), so SSJS is no longer an available technology. For those of you using SSJS, you should seriously consider moving to either Java servlets and JSP or Microsoft's ASP.NET (using JScript .NET as the language). Although this pretty much means a complete rewrite of your code, not doing so would ultimately lead to a dead end.

With Microsoft's .NET initiative on the forefront of today's technologies, JScript .NET is a perfect language to build .NET Web Services. But before we get into the details of building Web Services with JScript .NET, which is covered in the next chapter, we want to cover some basics about the server-side environment. It is important to understand how to build client/server applications.

Your ASP application that runs on a Microsoft Internet Information Server (IIS) represents the server in this client/server model, and the client is the browser or application to which information is being sent. This two-tier model can easily be extended to three or more tiers by simply adding a database or another application that your ASP code accesses and/or uses. A firm grasp on client/server architectures will accelerate your learning in the next chapter, so we will take a quick look at them here.

Web-Based Architectures

The client/server concept has evolved with the advent of the Internet. The Web brought with it a design whereby static, and some dynamic, information could be readily served to many different users from a single server, which allows servers to handle more users and requests.

Traditionally, the server was a database server used to store and process data requests from the client, which limited the amount of processing that it could handle. In a Web-based system, the server is not a database; it is just the Web server that is used for processing, administering, and performing the delivery of XHTML documents and other HTTP accessible resources. The capability still exists to split processing between client and server, but the processing is usually centralized on the server.

Before we get into the details of these multitier systems, let's first look at how this all started.

Two-Tier Application Structure

When developing such an application, you will partition it into two distinct pieces. This is the two-tier structure for client/server architecture. One piece is the graphical user interface (GUI), or front end, where the user can interact with the application (often a database or other datastore). The second is the server, the back end, where most of the processing capabilities reside.

The original client and server architected applications represented separate entities, as shown in Figure 26.1, relatively independent, with the exception of a connection, from each other until the client needed information from the database. In these early systems, which are still often in use today in large corporations, desktop applications connected to databases to access the data they needed for specific tasks.

In these traditional environments, it was reasonable to put more processing on the clients, because you usually have some control over the configuration and setup of those machines. You, the developer, could partition the application as you saw fit, moving more or less processing to the client side, depending on its capabilities, server processing load, and network traffic flow. The server was the processing engine for the data, and the desktop application performed any necessary presentation or manipulation. The server usually stored and managed the large amounts of data and performed the processor-intensive, large-scale calculations and system processing.

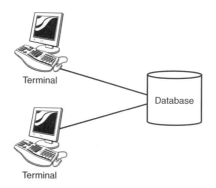

FIGURE 26.1   Two-tier client/server architecture.

The capability to segregate the two parts of a system, making them largely independent of each other, has contributed to significant advances in the development of large-scale database systems. The capability of splitting an application into two pieces gave the developer more flexibility in application design. However, this approach was considered limited because the database server would often be overwhelmed with requests or a high number of users. Quite simply, this type of system did not scale.

Three-Tier Application Structure

When information began to be available on the Web, we saw a movement from traditional client/server applications to three-tier applications. In these systems, as shown in Figure 26.2, client machines would talk to a Web server (or a farm of more than one server), which would then talk to the database. Also, users would simply connect just long enough to get the data, and then disconnect. This allowed more users and requests to be processed, without putting undue pressure on the database.

If you look at the design of these systems, the benefits are obvious. And with client-side scripting languages, like JavaScript, being widely used today, Web-based applications are able to offload some of the processing on the client itself, rather than the Web server.

N-Tier Application Structure

With Web Services taking a strong place in today's systems, n-tier applications are now more often used to overcome some of the limitations associated with the two- and three-tier systems. N-tier architecture, shown in Figure 26.3, involves splitting user interface, processing, and data storage into distinct levels, spreading the workload even further.

26

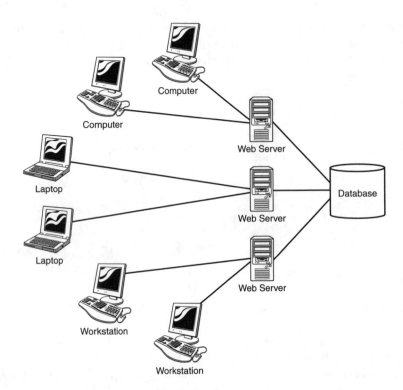

FIGURE 26.2   Three-tier Web-based architecture.

The front end remains responsible for the user interface and minor processing, and the back end is still responsible for data storage, but processing and calculations (or business rules as they are often referred to) have been moved to a middle layer. This allows changes to be made to the business rules without affecting the user interface or the database. Additionally, by taking this approach, you can also tap the power of other applications and systems that were not part of your original design. For instance, you integrate with a third-party system that can check the credit of an individual as they are purchasing something on your site.

You have far less control over the front-end computer (both Web browser and desktop workstation) in the Web environment than you do in the normal application environment. It is more difficult to judge how well processes run on the client side. This makes it more reasonable to run processes on the back end, because you have control over that environment and can predict the outcome.

On the other hand, normal client/server applications face some problems that a Web-based client/server doesn't. In a normal client/server database application, if the client-side module is modified, you might need to redistribute the entire application. With a Web-based client/server, because the client is a Web page, the new front end is just redistributed the next time the page is loaded.

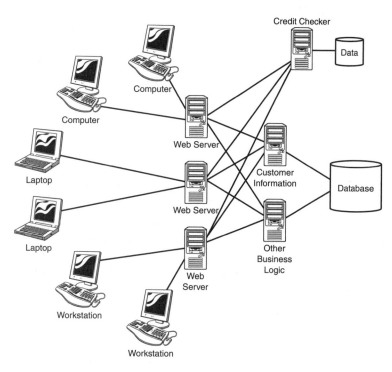

FIGURE 26.3   N-tier Web-based architecture.

The browser client initiates the transaction by sending a request to the server to perform some operation, database request, calculation, processing request, or other server-side function. The client then waits for a response from the server before continuing. Server-side processing allows code to remain on one centralized server for easier modification and also gives you the benefit of faster processing, because the processing occurs on the server.

Questions to Avoid Pitfalls

JavaScript presents you with client/server architecture questions as well. JavaScript processing can be distributed between the client and the server, depending on your preferences. Processing speed on the client is completely dependent on the client's environment, memory, speed, and other internal factors; processing on the server is dependent on the amount of traffic on the Internet as well as traffic and processing on the server. Dividing processing among multiple entities is a good idea, keeping intense processing on the more known quantity—the server.

> **NOTE**
>
> Thinking about architecture design early in the development phase of a Web application helps you build a more stable application that gives you the most processing power available.

Client/Server Communication

Communication between client and server in a Web-based environment is an important component to consider—one that presents a new hurdle to overcome. Unlike client/server environments on a normal network, the Web environment doesn't provide a constant connection to the server; instead, communication is through HTTP protocols using TCP/IP.

Client to Web Server

The first substantial exchange of information between client (browser) and Web server is the client request. Because of the nature of HTTP, it is necessary for browser clients to send requests to servers for all the information they want. Servers do not have a way of initiating an HTTP document transfer/connection.

The format for the HTTP request to the server can be a basic XHTML page request, or it can be a request that contains content information or data that needs to be processed or posted to the server. Additionally, a piece of information included in the request message, called the body, contains data (content) to be used by the server, either from functions or data-entry fields on the XHTML document.

The HTTP request contains three basic groups of information:

- Request line: Method (`GET`, `HEAD`, `POST`), URL, and HTTP version
- Name/value pairs for fields such as `accept`, `referer`, `if-modified`, `user-agent`, `content-type`, and `content-length`
- Content: Information (data) being sent to the server for processing

Web Server to Client

After a client has sent a request to a Web server for information, that server will in turn send a message back to the client containing information that the client has requested. HTTP responses take a similar format to HTTP requests, but they include the returned XHTML document (response) at the end.

The HTTP response contains three basic groups of information:

- Response line
- Response headers
- Response data

The response line from the server has the syntax of HTTP version, status code (a three-digit return code), and the response line of the text (not used by the browser, but it can be used for document interpretation). This might look like the following:

```
HTTP/1.1 200 OK
Connection: close
Server: Microsoft-IIS/6.0
Date: Wed, 19 Apr 2003 17:13:33 GMT
Content-Length: 30465
Content-type: text/html
Expires: Mon, 22 Jul 2003 01:31:18 GMT
Cache-control: private
```

The response line gives the browser some initial information about what it can expect to follow in the rest of the response. The HTTP version tells it how to begin interpreting the document response, and the status code tells it what to expect as far as the return. For example, a response status code of 200 is "OK."

> **NOTE**
>
> HTTP has a variety of response codes (such as 200, 302, and 404) that relate to the state and content of the document being returned. You can learn more about these codes by reading the HTTP 1.1 RFC 2616 at http://www.ietf.org/rfc/rfc2616.txt.

The response data, or body, is the final part of the HTTP response and is in the format defined by the content-type passed. The significance of this data depends on the status code that is returned in the response header. The response data is usually in the form of an XHTML document to be displayed in the client browser.

Session Management

One of the benefits of the Web and its design is also one of its biggest obstacles in applications that require client interaction with the server itself. Because a server operates in a stateless environment, it can run faster, but it has to rely on the client to remind it who the client is when a client makes a request. The evolution of XHTML from static pages to interactive applications has made a formerly stateless environment look for ways to maintain state.

Because the client is not continuously connected to the Web server, there is the problem of knowing how to tell a Web server who the client is when the client reconnects to send a request back to the server. If Web applications remained continuously connected to the server, Web development would be as uncomplicated as generic client/server applications—but Web applications aren't continuously connected.

Several techniques for session management are available, including the use of client cookies, URL encoding, and IP addresses on the server. The first two techniques can involve complete client-side state maintenance or help from the server. IP addresses require the server to maintain the information, and the client can help.

Cookies

Cookies provide a Web server with a mechanism, through identification, to save client information that can be used in future connections to the server. Cookies are a client-based state maintenance methodology. The server saves the information that it needs about the client on the client itself, and the client sends the information back with every HTTP request.

Cookies are stored in a text file on the client drive. The server, as a means of keeping track of the client's state, has the capability to set the information in a cookie as long as the browser allows it. Different browsers handle cookies different ways. Some have only one cookie file and all servers write cookie information to the same file, tagging sections in the cookie with the specific URL names as they are saved and updated. Others store cookie information in multiple files located in a cookie directory.

> **CAUTION**
>
> The size of the cookie file may be limited depending on the browser, so only a certain amount of information can be stored on any given client. This limits the amount of information that each server can store and the number of Web servers that can store information on a specific client computer.

With cookies, the possibility always exists that the user could delete the cookie file by mistake (after all, it's only a text file). Then every server would lose whatever state information it had been maintaining, and the client would need to start from scratch in establishing itself with the server.

Because cookie information is stored on the client side, it is not affected by server issues. It also allows the client to resend a request successfully, even if problems are encountered on the server side. Another benefit of cookies is that, because the server isn't required to store any information about the client, the server can forget about the client after the initial request for information, and no storage of information is required on the server.

Cookies increase the amount of Internet traffic, because the server is sending and receiving extra information with every client URL request; however, it is very minimal. Cookie information is transferred in the name/value pair methodology, using the cookie protocol for transferring cookie information with requests.

> **NOTE**
>
> If you would like to read more about cookies, refer back to Chapter 24, "Forms and Data Validation," or check out RFC 2965 at http://www.ietf.org/rfc/rfc2965.txt.

URL Encoding

The client URL encoding methodology for maintaining state information between client and server involves sending name/value pairs or unique key fields of information as part of the URL string at client HTTP request time. This method of storing state information has the same benefits for the server as cookies, in that no information needs to be stored on the server.

> **NOTE**
>
> Using this process to maintain client state requires that the URL be built dynamically, which can cause a significant increase in the size of the URL. Additionally, it means that every link in your document that links to another part of your site must also have this extra session-specific information to maintain the session.

Using client-side URL encoding allows more flexibility when the need for state maintenance exists. Unlike cookies, client URL encoding isn't browser-specific. Because you don't know which type of browser is accessing your server, this is a more reliable method of maintaining state.

IP Address on the Server

A third method of maintaining state is to store IP addresses and state information on the server. The server must have database access or shared memory in which to store the information. The state information of a client is stored based on the IP address of the client, and this information is held and usable only by this particular server.

Because of these drawbacks, this type of state maintenance is useful only if the following criteria apply:

- Clients are known to have fixed IP addresses.

- Only one server supports the application.

The practice of dynamically allocating IP addresses for machines that in turn run a Web browser makes this type of state maintenance impossible to implement. Multiple Web servers can't easily support this methodology, either.

Summary

Much thought needs to go into the architecture of the application before you can begin to build it for successful Internet use. Knowing your predicted audience and being able to anticipate access to your server helps when defining the methodologies and techniques that you choose to use to implement a client/server application. Adding JavaScript and database functionality brings on a whole new level of concerns and issues that must be accounted for.

Server-side versus client-side processing needs to be taken into account when deciding test speed and functionality of the JavaScript application. The two-tier and *n*-tier methodologies need to be evaluated for advantages and disadvantages on your particular application and its complexity and maintainability.

In this chapter, you learned some of the basics for creating Web-based applications and how they should be architected. We also talked about some of the approaches you should use to maintain sessions and track users. In the next chapter we are going to put some of this knowledge to use as we take a look at building pages and Web Services using JScript .NET.

Web Services with JScript .NET

The last chapter introduced and discussed the server-side environment. We not only talked about Web-based architectures, including the original client/server model, three-tier, and n-tier, but also the type of communication that exists between these clients and servers. We even spent some time on how to deal with user sessions, which is an extremely important aspect of building multitier applications. But more important than each of these individual topics, we laid the groundwork for covering the use of JavaScript on the server side.

As we discussed early in the last chapter, JavaScript on the server side has changed since its initial implementation. It is no longer present in the Netscape/iPlanet line of servers and it has changed dramatically within Microsoft's ASP environment. It is this second topic, however, that we want to discuss further in this chapter.

Since the last edition of this book, Microsoft has embarked on a great new initiative called .NET. Although the following sections cover some of the aspects of .NET, the importance as it relates to this book is that it has taken their JScript implementation to a whole new level—specifically the ability to create, among other things, Web Services.

Introducing Web Services

Web Services, by definition, represent software functionality exposed in XML (eXtensible Markup Language) as a service on the Web through SOAP (Simple Object Access Protocol), described by WSDL (Web Services Description Language), and registered in the UDDI (Universal Description, Discovery, and Integration) database. But what does this really mean?

> **NOTE**
>
> Microsoft's .NET initiative, which is where you find the majority of their Web Services push, is not the only approach to building and using Web Services. Sun Microsystems has their ONE (Open Net Environment), which is also based on XML, SOAP, WSDL, and UDDI, but adds ebXML (Electronic Business Extensible Markup Language). Because JavaScript is only used within Microsoft's implementation, however, we will only focus on the .NET implementation within this book.

Think of it this way. In much the same way that APIs and classes allow you to link together functionality into an application, Web Services represent building blocks of functionality that can be linked together to build Web-based applications. This is a very important concept to grasp and understand, because it represents a shift from approaches like DCOM (Distributed Component Object Model) and CORBA (Common Object Request Broker Architecture) to a method of accessing and reusing components across the Web.

For example, you work for a large company that maintains the master employee contact database in Dallas, Texas. At the same time, you are writing a very basic Web application for your department in San Diego, California. Part of the requirements for your application is that you only have it available to the users in your office location, although it is accessible on the open Internet. In order to do this, you must have a list of employees in the office and ask them to log in to your application.

Let's assume the database in Dallas has a Web service interface that allows other applications to authenticate employees. To perform this action, you simply pass the employee's name and password to the service. If the name and password authenticate properly, the service returns a Boolean true. If the authentication fails, false is returned.

This is a huge benefit to the programmers because it means they do not have to locally replicate data that is centrally stored in Dallas. Additionally, as names and passwords change, the application stays updated without any programming intervention.

Even through this very simple and basic example, it is easy to begin to see the power of Web Services. For instance, what if our application needed to include a search feature? Search technology can be an extremely complex process and something most people would rather avoid. Using a Web service powered by a popular Internet search engine, like Google, could cut your development time dramatically. And let's say you also need to add an auction powered by eBay, and a store front powered by Amazon—all through Web Services. It can be component sharing and reuse galore!

Now that you've had a quick introduction to Web Services and some of their uses, let's talk about the technologies that make up Web Services themselves.

XML

Within the context of Web Services, XML is used as the technology responsible for describing the software service that is being exposed on the Web. This is an extremely important aspect of Web Services in that XML has several inherent characteristics and features that allow for accurate descriptions. But before we talk about how XML is used within Web Services, let's take a general look at XML.

Schemas, which can be defined as an XML Document Type Definition (DTD) or XML Schema Definition (XSD), are created to define the languages used to describe data. In other words, they define the elements (that is, tags), attributes, and other characteristics that make up the language. Additionally, the purpose of schemas is not only to describe the content itself, but also the interrelationships, or hierarchy, within the data.

> **NOTE**
>
> The term "schema" is used in a generic context in this chapter to represent a definition—not necessarily XML Schema (W3C Recommendation). If we talk about XML Schema, we will refer to it specifically as an XSD schema.

At the same time, in almost a contradiction, schemas are not required to have XML documents. For instance, Listing 27.1 shows a sample XML document that does not have a schema associated with it.

LISTING 27.1   A Simple XML Document

```
<?xml version="1.0" encoding="utf-8" ?>
<book>
  <details>
    <title>JavaScript Unleashed</title>
    <edition>4th</edition>
    <publisher>Sams</publisher>
    <authorList>
      <author>R. Allen Wyke</author>
      <author>Jason D. Gilliam</author>
    </authorList>
  </details>
  <available>2002</available>
</book>
```

Although this XML document is not **valid** (verified against an XSD schema or DTD), it is **well-formed**. This means that it has the proper tag structure. For instance, the beginning tags have ending tags and there is no improper nesting.

Before we talk a little more about schemas, let's make sure you understand Listing 27.1. If you look at this example you can see there is a parent, or root, element called <book>. Within this element there are two child elements—<details> and <available>. Additionally, the <details> element has several other child elements, such as <title>,

<edition>, <publisher>, and <authorList>. And finally, <authorList> has two instances of an <author> element.

The purpose of these elements is to act as containers for data. For instance, the <title> element contains the data JavaScript Unleashed. This obviously takes great steps in describing what the data is.

At the same time, it is pretty easy to see the relationship of the elements. In other words, the title and the edition are actually on the same *level* as one another, which represents a sibling-like relationship. This provides even more information on the data. You can see a visual representation of this in Figure 27.1.

FIGURE 27.1   Visual representation of our schema.

As for the schemas that can be used to define XML documents and therefore be able to validate them, these are contained in different files. As mentioned before, these contain the actual code to create the language and structure. For instance, Listing 27.2 contains a DTD that could be used to govern our example from Listing 27.1.

LISTING 27.2   A DTD to Govern the Previous Example

```
<?xml version='1.0' encoding='UTF-8' ?>


<!ELEMENT book (details , available)>
<!ELEMENT details (title , edition , publisher , authorList)>
<!ELEMENT title (#PCDATA)>
<!ELEMENT edition (#PCDATA)>
<!ELEMENT publisher (#PCDATA)>
<!ELEMENT authorList (author+)>
<!ELEMENT author (#PCDATA)>
<!ELEMENT available (#PCDATA)>
```

Just as a quick overview, what Listing 27.2 shows is the definition of eight elements. The part that is contained in the parentheses represents the "content model" of a given element. When defining the <book> element, for example, this contains two other elements: <details> and <available>. The definition of <author> on the other hand, contains **PCDATA**, which means that it contains parse character data—basically any kind of character, with a few exceptions.

One of the things we mentioned earlier was the fact that schemas could be created in DTDs or XSD. As a comparison, we have included the XSD schema for Listing 27.1 in Listing 27.3. One of the things you will notice is that you can provide additional information, such as data types, that further defines the data.

LISTING 27.3   XSD Schema to Govern Our Previous Example

```
<?xml version = "1.0" encoding = "UTF-8"?>
<xsd:schema xmlns:xsd = "http://www.w3.org/2001/XMLSchema"
   elementFormDefault = "qualified">
  <xsd:element name = "book">
    <xsd:complexType>
      <xsd:sequence>
        <xsd:element ref = "details"/>
        <xsd:element ref = "available"/>
      </xsd:sequence>
    </xsd:complexType>
  </xsd:element>
  <xsd:element name = "details">
    <xsd:complexType>
      <xsd:sequence>
        <xsd:element ref = "title"/>
        <xsd:element ref = "edition"/>
        <xsd:element ref = "publisher"/>
        <xsd:element ref = "authorList"/>
      </xsd:sequence>
    </xsd:complexType>
  </xsd:element>
  <xsd:element name = "title" type = "xsd:string"/>
  <xsd:element name = "edition" type = "xsd:string"/>
  <xsd:element name = "publisher" type = "xsd:string"/>
  <xsd:element name = "authorList">
    <xsd:complexType>
      <xsd:sequence>
        <xsd:element ref = "author" maxOccurs = "unbounded"/>
```

27

LISTING 27.3   Continued

```
      </xsd:sequence>
    </xsd:complexType>
  </xsd:element>
  <xsd:element name = "author" type = "xsd:string"/>
  <xsd:element name = "available" type = "xsd:string"/>
</xsd:schema>
```

Going back to our first example, we can govern our XML document by simply adding in a reference to our schema, as you can see in Listing 27.4. You can see this loaded into an Internet Explorer browser in Figure 27.2.

LISTING 27.4   Referencing Our XSD Schema

```
<?xml version = "1.0" encoding = "utf-8"?>
<book xmlns:xsi = "http://www.w3.org/2001/XMLSchema-instance"
      xsi:noNamespaceSchemaLocation = " Listing27-03.xsd">
  <details>
    <title>JavaScript Unleashed</title>
    <edition>4th</edition>
    <publisher>Sams</publisher>
    <authorList>
      <author>R. Allen Wyke</author>
      <author>Jason D. Gilliam</author>
    </authorList>
  </details>
  <available>2002</available>
</book>
```

> **NOTE**
>
> XML DTDs and XSD schemas are well beyond the scope of this book; however, you can read the actual W3C Recommendations at http://www.w3.org/XML.

Even though we have not gone into a lot of detail on XML or schemas within this section, this should have given you a very basic idea of what it is and how it can be used. That is all you need at this point. Let's now move on to SOAP.

> **NOTE**
>
> To explore this topic further, see *XML and Web Services Unleashed* from Sams Publishing.

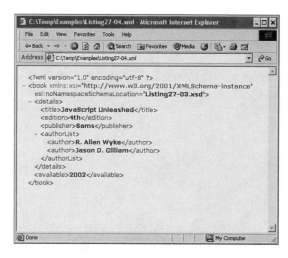

FIGURE 27.2 Loading our XML document into Internet Explorer.

SOAP

SOAP is a protocol for exchanging data in distributed and decentralized networks, such as the Internet. It is used to describe the XML format of the messages as well as the ability to invoke remote procedure calls (RPC). This, for instance, allows you to specify what function to call, what parameters to pass, and encoding rules.

SOAP is like the United Parcel Service (UPS) of digital data. It not only contains the data itself, but also the necessary instructions for what to do with the data and how to return the results of any necessary processing.

The SOAP document itself is made up of a header and a body. The body contains the XML document that is being passed between the SOAP-supporting applications. For instance, if we wanted to send our XML document (Listing 27.1) contained in a SOAP envelope, it would look like Listing 27.5.

LISTING 27.5 Sending Our Example in a SOAP Envelope

```
<?xml version="1.0" encoding="utf-8"?>
<soap:Envelope xmlns:xsi="http://www.w3.org/2001/XMLSchema-instance"
               xmlns:xsd="http://www.w3.org/2001/XMLSchema"
               xmlns:soap="http://schemas.xmlsoap.org/soap/envelope/">
  <soap:Body>
    <book>
      <details>
        <title>JavaScript Unleashed</title>
        <edition>4th</edition>
```

27

LISTING 27.5   Continued

```
        <publisher>Sams</publisher>
        <authorList>
          <author>R. Allen Wyke</author>
          <author>Jason D. Gilliam</author>
        </authorList>
      </details>
      <available>2002</available>
    </book>
  </soap:Body>
</soap:Envelope>
```

There is obviously a lot of other information that can be passed back and forth within a SOAP message, but we will not go into those details here. The good news for the .NET Web service developer is that Microsoft takes care of almost all of these details. All you have to do is properly author your code, and the tools build the appropriate SOAP messages for you.

> **NOTE**
>
> Comprehensive coverage of SOAP, which is maintained by the XML Protocol Working Group at the W3C, is beyond the scope of this book. However, additional information can be found at `http://www.w3.org/2000/xp/Group`.

WSDL

WSDL is essentially the IDL (Interface Definition Language) of Web Services. It is defined using an XSD schema and is used to describe Web Services. For instance, it defines where the service is available and what communication protocol should be used to communicate with the service. It is also used to describe the message contents and/or functionality.

As with SOAP, Microsoft has built the necessary development tools and environment within their .NET initiative to generate the necessary WSDL, which increases the ease of development. We are not going to show you any examples of what a WSDL document looks like just yet—we are going to wait and show you after we create an example of a Web service later in the chapter.

> **NOTE**
>
> Because Microsoft's tools generate the necessary WSDL for our examples and objectives in this book, we will not go into detail on the syntax of the language. However, you can read more information on WSDL, which now falls under the Web Services Description Working Group, at the W3C (`http://www.w3.org/2002/ws/desc`).

UDDI

The last item that we need to cover in our discussion of Web Services is the UDDI. We have talked about how to describe data, how to send it, and how to describe the service that is to act on it, but we have not talked about how developers are supposed to find Web Services.

Most developers would admit that finding the right control, class, or function to perform a given action is not always the easiest thing. Now, if you multiply the frustration that can cause just with the libraries on a single machine by the number of possible Web Services that could be built and connected across the entire world, it is easy to see the difficulty at hand. This is where the UDDI comes to the rescue.

The UDDI is essentially a searchable database of Web Services—like the Yellow Pages. It contains all the necessary information about the service to utilize it in your development. It is actually made up of three different types of information:

- Business Entity: Information about the business registering the Web service, such as various contact data.

- Business Service: Information about the services themselves, categorized by standard taxonomies.

- Template: Technical information about a given service.

There is an API available that is accessed and called within a SOAP message, which allows you to find various information on these services—to essentially search for a service. You can perform actions such as searching for a business, a specific service, bindings, and other details.

We are not going to use the UDDI for our examples, but we did want to expose you to the concept. If you plan on building Web Services that can then be utilized by others, you will definitely want to check out the UDDI site (`http://www.uddi.org`) for more information.

What Is .NET?

Now that you have a basic understanding of Web Services, let's take a few minutes to understand Microsoft's .NET. One of the important things we do want to point out is that .NET is not just about Web Services, which are technically made possible though ASP.NET. Web Services are core to the .NET framework, but the Web Services technology does not represent everything despite the attention and hype it is getting right now. .NET is, however, a great environment for writing Web services or consuming them.

Development Platform

.NET is a general-purpose application development platform that Microsoft has developed. Ultimately the entire OS will utilize this platform, which represents a layer of abstraction for many of the different Microsoft technologies. Essentially, it is a wrapper for technologies like COM (Component Object Model), GDI (Graphics Device Interface), BCL (Base Class Libraries), and others. At the same time, developers can still drop down into the lower-level APIs if need be.

These groups still have an organizational structure of their technologies that is relevant to how they have historically been. What .NET does is that it provides the wrapper/interface and a common organization of these wrappers, which are called namespaces. These 26 or so namespaces are not built on organizational structures, but rather on how developers would go about finding and using the functionality.

This initiative started at a time when all of these product groups at Microsoft were looking for the next big thing and where to take their technologies. There was an internal project that ultimately evolved into the CRL (Common Language Runtime), which really started to bring together the various groups. But the organization of the APIs and the CLR is not the only benefit.

Ease of Deployment

.NET also greatly simplified the deployment of applications. Are you familiar with "DLL hell?" This refers to the need to register DLL files within the Windows registry for applications that are built. DLLs often are overwritten, deleted, or even modified—all at the expense of the user's experience.

With .NET, you no longer have to write to the registry or worry about applications overwriting each other. The mentality going forward is literally to use the xcopy command (which copies entire directories) to deploy applications. Those of you who use Mac OS are familiar with the concept of moving applications simply by dragging them to another location. With .NET, building applications with this type of deployment method is also made possible.

Introducing JScript .NET

One of the key aspects of .NET, as it pertains to this book, is JScript .NET, which builds upon the third edition of the ECMAScript implementation Microsoft included in JScript 5.6. Since the release of 5.6, ECMAScript itself has progressed and is nearing the release of version 4 of the standard. This version is actually one of the largest steps it has taken to date to expand the context and potential of these JavaScript-type languages.

For instance, JScript .NET adds typed and typeless variables, packages, and full support of class-based objects, including inheritance, function overloading, property accessors, and more. In addition to these ECMAScript-based enhancements, the JScript .NET implementation also provides the ability to truly compile code into applications, cross-language support through Common Language Specification (CLS) compliance, and access to the .NET Framework.

So, what does all of this mean? Well, it means that ECMAScript is growing up and that JScript .NET has taken great strides to take ECMAScript from just a programming language syntax into the real world of application development, and not just browser scripting.

NOTE

Although we hate to say it because of the excitement it brings, coverage of JScript .NET is simply beyond the scope of this book. If you would like more information on JScript .NET and the specifics of its syntax and semantics, please check out `http://msdn.microsoft.com/library/en-us/jscript7/html/jsoriJScript.asp`.

Another useful resource is *Microsoft JScript .NET Programming* by Justin Rogers from Sams Publishing.

Building .NET Applications

One of the best ways to learn any technology or programming language is through the use of examples. In this part of the chapter we are going to take you through a brief example of building a Web service in JScript .NET. In this example we are going to create a service that allows you to enter an author's name. If the name matches one of the authors of this book, the service will return a message stating such. If the author is not an author of this book, it will return a message stating this is not a registered author.

ASP.NET Web Matrix

The first thing to do is download a free development tool from Microsoft called the ASP.NET Web Matrix, which can be seen in Figure 27.3. This tool, which is available from `http://www.asp.net`, will make it easy for us to develop and run our JScript .NET Web service.

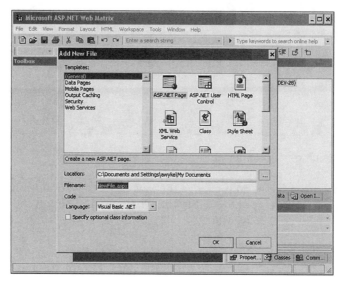

FIGURE 27.3   Microsoft's ASP.NET Web Matrix.

After you have downloaded and installed the application, which also requires the installation of the .NET Framework and Internet Explorer 5.5 or greater, go ahead and launch the program.

Initial Steps

On the initial screen that pops up, which you can see in Figure 27.3, click General under the templates and select XML Web Service as the template. Name the file `SimpleExample.asmx`.

One of the things you will notice is that this tool currently, as of the writing of this book, does not natively support JScript .NET—it only supports Visual Basic .NET and C#. But that is okay—we can still use it for our development. For now, just leave Visual Basic .NET as the selected language and enter `validateNames` as the class and `Sams` as the namespace. After you have done this, click OK. This will give you with some default code to work with, as you can see in Figure 27.4.

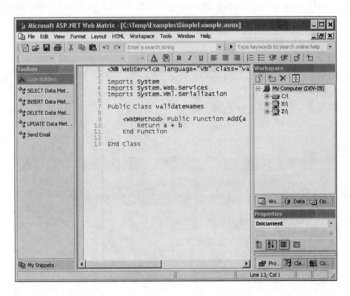

FIGURE 27.4   Result of starting our project.

The first thing we are going to do is change the language declaration in the first line from `"VB"` to `"JScript"`. Next we need to modify the syntax used to import the namespaces we want to work with. To do this, we will

- Change `"Imports"` to `"import"`

- Add a semicolon, `;`, to the end of each of the lines that contain the `"import"` statement

The final thing we are going to do is remove all of the code that defines the validateNames class. This means you will simply delete the following snippet from your code:

```
Public Class validateNames
  <WebMethod> Public Function Add(a As Integer, b As Integer) As Integer
    Return a + b
  End Function
End Class
```

At this point we have a clean and clear plate to add in the necessary JScript .NET code for our example.

Adding Code

As we discussed earlier in the chapter, a lot of the real power of JScript .NET comes from the Fourth Edition of the ECMAScript standard, which has not yet been released. So, for instance, the creating of a class in JScript .NET will seem a little foreign to you from the standpoint of what you have seen about JScript and JavaScript up to this point. However, if you have previously developed in languages such as Java or C++, this will look familiar.

The first thing we need to do is define our validateNames class, which will extend the built-in WebService class. This is accomplished by adding the following:

```
public class validateNames extends WebService{
  // Functions will go here.
}
```

Next, we will define a single function in our class called authorCheck() that will be used to take the name, which will be a String data type, passed to the service and return a String result. This will be declared inside our class wrapper that we just created, and it looks like this:

```
public class validateNames extends WebService{
  WebMethodAttribute public function authorCheck(name:String) : String {
    // Code defining function will go here.
  }
}
```

Now that this has been created, we can get back to some of the basic JScript code we are used to seeing. In this code we are going to first create a String variable that will hold a lowercase version of the original value of our name passed in. This looks like the following. Remember, from our previous function definition that name represents the name passed to the function.

```
// Create variable to store original value passed.
var orig = new String();
```

```
// Convert value to lowercase for comparisons.
orig = name.toLowerCase();
```

The final step is to simply add in the appropriate if..else statements to see if r. allen wyke or jason d. gilliam are passed to the service. If one of these names is passed, the service will return the original name passed in (no case change) followed by is a JavaScript Unleashed author! If the name passed in is not one of these names, the service will return the original name followed by is not a registered author.

Our final code for our service can be seen in Listing 27.6.

LISTING 27.6   Final JScript .NET Code to Build Our Web Service

```
<%@ WebService language="JScript" class="validateNames" %>

import System;
import System.Web.Services;
import System.Xml.Serialization;

public class validateNames extends WebService{
  WebMethodAttribute public function authorCheck(name:String) : String {

    // Create variable to store original value passed.
    var orig = new String();

    // Convert value to lowercase for comparisons.
    orig = name.toLowerCase();

    // Check to see if the name passed is one of the authors.
    if((orig =="r. allen wyke") || (orig == "jason d. gilliam")){
      return(name + " is a JavaScript Unleashed author! ");

    // If not, then tell the user that.
    }else{
      return(name + " is not a registered author.");
    }
  }
}
```

Testing Our Service

Now that we have our code written, we can use the ASP.NET Web Matrix application to execute it for us. You can do this by selecting View, Start or by pressing the F5 key. This will present you with a dialog, shown in Figure 27.5, to start a personal Web server to run the application.

NOTE

If you already have IIS running on your machine with the .NET Framework installed, you can also run this service using that Web server. To do so, simply place the SimpleExample.asmx file in the appropriate Web root directory and request it using your browser.

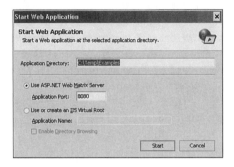

FIGURE 27.5   Starting a personal Web server to run our service.

Go ahead and select Start to run the server and open a browser with your application loaded. Doing so will present you with a screen like Figure 27.6 that details information about the service.

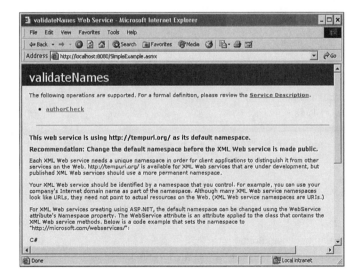

FIGURE 27.6   Viewing the service's details.

You can click on the Service Description link at the top of the page to see the actual WSDL that describes the service. Optionally, you can simply add ?WSDL to the end of the URL to see the WSDL code. We have included it here in Listing 27.7 for your review.

LISTING 27.7   WSDL Used to Describe Our Service

```
<?xml version="1.0" encoding="utf-8"?>
<definitions xmlns:http="http://schemas.xmlsoap.org/wsdl/http/"
             xmlns:soap="http://schemas.xmlsoap.org/wsdl/soap/"
             xmlns:s="http://www.w3.org/2001/XMLSchema"
             xmlns:s0="http://tempuri.org/"
             xmlns:soapenc="http://schemas.xmlsoap.org/soap/encoding/"
             xmlns:tm="http://microsoft.com/wsdl/mime/textMatching/"
             xmlns:mime="http://schemas.xmlsoap.org/wsdl/mime/"
             targetNamespace="http://tempuri.org/"
             xmlns="http://schemas.xmlsoap.org/wsdl/">
  <types>
    <s:schema elementFormDefault="qualified"
              targetNamespace="http://tempuri.org/">
      <s:element name="authorCheck">
        <s:complexType>
          <s:sequence>
            <s:element minOccurs="0" maxOccurs="1" name="name"
                       type="s:string" />
          </s:sequence>
        </s:complexType>
      </s:element>
      <s:element name="authorCheckResponse">
        <s:complexType>
          <s:sequence>
            <s:element minOccurs="0" maxOccurs="1"
                       name="authorCheckResult" type="s:string" />
          </s:sequence>
        </s:complexType>
      </s:element>
      <s:element name="string" nillable="true" type="s:string" />
    </s:schema>
  </types>
  <message name="authorCheckSoapIn">
    <part name="parameters" element="s0:authorCheck" />
  </message>
  <message name="authorCheckSoapOut">
    <part name="parameters" element="s0:authorCheckResponse" />
  </message>
  <message name="authorCheckHttpGetIn">
    <part name="name" type="s:string" />
  </message>
```

LISTING 27.7   Continued

```
<message name="authorCheckHttpGetOut">
  <part name="Body" element="s0:string" />
</message>
<message name="authorCheckHttpPostIn">
  <part name="name" type="s:string" />
</message>
<message name="authorCheckHttpPostOut">
  <part name="Body" element="s0:string" />
</message>
<portType name="validateNamesSoap">
  <operation name="authorCheck">
    <input message="s0:authorCheckSoapIn" />
    <output message="s0:authorCheckSoapOut" />
  </operation>
</portType>
<portType name="validateNamesHttpGet">
  <operation name="authorCheck">
    <input message="s0:authorCheckHttpGetIn" />
    <output message="s0:authorCheckHttpGetOut" />
  </operation>
</portType>
<portType name="validateNamesHttpPost">
  <operation name="authorCheck">
    <input message="s0:authorCheckHttpPostIn" />
    <output message="s0:authorCheckHttpPostOut" />
  </operation>
</portType>
<binding name="validateNamesSoap" type="s0:validateNamesSoap">
  <soap:binding transport="http://schemas.xmlsoap.org/soap/http"
                style="document" />
  <operation name="authorCheck">
    <soap:operation soapAction="http://tempuri.org/authorCheck"
                    style="document" />
    <input>
      <soap:body use="literal" />
    </input>
    <output>
      <soap:body use="literal" />
    </output>
  </operation>
</binding>
```

27

LISTING 27.7   Continued

```
<binding name="validateNamesHttpGet" type="s0:validateNamesHttpGet">
  <http:binding verb="GET" />
  <operation name="authorCheck">
    <http:operation location="/authorCheck" />
    <input>
      <http:urlEncoded />
    </input>
    <output>
      <mime:mimeXml part="Body" />
    </output>
  </operation>
</binding>
<binding name="validateNamesHttpPost" type="s0:validateNamesHttpPost">
  <http:binding verb="POST" />
  <operation name="authorCheck">
    <http:operation location="/authorCheck" />
    <input>
      <mime:content type="application/x-www-form-urlencoded" />
    </input>
    <output>
      <mime:mimeXml part="Body" />
    </output>
  </operation>
</binding>
<service name="validateNames">
  <port name="validateNamesSoap" binding="s0:validateNamesSoap">
    <soap:address location="http://localhost:8080/SimpleExample.asmx" />
  </port>
  <port name="validateNamesHttpGet" binding="s0:validateNamesHttpGet">
    <http:address location="http://localhost:8080/SimpleExample.asmx" />
  </port>
  <port name="validateNamesHttpPost" binding="s0:validateNamesHttpPost">
    <http:address location="http://localhost:8080/SimpleExample.asmx" />
  </port>
</service>
</definitions>
```

From the page shown in Figure 27.6, we can also test our service. To do so, simply click the validateNames link, which will take you to a screen like the one shown in Figure 27.7.

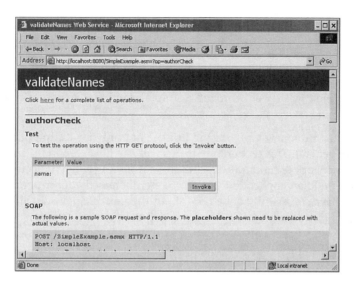

FIGURE 27.7 Testing our service.

All you have to do to test the service is to type in a name and click the Invoke button. Depending on the name you enter (which is not case sensitive), you will get a response either confirming it is a JavaScript Unleashed author or telling you that the name is not registered. In Figure 27.8, you can see the result of entering R. Allen Wyke as a test.

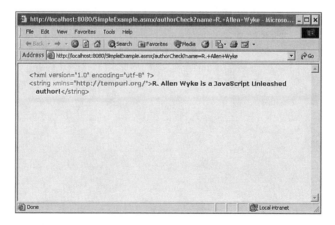

FIGURE 27.8 Results of testing our service.

We have obviously only touched on the power of Web Services and JScript .NET in this chapter. If you would like more information on .NET or JScript .NET, be sure to visit Microsoft's MSDN site at http://msdn.microsoft.com.

Summary

In this chapter we introduced you to Web Services and covered some of the specifics of what enables this powerful approach to building applications. We also introduced you to Microsoft's .NET initiative and went over some of the framework and how Web Services fit into the picture. Finally, we went through a simple example to expose you to developing and deploying Web Services using JScript .NET.

Web Services represent a new and exciting frontier not only for JScript, but application development in general. This technology truly takes the next step in utilizing the Internet as a connected network of functionality and turns it into an interconnected grouping of functionality to build an application. If this chapter increased your interest and desire to learn more, we have successfully done our job. In the next chapter we will look at another server-side use of JScript, within the Windows Script Host environment.

CHAPTER **28**

Windows Script Host

In this section of the book, we have really come to see how Microsoft has extended their use of JavaScript (JScript) to be much more than just a client-side programming language for browsers. We have talked about using it within the .NET environment to create Web Services, and now we are going to look at using it to perform everyday system tasks.

As many developers know, a big deficiency with Windows was its lack of scripting support for automating tasks. Most other operating systems had some type of built-in scripting engine, like AppleScript for the Mac OS and shell scripting for flavors of UNIX. There is batch file support in MS-DOS, but it is very limited in its capability and not very useful in the Windows environment.

Microsoft realized this limitation and introduced the Windows Script specification within Internet Explorer 3.0. This provided an interface for developers to build scripting engines for different browsers. From the Windows Script Interfaces grew, among other things, what is known today as the Windows Script Host (WSH).

> **NOTE**
>
> Complete coverage of WSH is well beyond the focus of this book, and the intention of this chapter is simply to expose you to some of its power. If you would like to read more information on WSH, then please check out the MSDN scripting site at `http://msdn.microsoft.com/library/en-us/script56/html/wsoriWSHLanguageReference.asp` for a language reference and details.

Windows Script Host

WSH provides the ability to automate tasks for the Windows environment. Before WSH, batch files were available in

MS-DOS; however, they weren't very powerful and provided little use in the Windows environment. A scripting language was needed for the system, and WSH was the answer. Suppose that you wanted to get the computer name, add a desktop shortcut, and map a network drive without doing each task individually. With Windows Script Host, all these tasks can be performed with a single script.

> **NOTE**
>
> WSH can be used with a few different programming languages—not just JScript. However, this chapter will focus on the JScript language.

The latest version of WSH is version 5.6. Although older versions are found in systems before Windows 2000, the scripting engine itself can be downloaded from Microsoft's Web site. The added benefits of this version are improved argument handling, remote script capability, treating processes as objects, access to the current working directory, and an improved security model.

The way the system works is that you create a script using various methods and properties from their object container and save these scripts in a file with the .wsf extension. This extension specifies that the file is a Windows Script Host file.

To better understand how this works, let's take a look at an example. Listing 28.1 shows a script that will display the username of the local machine on which the script is run.

LISTING 28.1   Example of a WSH File

```
<job>
  <script language="JScript">
    var WshNetwork = WScript.CreateObject("Wscript.Network");
    WScript.Echo("The User name is: " + WshNetwork.UserName);
  </script>
</job>
```

> **NOTE**
>
> To run this script, simply double-click it. There are other ways to run WSH scripts, which will be discussed later in the chapter.

You can see the results of running this example in Figure 28.1.

The syntax of a WSH script is fairly simple. You enclose your functionality between the <job> and <script> elements. This is similar to a normal JScript or JavaScript program, and is executed when the script is run.

FIGURE 28.1   Displaying the username of the person running the script.

Architecture

The architecture of the Windows Script Host is fairly basic as well, which will help those of you interested in using it. There are only a few components, which operate together, to make your scripts come alive. They are the scripts themselves, the Windows Shell, the Windows Registry, and the scripting engine. Figure 28.2 shows a diagram indicating how the components interact with each other to process the script.

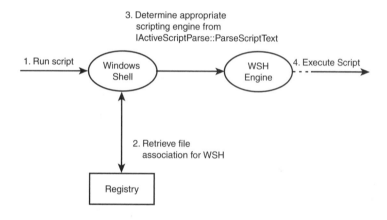

FIGURE 28.2   WSH architecture.

As you can see, the Windows Shell is the first component to encounter the script file. The shell must determine the file type by looking up the file association in the Registry. When it has the necessary information, it then passes the file to the Windows Script Host engine. This engine will use the `IActiveScriptParse::ParseScriptText` method to determine whether this particular script will go to a JScript engine, VBScript engine, or potentially other engines such as the PerlScript engine.

As we mentioned before, one of the benefits of the WSH is that it can support multiple languages, and it is able to accomplish this through its modular design.

28

Object Model

As with other aspects of JavaScript and JScript, WSH is based on an object model hierarchy. The majority of this hierarchy, which consists of 14 objects and can be seen in Figure 28.3, stems from the parent `WScript` object.

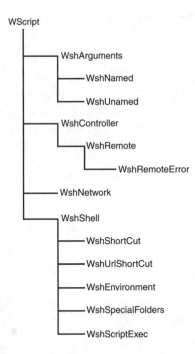

FIGURE 28.3   WSH object model hierarchy.

When looking at this figure, it is worth mentioning that not every object can be instantiated directly. The `WScript` object is available in every script and does not need to be explicitly instantiated. Other objects that are instantiated are the `WshController`, `WshNetwork`, and `WshShell`. To create instances of these objects, you use the `CreateObject()` method. All other child objects are indirectly created through the top-level objects. Additionally, the object model exposes various COM objects, which can be manipulated.

Benefits and Limitations

WSH has both benefits and limitations. Using JScript or VBScript, WSH provides you direct access to a Windows computer and its resources. You can directly manipulate the Registry, set default printers, run remote scripts, and more.

This low-memory scripting host works well with scripts that require little user interaction. So for things such as entering logon scripts and batch processes, and performing administrative tasks, WSH is a great tool to use. However, with this power come disadvantages.

Giving a script direct access to your local computer's resources can be very dangerous. Should a developer decide to write a malicious script, a lot of damage could be done. For this reason, many administrators choose to disable the WSH functionality in Windows.

Additionally, WSH is limited in other respects. The graphical components are limited because there are no custom dialogs or anything of that sort. So, if you want to add nice graphical interactions with users, your program will need to rely on the various tools available with whichever language you choose.

Windows Script Components

As you saw in Figure 28.2, many different components are tied together to create the whole Windows Script Host object model. Each of these components is important in terms of the capabilities that it provides. In this section we will discuss some of these objects and what they can be used for in more detail. But first, let's look at the various methods of executing these scripts.

Methods of Executing Scripts

To run a WSH script, you need to have the Windows Scripting Engine installed on your operating system. This is included in Windows 98/Me and 2000/XP. For earlier versions of Windows, the WSH engine can be downloaded and installed from the MSDN Scripting site at http://msdn.microsoft.com/scripting.

After scripts have been installed, they can be run in two different modes. These two modes are windows (wscript.exe) and command (cscript.exe) mode. The mode in which you run your scripts depends on what tasks you intend to accomplish. If you intend to have some user interaction and want to use graphical components, the windows mode is preferred. If your script needs to perform tasks that can be accomplished in MS-DOS or require little user interaction, the command mode should be used. Both of these modes can be started from the command line and have certain options that can be specified. These options are listed in Table 28.1.

TABLE 28.1   wscript.exe and cscript.exe Options

Type	Description
//B	Specifies batch mode, which suppresses user prompts and script error messages
//D	Enables the debugger
//E:engine	Runs the script with the specific script engine
//H:cscript	Uses cscript.exe as the default execution method
//H:wscript	Uses wscript.exe as the default execution method
//I	Specifies interactive mode, which displays user prompts and script errors

28

TABLE 28.1   Continued

Type	Description
//Job:<jobID>	Executes a specified jobID from within the .wsf file
//logo	Displays an execution banner
//nologo	Prevents display of the execution banner
//S	Saves the current command-line options
//T:nn	Sets the maximum number of seconds that a script can run
//U	Not available with wscript.exe
//X	Launches a program in the debugger
//?	Displays information for command parameters

To execute a script generically from the command line, adhere to the following syntax:

```
wscript <filename> [//options] [arguments]
cscript <filename> [//options] [arguments]
```

Arguments should be separated with a space. WSH also supports drag-and-drop for arguments, where you can drag and drop a file onto a WSH file, and—provided that your script is written to parse the argument—it will treat your dragged filename as an argument.

Windows-Based Scripts

Windows-based scripts allow you to take advantage of the limited graphical capabilities in WSH. This is particularly useful if your script requires visual user interaction. Keep in mind, though, that this environment doesn't have very complex dialog boxes. The graphical components are mostly limited to the tools available in VBScript or JScript such as pop-up dialogs.

There are three methods to execute scripts in the windows mode. The easiest is to simply double-click it. Alternatively, you could type the path to the file either in the Run dialog of the Start menu or from the command line. Any of these methods will work, and it is simply a matter of personal preference as to which one you use.

As an example, let's take a look at the script in Listing 28.2, which pops up a dialog with "Hello World!" written in it.

LISTING 28.2   Simple Hello World Script

```
<job>
  <script language="JScript">
    // Output the Hello World text.
    WScript.Echo("Hello World!");
  </script>
</job>
```

If we were to run the script by double-clicking on it, it will display a pop-up window as shown in Figure 28.4.

FIGURE 28.4   The WSH pop-up display box.

Command-Based Scripts

WSH scripts can also be run from the command prompt. This is performed at the command prompt using the `cscript.exe` executable. For example, if you wanted to run a script called `hello.wsf`, you would type the following at a command prompt:

```
cscript hello.wsf
```

This example, of course, assumes that you are running the script from the same directory where it is located. Otherwise, the path to the file will need to be specified. Any arguments or options passed to the script would be added after the script name. So, if you wanted to use the Interactive mode options and pass a string as the first argument, your script call would look similar to this:

```
cscript hello.wsf //I /arg1
```

Command-mode scripts can also display output, similar to running the script in windows mode. However, unlike the windows mode pop-up window, the command script output is suppressed to the same command-prompt window in which the script is run. This is one of the disadvantages to the command-mode scripts—no graphical components are provided.

In Figure 28.5 you can see the results of running Listing 28.2, which displays the Hello World text.

28

Objects

In the object model, you saw that many different objects compose the Windows Script Host. Each object has its own methods and properties associated with it, and the main objects from which all child objects stem are `WScript`, `WshController`, `WshNetwork`, and `WshShell`.

The three most commonly used ones that we'll discuss are `WScript`, `WshShell`, and `WshNetwork`. They provide the majority of the top-level functionality. Let us take a look at what each of them can do.

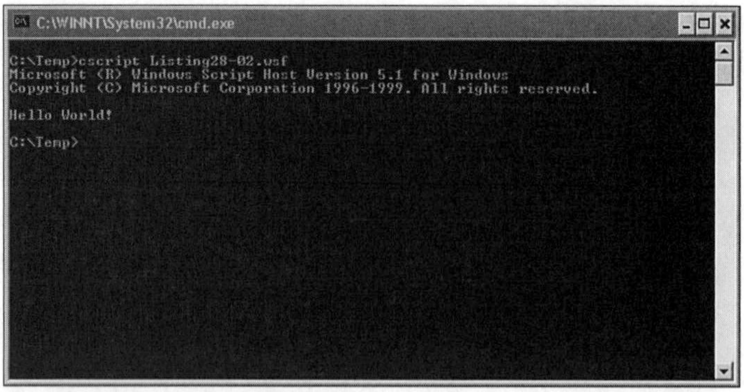

FIGURE 28.5   Command-based output display.

WScript

The WScript object is the root-level object, which does not need to be instantiated and is available from any script file. It can be used for a number of different tasks, including using it as an informational object to get script filenames, handle command-line arguments, as well as handle host information. It can also be used to create objects, connect to and disconnect from objects, sink events, stop script execution, and output information. Back in Listing 28.1, we used it in its simplest form by using its Echo() method to output the username of the person running the script.

As mentioned earlier, WScript can create any type of child object by using the CreateObject method.

Suppose that you wanted to create a new WshShell object. You could do so by using the following line.

```
WshShellObj = WScript.CreateObject("WScript.Shell");
```

By now you are probably saying to yourself, "This is great, but what can I do with a new WshShell object?" Let's take a look.

WshShell

WshShell is a very useful object for manipulating the Registry, creating shortcuts, starting new shell processes, and reading system information. It provides the ENVIRONMENT collection for your program, which allows you to access or manipulate environment variables. Let's look at a simple example to help illustrate this point.

In Listing 28.3, which creates a shortcut on the desktop to the Amazon.com Web site, we will use the CreateObject() method of the root WScript object and create a WshShell object named WshShellObj. Next we need to specify that the shortcut is to be created on the desktop. To accomplish this, the SpecialFolders() method is used with "Desktop" as the parameter. Then we call the `CreateShortcut()` method and pass it the path for our shortcut. Finally the target path for the shortcut is specified and the shortcut is saved.

LISTING 28.3   Example of Creating a Shortcut with the WshShell Object

```
<job>
  <script language="JScript">

    // Create a WshShell object.
    WshShellObj = WScript.CreateObject("WScript.Shell");

    // Specify the Desktop as a folder.
    myDesktop = WshShellObj.SpecialFolders("Desktop");

    // Create a shortcut to the Amazon.com website.
    var urlShortcut = WshShellObj.CreateShortcut(myDesktop + "\\Amazon.url");
    urlShortcut.TargetPath = "http://www.amazon.com";
    urlShortcut.Save();

  </script>
</job>
```

WshNetwork

The `WshNetwork` object is used to perform many different network-related tasks. With this object, you can add printer connections, obtain the computer name, map network drives, set default printers, get user domains, and more. These types of tasks can be very useful to a Windows network administrator.

Suppose, for example, a new network printer has been added and the network administrator wants to make it as easy as possible for users to add this printer to their machine. The administrator could create a script that all users could use to add the printer to their machines simply by running the script. In Listing 28.4, we see the code to add this new printer.

LISTING 28.4   Adding a Printer with WshNetwork Object

```
<job>
  <script language="JScript">

    // Create Arguments object.
    WshArgObj = WScript.Arguments;

    // Read in the username and password.
    var userName = WshArgObj.Item(0);
    var passwd = WshArgObj.Item(1);
```

28

LISTING 28.4   Continued

```
    // Create a new Network object and add printer.
    var WshNetwork = WScript.CreateObject("WScript.Network");

    // Contains the network path to the printer.
    var printer = "\\printers\NewPrinter";

    var localName = "myNewPrinter";

    WshNetwork.AddPrinterConnection(localName, printer, userName, passwd);

  </script>
</job>
```

Because user input is required for this particular script, it is recommended that the command-line method, cscript.exe, is used to execute the script. The user would specify his username and password as the arguments.

Assuming that the file is named addPrinter.wsf, the user's name was Betty, and the password was pass123, for example, you would be executing the script in an MS-DOS window as follows:

```
cscript addPrinter.wsf Betty pass123
```

Remote Scripting

With version 5.6 of the WSH, it is also possible to execute scripts remotely. This allows you to remotely administer various automation tasks to computers across the network. These tasks can even be executed simultaneously. You can remotely start, stop, and get the status of WSH scripts. If an error occurs through the WshRemoteError object, you can get the character, line number, error description, and even source code for the error. When a remote script is executed, the local machine actually copies the script to the remote machine before execution.

Before a remote script can be executed, though, the remote machine must be set up with the proper security settings. To set up remote scripting on your machine, you need to follow three simple steps.

1. Install WSH version 5.6 (if not already installed).

2. Add yourself to the remote machine's local administrators group.

3. Enable remote WSH through the Poledit.exe executable.

After this is taken care of, your machine is ready for remote scripting!

> **CAUTION**
>
> There is one caveat to remote scripting. Remote scripts can only be executed on the Windows NT/2000/XP environments. The scripting engine available for Windows 95/98/Me does not support this functionality, because you cannot properly authenticate users before running a script.

How to Use Remote Scripting

So how do you use remote scripting? The WSH has provided the `WshRemote` object and various properties and methods to control the execution of your remote scripts. The `WshRemote` object is created through the `WshController` object.

To use this object, you must first create an instance of the `WshController` with the `CreateObject()` method. After you have the controller object, you can use the `CreateScript()` method to specify which script you want to execute remotely. This method returns a `WshRemote` object instance that can be used with its `execute()` method to run the script remotely.

It is worth pointing out that, as with most computer programs, not all scripts run without errors. This is not, however, a problem within the WSH environment. The WSH object model includes the `WshRemoteError` object, which can be used to obtain error information in case of a problem. It is not an object that is directly instantiated, but is created when an error occurs and is accessible as a child of the `WshRemote` object. To better understand how this works, let's take a look at an example.

Remote Scripting Example

Let's imagine we have a maintenance script that is to be run remotely on a machine named `blue`. A controller object, `WshCtrlObj`, is first created. Then an instance of the `WshRemote` object is created using the `CreateScript()` method. The path of the script to be run and the machine name are passed as parameters. We specify some events to be caught and then execute the script.

After we execute the script, a print statement is added to output the status. Our current script sleeps while waiting for the remote script to finish execution. Should any errors occur, the function `remote_Error()` will display error information. The complete code for this example is contained in Listing 28.5.

LISTING 28.5   Remote Scripting Example

```
<job>
  <script language="JScript">

    // Create a WshController object.
```

28

LISTING 28.5 Continued

```
WshCtrlObj = WScript.CreateObject("WSHController");

// Create a WshRemote object.
remoteScript = WshCtrlObj.CreateScript("seturl.wsf", "\\blue");

// Catch events.
WScript.ConnectObject(RemoteScript, "remote_");

// Start the script.
RemoteScript.Execute();

// Print the current status.
WScript.Echo("The current status of the remote script is: " +
             ➥RemoteScript.Status);

while (remoteScript.Status !=5) {
  WScript.Sleep(100);
}

WScript.DisconnectObject(RemoteScript);

// Catch errors.
function remote_Error(){
  var myError = RemoteScript.Error;
  var errorString  = "Error (" + myError.Line + "): ";
  errorString += myError.Description + "\n";
  WScript.Echo(errorString);
  WScript.Quit(-1);
}

  </script>
</job>
```

Summary

In this chapter, we have discussed several aspects of the Windows Script Host. We have taken a look at the object model and a few specific objects in detail. We discussed the methods of running scripts and even how to run scripts remotely. Even though this chapter represented a brief introduction to WSH, you can quickly see the power of using it either at home or at work to automate tasks.

This chapter concludes our focus on using JavaScript on the server side. In our next and last section we are going to take a look at some essential JavaScript programming techniques, including how to perform regular expression pattern matching, error handling, and debugging.

PART VII

Essential Programming Techniques

IN THIS PART

Pattern Matching Using Regular Expressions

One of the most powerful attributes of JavaScript is its capability to perform pattern matching. In fact, JavaScript's implementation of pattern matching, called regular expressions, was taken directly from one of the best pattern-matching languages available today—Perl. In fact, pattern matching as defined in ECMAScript, third edition, was taken directly from Perl 5. Pattern matching allows you to find complex patterns in strings with just a line or two of code. To implement some of the simplest pattern-matching expressions without regular expressions would require many lines of code. In this chapter, you will learn the syntax used to create regular expressions and try your hand at creating a couple of JavaScript programs that make use of regular expressions.

Creating Regular Expressions

Although regular expressions may seem like a mystical power, you, as a JavaScript developer, will see them as little more than strings that contain letters, numbers, and symbols. You just create the pattern and JavaScript does the work. To make regular expressions easy to work with, they are conveniently contained in their own JavaScript object called RegExp. Creating regular expressions is very similar to creating strings in that regular expressions can be created with an object constructor or with just an assignment operator (=).

RegExp() Constructor

Because a regular expression is an object in JavaScript, you can simply pass in your pattern as an argument to a RegExp() constructor and then assign the resulting RegExp object to a variable. For example, the following line of code creates a `RegExp` object called `firstName` that contains the pattern `John`.

```
var firstName = new RegExp("John");
```

Do not worry about what the pattern means (that will be discussed shortly), but rather focus on the syntax used to create the `RegExp` object.

Assignment Operator

The second way to create a regular expression is to assign the pattern directly to a variable and let JavaScript determine that the variable should be a `RegExp` object. The following line of code also creates a `RegExp` object called `firstName` that contains the pattern `John`.

```
var firstName = /John/;
```

At this point, you may be wondering how JavaScript knows that you want `firstName` to be a `RegExp` object rather than a `String` object. The difference is that strings are enclosed in single or double quotes, whereas patterns are enclosed in forward slashes (/). Notice that the forward slashes (/) are not needed in the `RegExp()` constructor because it can be distinguished from the `String()` constructor.

Regular Expression Syntax

Now that you know how to create a regular expression object, the next step is to understand the syntax used to create the actual pattern. As mentioned earlier, the pattern syntax is taken directly from Perl. If you have used Perl before, this will look familiar. Table 29.1 lists all of the special pattern-matching characters.

TABLE 29.1   Pattern-Matching Characters

Character	Description
\w	Matches any word character (alphanumeric).
\W	Matches any non-word character.
\s	Matches any whitespace character (tab, newline, carriage return, form feed, vertical tab).
\S	Matches any non-whitespace character.
\d	Matches any numerical digit.
\D	Matches any character that is not a number.
[\b]	Matches a backspace.
.	Matches any character except a newline.
[...]	Matches any one character within the brackets.
[^...]	Matches any one character not within the brackets.
[x-y]	Matches any character in the range x to y.
[^x-y]	Matches any character not in the range x to y.
{x,y}	Matches the previous item at least x times but not to exceed y times.

TABLE 29.1   Continued

Character	Description
{x,}	Matches the previous item at least x times.
{x}	Matches the previous item exactly x times.
?	Matches the previous item once or not at all.
+	Matches the previous item at least once.
*	Matches the previous item any number of times or not at all.
|	Matches the string to the left or the right of the | character.
(...)	Groups everything inside parentheses into a subpattern.
\x	Matches the same characters that resulted from the subpattern in group number x. Groups that are designated with parentheses are numbered from left to right.
^	Matches the beginning of the string or beginning of a line in multi-line matches.
$	Matches the end of the string or the end of a line in multi-line matches.
\b	Matches the position between a word character and a non-word character.
\B	Matches the position that is not between a word character and a non-word character.

Some of the characters listed in the table are fairly straightforward, but others are bit cryptic. The following sections examine each one.

\w and \W

The lowercase w (\w) matches any word character. A word character is alphanumeric, which means it can be either an alphabetic character (a–z) or a number (0–9). The uppercase W (\W) is the opposite of its little brother (\w) in that it matches any non-word character. For example, in Listing 29.1 the search pattern

```
var regExpObj = /\w\W/;
```

finds b? in the search string but does not find ?b because the first character must be a letter or a number, and the second character cannot be a letter or a number. The test for a match is accomplished with the test method of the regular expression object. If the string that is passed in to the method has a match, true is returned; otherwise, false is returned. You can learn more about the test method as well as other methods in the section called "Using Regular Expressions" later in this chapter.

LISTING 29.1   Match Any Word or Non-Word Character

```
<html>
<head>
<title>Match Any Word or Non-Word Character</title>
</head>

<body>
```

29

LISTING 29.1   Continued

```
<h2>Match Any Word or Non-Word Character</h2>

Pattern = \w\W <br /><br />

<script type="text/javascript">

var regExpObj = /\w\W/;

//Test for "b?"
document.write("Test for String \"b?\" returns ");
document.write(regExpObj.test("b?"));
document.write("<br /><br />");

//Test for "?b"
document.write("Test for String \"b?\" returns ");
document.write(regExpObj.test("?b"));
document.write("<br /><br />");
</script>

</body>
</html>
```

\s and \S

The lowercase s (\s) matches any whitespace character. A whitespace character is a tab, newline, carriage return, form feed, or vertical tab. The uppercase S (\S) is the opposite of its little brother (\s) in that it matches any non-whitespace character. For example, in Listing 29.2 the search pattern

```
var regExpObj = /\s\S/;
```

finds a carriage return character that is followed by the letter g but does not find the letter g followed by a carriage return.

LISTING 29.2   Match Any Whitespace or Non-Whitespace Characters

```
<html>
<head>
<title> Match Any Whitespace or Non-Whitespace Characters </title>
</head>

<body>
```

LISTING 29.2   Continued

```
<h2> Match Any Whitespace or Non-Whitespace Characters </h2>

Pattern = \s\S <br /><br />

<script type="text/javascript">

var regExpObj = /\s\S/;

//Test for "\ng"
document.write("Test for String \"\\ng\" returns ");
document.write(regExpObj.test("\ng"));
document.write("<br /><br />");

//Test for "g\n"
document.write("Test for String \"g\\n\" returns ");
document.write(regExpObj.test("g\n"));
document.write("<br /><br />");

</script>

</body>
</html>
```

\d and \D

The lowercase d (\d) matches any number between zero (0) and nine (9). The uppercase D (\D) is the opposite of its little brother (\d) in that it matches any character that is not a number. For example, in Listing 29.3 the search pattern

```
var regExpObj = /\d\D/;
```

finds 4p in a search string but does not find p4 because the first character must be a number, and the second character cannot be a number.

LISTING 29.3   Match Any Numerical or Non-Numerical Characters

```
<html>
<head>
<title>Match Any Numerical or Non-Numerical Characters</title>
</head>

<body>
```

LISTING 29.3   Continued

```
<h2>Match Any Numerical or Non-Numerical Characters</h2>

Pattern = \d\D <br /><br />

<script type="text/javascript">

var regExpObj = /\d\D/;

//Test for "4p"
document.write("Test for String \"4p\" returns ");
document.write(regExpObj.test("4p"));
document.write("<br /><br />");

//Test for "p4"
document.write("Test for String \"p4\" returns ");
document.write(regExpObj.test("p4"));
document.write("<br /><br />");

</script>

</body>
</html>
```

[\b]

A lowercase b in brackets ([\b]) is used to match the backspace character. There are not very many instances when you would want to search for a backspace character, but if you do, this is the search pattern syntax to use. For example, in Listing 29.4 the search pattern

```
var regExpObj = /[\b]\d/;
```

finds a backspace character that is followed by the number 5 but does not find the number 5 followed by a backspace character.

LISTING 29.4   Matching the Backspace Character

```
<html>
<head>
<title>Matching the Backspace Character</title>
</head>

<body>
```

LISTING 29.4   Continued

```
<h2>Matching the Backspace Character</h2>

Pattern = \b\w <br /><br />

<script type="text/javascript">

var regExpObj = /\b\w/;

//Test for "/bg"
document.write("Test for String \"//bg" returns ");
document.write(regExpObj.test("g/b"));
document.write("<br /><br />");

//Test for "g/b"
document.write("Test for String \"g//b" returns ");
document.write(regExpObj.test("g/b"));
document.write("<br /><br />");

</script>

</body>
</html>
```

The Period

A period (.) by itself is used to match any character except a newline character. For example, in Listing 29.5 the search pattern

```
var regExpObj = /good.bye/;
```

finds the string "good bye" because the two words are separated by a space but no match is found when the two words are separated by a newline character.

LISTING 29.5   Matching Any Character Except A Newline Character

```
<html>
<head>
<title>Match Any Character except A Newline Character</title>
</head>

<body>
<h2>Match Any Character except A Newline Character</h2>
```

LISTING 29.5   Continued

```
Pattern = good.bye <br /><br />

<script type="text/javascript">

var regExpObj = /good.bye/;

//Test for "good bye"
document.write("Test for String \"good bye\" returns ");
document.write(regExpObj.test("good bye"));
document.write("<br /><br />");

//Test for "good\nbye"
document.write("Test for String \"good\\nbye\" returns ");
document.write(regExpObj.test("good\nbye"));
document.write("<br /><br />");

</script>

</body>
</html>
```

[...] and [^...]

Brackets are used to match any one character that appears within the brackets. If a caret
(^) appears directly after the left bracket, any characters that do not appear within the
brackets are matched. For example, in Listing 29.6 the search pattern

```
var regExpObj = /[abc][^def]/;
```

finds ag in a search string but does not find ge because the first character must be either a,
b, or c, and the second character cannot be d, e, or f.

LISTING 29.6   Matching Any One Character

```
<html>
<head>
<title>Matching Any One Character</title>
</head>

<body>
<h2>Matching Any One Character</h2>

Pattern = [abc][^def]<br /><br />
```

LISTING 29.6   Continued

```html
<script type="text/javascript">

var regExpObj = /[abc][^def]/;

//Test for "ag"
document.write("Test for String \"ag\" returns ");
document.write(regExpObj.test("ag"));
document.write("<br /><br />");

//Test for "ge"
document.write("Test for String \"ge\" returns ");
document.write(regExpObj.test("ge"));
document.write("<br /><br />");

</script>

</body>
</html>
```

[x-y] and [^x-y]

A dash can be used within the bracket syntax to specify a range rather than having to type a long list of characters. Any character in the range x to y that appears in the search string, where x and y are characters that you specify, will result in a positive match. If a caret (^) appears directly after the left bracket but before the range, any characters that are not in the range specified are matched. For example, the previous bracket example could have been written using

```javascript
var regExpObj = /[a-c][^d-f]/;
```

as shown in Listing 29.7. In this example the pattern would find ag in a search string but would not find ge because the first character must be either a, b, or c, and the second character cannot be d, e, or f.

LISTING 29.7   Match Any Character in Range

```html
<html>
<head>
<title>Match Any Character in Range</title>
</head>

<body>
<h2>Match Any Character in Range</h2>
```

29

LISTING 29.7   Continued

```
Pattern = [a-c][^d-f]<br /><br />

<script type="text/javascript">

var regExpObj = /[abc][^def]/;

//Test for "ag"
document.write("Test for String \"ag\" returns ");
document.write(regExpObj.test("ag"));
document.write("<br /><br />");

//Test for "ge"
document.write("Test for String \"ge\" returns ");
document.write(regExpObj.test("ge"));
document.write("<br /><br />");

</script>

</body>
</html>
```

{x,y}, {x,}, and {x}

There are a few variations of the curly braces syntax, but all are associated with the repetition of the character preceding the left curly brace. In this syntax, x and y represent numbers. If both x and y are used in the syntax, the preceding character is matched at least x times but not to exceed y times. If only x is provided followed by a comma, the preceding character is matched at least x times. Finally, if x is provided by itself (without a comma), the preceding character is matched exactly x times. For example, in Listing 29.8 the search pattern

```
var regExpObj = /cho{1,2}se/;
```

finds chose or choose in a search string but does not find chooose because the character o must be matched at least 1 time but must not exceed 2 times.

LISTING 29.8   Match Character Repetition

```
<html>
<head>
<title>Match Character Repetition</title>
</head>
```

LISTING 29.8   Continued

```
<body>
<h2>Match Character Repetition</h2>

Pattern = cho{1,2}se<br /><br />

<script type="text/javascript">

var regExpObj = /cho{1,2}se/;

//Test for "chose"
document.write("Test for String \"chose\" returns ");
document.write(regExpObj.test("chose"));
document.write("<br /><br />");

//Test for "choose"
document.write("Test for String \"choose\" returns ");
document.write(regExpObj.test("choose"));
document.write("<br /><br />");

//Test for "chooose"
document.write("Test for String \"chooose\" returns ");
document.write(regExpObj.test("chooose"));
document.write("<br /><br />");

</script>

</body>
</html>
```

?, +, and *

There are three operators that perform some specific tasks associated with the curly braces. They are the question mark (?), the plus sign (+), and the asterisk (*). The question mark (?) matches the preceding character once or not at all. The plus sign (+) matches the preceding character at least once. Finally, the asterisk (*) matches the preceding character any number of times or not at all.

Listing 29.9 demonstrates how to use the question mark by creating the search pattern

```
var regExpObj = /ab?a/;
```

29

This expression finds a match within the strings aba and aa but not in the string abba because there are two b's.

LISTING 29.9   Match Once or Not at All

```
<html>
<head>
<title>Match Once Or Not At All</title>
</head>

<body>
<h2>Match Once Or Not At All</h2>

Pattern = ab?a<br /><br />

<script type="text/javascript">

var regExpObj = /ab?a/;

//Test for "aa"
document.write("Test for String \"aa\" returns ");
document.write(regExpObj.test("aa"));
document.write("<br /><br />");

//Test for "aba"
document.write("Test for String \"aba\" returns ");
document.write(regExpObj.test("aba"));
document.write("<br /><br />");

//Test for "abba"
document.write("Test for String \"abba\" returns ");
document.write(regExpObj.test("abba"));
document.write("<br /><br />");

</script>

</body>
</html>
```

Listing 29.10 demonstrates how to use the plus sign by creating the search pattern

```
var regExpObj = /ab+a/;
```

This expression finds a match within the strings aba and abba but not in the string aa because there was no b.

LISTING 29.10   Match at Least Once

```
<html>
<head>
<title>Match At Least Once</title>
</head>

<body>
<h2>Match At Least Once</h2>

Pattern = ab+a<br /><br />

<script type="text/javascript">

var regExpObj = /ab+a/;

//Test for "aa"
document.write("Test for String \"aa\" returns ");
document.write(regExpObj.test("aa"));
document.write("<br /><br />");

//Test for "aba"
document.write("Test for String \"aba\" returns ");
document.write(regExpObj.test("aba"));
document.write("<br /><br />");

//Test for "abba"
document.write("Test for String \"abba\" returns ");
document.write(regExpObj.test("abba"));
document.write("<br /><br />");

</script>

</body>
</html>
```

Finally Listing 29.11 demonstrates how to use the asterisk by creating the search pattern

```
var regExpObj = /ab*a/;
```

This expression finds a match in the strings aa, aba, and abba because the character b can exist any number of times or not at all.

29

LISTING 29.11   Match Any Number of Times or Not at All

```
<html>
<head>
<title>Match Any Number Of Times Or Not At All</title>
</head>

<body>
<h2>Match Any Number Of Times Or Not At All</h2>

Pattern = ab*a<br /><br />

<script type="text/javascript">

var regExpObj = /ab*a/;

//Test for "aa"
document.write("Test for String \"aa\" returns ");
document.write(regExpObj.test("aa"));
document.write("<br /><br />");

//Test for "aba"
document.write("Test for String \"aba\" returns ");
document.write(regExpObj.test("aba"));
document.write("<br /><br />");

//Test for "abba"
document.write("Test for String \"abba\" returns ");
document.write(regExpObj.test("abba"));
document.write("<br /><br />");

</script>

</body>
</html>
```

Logical OR (|)

The vertical bar character (|) acts like a logical OR by matching the string on either the left or right of the vertical bar (|). For example, in Listing 29.12 the search pattern

```
var regExpObj = /cat|dog/;
```

finds cat in the string "A hungry cat" and dog in the string "A hungry dog" but does not find dog or cat in the string "A hungry cow".

LISTING 29.12   Match Either String

```html
<html>
<head>
<title>Match Either String</title>
</head>

<body>
<h2>Match Either String</h2>

Pattern = cat|dog<br /><br />

<script type="text/javascript">

var regExpObj = /cat|dog/;

//Test for "A hungry dog"
document.write("Test for String \"A hungry dog\" returns ");
document.write(regExpObj.test("A hungry dog"));
document.write("<br /><br />");

//Test for "A hungry cat"
document.write("Test for String \"A hungry cat\" returns ");
document.write(regExpObj.test("A hungry cat"));
document.write("<br /><br />");

//Test for "A hungry cow"
document.write("Test for String \"A hungry cow\" returns ");
document.write(regExpObj.test("A hungry cow"));
document.write("<br /><br />");

</script>

</body>
</html>
```

29

(...)

Parentheses allow you to subnest search patterns inside other search patterns. For example, in Listing 29.13 the search pattern

```
var regExpObj = /f(a|o)r/;
```

finds far or for but does not find fmt.

LISTING 29.13   Match Grouping

```
<html>
<head>
<title>Match Grouping</title>
</head>

<body>
<h2>Match Grouping</h2>

Pattern = f(a|o)r<br /><br />

<script type="text/javascript">

var regExpObj = /f(a|o)r/;

//Test for "far"
document.write("Test for String \"far\" returns ");
document.write(regExpObj.test("far"));
document.write("<br /><br />");

//Test for "for"
document.write("Test for String \"for\" returns ");
document.write(regExpObj.test("for"));
document.write("<br /><br />");

//Test for "fmt"
document.write("Test for String \"fmt\" returns ");
document.write(regExpObj.test("fmt"));
document.write("<br /><br />");

</script>

</body>
</html>
```

\x

You can use the \x in conjunction with parentheses to match the same characters that resulted from the subpattern in group number x. Groups are designated with parentheses and are numbered from left to right. For example, in Listing 29.14 the search pattern

```
var regExpObj = /f(a|o)r\1/;
```

finds fara or foro but does not find faro or fora.

LISTING 29.14   Match Group Number

```html
<html>
<head>
<title>Match Group Number</title>
</head>

<body>
<h2>Match Group Number</h2>

Pattern = f(a|o)r\1<br /><br />

<script type="text/javascript">

var regExpObj = /f(a|o)r\1/;

//Test for "fara"
document.write("Test for String \"fara\" returns ");
document.write(regExpObj.test("fara"));
document.write("<br /><br />");

//Test for "foro"
document.write("Test for String \"foro\" returns ");
document.write(regExpObj.test("foro"));
document.write("<br /><br />");

//Test for "faro"
document.write("Test for String \"faro\" returns ");
document.write(regExpObj.test("faro"));
document.write("<br /><br />");

//Test for "fora"
document.write("Test for String \"fora\" returns ");
document.write(regExpObj.test("fora"));
document.write("<br /><br />");

</script>

</body>
</html>
```

^

When the caret character (^) is placed in front of text, a match will only be found if the text appears at the beginning of a search string or the beginning of a line in multi-line matches. For example, in Listing 29.15 the search pattern

```
var regExpObj = /^The/;
```

only finds the word The when it appeared at the beginning of the line string "The Big House". The word The could not be found in the string "He Lived In The Big House" because it did not occur at the very beginning of the string.

LISTING 29.15   Match Beginning of Line

```
<html>
<head>
<title>Match Beginning Of Line</title>
</head>

<body>
<h2>Match Beginning Of Line</h2>

Pattern = ^The<br /><br />

<script type="text/javascript">

var regExpObj = /^The/;

//Test for "The Big House."
document.write("Test for String \"The Big House.\" returns ");
document.write(regExpObj.test("The Big House."));
document.write("<br /><br />");

//Test for "He Lived In The Big House."
document.write("Test for String \"He Lived In The Big House.\" returns ");
document.write(regExpObj.test("He Lived In The Big House."));
document.write("<br /><br />");

</script>

</body>
</html>
```

$

The dollar sign ($) is the opposite of the caret character (^) in that when it is placed in after some text, a match will only be found if the text appears at the end of a search string or the end of a line, in multi-line matches. For example, in Listing 29.16 the search pattern

```
var regExpObj = /House$/;
```

finds the word House only when it appears at the end of the string "The Big House".

LISTING 29.16   Match End of Line

```html
<html>
<head>
<title>Match End Of Line</title>
</head>

<body>
<h2>Match End Of Line</h2>

Pattern = House$<br /><br />

<script type="text/javascript">

var regExpObj = /House$/;

//Test for "The Big House"
document.write("Test for String \"The Big House\" returns ");
document.write(regExpObj.test("The Big House"));
document.write("<br /><br />");

//Test for "House On The Hill"
document.write("Test for String \"House On The Hill\" returns ");
document.write(regExpObj.test("House On The Hill"));
document.write("<br /><br />");

</script>

</body>
</html>
```

29

\b and \B

The lowercase b (\b) matches a position between a word character and a non-word charac-ter. Keep in mind that a word character is alphanumeric, which means it can be either an alphabetic character (a–z) or a number (0–9). The uppercase B (\B) is the opposite of its little brother (\b) in that it matches the position that is not between a word character and a non-word character. For example, in Listing 29.17 the search pattern

```
var regExpObj = /cat\b/;
```

finds the word cat in the string "The cat is sleepy" because the word cat is followed by a space, which is a non-word character. But the word catch can not be found in the string "Please catch the bus" because the c after the t in the word catch is a word character.

LISTING 29.17   Match Position Between Word and Non-Word Character

```
<html>
<head>
<title>Match Position Between Word And Non-Word Character</title>
</head>

<body>
<h2>Match Position Between Word And Non-Word Character</h2>

Pattern = cat\b <br /><br />

<script type="text/javascript">

var regExpObj = /cat\b/;

//Test for "The cat is sleepy"
document.write("Test for String \"The cat is sleepy\" returns ");
document.write(regExpObj.test("The cat is sleepy"));
document.write("<br /><br />");

//Test for "Please catch the bus"
document.write("Test for String \"Please catch the bus\" returns ");
document.write(regExpObj.test("Please catch the bus"));
document.write("<br /><br />");

</script>

</body>
</html>
```

Maybe you are starting to ask yourself, "What if I want to match a character that has special meaning such as a dollar sign?" All the characters that have special meaning to the regular expression object can be used literally (escaped) by using a backslash (\) followed by the character in question. Table 29.2 lists all the characters that conflict with pattern-matching symbols.

TABLE 29.2   Escaped Characters

Character	Description
\f	Form feed
\n	Newline
\r	Carriage return
\t	Tab
\v	Vertical tab
\/	Forward slash (/)
\\	Backward slash (\)
\.	Period (.)
*	Asterisk(*)
\+	Plus (+)
\?	Question mark (?)
\¦	Vertical bar (I)
\(	Left parenthesis (()
\)	Right parenthesis ())
\[	Left bracket ([)
\]	Right bracket (])
\{	Left curly brace ({)
\}	Right curly brace (})
\XXX	ASCII character represented by the octal number XXX
\xHH	ASCII character represented by the hexadecimal number HH
\cX	The control character represented by X

There is one final piece of syntax that allows you to set some attributes associated with the regular expression. The attributes are shown in Table 29.3.

TABLE 29.3   Pattern-Matching Attributes

Character	Description
g	Global match. Find all possible matches.
i	Make matching case-insensitive.
m	Multi-line match. Search in string across multiple lines.

Unlike the syntax covered so far, these attributes are set outside the forward slashes that define the pattern when creating a regular expression with just an assignment operator.

29

For example, a regular expression that is to search globally for the word "bear" would look like the following:

```
var animalSearch = /bear/g;
```

If you are creating a regular expression using the `RegExp()` constructor, store the attributes as a string and pass the string in as the second argument of the constructor. For example, a regular expression that is to perform a case-insensitive search for the word "bear" would look like the following:

```
var animalSearch = new RegExp("bear","i");
```

Using Regular Expressions

Now that you have this really useful pattern assigned to a `RegExp` object, what do you do with it? There are two ways to utilize regular expressions. One way is through methods provided by the `RegExp` object, and the other is through methods provided by the `String` object. After all, the whole point of regular expressions is to have the ability to search for patterns within strings. The pattern-matching methods provided by the `RegExp` object are shown in Table 29.4, and the associated properties are shown in Table 29.5. Notice that these methods require that the `String` object to be searched be passed in as an argument.

TABLE 29.4   Pattern-Matching Methods in the RegExp Object

Method	Description
exec(*str*)	Searches for pattern in *str* and returns result
test(*str*)	Searches for pattern in *str* and returns true if match found; otherwise, false is returned
toString()	Returns a string value of the pattern formed by concatenating the strings "/", *source*, and "/"; plus any of the flags "g", "i", "m" that were set
(*str*)	Same as exec(*str*) method

TABLE 29.5   Pattern-Matching Properties in the RegExp Object

Property	Description
source	A string representation of the pattern associated with the current regular expression
global	The value of the global flag "g"
ignoreCase	The value of the ignorecase flag "i"
multi-line	The value of the multi-line flag "m"
lastIndex	Specifies the string position at which to start the next match

The pattern-matching methods provided by the `String` object are shown in Table 29.6. Notice that these methods require that the `RegExp` object for which you are searching be passed in as an argument.

TABLE 29.6   Pattern-Matching Methods in the String Object

Method	Description
`match(regExpObj)`	Searches for *regExpObj* pattern in string and returns result.
`replace(reqExpObj,str)`	Replaces all occurrences of the *regExpObj* pattern with *str*.
`search(reqExpObj)`	Returns the position of matching *regExpObj* pattern within the string.
`split(regExpObj,max)`	The string is split everywhere there is a matching *regExpObj* pattern up to *max* splits. The substrings are returned in an array.

Regular Expression Tester

The cryptic syntax used to create patterns for regular expressions can be a bit confusing, especially when you begin to mix and match functionality to create a complex search pattern. For this reason, this chapter includes a program for testing regular expressions. This program will not only help you learn how to create regular expressions using the `RegExp()` constructor, but it is also a great utility for creating and testing your own search patterns.

The utility performs either a search or a replace on the search string, replace string, and pattern that you enter, as shown in Figure 29.1. The power of this utility is that you can create a search string and a pattern, and then quickly verify that your pattern works as you intended. The code for the program is shown in Listing 29.18.

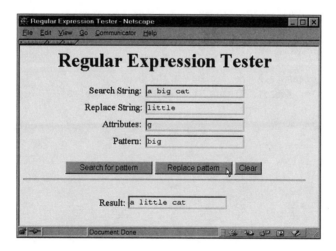

FIGURE 29.1   The Regular Expression Tester.

LISTING 29.18   The Regular Expression Tester

```
<html>
<head>
```

LISTING 29.18   Continued

```
<title>Regular Expression Tester</title>

<script type="text/javascript">

// The function searches for the pattern in searchStr.
function searchForPattern(searchStr,pattern,REattributes,theResult)
{
  //Create Regular Expression Object.
  var regExpObj = new RegExp(pattern,REattributes);

  //Populate the result field with the result of the search.
  theResult.value = regExpObj.exec(searchStr);
}

// This function replaces all occurrences of the pattern in
// searchStr with replaceStr.
function replacePattern(searchStr,replaceStr,pattern,REattributes,theResult)
{
  //Create Regular Expression Object.
  var regExpObj = new RegExp(pattern,REattributes);

  //Populate the result field with the result of the search.
  theResult.value = searchStr.replace(regExpObj,replaceStr);
}

// This function clears all the fields in the page.
function clearFields(field1, field2, field3, field4, field5)
{
  field1.value = "";
  field2.value = "";
  field3.value = "";
  field4.value = "";
  field5.value = "";
}

</script>
</head>

<body style="text-align:center">
<h1>Regular Expression Tester</h1>
<form name="myForm"">
<table border="0">
```

LISTING 29.18   Continued

```
  <tr align="right">
    <td>Search String:</td>
    <td><input type="text" name="searchString"></td>
  </tr>
  <tr align="right">
    <td>Replace String:</td>
    <td><input type="text" name="replaceString"></td>
  </tr>
  <tr align="right">
    <td>Attributes:</td>
    <td><input type="text" name="REattributes"></td>
  </tr>
  <tr align="right">
    <td>Pattern:</td>
    <td><input type="text" name="pattern"></td>
  </tr>
</table>
<br />
<input type="button"
       value="Search for pattern"
       onclick="searchForPattern(searchString.value,
                                 pattern.value,
                                 REattributes.value,
                                 result)">
<input type="button"
       value="Replace pattern"
       onclick="replacePattern(searchString.value,
                                 replaceString.value,
                                 pattern.value,
                                 REattributes.value,
                                 result)">
<input type="button"
       value="Clear"
       onclick="clearFields(searchString,
                                 replaceString,
                                 pattern,
                                 REattributes,
                                 result)">
<br /><hr /><br />
Result: <input type="text" name="result">
```

29

LISTING 29.18   Continued

```
</body>
</html>
```

The Regular Expression Tester can be broken down into four major parts: user interface, search function, replace function, and clear fields function.

User Interface

The user interface for the Regular Expression Tester consists of a form with five text boxes and three buttons. The searchString text box provides a place for you to enter the string that is to be searched for the specified pattern. The replaceString text box provides a place for you to enter the string that is to be used to replace parts of searchString where a pattern match is found. This field is only used when the Replace Pattern button is clicked. Pattern-matching attributes, such as global search/replace and case insensitivity, are placed in the attributes text box. The pattern text box provides a place for you to enter the regular expression search pattern that is to be searched for in the searchString. When the Search for Pattern or Replace Pattern button is clicked, the result of the search or replace is inserted into the result text box.

Search Function

When the Search for Pattern button is clicked, the onClick event handler calls the searchForPattern() function. This function passes the pattern and attributes information entered in the HTML form into the RegExp() constructor to create a RegExp object called regExpObj. The RegExp exec() method is then used to search for the pattern in the search string that was entered in the form. The result of the search is then placed into the result text box. If no match was found, the result text box will be empty.

Replace Function

When the Replace Pattern button is clicked, the onClick event handler calls the replacePattern() function. This function passes the pattern and attributes information entered in the HTML form into the RegExp() constructor to create a RegExp object called regExpObj. The replace() method of the searchStr object is then used to replace occurrences of the pattern in the searchStr with the replaceStr. The result of the search and replace is then put into the result text box. If no match was found, the searchStr will be placed into the result text box.

Clear Function

When the Clear button is clicked, the onClick event handler calls the clearFields() function. This function simply clears all of the text boxes.

Example: Phone Number Validation Program

So far, I have introduced regular expressions and discussed how to create them, as well as providing a program for helping you create your own search patterns. But how would you use regular expressions in a real-life programming situation? For e-commerce sites, it is important that phone numbers, addresses, and credit card numbers be validated before allowing a customer to place an order. Some validations, such as credit cards, must be processed on the server side, but other relatively static information can be validated on the client side. One such piece of information that lends itself to client-side validation is area codes. Because they do not change that often, area codes can be placed into Web pages and validated using the searching capability of JavaScript's regular expressions.

In this section, you will see how regular expressions can be used to validate area codes before allowing a customer to proceed. For the sake of this example, assume that you are building a Web site for a North Carolina–based company that sells widgets. Before you process a customer's online order, you want to make sure that the company has a valid North Carolina phone number, so that you do not have to make an out-of-state call should there be shipping problems.

Obviously, it would not be reasonable to put every North Carolina phone number into your Web page to validate phone numbers, but you can check to see if the customer's area code is a valid North Carolina area code. If it is not valid, you want to alert the user that he must enter a North Carolina phone number. If the area code is valid, you want to proceed with the order.

By creating a search pattern for North Carolina phone numbers, you could quickly determine if the phone number entered by the customer is valid. Given that all phone numbers have a 3-digit area code, followed by a 3-digit prefix, followed by a 4-digit extension, you see a pattern that looks like this: ###-###-####. Because the # characters represent digits, you could use the regular expression syntax \d to search for just numbers in these positions. At this point, the search pattern would look like the following:

```
/\d\d\d-\d\d\d-\d\d\d\d/
```

Notice that forward slashes (/) were used to represent the beginning and end of the pattern. Because you know there are currently only six valid area codes for North Carolina (828, 252, 704, 919, 910, 336), you can add this to your search pattern as follows:

```
/(828|252|704|919|910|336)-\d\d\d-\d\d\d\d/
```

You add a subsearch to the search pattern by placing all the possible area codes inside parentheses and separating each area code with a vertical bar character (|). The vertical bar tells the regular expression to try to match the number to the left or the right of the | character. This is essentially a logical OR operation. If the customer enters an area code that is specified in the subsearch, a positive match will be made.

29

Now that you have a search pattern for North Carolina phone numbers, all you have to do is create a user interface and test the pattern against phone numbers that customers enter. If you search for the search pattern in a string containing a valid phone number, the matching phone number will be returned. On the other hand, if you search for the search pattern in a string that does not contain a valid phone number, NULL will be returned. By testing for NULL, you can determine if the customer's phone number is valid. The following JavaScript function will perform the logic that was just described.

```
function validatePhone(areaCode,prefix,extension)
{
  //Assemble phone number.
  var phoneNum = new String(areaCode + "-" + prefix + "-" + extension);

  //Create a regular expression pattern that searches for
  //phone numbers with an area code of: 828, 252, 704, 919, 910, or 336.
  var regExpObj = /(828|252|704|919|910|336)-\d\d\d-\d\d\d\d/;

  if(regExpObj.exec(phoneNum) == null)
  {
    alert(phoneNum + " does not contain a valid North Carolina area code!");
  }
  else
  {
    alert("Thank you for your order!");
  }
}
```

By adding some additional HTML code to accept the customer's phone number and pass it to this function, you can create a full-blown phone number validation program. Listing 29.19 shows the completed phone number validation program.

LISTING 29.19   Phone Number Validation

```
<html>
<head>
<title>Phone Number Validation</title>
<script type="text/javascript">
function validatePhone(areaCode,prefix,extension)
{
  //Assemble phone number.
  var phoneNum = new String(areaCode + "-" + prefix + "-" + extension);

  //Create a regular expression pattern that searches for
  //phone numbers with an area code of: 828, 252, 704, 919, 910, or 336.
```

LISTING 29.19   Continued

```
  var regExpObj = /(828|252|704|919|910|336)-\d\d\d-\d\d\d\d/;

  if(regExpObj.exec(phoneNum) == null)
  {
    alert(phoneNum + " does not contain a valid North Carolina area code!");
  }
  else
  {
    alert("Thank you for your order!");
  }
}
</script>
</head>

<body style="text-align:center">
<h1>NC Sales Company</h1>

Thanks for your order.  Please provide us with your North
Carolina phone number so we can contact you if there are
any problems shipping your order.

<form name="form1">
Phone Number: <input type="text"
                     size="3"
                     maxlength="3"
                     name="area">-
              <input type="text"
                     size="3"
                     maxlength="3"
                     name="prefix">-
              <input type="text"
                     size="4"
                     maxlength="4"
                     name="extension">
<br /><br />
<input type="button"
       value="Submit"
       onClick="validatePhone(area.value,
                              prefix.value,
                              extension.value)">
</form>
```

29

LISTING 29.19   Continued

```
</body>
</html>
```

Now that the program is complete, give it a try. If you enter a valid phone number, such as 919-293-4444, and click the Submit button, you are presented with an alert box that tells you that your order is being processed. If you enter an invalid area code, such as 918-293-4444, and click the Submit button, the search fails and you are presented with the error message shown in Figure 29.2.

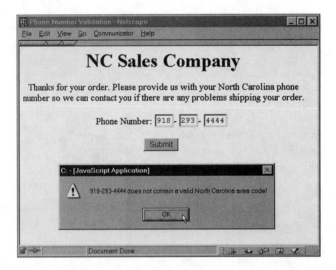

FIGURE 29.2   The Phone Number Validation program.

Example: Email Address Validation Program

Another possible real-life programming situation for regular expressions would be to validate the format of an email address on an e-commerce site. This email address might be used to let the user know of special deals or new items. The format of an email address is governed by a set of complex rules defined in a standard called RFC 882. To keep things simple, we will use a more rigid format.

The format we will code will be one that looks like this:

```
[username]@[domain prefix].[domain suffix]
```

In this case the username and domain prefix will be allowed to contain an unlimited number of alphanumeric characters. The domain suffix will be restricted to the strings com and net. An at character (@) will separate the username and the domain prefix, and a period (.) will separate the domain prefix from the domain suffix.

So how might a regular expression look that represents this format? Let's begin with the username. The username must contain one or more alphanumeric characters followed by the at character (@). This would be represented with the following regular expression syntax:

```
var regExpObj = /^\w{1,}@/;
```

Notice that the caret (^) is added to ensure that there is nothing in front of the username. Next we need to test for the domain prefix. The domain prefix must contain one or more alphanumeric characters followed by a escaped period (.) as shown in the following regular expression syntax:

```
var regExpObj = /^\w{1,}@\w{1,}\./;
```

Finally, we need to add the domain suffix. In this example we are going to restrict the domain suffix to either com or net although there are many others in the real world. The test for these two strings is done using a subquery and OR logic. The final result is shown in the following regular expression syntax:

```
var regExpObj = /^\w{1,}@\w{1,}\.(com|net)/;
```

Now that we have a search pattern for email addresses, all you have to do is create a user interface and test the pattern against email addresses that customers enter. If you search for the search pattern in a string containing a valid email address, the matching email address will be returned. On the other hand, if you search for the search pattern in a string that does not contain a valid email address, NULL will be returned. By testing for NULL, you can determine if the customer's email address format is valid. Of course there is no way to determine if the address is a valid address. The following JavaScript function will perform the logic that was just described.

```
function validateEmail(emailAddress)
{
  // Create a regular expression pattern for verifying an email address.
  var regExpObj = /^\w{1,}@\w{1,}\.(com|net)/;

  if(regExpObj.exec(emailAddress) == null)
  {
    alert(emailAddress + " is not a valid email address format!");
  }
  else
  {
    alert("Future specials and news will be sent to this email address.");
```

29

```
      }
}
```

By adding some additional HTML code to accept the customer's email address and pass it to this function, you can create an email address format validation page. Listing 29.20 shows the completed email address format validation program.

LISTING 29.20   Email Address Format Validation

```
<html>
<head>
<title>Email Address Format Validation</title>
<script type="text/javascript">
function validateEmail(emailAddress)
{
  // Create a regular expression pattern for verifying an email address.
  var regExpObj = /^\w{1,}@\w{1,}\.(com|net)/;

  if(regExpObj.exec(emailAddress) == null)
  {
    alert(emailAddress + " is not a valid email address format!");
  }
  else
  {
    alert("Future specials and news will be sent to this email address.");
  }
}
</script>
</head>

<body style="text-align:center">
<h2>Email Address Format Validation</h2>

Please provide us with your email address so we can notify you of
special deals and news in the future.

<form name="form1">
Email: <input type="text"
                    size="25"
                    name="email">
<br /><br />
<input type="button"
      value="Submit"
```

LISTING 29.20   Continued

```
        onClick="validateEmail(email.value)">
</form>
</body>
</html>
```

Now that the program is complete, give it a try. If you enter a valid email address format, such as Jason@mydomain.com, and click the Submit button, you are presented with an alert box informing you that future specials and news will be sent to this email address, as shown in Figure 29.3. If you enter an invalid email address format, such as Jason.mydomain.org, and click the Submit button, the search fails and you are presented with the error message.

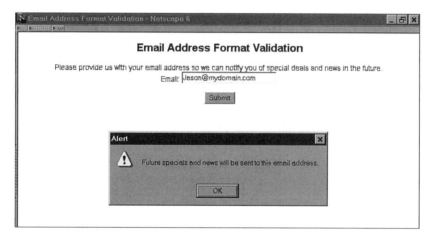

FIGURE 29.3   The Email Address Format Validation program.

Summary

In this chapter, you were introduced to the JavaScript regular expression object. You learned how to create search patterns and the RegExp objects that hold them. You also learned how to use the patterns you create to perform text searches using methods built into the RegExp and String objects.

To show you how to work with regular expressions in JavaScript, a Regular Expression Testing utility was outlined. This tool is especially handy in helping you create and test your own complex search patterns. Finally, a phone number validation program and an email address format validation program were created to demonstrate how regular expressions can be used in real-life programming situations.

29

CHAPTER **30**

Error Handling

Error handling in general is a combination of preventive controls (identifying and fixing errors before execution), detective controls (identifying errors during execution), and corrective controls (fixing errors found during execution). JavaScript—or, more accurately, the JavaScript interpreter built into JavaScript-compliant browsers—provides automated detective error control in the form of dialog boxes that display information when an error occurs. Although the newest browsers on the market allow you to specify a preference to suppress these alerts, they are still present and can be viewed when debugging a script.

Additionally, the introduction of new JavaScript scripting and debugging tools has helped developers take advantage of more automated preventive and—to a lesser extent—corrective controls. This chapter discusses some of the methods of identifying, fixing, and testing your JavaScript, as well as techniques for writing solid and maintainable code.

Types of Errors

JavaScript errors are identified by the JavaScript-compatible browser as the XHTML document is loaded and can be classified in the following three types:

- Syntax errors
- Runtime errors
- Logical errors

Over the next few sections we are going to look into each of these and understand how you can identify them when encountering problems. This will ultimately allow you to correct the problem, and create error-free code.

Syntax Errors

Syntax errors, which stem from incorrectly constructed code, are often caused by typographical errors, spelling mistakes, missing punctuation, and unmatched brackets. The following snippet demonstrates several common syntax errors, which we have specified in the comments:

```
// "function" is misspelled
fuction errorProne(){

  // should be initialized to zero "0"--not letter "o"
  var i = o;

  // variable "I" is not defined (should be small "i")
  for (i >= 0; I =< 10; i++) {
    document.write("The square of " + i + " is " + (i*i) + "<br>")

    // double quote expected after "is"
    document.write("The cube of " + i + " is ' + (i*i*i) + "<hr>");
  // missing closing braces to end for loop

}
```

Syntax errors are the most commonly made and most easily correctable errors in JavaScript. The JavaScript interpreter often does a good job of identifying the exact source of these errors in your code, and the resolution generally requires no more than a simple edit.

Another thing you need to be cautious of when writing code is that JavaScript is case sensitive. In particular, when you're using JavaScript's built-in objects—and their properties, methods, and events—be sure to use the exact syntax. If you are unsure of the syntax, check the resources provided in Chapter 1, "Introducing JavaScript," for links to both Microsoft, Netscape/Mozilla, and ECMA's sites for language reference information.

Runtime Errors

Runtime errors occur when a syntactically correct statement attempts to do a task that is impossible to perform. Common runtime errors include invalid function calls, mismatched data types, undeclared variable assignment, and arithmetic impossibilities (such as division by zero).

Runtime errors are reported by the browser much as syntax errors are reported; however, their resolution often requires a more thorough investigation of the code. The following snippet demonstrates a runtime error caused by a division by zero:

```
function mismatched() {
  var i = 10;
```

```
// this loop will cause a division by zero and unpredictable results
for (i <=10; i >= 0; i--) {
   document.write(i + " divided by twice its square (" +
                 (i*i*2) + ") = " + (i/(i*i*2)) + "<br>");
}
}
```

Logical Errors

Logical (or logic) errors occur when an application or function doesn't perform the way its users or designers intended. In other words, an application that has syntactically good code and is free of runtime errors but still produces incorrect results has logical errors.

Logical errors are the hardest type to identify and fix and usually demand a thorough test of the application, analysis of the result, and a review of the design. Many logical errors are generated from a poor understanding of the requirements, bad design, and subsequent incorrect code. Listing 30.1 demonstrates a logical error caused by evaluation of mismatched data types.

LISTING 30.1   Logical Error Example

```
<?xml version="1.0" encoding="UTF-8"?>
<!DOCTYPE html PUBLIC "-//W3C//DTD XHTML 1.0 Transitional//EN"
                      "DTD/xhtml1-transitional.dtd">
<html xmlns="http://www.w3.org/1999/xhtml" xml:lang="en">
<head>
   <title>JavaScript Unleashed</title>
</head>
<body>
   <script type="text/javascript">
   function mismatched() {
     var Constant = "10";
     var i = 10;
     for (i <=10; i > 0; i--) {
        document.write(i + " + " + Constant + " = " + (i + Constant) + "<br>");
     }
   }
   </script>
</body>
</html>
```

30

You can see in Figure 30.1 that the results displayed are clearly incorrect, even though the code ran successfully. In this case, JavaScript evaluates the result of the expression (i + Constant) as a string and concatenates the two operands.

> **NOTE**
>
> The JavaScript interpreter doesn't identify logical errors. You must test the functionality of your code to identify potential errors in your program logic.

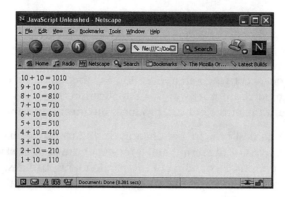

FIGURE 30.1   An example of a logical error.

Interpreting Error Messages

When the browser recognizes an error (syntax or runtime), it may then display a large dialog box, as shown in Figure 30.2. The information contained in this dialog box helps identify the approximate source and location of the error. These dialog boxes, which vary depending on your preferences and the browser, often contain some combination of the following information:

- The URL or filename where the error occurred.

- The line number in the file where the error occurred. This is a sequential line count from the beginning of the XHTML (or JS) file—not just the JavaScript code.

- A description of the error. This is valuable information in identifying the type of fix required.

- The actual code that contains the error. This is not always reliable information, because the source of the error might well occur before this line.

- A pointer indicating where on the line the error occurred. Again, don't rely on this too heavily; try to follow the flow of nearby code.

To better understand errors, let's look at some of the most common ones. Table 30.1 summarizes common JavaScript error messages and their potential causes.

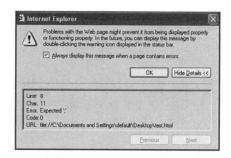

FIGURE 30.2   A JavaScript error message reporting a syntax error.

TABLE 30.1   Common JavaScript Error Messages

Error Message	Potential Causes
item is not defined	Named variable is not defined. Variable is misspelled. Named function is not defined. Unterminated string (regarded as an undefined variable by JavaScript).
item is not a function	Function is not defined. Function is misspelled. Other errors exist before function definition.
item cannot be converted to a function	Variable is misstated as a called function. Function (or a built-in object's method) is misspelled.
item has no properties	Object property is referenced incorrectly. Array is referenced incorrectly.
item is not a numeric literal	Variable does not contain numeric data. Other errors exist before variable assignment.
unterminated string literal	Missing quotes around string. String value has more than 250 characters. String values include a line break.
missing) after argument list	Missing parenthesis, brace, or semicolon.

Fixing Errors in Your Code

Even though JavaScript's error messages are helpful in identifying many program bugs, you usually need to do more investigative work yourself to fix all the errors—especially logical ones. This section outlines some common things you can do to make your investigative work both easier and a little more systematic. In Chapter 31, "Debugging," we will discuss how the debuggers from `Mozilla.org` and Microsoft can help you find problems in your code.

Checking the XHTML

Because JavaScript commonly interacts with XHTML code, you must first make sure that the file has no XHTML errors. These can often lead to hard-to-diagnose problems, so special consideration should be placed on this easily overlooked check. Use the following list as a starting guideline:

- Check for starting and ending <script> tags.

- Check for the attribute type = "text/javascript" inside the <script> element.

- Check for missing or misspelled XHTML elements.

- Check for angle brackets (<>) to open and close a tag.

- Check for matching pairs of tags (for example, <script>...</script>).

- Check for correct use of comments (<!--...-->) if you are hiding your JavaScript.

- Make sure you test your code thoroughly on the browsers you want to support.

- Make sure the form and frame names called in your JavaScript code match the names defined in the XHTML elements.

One quick check you can perform to help ensure that your XHTML documents do not have any errors is to have it validated. One of the nice things about XHTML now that it is officially an application of XML is that you can run the document through a parser to check for syntactical errors. One of our favorite tools is the HTML Validation Service, which does verify XHTML documents as well, at the W3C (http://validator.w3.org). It will allow you to either specify a URL or upload a specific file for validation.

Controlling and Identifying Problems with Comments

You can also use comments to systematically block out various lines and, therefore, functionality in your code to help identify the source of errors. This is an iterative process, whereby you simply prevent one or more lines of your script from executing. By doing so you can narrow your search for the source of the error, and therefore the time necessary to fix it. The following list outlines the steps involved in using this approach:

1. Comment out one or more lines from your code.

2. Save the code.

3. Reload the page in the browser.

4. Note the effect.

5. Modify the code to fix the issue or comment out more lines to further restrict your focus area.

6. Repeat until you've fixed the error.

Using the alert() Method

To identify runtime and most logical errors in your code, you must be able to follow the flow of the code and imagine how it processes its data. Many debugging tools let you step into your code, execute it one line at a time, and see the results of the executed code. Although these larger programs will be discussed in Chapter 31, "Debugging," you can use the alert() method to simulate a similar approach.

The alert(), as you learned earlier, displays a dialog box with information that you specify, such as the value of a variable. You can easily use this to show various types of useful messages and values that help trace your code's progress. Here are some techniques for using the alert() method successfully for this type of troubleshooting:

- Use something such as alert("Starting Check") to identify the starting point for debugging. As you progress through your code and fix errors, you can move this down in the code.

- Use alert() to display values of variables, arrays, and function returns. By running some simple test scenarios, you can quickly determine whether the values displayed are what you expect.

- Use alert() to display the results of expressions after processing. This is particularly helpful for tracking logical errors, because many of them come from using expressions incorrectly.

Testing Your Code

Traditionally, testing code means that you are preparing your application for production. This concept is equally true when it comes to publishing JavaScript-enhanced Web pages on the Internet—except that your "production" is now a worldwide stage with many potential users on a variety of platforms.

With that as a premise, you can use many common testing techniques to help test your JavaScript code. You need to make some modifications to cater to the special world of JavaScript and the Internet, but not many. JavaScript is a programming language capable of producing sophisticated applications that, like applications in traditional programming languages, demand solid testing.

> **NOTE**
>
> Testing is different from debugging. Testing is a means of finding errors. Debugging is a means of determining the source of errors and correcting them.

When you test your code, you should go in with the mindset that you will find errors. If you believe there are no errors at all, you will probably not find any! In practice, even the most thorough tests can never prove the absence of errors; you can only prove their existence.

To help test your code, you should write a formal test plan—one that contains both a checklist (one-page list of testing activities) and detailed test-case scenarios (detailed steps to perform the testing activities)—to test the code. Test-case scenarios should list specific and systematic test steps that you can perform on the application, along with expected results. The objective of doing this is to provide a documented and systematic approach to testing your code.

Consider the following items when devising test scenarios:

- Application requirements: Tests to make sure the application satisfies the original functional requirements. Tests should include getting feedback on how closely the application functions to the original requirements. Users' knowledge of the underlying model for the application should lead to identification and correction of many logical errors caused by the implementation of incorrect business rules.

- Design requiremênts: Tests to make sure the application conforms to its proposed design. These tests should include getting feedback from the application designers on how closely the application follows their design. These tests can also identify potential flaws in the design.

- Data flow patterns: Tests to check the validity of data flow in the system, especially with respect to the design. These tests should validate the integrity of the data that is processed by your application. You need to sketch the data flow in the application from input through processing to output and trace how data is affected at each phase.

- Functions: You should test each function in the application for correct functionality. These tests should validate the functionality of individual functions, irrespective of the rest of the code. The success of these tests often depends on how modular (single-focused in purpose, with zero dependencies) the functions are. (Modular programming is explained in more detail later in this chapter, in the section "Modular, Loosely Coupled, and Reusable Code.")

- Lines of code: You should test each line of code in the application for correct functionality. This can be done by stepping through each line of code and checking the result (for example, by using comments to isolate code or the `alert()` method to show values of variables).

- Bad data: Tests to see how the application performs when it receives bad data (for example, too little data, too much data, the wrong type of data, and the wrong size of data). These tests should also test for application behavior when required or optional data is missing (for instance, blank data entry fields on a form). Tests should confirm the existence of error-handling techniques to deal with these situations.

- Boundary analysis: Tests to see how the application performs at boundaries of data types, loops, and iterative function calls. These tests should ensure that the application can correctly cope with minimum and maximum values of variable ranges, and that error handling is built for the values that the application can't handle.

- Common values: Tests to see how the application performs when given information commonly entered by the user. These tests should ensure that the application works flawlessly for common data, because its failure to do so will affect the majority of users.

- Common errors: Tests common or previously occurring errors to ensure they have been corrected. Tests must be run to ensure that bugs that were corrected earlier don't reappear in a later version of the code. The most common potential cause of this type of errors is poor change management (version control), which might require follow-up tests of those procedures to identify and correct the root cause.

- Different platforms: Tests the application on various hardware and software platforms. The Internet consists of many users working on many different systems (such as Intel, Macintosh, and Sun) and operating systems (such as Windows, different flavors of UNIX and Linux, and versions of Mac OS). Your code should be tested on as many different platforms as possible so you can understand its behavior and, if necessary, modify it.

- Minimum configurations: Tests the application on a client desktop with the minimum configuration. Users will have different resources to access the Internet and you should, if possible, test to see how much demand (for example, memory, bandwidth, and so forth) your application puts on a machine. The test should be developed to check how the code will perform under the recommended minimum configurations and how error handling for users with less than minimum configuration is handled.

- Different browsers: Tests the application on different JavaScript-compatible browsers, such as various versions of Internet Explorer, Netscape/Mozilla, and Opera. These tests should help you identify how each browser handles your code and whether the code performs consistently. If the code doesn't perform consistently, you might need to modify your code or write some error-handling code.

- Compatibility with old browsers: Tests the application to ensure that files can be read by older (non–JavaScript-compatible) browsers. You should test your code with text-only or older browsers to see how the lack of JavaScript compatibility affects the user's experience—for instance, if the browser locks up or crashes, or if the page simply fails to load. Test for whether an alternative way of reading your content is available and how effective and reliable it is.

> **TIP**
>
> In many cases, because of the functionality desired, it makes sense to consciously design and implement a site around a specific base (or minimum) browser. For instance, you might decide that the user must have at least Navigator 4 or Internet Explorer 4 in order to effectively use your application.

- Reloading: Tests application behavior when the page is reloaded. These tests make sure that your code doesn't crash or behave oddly if the page is reloaded. If reloading affects the code, tests should confirm the existence of error-handling code and instructions to help the user avoid the problem.

- Resizing: Tests application behavior when the browser window is resized. These tests confirm that your code doesn't crash or behave oddly if the page is resized. If there is an effect, your tests should confirm the existence of error-handling code and instructions to help the user avoid the problem.

- Stress testing: Tests application behavior when many people use it at the same time. These tests can be done either by having several users running your code following a specific and detailed script or by setting up some type of automatic site launcher. You should monitor, record, and analyze the results of all tests (including response times and behavior glitches). You should also make note of how your code affects the rest of your site. If necessary, modify your code, and retest the affected code.

- Lost connections: Tests application behavior when the Internet connection is lost or the page is stopped. Users commonly lose connection to a site or manually force a halt in data transmission. Your code must be able to cope with this and exit gracefully (without locking up or crashing the browser) when needed.

Solid Programming Techniques

Like any other programmers, JavaScript authors can benefit greatly from learning and using solid programming techniques to code their applications. Even though JavaScript is still too immature to have a wealth of its own material on solid coding practices, you can adopt a good set of general guidelines from proven techniques used in other programming languages, especially object-oriented languages. The following list shows some of the techniques adopted for JavaScript:

- Coding from high-level and detailed designs

- Writing modular, loosely coupled, and reusable code

- Writing strongly cohesive code

- Writing error-handling code

- Using strong naming conventions

- Using comments

- Declaring and initializing variables

Each of the techniques listed here is explained briefly in the following sections. Be warned, however: Consistently performing such techniques involves a stiff learning curve, not only because of the level of discipline required, but also because you might need to forget some previous bad habits and learn some new good ones!

Coding from High-Level and Detailed Designs

Building code from a high-level and detailed design is the first step in constructing good code. A high-level design should help you identify the types of functionality required across different functions in the application. A detailed design should help you identify and name individual functions and sketch out their processes.

Good detailed design, especially if written in pseudocode, can be transformed into code and comments without too much difficulty. You should at least be able to write function and variable declarations straight from the design. Following that, you should be able to iteratively break down the rest of the detailed design and convert each section into code.

Modular, Loosely Coupled, and Reusable Code

Writing modular code means dividing your application into several individual functions or modules, where each function performs only specific tasks and communicates with other functions through function calls. You gain several benefits from such modular coding:

- Reduced complexity: Each module focuses on only one task, so most modules remain simple.

- Reduced duplication: If one type of functionality occurs in several different places, the code to make that happen needs to be written only once.

- Reduced effect of change: You can change a commonly used functionality in only one place instead of several places.

- Increased process hiding: Implementation details of functions are hidden from other functions. This means that you can change the way a function works without changing the rest of your code.

- Increased code reusability: You can reuse individual functions in other programs requiring the same type of functionality.

- Improved readability: Modular programming leads to simpler and more focused components in a program, which in turn makes the program more readable and easier to maintain.

30

Coupling relates to how closely two functions are related. Loosely coupled code means that the relationship between two functions is small, visible, and direct. This provides flexibility for either function to call the other but not depend on the other for much of its own functionality.

Modular programming, along with module code and loose coupling, provides the ideal recipe for creating reusable code. You can essentially plug this code into any other code to provide a known functionality. Writing reusable code has many benefits:

- High reliability: Reusable functions are proven and tested many times.

- Low cost: There's no need to write a new function.

- Portability: You can make code available to other platforms more easily.

- Information hiding: The code's internal operations are hidden from calling objects.

Writing Strongly Cohesive Code

Cohesion relates to how closely activities in a function are related. A strongly cohesive code means that the function is almost entirely dedicated to just one purpose. The goal is to do only one thing and do it well. An example of a perfectly cohesive function is JavaScript's `sqrt()` method of the Math object. This method simply performs the square root of the value it receives as an argument and returns the result.

Strong cohesion leads to high reliability because the scope of each function is very narrowly defined and the number of tasks it performs is extremely limited.

Error-Handling Code

A good program must be able not only to anticipate uncommon and erroneous events, but also to deal with them all gracefully. For example, bad input data, unusual user behavior, and interruption of transfer represent uncommon and error-producing events that need to be considered. This is where writing good error-handling code becomes a vital issue. Error handling should be built into your code to perform at least some of the following tasks:

- Check the values of all data input from external sources: You should check for the validity of the data, including data types, value ranges, and completeness. If an error occurs, the program should discard the current data and request a new submission.

- Check the value of all function parameters: You should check the validity of data coming from other functions. In case of error, the receiving function should discard the erroneous data and send a new request to the sending function.

- Perform exception handling: Exceptions should be noted by the program and logged in an exceptions log. If no solution exists, the function should exit gracefully.

- Check for other important errors: If possible, the error-handling code should prevent errors from occurring.

- Perform graceful exits: If your code crashes or the user stops the file transmission before the page is completely loaded, the browser should not crash or lock up. This can be performed by writing an error-handling routine to check if the page is successfully loaded or by opening a new browser window for your application, so that if it crashes it brings down only its >own window.

Naming Conventions

Using strong naming conventions refers to using appropriate, consistent, and meaningful names for all the declarations in your code. For example, objects, properties, methods, and variables should have strong naming conventions to help reduce code maintenance, improve readability, increase understanding, and eliminate confusing name proliferation (calling the same thing by two different names).

You can use many variations to develop a strong naming convention in your code. Here is a suggested list of things to identify distinctly in your code:

- Global variables

- Local variables

- Named constants

- Function names

- Function arguments

> **TIP**
>
> Use formatted compound words to enhance the meaning and readability of your names. For example, use `MaximumWeight = 200` for a variable or `findHeightInMeters(Height) { ...` for a function.

Using Comments

Comments can be a very effective form of source code communication from a programmer to the rest of the world, including other programmers who might maintain the code later. As much as good comments help increase a program's readability, bad comments can be wasteful and misleading. A certain amount of care and attention is required to write useful comments. Here are some guidelines for writing good comments:

- Include important and general program information with the source code. For example, author, date of last update, purpose of the function, and last changes. It might be the only source of documentation that is readily available or up-to-date.

- Write comments about the code that the source code itself can't easily explain. Comments should add value so the user can understand more than what is already apparent.

- Write comments at the level of intent of the code to explain why something is done. This means writing comments in an appropriate location to explain the purpose of code, and not just how the code does its processing. For example, place comments right before or after the line of code to which they apply.

- Comment on global variables. What do they contain? When are they updated?

- Comment on unusual or hard-to-follow pieces of code. What do they do? Why are they used?

- Keep in mind that those who load your Web page can see the JavaScript comments by simply viewing the source, so do not put information in JavaScript comments that you do not want others to see.

Declaring and Initializing Variables

Even though JavaScript lets you use undeclared and uninitialized variables in your code, it is good programming practice to consistently declare and initialize your variables. Declaring variables in one common place, like the beginning of a function or a centralized global area, makes tracking and maintaining them relatively easy. Initializing variables ensures that the variables contain the correct data type throughout the remainder of the program. For example, if var Counter = 0;, the variable Counter is set to a numeric data type.

CAUTION

You can't use JavaScript's reserved keywords as variable names, because these result in an error. Check JavaScript's reference guide for a list of reserved keywords.

Bulletproofing Your Code

JavaScript, like other programming languages, has nuances—including language bugs, obscure features, and strange behavior—that you need to recognize to write really solid code. You also need to be aware of the differences between JavaScript, as implemented in Netscape and Mozilla-based browsers, and JScript, implemented in Microsoft's browsers. Even though they are fundamentally identical, each has functionality that the other does not have. Rather than spend page after page listing bugs, obscure features, and strange behaviors of various browsers only to find out that they were fixed in the last release of the code, we just emphasize that JavaScript is always evolving. This means that you should know and understand, in detail, the level of the browser(s) you want to support as your base site requirement and how those browsers differ from other browser versions.

If you are ever unable to find answers to your questions, participate in a JavaScript discussion group such as `comp.lang.javascript`. Finally, to significantly improve your chance of writing code that works on both browsers, you must be sure to test your code thoroughly on both browsers and avoid JavaScript that seems to work in one but not the other.

Summary

This chapter introduced you to the three types of JavaScript errors—syntax, runtime, and logic—and described common JavaScript error messages and their possible causes. You also looked at ways to fix your code and identify errors—including specific things, places, and techniques to look for to help you do so. In addition, we discussed a systematic approach for testing your code, consisting of a test plan and detailed test scenarios, including specific items to consider in creating detailed test scenarios.

We showed you ways to build more preventive control into your code, so that you can spend less time debugging, with proven techniques for writing solid and maintainable code. These techniques will save you many hours of work in the long run and will help you write better code. To wrap up, we briefly covered how you can bulletproof your code.

CHAPTER **31**

Debugging

Although it is sometimes underestimated as a programming activity, debugging source code is a fundamental element of developing applications in any programming language. JavaScript is no exception.

Now that JavaScript has found its place in the coding community, we are seeing support of native and comprehensive third-party scripting and debugging environments that are similar to those of mature programming languages (such as C++, Visual Basic, and Java). I like to think of these tools as falling into one of the following three categories:

- Integrated Development Environment (IDE) tools: These help you quickly construct rich and dynamic Web sites, including JavaScript-enabled pages.

- JavaScript scripting tools: These help you more efficiently develop JavaScript-enabled pages through the use of intuitive visual interface and editing techniques.

- JavaScript debugging tools: These help you more effectively debug, fix, and test your code with the use of a graphical interface and commonly practiced debugging techniques (such as breakpoints and stepping into or out of code). An example of such tools is Netscape's JavaScript Debugger.

The availability of JavaScript scripting and debugging tools helps the developer take advantage of more automated preventive and, to a lesser extent, corrective controls. When you do not have access to JavaScript debugging tools, or the debugging job is very small, a simple JavaScript alert box can work as a debugging tool. In this chapter, three free JavaScript debugging options will be examined that are at your disposal.

Using the Microsoft Script Debugger

The Microsoft Script Debugger (MSSD) is a freely downloadable script debugging tool that works as an integrated part of Internet Explorer. You can use MSSD to write and, more importantly, debug your JavaScript (known as JScript with the Microsoft implementation) or Visual Basic Script (VBScript) code. MSSD has the advantage of being able to handle the debugging demands of ActiveX, Java, JScript, and VBScript. You can download it from `http://msdn.microsoft.com/scripting`.

An Overview of Microsoft Script Debugger Features

The following are the main features of the Microsoft Script Debugger:

- A dynamic view of XHTML structure: MSSD lets you view the whole structure of your page from the Project Explorer window and view the individual HTML files (for example, in a frameset) within their own windows.

- Multiple language integration: You can seamlessly debug JavaScript, VBScript, and Java within the same document.

- Color coding: MSSD displays your code with standard debugging color coding to help you better identify the composition of your code and ease debugging.

- Breakpoints: You can set breakpoints anywhere in your script to stop the debugger from executing at that point.

- Stepping into code: MSSD allows you to step (execute and pause) through your code one line at a time.

- Stepping over code: This feature lets you step into your code, but it executes procedure calls as one unit (rather than stepping into them) and returns to the next statement.

- Stepping out of code: As opposed to stepping over, this feature allows you to execute the remaining lines (from the point of execution) of a called procedure, and then it returns you to the next statement after the procedure call.

- Integrated call stack: MSSD seamlessly integrates the call stack from both VBScript and JScript in your code into a single call stack.

- Immediate expression window: This allows you to immediately evaluate an expression within the call stack or test new code. The result from executing the line of code is displayed in the immediate window.

Using the Microsoft Script Debugger to Debug a File

We will now walk through the steps of a sample debugging session using MSSD. During this exercise, we will be more concerned about the features of MSSD and their application than the content or functionality of the sample files. The remainder of this section assumes that you are using Microsoft Internet Explorer as your current browser and that you have already successfully downloaded and installed MSSD.

Starting the Microsoft Script Debugger

To start MSSD, first open Internet Explorer and load the desired HTML source file. Select View, Script Debugger, Open. This will open the debugger in its own window.

Alternately, you can immediately start the debugging process, by choosing View, Script Debugger, Break at Next Statement. To start debugging in the debugger, choose Break at Next Statement and execute the script. This starts the debugger and stops it at the first statement in the current script.

Using the Break at Next Statement Command

The Break at Next Statement command (which appears on the Script Debugger option of the View menu of Internet Explorer and the Debug menu of MSSD) is similar to a step command, in which the debugger executes the next statement in the script and then breaks, except that you can also use it when you aren't currently running the script.

This is an important debugging feature of MSSD, because a lot of JavaScript code is commonly declared in the header (or <HEAD>) section of an HTML file, and this command is the only way to debug that code. This is because the code in the header of the file has already been executed by the time the HTML file is loaded (remember that JavaScript is interpreted). Also, any breakpoints set after the HTML file has been loaded are lost if you reload the page.

Evaluating Expressions

An expression can be evaluated with the aid of MSSD's Command window and the following two methods during debugging of a script:

- Debug.write(string): This method writes a specified string—commonly, the value of a variable—to the immediate window, with no intervening spaces or characters between each string.

- Debug.writeln([string]): This method is identical to the preceding method, except that a newline character is inserted after each string. Also, the string argument is optional. If it's omitted, only a newline character is written to the immediate window.

Walking Through an Example

To better understand the capabilities of MSSD, you should practice using it to debug your code. The following exercise should provide you with a good starting point:

1. Open Internet Explorer.

2. Select View, Break at Next Statement.

3. Open the HTML file that contains Listing 31.1. You can type its URL, drag and drop the file into the browser window, or select File, Open. The content of this file is shown in Listing 31.1 (note that you should replace the names of the WAV files mentioned with the names and paths of sound files that you have available on your system).

LISTING 31.1   Using JavaScript Events to Play Sounds

```html
<html>
<head>
<title>Sound on JS events</title>
<script type="text/javascript">

function playSound(sfile)
{
  //Load a sound and play it
  window.location.href=sfile;
}
</script>
</head>

<body onLoad="playSound('Type.wav');"
      onUnLoad="playSound('Glass.wav');">
<h2>Sounds on JS Events</h2>
<br />
<hr />
The following are examples of JS event handlers used
to play sounds.
<hr />
<a href="#" onclick="playSound('Cashreg.wav');">
Click here for sound</a>
<br /><br />
<form name="form1">
<input type="button" value="Click Button to play a sound"
      onclick="playSound('Gunshot.wav');">
</form>
</body>
</html>
```

4. As the file is opened, MSSD is simultaneously activated, and a break occurs after the first statement is executed, as shown in Figure 31.1.

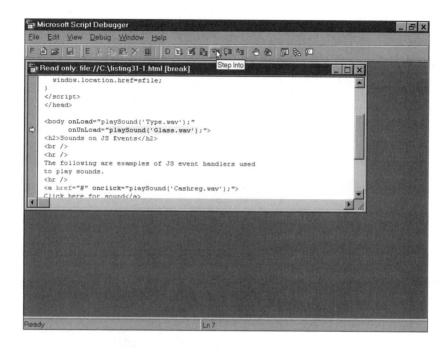

FIGURE 31.1   MSSD breaks after reading the first statement.

5. You can now step through your code to see the next sequence of program flow activities. Use the Step Into, Step Over, and Step Out toolbar icons to step through your code.

> **TIP**
>
> You can view the names of the icons on the MSSD toolbar by holding the mouse pointer—but not clicking—over any icon for a second or so. You can also read more detailed descriptions of all the icons and features of MSSD on the online help menu.

6. After you have stepped through (or used the Continue icon) to where the onLoad event call has been completed, you should hear a sound file played by your system (if your computer has audio capabilities). You may need to explicitly permit the browser to open the sound file, depending on how you have your Internet Explorer browser configured. This is a security measure to safeguard you from opening unknown and potentially dangerous (virus-containing) non-HTML files. Figure 31.2 shows the file after it is completely loaded into the browser.

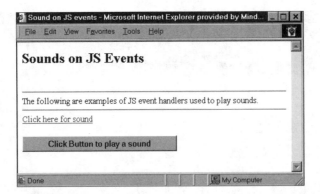

FIGURE 31.2   The result of loading Listing 31.1.

A Final Word on the Microsoft Script Debugger

The Microsoft Script Debugger provides a very helpful environment for you to kick start your JavaScript debugging and testing. The tools provided in MSSD are much like tools usually found in full-blown programming language environments such as Visual Basic and C++. Also, MSSD's interface, setup, and installation are all very user friendly and intuitive. However, MSSD has some limitations in that you need to switch frequently between Internet Explorer and MSSD to conduct debugging, and you can't print source code. At the least, MSSD is certainly a good tool to have in your arsenal, and it's a great value to boot because it's free. However, it can't take the place of writing solid code and systematically testing it.

Using the Netscape JavaScript Debugger

Like the Microsoft Script Debugger, the Netscape JavaScript Debugger (code named Venkman) is a freely downloadable JavaScript debugging tool that works as an integrated part of Netscape Navigator. You can download it from
`http://www.mozilla.org/projects/venkman/index.html`.

Examining Netscape JavaScript Debugger Features

The following are the main features of the Netscape JavaScript Debugger:

- Source View window: Lets you view the source of the HTML page being debugged.

- Breakpoints: Lets you insert breakpoints anywhere in your script to stop the debugger from executing at that point.

- Stepping into code: Allows you to step (execute and pause) through your code one line at a time.

- Stepping over code: Lets you step into your code, but executes function calls as one unit (rather than stepping into them) and returns to the next statement.

- Stepping out of code: Allows you to execute the remaining lines (from the point of execution) of a called function, and then returns you to the next statement after the procedure call.

- Call stack: Displays the current execution location.

Using the Netscape JavaScript Debugger to Debug a File

We will now walk through a sample debugging session using the Netscape JavaScript Debugger. The remainder of this section assumes that you are using Netscape Navigator as your current browser and that you have already successfully downloaded and installed the Netscape JavaScript Debugger.

Starting the Netscape JavaScript Debugger

To open an HTML source file for debugging in the Netscape JavaScript Debugger, follow these steps:

1. Begin by selecting Tasks, Tools, JavaScript Debugger in Netscape Navigator.

2. Open the page you want to debug in Netscape Navigator.

3. In the debugger, set breakpoints in the code where you want the debugger to stop.

4. Click the Reload button in Netscape Navigator to start debugging the page.

> **NOTE**
>
> Any time you stop the Netscape JavaScript Debugger, you cannot use Netscape Navigator to browse Web pages.

Walking Through an Example

To better understand the capabilities of the Netscape JavaScript Debugger, you should practice using it to debug your code. The following exercise should provide you with a good starting point:

1. Open the HTML file that contains Listing 31.2 by typing its URL in Netscape Navigator. Open the same file in the Netscape JavaScript Debugger.

LISTING 31.2   Problem Code

```
<html>
<title>vehicle_test.html</title>
<body>
```

LISTING 31.2   Continued

```
<script type="text/javascript">

//Create two global variables used to describe the vehicles
var vehicleColor;
var vehicleType;

//Set the type of vehicle
function setType()
{
  return(vehicleType="truck");
}

//Set the color of the vehicle
function setColor()
{
  return(vehicleColor="blue");
}

//If the vehicle type and color were not properly set, alert the user.
if(setType() || setColor())
  document.write("The " + vehicleType + " is " + vehicleColor);
else
  alert("The vehicle type and color could not be set");

</script>

</body>
</html>
```

2. After the file is open and executed, the resulting Web page should look similar to Figure 31.3. One look at the result and you can see something went wrong. The script was supposed to set the vehicle type to truck with the setType() function and the vehicle color to blue with the setColor() function. If these two functions had worked properly, a string would be written to the screen; otherwise, an alert message would be displayed to let you know one of the assignment operations failed. No alert message was displayed, yet the variable representing the vehicle's color was never set to blue.

3. We don't know where the problem lies, so let's set breakpoints in each of the functions to help locate the problem. Set a breakpoint in the setType() function and the

setColor() function because these should have been called to set the vehicleType and vehicleColor.

FIGURE 31.3   The result of loading Listing 31.2.

4. To start debugging, pause the debugger by clicking the Stop icon. Refresh the Netscape Navigator window to start debugging.

5. At this point the debugger will stop at the first breakpoint it encounters, which is the setType() function. From here, step through the code line by line by clicking the Into icon. As each line is executed, keep an eye on the value of the two variables in the lower window. Before the if statement is reached, both variables are undefined as you would expect. Because you are in the setType() function, vehicleType is properly set to truck. At this point, you would expect to step into the setColor() function, but instead you step into the document.write() method, as you see in Figure 31.4. What caused the if statement to not call the setColor() function? A closer look at the if statement reveals that if the first argument in a logical OR operation evaluates to true, the second argument is never evaluated. Because the setType() function returned true, the setColor() function was never executed. To correct the problem, simply change the logical OR operator to a logical AND operator. The correct version of the script is shown in Listing 31.3. The result of executing the file is shown in Figure 31.5.

LISTING 31.3   Corrected Code

```
<html>
<body>

<script type="text/javascript">

//Create two global variables used to describe the vehicles
var vehicleColor;
```

LISTING 31.3   Continued

```
var vehicleType;

//Set the type of vehicle
function setType()
{
  return(vehicleType="truck");
}

//Set the color of the vehicle
function setColor()
{
  return(vehicleColor="blue");
}

//If the vehicle type and color were not properly set, alert the user.
if(setType() && setColor())
{
  document.write("The " + vehicleType + " is " + vehicleColor);
}
else
{
  alert("The vehicle type and color could not be set");
}

</script>

</body>
</html>
```

A Final Word on the Netscape JavaScript Debugger

The Netscape JavaScript Debugger provides a very helpful environment for you to kick start your JavaScript debugging and testing. The tools provided in the Netscape JavaScript Debugger are much like tools usually found in full-blown programming language environments, such as Visual Basic and C++.

However, the Netscape JavaScript Debugger has some limitations. Among the most noticeable are that you need to switch frequently between Netscape Navigator (the browser) and the debugger to conduct debugging, and that you cannot create, modify, or print source code.

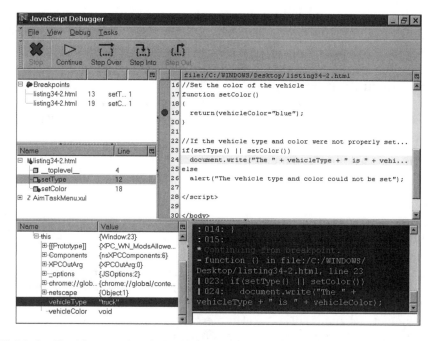

FIGURE 31.4   The Netscape JavaScript Debugger after an action.

FIGURE 31.5   The result of loading Listing 31.3.

Using the alert() Method

When you cannot get your hands on a full-featured JavaScript debugger or you are short on time and don't want to fire up a JavaScript debugger to solve a simple functionality problem, there is hope. If you have coded in any language for any length of time, you know that one of the simplest and quickest ways to debug functionality problems is to display the content of important variables at various stages of your program's execution. By doing so, you can determine if your code is executing as you intended.

JavaScript has a handy method called `alert()` that lends itself well to stopping the execution of your script to see the value of a variable. With a little thought and proper placement of this method, you can quickly track down functionality problems in scripts.

Walking Through an Example

To illustrate how to use the `alert()` method to debug JavaScript code, the same script that was used in the Netscape JavaScript Debugger example (see Listing 31.3) will be used again so that you can compare the two methods.

1. Open a JavaScript-enabled browser.

2. Open the HTML file that contains Listing 31.2 by typing its URL in Netscape Navigator.

3. When the file is open and executes, the resulting Web page should look similar to Figure 31.3, earlier in the chapter. One look at the result and you can see something went wrong. The script was supposed to set the vehicle type to `truck` with the `setType()` function and the vehicle color to `blue` with the `setColor()` function. If these two functions had worked properly, a string would be written to the screen; otherwise, an alert message would be displayed to let you know that one of the assignment operations failed. No alert message was displayed, but the variable representing the vehicle's color was never set to `blue`.

4. Because you are concerned with the values of the `vehicleType` and `vehicleColor` variables, you should display their values in `alert()` methods. You should carefully place these `alert()` methods at points in the code that will help you pinpoint the problem area. For example, an `alert()` method in each of the variable-setting functions will let you know that each function is being executed. An `alert()` method before and after the `if` statement will tell you how the conditional evaluates. Listing 31.4 contains these extra `alert()` methods and can be opened by typing its URL into the browser.

LISTING 31.4   Debugging Using alert() Methods

```
<html>
<title>vehicle_debug.html</title>
<body>

<script type="text/javascript">

//Create two global variables used to describe the vehicles
var vehicleColor;
var vehicleType;

//Set the type of vehicle
```

LISTING 31.4 Continued

```
function setType()
{
  alert("Inside the setType function.");  //Debug statement
  return(vehicleType="truck");
}

//Set the color of the vehicle
function setColor()
{
  alert("Inside the setColor function.");  //Debug statement
  return(vehicleColor="blue");
}

//Debug statement
alert("Before if statement: type="+vehicleType+" color="+vehicleColor);

//If the vehicle type and color were not properly set, alert the user.
if(setType() || setColor())
{
  //Debug statement
  alert("After if statement: type="+vehicleType+" color="+vehicleColor);

  document.write("The " + vehicleType + " is " + vehicleColor);
}
else
  alert("The vehicle type and color could not be set");

</script>

</body>
</html>
```

> **TIP**
>
> Make sure that you include enough information in each `alert()` method so that you can tell where you are in the code just by reading the text in the alert box.

5. After the file is open and executes, notice which alert boxes are displayed and which ones are not, as well as the variable values at each stage. The first alert box that is displayed shows that both variables are undefined before the execution of the

if statement, as you would expect. The next alert box shows that the setType() function was executed. The final alert box shows the vehicle type set to truck, but the color is still undefined after the if statement, as you can see in Figure 31.6. What happened to the setColor() function? The alert() method in the setColor() function was never executed, which tells you that the setColor() function was never called from within the if statement. There is something wrong with the if statement.

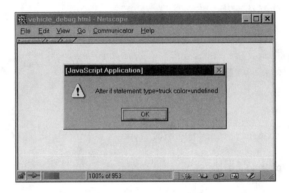

FIGURE 31.6   The result of loading Listing 31.4.

6. A closer look at the if statement reveals that if the first argument in a logical OR operation evaluates to true, then the second argument is never evaluated. Because the setType() function returned true, the setColor() function was never executed. To correct the problem, simply change the logical OR operator to a logical AND operator. Don't forget to remove the alert() methods that you added for debugging. The working version of the script is shown in Listing 31.3, which appeared earlier in this chapter. The result of executing the file is shown in Figure 31.5, which appeared earlier in the chapter.

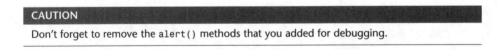

CAUTION

Don't forget to remove the alert() methods that you added for debugging.

A Final Word on Using the alert() method

As you have seen from the example, the alert() method can be a handy debugging tool for quickly solving small functionality problems. If you are debugging complex functionality problems or syntax problems, the alert() method will be more of a hindrance than a timesaver. Although useful, the alert() method should not be considered a replacement for a full-featured debugging tool, such as Netscape's JavaScript Debugger.

Summary

This chapter introduced you to three debugging tools that you can use to debug your JavaScript code. The Microsoft Script Debugger and the Netscape JavaScript Debugger allow you to debug complex JavaScript code. Both tools are good to have in your arsenal and, because they are free, they are great values to boot. Although not covered in this chapter, there are a number of full-blown development tools on the market that handle debugging, but they often come with a steep price tag. The last part of the chapter focused on using the alert box as an alternate debugging tool when you don't have access to a debugging tool such as Netscape's or Microsoft's. Even with these new tools, thoroughly testing and debugging JavaScript code is still the responsibility of the developer. However, none of the debugging tools discussed in this chapter can take the place of writing solid code and systematically testing it.

31

Index

Symbols

A

B

How can we make this index more useful? Email us at indexes@samspublishing.com

How can we make this index more useful? Email us at indexes@samspublishing.com

G

H

//H[colon]cscript (wscript.exe and cscript.exe option), *657*

//H[colon]wscript (wscript.exe and cscript.exe option), *657*

handling

errors. *See* errors, handling

events. *See* event handlers

height attribute, **486-488**

iframe tag, 505

layer/ilayer tags, 507

open() method, 216

Hello World, **658-659**

Help window, **444**

hidden form variables, maintaining state (Web pages), **620**

Hidden object, **295**

code examples, 298

defining, 295

hidden value, visibility property, **493**

hiding

layers, 494-496

scripts from Web browsers, 34-35

hierarchies

frames, 336

WSH (Windows Script Host) object model, 656

highlightButton() function, **526**

History list, navigating, **348-349**

History object, **564**

back() method, 565

code example, 565-566

forward() method, 565

History list, navigating, 348-349

list length, 347-348

methods, 347

properties, 347

Home button, **541**

host objects

MimeType object, 205

navigator object, 201-204

methods, 204-205

properties, 204-209

Plugin object, 205-207

HTML

browsers, 711

cascading style sheets. *See* CSS

color changes, Document object properties, 245-249

creating documents, Document object methods, 241-245

DHTML, 376-377

forms. *See* forms

Netscape layers, 376

structure view, 720

tags. *See* tags

HTTP

requests, 628

responses, 628

Hypertext Markup Language. *See* HTML

I

I character, pattern-matching, **689**

//I (wscript.exe and cscript.exe option), *657*

icon names, MSSD toolbar, **723**

M

How can we make this index more useful? Email us at indexes@samspublishing.com

How can we make this index more useful? Email us at indexes@samspublishing.com

options property, Select object, 290

OR (| |) logical operator, 98

ordering layers, 489-493

originalString parameter, stringReplace()
  function, 169

outerHeight attribute, open() method, 216

outerWidth attribute, open() method, 216

P

p tag, accessing, 397

padding, style sheets, 468

page loads, 30-31

pages. *See* Web pages

parameters

  cookies

    expiration date, 601-604

    name, 601

    null, 604

    path, 602-604

    secure, 604

    value, 601

  Date object, 189-190

  location, specifying URLs, 349

  message, 227

  open() method, 213

  stringReplace() function, 169-170

  URL, browser window content, 215

  windowFeatures

    attributes, 215-216

    displaying windows, 215

parent frames, referencing, 333-336

parent nodes, DOM navigation, 404-407

parent property, 337-339

parent windows, 214, 331

parentheses (), 354

parse() method, Date object, 188

parseFloat() method, 180

  Global object, 164

  Window object, 233

parseInt() method

  Global object, 164

  String object, 180

passCheck() function, 48

Password object, 294

path parameter, 602-604

pattern matching

  Perl, 669-671

  RegExp object

    methods, 690

    properties, 690

  regular expressions

    creating, 669-670

    email address validation program, 698-701

    pattern-matching attributes, 689-690

    phone number validation program,
      695-698

    syntax, 670-679, 682-690

    tester program, 691-694

    uses, 690

  String object methods, 691

pattern mining, 263

Perl, 669-671

PerlScript, 11

persistence (objects), 355, 601-604

Q

R

Refreshing dynamic toolbars, 562-563

RegExp object, 182, 669-670

methods, 182-183

pattern-matching methods, 690

pattern-matching properties, 690

properties, 182-183

RegExp,$* property, RegExp object, 183

RegExp.$ property, RegExp object, 183

RegExp.$& property, RegExp object, 183

RegExp.$' property, RegExp object, 183

RegExp.$+ property, RegExp object, 183

RegExp.$1,$2, $9 property, RegExp object, 183

RegExp.$` property, RegExp object, 183

regular expressions

creating, 669

assignment operator, 670

RegExp() constructor, 669-670

email address validation program, 698-701

pattern-matching attributes, 689-690

phone number validation program, 695-698

syntax, 670-671, 673, 675-689

escaped characters, 689-690

logical OR, 682

parentheses, 683

period (.),

tester program, 691-694

uses, 690

relative value, position property, 482

Reload/Refresh button, 541

reloading HTML pages, 712

remote scripting, 662-664

removeAttribute method, 411

removeAttributeNode method, 411-412

removeChild method, 409

removeItems function, 410

removing

alert() methods, 732

border attribute from table tag, 411

focus, 225

replace() method

adding to String object, 170-172

String object, 166

replaceChild method, Node object, 422-423, 426

replaceText parameter, stringReplace() function, 169

request line, HTTP requests, 628

requests, HTTP, 628

reserved words, 58-59

Reset button, 278

resetting forms, 448-449

resizeable attribute, open() method, 216

resizing browser windows, testing, 712

resources, 15-16

responses, HTTP, 628

reusable code, 140, 154-156, 584

best practices for constructing code, 713-714

credit cards, 591, 594

date, 587-588

dollar, 589-591

integer, 584-585

string, 586-587

reverse() method, Array object, 183

RFC 822, 601

RGB triplet, 246

right property, 484-486

right-shift (>>) operator, 103

How can we make this index more useful? Email us at indexes@samspublishing.com

Z

Your Guide
to Computer
Technology